D0743187

SHAKESPEARE SURVEY

ADVISORY BOARD

JONATHAN BATE

MARGRETA DE GRAZIA

MICHAEL DOBSON

INGA-STINA EWBANK

R. A. FOAKES

ANDREW GURR

TERENCE HAWKES

JOHN JOWETT

A. D. NUTTALL

LENA COWEN ORLIN

RICHARD PROUDFOOT

R. L. SMALLWOOD

ANN THOMPSON

STANLEY WELLS

Assistant to the Editor PAUL EDMONDSON

1 Shakespeare and his Stage
2 Shakespearian Production
3 The Man and the Writer
4 Interpretation
5 Textual Criticism
6 The Histories
7 Style and Language
8 The Comedies
9 *Hamlet*
10 The Roman Plays
11 The Last Plays (with an index to *Surveys 1–10*)
12 The Elizabethan Theatre
13 *King Lear*
14 Shakespeare and his Contemporaries
15 The Poems and Music
16 Shakespeare in the Modern World
17 Shakespeare in his Own Age
18 Shakespeare Then Till Now
19 *Macbeth*
20 Shakespearian and Other Tragedy
21 *Othello* (with an index to *Surveys 11–20*)
22 Aspects of Shakespearian Comedy
23 Shakespeare's Language
24 Shakespeare: Theatre Poet
25 Shakespeare's Problem Plays
26 Shakespeare's Jacobean Tragedies
27 Shakespeare's Early Tragedies
28 Shakespeare and the Ideas of his Time

29 Shakespeare's Last Plays
30 *Henry IV* to *Hamlet*
31 Shakespeare and the Classical World (with an index to *Surveys 21–30*)
32 The Middle Comedies
33 *King Lear*
34 Characterization in Shakespeare
35 Shakespeare in the Nineteenth Century
36 Shakespeare in the Twentieth Century
37 Shakespeare's Earlier Comedies
38 Shakespeare and History
39 Shakespeare on Film and Television
40 Current Approaches to Shakespeare through Language, Text and Theatre
41 Shakespearian Stages and Staging (with an index to *Surveys 31–40*)
42 Shakespeare and the Elizabethans
43 *The Tempest* and After
44 Shakespeare and Politics
45 *Hamlet* and its Afterlife
46 Shakespeare and Sexuality
47 Playing Places for Shakespeare
48 Shakespeare and Cultural Exchange
49 *Romeo and Juliet* and its Afterlife
50 Shakespeare and Language
51 Shakespeare in the Eighteenth Century (with an index to *Surveys 41–50*)
52 Shakespeare and the Globe
53 Shakespeare and Narrative

Aspects of *Macbeth*
Aspects of *Othello*
Aspects of *Hamlet*
Aspects of *King Lear*
Aspects of Shakespeare's 'Problem Plays'

PR
2888
C3
V.53

SHAKESPEARE SURVEY

AN ANNUAL SURVEY OF

SHAKESPEARE STUDIES AND PRODUCTION

53

Shakespeare and Narrative

EDITED BY

PETER HOLLAND

CAMBRIDGE
UNIVERSITY PRESS

University of Winnipeg, 515 Portage Ave., Winnipeg, Manitoba, Canada DISCARDED

PUBLISHED BY THE PRESS SYNDICATE OF THE UNIVERSITY OF CAMBRIDGE
The Pitt Building, Trumpington Street, Cambridge CB2 1RP, United Kingdom

CAMBRIDGE UNIVERSITY PRESS
The Edinburgh Building, Cambridge CB2 2RU, United Kingdom   http://www.cup.cam.ac.uk
40 West 20th Street, New York, NY 10011–4211, USA   http://www.cup.org
10 Stamford Road, Oakleigh, Melbourne 3166, Australia
Ruiz de Alarcón 13, 28014 Madrid, Spain

© Cambridge University Press 2000

This book is in copyright. Subject to statutory exception and to the provisions
of relevant collective licensing agreements, no reproduction of any part may
take place without the written permission of Cambridge University Press.

First published 2000

Printed in Great Britain at the University Press, Cambridge

Typeset in Bembo 10/12pt [CE] System [3b2]

A catalogue record for this book is available from the British Library

ISBN 0 521 78114 0 hardback

Shakespeare Survey was first published in 1948. Its first
eighteen volumes were edited by Allardyce Nicoll.
Kenneth Muir edited volumes 19 to 33.
Stanley Wells edited volumes 34 to 52.

DISCARDED

EDITOR'S NOTE

The previous volume of *Shakespeare Survey* carried a brief note that 'Future volumes . . . will be edited by Professor Peter Holland.' And with that characteristically modest comment Stanley Wells bowed out as Editor. He took over as Editor from Kenneth Muir with volume 34, though he had been closely associated with *Survey* prior to that. He has edited nineteen issues of the volume, amounting to many thousands of pages of comment on Shakespeare, and Shakespearians recognize the immense contribution that is represented by that work, itself only a small part of Stanley Wells' own achievements as a Shakespeare scholar across that period. Every contributor to *Shakespeare Survey* during his editorship has valued the attention, tact, advice and, occasionally, welcome correction which he has offered them for their articles. Every member of the Advisory Board has known that he has been a model editor, valuing the Board's support in the often difficult decisions an editor needs to make. Everybody at Cambridge University Press who has been connected with *Shakespeare Survey* in these years has found Stanley Wells always calmly unflappable and scrupulously on time with each stage of the arduous process of publication. The international community of Shakespeare scholars owes Stanley Wells an immense debt of gratitude for his years as Editor of *Shakespeare Survey*.

Volume 54, on 'Shakespeare and Religions', including papers from the International Shakespeare Conference held in August 2000, will be at press by the time this volume appears. The theme of Volume 55 will be '*King Lear* and its Afterlife'.

Submissions should be addressed to the Editor at The Shakespeare Institute, Church Street, Stratford-upon-Avon, Warwickshire CV37 6HP, to arrive at the latest by 1 September 2001 for Volume 55. Pressures on space are heavy; priority is given to articles related to the theme of a particular volume. Please either enclose postage (overseas, in International Reply Coupons) or send a copy you do not wish to be returned. Submissions may also be made via email attachment to p.d.holland@bham.ac.uk. All articles submitted are read by the Editor and at least one member of the Advisory Board, whose indispensable assistance the Editor gratefully acknowledges.

Unless otherwise indicated, Shakespeare quotations and references are keyed to the modern-spelling Complete Oxford Shakespeare (1986).

Review copies should be addressed to the Editor, as above. In attempting to survey the ever-increasing bulk of Shakespeare publications our reviewers inevitably have to exercise some selection. We are pleased to receive offprints of articles which help to draw our reviewers' attention to relevant material.

P. D. H.

CONTRIBUTORS

HERBERT BERRY, *University of Saskatchewan*
HELMUT BONHEIM, *University of Cologne*
MICHAEL BRISTOL, *McGill University*
BARABARA EVERETT, *Somerville College, Oxford*
ALISON FINDLAY, *Lancaster University*
DAVID GEORGE, *Urbana University*
REX GIBSON, *Cambridge Institute of Education*
JULIA GRIFFIN, *Tsuda College, Tokyo*
E. A. J. HONIGMANN, *University of Newcastle*
JILL L. LEVENSON, *Trinity College, Toronto*
JOHN LYON, *University of Bristol*
CYNTHIA MARSHALL, *Rhodes College, Memphis*
PHYLLIS MCBRIDE, *Texas A&M University*
RUTH MORSE, *University of Paris 7*
A. D. NUTTALL, *New College, Oxford*
EDWARD PECHTER, *Concordia University*
ADRIAN POOLE, *Trinity College, Cambridge*
ERIC RASMUSSEN, *University of Nevada*
NIKY RATHBONE, *Birmingham Shakespeare Library*
EDWARD L. ROCKLIN, *California State Polytechnic University*
ROBERT SHAUGHNESSY, *Roehampton Institute, University of London*
ROBERT SMALLWOOD, *The Shakespeare Birthplace Trust*
PETER J. SMITH, *Nottingham Trent University*
MARGARET TUDEAU-CLAYTON, *University of Zürich*

CONTENTS

vii

CONTENTS

ILLUSTRATIONS

SHAKESPEARE'S NARREMES

HELMUT BONHEIM

In Shakespeare's plays the chief figures are often separated, usually at sea, and united again. In *Twelfth Night* it is Sebastian and Viola (brother and sister) who are separated by shipwreck; in *Pericles* it is Pericles and Marina (father and daughter); in *The Comedy of Errors* it is Aegeon and Aemilia (husband and wife). The separation-and-reunion pattern spans the play, the span varying from days to decades. Variations of the pattern occur in *Antony and Cleopatra*, *King Lear*, *Much Ado* and rather more marginally in *Hamlet*, *The Merchant of Venice* and in *Richard II*, again more obviously in *Cymbeline*, *The Tempest* and *The Winter's Tale*. Such recurring patterns of action, place and time we call *narremes*.

Oddly enough, although the major playwrights of the following centuries hardly use the separation-and-reunion narreme, modern drama still flirts with it: at the end of Arnold Wesker's *Roots*, for instance, Beatie's friend fails to arrive: the reunion expected but not achieved characterizes the play; the old narreme, in other words, is present but reversed. Another example: at the conclusion of Peter Nichols' *Passion Play* James says to Eleanor: 'I think we can make a go of it, don't you?' and she answers, 'No'.[1] In the conscious rejection of a reunion of husband and wife, then, the old narreme lives on. To spin this thread a little further, we might conclude that according to the accepted narremes of our day, Shakespeare is rather outmoded: in a modernization of *Measure for Measure*, the Duke would not offer his hand in marriage to Isabella, in *The*

Winter's Tale the statue of Hermione would not come to life. The narremes of closure today are not those of Shakespeare's time. Some patterns seem merely conventional or arbitrary, others reflect systematic changes both of taste and the current sense of fitness and closure, yet others appear to be systematic, but elude explanation.

Narremes in prose and drama. The concept of the narreme was developed three decades ago by Eugene Dorfman,[2] who saw the narreme as a basic unit or quality of narration. His concept was expanded by Henri Wittmann,[3] but Shakespeare criticism has given it scant notice.[4] One reason is that narratologists concentrate on narrative prose and largely ignore drama, and thus have developed few tools that apply to it. After all, a basic narratological model has it that a story has four constituents: two dynamic ones, namely *report* and *speech*, and two static ones, *comment* and *description*.[5] But in drama one *shows* rather than *reports* (ignoring the occasional ex-

---

[1] Peter Nichols, 'Passion Play', in *Landmarks of Modern British Drama; The Plays of the Seventies* (London, 1986), p. 442.

[2] Eugene Dorfman, *The Narreme in the Medieval Romance Epic: An Introduction to Narrative Structures* (Toronto, 1969).

[3] Henri Wittmann, 'Théorie des Narrèmes et Algorithmes Narratifs', *Poetics* 4 (1975), 19–28.

[4] Rawdon Wilson, *Shakespearian Narrative* (London, 1995), refers to but makes no particular use of the term (pp. 35ff., 52 and 261) and does not explain it.

[5] The model is that advanced in my *Narrative Modes* (Cambridge, 1982).

ception), and the work of *description* is carried by scene and costume, only marginally by the text ('This castle hath a pleasant seat'). As to *comment*, especially in the extended forms it can take in the novel, it is rarely the staple of the play, and can even be frowned on. If E. M. Forster was right to suggest that showing is better than telling, and if that applies to fiction, it applies to drama all the more. The narremes of modern prose, in other words, look to be marginal in a genre composed almost exclusively of *speech*.

A play has constituents of its own: the task of casting, the ball and chain of the set (largely irrelevant to the novelist), and the iron cage of an evening's performance time, although the actions presented can range from minutes to decades. Shakespeare can also play effectively with contradictory elements of time, as Brian Richardson has shown with reference to *A Midsummer Night's Dream*.[6] What we need now is a proper narratology of drama, for the narremes that critics of drama have discussed tend to be borrowed from the analysis of prose fiction, indeed; dialogue (the staple of drama, of course) has tended to be considered out of bounds, the assumption being that narration is largely a matter of inserted reports (like that of the ghost of Hamlet Senior or Othello's wooing of Desdemona), stories within stories.[7] But of course dialogue is also a form of narration: who would analyse a novel and ignore everything in quotation marks? So narratology ought to help us to analyse drama, but has done so very little. One reason is that the field is constantly in flux, so that a number of recent developments, such as chaos theory,[8] frame theory or Gricean maxims have yet to be properly applied to Shakespeare's texts. Then, too, narratology became popular only a few decades ago, and its tools require further honing. This applies to prose, and all the more to dramatic art.

Macrostructures and microstructures. Drama has a special structuredness, in part because of its comparative brevity, that offers opportunities to narreme-hunters. Indeed, we see countless attempts to define the governing macrostructures of Shakespeare's plays, although structuralism has fallen out of fashion. Summaries of Shakespeare's plays tend to assume that it is respectable to posit (or impose) an over-all pattern. For example: an aristocrat is disappointed in the behaviour of one or more members of the family and the court. He feels threatened, is forced to leave home and is exposed to victimization. He has, however, a loyal dependant, who accompanies him even in a final confrontation with his enemies. He cannot hinder a plot against him, and although he himself as well as the female closest to him dies a violent death, his enemies are finally exposed and killed. The hero is praised by a survivor and justice restored to the land. A successor to the throne brings the country back to normality and peace; thus family drama goes hand in hand with political drama.

Of course this is a summary of *Hamlet*. But others may say: 'Surely this is the story of *King Lear*!' Which is also correct. The two plays share a set of constituent narremes: configurations of character, plots, themes. Indeed, some

---

6 Brian Richardson, ' "Time is out of joint": Narrative Models and the Temporality of the Drama', *Poetics Today*, 8 (1987), 299–309.

7 See for instance N. Delius, 'Die epischen Elemente in Shakespeares Dramen', *Shakespeare Jahrbuch*, 1877; Kurt Schlüter, *Shakespeares dramatische Erzählkunst* (Heidelberg, 1958); Joan Rees, *Shakespeare and the Story: Aspects of Creation* (London, 1978); W. T. Jewkes, ' "To Tell My Story": The Function of Framed Narrative and Drama in *Hamlet*', in *Shakespearian Tragedy*, ed. Malcolm Bradbury and David Palmer (London, 1984), pp. 31–46; Catherine Bates, 'Weaving and Writing in Othello', *Shakespeare Survey* 46, (1994), pp. 51–60; Eduard Costigan, 'Aspects of Narrative in Some Plays by Shakespeare', *English Studies*, 77 (1996), 332–42; Barbara Hardy, *Shakespeare's Storytellers: Dramatic Narration* (London and Chester Springs, 1997).

8 Although the author has made an attempt to apply chaos theory to a modest range of literary works and authors, including Shakespeare: 'The Nature/Culture Dyad and Chaos Theory' in *Das Natur/Kultur-Paradigma*, Festschrift Paul Goetsch (Tübingen, 1994), pp. 8–22.

of these also apply to *Antony and Cleopatra*, *The Tempest*, *As You Like It* and *The Winter's Tale*. No doubt narremes are in the eye of the beholder; alternative summaries might emphasize or attempt to eradicate the common narremes. Theodore Spencer's definition of the macrostructure that governs all of the history plays also sounds very like a narratological definition: 'An existing order is violated, the consequent conflict and turmoil are portrayed, and order is restored by the destruction of the force or forces that originally violated it.'[9] Having gone thus far, one wonders if this super-narreme does not apply to most of the tragedies – and some of the comedies too, except that there we often see the 'destruction of the force or forces' that attempt to block the happy ending, a rather foreign body of characters who display 'motiveless malignity', like the antagonist in a punch-and-judy play: Lucio in *Measure for Measure*, for example, or Don John in *Much Ado*, Caliban in *The Tempest*, perhaps Maria in *Twelfth Night*. In contrast to most dramatists now, Shakespeare prefers sets of characters in opposition, irrespective of the dramatic genre.

Patterns and solitaires. The repertoire of possible narremes might also be divided into repeated and thus comparable events – as opposed to singular narremes or microstructures. A checklist of these might include countless entries: *aberrant* or *abrasive* behaviour; *absurd* speech; *accusation*; *actantial* roles; *acrimonious* dialogue; *adultery*; *affectated* and *agitated* behaviour; *alcoholic excess*; *ambassadors* (treatment of); *ambiguity*, play with; *betrayal*; *blaming*; *character* types; *chivalry*; *coincidences*; *complicity* in crime; *confession*; *conflictual* behaviour; *corpus alienum* (such as comic interlude, dance, play within play, song, pageant, sword fight, wrestling match, etc.) In other words, we might scan the plays to take account of the 'infinite variety' but also forms of action and behaviour otherwise hardly noticed (for instance, the remarkable attachment of Aaron to his bastard child in *Titus Andronicus*). A *solitaire* like this, lacking an analogy (although we might construct a parallel to the shepherd's adoption of Perdita in *The Winter's Tale*), constitutes a one-off phenomenon: *interpretation* lacks its *-inter*. An apt image of the *solitaire* is the definition of a pier as 'a disappointed bridge' on the part of Joyce's Stephen Daedalus. Even as few as two examples of a phenomenon, like the bed-trick in *All's Well* and in *Measure for Measure*, give more rise to scholarly discussion than does the 'pier' of a *solitaire*. Often enough, however, once we hit on a seeming solitaire, we find parallels and analogies after all.

This is to say that significant narremes continue to be discovered. Shakespeare's penchant for elopements, for instance, deserves scrutiny – in *A Midsummer Night's Dream*, *Romeo and Juliet*, *Othello* and *The Winter's Tale*. This narreme carries on its back an ideologeme:[10] all of these elopements apparently have the approval of the playwright. Does this conclusion fit our concept of the Elizabethan world? Of a piece with this narreme are the marriages in which husband and wife-to-be hardly know one another. Yet this rarely seems to jeopardize their happiness: consider Proteus, Berowne, Bassanio, Orlando, Claudio, Orsino, Petruchio, and Cordelia's husband, the King of France. We might elevate the oddity of brief or non-courtship to the status of a narreme. It may be the very brevity of the plays in general that imposes it, although some of the plays encompass months if not years, even decades. Hand in hand with this narreme of strangers marrying goes the unnatural speed with which fathers reject their daughters: Leonato/Hero, Brabantio/Desdemona, Lear/Cordelia, Cymbeline/Imogen. One theory has it that in Shakespeare's time the average life span was by present standards relatively brief, so that we must expect to find a distance within

---

9 Theodore Spencer, *Shakespeare and the Nature of Man* (London, 1949), p. 72.

10 Cf. H. Bonheim, 'Ideologemes, Culturemes and other Emes', in *Studies in English and American Literature*, Festschrift Jerzy Strzetelski (Krakow, 1995), pp. 241–53.

the family, which from a contemporary perspective suggests a lack of emotional warmth.[11] But the argument is weak: we might just as well expect that a brief life span would make family attachments all the more precious, closer rather than distant. A narratological explanation of this narreme is perhaps more plausible: the five-act play favours a compression of events, not a depiction of lingering relationships, and some modern narremes, like the husband/mother-in-law conflict, had not been invented.

The microstructural narreme of the flashback also repays scrutiny. Often as not, flashbacks are dramatic 'cameos', stories within stories, like Gertrude's description of Ophelia's death, Clarence's dream in *Richard III*, or Enobarbus' description of Cleopatra: 'The barge she sat in, like a burnished throne. . .' (2.2.198). Interludes include dances, poems, inset plays (in *Hamlet*, *A Midsummer Night's Dream*, *The Tempest*), the first two of these clearly functional. Endings also run according to pattern.

The critic who fails to see the pattern and interprets a dramatic element as a solitaire may be misled. An example: at the end of *Hamlet*, Fortinbras, who seems hardly to know Hamlet, praises him: 'For he was likely . . . / To have proved most royally' (5.2.351-2). An assessment of Fortinbras' judgement would go astray if the governing narreme here were not recognized: the *laudatio* on the dead protagonist, the curious convention being that the praise comes either from an enemy or a person who hardly knew the protagonist. Only a voice of authority makes plausible an end to conflict: there is Antony on Caesar: 'This was the noblest Roman of them all. . .' (5.5.67), Caesar on Antony and Cleopatra: 'No grave upon the earth shall clip in it / A pair so famous. . .' (5.2.353-4), Cassio on Othello: 'For he was great of heart . . .' (5.2.371), Alcibiades on Timon of Athens: 'Dead / Is noble Timon, of whose memory / Hereafter more.' (5.5.84–6) or Aufidius on Coriolanus: '. . . he shall have a noble memory' (5.6.154). One critic has noticed the oddness of the latter example,

taking it to be a solitaire, '. . . the epitaph [on Coriolanus] being pronounced by his murderer with a sudden and unconvincing volte-face'.[12] But Caesar also evidences such a volte-face; the parallel suggests the problem of finding someone among the dramatis personae with sufficient authority to lend the *laudatio* weight. To recognize the narreme is not to explain it, but a safety net that may protect the critic from unfounded speculation concerning a single case.

The stage death of the person who has spun the plot has a kind of parallel in the comeuppance of the plot-spinners in the comedies and romances, the machinations of which, however, are punished lightly if at all: Don Pedro in *Much Ado*, Maria in *Twelfth Night*, Leontes in *The Winter's Tale*, or Antonio, the usurper of Prospero's dukedom in *The Tempest*. Such patterns should remind us of Vladimir Propp's thesis that a tale consists of a standard set of functions in a standard sequence.[13] Like the fairy tale, Shakespeare's plays tend to move toward a conclusion which supports a repertoire of *ideologemes* and *culturemes*[14] as well as patterns of closure. The light or non-punishment of characters such as Don Pedro and Maria is one such, and also a gross injustice that goes with the comic genre: in the tragedies, by contrast, the injustice is that the innocent are punished as much as the guilty. As to the narreme that there be a closing *laudatio* and that it be spoken by a person of authority, perhaps this is meant to suggest the likelihood that strife will now give way to peace, that whoever had a position of honour in the state also had special qualities that justified this honour, that the dead person deserved to have his story told etc. But

---

11 Marianne Novy, 'Shakespeare and Emotional Distance in the Elizabethan Family', *Theatre Journal*, 33 (1981), p. 24.

12 Brian Vickers, *The Artistry of Shakespeare's Prose* (London, 1968), p. 403.

13 Vladimir Propp, *Morphology of the Folktale* (Bloomington, 1958).

14 The term is that of Fernando Poyatos, *New Perspectives in Nonverbal Communication* (New York, 1983), p. 35.

here, again, we can identify a narreme, but fail to find a good explanation: we can surmise a dramatic but not a psychological or ideological function.

The narreme of the threatened child, too (for instance Aaron's infant, Perdita in *The Winter's Tale*, Banquo's Fleance and Macduff's children in *Macbeth*) presumably has the function of appealing to the audience for sympathy. Audiences are likely to sympathize with characters caught between conflicting loyalties (Desdemona in *Othello*, Octavia in *Antony and Cleopatra* or the Duke and Duchess of York in *Richard II*), a narreme native to classical Greek drama, now as good as extinct. Fighting to the death, though against the odds, is another narreme which Shakespeare favoured; he imposes it even on villains like Richard III and Macbeth. If villains could choose the genre in which to appear, it should be comedies, for there the rule pertains that justice will *not* be done.

Some of the narremes noted thus far are well-known patterns, and we call such a pattern a *locus communis* or *topos*. The *narreme* is a more encompassing term, including those patterns of event which to our knowledge have *not* been identified or explained. A narreme, then, might be thought of as a topos *in spe*.

Interestingness. We know approximately, however, what we are looking for: we search the texts for narrative elements which have 'interestingness'[15] – the quality of data that invites repeated attention. For example, the conflicts between some of the characters mentioned above adhere to a common pattern: unlike the situation of Aaron, they tend to have both a private and a political character. This doubling of function is itself a *narreme* and gains interestingness because it is obvious in usurpers like Macbeth and Claudius, perhaps less so in advisers and critical commentators: Kent in *King Lear*, Gonzalo in *The Tempest*, Enobarbus in *Antony and Cleopatra*, Menenius in *Coriolanus*. The very diversity of the fields to which a conflict pertains – psychological, ethical, poli-

tical, military, domestic – is also a peculiarly Shakespearian narreme: this diversity is evident in Shakespeare's plays, whereas we hardly find it in Restoration drama (Dryden is an exception) nor in major eighteenth or nineteenth-century plays, which tend to be unpolitical, until the advent of G. B. Shaw. Another victim of time is the revenge narreme, now practically extinct (although Ayckbourn has written an *The Revengers' Comedies*).

Such historical *culs de sac* suggest the value of an approach to Shakespeare via narremes. A narreme is 'interesting' not only because it puzzles us but because it functions as a 'search-engine': seeing a sequence of events in one play, we can search for it elsewhere and examine it in the sources, in the works of predecessors and successors. This is also what we do with the more familiar *topoi* and with genre distinctions like tragedy and comedy. The very idea of a tragedy–comedy–history triad suggests specific chains of events and reflects the common assumption that such categories, though questionable, may have explanatory value.

Of course we know how fuzzy such categories are: our editions of Shakespeare tend to ride roughshod over the *Tragedy* (not the *History* that it is called nowadays) of Richard III, the *History* of Othello and *All is True* (not *Henry VIII*), and when we come to Congreve or Sheridan, these categories no longer apply. There is surely more explanatory value in the micro-narremes of drama like confrontation and conciliation scenes, threats and placating gestures, cycles of conflict and unexpected compromise (as in the final scenes of *Cymbeline* and *Pericles*) than in supposed sub-genres.

The narreme, in other words, like the *topos*, is a heuristic tool. It allows us better to identify, contrast, compare. Its ahistoric nature should not bother us: there is no shame in imposing

---

[15] Suzanne Hidi and William Baird, 'Interestingness – A Neglected Variable in Discourse Processing', *Cognitive Science*, 10 (1986), 179–84.

narremes and ideologemes on Shakespeare in anachronistic fashion: after all, we see proto-Marxist elements in *King Lear* and Lacanian ones in *Hamlet*, we recognize in Shakespeare's *oeuvre* 'down-with-authority-plays' (*Coriolanus* and *The Winter's Tale*), usurpation plays (*Richard III, Hamlet, Macbeth, The Tempest*), and see that these plays share macro-narremes like transgression and punishment, guilt and absolution. For forensic purposes we can generate categories as we go along, giving each narreme a label, like 'usurpation play': labels have explanatory value and help identify and pin down the interestingness of phenomena, to see not only a tree but also the forest it grows in. Forster's battle-cry, 'Only connect' becomes 'Only compare!'

Thus, for instance, the pirate attack in *Hamlet* has little interest as a *solitaire* and might be seen as a foreign body in the tragedy. It gains interest when we consider the ubiquity of 'trouble on the high seas', from *The Merchant of Venice, Pericles* and *Twelfth Night* to *Antony and Cleopatra, Cymbeline, The Winter's Tale* and *The Tempest*, a list which includes some of the earliest but also latest of Shakespeare's plays. This narreme tends to be connected with other narremes: loss and recovery, exile and return, even when sea-crossings are only incidents which, as in *Hamlet, Othello, Lear* or *The Winter's Tale*, might be elided without serious damage.

The solitaire, as we have seen, is comparatively hard to interpret: what do we make of Hamlet's chance-medley killing of Polonius, his potential father-in-law? Is this an important action? True, it has functions in the plot: it gives Claudius an excuse to send Hamlet abroad and, if Claudius is to be trusted, causes Ophelia's madness. Shakespeare found it in the *Historiae Danicae*, but there the victim is neither named nor relevant except as an example of cunning and ruthlessness on the part of 'Amleth'.[16] More interesting criticism is produced from the focal areas of literary discourse which concentrate on recurring partials or 'fractals' (as they are called in chaos theory),[17] like

sources and analogues, encounters and actions, narrative techniques and configurations of character.

Narremes of time and character. Shakespeare not only had to convert his sources into dialogue but also to compact the events of years into a performance time of hours: in narratological terms, Shakespeare had to cut story time down to discourse time. Thus a scene which takes ten minutes to act out would also convey a scene which might in real life take ten minutes to unfold – at least in theory. When we trace such a scene back to its source, we see how Shakespeare blew up a mere detail into a full-fledged scene, or took the opposite direction, converting the panoramic time structures into an event occupying minutes on stage.

Between the scenes, on the other hand, we have broad gaps of time: from hours to days, years or decades, gaps which Shakespeare often leaves unspecified. Thus a reading time of ten minutes in Holinshed can catapult the *dramatis personae* through a year of events, whereas stage presentation demands that narrated and narrative time be more or less conflated and then divided up into parcels of action delimited by a grouping of the characters concerned. The year which Saxo Grammaticus has *Amleticus* spend on the way to and in Britain is as good as obliterated in the letter of ten sentences in which Hamlet tells Horatio of the pirate attack

---

16 '[Amleth] mounted the straw and began to swing his body and jump again and again, wishing to try if aught lurked there in hiding. Feeling a lump beneath his feet, he drove his sword into the spot, and impaled him who lay hid. Then he dragged him from his concealment and slew him. Then, cutting his body into morsels, he seethed it in boiling water, and flung it through the mouth of an open sewer for the swine to eat, bestrewing the stinking mire with his hapless limbs.' Geoffrey Bullough, *The Narrative and Dramatic Sources of Shakespeare* vol. 7, (London, 1994), p. 65.

17 This avenue is pursued in my paper, 'The Nature/Culture Dyad and Chaos Theory' in *Das Natur/Kultur Paradigma*, Festschrift Paul Goetsch (Tübingen, 1994), pp. 8–22.

and in the forty-line description of his rewriting Claudius' letter to the English king.

Turning chronicle into play-text, then, required a concept of scene lacking in most of the sources. For the chronicles (but also the verse sources such as those Shakespeare used for *Romeo and Juliet*) tend to panoramic, not scenic, narration. Macbeth's career after the murder of Duncan occupies seventeen years in Holinshed, of which Shakespeare took over a fraction, expanded into a playing time of three hours. In the terms of E. M. Forster,[18] the playwright has by and large to convert *panoramic* into *scenic* narration. In principle, the playwright effects a decompression of story time and a compression of presentation time.

Odd is the frequency with which the jumps between scenes are (or are not) signalled. For instance, the spectator may or may not recognize that when Hamlet comes across the grave-diggers, a month or even (as in the source) a year has elapsed since he had consigned Rosencrantz and Guildenstern to their deaths. Similar gaps occur in *King Lear*: we have hardly more than an hour's playing time between France's offer to marry Cordelia and Cordelia's return to England at the head of a French Army. In model theory, one might posit that the would-be dramatist's sources confront him with a bolus of intransigent materials which had to be translated into theatre: insignificant details had to be endowed with interest, plain narrative had to be converted into dialogue, mere hints developed into scenes. The epic surveys of chronicle must be hugely cut but also augmented so as to yield a more or less one-to-one relationship between narrative and narrated time (not that Shakespeare always manages this successfully; Richardson [cf. note 6] is most acute in tracing the multiple contradictions in *A Midsummer Night's Dream*). The largely unsegmented flow of events in the chronicles had to be encased anew in separate pillows (called scenes, then amalgamated into acts), between which the spectator is invited to imagine unspecified gaps of time, be it hours or decades,

only occasionally invited to jump such gaps by a character called 'Time' or 'Gower'.

As to character, Shakespeare excised some and added others. Roderigo, for instance, was not part of Cinthio's story of Othello: Iago would be condemned to monologues and asides without Roderigo (Henry James called such a crutch of narrative a *ficelle*). Only some of the figures, as an assessment of Roderigo or Lodovico would show, had to be invested with character. One would think that Shakespeare was hampered rather than inspired by the crude *pastoso* depictions of persons in his sources, but in fact he fashioned vivid and memorable ones (the nurse in *Romeo* and Beatrice in *Much Ado*) from the merest hints, or developed new ones, like Lear's Fool. He turns a rusty handsaw into an army of hawks, converting an indeterminate set of participants into memorable characters, investing them with variety and 'presence'. But he also creates characters of remarkable inconsistency: Polonius is honoured at court for his sage advice but also the 'busy old fool', so that one must concur with Dr Johnson's diagnosis of Polonius, 'dotage encroaching upon wisdom'. But do we not find even greater contradictions in Lear, in Antony, in Leontes? As to Hamlet, he is a proper scholar, incapable of action, scrupulous about not killing Claudius (supposedly at his prayers), but then he kills Polonius without regret and proves absolutely ruthless about the corpse. At the end of the play he becomes a bloodthirsty and practised 'sworder'. Despite his ill treatment and abandonment of Ophelia in Act 3, Hamlet turns out in Act 5 to claim that 'Forty thousand brothers / Could not, with all their quantity of love' (5.1.266–7) equal his love of her, but then kills Ophelia's brother as well. On the other hand, perhaps modern fiction is sworn to a narreme of character consistency equally untenable, at odds with newspaper reports of men butchering wife and children because of an impending

---

[18] Forster, *Aspects of the Novel* (London, 1927).

7

bankruptcy; and we find among commanders of concentration camps loving husbands and doting fathers. Perhaps our present-day assumption that character is consistent has even less plausibility than do the inconsistencies of Polonius and Hamlet.

Conventions of space. Some of the conventions of space-jumping in Shakespeare are as odd as those pertaining to time and character, and tend to be intimately connected with them. In *Othello*, for instance, Desdemona waits in Cyprus for her husband to arrive from Venice, afraid that he has been caught up in a 'high-wrought flood' (2.1.2). It is left to the literally-minded audience to assume that Othello's ship was delayed by a storm.[19] The scene on shore has several functions. First it affords the comic relief of the bawdy banter of Desdemona and Iago. Second, Desdemona reveals her affection for Othello by worrying about him. As is well known, the time-scheme of the play is as quirky as in *Hamlet*, in *Lear* or in *Antony and Cleopatra*. We must grant Othello reason to think that Desdemona might have been untrue to him, just as Hamlet has reason to believe that Ophelia is a tool of the court and the entertainment with which Hermione provides Polixenes makes it not quite preposterous that Leontes should accuse her of infidelity. The supposed affair of Hero in *Much Ado* is shored up by a similar substructure of situation and event. The narremes which all these situations have in common is that a woman's honour is compromised but then vindicated. A further narreme in this scene is its echo of the European ur-romance, the *Aethiopica* of Heliodorus. This work opens onto a similar scene on a seashore: a girl, Chariclea, worries about the fate of Theagenes, her lover. A variant of this narreme was used earlier on in *As You Like It* and much later again in the opening scene of *The Tempest* – there it is Miranda that fears for the safety of the voyagers. A corollary to the separation of lovers or family members is naturally the reunion, as in Pericles' meeting Marina at the end of *Pericles* or Egeon's with Emilia in *The*

Comedy of Errors. The happy arrival by sea, then, is a macro-narreme, a resolution-and-lover's-reunion sequence of ancient lineage. Behind the lovers there is often as not a family, so we might posit the relevant narreme (in parallel to Chekhov saying if a gun is hanging on the wall in the first act, someone has to shoot with it before the play is over): if Shakespeare shows us a family, its members will soon be separated. A majority of Shakespeare's plays, certainly the comedies, are constructed on variants of this narreme, which falls into disuse in the eighteenth century. Some form of 'family gathering,' whether happy, as in *The Winter's Tale*, or in the form of a sequence of deaths, as in *Hamlet* and *King Lear*, characterizes all ten tragedies and some of the histories as well, such as *King John*, *Henry VI* and *Richard II*. Shakespeare seems to have favoured 'family values', for his plot structures enforce the relevant cultureme to a degree to which English drama was not to return before the Victorian period.

Narremes as recurring partials. We can call the family separations and reunions in Shakespeare *narremes* or employ a term from linguistics: the 'recurring partial'. This is a textual element that appears repeatedly, like the English suffixes *-ed* and *-ing*. Linguists argue that recurring partials repay study: grasp the essential design of one and you have a ready-made category for the next one that presents itself. By contrast, linguists profess little interest in the phenomena of rhetoric, which are judged to be *exceptions* to or even *contraventions* of standard usage, and thus of little interest. Poets and critics may want to

---

19 Graham Bradshaw's article ('Obeying the Time in Othello: The Myth and the Mess it Made' in *English Studies*, 73 (1992), 211–28) argues that the problem has been imposed on the play by overly zealous dissectors of the text and poses no problem in performance, but his reading supersedes neither T. G. Nelson and Charles Haines, 'Othello's Unconsummated Marriage' in *Essays in Criticism*, 33 (1983), 1–18, nor Karl P. Wentersdorf, 'The Time Problem in Othello: A Reconsideration' in *Jahrbuch der Deutschen Shakespeare-Gesellschaft West* (1985), 63–77.

collect rhetorical figures and memorize them, but no systematic knowledge will be gained: these figures are remarkable exactly because of their singularity; narremes deserve attention because of their recurrence.

If narremes occur repeatedly in the plays this must be because Shakespeare found them attractive. We profit from examining them because we frequently locate in them central issues and motifs, as in Shakespeare's more or less unstageable passages showing adventures at sea or on shore. But the genuinely unstageable action in the sources is also a potential narreme, for Shakespeare had to excise or replace it, or try to make do with it after all. In Cinthio's version of *Othello*, the Moor pulls the ceiling down on his wife,[20] a method which Shakespeare's Globe would hardly allow. Iago's attack on Cassio involves problems of staging as well. Cassio's leg is cut off, and Shakespeare retains Cassio's 'My leg is cut in two' (5.1.73) – hardly possible on stage. Indeed, later that evening, Cassio comes on stage again: he is needed to explain that the handkerchief with the strawberry mark was found in his chamber and also to accept the rule of Cyprus at Lodovico's hands. Some modern editors show their awareness of the problem of the missing leg by adding a note: Cassio is to be carried in on a chair. But perhaps Shakespeare had no such help in mind, assuming the amnesia of the audience in the matter of a missing leg. Remarkable is the gratuitous violence in Shakespeare generally, a hallmark not only of his work: much of Jacobean drama is tainted, if we may dare such a subjective judgement, by it – another Elizabethan/Jacobean cultureme?

The pirate attack during Hamlet's voyage to England will serve as a further instance of a narreme, one particular to the stage, although only reported, not staged. The piracy- and shipwreck-narremes were derived from the so-called 'separation romances', and were indeed elements essential to the Greek romance from the *Aethiopica* of Heliodorus on. Hamlet could surely have exchanged the letter of Claudius to

the British king without such an addition. Scenes on board ship, like pulling down ceilings, tend to cause expense and are from a utilitarian point of view expendable. But the narreme of the sea voyage is repeatedly used not only in the ten plays which Shakespeare based on Elizabethan works of narrative prose, and we must admit that theatre versions often manage to stage storm and shipwreck in impressive ways.

The event as narreme. A narrower concept of the narreme focuses on what Lotman called an *Ereignis* ('event') in a narrative.[21] This is not an occurrence like a shipwreck or a duel but the psychologically essential turning point in a series of actions, the crossing of a 'semantic boundary'. It need not be staged at all: for instance, it may consist of a decision, a crossing from innocence to experience or ignorance to knowledge. In *Othello* the first event in Lotman's sense is Othello falling in love with Desdemona. But this does not 'happen' on stage. The next 'event' is the revelation of the animus which Iago bears against Othello – again, not an 'event' in common parlance. Next there is Othello's entrance and the words, 'Keep up your bright swords for the dew will rust 'em', which convey his self-confidence, his sovereign nature, the respect he commands. But he *does* nothing. The next event is the realization on the part of Brabanzio that he has lost his daughter to Othello. In the Lotmanesque sense, by contrast, Iago's cutting off Cassio's leg is no event: a director could excise the passage. It only confirms what we know about Iago's ruthlessness.

Lotmanesque 'events' are potential narremes, usually fabricated by audiences and readers.

---

20 In Cinthio's version (Bullough, *Sources*, vol. 7, p. 250f), 'Disdemona' is struck several times by the Ensign (whom Shakespeare calls Iago) until she is dead, and then, 'placing her in the bed, and breaking her skull, he and the Moor made the ceiling fall as they had previously planned . . .'

21 Juri M. Lotman, *Die Struktur Literarischer Texte* (Munich, 1972), p. 232.

Thus we might assign them to reader response theory as much as to the analysis of a dramatic plot. What speaks for Lotman's concept of the *event* is the agreement of the commentators as to what 'happens' in the plays. The action of *King Lear* is triggered off by Lear's terrible mistake in 'reading' Cordelia's 'Nothing'. Yet the text itself refers to it only slantingly – in Kent's 'What wouldst thou do, old man?' (1.1.146), and in Regan's judgement, 'He hath ever but slenderly known himself' (1.1.292–3) By definition, the narreme is a recurring phenomenon: here the concept of the event is expanded to include focal points of a psychological or moral kind which are not to be seen on stage but on which audiences and readers are nevertheless likely to agree.

In contrast to the narreme of the shipwreck, then, a marginal element in some of the plays, the 'event' in Lotman's sense is an essential narreme of the play; indeed, the concept allows a fresh look at what happens in any and all of Shakespeare's plays. The first event in *Lear* might then be signalled by Lear's question, 'Are you our daughter?' (1.4.201) and later on his line, quite out of context, emerging as it were out of some subterranean level of consciousness, 'I did her wrong.' (1.5.25). The overt action in this scene is comparatively trivial.

In the light of Lotman's view, we might question the view that Shakespeare's words, not his 'events', constitute the essential ingredient of his genius. We have the fact that Verdi's *Otello* dispenses with every syllable of the original text, and might be seen as a travesty of the original, yet continues to captivate audiences all over the world. As John Russell Brown put it recently, the plays 'survive without the advantage of his verbal brilliance when translated into many other languages'.[22] Indeed, the opera dispenses not only with Shakespeare's text but also with much of the action of the play. Presumably it continues to grip us because the narremes encapsulated in the Lotmanesque 'events' are successfully translated into the opera. As Brown puts it, 'seeing his plays performed in other languages than English is to realize how much of their vitality and viability is due to popular showmanship and an imaginative use of the physical elements of the actors' performances . . .'[23] An alternative hypothesis might have it that Shakespeare's words are gone, but not his narremes, especially those patterns of experience and insight which constitute the 'viability' of the plays.

At this point we can explain more exactly what a *narreme* is in relation to our analysis of Shakespeare's narrative. It is a *type* of event in a text, and belongs to a category of phenomena which we can better understand by comparing and contrasting a number of examples. The idea that we have to do with a collection of similar phenomena can inspire us to organize or reorganize our perception of the work and of our considered responses to it. This is a process to which the solitaire does not readily lend itself: for the standards to be applied have to be drawn from nonliterary fields, such as psychology, sociology, history, and so on, as well as our own life experience. But the latter probably fails to include sword fights, piracy on the high seas, oracles and such mortal family feuds as those between the Montagues and the Capulets.

Thus the relevant standards of comparison cannot be derived from literature but only from those elements in the drama that can or perhaps must be captured in the opera version. The event survives translation into a foreign tongue and into genres of which Shakespeare knew nothing, like the children's tales which Charles and Mary Lamb based on Shakespeare.

The success of the Lambs' retelling of Shakespeare's plots is presumably (since the language and imagery are largely their own and the plots are much simplified), also due to the narremes retained. One of the narremes which the Lambs generally rescue is the over-all structure which

22 John Russell Brown, 'Shakespeare's International Currency', *Shakespeare Survey 51* (1998), p. 193.
23 Brown, 'Shakespeare's International Currency', p. 195.

contemporary criticism has identified as being that of the tale *per se*, identified by Vladimir Propp,[24] sometimes encapsulated as the narreme called the 'lack-and-its-liquidation' narreme, said to be basic to the folk tale. The same claim can be made for the model of the French narratologist Claude Bremond,[25] who offers us a very simple pattern of events which we can also claim to be a narreme, and one that applies to some of Shakespeare's works: a folk-tale consists often as not of a cycle of movements across four poles, from *stasis* to *degradation* to *deficiency* and back through *amelioration* to stasis once more (see figure).

$$
\begin{array}{ccc}
\leftarrow \leftarrow \leftarrow & \text{Satisfactory} & \leftarrow \leftarrow \leftarrow \\
\downarrow & \text{state} & \uparrow \\
\text{Procedure of} & & \text{Procedure of} \\
\text{degradation} & & \text{amelioration} \\
\downarrow & \text{State of} & \uparrow \\
\rightarrow \rightarrow \rightarrow & \text{deficiency} & \rightarrow \rightarrow \rightarrow
\end{array}
$$

The Winter's Tale will serve to illustrate this model. We begin with a pleasant scene at the court of Leontes. This image of harmony clouds over as Leontes' suspicion of Hermione's infidelity grows. Here the 'event' is the change of Leontes' attitude to his wife and then in paranoid succession to his son Mamillius, his friend Polixenes and his adviser Camillo. A series of tragic events follows: the deaths of Mamillius and Hermione, the flight of Polixenes and Camillo. Here the cycle stops at the 'deficiency' way-stage. The second cycle is completed. The sheep-shearing feast shows a pleasant scene of social life and a seemingly

stable society, which then moves via an accusation scene toward disintegration. Finally, the two kings are reconciled, their children reunited, and Hermione turns out to be alive after all.

The play, in other words, follows a version of the Bremond cycle, moving from stasis to deterioration and then to amelioration and stasis again. Each section is punctuated by some kind of revelation: in the first cycle it is truth brought in by an oracle, in the second cycle it is the 'fardel' that proves Perdita to be Leontes' daughter. Thus we have a double narreme consisting of two interlocked Bremond-like patterns of character and event.

The structural narremes of *Othello* or of *Troilus and Cressida* can be similarly charted, except that 'chaos is come again' in the finale of each. Other plays, such as *Measure for Measure* and *Cymbeline*, are more complex, so that the Bremond model can help elucidate sections of the work, not the over-all pattern. For the *aficionado* of plot structures, however, this is no great drawback: if a narreme helps us better to grasp minor patterns between the greater ones, it is illuminating. For the student of Shakespeare seeking to identify and sort out characters, themes, motivations, or patterns of time and action, the Bremond model, like that of Propp, helps to make the concept of the narreme a useful tool.

---

24 Vladimir Propp, *Morphology of the Folktale* (Bloomington, 1958).
25 Claude Bremond, 'Morphology of the French Folktale', *Semiotica*, 2 (1970), 247–76.

STEPPING OUT OF NARRATIVE LINE: A BIT OF WORD, AND HORSE, PLAY IN *VENUS AND ADONIS*[1]

MARGARET TUDEAU-CLAYTON

Imperiously he leaps, he neighs, he bounds,
And now his woven girths he breaks asunder;
The bearing earth with his hard hoof he wounds,
Whose hollow womb resounds like heaven's
    thunder;
  The iron **bit** he crusheth **'tween** his teeth,
  Controlling what he was controllèd with.[2]

Picked out in bold type here is a piece or 'bit' of word-play in Shakespeare's erotic narrative poem *Venus and Adonis*, which has not been noticed, or at least not recorded, and which has ramifications far and beyond its immediate context which I shall explore in what follows. Briefly, it consists in a verbal mimesis of the violence done by the horse to its 'iron bit', an image which thus acquires an emblematic metatextual significance as well as inter- and extra- textual significances.[3] More precisely, the formation of 'tween' from *between* – a formation exemplary of poetic linguistic licence, as I shall indicate – is reactivated by a virtual homophone of the elided syllable or 'bit' before the verbal phrase 'he crusheth'. Releasing the polyvalency of the word *bit* this evokes at the same time its relation to the word *bite*, from which it is formed (again by elision), together with the relation of both to the body's organs of articulation ('tween his teeth'). Evoking these relations this bit of word-play makes them new, illustrating a poetics of re-creative licence, a stepping out from narrative and syntactic linearity in a discursive equivalent to the intemperance of holiday, which, breaking with common or ordinary discourse, liberates and regenerates desire in a pleasurable re-creation of relations, especially of the word to the body.

In her pioneering work on Shakespearian word-play Patricia Parker has pointed to the ideological implications of such discursive stepping out of line for class and gender relations.[4] These are indeed made explicit in the retrospective version of the horse's act by the poem's embodiment of unruly female desire, who describes the act as an heroic '[e]nfranchising' of 'his mouth, his back, his breast' from the 'petty bondage' of his prior condition as

---

[1] What follows was first presented at the Universities of Fribourg (Switzerland) and Chambéry (France). I am much indebted to suggestions made by the distinguished company present on both occasions. I record specific acknowledgements below; aberrations remain my own.

[2] *Venus and Adonis*, lines 265–70 in William Shakespeare, *The Poems*, edited by John Roe (Cambridge, 1992). Citations (henceforth given in parentheses) will be from this edition. Citations from the plays will be from *The Riverside Shakespeare*, edited by G. Blakemore Evans et al. (Boston, 1974).

[3] My thanks to Brian Vickers for pointing out the strictly impossible character of the horse's action here. This failure of verisimilitude in a poem traditionally much praised for its 'truth to nature' strengthens the case for motivation by another mode of mimesis.

[4] Patricia Parker, *Literary Fat Ladies. Rhetoric, Gender, Property* (London and New York, 1987); *Shakespeare from the Margins* (Chicago and London, 1996). Parker's superb analyses show how various kinds of linearity inside and outside the text are interrogated both by the mode of signification of Shakespearian word-play and its exposure of extra-textual structures.

'[s]ervilely mastered' (lines 396, 394, 392). Though necessarily attending to these ideological implications, I want to focus primarily on the intertextual as well as formal – and metatextual – aspects of our example. For this bit of word, and horse, play has an intertextual significance, which we may describe as an 'enfranchising' of the 'mouths' of Ovid and Virgil from the constraints of the imperative to moral instruction and, more specifically, the imperative to temperance, an imperative which the Ovidian and Virgilian intertexts in play here had been made to serve by a dominant moralizing interpretative discourse. The liberation from this imperative – for poetic discourse more generally as well as for Ovid and Virgil specifically – is indeed signalled in the meaning/function of the preposition which the verbal phrase 'he crusheth' divides (and iconically usurps the place of). For the place *between* is the place at once of interpretation (that which comes between the reader and the text), and temperance, the virtue which Edmund Spenser, for instance, in the second book of *The Faerie Queene*, 'Of Temperaunce', represents as the place between when he describes Medina in relation to her two sisters: '*Betwixt* them both the faire *Medina* sate'.[5] The image and its word-play emblematize, finally, a rupture which may be taken, I shall suggest, as the rupture, at once of Renaissance and of modernity.

Technically or formally, 'tween' is an example of *Aphaeresis*, which Thomas Wilson and Henry Peacham both place in the first group of rhetorical schemes – defined by Peacham (following Susenbrotus) as 'a fashion of writing or speaking, *made new* by some Art'.[6] The group is classified by Wilson as 'Figures of a worde' and by Peacham more specifically as 'Schemats Orthographicall', 'which be occupyed about letters, and sillables of wordes, *lawfull only to Poets . . . unlawfull in prose*'.[7] That such figures of the word are peculiar to the poet – instances of poetic licence – is reiterated by George Puttenham, who, without distin-

guishing them as schemes, likewise treats them first in his '*division of figures*' describing them as '*auricular figures apperteining to single wordes*'[8] True to his advertised intention to exercise his own bit of 'licence' by imitating the 'liberty' of the Greeks and inventing '*new names for every figure*' (*The Arte*, pp. 157, 156), he coins his own vernacular term for the figure of *aphaeresis*:

---

5 E. Spenser, *Poetical Works*, edited by J. C. Smith and E. De Selincourt (Oxford, 1970), p. 80 (book 2, canto 2, stanza 38) (my emphasis).

6 Henry Peacham, *The Garden of Eloquence* (1577), reprint (Menston, 1971), fol. EIV (my emphasis) and fol. E2r. All citations will be from this edition (contracted forms normalized, i/j u/v spellings modernized). Compare Thomas Wilson, *The Arte of Rhetorique 1553*, reprint (Amsterdam and New York, 1969), fol. 94v (where *Aphaeresis* is translated as 'Abstraction'). My thanks to Maya Mortimer for suggesting the relevance of *tmesis*, which Peacham, again following Susenbrotus, defines: 'when a compounded worde is parted by the interposition of another word, and sometyme of many', giving his own vernacular example, 'you ryse I perceyve early up . . . here the compounded word, ryseuppe is parted, and other wordes put *betweene the partes*' (fol. F4v, my emphasis). For Peacham (as for Servius (see note 32)) *tmesis* may be used only with a compound of two complete words, which *between* is not. Nevertheless, inasmuch as it is turned into a virtual compound by the word-play, we may say that we have a twofold figure, which, moreover, iconically reflects on *tmesis* as well as on *aphaeresis*. Though not mentioned by Wilson or Puttenham, *tmesis* is included by Richard Sherry, who also includes *aphaeresis*. Richard Sherry, *A Treatise of Schemes and Tropes* (1550), introduced by Herbert W. Hildebrandt (Gainesville, Florida, 1961). pp. 26, 31.

7 Wilson, *The Arte*, fol. 94r. Peacham, *The Garden*, fol. EIV (my emphasis). In the 1593 edition of *The Garden* this group has been dropped as has the group of syntactic schemes which include *tmesis*. See William G. Crane, 'Introduction' in Henry Peacham, *The Garden of Eloquence* (1593), (Gainesville, Florida, 1954), p. 10. Quintilian treats the addition or omission of a letter or syllable as a poetic licence ('poetico iure'), which should otherwise be shunned as a barbarism. See *The Institutio Oratoria of Quintilian*, translated by H. E. Butler, rep. 4 vols. (London and Cambridge, Mass., 1980), vol. 1, pp. 82–85 (Book 1, v. 10–14).

8 George Puttenham, *The Arte of English Poesie*, edited by Gladys Doidge Willcock and Alice Walker, reprint (Cambridge, 1970), pp. 158, 161. All citations will be from this edition (u/v i/j spellings modernized).

rabbate. A word, he writes, may be altered in poetic discourse, 'sometimes by *adding* sometimes by *rabbating* of a sillable or letter . . . either in the beginning, middle or ending . . .' (ibid. p. 161). Having illustrated the figures of addition he goes on: 'And your figures of *rabbate* be as many, videl. From the beginning, as to say [*twixt* for *betwixt*] . . .' (p. 162), which is, almost, to say *tween* for *between*.[9]

Puttenham's term *rabbate* is formed from the French *rabat*, a noun closely linked to (and in modern French largely replaced by) *rabais*, both derived from the verb *rabattre* (cf. Puttenham's verbal form *rabbating*). The semantic overlap of the two nouns is signalled in Randle Cotgrave's French–English dictionary, which glosses *rabat* first '*as* Rabais', which is, in turn, glossed '[*a*]*n abatement, deduction, defalcation, diminution, extenuation;*' a gloss echoed by the gloss to *rabattre*: '*To abate, deduct, defaulke, diminish, lessen, extenuate;*'[10] It is clearly these first senses of *rabat/rabais/rabattre* that Puttenham had in mind when he coined his term for the figure of *aphaeresis*. But both the noun *rabat* and the verb *rabattre* carried other specific (no longer extant) senses which bear directly on our Shakespearian bit of word-play. While under *rabat* Cotgrave gives the idiom 'Un rabat de bride', which he translates, '*A job, or checke which a horse gives himselfe with his bridle*', he concludes the gloss to *rabattre*, '*also, a horse to rebate his curvet*'. According to the *OED* this expression means simply to perform the *curvet*, a term which has a specific technical sense in the lexicon of manège as well as a more general sense of prancing. Either of these may be intended when *curvet* is used, as a verb, of Adonis' horse nine lines after our bit of word-play: 'Anon he rears upright, curvets and leaps' (line 279).

These adjacent senses of *rabat/rabattre* and the implied discourse of manège invite us to understand Shakespeare's reactivation of what is virtually Puttenham's instance of *rabbate* as a self-conscious bit of verbal curvetting done in the spirit of Puttenham's creative 'licence'. It is,

in short, another instance of the Shakespearian 'paranomastic play on tropes' to which Parker's work has drawn our attention.[11] Indeed, word-play is explicitly figured as the curvet in *As You Like It:* Celia, finding her communications with regard to Rosalind's object of desire, Orlando, constantly interrupted by her cousin's diversionary and often punning glosses, attempts to curb her with the rider's verbal equivalent or supplement to the bit: 'Cry 'holla' to thy tongue, I prithee; it curvets unseasonably'.[12] Rosalind's verbal curvetting is done under the pressure of what Montaigne calls 'cette naturelle violence de leur desir', the natural violence of women's sexual desire, which is held in check 'tenu . . . en bride' (like a horse) only by a learnt fear of dishonour; nature, that is, is restrained by forms of socialization.[13] A similar point is made by Myrrha, mother of Adonis, in Ovid's *Metamorphoses* 10 (principal source for *Venus and Adonis*), in her speech justifying her incestuous desire for her father. Her justification rests on examples from the animal world where there is a happy freedom not allowed humankind, for, to quote Golding's translation,

---

9 Presumably Shakespeare opted for 'tween' because of the assonance with 'teeth' (discussed below). In a modern grammar the two forms are grouped in a note as 'reduced forms' that 'may occur' in 'poetic style'. They remain, that is, grammatical anomalies specific to poetic discourse. Randolph Quirk, Sidney Greenbaum, Geoffrey Leech, Jan Svartik, *A Comprehensive Grammar of the English Language* (London and New York, 1985), p. 667, note c. (My thanks to Liliane Haegeman for this reference.) There is no typographic sign of the elided syllable either in Puttenham's text or in the quarto text of Shakespeare's poem.

10 Randle Cotgrave, *A Dictionarie of the French and English Tongues* (1611), introduced by William S. Woods, reprint (Columbia, 1968) (u/v i/j spellings modernized).

11 Parker, *Literary Fat Ladies*, p. 2.

12 *As You Like It*, 3.2.239–40. The figure of the horse that 'gambol(s)' is also used of the verbal symptoms of 'madness' by Hamlet, who elsewhere practises such verbal 'gambols' himself. *Hamlet*, 3.4.135.

13 Michel de Montaigne, 'Sur des vers de Virgile', in *Essais*, 3 vols. (Paris, 1979), vol. 3, pp. 56–112 (p. 72).

'mans malicious care /Hath made a brydle for itself, and spyghtfull lawes restreyne / The things that nature setteth free'.[14] Significantly, Golding has exercised a bit of translator's licence here, for the Ovidian text runs, 'humana malignas / cura dedit leges, et quod natura remittit, / invida iura negant'.[15] Though the image of the bridle may be implied in 'remittit' since the verb is used, especially by Ovid, in collocation with *frenum* (Latin for bit or bridle), it is Golding who inserts it explicitly as a figure for the laws introduced by human-kind, laws which divide humans from the animal world as well as from their own sexual impulses.

Bit, bridle and reins are of course recurrently used in Western forms of representation from Plato on to figure constraints on the body's natural, especially sexual, impulses, as other scholars have amply illustrated, including, most pertinently, Robert P. Miller, who reads the episode of the horses in *Venus and Adonis* as an endorsement of 'conventional Renaissance morality' advocating control of the body's affections by reason, which is to say temper-ance.[16] It is indeed with this cardinal virtue that bit and bridle are specifically associated in what Emile Mâle called the new iconography of the virtues, which, spreading from fifteenth-century France, manifested itself in various forms of visual representation in Europe in-cluding, in England, the emblems of Henry Peacham (the younger), who, like Ripa, repre-sents Temperance with a bridle in her hand, though not with a bit in her mouth, as in the earliest examples mentioned by Mâle, and as in what is perhaps the most well-known example by Peter Bruegel (dated 1560) (illustrations 1 and 2).[17] Like Mâle's earlier examples, Bruegel's figure advocates a stopping both of the (woman's) mouth – a constraint on speech which is explicit, though not gender specific, in the gloss quoted by Mâle[18] – and of female libidinal desire – the shape of the bit, bridle and reins as well as their suggestive relation to the woman's body underscoring the association of

mouth and genitalia which is a commonplace in modern psychoanalytic discourse as it is in a wide range of earlier discourses.[19] Indeed, the

---

14 *The XV Bookes of P. Ovidius Naso, entytuled Metamor-phosis, translated . . . by Arthur Golding* (London, 1567) reprint (Amsterdam, 1977), fol. 128r. All citations will be from this edition (u/v i/j spellings modernized).

15 Publius Ovidius Naso, *Metamorphoses*, translated by Frank Justus Miller, 3rd edn 2 vols. (Cambridge, Mass and London,1977), vol. 2, p. 86 (book 10, lines 329–31). All citations will be from this edition.

16 Robert P. Miller, 'Venus, Adonis, and The Horses', *ELH*, 19 (1952), 249–64 (p. 263).

17 Emile Mâle, *L'Art Religieux de la Fin du Moyen Age en France* (Paris, 1908), pp. 334–43; Henry Peacham, *Minerva Britanna* (London, 1612), reprint (Amsterdam and New York, 1971), p. 93; Cesare Ripa, *Iconologia* (Padua, 1611), in *The Renaissance and the Gods* (New York and London, 1976), p. 509; *Bruegel. The Drawings*, edited by Ludwig Müntz (London, 1961), plate 145. For the iconography of temperance and its 'submerged' presence in Renaissance literature, see Bart Westerweel, 'The Well-Tempered Lady and the Unruly Horse: Convention and Submerged Metaphor in Renaissance Literature and Art' in Teo D'haen, Rainer Grübel and Helmut Lethen (eds.), *Convention and Innovation in Literature* (Amsterdam and Philadelphia, 1989), pp. 105–21. For literary uses of the figure of the uncontrollable steed, with a focus on later German literature, see Sander L. Gilman, 'The Uncontrollable Steed: A Study of the Metamorphosis of a Literary Image', *Euphorion*, 66 (1972), 32–54. Some of the same ground, though with a focus on the association of the horse with the body, the rider with the soul, is covered in Joan Hartwig, 'Donne's Horse and Rider as Body and Soul', in Raymond-Jean Frontain and Frances M. Malpezzi (eds.), *John Donne's Religious Imagination. Essays in Honor of John T. Shawcross* (Conway, 1995), pp. 262–81. For the association of women and horses and their 'management' in the Shakespearian corpus, especially *The Taming of the Shrew*, see Joan Hartwig, 'Horses and Women in *The Taming of the Shrew*', *The Huntington Library Quarterly*, 45 (1982), 285–94.

18 Mâle, *L'Art Religieux*, p. 336; cf. Westerweel, 'The Well-Tempered Lady', p. 108.

19 See Ivan Fonagy, *La vive voix. Essais de psycho-phoné-tique*, reprint (Paris, 1991), pp. 85–88; Parker, *Literary Fat Ladies*, especially pp. 26–7, 106–7; Lynda E. Boose, 'Scolding Brides and Bridling Scolds: Taming the Woman's Unruly Member', *Shakespeare Quarterly* 42 (1991), 179–213 (my thanks to François Laroque for this reference); Ann Rosalind Jones, 'Nets and Bridles: Early Modern Conduct Books and Sixteenth-Century

1 'Temperantia' by Peter Bruegel (the elder) (1560).

figure implicitly calls for, even as it endorses, the social practice of the 'scold's bridle', 'a kind of chastity belt for the tongue', as Patricia Parker calls it, which, as Lynda E. Boose has shown, was one of the more brutal material instruments of 'women's socialization into shame' (and silence) in early modern England.[20]

It is in the mutually implicated contexts of this social practice and the iconographic tradition that Golding's insertion of the 'bridle' of the law into the mouth of Myrrha acquires its full significance. More immediately, it recalls his own earlier elaboration of the Platonic instance, done perhaps with the narrative of Phaethon as well as the iconographic tradition in mind,[21] in lines in the dedicatory epistle

which at once rehearse moral readings of particular tales and aspire to assert control over '[t]he

Women's Lyrics', in Nancy Armstrong and Leonard Tennenhouse (eds.), *The Ideology of Conduct. Essays on Literature and the History of Sexuality* (New York and London, 1987), pp. 39–72.

20 Parker, *Literary Fat Ladies*, p. 27; Boose, 'Scolding Brides', p. 189. See too Hartwig, 'Horses and Women', pp. 289–91. Both Hartwig and Boose relate this social practice to *The Taming of the Shrew*, which they see as endorsing the gender hierarchy it enforces.

21 Gilman suggests that Plato's image of the uncontrolled steed may itself owe something to the myth of Phaethon (Gilman, 'The Uncontrollable Steed', p. 34). The most influential version is Ovid's in *Metamorphoses* 2. The myth is used by Shakespeare to represent 'unbridled' female desire in *Romeo and Juliet*, 3.2.1–4.

2 'Temperantia' in Henry Peacham, *Minerva Britanna* (London, 1612), p. 93.

use of this same booke' (*The XV Bookes*, fol. b3v). They attempt, that is, to control – or manage – readers' responses to the tales of sexual licence which follow, including the particularly dangerous story of the incestuous desires of Myrrha.

> The use of this same booke therfore is this: that every man
>
>   . . . should direct
> His mynd by reason in the way of vertue, and correct
> His feerce affections with *the bit of temprance*, least perchaunce

> They *taking bridle in the teeth* lyke wilfull jades doo praunce
> Away . . .   (ibid. my emphasis)[22]

---

22 The tale of Tereus is earlier moralized as illustrating 'the man in whom the fyre of furious lust dooth reigne / Dooth run too mischeefe like a horse that getteth loose the reyne' (ibid. fol. a3r; see Miller, 'Venus, Adonis and the Horses', p. 256). Compare Prospero: 'Do not give dalliance / Too much the rein' (*The Tempest*, 4.1.51–2) – a paternal imperative which uses the same imagery as Golding's authorial prescriptions to attempt to assert as well as to represent control over (in this instance male) sexual desire .

17

The licence Golding allows himself as translator in putting the 'bridle' into Myrrha's mouth serves then his controlling aspirations as moralizing interpreter coming between the reader and the Ovidian text to draw Myrrha's speech within the framework of the exhortation to temperance. This clearly bears on the Shakespearian image and its word-play, all the more so given that Shakespeare's embodiment of 'unbridled' female desire identifies with the argument from nature made by Ovid's when she appeals to Adonis, 'O, had thy mother borne so hard a mind, / She had not brought forth thee, but died unkind' (lines 203–4).

There is in short an intertextual significance here, which, like the implied poetics of re-creative licence, aligns immanent (male) authorial agency with these unbridled female voices, and which I have suggested we might describe, in the words of Venus, as an 'enfranchising' of the 'mouth' or voice of Ovid. For the material Ovidian poetic texture dense, as Frederick Ahl has demonstrated, with word and syllable play, is thus symbolically liberated from the 'woven girths' (line 266) or textual strait-jackets of the dominant, moral interpretative discourse, exemplified by Golding's translation and practised in the grammar schools.[23] More generally, the image represents an enfranchising or liberation of libidinal desire, while the (male) narrator's verbal mimesis together with the example of Rosalind's verbal curvets cited earlier, make the material turns, or swerves, of poetic figuration and word-play privileged occasions for this liberation of desire – male as well as female – in language. This is especially important because, although, as Thomas Laqueur remarks, 'libido . . . had no sex' in the dominant one-sex model of the body, the vagaries of figuration, especially word-play, were frequently sexed in discourse on rhetoric, as Parker points out, a sexing which is merely more specifically inflected by critics from Samuel Johnson to William Empson who disparagingly characterize Shakespeare's 'unbridled' word-play as 'feminine'.[24] The frequently expressed imperative to control figuration is thus tied up, often explicitly in discourse on rhetoric, with the imperative to control gender relations, as, more generally, linguistic 'licence' is tied up with social disorder – and loss of control – as, for example, in Ben Jonson's exhortation against excessive use of figures, especially word-play: 'Marry, we must not play, or riot too much with them, as in *Paranomasies*.'[25]

In our instance, however, it is not loss of control but, on the contrary, its achievement that is affirmed: 'The iron bit he crusheth 'tween his teeth / Controlling what he was controllèd with.' In order to think about this affirmation of control in relation to the performed bit of word-play I want to return to the point I made at the outset, namely, that it has not been recognized by editors and critics, and consider the obstacles to recognition. These are formal as well as ideological for, as John Roe notes, the episode of the horses 'conduct[s] the narrative', thus adding the momentum of narrative to the relentless linearity of English syntax.[26] To recognize the word-play requires

[23] Frederick Ahl, *Metaformations. Soundplay and Wordplay in Ovid and other Classical Poets* (Ithaca and London, 1985). For the moral emphasis in the teaching of classical authors, see Margaret Tudeau-Clayton, *Jonson, Shakespeare and Early Modern Virgil* (Cambridge, 1998), pp. 72–6.

[24] Thomas Laqueur, *Making Sex. Body and Gender from the Greeks to Freud* (Cambridge, Mass. and London, 1990), p. 43; Parker, *Literary Fat Ladies*, pp. 107–13; on Johnson, see Christopher Norris, 'Post-Structuralist Shakespeare: Text and Ideology', in John Drakakis (ed.), *Alternative Shakespeares* (London, 1985), pp. 47–66 (p. 51); on Empson, Frederick Ahl, 'Ars Est Celare Artem', in Jonathan Culler (ed.), *On Puns* (Oxford, 1988), pp. 17–43 (p. 22). Contrast the affirmation of Rosalind's affinity to her author in Harold Bloom, *Shakespeare. The Invention of the Human* (New York, 1998), pp. 206–9, 225.

[25] Ben Jonson, *Timber: or Discoveries*, in *Ben Jonson*, edited by C. H. Herford, Percy and Evelyn Simpson, 11 vols. (Oxford, 1925–52), vol. 8, p. 623.

[26] *Venus and Adonis*, note to lines 263–70. Roe's point needs nuancing inasmuch as, although the episode does

an openness to diversion by relations of sound and sense counter to narrative and syntactic linearity. The horse, writes John Eliot in 1593, that 'plaieth . . . with his bit' 'sheweth that the bit is not his maister'.[27] Stopping or tarrying out (see note 26) to play with the bit, which actually requires reading backwards, readers may enjoy an enfranchisement, if a small and temporary one, from the laws of narrative and English syntax, and the linear, sequential sense of time they dictate. In the alternative temporal and spatial economy of word-play, which we might call, again quoting Venus, the 'time-beguiling sport' (line 24) of the curve[t], they are called upon to dwell upon the pleasurable proliferation of relations of signification as well as on the material excess to signification of the signifier. In short, they are called upon to take a holiday – or stop out – and delight in verbal intemperance.[28] An original intervention in language such verbal intemperance not only liberates from linearity – and so from the imperative to closure/containment – but regenerates desire in a re-creation of relations, especially of the word to the body (recurrently figured by the horse in early modern discourses[29]) with the effect, for reader as well as writer, precisely of controlling or managing where they feel habitually controlled.[30]

Indeed Frederick Ahl has argued that the practice of word-play not only offers 'a measure of freedom from the constraints that our societies and linguistic training impose upon us', and a sense of controlling rather than of being controlled, especially in relation to the 'tyrant' sequential time, but works 'to destroy death or at least our subservience to death', our subservience, that is, to a sense of (and drive towards) closure.[31] Still more importantly for our purposes, he shows definitively that the practice is not merely incidental but germane to Ovid's poetry. For this bears out my point that this word-play is not only exemplary of the re-creative licence of poetic intervention, but an intertextual intervention, symbolically enfranchising the material Ovidian poetic texture

from the controlling moralizing interpretative discourse, emblematized in Golding's 'bit of temprance'.

Still more prominent here, however, than the voice of Ovid is the voice of Virgil, whose practice of word and syllable play has again been underscored by Ahl.[32] Scholars have

---

not (*pace* Miller) suspend the time of the main narrative (Miller, 'Venus, Adonis and the Horses', p. 251), it has its own internal structure and rhythm as a narrative within the narrative. Formally, it may be classed as a *digressio*, which, according to Peacham, is a virtue if properly used, but otherwise a vice 'that doth diforme and patch . . . with broken peeces' the whole of which it is a part and from which it should not be a 'longe taryaunce out' (Peacham, *The Garden*, fols. U4r–U4v). In its evocation of a temporal delay, or stopping out, this bears on the episode (or interlude, as Miller calls it) of the horses, as we shall see.

27 John Eliot, *Ortho-epia Gallica* (1593), reprint (Menston, 1968), p. 89.

28 That sequential time is a manifestation or function of temperance is signalled by the clock of the iconographic tradition (illustration 1). See too the passage from *Hamlet* cited in note 12, where a condition of health, in contrast to a condition of madness marked by verbal gambols, is marked by temporal regularity: 'My pulse [. . .] doth temperately keep time' (*Hamlet*, 3.4.131).

29 Joan Hartwig, 'Donne's Horse and Rider as Body and Soul', *passim*.

30 The economy outlined here is an open, expansive and non-teleological alternative to the end-oriented economy of desire augmented by the constraints of resistance/delay which according to Joel Fineman motivates the narrative as well as the rape in *The Rape of Lucrece*. Joel Fineman, 'Shakespeare's Will: The Temporality of Rape', in *The Subjectivity Effect in Western Literary Tradition* (Cambridge, Mass. and London, 1991), pp. 165–221. It is, we might say, an economy of flirtation rather than rape, an economy, moreover, in which the imperative to linearity and the will to consummation/closure themselves constitute constraints augmenting desire.

31 Ahl, *Metaformations*, pp. 291–2.

32 Ahl, *Metaformations*, *passim*. Worth noting specifically is the example of mimetic *tmesis* in *Aeneid* 1 (which Ahl does not mention): 'et multo nebulae *circum* dea *fudit* amictu' (and round them, as goddess, she poured a dense cloak of cloud) (*Aeneid* 1, line 412; split verb emphasized). The figure is pointed out in the early commentary by Servius (usually included in larger sixteenth-century editions of Virgil), who recommends

19

indeed recognized a relation between this Shakespearian episode and the passage on the rearing of horses in *Georgics* 3, although they have confined their comments to noting parallels between the poets' descriptions of the ideal horse and, in the case of T. W. Baldwin, what he sees as a shared emphasis on the aggressive sexuality of mares.[33] What has not been recognized is the shared association of the figure of the horse (male as well as female) liberated from the constraints of bit/bridle/reins with the release of libidinal energy in a transgressive, material and mimetic poetic texture. To reproduce this association in a 'Virgilian' episode is again to 'enfranchise' the voice of a poet, who was bound, more tightly still than Ovid, within the terms of a dominant moralizing interpretative discourse. For, if Ovid was sometimes represented, as by Jonson in *Poetaster*, as '[l]icentious' – both sexually and linguistically – Virgil was almost always portrayed, as by Jonson, as 'grave Maro', of 'chaste . . . ear'.[34] More specifically, this passage in *Georgics* 3 had been drawn within the frame of a moral discourse advocating temperance by Gavin Douglas, in the prologue to his translation of *Aeneid* 4, an interpretation of the passage which was doubtless echoed throughout the sixteenth century by English schoolmasters trained in morally oriented Erasmian pedagogic strategies.[35]

Virgil first yokes the figure of the horse to his own writing through the unusual trope (of unyoking) with which he represents the closure of *Georgics* 2 as: 'time t'unlose the smoking necks of sweating horses'.[36] It is then in the passage on the raising of racehorses (*Georgics* 3, lines 197–208) that the writing is twined, sensibly, with riding, for, as R. A. B. Mynors points out, the stages of the colt's education 'are marked out in decreasing detail and with increasing intensity, until as though it could be controlled no longer the narrative erupts into a six-line simile',[37] a simile which is without end-stops for four of its six lines. Comparing to fierce northern winds the colt released from hard training, galloping 'liber habenis' (line 194)

– suggestively glossed by Fleming, 'Free or discharged of his rains, unbridled, loose and at libertie' (Fleming, *The Bucoliks*, p. 43, note 'd') – the simile suspends the narrative to mime the liberated energy it describes.

Something of the same effect is produced in lines describing mares under the influence of Venus: 'Love leads them' (Fleming, *The Bucoliks*, p. 45) over rivers and mountains, especially in spring, when they turn towards the winds by which they are impregnated and flee, a frenzied flight mimed again by six run-on lines (*Georgics* 3, lines 271–7). These lines constitute the climax of the passage (lines 209–83) following the description of the education of the colt, which Mynors summarizes as '[t]he effects of Sex on the animal kingdom', although the animals of course include humans whose sub-

---

it be used only with compounds made of two complete words. See *P. Virgilii Maronis Opera* (Venice, 1544), in *The Renaissance and the Gods*, 2 vols. (New York and London, 1976), vol. 1, fol. 181r. Citations from Virgil are taken from *Virgil*, translated by H. Rushton Fairclough, 2nd edn. reprint, 2 vols. (Cambridge, Mass: and London, 1974). Unless otherwise stated translations are my own.

33 Carleton Brown, 'Shakespeare and the Horse', *The Library*, third series iii (1912), 152–80; T.W. Baldwin, *The Literary Genetics of Shakespere's Poems and Sonnets* (Urbana, 1950), pp. 23–6.

34 Ben Jonson, *Poetaster*, edited by Tom Cain (Manchester, 1995), IV.vi.52; v.iii.160, v.i.108. See Tudeau-Clayton, *Jonson, Shakespeare and Early Modern Virgil*, pp. 151–2, 169–71, 176.

35 Gavin Douglas, *Virgil's 'Aeneid' translated into Scottish Verse*, edited by D. F. C. Coldwell, Scottish Text Society, 4 vols. (Edinburgh and London, 1957–64) vol. 2, pp. 147–54 (pp. 148–9). On the teaching of Virgil, especially the *Georgics*, as moral discourse, see Tudeau-Clayton, *Jonson, Shakespeare and Early Modern Virgil*, pp. 72–7.

36 Abraham Fleming's translation of: 'iam tempus equum fumantia solvere colla' (*Georgics* 2, line 542). *The Bucoliks of Publius Virgilius Maro, . . . Together with his Georgiks . . . translated into English verse by A.F.* (London, 1589), p. 36. (Spellings have been modernized where necessary.) My warmest thanks to Jane Griffiths for getting this material to me.

37 Virgil, *Georgics*, edited by R. A. B. Mynors (Oxford, 1990), p. 210.

jection to Venus is illustrated by the story of Leander (lines 258–63). As Mynors comments, the second half of the passage (from line 241) 'is broken up into a series of separate attacks on our feelings, and is full of rhetoric and allusion and in places almost febrile; the whole thing designed to give us the sense that the subject is getting out of hand, so that at 284 the poet has, as it were, to come to our rescue and openly resume control . . .'.[38] He does not, however, remark how, in performing this intervention, the poet represents himself as writing 'capti . . . amore' (line 285), in the grip of the desire driving the animal kingdom – not only the frenzied mares, but also the steeds which 'neither bit and bridle' ('frena') '[n]or cruell yerkings' 'do stop or stay' ('retardant') once they have felt desire (lines 250–4; Fleming, *The Bucoliks*, p. 45). Thus possessed, the poet lingers over ('circumvectamur'; literally: circles round) particulars ('singula'), while time flies ('fugit . . . tempus') (lines 285, 284), a representation of what precedes as a temporal diversion which clearly bears on the Shakespearian episode and its word-play, both forms of diversion or 'tarrying out' which 'circle round' particulars, whether the physical features and actions of the horse or the singular verbal event of the word-play with its cluster of sound and sense relations. As I suggested in relation to the second, readers are invited likewise to 'tarry out', 'capti . . . amore' (and Virgil actually uses this phrase of readers in *Eclogue* 6 (line 10)[39]), infected by the same love or desire, which both poets represent as released in the intemperance – temporal as well as formal curves – of a specifically poetic writing breaking the constraints of linearity in a miming of the action of the figure of this release – the horse liberated from reins, bridle and bit. Thus to represent poetic discourse as inspired by and inspiring desire is to enfranchise it from the inherited imperative to moral instruction, as it is, more specifically, to enfranchise the mouths of Virgil and Ovid from the 'bit of temprance' inserted by the dominant moral interpretative tradition exemplified by Golding and Douglas. While the second suggests Re-naissance, inasmuch as it invites a new response to the ancients, the first suggests rather modernity, inasmuch as, breaking with the inherited imperative to moral instruction, it promotes, as the purpose of poetic discourse, re-creative pleasure and the renewal of desire rather than its containment or what we now call repression.

Readers are indeed invited to regard 'this horse' (line 293) as exemplary of poetic discourse by the comparison with painting, which is introduced in a stanza exactly in the middle of this episode – another bit between which summons readers to step out ('[l]ook when' (line 289)), here in order to contemplate two forms of art in their differently inflected relations to nature. Specifically, the representation of the difference of 'this' – the poet's singular – 'horse' from nature's 'common one' (line 293) echoes the terms of a tradition of writing about the difference of poetic language which goes back to Aristotle, as Derek Attridge has shown, and which he illustrates, in a first case study, from *The Arte of English Poesie*.[40] Puttenham does indeed rehearse these terms, notably in his description of figures as at once 'trespasses in speech, because they passe the *ordinary* limits of *common* utterance', and 'requisite to the perfection of this arte', constitutive of the very texture of poetic discourse (Puttenham, *The Arte*, pp. 154, 137 (my emphasis)). He reiterates the point in the introduction to the figures (ibid. p. 159), which he then divides into three broad classes, the first being 'auricular figures', which, as we have seen, he prescribes as proper (or, as Peacham puts it, lawful) to poetic discourse only. Auricular figures are, that is, those deviations from 'common utterance' which especially serve to differentiate poetic discourse.

---

[38] Ibid. p. 214.
[39] Ibid. p. 226.
[40] Derek Attridge, *Peculiar Language. Literature as Difference from the Renaissance to James Joyce* (Ithaca, New York, 1988), pp. 17–45.

As we have seen, Puttenham's first 'division' of this class groups the figures of *addition* and *rabbate*, the second being illustrated by *twixt* from *betwixt*, virtually the example reactivated in Shakespeare's bit of word, and horse, play. This underscores its significance as emblematic of the licence – or curvetting – of poetic discourse which distinguishes it from nature's 'common utterance'.

Auricular figures are of course designed, as Venus puts it, to 'enchant' the 'ear'. 'Bid me discourse' she urges, 'I will enchant thine ear' (line 145), appealing to readers as well as to Adonis to attend to the aural texture of her discourse, a discourse which makes up much of the poem, and to be held 'capti . . . amore', as the languid object of her desires within the world of the poem is not.[41] For Puttenham the pleasure procured by such figures falls within a more general view of poetry as (courtly) recreation. More implicitly, his 'recognition of the sensory apparatus by which poetry works her (sic) spell' suggests re-creation of the word's relation to the body.[42] In our Shakespearian instance this is done by a conjunction of sound and imagery, notably the assonance of 'tween his teeth' which invites readers to recognize experientially the physical organs/origins which 'let' – allow as well as impede and allow by impeding – the production of sound, especially the initial sound of 'bit', 'utterd', as Jonson puts it, 'with closing of the lips'.[43]

Insisted upon throughout by the poem's aural texture, these organs/origins are also thematized, sometimes to comic effect, as in the lines describing how the language of Venus breaks, as she seeks to stop the lips of Adonis with a kiss (lines 46–8), sometimes more movingly, as: 'And now she weeps, and now she fain would speak, / And now her sobs do her intendments break' (lines 221–2). Language is broken by the body's modes of expression in kissing and sobbing, which compete for the same organs. That language itself may function, like sobbing, as a mode of physical release is suggested by the stanzas immediately following

the horse episode, which recall its image of the release of libidinal energy. Adonis sits, '*swoln* with chafing' '[*b*]anning his *b*oist'rous and unruly *b*east' (lines 325, 326 my emphasis), and the narrator comments, if ironically, that it is once more 'the happy season' for Venus to plead her cause: 'For lovers say, the heart hath treble wrong, / When it is *b*arred the aidance of the tongue.' (lines 329–30 my emphasis). In the next stanza 'barred' emotion is likened to the confinement of fire and water in '[a]n oven . . . stopped, or river stayed', which, under such confinement, '*b*urneth more hotly, *swelleth* with more rage;' (lines 331, 332 my emphasis). The release afforded by words is likened to the release of the 'vent', a release which, in the description of Adonis, 'swoln', like the river, with 'rage', is performed by another figure of sound, which, as it happens, echoes the initial sound of 'bit'. This echo, together with the (ex)plosive character of the sound and the sexual overtones of 'swoln' and 'swelleth', suggest that rather than simply a contrast to his horse, as critics have thought, Adonis shares his mount's 'unruly' libidinal energy, though it manifests itself as rage rather than desire.[44] This

---

41 Compare Montaigne (in the essay cited above (note 13)): '*Venus* is not so faire, nor so alluring all naked, quick and panting, as she is here in *Virgill*.' John Florio, *Essays by Michel Lord of Montaigne* 3 vols, rep. (London, 1946), vol. 3, p. 72. Montaigne is referring to Virgil's description of the seduction of Vulcan by Venus (in *Aeneid* 8), which he aligns with the description of her seduction of Mars by Lucretius (in *De Rerum Natura*), both passages illustrating precisely the seductive power of a material, poetic texture.

42 Willcock and Walker, 'Introduction', *The Arte*, p. lviii.

43 Ben Jonson, *The English Grammar*, in *Ben Jonson*, edited by Herford and Simpson, vol. 8, p. 480. The paradoxical operations of the Shakespearian 'let', though in relation to the production of narrative rather than sound, are brilliantly explored in Fineman, 'Shakespeare's Will' (cited above, note 30).

44 In contemporary terms rage and inordinate desire are both manifestations of distemper, a condition which may signal bad horsemanship. The contemporary expert, Thomas Blundeville, advises 'a temperate hand' in using the bit, not the 'rough' 'bit' used by English

energy is, moreover, released in a figure of sound which, 'let' by the lips, mimes the condition of the 'let' or obstacle said to augment (or swell) desire/rage.[45]

As the 'vent' of words is said here to 'assuage' (line 334) such energy, it is 'their violent passions to asswage' that frustrated lovers of Hero are said, if with a touch of irony, to have recourse to writing poetry in *Hero and Leander* by Christopher Marlowe, who later uses the image of the horse and bit as the images of stopped oven and stayed river are used by Shakespeare, to represent the same erotic economy.[46] Again, 'swollen' desire finds release in a breaking of the forms of restraint, represented again by bit and reins. Significantly, it is the words of Leander's father that are specifically associated with this restraint. For the image of the horse, which here takes the form of a simile, follows a brief scene in which Leander's father seeks 'to quench the sparckles' (line 622) of love's fire with a mild rebuke. The violence done to bit and reins thus represents at once a breaking of paternal law and a release of libidinal energy 'swollen' by the law. As we have seen, Shakespeare likewise associates the 'iron bit' with the obstacle or 'let' of paternal law, including the imperative (of narrative and syntax) to linearity and closure, and the (linked) moral imperative to temperance. Like Shakespeare, and Virgil, too, Marlowe formally mimes his meaning, using assonance together with (ex)plosive consonance, like Shakespeare, and, like Virgil, breaking the line stop as well as suspending the narrative with a simile:

For as a hote prowd horse highly disdaines,
To have his head control'd, but breakes the raines,
Spits foorth the *ringled bit*, and with his hoves,
Checkes the submissive ground: so he that loves,
The more he is restrain'd the woorse he fares, . . .
(lines 625–9, my emphasis)

It is not only for this mimetic representation of liberated libidinal energy that these poems ask to be read together. For Shakespeare's narrative is told at the outset of Marlowe's poem in a part – or bit – of the description of Hero's baroque outfit (lines 9–36):

Her wide sleeves greene, and bordered with a grove,
Where *Venus* in her naked glory strove,
To please the carelesse and disdainfull eies,
Of proud *Adonis* that before her lies.
(lines 11–14)

Like Shakespeare in the stanza discussed earlier, Marlowe brings together a material, visual texture, here embroidered cloth, and the verbal form of art exemplified by his own text,[47] which he then elaborates in an exploration of the relation of art to nature (lines 19–24), though it is not their difference but their likeness, their confusion even, that is pointed up, a confusion which is underscored for readers by the use of the word 'workmanship' (line 20) for the achievements of art, which Shakespeare uses rather of the achievements of nature. Shakespeare's own workmanship consists in the

---

horsemen, which produces a 'distempred' 'mouth' and 'headstrong Jades'. In short, as is the (distempered) master so is the (distempered) horse, which appears to be Adonis' case. Thomas Blundeville, *The Arte of Ryding and Breakinge Greate Horses* (London, 1560), reprint (Amsterdam and New York, 1969), Book I, cap x; Book III, cap. xx, cap xxii.

45 Compare the economy described here to that explored in Fineman, 'Shakespeare's Will' (see notes 30 and 43).

46 Citations from *Hero and Leander* are from *The Complete Works of Christopher Marlowe*, edited by Roma Gill (Oxford, 1987), vol. I, pp. 175–209 (here lines 126, 625–29). While Gill simply quotes the relevant stanza from *Venus and Adonis* (p. 304), Brown asserts that Shakespeare is consciously copying Marlowe (Brown, 'Shakespeare and the Horse', p. 179). It is as likely that both are drawing on the passage in *Georgics* 3 where the figure of the sexually aroused (male) horse that cannot be restrained by bit/bridle (cited above, p. 21) comes a mere four lines before the example of Leander.

47 He is also playing on a commonplace trope for rhetorical embellishment, as Gill unwittingly points up in the comment that the 'simple story is heavily embroidered . . .' (p. 179). The difference between the forms of art is suggested by the (comic) discrepancy between the immediacy of the visual and the necessary temporal extension of the verbal.

explication, or unfolding, of Marlowe's hem/ bit of three lines, in an expansion which at once releases and manages libidinal energy through the transgressive and re-creative aural figures of a specifically poetic texture.

I use the verb 'manage' here, as I have throughout, in order to evoke the semi-technical term of manège, or 'manage' as Philip Sidney calls it, in a sonnet in which he brings together the two noble arts of poetry and manège, as he does in the opening of the *The Apology for Poetry*, which indeed dwells at such length on Pugliano's praise of horsemanship that one of the earliest manuscript copies was miscatalogued at an early date as 'A treatise of Horsman Shipp' and so not discovered until the 1960s.[48] In the sonnet Sidney yokes together what he calls 'our horsemanships' – he on his horse, Love on him as horse – in a conceit which he acknowledges to be 'strange' in the phrase 'by strange work' (line 2), which implies a third level of 'manage' – that done by his verbal work as poet. The pleasure in the achieved management of desire in such 'strange work' is in turn included in the affirmation with which the sonnet closes: 'in the manage my self takes delight' (line 14). The strengthening of the sense of self in the pleasure of 'manage', which in the case of Sidney resonates with the meaning of his own first name,[49] is the aspect of the Shakespearian bit of word, and horse, play with which I shall close. I have argued that this illustrates the licence of a specifically poetic texture which 'steps out of line' in an alternative temporal and spatial

economy, releasing libidinal energy in pleasurable re-creation, especially of the word's relation to the body, through the strange, transgressive, even violent swerves of its singular, material and mimetic figures. In this pleasurable re-creation the writer/reader, like the rider (homonym of writer/reader taken together), acquires a strengthened sense of self in controlling, or managing, rather than being controlled by the otherness within (the body's desires) and without (the given forms of language). It is in its implied model of selfhood as well as in its implied poetics of re-creative licence that this bit of word, and horse, play announces the rupture that is modernity.[50]

---

48 *The Norwich Sidney Manuscript. The Apology for Poetry*, edited by Mary R. Mahl (Northridge, California, 1969), p. xiv. Citations from the sonnet are taken from Philip Sidney, *Astrophil and Stella*, edited by Max Putzel (New York, 1967), p. 49.

49 Geffrey Whitney exploits this in an emblem for Sidney which features a horse 'that champes the burnish'd bitte', 'mannag'd' by a rider (Sidney), one of the 'grave' men of 'highe estate' fit to rule. Geffrey Whitney, *A Choice of Emblemes and Other Devises* (Leyden 1586), reprint (New York and Amsterdam, 1969), p. 38 (u/v spellings modernized). This points up the ideological and political implications of Shakespeare's image of a horse seizing control of its bit and the performed verbal mimesis, done by one not of 'highe estate'.

50 And, perhaps, postmodernity: the cluster *mors* (horse's bit)/ *morsure* (bite) /*morceau* (fragment/bit) is recurrently exploited for significant word-play in relation to a self-conscious practice of writing disruptive of linearity by Jacques Derrida, who also uses the writer/rider analogy. Jacques Derrida, *Glas*, 2 vols. (Paris, 1981), especially, vol. 1, pp. 48, 166.

A 'CONSUMMATION DEVOUTLY TO BE WISHED': THE EROTICS OF NARRATION IN *VENUS AND ADONIS*[1]

PETER J. SMITH

In a poem written no more than four years after the publication of *Venus and Adonis*, Thomas Nashe dramatizes that most humiliating of masculine moments – premature ejaculation. In the poem, variously known as 'The choise of valentines' or, more popularly (and in the early MSS), as 'Nashe his Dildo', the first-person narrator visits 'mistris Francis', a high-class and expensive prostitute, who 'in hir velvet goune's, / And ruffs, and periwigs as fresh as Maye / Can not be kept with half a croune a daye' (lines 64–6).[2] The narrator, deciding that this is money well spent, describes her overwhelming performance:

> . . . she sprung full lightlie to my lips,
> And fast about the neck me colle's and clips.
> She wanton faint's, and falle's upon hir bed,
> And often tosseth too and fro hir head.
> She shutts hir eyes, and waggles with hir tongue:
> Oh, who is able to abstaine so long?
> I com, I com; sweete lyning be thy leave,
> Softlie my fingers, up theis curtaine, heave
> And make me happie stealing by degreese.
> . . .
> A prettie rysing wombe without a weame
>   [blemish],
> That shone as bright as anie silver streame;
> And bare out lyke the bending of an hill,
> At whose decline a fountaine dwelleth still,
> That hath his mouth besett with uglie bryers
> Resembling much a duskie nett of wyres.
> A loftie buttock barred with azure veine's,
> Whose comelie swelling, when my hand
>   distreine's,
> Or wanton checketh with a harmeless stype,

> It makes the fruites of love eftsoone be rype;
> And pleasure pluckt too tymelie from the stemme
> To dye ere it hath seene Jerusalem. (lines 93–120)

Her exuberant eroticism and the narrator's trembling gaze bring him to sexual climax before he is ready or she is willing. Despite his attempts to check his own wantonness he comes before he is able to penetrate the heavenly city.[3] Immediately he registers this incapacity as an anxiety about masculine identity, 'What shall I doe to shewe my self a man?' (line 127). The narrator's penis lies spent and impo-

---

[1] The title comes from *Hamlet* (3.1.65–6). I am grateful to Neal Curtis, Michael Davies, Peter Holland, David Salter, Greg Walker, Pip Willcox and *Shakespeare Survey*'s anonymous reader for commenting on earlier drafts. This essay was composed at the invitation of the *Centre d'Études Supérieures de la Renaissance* in Tours and my warm thanks go to Michel Bitot and his colleagues for their hospitality during November 1998.

[2] *The Penguin Book of Renaissance Verse*, ed. H. R. Woudhuysen and introd. David Norbrook (Harmondsworth, 1992), pp. 253–63.

[3] The rebellious character of the penis had been noted by Plato: 'the male member is mutinous and self-willed, like a beast deaf to the voice of discourse, and fain to carry all before it in a frenzied passion'. (*Timaeus*, 91b, in *Timaeus and Critias*, trans. A. E. Taylor (London, 1929).) For Augustine its unruliness was a consequence of The Fall of Adam and Eve: 'why should we not believe that the sexual organs could have been the obedient servants of mankind, at the bidding of the will, in the same way as the other [organs], if there had been no lust, which came in as retribution for the sin of disobedience?' (*Concerning the City of God Against the Pagans*, trans. Henry Bettenson (Harmondsworth, 1984), 14.585.)

tent but Francis, remember, costs more than the going rate, and it is here that she demonstrates why it's worth paying that little bit extra:

> Unhappie me, quoth shee, and wil't not stand?
> Com, lett me rubb and chafe it with my hand.
> Perhaps the sillie worme is labour'd sore,
> And wearied that it can doe no more.
> If it be so (as I am greate a-dread)
> I wish tenne thousand times, that I were dead.
> How ere it is; no meanes shall want in me,
> That maie availe to his recoverie.
> Whiche saide, she tooke and rould it on hir thigh,
> And when she look't on't, she would weepe and
>   sighe,
> And dandled it, and dance't it up and doune,
> Not ceasing, till she rais'd it from his swoune.
>
> (lines 131–42)

Fortunately for them both (and just as fortunately for the voyeuristic, heterosexual, male reader), her sensual ministrations have the desired effect: 'Now high, now lowe, now stryking short and thick; / Now dyving deepe he toucht her to the quick' (lines 147–8). The job well finished, in a disturbingly familiar combination of self-satisfaction and post-coital exhaustion, the narrator makes to turn over and start snoring: 'I faint, I yeald; Oh death rock me a-sleepe; / Sleepe – sleepe desire, entombed in the deepe' (lines 203–4). But not so fast – Francis is not so easily satisfied: 'Not so my deare; my dearest Saint replyde; / For, from us yett thy spirit maie not glide . . . Why shouldst thow fade, that art but newelie borne?' (lines 205–14). Already too late, her love snoozing next to her, Francis apostrophizes first him and then his all too readily wearied member:

> Adiew unconstant love, to thy disporte,
> Adiew false mirth, and melodie too-short.
> Adiew faint-hearted instrument of lust,
> That falselie hast betrayde our equale trust.
> Hence-forth no more will I implore thine ayde,
> Or thee, or men of cowardize upbrayde.
> My little dilldo shall suplye their kinde:
> A knave, that moves as light as leaves by winde;
> That bendeth not, nor fouldeth anie deale,
> But stands as stiff, as he were made of steele,
> And playes at peacock twixt my leggs right blythe,

And doeth my tickling swage with manie a sighe;
For, by Saint Runnion he'le refresh me well,
And never make my tender bellie swell.

(lines 233–46)[4]

Her solution to the problem of masculine failure is to employ a sex aid, and the benefits of this device are several. First it will never let her down and secondly, no matter how frequently it be put to use, it will never impregnate her. Finally, it awaits her convenience and may be used even while her lover slumbers next to her: 'How slye he creepe's betwixt the barke and tree, / And sucks the sap, whilst sleepe detaineth thee' (lines 251–2).

In the sonnet epilogue to this poem (which is in excess of three hundred lines), Nashe addresses his patron, Lord Strange, with chummy candidness and further innuendo, precluding any objections that might arise in response to the poem's obscenity by foregrounding his literary debt, 'Thus hath my penne presum'd to please my friend; / . . . Yett Ovids wanton Muse did not offend. / He is the fountaine whence my streames doe flowe' (lines 1–5).[5]

---

4 Woudhuysen glosses 'Runnion' as 'a mangy or fat woman' (p. 260) and though the first of *OED*'s definitions accords with this, it also defines *runnion* as 'The male organ' which seems far more appropriate here. Though *OED*'s first recorded use of this definition is 1655, in *Musarum Deliciae* (by John Mennes and James Smith), it notes that the poem in which it occurs 'is written in imitation of Chaucer' – the term appears twice in the *Introduction to the Pardoner's Tale*. Here, allusion to 'Seint Ronyan' follows mention of 'urynals' and 'jurdones' (lines 305–20) which would reinforce the penile meaning. Note also its derivation from the Latin *runa* meaning 'lance'.

5 Nashe is alluding to Ovid's *Amores*, 3.7.13–14: 'My member hung slack, as though frozen by hemlock / A dead loss for the sort of game I'd planned' (*The Erotic Poems*, trans. Peter Green (Harmondsworth, 1982), p. 150). The first Loeb edn excludes 3.7 completely: 'The translator has felt obliged to omit one poem entire, and to omit or disguise a few verses in other poems where, in spite of the poet's exquisite art, a faithful rendering might offend the sensibilities of the reader, if not the literary taste' (trans. Grant Showerman, Cambridge, Mass. and London, 1947, p. 317). In the second

And in a back-slapping gesture of male camaraderie, the poet blames any tendency he may have to blurt out indelicate details on the woman's part: 'Forgive me if I speake as I was taught, / A lyke to women, utter all I knowe, / As longing to unlade so bad a fraught' (lines 6–8). This disarming attempt to ingratiate the poet with his patron raises an intriguing paradox about 'Nashe's Dildo' for it both dramatizes a masculine anxiety in regard to woman's apparently inexhaustible physical expectations (by illustrating the ease with which his sexual role can be usurped by an inanimate sex toy) while, at the same time, demonstrating that the poem is composed for a male readership.[6]

Not until some eighty years later, with the ebullient obscenity of Rochester's 'The Imperfect Enjoyment' is the subject of premature ejaculation treated with such explicit licentiousness:

> In liquid raptures I dissolve all o'er,
> Melt into sperm, and spend at every pore:
> A touch from any part of her had don't,
> Her hand, her foot, her very look's a cunt.
> Smiling, she chides in a kind murmuring noise,
> And from her body wipes the clammy joys.
>
> (lines 15–20)[7]

Again in 'On his Prick' and 'A Curse on his Pintle', Rochester meditates upon his all too pliant manhood. Unlike 'Nashe's Dildo' however, Rochester's poems are nauseated by masculine impotence. Whereas Nashe's speaker gleefully details the efforts Francis makes to arouse him (and we remember that in this she is spectacularly successful), Rochester's narrator is utterly disgusted by his own sexual incapacities. Try as he might, he can only rant at his inadequacy, and this anger leads to a vicious circle of self-contempt and further ineptitude: 'Eager desires confound my first intent, / Succeeding shame does more success prevent, / And rage, at last, confirms me impotent' ('The Imperfect Enjoyment', lines 28–30). 'On his Prick' has the poet curse his own penis for its

flaccidity and ends with a warning that unless it improve its performance in future, it will be used only for pissing: 'Henceforth stand stiff, regain thy credit lost, / Or I'll ne'er draw thee but against a post' (lines 19–20). 'A Curse on his Pintle' ends in the humiliating scene of his mistress making the best of a bad job: 'Yea, though she took it in her warm moist hand / And crammed it in, dull dog, it would not stand' (lines 17–18). There is no satisfaction for a male readership in this moment of obdurate failure and sexual humiliation.

The contrast then is clear: whereas Nashe uses male impotence as a pretext to describe the intricacies of foreplay in pornographic detail, Rochester's limp masculinity is a dead end in itself. While the anonymous girls display themselves to him, the poet's focus remains directed into his own lap, stultified and disconsolate. Whereas Francis's antics are lustfully detailed for a voyeuristic male reader, the blunt and trashy pornography of Rochester's women – 'Her legs stretched wide, her cunt to me did show' ('A Curse on his Pintle', line 6) – impresses the reader only with the amplitude of masculine self-absorption and the vehemence

---

Loeb edn (rev. G. P. Goold, 1977), 3.7 is included though not without bowdlerization. The lines are rendered, 'my body, as if drugged with chill hemlock, was paralysed and failed to achieve my intent' (p. 475).

6 Over a quarter of a century ago, David O. Frantz registered the importance of the 'male gaze' to the reading of this poem: 'Nashe's . . . *Choise of Valentines* is certainly the most overtly pornographic poem of the English Renaissance; lust is glorified or at least displayed in a fashion meant to arouse the salacious reader's sensibilities.' Later he notes that the poem's lascivious sections 'exist to appeal to the licentious reader' ('"Lewd Priapians" and Renaissance Pornography', *Studies in English Literature*, 12 (1972), 157–72, pp. 168, 170).

7 Rochester, *Complete Poems and Plays*, ed. Paddy Lyons (London, 1993), p. 50. For a poem on a similar event but described from the female perspective, see Aphra Behn's 'The Disappointment' (*Oroonoko, The Rover and Other Works*, ed. Janet Todd (Harmondsworth, 1992), pp. 331–5). This poem, long thought to be by Rochester, was published along with 'The Imperfect Enjoyment' in his *Poems on Several Occasions* in 1680.

of self-loathing. Rochester's *The Farce of Sodom* alike is racked by instances of masculine inadequacy. Like that of Nashe's narrator, Prickett's premature ejaculation is followed by a desire to sleep – 'I've spent my last, and would fain retire, / To sleep an hour' (2.1.122–3) – but this time, instead of ministering to his ailing manhood, the girls (one of whom with an egregiously Rochesteresque twist, is his own sister) are resigned to his ineptitude: 'You see his spirits with our hopes are fled. / Though he be living, he's as bad as dead' (lines 127–8) and the stage direction reads '*Exeunt, leading him mournfully.*' Buggeranthus contrasts the insatiable longing of Cuntigratia with his own impotence: 'Your menstr'ous blood does all your veins supply / With unexhausted lechery, whilst I / Like a decrepit lecher, must retire, / With prick too weak to act what I desire' (3.1.50–3). In this alarming world of female rampancy, even a dildo is inadequate: 'This dildo by a handful is too short . . . Short dildos leave the pleasure half begun' (1.2.70–4).

In the case of the Nashe poem then, the (male) reader is drawn to / into the foreplay of Francis as a willing spectator / participant even if, in order to get there, he has to admit that he has occasionally experienced the same debilitating misfortune. The twisted misanthropy of Rochester's narrator, on the other hand (which is writ large in *Sodom*) compels the reader to differentiate himself from this socially and, more centrally, sexually dysfunctional individual, to register himself as separate from this incorrigible cynicism. Nashe's narration appeals to and binds together a male readership; Rochester's fulminates on masculine deficiency and urges its reader to distance himself from the narrative voice.

In Shakespeare's *Venus and Adonis* we have the nearest thing to a happy medium. Tonally the poem partakes both of Nashe's sexual comedy, dealing as it does with the vagaries of lust and the apparent absurdities of desire while, in its later stages in particular, it adumbrates Rochester's post-Restoration neuroses with de-

spondency, tragedy and failure. Shakespeare's poem ends in death and impotence, the comfort of the early comic scenes of failed seduction having been punctured by the horrid violence of Adonis' ghastly death and Venus' grief-stricken retirement. But what it shares with both Nashe's and Rochester's poems is its paradoxically tantalizing and alarming prospect of a seductive and authoritative woman, a dominatrix, a 'woman on top'.[8] As Barry Pegg's unabashed assertion puts it, 'One of the first things that is likely to strike the reader, as it has struck most critics, is how *sexy* Venus is. Few classes in Renaissance English poetry can be visited by [such] a sex-symbol'.[9] The figure of the sexually demanding woman, in these cases, is both a standard comic caricature and a threat. On the one hand, female sexual expectation need not be taken seriously, its genuine demands can be defused by the mechanisms of patriarchy and rendered laughable. On the other hand, such a predatory appetite threatens to invert the patterns of male supremacy and female submission upon which a society like that of early modern England is predicated.

Such a complicated amalgam of comedy and threat is Chaucer's Wife of Bath. She candidly acknowledges her own sexual appetites and the manner in which they draw her to a man half her age:

> He was, I trowe, twenty wynter oold,
> And I was fourty, if I shal seye sooth;
> But yet I hadde alwey a coltes tooth.

---

[8] Much of what follows relies upon the assumption of the ubiquity of a (juvenile) male fantasy about being sexually initiated by an 'older woman'. While Katherine Duncan-Jones's discussion of the poem deploys the same assumption, it is, for her, distinctly transatlantic: 'many American male sexual fantasies focus on powerful, sexually dominating women, and "Oedipal" unions'. ('Much Ado with Red and White: The Earliest Readers of Shakespeare's *Venus and Adonis* (1593)', *Review of English Studies*, 44 (1993), 479–501, p. 501.)

[9] Barry Pegg, 'Generation and Corruption in Shakespeare's *Venus and Adonis*', *Michigan Academician*, 8 (1975), 105–15, p. 107.

Gat-tothed I was, and that bicam me weel;
I hadde the prente of seinte Venus seel.
As help me God, I was a lusty oon,
And faire, and riche, and yong, and wel bigon,
And trewely, as myne housbondes tolde me,
I hadde the beste *quoniam* myghte be.

(lines 600–8)[10]

Such public declaration of sexual appetite is at once comical, including as it does the mock fatalism of her physiognomy (a gap between the front teeth indicated a lecherous disposition), and dangerously subversive (the Wife admits elsewhere how she would render or withhold sexual favours in exchange for new clothes and other trinkets). The Wife is able to indulge or deny her husbands as she chooses and thus occupies a position of sexual autonomy wholly in defiance of the Pauline doctrines which both exhort and extort wifely obedience. The necessity of bringing such froward women into line is seen at its most unpalatable in plays like *The Taming of the Shrew* wherein Katherine is reified into the concrete possessions of a capitalist economy:

I will be master of what is mine own.
She is my goods, my chattels. She is my house,
My household-stuff, my field, my barn,
My horse, my ox, my ass, my anything,
And here she stands, touch her whoever dare.

(3.3.101–5)

Katherine's final submission ensures that the presiding social structures are finally reinforced; such comical insubordination can only ever be temporary. In the case of the Wife of Bath, however, she retains the much sought for 'maistrie' – she 'wears the trousers' – though she adds that she was 'to hym as kynde / As any wyf from Denmark unto Ynde' (lines 823–4). Nonetheless, she possesses a good deal more authority in their relationship than the tamed shrew who, at the end of the play, publicly abases herself by placing her hand beneath her husband's foot.

The Venus of Shakespeare's poem is a version of Francis and Alisoun. Although her age is unspecified, as befits a goddess, the poem seems to construct her as a predatory 'older woman'. In addition, her physical superiority to the wimpish Adonis makes her a version of the sexually demanding woman that Rochester's speaker finds so threatening.[11] Her kinship with Alisoun is clear in the Wife's acknowledgement of the goddess's astrological influence: 'For certes, I am al Venerien / In feelynge, and myn herte is Marcien. / Venus me yaf my lust, my likerousnesse, / And Mars yaf me my sturdy hardynesse' (lines 609–12). The combination of love and martial stamina in the union of Venus and Mars represented the kind of golden mean that appealed to a neoplatonic period hungry for evidence of cosmological harmony. For example, Pico della Mirandola noted in his *On the General Nature of Beauty* that 'according to the ancient astrologers, whose opinion Plato and Aristotle follow . . . Venus was placed in the centre of heaven next to Mars, because she must tame his impulse which is by nature destructive and corrupting'.[12] It is during her attempted seduction of Adonis that Venus recalls her affair with the god of war:

'I have been wooed as I entreat thee now
Even by the stern and direful god of war,
Whose sinewy neck in battle ne'er did bow,
Who conquers where he comes in every jar.
Yet hath he been my captive and my slave,
And begged for that which thou unasked shalt
  have.

'Over my altars hath he hung his lance,
His battered shield, his uncontrollèd crest,
And for my sake hath learned to sport and dance,
To toy, to wanton, dally, smile, and jest,
Scorning his churlish drum and ensign red,
Making my arms his field, his tent my bed.

'Thus he that over-ruled I overswayed,

---

10 *The Riverside Chaucer*, ed. Larry D. Benson *et al.* (Oxford, 1988), p. 113.
11 For further versions of this misogynous anxiety see, for instance, 'A Letter fancied from Artemisa in the Town to Chloe in the Country', lines 226–51, and 'A Ramble in St James's Park', lines 83–142 (pp. 21–2 and 48–9).
12 Cited in Edgar Wind, *Pagan Mysteries in the Renaissance* (Oxford, 1980), p. 89.

Leading him prisoner in a red-rose chain.
Strong-tempered steel his stronger strength
 obeyed,
Yet was he servile to my coy disdain.
O, be not proud, nor brag not of thy might,
For mast'ring her that foiled the god of fight.

(lines 97–114)

Botticelli's *Mars and Venus* captures the supine exhaustion of the god of war. Above his naked, sleeping form, satyrs toy with his phallic lance and helmet while Venus sits erect, gazing across to Mars, dressed and fully in command. The episode looks forward to the moment in *Antony and Cleopatra* in which, following a night of drunken debauchery, the empress attires her lover in her own clothes and straps on 'his sword Philippan' (2.5.23). In both cases sexual congress is a kind of conquest. But the over-whelming of the god of war (and his incarnation, Antony) represents an out-Marsing of Mars; this is not the *discordia concors* of which Pico writes, but rather the 'distortion of the image of harmony into one of inequality. Here concupiscence *rules*.'[13] This masochistic subjugation may be good news for the warrior Antony but unsurprisingly it only alarms the *petit* and timid Adonis. If the poem is to succeed in its appeal, its narration must cast the reader in the role of an Antony rather than an Adonis. Unsurprisingly, of the two roles – the macho and the wimp – the former is the preferable, but an indication of how wildly inappropriate a reading of the poem would be, were one to side with Adonis, is provided by the uncharacteristic misprision of C. S. Lewis. Perhaps prudishness should be blamed for his obtuse response which perversely misses the point of the narrative's fantasy of the dominant woman:

Venus and Adonis reads well in quotation, but I have never read it through without feeling that I am being suffocated. I cannot forgive Shakespeare for telling us how Venus perspired (175), how 'soft and plump' she was, how moist her hand, how Adonis pants in her face, and so forth. I cannot conceive why he made her not only so emphatically older but even so much larger than the unfortunate young man. She is so large that she can throw the horse's rein over one arm and tuck the 'tender boy' under the other. She 'governs him in strength' and knows her own business so badly that she threatens, almost in her first words, to 'smother' him with kisses. The word 'smother,' combined with these images of female bulk and strength, is fatal: I am irresistibly reminded of some unfortunate child's efforts to escape the voluminous embraces of an effusive female relative . . . Shakespeare shows us far too much of Venus' passion as it would appear to a third party, a spectator – embarrassed, disgusted, and even horrified as any spectator of such a scene would necessarily be.[14]

Lewis's 'horrified' response is a retreat from the raw physicality detailed by the corporeal descriptions of the goddess. It is not that Antony and Adonis see different things; it is rather that Antony (the reader) and Adonis (Lewis) respond differently to the same woman: a Venus who is Rubenesque, dominant and sexually demanding. What for the former is thrilling is, for the latter, dreadful.[15]

---

13 Donald G. Watson, 'The Contrarieties of *Venus and Adonis*', *Studies in Philology*, 75 (1978), 32–63, p. 35.

14 C. S. Lewis, 'Hero and Leander', in *Elizabethan Poetry: Modern Essays in Criticism*, ed. Paul J. Alpers (Oxford, 1967), 235–50, pp. 236–7. Like Lewis a number of critics belittle Venus. Don Cameron Allen calls her 'Shakespeare's finished caricature of the frustrate lady, flushed and sweating [and] a fluttery and apprehensive Doll Tearsheet of forty' ('On *Venus and Adonis*', in *Elizabethan and Jacobean Studies Presented to Frank Percy Wilson* (Oxford, 1959), 100–11, pp. 100, 111). J. W. Lever (writing probably with Lewis and Allen in mind) is even less flattering: 'Shakespeare, it would seem, viewed her as thoroughly absurd, a fat white woman whom nobody loved. Forty years old, fluttery and apprehensive, loquacious and perspiring: such is the impression which the heroine of his first poem has made upon several distinguished scholar-critics' ('Venus and the Second Chance', *Shakespeare Survey 15* (1962), 81–8, p. 81).

15 Incidentally, it is a female critic who sensuously identifies Venus' voluptuousness: '*Venus and Adonis* is a great work of release, an assertion of natural energies. . . . the emancipation of the flesh' (Muriel C. Bradbrook, 'Beasts and Gods: Greene's *Groats-Worth of Witte* and the Social Purpose of *Venus and Adonis*', *Shakespeare Survey 15* (1962), pp. 62–72, p. 70).

The fear of Adonis (Lewis) is exacerbated by the tangible physicality of the goddess – her fleshiness – and this is achieved, in part, by the virtual absence of the narrator as an intrusive presence in the poem. Whereas Nashe's and Rochester's narrators took the leading roles in their own pornographic scenarios, the narrator of *Venus and Adonis* allows the reader intimate contact with the goddess without getting in the way. For Coleridge the physical presence of both the poem's settings and characters was symptomatic of this narrative distance or, as he called it, 'the utter *aloofness* of the poet's own feelings from those of which he is at once the painter and the analyst'.[16] He writes that Shakespeare's 'Venus and Adonis seem at once the characters themselves . . . You seem to be *told* nothing, but to see and hear everything.'[17] This almost-tactile materiality is both the source of erotic excitement and anxiety in the male, heterosexual reader and Adonis respectively: 'My flesh is soft and plump, my marrow burning' (line 142). This bodily presence works in tandem with the poem's more mythical and allegorical fictions to manipulate the reader into a state of sexual arousal.

Following her account of the subjection of the god of war, Venus encourages Adonis to enjoy her: 'Be bold to play – our sport is not in sight' (line 124). What she omits to tell Adonis (and any of Shakespeare's contemporary readers, familiar with the *Metamorphoses*, would have been struck by such an omission) was that her congress with Mars took place in front of a packed house. Ovid tells how Phoebus, the sun god, informed Vulcan, the blacksmith, that his wife, Venus, was planning a tryst with Mars. Arthur Golding translates the episode thus:

> It is reported that this God did first of all espie,
> (For euery thing in heauen and earth is open too his eye)
> How *Venus* with the warlike *Mars* aduoutrie did commit.
> It grieued him to see the fact and so discouered it.
> He shewed her husband *Junos* sonne th' aduoutrie and the place

> In which this priuie scape was done. Who was in such a case
> That heart and hand and all did fayle in working for a space.
> Anon he featly fordge[d] a net of Wire so fine and slight,
> That neither knot nor nooze therein apparant was to sight.
> This piece of worke was much more fine then any hand-warpe woofe,
> Or that whereby the Spider hangs in sliding from the roofe.
> And furthermore the suttlenesse and slight thereof was such,
> It followed euery little pull and closde with euery touch.
> And so he set it handsomely about the haunted couch.
> Now when that *Venus* and her mate were met in bed togither,
> Her husband by his new-found snare before conueyed thither
> Did snarle them both together fast in middes of all their play,
> And setting ope the Iuorie doores, cald all the Gods straight way
> To see them: they with shame ynough fast lockt together lay.
> A certaine God among the rest disposed for to sport,
> Did wish that he himselfe also were shamed in that sort.
> The resdue laught, and so in heauen there was no talke a while,
> But of this Pageant how the Smith the louers did beguile.[18]

Venus and Adonis signals its debt to the *Metamorphoses* by having Titan, the sun god, wish that he were in Adonis' place 'by Venus' side' (line 180) just as the unidentified 'certaine God' (line 225) in Golding wishes he were in Mars'

[16] Coleridge, *Biographia Literaria*, ed. George Watson (London, 1956), p. 177.
[17] *Ibid.*, p. 177.
[18] *The. XV. Bookes of P. Ouidius Naso, Entituled, Metamorphosis. Translated out of Latine into English Meeter, by Arthur Golding, Gentle-man. A Worke very pleasant and delectable* (London, 1603), pp. 45r–45v.

place. The dreadful embarrassment of sexual display reduces the gods to laughter; sexuality is about indignity. The episode insists on the inherent absurdity of the sex act with its postures so ridiculous that Mercutio can refer to 'this drivelling love . . . that runs lolling up and down to hide his bauble in a hole' (*Romeo and Juliet*, 2.3.84).[19] Venus' account of her conquest of Mars, then, is silent on their discovery and humiliation yet the poem nudges its reader to remember Vulcan's trap when it commands him to 'Look how a bird lies tangled in a net, / So fastened in her arms Adonis lies' (lines 67–8).

As Ben Jonson's Volpone attempts to seduce the unyielding Celia, he too assures her of the privacy that they enjoy:

> Come, my Celia, let us prove,
> While we can, the sports of love;
> . . .
> Cannot we delude the eyes
> Of a few poor household spies?
> Or his easier ears beguile,
> Thus removèd by our wile?
> 'Tis no sin love's fruits to steal,
> But the sweet thefts to reveal:
> To be taken, to be seen,
> These have crimes accounted been.
>
> $(3.7.166–83)^{20}$

Ironically, the playwright has gone to some trouble to ensure that Bonario is hidden on stage ready to burst in and prevent Celia's rape (which he does at line 267). Like Venus, Volpone is urging sexual congress on the grounds that no one is watching, unaware that he is the subject of Bonario's secret surveillance. Both moments chime with the episode in Eden when the fallen Adam and Eve attempt to hide from God:

And the LORD God called vnto Adam, and said vnto him, Where *art* thou? And he said, I heard thy voice in the garden: and I was afraid, because I *was* naked, and I hid my selfe. And he said, Who told thee, that thou *wast* naked? Hast thou eaten of the tree, whereof I commanded thee, that thou shouldest not eate? (Genesis, 3.9–11)

Their embarrassment proves their guilt. Volpone unwittingly draws attention to this biblical parallel at ' 'Tis no sin love's fruits to steal' which resonates with the fruit of that forbidden tree. With similar recklessness, Venus undermines her rhetoric of seduction by reminding us of the snake in the grass: 'Here come and sit where never serpent hisses; / And, being sat, I'll smother thee with kisses' (lines 17–18). The strong sibilance – 'sat', 'smother' – and rhyme – 'hisses', 'kisses' – make her not only a version of Eve, but an embodiment of the Satanic viper itself. Both classically, then, in the myth of Mars and Venus, and biblically, in the story of Adam and Eve, such temptation is literally overseen. Of course for the narrator and his narratee *the whole point* of the seduction is that it be observed; that is what scopophilia is all about. Without an audience, pornography is just private sex and no sponsorship deals that way lie. Shakespeare's dedication relies on the congruency of voyeurism and arousal: 'I leave it to your honourable *survey*, and your honour to your heart's content' (my emphasis).

Shakespeare's poem relishes the erotic wrestling of Venus and Adonis, her clumsy groping and his nervous dodging. Variously we see the goddess carrying him off, tucked under her arm like a screaming kid in a supermarket, we see her press him to the floor and roll him on top of her. Images of bondage (she has already referred to Mars as 'my captive and my slave . . . in a red-rose chain'), of reins, of folding arms and clasping hands terrify Adonis at the same time as they thrill the reader (lines 40, 101, 110, 226, 264, 392, 579, 812 etc.). Even the landscape clutches and caresses (lines 705, 872–4, 924). Yet buried in these moments of titillation are hints of a more dangerous kind.

As they kiss goodnight they 'fall to the earth' (line 546) and later, as she seizes him and rolls backwards, 'He on her belly falls, she on her back' (line 594).[21] As in Ralegh's reply to Marlowe's 'Come live with me, and be my love' or Marvell's 'The Garden', 'fall' here resounds with Edenic overtones.[22] As Adonis takes his leave he is anxious that it being dark, 'going I shall fall' (line 719), and this crepuscular wobbliness casts a threatening shadow over his masculine bravado. Yet this subtextual apprehension is allowed to coexist alongside the sexual euphoria without marring it. The poem maintains a delicate balance between the kinds of rough comedy personified by the Wife of Bath and made explicit in 'Nashe's Dildo', and the distrustful cynicism represented in Rochester. As John Klause puts it, 'The voice of comic and sometimes critical irony is resilient, able to coexist on its own terms with the swelling tones of pity, even to the end.'[23] How else could we cope with such a rapid transference between the arousing mud wrestling of the two protagonists and such sombre sentiments as 'What is thy body but a swallowing grave' (line 757)?

The vehemence of the *carpe florem* imagery is a function not just of a tried and tested seduction technique, but an intensely consumptive obsession with the imminence of extinction and even putrefaction. The couple's first physical contact involves Venus 'pluck[ing] him from his horse' (line 30) and the significance of the verb burgeons with the floral imagery of the poem. As Venus takes the flower-transmuted Adonis away with her to Paphos, the reader relishes the final climax of nestling between her breasts, yet even she acknowledges that this state of ecstasy must be short-lived for she has 'crop[ped] the stalk' and the flower will of necessity 'wither in my breast' (lines 1175–82). Golding's Ovid too is insistent on the brevity of floral vitality, 'Howbeit the vse of them [flowers] is short. / For why the leaves do hang so loose through lightnesse in such sort, / As that the windes that all things pierce, with

euerie little blast / Do shake them off, and shed them so, as that they cannot last.'[24] George Sandys in his 1632 commentary on Ovid agreed with this, reading Adonis' floral metamorphosis allegorically as an expression of 'the fraile condition and short continuance of Beautie'.[25] On the morning after Juliet's feigned death, Capulet informs Paris of her untimely plucking: 'O son, the night before thy wedding day / Hath death lain with thy wife. See, there she lies, / Flower as she was, deflowerèd by him' (4.4.62–4). In the poem, following the death of Adonis, Venus insists that all future love shall 'Bud, and be blasted, in a breathing-while' (line 1142).

Venus and Adonis is both a riotous male fantasy of being seduced by the goddess of love and a deeper interrogation of Ralegh's overwhelming question, 'What is our life?'[26] On this level it probes the same nebulous profundities as the Sonnets – doubts about progeny, about art outliving life and about the indiscriminateness and hopelessness of love, love between a mortal boy and an immortal goddess which, in the relationship of Bottom and Titania is a vehicle for obscene humour, but which, in the attraction of Venus to Adonis is 'begotten by despair / Upon Impos-

---

21 Shakespeare's use of the term 'belly' again highlights an analogy between the goddess and the Edenic snake who is cursed by God in the following terms: 'upon thy belly shalt thou go' (Genesis, 3.14).

22 Ralegh puns on *fall* meaning both 'autumn' (as in modern American) and The Fall when he talks of 'fancy's spring, but sorrow's fall' (*Silver Poets of the Sixteenth Century*, ed. Gerald Bullett (London, 1947), p. 285). Marvell's Edenic hedonism collapses under its own sensual weight: 'Stumbling on Melons, as I pass, / Insnar'd with Flow'rs, I fall on Grass' (Andrew Marvell, *The Poems*, ed. Hugh MacDonald (London, 1956), p. 52).

23 John Klause, '*Venus and Adonis*: Can We Forgive Them?', *Studies in Philology*, 85 (1988), 353–77, p. 368.

24 Golding, *Metamorphosis*, p. 130v.

25 George Sandys, *Ovids Metamorphosis Englished, Mythologized, and Represented in Figures*, ed. Karl K. Hully and Stanley T. Vandersall (Lincoln, Nebr., 1970), p. 493.

26 *Silver Poets of the Sixteenth Century*, p. 296.

sibility'.[27] The poem enjoys a calm resolution but its resolve is fragile and barren, and it is for this reason that Jonathan Bate can describe *Venus and Adonis* as 'a celebration of sexuality even as it is a disturbing exposure of the dark underside of desire'.[28] It is this 'dark underside' which is (in the story of the poem) the final bitter bequest of the exiting goddess. Since her love remains unconsummated, she prophesies 'Sorrow on love hereafter' (line 1136). It shall be racked with jealousy, 'fickle, false, and full of fraud . . . raging-mad, and silly-mild' (lines 1141–51). At its worst, anticipating the fall of Troy, 'It shall be cause of war and dire events' (line 1159). With a petulance characteristic of the worst moments of Adonis' puerile narcissism, she denies to all subsequent lovers the state of satisfaction that was denied her by the boar's intervention. The ending of the poem then is riven with ambiguity. On the one hand it enjoys the transcendental calm of Venus cutting the clouds noiselessly towards Paphos. On the other, its very quiet is a symptom of its sullen disappointment. As Coppélia Kahn notices, there is a fearful symmetry in each of the protagonists being satisfied on one count and frustrated on another: 'Venus loses her lover to the boar, but wins symbolic possession of him as a flower. Adonis successfully fights off Venus' sexual demands, but surrenders to her all-embracing love after death.'[29]

The idea of gain and loss, of an emotional exchange, of possession, surrender and ultimately of complete and mutual self-abrogation is a customary, even hackneyed, way of describing love in the literature of the period. In Shakespeare's Sonnet 10, for instance, love is nothing less than the exchange of identities: 'Make thee another self for love of me' (line 13). The replica of self, of course, refers here to the offspring that the sonneteer demands of the loved one, but the line also hints at a mutual exchange that love confers. In Sonnet 135 this interchange of identities is specifically genital: 'So thou, being rich in Will, add to thy Will / One will of mine to make thy large Will more'

(lines 11–12). Like a pair of Shakespearian twins, lovers swap places and assume each other's persona: 'Do I stand there?' (*Twelfth Night*, 5.1.224). Often, in Renaissance literature, this exchange takes place in terms of twisting eye beams or mutual reflection: 'My face in thine eye, thine in mine appears.'[30] Unsurprisingly, therefore, in *Venus and Adonis* this idea is rehearsed against the backdrop of the Narcissus myth in which mirroring is an index of self-absorption. It is Venus' job, as the wooer, to wean Adonis off self-love and to persuade him to surrender his self to her. Losing her patience, she challenges him to acknowledge the solipsism of his vanity, 'Is thine own heart to thine own face affected?' (line 157), before going on to point out the lethal consequences of such egotistical fascination, 'Narcissus so himself himself forsook, / And died to kiss his shadow in the brook' (lines 161–2). The moral is clear: love involves submission and surrender of the self to another. It is this that enables Venus to equate meagreness in love and self-love so readily; in the same breath she mocks both 'Love-lacking vestals and self-loving nuns' (line 752). This kind of barren self-love had already been devastatingly dramatized by Shakespeare in a play probably first performed in the same year as the publication of *Venus and Adonis*. On the eve of the battle of Bosworth, Richard III ponders his own schizophrenic evil:

> What do I fear? Myself? There's none else by.
> Richard loves Richard; that is, I am I.
> Is there a murderer here? No. Yes, I am.
> Then fly! What, from myself? Great reason. Why?
> Lest I revenge. Myself upon myself?
> Alack, I love myself. Wherefore? For any good
> That I myself have done unto myself?

---

27 Marvell, 'The Definition of Love', lines 3–4.
28 Jonathan Bate, 'Sexual Perversity in *Venus and Adonis*', *Yearbook of English Studies*, 23 (1993), 80–92, p. 92.
29 Coppélia Kahn, 'Self and Eros in *Venus and Adonis*', *The Centennial Review*, 20 (1976), 351–71, p. 371.
30 'The Good Morrow', line 15. *John Donne*, ed. John Carey (Oxford, 1990), p. 90.

O no, alas, I rather hate myself
For hateful deeds committed by myself.
I am a villain. Yet I lie: I am not.
. . .
There is no creature loves me,
And if I die no soul will pity me.
Nay, wherefore should they? – Since that I myself
Find in myself no pity to myself.   (5.5.136–57)

The tortured attempt to assert self-love and self-respect is flawed by the insistently fractured speaker. Richard is both grammatical subject and object of his own language even as he is both individual subject and object of his own desire. But what makes him autonomous also makes him lonely; his independence is an index of his isolation – 'There is no creature loves me' (line 154). Fifty lines later, as he rallies his troops, Richmond's co-operative spirit could not be more blatantly contrastive: 'if I thrive, to gain of my attempt, / The least of you shall share his part thereof' (lines 221–2). As Venus recounts the Orphic empathies between Adonis and the creatures that surrounded him, she notes plangently that fish would gild his reflection with their scales: 'When he beheld his shadow in the brook, / The fishes spread on it their golden gills' (lines 1099–100). It is as though nature has, albeit temporarily, communed with Adonis' beauty. The repeated pronoun which characterizes the vanity of Narcissus ('himself himself forsook') demonstrates grammatically the youth's self-regard and so when Venus chastises Adonis for his refusal to reproduce himself through her, the grammar (as in the example from *Richard III* above) becomes folded in on itself: 'So in thyself thyself art made away' (line 763). After his death, it is with fitting and devastating poignancy that his dead eyes no longer throw back her own reflection: 'Two glasses, where herself herself beheld / A thousand times, and now no more reflect, / Their virtue lost' (lines 1129–31). These internal resonances are a kind of poetic onanism, self-regarding and ultimately sterile; they lead nowhere but turn back on themselves.

The poem captures Venus' sexual frustration by toying with this linguistic masturbation, 'She's Love; she loves; and yet she is not loved' (line 610), while Adonis himself cruelly taunts her with a mockery of her entreaties which shares this sense of language as being circular and therefore ineffective: 'My love to love is love but to disgrace it' (line 412). This is a flirtatious, teasing language, a discourse that repudiates intercourse, an unfulfilling jargon, the aim of which is to turn vital physicality into petrified rhetoric. For Pauline Kiernan, the futility of love's oration in the poem is not just a symptom of Adonis' sexual reluctance, but actually has its origins in the rhetoric of seduction itself, a rhetoric which, she argues, Shakespeare is attacking:

Shakespeare in this poem writes about the form he writes in in order to make an implied criticism of the way the poetic written word turns everything which has life, warmth and movement in its immediate presence into an iconographical stasis, irretrievably lost to the present. Adonis' life, in Venus' hands, becomes a dead, literary image so that the only progeny he will be capable of begetting is sterile rhetorical tropes.[31]

The language of love *beyond* the poem is shown *by* the poem to be corrupt in this way. Adonis rejects Venus' suit on the grounds that her seduction speeches have been used on all and sundry, 'I hate not love, but your device in love, / That lends embracements unto every stranger' (lines 789–90). Yet, in a moment of embarrassed self-consciousness the reader registers himself as one of these 'stranger[s]' who is both origin and destination of the language of love – a language that is both intimate and private while being, simultaneously, conventional and public: the sentence 'I love you' must be the most heavily quoted utterance of all time.[32]

35

In *Venus and Adonis* the necessity of deferring the sexual act is of course essential in order to maintain the poem's erotic narrative. Narration is thus a device for prolonging arousal while it defers climax. After all, were sexual union to be achieved, the reader, like the narrator of Nashe's poem, cited above, would turn over and go to sleep. In *Venus and Adonis* therefore rhetoric is a kind of linguistic foreplay, both a means of exciting *and* deliberately frustrating the reader. This *jouissance* can be readily seen in the poem's insinuations surrounding the couple's physical contact. With almost schoolboy suggestiveness the poem describes Adonis as 'All swoll'n with chafing' (line 325) and the word reappears as he attempts to resuscitate the fainting goddess, 'He chafes her lips' (line 477) where the labial insinuation is only thinly masked. The risqué connotations of 'chafe' are obvious when we recall Francis's manipulative prowess with the wilting manhood of the narrator of 'Nashe's Dildo': 'Com, lett me rubb and chafe it with my hand' (line 132). With trenchant irony, the word reappears in *Venus and Adonis* linked to the agent of Adonis' death: in her vision of the hunt, Venus imagines 'The picture of an angry chafing boar' (line 662). But this chafing is unable to arouse; in an image of floral impotence, the blood drawn by the boar 'upon the fresh flowers being shed / Doth make them droop with grief, and hang the head' (lines 665–6). The post-orgasmic exhaustion from which Nashe's narrator recovered and against which Rochester's railed, has deadened Adonis too, for there is no doubt that the union of the hunter and the hunted is a kind of sexual congress.

For Shakespeare the boar seems always to have acted as a figure of violent sexual malevolence. For instance, in the earlier plays, the 'boar with bristled hair' is one of the prospective sexual partners Oberon wishes on the bewitched Titania when she wakes under the influence of his love charm (2.2.37). There is something uncannily appropriate about the association of the animal with the sexually pre-

datory Richard III (though the association is, of course, heraldic), and Aaron describes his own penchant for savagery by likening himself to 'The chafèd boar' (*Titus Andronicus*, 4.2.137). Near the end of the playwright's career, in *Cymbeline*, Posthumus imagines the lascivious Giacomo covering his yielding wife: 'Perchance he spoke not, but / Like a full-acorned boar, a German one, / Cried 'O!' and mounted' (2.5.15–17). In *Venus and Adonis* the boar, we are told, 'trenched [his tusk] / In [Adonis'] soft flank' (lines 1052–3) and the consequent bleeding is figured as a kind of hymeneal wounding: the 'wonted lily-white / With purple tears that his wound wept was drenched. / No flower was nigh, no grass, herb, leaf, or weed, / But stole his blood, and seemed with him to bleed' (lines 1053–6). The word 'flower', with its early modern resonances of vaginal bleeding, reinforces this wounding as a version of a sexual rite of passage.[33] Ten stanzas later the contact is explicitly sexualized. The boar, we are told, 'by a kiss thought to persuade

---

love you madly', because he knows that she knows (and that she knows that he knows) that these words have already been written by Barbara Cartland' ('Postmodernism, Irony, the Enjoyable', in *Modernism / Postmodernism*, ed. Peter Brooker (London, 1992), pp. 225–8, p. 227).

33 William Whately uses the word, *flowers*, as he proscribes intercourse during menstruation: 'this redundant humour (called their flowers or terms) hath (if no conception be) its monthly issue or evacuation . . . Now in all these . . . times and occasions, it is simply unlawful for a man to company with his own wife' (*A bride bush* (London, 1617), in *Renaissance Woman: Constructions of Femininity in England*, ed. Kate Aughterson (London, 1995), p. 35). Unsurprisingly, this is a taboo which Rochester relishes: 'By all love's soft, yet mighty powers, / It is a thing unfit, / That men should fuck in time of flowers, / Or when the smock's beshit' (*Complete Poems and Plays*, p. 34). Thomas Heywood in *The Brazen Age* (1613) attributes menstrual bleeding to Venus' lament following the death of Adonis: 'But thy liues bloud I'le turne into a flower, / And every Month in sollemne rights deplore / This beauteous *Greeke* slaine by *Dianaes* Boare' (cited by Duncan-Jones, 'Much Ado with Red and White', p. 496).

him there, / And, nuzzling in his flank, the loving swine / Sheathed unaware the tusk in his soft groin' (lines 1114–16). The equivalence of sex and murder is forged by a correspondence between Venus and the hog. At one point, she is described with the kind of untamed craving that verges on the bestial:

> And, having felt the sweetness of the spoil,
> With blindfold fury she begins to forage.
> Her face doth reek and smoke, her blood doth
>   boil,
> And careless lust stirs up a desperate courage,
> Planting oblivion, beating reason back,
> Forgetting shame's pure blush and honour's
>   wrack.   (lines 553–8)

The idea of Venus 'forag[ing]' for Adonis, looks forward to the image of the boar turning over the earth with his foraging snout (lines 622, 636). The parallel between hog and goddess is elaborated upon by Venus who exculpates the boar from blame on the grounds that, given half the chance, she would have behaved just the same: 'Had I been toothed like him, I must confess / With kissing him I should have killed him first' (lines 1117–18) where the kiss is both a fulfilment of desire and a Judas-like murder.[34] Golding's version of the carnage is even more explicitly phallic, the location of the fatal injury even more specifically testicular: the boar 'hiding in his cods, his tuskes as farre as he could thrust'.[35] The shedding of Adonis' seed at the same time as his blood is testified by the mixture of sperm and gore that lace the boar's jaws; his 'frothy mouth, bepainted all with red, / Like milk and blood being mingled both together' (lines 901–2).[36] The colours of white and red, the lily and the rose, with which Adonis is repeatedly identified (lines 3, 10, 21, 36, 346, 451, 506, 516, etc.) here take on a horrific resonance. The episode seems to insist, with Rochester-like disgust, on the destructiveness of sex, its capacities to destroy and devastate. For all its flirtatious promise, *Venus and Adonis* ends with perdition. Consummation may only be wished for; once that wish is granted, disaster will follow.

It is in Sonnet 129 that Shakespeare, at his most Rochester-like, remarks on the vanity of sexual congress at the same time as registering its irresistible appeal:

> Th' expense of spirit in a waste of shame
> Is lust in action; and till action, lust
> Is perjured, murd'rous, bloody, full of blame,
> Savage, extreme, rude, cruel, not to trust,
> Enjoyed no sooner but despisèd straight,
> Past reason hunted, and no sooner had
> Past reason hated as a swallowed bait
> On purpose laid to make the taker mad;
> Mad in pursuit and in possession so,
> Had, having, and in quest to have, extreme;
> A bliss in proof and proved, a very woe;
> Before, a joy proposed; behind, a dream.
> All this the world well knows, yet none knows
>   well
> To shun the heaven that leads men to this hell.

The sonnet demonstrates the overwhelming and all-consuming nature of sexual desire – 'Had, having, and in quest to have' – desire which occupies every waking moment.[37] Yet immediately this desire is indulged, the kinds of self-contempt and despair by which Rochester was so tormented inevitably follow – 'no sooner had / Past reason hated'. The kinds of deferral which invigorate desire are spoken of in *Venus and Adonis* in elemental metaphors of fire and water: 'An oven that is stopped, or river stayed, / Burneth more hotly, swelleth

---

[34] J. W. Lever notes that 'by reversing the usual role of lovers, Shakespeare had made Venus and the Boar into rivals for Adonis' ('The Poems', *Shakespeare Survey 15* (1962), pp. 18–30, p. 21).

[35] Golding, *Metamorphosis*, p. 130r.

[36] According to Pico the birth of Venus was itself a product of a castration: 'Venus could not be born if the testicles of Uranus did not fall into the waters of the sea' (cited in *Pagan Mysteries in the Renaissance*, p. 133).

[37] The ubiquity of desire is hinted at in the poem's mingling of tenses. In the opening stanza Adonis 'hied him to the chase' while three lines later, Venus ''gins to woo him' (lines 3–6). Venus' curse on love is phrased in the future tense (lines 1135–64). She, being a goddess, is above the rags of time that govern dull sublunary lovers.

with more rage' (lines 331–2).[38] The function of denial is, perversely, to intensify arousal because the sorts of exquisite foreplay that Milton refers to as 'sweet reluctant amorous delay' are cut short by full sexual intercourse.[39] The sonnet's closing couplet insists upon the vicious circle that is desire – a mixture of self-knowledge and profound ignorance: 'All this the world well knows, yet none knows well . . .' (line 13). It is this hopeless situation in which Venus is described, 'Now quick desire hath caught the yielding prey, / And glutton-like she feeds, yet never filleth' (lines 547–8). Her desire 'beat[s] reason back' (line 557) in just the same way as lust is described in the sonnet as 'Past reason hunted, and . . . Past reason hated'. Desire, then, is inherently irrational because it can never be fully satisfied and that is why the poem insists on her being unhinged by carnality. In the very first stanza Venus is described as 'Sick-thoughted' (line 5) and later her fervid imaginings seem to result in physical symptoms: 'the lovesick queen began to sweat' (line 175).[40] The closer Adonis gets to the goddess, the more intense is her sense of frustration. Even with Adonis straddling her, 'worse

than Tantalus' is her annoy, / To clip Elysium, and to lack her joy' (lines 599–600). The more phallic her craving, the more fallacious it is shown to be. Finally, then, the narrative logic of *Venus and Adonis* demands that consummation remain devoutly to be wished because its satisfaction must lead perpetually and inexorably to extinction.

---

38 Whereas Venus is associated throughout with moist and warm, the boar is imaged in terms of dry and cold. Thus his element is the earth. Note for example how his snout is always foraging in the earth – 'His snout digs sepulchres where'er he goes' (line 622).

39 *Paradise Lost*, 4.311, in *Complete English Poems, Of Education, Areopagitica*, ed. Gordon Campbell (London, 1990), p. 230.

40 Tita French Baumlin notes the necessity (according to Renaissance medicine) of heating the woman's naturally colder body in order to make it productive but since Venus and Adonis do not copulate let alone produce offspring, this is an unlikely reading of the sweating. ('The Birth of the Bard: *Venus and Adonis* and Poetic Apotheosis', *Papers on Language and Literature*, 26 (1990), 191–211, p. 200). See also, which she cites, Stephen Greenblatt's 'Fiction and Friction', in *Shakespearian Negotiations* (Oxford, 1988), pp. 66–93.

University of Winnipeg, 515 Portage Ave, Winnipeg, Manitoba, Canada

DISCARDED

ECHOES INHABIT A GARDEN:
THE NARRATIVES OF *ROMEO AND JULIET*

JILL L. LEVENSON

Sequences move in counterpoint; functionally, the structure of narrative is fugued: . . .

. . . if there is to be an articulated patterning of representations, there must be a murmur of analogies rising from things, . . .[1]

Despite its origins in Aristotle's exposition of tragedy, recent narrative theory neglects drama. Narratologists refer to *Oedipus the King* and Shakespeare plays for illustrations, assuming artistic mastery of narrative which they rarely demonstrate. In critical literature on Shakespeare and narrative, there are conspicuous gaps between Barbara Hardy's essay on 'Shakespeare's Dramatic Narrative' (1981) and J. Hillis Miller's chapter on *Troilus and Cressida*, 'Ariachne's Broken Woof' (1998).[2] Hardy has done the most to fill out this inquiry, a series of lectures and articles culminating in her book *Shakespeare's Storytellers: Dramatic Narration* (1997). She makes it clear that Shakespeare's interest in narrative extended throughout his career, from *The Rape of Lucrece* and *Titus Andronicus* to *The Winter's Tale* and *The Tempest*: there are explicit signs of this interest in references to other narrators like Virgil, and implicit signs in passages of exaggeration and parody.[3] This essay will extend Hardy's argument through an analysis of narration in *Romeo and Juliet*. She has examined discrete narrative forms within the play; I shall consider additional examples of these, as well as the relation of all inner forms to the narrative whole.[4]

'[B]ut narrative is not a very reasonable

subject', as Frank Kermode observed in writing about it two decades ago;[5] and narratologists have not yet found a single model with which to explain it. When Barthes began to search for a theory he described the obstacles in terms of scope, not only the vastness of the subject but also the wide range of critical strategies available for understanding it.

. . . under [an] almost infinite diversity of forms, narrative is present in every age, in every place, in every society; . . . narrative is international, transhis-

---

1 Roland Barthes, 'Introduction to the Structural Analysis of Narratives', in *Image-Music-Text*, trans. Stephen Heath (New York, 1977), p. 103; Michel Foucault, *The Order of Things: An Archaeology of the Human Sciences*, trans. of *Les Mots et les choses* (New York, 1970), p. 119.

2 Hardy's essay appears in *Papers from the First Nordic Conference for English Studies*, Oslo, 17–19 September 1980, ed. Stig Johansson and Bjørn Tysdahl (Oslo, 1981), pp. 1–17; Miller's chapter is part of his book *Reading Narrative*, Oklahoma Project for Discourse and Theory, vol. 18 (Norman, Okla., 1998), pp. 129–45.

3 See Hardy, 'Shakespeare's Dramatic Narrative', pp. 2–3, and the Introduction and fourth chapter of *Shakespeare's Storytellers* (London and Chester Springs, 1997).

4 In her book Hardy returns more than once to five narrative moments in *Romeo and Juliet*: the Prologue, second Chorus, and conclusion; Juliet's fantasy as she takes the potion in 4.3; and the Nurse's anecdote about Juliet's weaning in 1.3. She also refers to Romeo's dream in 5.1; Juliet's vision of Romeo at the bottom of a tomb in 3.5; Mercutio's Queen Mab speech in 1.4; and Juliet's anticipation of her wedding night in 3.2.

5 *The Genesis of Secrecy: On the Interpretation of Narrative*, The Charles Eliot Norton Lectures, 1977–1978 (London and Cambridge, Mass., 1979), p. 38.

torical, transcultural: it is simply there, like life itself. . . . [The analyst is] faced with the infinity of narratives, the multiplicity of standpoints – historical, psychological, sociological, ethnological, aesthetic, etc. – from which they can be studied, . . .[6]

As critics of narrative continue to examine their subject, they have produced a variety of paradigms and techniques for analysing it. The result is what Leah S. Marcus calls a 'tool box' for literary scholars, an eclectic mix of ideas and methods serviceable for managing unwieldy theses or texts.[7] In what follows I have made ample use of this resource.

Since a number of commentators distinguish between narrative and drama, contrasting diegetic representations with mimesis, it should be established at the start that this analysis makes no such distinction. It operates from the premise that drama is a form of narrative which, like all the other forms, takes shape through a sequence, a series of events connected in temporal and causal relationships.[8] 'Only one kind of thing can be narrated: a time-thing, or to use our normal word for it, an "event" . . . something that happens'.[9] Without succession, these units may be disposed as description, deduction, lyrical moments, or lists.[10] With it, they have an order which determines the deep structure of narrative. Earl Miner defines narrative sequence in the most fundamental terms: 'a central feature . . . derives from our simple sense that of two events not occurring simultaneously one must precede the other'. Generated by the most rudimentary logic, that central feature assumes a form in our minds, 'becoming intelligible, significant, meaningful'.[11] Aristotle gave sequence limits, a beginning and end, which some modern writers have adopted: 'the sequence opens when one of its terms has no solidary antecedent and closes when another of its terms has no consequent'.[12]

If standard definitions of narrative sequence make it sound for the most part linear and elementary, many late twentieth-century redefinitions stress its potential for complication.[13]

In the first place, many narrations are themselves revisions of earlier sequences, repetitions which interpret the originals by reorganizing events, creating fissures, or making additions. 'Always already', claims Jacques Derrida, '[e]verything begins with reproduction'. Kermode makes a similar point by citing the tradition of midrash: 'narrative interpretation of a narrative, a way of finding in an existing narrative the potential of more narrative'.[14] In the second place, structural repetitions of all kinds can interrupt a given series: one or more related sequences, whole or fragmentary, may

[6] 'Introduction to the Structural Analysis of Narratives', pp. 79–80.

[7] 'Renaissance/Early Modern Studies', in Redrawing the Boundaries: The Transformation of English and American Literary Studies, ed. Stephen Greenblatt and Giles Gunn (New York, 1992), p. 51.

[8] Among narratologists, Peter Brooks argues at greatest length for maintaining and using the concept of narrative sequence: see Reading for the Plot: Design and Intention in Narrative (New York, 1984), and Psychoanalysis and Storytelling, The Bucknell Lectures in Literary Theory, 10 (Oxford and Cambridge, Mass., 1994).

[9] Robert Scholes, 'Language, Narrative, and Anti-Narrative', in On Narrative, ed. W. J. T. Mitchell (Chicago and London, 1981), p. 205.

[10] These alternatives are mentioned by Claude Bremond, 'The Logic of Narrative Possibilities', New Literary History, 11 (1980), trans. Elaine D. Cancalon, rpt. Narratology: An Introduction, ed. Susana Onega and José Angel García Landa (London and New York, 1996), pp. 63–4; Brooks, Psychoanalysis and Storytelling, pp. 123–4; and Scholes, 'Language, Narrative, and Anti-Narrative', p. 205.

[11] 'Distributing the Middle: Problems of "Movement" in Narrative Poetry', in To Tell a Story: Narrative Theory and Practice, Papers read at a Clark Library Seminar February 4, 1972, introd. Robert M. Adams (Los Angeles, 1973), pp. 7, 8.

[12] Barthes, 'Introduction to the Structural Analysis of Narratives', p. 101.

[13] Again modern theory may have a source in Aristotle, who construed the middle of narrative sequence pluralistically as several episodes (see Miner, 'Distributing the Middle', pp. 4–5).

[14] Derrida, 'Freud and the Scene of Writing', trans. Jeffrey Mehlman, Yale French Studies, 48 (1972), 92; Kermode, The Genesis of Secrecy, p. xi.

be 'intercalated', 'imbricated', within the main sequence.[15] Each sequence has what Miner calls 'consequences', the effects of 'recognizable rhythms, iterations, parallels, echoes, and the like';[16] each resonates, in all of its frequencies, with the others.

Consequences include not only structural repetitions but linguistic ones, part of narrative's semantic component with its unlimited means to disturb the sequence: rhetorical figures can act as 'silent interpreters, straight-faced in their structural or their subversive force'; single words with more than one referent may supply texts with contradictory subtexts; mnemonic elements and tropes set up unexpected connections between different parts of a sequence.[17] Moreover the design of the whole, sequence and consequences, is never finalized. Because narrative is part of a 'social transaction', a dynamic requiring an audience, each of its parts is always open to new interpretations.[18] Every member of an audience responds differently, the variable effects of culture and temperament: familiarity with the allusions is one determinant, as every component of a narrative refers to something else; and perception of time is another, as it is individually conditioned by memory and expectation.[19] In view of these complexities − each member of every audience producing a new narrative from many components − it is no wonder that theorists are questioning concepts of narrative opening, closure, and linearity. Narratives are 'studded' with interpretations, deliberately put in place by their authors or discovered by members of an audience, and criticism can only begin to detect 'what [they] originally meant and what they originally mean'.[20] With dramatic narratives, the semiotic media of performance add another interpretative dimension: the actor's voice and gestures, visual imagery, non-vocal sound.

The unreasonable subject contains multitudes, and inevitably an analysis of narrative in *Romeo and Juliet* must be a study of narratives, or at least the start of one. In launching what could be a much larger project, the prelimin-

aries will centre on two of the means by which Shakespeare complicates his main sequence: other narratives and diction. They will bring into focus the effects of these strategies on both early versions of *Romeo and Juliet*, the familiar second quarto of 1599 (Q2), just over 3,000 lines, and the usually marginalized first quarto of 1597 (Q1), 2,364 lines. As a critical economy, the analysis will concentrate on the longer version to set up the basis for a comparison.[21]

It will quickly become apparent that *Romeo and Juliet* is constantly preoccupied with its own narration, an account enriched by various stories and fragments of stories. In Hardy's two catalogues − 'psychological and sociological life-forms of narrative' and 'narrative forms of theatre' − there are two dozen entries ranging from memory, fantasy, and report to exposition, summary, and message.[22] All of these are different in kind; most occur in *Romeo and Juliet*. Moreover, there are one or two examples not on the lists, such as Friar Laurence's allegory of weeds and flowers in his first soliloquy (2.2.5−30). I shall consider narrative forms

---

[15] The quoted terms come (respectively) from Kermode, the sixth chapter of *The Genesis of Secrecy*, and Barthes, 'Introduction to the Structural Analysis of Narratives', p. 103.

[16] 'Distributing the Middle', p. 10. See also Miller, *Reading Narrative*, p. 64.

[17] On the interpretative effect of rhetorical figures see Patricia Parker, *Literary Fat Ladies: Rhetoric, Gender, Property* (London and New York, 1987), quotation from p. 94; on mnemonic devices and tropes see Brooks, *Reading for the Plot*, p. 99.

[18] Barbara Herrnstein Smith, who uses the quoted phrase, emphasizes the continuity of narrative with other kinds of discourse ('Narrative Versions, Narrative Theories', in *On Narrative*, ed. Mitchell, pp. 209−32, quotation from p. 228).

[19] On the determinants see Derrida, *Positions* (Paris, 1972), pp. 37−9, and Kermode, *The Sense of an Ending: Studies in the Theory of Fiction* (New York, 1967), p. 46.

[20] Kermode, *The Genesis of Secrecy*, pp. 101, 99, 126.

[21] References to the longer version come from John Jowett's edition in *William Shakespeare: The Complete Works* (Oxford, 1986).

[22] Hardy, *Shakespeare's Storytellers*, pp. 13−14.

which are striking, either because they recur or because their length and elaboration call attention to themselves.

Both original texts of *Romeo and Juliet* adopted their sequences from narrative fiction, the popular version of a story which had circulated in Italy, France, and England through the sixteenth century and which was 'international, transhistorical, transcultural' as Barthes conceived narrative. Originally derived from myth, the early modern fictions took shape from the pressures of the times and places in which they were composed, but they always put the same dozen events in the same order: Romeo's initial, abortive love affair; the Capulet feast, where Romeo and Juliet first encounter each other and immediately become enamoured; the meeting at Juliet's house, when they plan to marry; the carrying out of these plans with the assistance of a friar; the brawl between the Montagues and Capulets which leads to Romeo's banishment; Romeo and Juliet's leave-taking of each other; the Capulets' arrangement for Juliet to marry a man of their choice; Juliet's appeal to the friar for help, resulting in the potion scheme; Juliet's false death, reported to the exiled Romeo as true; the scene in the tomb, where both lovers die; the governor's distribution of justice; and the reconciliation of the two families.[23]

Shakespeare's adjustments of this sequence, particularly his additions and accelerated tempo, have been documented often. Less obvious, his play on and with the series of incidents has yet to be noticed. In Q2 these manoeuvres begin with the Prologue, who pointedly carries out the role of expositor: the introductory sonnet contextualizes the action and delineates the principal characters. Ingeniously the Prologue delivers this compact exposition with a synopsis of the fictional sequence which rearranges the order of events and opens it to new interpretation. As organized here, the series begins with brawling, proceeds to the suicides and reconciliation, and collapses other episodes involving

the protagonists into scattered phrases: 'star-crossed lovers' (line 6), 'misadventured piteous overthrows' (line 7), 'fearful passage of their death-marked love' (line 9). In this telling violence engulfs the love-story.[24]

The Prologue relates the sequence in its first two quatrains; the rest of the sonnet is reiterative. In the sestet, the ninth line turns again to the lovers' story; the tenth and eleventh lines recapitulate the feud and the sacrifice necessary to end it. The well-known fictional sequence, leisurely and circumstantial, allowed for careful rationalizing of each event. With its Prologue the dramatization does away with circumstance and reason, emphasizing the passions which drive the narrative. At the same time it maintains that the narrative it has just summarized, the fiction it will perform, is a collaborative enterprise for audience and actors. It invites the spectators to participate in making the play, by implication a new form of the narrative with every performance.

What the Prologue says destabilizes the established sequence in other ways. As M. M. Mahood has shown, this speech anticipates many others in the text through its word-play: she finds six puns in the ninth line alone.[25] Ambiguities, apparently intentional, unsettle diction from the first line to the last; they add not only nuance but also uncertainty as the verses flicker with more than one meaning. While 'dignity' (line 1) indicates social rank, for

---

23 For the background of the sixteenth-century fiction see 'The Romeo and Juliet Narrative Before Shakespeare', in the Introduction to my edition (Oxford, 2000), pp. 1–15.

24 The Prologue's organization differs from the sonnet 'Argument' of Shakespeare's immediate source, Arthur Brooke's *Tragicall Historye of Romeus and Juliet*, which may have inspired it. In his fourteen lines Brooke lists almost all of the incidents related to the love-story, omitting Romeo's early infatuation and events after the suicides. (See Brooke's version in Geoffrey Bullough's edition, *Narrative and Dramatic Sources of Shakespeare*, vol. 1 (London and New York, 1957), p. 286.)

25 *Shakespeare's Wordplay* (London, 1957), pp. 56–7.

instance, it signifies nobleness of character as well. 'Mutiny' (line 3) denotes both a revolt against authority and a quarrel; 'fatal loins' (line 5) are both fateful and deadly. The double-edged phrase 'take their life' (line 6), 'derive their life' or 'deprive themselves of life', fuses the preconditions of the sequence with its ending. In the twelfth line *OED* cites 'traffic' as an illustration for 'business', but the word retains its more literal associations of trade, merchandise, and journey. The subtleties of the closing couplet – the elusiveness of terms like 'attend', 'here', 'miss', 'mend' – encourage more than one reading: what sounds like closure is really elaboration. Comparable to the rhetorical devices which appear to impose symmetry on the lines, the antitheses and *ploce* identified by Harry Levin, the sonnet formula only seems to contain the sequence of the Romeo and Juliet narrative. Diction continually undermines what had become formulaic, creating two or three impressions with almost everything the Prologue speaks.[26]

In Q2 the Chorus appears for a second time between the fifth and sixth scenes. Its sonnet here is less ambitious, reprising two-thirds of the party episode in a quatrain before previewing the next four scenes. Interrupting the sequence – Romeo and Juliet's first encounter and their meeting at Juliet's house – it explicates what the audience has just witnessed without conveying its speed or matching its intensity. The rest of this sonnet is similarly out of phase with events to come. In its position the narrative fragment contrasts with the audience's experience of the dramatized sequence, calling attention to Shakespeare's revisions, engaging spectators in generation of the narrative. Despite word-play, and echoes of the Prologue,[27] this speech simplifies the developing sequence. The Prologue maintained that narrative was a co-operative activity; the Chorus now illustrates what happens when narrative becomes prescriptive. With its prominent devices of repetition this sonnet offers an emphatic

description of events, reducing the possibilities for interpretation.

On his second exit the Chorus disappears from *Romeo and Juliet*, although Benvolio and Friar Laurence continue to carry out one of his functions each time violence erupts: they reprise events in speeches which call attention to the processes of narration. Benvolio gives the first of three such accounts at 1.1.103–12, summarizing action just seen by the audience. As James Black has noticed, the summary narratives counterpoise strong refutative visual impressions;[28] they contrast and increase the complexity of Shakespeare's narration. Benvolio stands among discarded weapons during the first scene – swords, clubs, and halberds – addressing Montague and his wife in the aftermath of a public brawl. Within its context the speech sounds logical, an exposition which partly clarifies the preceding disorder: Benvolio identifies Tybalt by name and character note. At the same time its tone of equanimity helps to make the transition from active feud to nascent love-story. Whatever purposes it serves, however, Benvolio's presentation of the fight is curiously static and flat, a triptych of descriptions in three different styles. The stage-properties tell another story while Benvolio sums up the most chaotic events so far in the most carefully proportioned lines of the speech, the closing heroic couplet balanced by rhetorical devices of repetition.

---

[26] Annotations are borrowed from the Commentary to my edition; Levin identifies the rhetorical devices in his seminal essay 'Form and Formality in *Romeo and Juliet*', *Shakespeare Quarterly*, 11 (1960), rpt. *'Romeo and Juliet': Critical Essays*, ed. John F. Andrews (New York, 1993), pp. 41–53.

[27] In line 3, 'for' (in 'groaned for') means 'because of' and 'in order to have'; in line 6, 'looks' signifies both appearances and glances; in line 7, 'he must complain' can be construed as 'he must make moan' or 'he must compose laments'. 'Fearful' in line 8 echoes the Prologue, line 9.

[28] 'The Visual Artistry of *Romeo and Juliet*', *Studies in English Literature*, 15 (1975), rpt. *Critical Essays*, ed. Andrews, pp. 149–61.

If inanimate objects qualify Benvolio's first summary, a more diversified and kinetic stage-picture raises questions about his next one. When Benvolio delivers his second, longer narration (3.1.151–74), again he describes violence witnessed moments before by the audience: the fatal duels between Mercutio and Tybalt, and between Tybalt and Romeo. This time the body of Tybalt is one of the visual impressions, and the agitated auditors are another. As much a defence as an eyewitness account, this narrative slants events to exonerate Benvolio's two friends. It argues his point of view with straightforward, monosyllabic diction and rhetorical devices, especially repetition, but its breathlessness testifies to its subjectivity. What Benvolio says is inconsistent with what the audience knows: he omits Mercutio's provocation of Tybalt, and he heightens Romeo's gestures of peaceful intervention. In this instance facts resist Benvolio's construction, evidence weakens his dialectic. Charges of falsehood by Capulet's Wife immediately follow the monologue; they are not entirely unjustified.

Shakespeare invented Benvolio's narrations, but he derived Friar Laurence's lengthy account at 5.3.228–68 from an even longer passage in his source.[29] Perhaps early narrative fiction needed summaries like this to help unpractised readers through newly extended sequences; however the staging of Friar Laurence's lines, like that of Benvolio's, provides assistance of a different type. With the bodies of Romeo, Paris, and Juliet near at hand, and a crowd of bewildered auditors, Friar Laurence gives a synopsis of the plot from the marriage of the lovers to the death of Juliet. Q2 punctuates the verse lightly, allowing it a faint gasp here and there; otherwise the rhetorically balanced speech, with its relatively unadorned diction, gives a matter-of-fact outline of events. Finally Friar Laurence's version of the sequence stands in counterpoint to Shakespeare's even as it interrupts Shakespeare's dénouement. Together with the Chorus's sonnet between episodes and

Benvolio's two explanations, it represents another interpretation of the story far simpler than what the playwright has made possible. These secondary characters, caught up by or in the 'traffic of our stage', occasionally enact the parts of narrators with imperfect skills; they remain unaware of the dynamic which determines their very speeches. In their summaries Shakespeare displays imagination inhibited by other faculties of thought. He may also be giving his own auditors discreet prompts about the artfulness of the play's narration and the imaginative synergy essential to completing his design.

There are many similar passages throughout the text, invented or adapted narratives which diminish in various ways the events they re-create. During the first meeting between Romeo and Friar Laurence, for example, Friar Laurence summarizes the love-story of Romeo and Rosaline (2.2.69–78). His diction is hyperbolic and playful, a comic account of Romeo's loverlike posturing in earlier scenes which omits the signs of true passion and complexity. Several times the Nurse relates incidents which the audience has witnessed; each narration represents what happened in partial terms which reveal more of her personality than the event. On her errand to Romeo in 2.3, a typical occasion, she describes Paris's courtship of Juliet to enlarge her own role, embellishing information from 1.2 and 1.3 until it no longer corresponds with the facts or chronology of the play:

O, there is a nobleman in town, one Paris,
That would fain lay knife abroad; but she, good
  soul,
Had as lief see a toad, a very toad,
As see him. I anger her sometimes,
And tell her that Paris is the properer man;
But I'll warrant you, when I say so she looks
As pale as any clout in the versal world.

(lines 190–6)

---

[29] Brooke, *Tragicall Historye*, in Bullough, ed., *Narrative and Dramatic Sources*, lines 2837–964.

44

When the Nurse returns to Juliet with the 'news' of this meeting in the next scene, she releases the narrative in bits and pieces: her wearying journey to find Romeo (2.4.26); a list of his features and a sentence about his behaviour (lines 39–44); a description of the message's delivery (lines 55–7); and at last the message itself, indirectly (line 66) and directly (lines 68–9), with some details about her part in the secret plans (lines 72–5). Here the playwright recasts the end of a scene as a series of impressions in the mind of one character; and the character's report is particularized by her age, sexuality, and self-interest.

After the crises in 3.1 – the deaths of Mercutio and Tybalt, and the banishment of Romeo – two scenes re-create these violent events as the Nurse and Friar Laurence perceive them. Initially the Nurse conveys disaster to an oblivious Juliet. She begins *in medias res*, with a graphic but ambiguous portrayal of Tybalt's death coloured by her reaction to the sight of the corpse (3.2.37–9, 40–2, 52–6, 61–3); she then conflates duel and outcome in one line, 'Romeo that killed him – he is banishèd' (line 70). From the general incoherency Juliet reconstructs a crucial part of 3.1, correctly interpreting the sequence:

> But wherefore, villain, didst thou kill my cousin?
> That villain cousin would have killed my
> > husband.   (lines 100–1)
>
> My husband lives, that Tybalt would have slain;
> And Tybalt's dead that would have slain my
> > husband.   (lines 105–6)

Finally Juliet expounds the meaning of 'banishèd', transforming the Nurse's word for an act into a personal theme expressing her grief.

In the following scene Friar Laurence reviews events at much greater length than the Nurse. First he tells Romeo what happened in 3.1 after the second duel and Romeo's exit: 'I bring thee tidings of the Prince's doom' (3.3.8). Then he repeats the judgement of banishment four times (lines 10–11, 15, 25–7, 56), urging patience but moving Romeo to a brief and

focused narration of the love-story which epitomizes his despair (lines 65–7). As he responds to Romeo's suicide attempt, Friar Laurence weaves circumstances from 3.1 and the scene before us into a prolonged argument which not only rationalizes events but gives them a happy ending (lines 107–57). Philosophy, complacent and rhetorical, invents an impossible conclusion for its rendering of the sequence.

Several other narratives in *Romeo and Juliet* draw attention to imaginations which are somehow inhibited: the Prince's balanced review of three previous brawls between the rival houses (1.1.86–92); Capulet' enumeration of his efforts to find Juliet a suitable husband and of their results (3.5.176–86); Friar Laurence's recital of the potion scheme (4.1.91–120). If these passages define boundaries, however, others venture through or beyond them. During the third act the lovers, impatient with the Nurse and Friar Laurence, create meaningful versions of their own narratives. Juliet's soliloquy as she takes the potion in 4.3 exposes and finally risks the possibility of fault-lines in the Friar's logic: 'What if this mixture do not work at all?' (line 20); 'What if it be a poison [?]' (line 23).

> How if, when I am laid into the tomb,
> I wake before the time that Romeo
> Come to redeem me? There's a fearful point.
> > (lines 29–31)

Romeo's narratives about his dream and the Apothecary's shop, very recent memories, become densely figurative interpretations as he speaks them (5.1.1–11, 38–55).

In the space beyond rationalization Shakespeare exploits the mythical component of his narrative sequence, *Liebestod* and related stories. The *Liebestod* myth, linking passion with death, sets the limits of desire at the highly charged point where lovers feel they have transcended ordinary human experience, driven to union which means dissolution of self, a permanent metamorphosis. Paradox dominates this narrative in which the compulsion to love is a compulsion to die, and death is the price for an absolute. Again and again *Romeo and Juliet* calls attention to its ultimate source and profound subtext. Sometimes the allusions are direct: the motif of death as Juliet's bridegroom, identified by Mahood and T. J. B. Spencer, is introduced at the end of the fifth scene (lines 133–4) and repeated until its enactment in 5.3.[30] Elsewhere the play alludes to other myths, not only with references to Cupid and Venus but with citations of unrelated Ovidian stories connecting disaster and transformation: Phaëton, the most prominent (2.2.4, 2.4.9, 3.2.1–4, 5.3.305), as well as Danaë (1.1.211), Echo (2.1.206–8), Julius Caesar (3.2.22–5), Philomel (3.5.4), and Proserpine (5.3.104–5). Now and then quotations of supporting myth and legend appear in unlikely places, such as Mercutio's catalogue of five tragic heroines in his mockery of Romeo as lover (2.3.39–41). Wherever they occur they call to mind whole narratives of another order, timeless and eloquent, which correspond with the dramatic narrative in progress.

At every level the dramatic narrative in progress seems to take its bearings from other narratives. It moves forward in uneven steps, pausing over its own implications. Twice it comes to a halt in famous speeches, largely invented, which display the idiosyncrasies of both narratives and narrators: the Nurse's story of Juliet's weaning at 1.3.18–59, and Mercutio's fantastic account of Queen Mab at 1.4.56–96. The narrative in each instance communicates a striking impression of the speaker's personality; it is voiced in the fullest sense.

The Nurse conflates a traumatic event in Juliet's life with her own history, fusing the losses of the child with her own losses. In a narrative where consequences overwhelm sequence, she registers the end of Juliet's total dependency with the deaths of her daughter and husband. The style anticipates her speeches later in the play – redundant, unstructured, ambiguous, edged with ribaldry – but here it is

thoroughly purposeful. As Shakespeare's narrative gets underway, the Nurse's speech accentuates a few of its key features: it sets the season of the play and Juliet's birth in high summer, with its attendant rituals and symbolic associations; it emphasizes the strong element of surrogation in the Nurse's bond with Juliet; and in the repeated prediction of the Nurse's husband – 'Thou wilt fall backward when thou hast more wit' (line 44) – it draws attention to the adolescent Juliet, poised on the border of innocence and experience. Of course the Nurse's story provides a key at once to the Nurse's mentality, described by Coleridge as her 'childlike happy, humble ducking under, yet resurgence against the check'.[31] What Barbara Hardy concludes about Mistress Quickly in *2 Henry IV* applies as well to this prototype: 'There is a brilliant tension between the seemingly incompetent telling of the character and the competence and cunning of the dramatist.'[32] The Nurse's telling is determined by memory and therefore removed from the immediate occasion in every sense but one: the character retrieves the past in her present state of mind, inevitably the source not only of inaccuracies but of emotional colouring.

Mercutio's is another story, a narrative fantasy on Romeo's line 'I dreamt a dream tonight' (1.4.50). It is a display of imagination playing on the concept of wish-fulfilment, and it identifies Mercutio as one of those Shakespearian characters who are 'centres and models of creativity', like their author.[33] In a sequence related by causation more than regular chronology, Mercutio portrays the acts of the folkloric Mab through their manifestations in human behaviour. The exposition, a catalogue

[30] Mahood, *Shakespeare's Wordplay*, p. 57, and Spencer, ed., *Romeo and Juliet*, New Penguin Shakespeare (Harmondsworth, 1967), 1.5.135 n.

[31] *Coleridge on Shakespeare*, ed. Terence Hawkes (Harmondsworth, 1969), p. 135.

[32] 'Shakespeare's Dramatic Narrative', pp. 8–9; quotation from p. 9.

[33] See Hardy, *Shakespeare's Storytellers*, p. 144.

of images, gives material presence to the abstractions Mab represents and the logic of fairy-tale to her effects. An alternative reality, the world of Mab exists in its own time, not measured by the usual instruments, 'Time out o' mind' (line 70): it is perpetual night when she travels, 'sometime' here, 'sometime' there. But the desires she activates, the appetites which impel human conduct, belong together in the series Mercutio constructs which advances gradually from personal to social and from benign to damaging.

In this version of the topos *somnium animale*, or dream which arises from disturbance of the waking mind, presentation of the sequence is notable for its rhetoric: Mercutio amplifies the subject of dreams for forty lines. Robert O. Evans calls Mercutio's performance 'a demonstration of rhetorical fireworks', and he maintains that no Elizabethan writer would employ so many figures without intending to make the passage conspicuous.[34] Among these figures word-play is emphatic from beginning to end. Occasionally it sounds respectable: 'wat'ry' means 'connected with water' and 'pale' (line 62); 'collars' puns on 'colours' (line 63), 'curtsies' on 'courtesies' (line 73). More often it does not, betraying an obsession with sexual organs ('stone' (line 56), 'forefinger' (line 57), 'tail' (line 79), 'nose' (line 80), 'breaches' (line 85)) and with sexual intercourse ('lie on their backs' (line 92), 'learns them first to bear' (line 93), 'women of good carriage' (line 94)). The mentality revealed here is complex and subversive, distant enough from the narrative that E. Pearlman considers it an interpolation:

Mercutio's excursus is not articulated with the remainder of *Romeo and Juliet* in terms of plot, context, language, or intellection. There is no overlap between the realist, materialist Mercutio and the Mercutio who celebrates Queen Mab in elaborate, imaginative, and romantic terms.[35]

Arguments along these lines could dispense with other narratives in *Romeo and Juliet*; Pearlman himself rationalizes the Chorus as a

technique which Shakespeare abandoned.[36] But there is evidence that the unusual harmonies and changing chords are intrinsic to this play. Q1, despite its expeditiousness, also pauses over its own narration: it hovers less often, more briefly. In this version the Prologue, two quatrains and two couplets, corresponds significantly to the sonnet which opens Q2. It reorganizes the fictional sequence with additional stress on the violence which destroys the lovers: 'Through the continuing of their fathers' strife / And death-marked passage of their parents' rage' (lines 8–9).[37] Many ambiguities occur here too, ('dignity' (line 1), 'fatal loins' (line 5), 'took their life' (line 6), 'traffic' (line 10)); and the closing couplet is an invitation to the audience:

The which if you with patient ears attend,
What here we want, we'll study to amend.

As the Q1 narrative proceeds, the Chorus does not reappear.[38] Some descriptions of events already witnessed are more concise than their parallels in Q2, or they are absent. In the first scene, for example, Benvolio speaks only two lines about the beginning of the street fight; and in 3.1 his account of the duels is several verses shorter than his speech in Q2. Nevertheless, Q1 allows space for Friar Laurence's lengthy summation in 5.3, as well as his reductive moralizing in 2.2 and 3.3. Many of the same mythological allusions enhance this text; Romeo summons his dream and (less

---

[34] *The Osier Cage: Rhetorical Devices in 'Romeo and Juliet'* (Lexington, Ky., 1966), pp. 81, 86.

[35] 'Shakespeare at Work: *Romeo and Juliet*', *English Literary Renaissance*, 24 (1994), rpt. *Critical Essays on Shakespeare's 'Romeo and Juliet'*, ed. Joseph A. Porter (New York, 1997), p. 119.

[36] 'Shakespeare at Work', pp. 112–15.

[37] Quotations of Q1 come from the modern-spelling version in my edition.

[38] The Chorus is certainly anomalous. Its role as Prologue in both quartos suggests that the opening speech was performed in the theatre. The Folio omits the Prologue, perhaps through an error in casting off copy, but includes the second Chorus.

imaginatively) the Apothecary's shop in 5.1; and the third and fourth scenes halt for the Nurse's story and Mercutio's account of Queen Mab.[39]

In both of its sixteenth-century forms, the play so frequently appraised by literary critics as an experiment – a testing of conventional genres, verse, and rhetoric – listens more or less attentively to its own narration in an echo chamber of its own constructing. One result of the process is irony as the concept was formulated by Friedrich Schlegel and reformulated by Paul de Man: suspension of the narrative line, fragmentation of its continuity to make meaning uncertain.[40] Through its structural correspondences, as well as its verbal play, *Romeo and Juliet* inflects a familiar narrative sequence with multiple, ambiguous implications.

The new multiplicity has at least two notable effects. It suggests that narratives, like life, are 'necessarily unfinished, processual, contradictory';[41] and it postpones the tragic ending of this narrative with many digressions. If the stories we tell ourselves are detours to death, as Freud claimed in *Beyond the Pleasure Principle*, Shakespeare's dramatized telling of this particular story circumvents the inevitable through countless byways. In its pluralities the dramatic narration asserts that the meanings of events and words are never final; it implies that even death lacks finality. 'Death is the most enigmatic ending', as Miller claims, 'the darkest

dramatization of the way an ending always recedes, escapes, vanishes as a clarifying telos'.[42] Like the other events along its narrative line, the suicides in *Romeo and Juliet* provide no closure: dialogue continues for more than 100 verses in both texts; dawn rises; and the actors depart as the Prince calls for 'more talk of these sad things' (5.3.306). The tragedy ends, as it started, in irony that allows the possibility of new beginnings.[43] If the younger generation has been eradicated, their narrative promises to revive, as it has infinite times in the Shakespearian format and others. Over four centuries many performances and adaptations of *Romeo and Juliet* – drama, fiction, cinema, ballet, opera – have invited new constructions of the play's events, allowing each audience to re-create the story whose sequence and ending they already know.

---

[39] Part of the Nurse's story is virtually identical in the two quartos, since it belongs to a passage of Q2 printed from Q1. Mercutio's speech, approximately twenty-five per cent shorter than the Q2 monologue, is similarly complex and disturbing.

[40] See Miller, *Reading Narrative*, pp. 36–7, 44.

[41] The quotation is borrowed from Terry Eagleton, who describes the 'nature of historical affairs' in these terms and admits that irony can point such complexities (*Against the Grain* (London, 1986), p. 162).

[42] *Reading Narrative*, p. 55. On Freud's claim about storytelling, see pp. 228–9 and 253.

[43] Kierkegaard defines irony in these terms, and Miller paraphrases the definition (*Reading Narrative*, p. 229).

A MIDSUMMER NIGHT'S DREAM: COMEDY AS *APOTROPE* OF MYTH

A. D. NUTTALL

Hippolyta, I wooed thee with my sword,
And won thy love doing thee injuries.
But I will wed thee in another key –
With pomp, with triumph, and with revelling.

(1.1.16–19)

Thus Theseus, benignly, to Hippolyta in the opening scene of *A Midsummer Night's Dream*. Everyone watching, in 1595 or 1596, would have known that the speaker was an important personage. He enters, splendidly dressed (we may be certain) and, according to the Folio stage direction, 'with others' (rightly interpreted by Theobald as implying a train of attendants). His speech contrives, within a small compass, to be stately. It at once receives from Egeus, a kind of underlining, a graceful, articulate equivalent of loyal (servile?) applause: 'Happy be Theseus, our renowned Duke.' Now we are clearly aware of the exact social status of Theseus, which is of course very high. The cadence of Egeus' words anticipates that of the courtier Amiens in *As You Like it*, 'Happy is your grace', after Duke Senior's similarly stately (if deeply implausible) speech on the merits of the simple life, although, interestingly, Amiens' 'happy' carries, as Egeus' 'happy' does not, a connotation of stylistic felicity. Theseus, then, is a grand fellow of whom we should all take notice. Do we know anything else? Do we know – to put the question more precisely – who he is?

A little more than eighty years after the London audience listened to the words of Shakespeare's Duke of Athens, another audience in another country could be found listening to the words of one Thésée (or Theseus) in another play. This other play - Racine's *Phèdre* – is, to put it mildly, different from Shakespeare's. It is black tragedy. This Theseus is a harsh figure of sexual violence. Racine builds explicitly on Euripides and Seneca.

The full mythological information is made available. Indeed it impregnates the semantic fabric of the drama. This, we are left in no doubt, is the Herculean hero who with his sword defeated the army of women, the Amazons, and afterwards carried off their queen, Antiope, begetting on her his son, Hippolytus – that Hippolytus who describes his father as the deliverer of Crete, 'fumant du sang du Minotaure' (1.i.82). Behind this line stands a passage in Shakespeare's favourite poet, Ovid, beginning,

Te, Maxime Theseu,
Mirata est Marathon, Cretaei sanguine tauri
(*Metamorphoses*, vii.433–4)

You, greatest Theseus, Marathon adores for the blood shed of the Cretan bull.

Racine, however, has actually darkened the bestial allusion. Where Ovid evokes the slaying of the Marathonian bull, Racine slides to the far more frightening Minotaur, half bull, half man (equally part of the Theseus myth). The Minotaur was the creature who lived in the labyrinth, the monstrous issue of the unnatural coupling of Pasiphae with a bull. We now meet perhaps the most grotesque, the most disturbing, of all the Greek myths. When Pasiphae was overcome with lust for the beautiful bull she was at first at a loss how to contrive physical intercourse with the brute. To solve her problem she had a wooden cow constructed, to attract the bull. He mounted the wooden cow and she, straddling within, received the bull's member. The story is so gross that even Ovid seems to flinch from it, in his uncharacteristically hurried account of Pasiphae 'quae torvum ligno decepit adultera taurum', literally, 'who, unchaste, deceived the savage bull with wood' (*Metamorphoses*, viii.132). Theseus was aided in his defeat of this monster by a daughter of the same Pasiphae, Ariadne, whom he later ditched in Naxos. After the death of the Amazon queen Antiope he married (in the normal version of the myth) Phaedra (Racine's Phèdre), another daughter of Pasiphae. She it is, in Racine, who, infected by her terrible lineage ('la fille de Minos et de Pasiphaé', 1.i.36) is incestuously drawn to her son-in-law, Hippolytus. We are, quite obviously, in another world. On the one hand, in the English comedy, we have moonlight, fairies and happy love. On the other, in the French tragedy, we have sexual horror. Can Shakespeare's Theseus be in any sense the same person as the one we meet in Racine?

When we passed from Racine to Ovid we crossed over from drama to narrative poetry. Yet the answer, from the point of view of a mythographer, is, 'Yes, Shakespeare's Theseus is quite clearly the Theseus of Greek myth; it is the same man.' Racine's tragedy is in immediate accord with ancient story. Shakespeare's comedy, perhaps, is not. The first thing Shakespeare's Theseus tells us, however, is that he wooed Hippolyta 'with my sword' (1.1.16). This is – must be – an allusion to the war with the Amazons. Good scholarly editions of the play accordingly cite at this point Shakespeare's source, which is, once more narrative: North's Plutarch.

Touching the voyage he made by the sea Major, Philochorus, and some other holde opinion, that he went thither with Hercules against the Amazones: and that to honour his valiantnes, Hercules gave him Antiopa the Amazone. But the more part of the other Historiographers, namely Hellanicus, Pherecydes, and Herodotus, doe write, that Theseus went thither alone, after Hercules voyage, and that he tooke this Amazone prisoner, which is likeliest to be true.[1]

At this point we have in North's margin the shoulder-note, 'Antiopa the Amazone ravished by Theseus'. Then, a little later, after the shoulder-note, 'Theseus fighteth a battell with the Amazones', we are told how

The graves of the women which dyed in this first encounter, are founde yet in the great streete, which goeth towards the gate Piraica, neere unto the chappell of the litle god Chalcodus. And the Athenians . . . were in this place repulsed by the Amazones, even to the place where the images of Eumenides are, that is to saye, of the furies. But on th'other side also, the Athenians comming towards the quarters of Palladium, Ardettus and Lucium, drove backe their right poynte even to within their campe, and slewe a great number of them. Afterwards, at the ende of foure moneths, peace was taken betwene them by meanes of one of the women called Hypollita. For this Historiographer calleth the Amazone which Theseus maried, Hyppolita, and not Antiopa . . . It is very true, that after the death of Antiopa, Theseus maried Phaedra, having had before of Antiopa a sonne called Hippolytus . . .[2]

Far more lightly than Racine but nevertheless unmistakably Shakespeare is touching on this Greek story. Near the beginning of Act 2 Oberon and Titania are squabbling, each half-accusing the other of adulterous desires. Oberon says,

How canst thou thus for shame, Titania,
Glance at my credit with Hippolyta,
Knowing I know thy love to Theseus?
Didst thou not lead him through the glimmering
night

50

From Perigouna, whom he ravishèd,
And make him with fair Aegles break his faith,
With Ariadne and Antiopa?   (2.1.74–80)

The myth wobbles as myths do. Antiope, queen of the conquered Amazons can, as we saw already in Plutarch, reappear with another name, Hippolyta – a name which seems somehow to have moved, with the necessary change of gender, from Hippolytus, Theseus' son. Shakespeare went for 'Hippolyta' in his main action, yet Antiopa is still there in Oberon's speech. Theseus appears alternately as ravisher and bridegroom. Most wonderfully, when the story is told by the king of the fairies, the myth itself is drawn into the distinctive magic of Shakespeare's comedy: Theseus, we learn, was led through a 'glimmering night' by a fairy to his harsh conquests. Titania, it seems, played Robin Goodfellow to the erotic Hercules of antiquity.

Obviously the scholars are not wrong to cite North's Plutarch. But still, it might be said, the source, though certainly that, a source, remains poetically extraneous. Does the Theseus of myth figure in the *theatrical* experience of *A Midsummer Night's Dream*? I think the answer to this question must be blurred. The mythological Theseus will be there for some, not there for others. Those who see only the benign conquering bridegroom will be happy. Others, however, will not be able to help knowing more (and Shakespeare knows that some will know more). The flowery train of names in Oberon's speech especially will be largely dead matter to the former class. To the latter it will work, as allusive poetry properly works, as a series of casements opening on the wild foam of European story. Shakespeare, I am sure, would not have allowed Theseus his reference to the sword used in winning Hippolyta if he had not wanted such thoughts to arise. He reminds us – very swiftly, I grant – of past violence in the opening sequence of the play; it is a prominent, *mind-setting* speech.

And of course if we admit the ravisher

Theseus we at once let in a strand of meaning which is as congenial to feminist criticism as it is uncongenial to old-fashioned bardolatry. It is, I suppose, a good rule in criticism to be especially mistrustful of anything you find with delight and, conversely, to be prepared to concede, as it were, with clenched teeth, the presence of undesired matter. It is for the reader to judge which of these injunctions (if either) is being followed in the rest of this essay.

Surely nothing can be more evident – and more obstinately irremovable – than the contrast to which I carefully alluded at the outset. Racine's *Phèdre* and Shakespeare's comedy, whatever off-stage links may be discovered in the hinterland of sources, present substantially different universes. Mythologically this may be the same Theseus, but poetically this is another person altogether. What happens in Theseus' wholly benevolent speech to Hippolyta is a *successful* banishing of the old dark narrative from the play. With these words the myth is turned on its head; the harsh Theseus drops out of sight and the smiling Duke of Athens springs up in its place. What we see is a verbal equivalent of a visual transformation in a masque. Still more it resembles a transition in music (Theseus himself says 'in another key', 1.1.18). The whole point of *A Midsummer Night's Dream* is its gossamer beauty. The twentieth century is marked by a prejudice in favour of the discordant. Shakespeare is saying, as clearly as it can be said, that this is not what he is after. *Préjudice de siècle* is nowhere so evident as in Jan Kott. His notorious description of Titania as 'longing for animal love'[3] (as if Titania were Pasiphae) is simply ludicrous. Has he not noticed that Titania is deluded? She is attracted by what she sees as a wise and beautiful being. She cannot see the grotesque half-donkey available to the rest of us. A play in which Titania said, 'Give me a beast to make love to me' would be essentially different from

---

[3] Jan Kott, *Shakespeare Our Contemporary* (2nd edn (London, 1967)), p. 183.

Shakespeare's. In his words to Hippolyta Theseus actually changes the story itself; it is now another story, one (why should we be so reluctant to receive it?) of happy love.

All of that sounds like good sense. It is, I think, 90 per cent true. This leaves, the alert will perceive, a troubling 10 per cent which I propose now to consider. I have just said that Shakespeare has changed the myth and moved on to new territory. If he had wished simply to produce a new story why did he allow Theseus to mention his sword at all? Why, after the great switch, did he let the word 'ravished' appear in Oberon's speech? Why did he not present a smiling wooer who could quite easily have been called by some other name than Theseus?

When I was trying to describe the transformation of the myth the phrase 'turns all to favour and to prettiness' came into my mind. These of course are the words of Laertes as he looks at Ophelia. The full speech runs,

> Thought and affliction, passion, hell itself
> She turns to favour and to prettiness.
>
> (*Hamlet* 4.5.186–7)

Laertes is responding to a speech by Ophelia which is, in fact, faintly evocative of the world of *A Midsummer Night's Dream*: it is all flowers and greenery and ends with a snatch from the song 'Sweet Robin'. There is a robin – Robin Goodfellow – in *A Midsummer Night's Dream*. The effect of this sequence of speeches in *Hamlet* is not to enforce the absolute division of tragedy from comedy, *Phèdre* from the *Dream*, but to mediate between them. Just as triple Hecate, goddess of hell in Ovid and Seneca[4] finds her way into *A Midsummer Night's Dream*, drawing the fairies after her from the rising sun (5.2.14), so hell and passion, the stuff of *Phèdre* are the matter of Ophelia's feat of transformation. If we had no sense of the material, we would not know that a feat had been performed. Of course in the tragic world of *Hamlet*, confronted as we are by the wreckage of Ophelia's mind, we cannot forget these

things. In *A Midsummer Night's Dream* it is all so much lighter, so much swifter, that we can forget. Nevertheless *A Midsummer Night's Dream*, likewise, presents not the accomplished fact of terror disarmed but a feat of disarming. To understand the feat, to feel the proper energy within the lines, we must be aware in some degree, if only for a moment, of background terror.

George Herbert in his 'Jordan' poems did not make an editorial decision in advance to exclude all artful ingenuity from his divine poems; instead he risked his soul and made poetry from the act of exclusion. Shakespeare similarly did not decide in advance not to use the old myth. Instead he chose to exhibit the exclusion, as a process within the drama. Having said this, I will now push the thesis a little further. The suppression of dark forces is not only incomplete at the beginning of the play; there is a sense in which it remains incomplete throughout. The play is haunted to the end by that residual ten per cent.

Listen again to Theseus:

> Hippolyta, I wooed thee with my sword,
> And won thy love doing thee injuries.
> But I will wed thee in another key –
> With pomp, with triumph, and with revelling.

I wish now to draw attention to the fact that a certain disquiet can persist, even in the latter, supposedly joyous half of this 'over-turning' speech. Instead of making Theseus say 'I won you by violence but now I will seek to gain your trust by a loving devotion', Shakespeare makes him say, 'I won you with my sword, but now we will proceed in joyous triumph.' The second half of the antithesis actually fails to achieve a fully antithetical status. 'Triumph' remains, obstinately, an arrogant, masculine word. It carries the idea of military victory into the new world of marriage. The actor who delivers this speech is in no danger of kneeling

---

4 Ovid, *Metamorphoses*, vii.194; Seneca, *Hippolytus*, 406–17.

to his lady, as Lear would have knelt to Cordelia. Rather the very words will cause him almost to strut.

Later in the play, in the famous dialogue about the lunatic, the lover and the poet, Theseus (who certainly won the battle of the citations-index since his are the words endlessly quoted in anthologies) uncomprehendingly occludes the far subtler observations of Hippolyta. It is not too much to say that the entire 'Coherence Theory' of truth is sketched in her phrase 'grows to something of great constancy' (5.1.26). Her IQ is as far above Theseus' as her real status is, quite evidently, below. As Graham Bradshaw saw, there is a delicious *gaucherie* in a lover telling his lady, *de haut en bas*, that all lovers are crazy.[5] It is not *galant*.

Thus the new, smiling Theseus remains oddly stiff. He is indeed no longer the ravisher. Nor does he ever come close to bullying Hippolyta. But he is still harshly masculine. We cannot quite say, with a whole heart, 'Now all is well!' It is as if, after all, Shakespeare wants a half-memory to continue, at the edge of consciousness.

Another work famous for turning enmity into beauty and lightness is Pope's *Rape of the Lock*, written, it is said, to laugh quarrelling parties out of their difference. The very title enacts, within a monosyllable, the healing transformation. The word 'rape', then as now, applied to forced sexual intercourse. But as we reach the words 'of the lock' we begin to guess, with relief, that the word is being used in its milder, Latin sense: 'seizure', 'carrying off'. Nevertheless, having achieved the soothing modification and dispelled all anxieties (we might suppose), Pope keeps the harsher meaning alive, at the back of the reader's mind, through imagery of cracked porcelain, scissors ('the glittering forfex') and the like. The alternatives before us are, first, that *A Midsummer Night's Dream* enacts a complete suppression of sexual violence, replacing it with unbroken felicity and, second, that there is indeed just such a suppression but it is laced with a

nervous, intermittent memory of the matter suppressed. It will be obvious by now that I am going for the second alternative.

I want at this point to shift focus from Theseus to the fairies. If Theseus is, by mythological birthright, the figure who could have brought a Greek violence into the play had he not been softened, the very English fairies are surely the obvious agents of that softening, powerfully assist the change of tone, embody the opposite principle, the principle of beauty. Once more, however, the absoluteness of our initial distinction will not survive close inspection. The fairies, no less than Theseus, carry the burden of a dark history. Shakespeare's fairies, indeed, are miniature, pretty creatures, but to say this is very like saying that Shakespeare's Theseus is a benign figure. We can no longer assert with Latham that Shakespeare was the first to present minuscule fairies, since earlier examples have been found, but we can say that he chose the then unusual miniature fairy, in preference to the more usual version. And of course Titania, herself a fairy, is clearly full-size; she can entwine Bottom the Weaver in her arms. Even if Peaseblossom and the rest were played by children, children are not nearly small enough to lie in a cowslip's bell (from *The Tempest*, I know, but really a bit of *A Midsummer Night's Dream* which has somehow strayed into *The Tempest*, at 5.1.89). The truth is that Shakespeare knows that one element in the pleasure taken in all this pretty flimsiness will be relief. The fairies of *A Midsummer Night's Dream*, with their redemptive beauty chasing away all tragic elements may be the same people as the fairies who were once feared. At the end of the play Oberon has to promise that no child born from the marriages forged on that magic night will be deformed:

Never mole, harelip, nor scar,
Nor mark prodigious, such as are
Despisèd in nativity

---

[5] *Shakespeare's Scepticism* (Brighton, 1987), p. 44.

Shall upon their children be.   (5.2.41–4)

The promise is urgently required because the fear of these effects is still there – fairies are notorious for pranks, but the infliction of a hare-lip on a new born child is something worse than a prank.

In a way everything I have been saying is already present in the phrase, 'The Good Folk', a minor anthropological curiosity in its own right. The fairies were called 'The Good Folk' not because they were benevolent but in the hope of making them so – we can almost say, because they were in fact the reverse of benevolent. The phrase does not occur in *A Midsummer Night's Dream* but 'Goodfellow' does, as another name for Puck. There is a seventeenth-century woodcut of Robin Goodfellow which shows him with horns, shaggy thighs, cloven hooves and graphically emphasized animal genitalia.[6] 'Good Folk', then, is a conciliating, propitiatory description, which can be paralleled in other languages. For example the avenging Furies whom we have already met in Plutarch and can find again in Aeschylus were called the 'Eumenides', 'The Kindly Ones'. In Sophocles' *Oedipus at Colonus* the chorus sings

ὥς σφας καλοῦμεν Εὐμενίδας, ἐξ εὐμενῶν
στέρνων δέχεσθαι τὸν ἱκέτην σωτήριον   (486–7)

As we call them the kindly ones, that they may receive the supplicant safe, with kindly heart.[7]

Near the end of the seventeenth century Robert Kirk wrote in *The Secret Commonwealth of Elves, Fauns and Fairies*, 'These sith's or Fairies, they call sluagh-maith or the good people (it would seem, to prevent the dint of their ill attempts: for the Irish use to bless all they fear harme of)'.[8]

We are dealing with a kind of euphemism, but not the kind we employ simply to avoid an undesired image (as in 'passed away' for 'died'). Rather, this euphemism is *put to work* (presumably in the hope of inducing the hearer to conform to the flattering description) with the design of *turning away* hostility. It is therefore an apotropaic euphemism, from the Greek

ἀποτροπή, 'turning away'. Richard Wilson applies the term 'apotropaic' to this comedy in his brilliant essay, 'The Kindly Ones: The Death of the Author in Shakespearian Athens'.[9] He observes that the play procedes through a series of rejected scripts, 'Seneca's *Hercules*, Euripides' *Bacchae* . . . all are evaded during the action'.[10] Of course I want to say 'not quite rejected, not exactly evaded', but Wilson is basically right. Duke Theseus performs an *apotrope* of his former self at the beginning of the play. Could *A Midsummer Night's Dream* constitute, as a whole, an *apotrope*? Myths are essentially recounted; the story of the things that happened long ago is told, and re-told. But apotrope is not narrative but action upon those very beings whose exploits are set forth in myth. It is the product of efficacious ritual. Remember here how *drama* in Greek once meant 'doing'. When Theseus re-describes himself in that opening *volta*, in a euphemism which we hope will 'take', like an inoculation, Shakespeare is perhaps banishing, or 'praying-away' from his drama that mythic darkness which Racine will later let back in. But Shakespeare also knows that the joy and relief consequent upon the *apotrope* will lose their keenness if all sense of danger is lost. Hence the

---

6 Reproduced in Marina Warner, *From the Beast to the Blonde* (London, 1994), p. 257.
7 The Greek is tricky. The purposive colouring of δέχεσθαι, basically an epexegetic infinitive explaining Εὐμενίδας, is given by λιτάς, 'prayers' in line 484. See Sir Richard Jebb's edn (Cambridge, 1885), p. 85.
8 Ed. Stewart Anderson (Cambridge, 1976), p. 49.
9 In *A Midsummer Night's Dream*, 'New Casebooks', ed. Richard Dutton (London, 1996), pp. 198–222, at p. 213. See also D'Orsay W. Pearson, '"Unkinde Theseus'. A Study of Renaissance Mythography', *English Literary Renaissance*, 4 (1974), 276–98; M. E. Lamb, '*A Midsummer Night's Dream*: The Myth of Theseus and the Minotaur', *Texas Studies in Literature and Language*, 21 (1979), 478–91; David Ormerod, '*A Midsummer Night's Dream*: The Monster in the Labyrinth', *Shakespeare Studies*, 11 (1978), 39–52; Barbara A. Mowat, '"A Local Habitation and a Name": Shakespeare's text as construct', *Style*, 23 (1989), 335–51.
10 Ibid., p. 205.

keeping-alive of the disquiet after the opening *apotrope*.

How does Bully Bottom figure in this play of nervous delight? The answer (which may strike the reader as vacuously pious) is 'With a deep, very Shakespearian complex coherence'. Once more, the first thing to be said is that Bottom, translated into the form of a beast, is (hilariously) innocent. He lolls, like some degenerate Roman emperor, in the midst of a feast, as a beautiful woman climbs all over him, and his great hairy head is full of thoughts of food, not sex. He is like a small boy. Yeats famously said (in 'Ego Dominus Tuus') that Keats was like a schoolboy 'with face and nose pressed to a sweetshop window', which makes some sense if one thinks of *The Eve of Saint Agnes*. But, in spite of the notorious 'feast in the dorm' passage, we are in fact clearly aware that Porphyro in that poem is interested in sex as well as food. Bottom is interested only in the jellies and ice-creams (or rather, since the donkey is beginning to take over, in hay).

I am now repeating the move I made at the beginning of this essay. I said then that the most obvious thing - and the most obvious thing can be the most important thing − about Shakespeare's Theseus is that he differs from Racine's Thésée, as *A Midsummer Night's Dream* differs from *Phèdre, toto coelo*. But then I admitted a darker penumbra of meaning. So here, having asserted the comic innocence of Bottom, I must acknowledge that the mere sight of a woman entwined with a beast or half-beast of itself suggests monstrosity. Again I have to ask, are the demons completely removed? Is our laughter simple, unmixed, or is it the louder because energized by a surviving anxiety? Again, I go for the second alternative.

While the 'primary move' of Theseus is from hostility to benevolence, the 'primary move' of Bottom, at the level of action, is in the opposite direction, from human being to beast. That is why the Bottom sequence is immediately funny, as Theseus is not. In Bottom's case there is an element of shock to be surmounted and

this supplies the incongruity needed. 'Jupiter / Became a bull, and bellowed', says Florizel in *The Winter's Tale*, (4.4.28) (apparently in the hope of cheering up the rustic Perdita with august precedents of sexual condescension). But Bottom, who becomes not a bull but half an ass, is no Jupiter but a hard-handed mechanical. Yet Europa and the bull, Leda and the swan and all the other ancient stories of bestial coupling remain critically relevant. They are part of the material to be comically inverted or apotropaically defused. Again, a quantum of anxiety survives the *apotrope*. As I have said, it is difficult to look at a woman entwined with something which is turning, as we watch, into an animal − Beauty and the Beast − without worrying. The worry, at the back of one's mind, may be partly about physiology. 'Will she be hurt if they have sexual intercourse? Oh, no danger of that, I see' (laughter here) − but then the thought returns.

This obstinate refusal ever quite to go away is admirably caught by Peter Holland in his essay, 'Theseus' Shadows in *A Midsummer Night's Dream*'.[11] Holland quotes the sinister jingle of Hughes Mearns,

> As I was going up the stair
> I met a man who wasn't there,
> He wasn't there again today.
> *I wish, I wish he'd stay away.*

For Holland, Seneca's Hippolytus is a shadow - an absence-presence - in the play, 'a man on the stair'. Surely sane persons take care not to be seriously distracted by such things? Holland writes, 'Hippolytus cannot be ignored, but does that mean he should be noticed?' It is a good question. That criticism which solidifies the properly fluid, changes glimpses into full percepts, must be falsifying its material. But meanwhile it remains just (as Holland sees) to register shadows as − merely − shadows. Moreover our relation to these shadows may be more dynamically charged than at first appears. The last line

---

[11] *Shakespeare Survey 47* (Cambridge, 1994), pp. 139–51.

of the jingle expresses a wish. Translate that wish into magical action and you have, once more, *apotrope*.

As the Plutarchian Theseus stands behind the Duke of Athens, so the Golden Ass of Lucius Apuleius stands behind Bottom the Weaver. Once more, the scholarly editions rightly cite Adlington's translation of 1566 as a source. Here is Lucius' account of how he, transformed into an ass, became involved with a lustful matron. In this passage all the anxieties I was just alluding to are explicit.

Then she put off all her Garments to her naked skinne, and taking the Lampe that stood next to her, began to anoint her body with balme, and mine likewise, but especially my nose . . . Then she tooke me by the halter and cast me downe upon the bed, which was nothing strange unto me, considering that she was so beautifull a matron and I so wel boldened out with wine, and perfumed with balme, whereby I was readily prepared for the purpose: But nothing grieved me so much as to think, how I should with my huge and great legs imbrace so fair a Matron, or how I should touch her fine, dainty and silken skinne, with my hard hoofes, or how it was possible to kisse her soft, pretty and ruddy lips, with my monstrous mouth and stony teeth, or how she, who was young and tender, could be able to receive me.[12]

That last word, 'me' is a euphemism, on Adlington's part, a euphemism of the ordinary kind. The Latin at this point (x.22) is 'Tam vastum genitale'. Remember Pasiphae, within the wooden cow, receiving the organ of the bull. Apuleius, certainly, has not forgotten. He writes how the matron 'had her pleasure with me, whereby I thought the mother of Minotarus [sic] did not causelesse quench her inordinate desire with a Bull'.[13] Earlier, when the matron is introduced, she is likened to Pasiphae. Here Adlington says, simply 'as Pasiphae had with a Bull', eliding the note of comic incongruity, essential to the Shakespearian version, which is present in the Latin, *instar asinariae Pasiphaae* 'like some *asinine* Pasiphae'.

With Bottom, as with Theseus, if we read backwards into prior myth, we are led into the world of *Phèdre*. Bottom is a happily averted Minotaur, or Bull, Titania Pasiphae. In Peter Holland's essay the Minotaur is the second major 'shadow' of the play, after Hippolytus.[14] It will be said, 'There is nothing in Shakespeare about a huge penis.' True. But this thought must lie behind the physiological anxiety, the physiological comic incongruity. Titania's words,

While I thy amiable cheeks do coy,
And stick musk-roses in thy sleek smooth head
(4.1.2–3)

are funny because, as she speaks, we are looking at a monstrous, hairy head. She herself betrays, a line later, that even to the eye of infatuation Bottom's ears are oddly large. A moment afterwards he says himself, 'I am marvellous hairy about the face' and the scratchy word 'scratch' appears twice in the same speech (4.1.22–5). A sense of physical incompatibility is present in the faint Ovidian surrealism of Titania's image of 'the female ivy' encircling 'the barky fingers of the elm' at 4.1.42–3. Think of Apollo feeling the breast of Daphne as the bark began to form over it, the heart fluttering under the roughened surface, at *Metamorphoses*, i.554. Horror is successfully averted. We laugh and we are happy. But the horror is there, to be averted, and in some degree survive the act of aversion. The director who caused Bottom to cast on the backcloth a shadow (Peter Holland's word!) that looked for a moment more like a minotaur than a donkey would not, I suggest, be exceeding his interpretative brief.

There is a nasty poem by Martial about a promiscuous lady, one Marulla, whose children can be seen by their looks to have many fathers,

---

12 *The Golden Ass of Apuleius*, translated by William Adlington. The Tudor Translations, ed. W. E. Henley, iv (London, 1893), p. 218.

13 Ibid., p. 217.

14 'Theseus' Shadows in *A Midsummer Night's Dream*', pp. 149 f.

none of which is the lady's husband. One with frizzy hair looks like the African cook; another, with flat nose and thickened lips is the very image of Pannicus, the wrestler and so on. The poem includes these lines,

> Hunc vero acuto capite, et auribus longis,
> Quae sic moventur ut solent assellorum
> Quis morionis filium neget Cyrrhae?[15]

And this one with his tapering head and long ears which have a way of twitching like those of an ass, who will deny that he is the son of the idiot Cyrrha?

No grand mythology now, but a sneer at the woman who will go with anyone, even a cretin. Bottom may not be an idiot, which seems to be the sense of *morio* here. But another sense of *morio* is 'one kept as a laughing stock, a fool', and this is not a million miles away from Bottom's function in relation to the grand persons of the play. Although Shakespeare gives him the most profound speech in the comedy, 'It shall be called "Bottom's Dream", because it hath no bottom' (4.1.213–4), his best friend could not call him wise. When the love-crazed Titania applies this word to him at 3.1.140 ('Thou art as wise as thou are beautiful'), it always gets a laugh. I cite Martial's donkey-man not because I am sure – or even think – that Shakespeare read this poem but because it highlights discomforts of a more trivial kind than those broached in the more ancient myths – discomforts arising from perceived social and intellectual disparity. This is also relevant to the comedy of *A Midsummer Night's Dream*. But the myths, with their deeper violence, though they may seem more remote from comedy, really are more deeply pertinent to the major effects of this play.

It is often said that Shakespeare continued to be an adventurous, experimental poet to the very end. *The Tempest*, his last complete play, is a very strange pastoral. A displaced duke and his entourage find themselves in an uncivilized place, where the issues of nature and nurture are debated and all are sorted out, so that they can begin their lives afresh at the end. Thus far I could be describing *As You Like it*. But we are not in Arden or Arcadia. We are on a supposedly Mediterranean island which is removed by more than Atlantic distances from the North African coast, in a place having its own physical laws and lawlessness – almost an alternative, science-fiction world. *The Tempest*, therefore, is transposed pastoral. But long before all this, *A Midsummer Night's Dream* was also, in its own way, a transposed pastoral. The transposition is achieved by darkening, and by placing the trees closer together. In ordinary pastoral there are spaces for the sheep to crop the grass, spaces for reflection, singing-competitions and so on. But the dense, tangled wood – an Athenian labyrinth to answer that of Crete – is frightening. This is the same wood that we find in Milton's *Comus* or in Kenneth Graham's *The Wind in the Willows* – the Wild Wood. Shakespeare has in this early play given us a Nocturnal Pastoral, itself, generically, a strange thing. Even the weather is unpastorally bad. You hear people say 'Oh, we don't have summers now like the summers I remember in my childhood.' *A Midsummer Night's Dream*, if indistinctly remembered, can seem (there are so many flowers in it) to embody this golden world. Yet if we re-enter the play we meet people complaining, exactly as people complain today, about the rotten weather this year.

> Therefore the winds, piping to us in vain,
> As in revenge have sucked up from the sea
> Contagious fogs which, falling in the land,
> Hath every pelting river made so proud
> That they have overborne their continents.
> The ox hath therefore stretched his yoke in vain,
> The ploughman lost his sweat, and the green corn
> Hath rotted ere his youth attained a beard,
> The fold stands empty in the drowned field,
> And crows are fatted with the murrain flock.
> The nine-men's morris is filled up with mud,
> And the quaint mazes in the wanton green
> For lack of tread are indistinguishable
>
> (2.1.88–100)

---

15 Epigrams. vi.39. 'To Cinna'.

57

Even this speech, which might seem the purest contemporary realism, has its roots in ancient materials. There is a running reference to ancient plague: the plague of Aegina in Ovid (*Metamorphoses*, vii), the plague of Thebes in Seneca's *Oedipus*, *Medea* and *Hippolytus* (the last of these is of course Seneca's 'Phèdre'). But the reader may say, 'Stop! You are reading backwards again'.

In what sense is *A Midsummer Night's Dream* an apotropaic work? Shakespeare has performed an active, suasive euphemism upon ancient myth, and this, I have suggested is in accord with the element of quasi-ritual efficacy still present in comic drama but absent from pure narrative. But presumably in this irreligious, unsuperstitious age we cannot believe that a full *apotrope*, in the old sense, has occurred. We cannot believe that demons have been driven off, because we do not believe in demons. Could the play, nevertheless, have been a full *apotrope* for the original audience, in the 1590s? I am not sure, but I suspect not. The magic of *A Midsummer Night's Dream* is not like the magic of *The Tempest*. Prospero is a serious (highly fashionable) proto-scientific magician, a little like the real Dr Dee, but the magic and fairies of the earlier play are perceptibly becoming picturesque, the stuff of the old tales at which city people now smile. If that is right, this *apotrope* never had the status of an efficacious ritual, actually turning aside malign spirits. Weakening of belief makes inversion of tone easier. It is obviously a simpler matter to vary a mere tale than to alter a known, inherited truth. If people in the seventeenth century had really believed that, once, Apollo pursued Daphne, it would have been harder for Andrew Marvell in 'The Garden' to turn the myth on its head, suggesting that the god, so far from being frustrated when Daphne was turned into a laurel, was actually pursuing her, with dendrophiliac intent, *because* she was turning into a very attractive plant.

It might be thought that Theseus would have been history not myth for Shakespeare because he is in Plutarch. But it is pretty evident that we are not in the historically constrained environment of *Julius Caesar*. Shakespeare knows his audience will have some notion of Theseus as a character but will have few rigid expectations. But all of this, while it facilitates the transformation we see in *A Midsummer Night's Dream*, seems at the same time to deprive it of apotropaic force.

Indeed, we have made it all too easy. While we may not believe in demons, we still believe in what those demons mean. The fears remain. Could Shakespeare have performed a real *apotrope* not at the level of spirits and demons but at the psychological level? Has he turned away fear, not only within his fiction but in the minds and hearts of those who watch?

Within the fiction he has turned aside not only ancient myth but also incipient tragedy. We have the *Hippolytus* of Euripides and Seneca, the *Phèdre* of Racine, but we know, when we see Duke Theseus smiling on Hippolyta, that we are not going to get Shakespeare's - I suspect that it would have been called - *Hippolytus and Phaedra*. While Shakespeare is carefully *not* writing *Phèdre* the mechanicals are carefully *not* performing *Romeo and Juliet*. 'I believe we must leave the killing out, when all is done,' says Starveling (3.1.12−13) and they all assent. At the same time Shakespeare is concerned not simply that his audience should be happy but that it should experience the more specific pleasure of relief. The myths, though not felt to be literally true, are still full of meaning and that meaning is black. Shakespeare triumphs over horror not only with humour but with a still-ambiguous beauty, a beauty mediated by the pale fire of moonlight, itself somehow half-way between darkness and day. In America at Halloween little children shriek with alarm at the first appearance of witches and goblins and then the shrieks turn to peals of laughter. Most of them (not all) are, I think, psychically strengthened and protected by the process. A successful *apotrope* of fear is performed. We seem now very close indeed to the real *apotrope* of *A Midsummer Night's Dream*.

It is, however, one thing to comfort a person by saying 'It's all right – wake up – the thing you feared was never real at all' and another to say, 'You can deal with your fear if you *pretend* it isn't there – tell a different story to yourself – give the demons smiling faces.' The former kind gives the more complete victory; indeed it is not so much an *apotrope* as a complete exorcism, or abolition. There is no need, in this scheme, to evoke the notion of suasive euphemism, for there is no malign entity to be flatteringly re-described. But the latter scheme – 'Give the demons smiling faces' – implicitly allows that the dark forces continue in existence. We turn them aside, keep them off, at least for a while, by pretending in their hearing – as a placating courtesy – that they are benevolent. Which of these is the scheme of *A Midsummer Night's Dream*? Puck's epilogue in which he draws a line under the whole experience by terming it a *mere* dream – 'you have *but* slumber'd here' (Epilogue.3) – is the first. The logic is the re-assuring logic of Theseus' 'lunatic/lover' speech, always obscurely annoying to lovers of poetry. But Hippolyta's reply to Theseus, Bottom's 'It hath no bottom' and Demetrius' love for Helena, which, wonderfully, spills over from the enchanted night into the following, civil day, are the other. These powers and their effects are not, after all, so easily erased. Thus a sense of euphemism survives the close of the play. This entails a negotiation – with a long spoon, as it were – between comedy and tragedy, between comedy and myth, a negotiation, that is, between joy and fear, resulting in an *apotrope* of the latter. Just that, *apotrope*, not abolition.

PLUTARCH, INSURRECTION, AND DEARTH IN *CORIOLANUS*

DAVID GEORGE

'The rising of the peasants has gone on growing from day to day to such an extent that they only required a leader to make it formidable and open rebellion'. (Venetian Ambassador to England, to the Doge and Senate, 26 June 1607)[1]

Back in 1876, an anonymous critic in *The Cornell Review* pronounced *Coriolanus* 'biography dramatized'.[2] Brander Matthews said much the same thing about the play in 1913: 'Shakespeare rarely contradicts Plutarch whereas he often contradicted Holinshed; he speeds up Plutarch's passage of time, however, and makes no attempt to recreate the ancient world.'[3] For John W. Draper in 1939, Plutarch's story is retold in *Coriolanus* in contemporary terms.[4] Recently, in 1996, David Farley-Hills has repeated the idea that 'the sources of *Coriolanus* are . . . followed with considerable fidelity, with only those changes that help convert prose narrative into effective verse drama'.[5]

Certainly Shakespeare followed the main events of Plutarch's 'Life of Caivs Martius Coriolanus': the citizen unrest in Rome, the war with Corioli, Coriolanus' standing for consul, his opposition to the tribunes and free corn, the mob violence, his trial and banishment, his alliance with the Volscians and attack on Rome, the embassy of women, his yielding to Volumnia, and assassination in Antium.[6] Yet in Acts 1 and 3, particularly, Shakespeare added current and exciting material from 1607–8.

As Plutarch tells the story of unrest in Rome, the commoners returned from the Sabine war only to find that they were at the mercy of their creditors. (This might have been about 491 BC, the date at which the Roman republic was founded.)[7] The commoners therefore rebelled and stirred up tumults in the city. Rome's enemies immediately attacked. Recruitment of the plebeians failing, some senators counselled forgiveness of their debts, but Martius argued that lenity towards them would foment disobedience. The commoners retreated to Mons Sacer, about three miles from the city, and to them the senators sent Menenius Agrippa, who told them the fable of the belly and its dependent members. The pacified commoners agreed to return to Rome if they could have five representatives or tribunes in the Senate. Two were chosen, Junius Brutus and Sicinius Vellutus. Recruitment of the commoners now pro-

---

[1] *Calendar of State Papers and Manuscripts: Venice*, ed. Horatio F. Brown vol. 11 1607–1610 (London, 1904), p. 8.

[2] Reported in John Velz, *Shakespeare and the Classical Tradition* (Minneapolis, 1968), pp. 200–1.

[3] *Shakspere as a Playwright* (London, 1913), pp. 257–8.

[4] '*Coriolanus* and Plutarch', *West Virginia University Bulletin Philological Studies*, 3 (1939), 22–36.

[5] '*Coriolanus* and the Tragic Use of History', *Shakespeare Yearbook*, 6 (1995), 205.

[6] Geoffrey Bullough, ed., *Narrative and Dramatic Sources of Shakespeare*, vol. 5 (London, 1964), p. 477.

[7] William Warburton, *The Plays of William Shakespeare*, eds. Samuel Johnson and George Steevens (London, 1778), vol. 7, p. 381.

ceeded, and the battle for Corioli took place, in which Martius entered the city 'with very fewe men'. He took the city and helped win the field. However, when the soldiers returned to Rome, they faced a lack of corn, since the retreat to Mons Sacer had taken place in the ploughing season. Coriolanus stood for consul and was rejected. Rome eventually purchased some corn and received a gift of more from Sicily. Coriolanus opposed a corn dole and the tribunes' appointment. He was forced to answer the plebeians' accusations concerning this opposition on two separate occasions, and sentenced to banishment. After that, Plutarch's narrative and *Coriolanus* follow the same sequence. From the Sabine war to Martius' assassination seems to have taken four years, 491–487 BC or 262–266 AUC.[8]

This narrative is too bald for dramatization on two counts: it fails to follow up the acute psychological remarks which open 'The Life of Coriolanus', and it has only historical interest. Shakespeare therefore turned to Livy's 'Romane Historie' to fill in the key influences on Martius, and to the Midlands insurrection and dearth of 1607–8 to create popular interest. Plutarch notes that Martius was an orphan, and 'orphanage bringeth many discommodities to a childe, but doth not hinder him to become an honest man'; but 'for lacke of education, he was so chollericke and impacient, that he wold yeeld to no liuing creature: which made him churlishe, vnciuil, and altogether vnfit for any mans conuersation'. 'Education' here is used in an obsolete sense, 'proper upbringing', and Shakespeare demonstrates Martius' lack of it by analogy, in the report of the wilful behaviour of Young Martius, the mammocker of butterflies. Martius was also 'too much giuen to ouer selfe will and opinion' and he 'lacked the grauitie, and affabilitie that is gotten with iudgement of learning and reason'; and to 'wilfulnesse . . . , that which *Plato* called solitarinesse'.[9] His defective upbringing is linked with Volumnia's domination and Menenius' surrogate father-

hood. Shakespeare found Volumnia's high temper in Livy, where, refusing to plead for the sparing of Rome, she fell instead into 'a fit of choller' and berated her son. He found Coriolanus' deep reverence for her in Plutarch, where Martius kissed and embraced her before turning to his wife when the women came to plead for Rome. As for Menenius, Livy calls him 'a faire spoken and eloquent man, gratious withall and welbeloved among the commons, for that he was from them descended'; he died soon after the battle of Corioli, known only as a mediator, but not as a friend to Martius.[10] Somehow Shakespeare had to insert scenes into Acts 1 and 2 that would indicate Volumnia's domination and Menenius' fatherly indulgence of Coriolanus. Thus the swift Plutarchan narrative is slowed by 1.3 (the 'sewing scene') and the dialogue between Volumnia and Menenius in 2.1 about Coriolanus' wounds (95–159). These episodes may be called psychological exposition. Menenius, of course, is necessary throughout the entire play, and outlives his Livian model by years. Yet there was still something to do to enliven Plutarch's early scenes. Sabines, creditors, Mons Sacer, failure to plough, purchase of corn in Italy – all these Shakespeare omitted. He had before him something that would make Act 1 as recognizable to the audience as the back of their hands. Violent insurrection had taken place in the Midlands in June 1607, and severe dearth in all England in 1608. Most of 1.1 of *Coriolanus* is devoted to England's two troublesome years.

Dearth in Tudor and Stuart England was not unusual. Shakespeare lived through grain shortages in 1563–4, 1573–4, 1586–7, and 1595–7, all years when harvests were bad and

---

8 Warburton, *Plays*, p. 381.

9 'Life of Caivs Martius Coriolanus', *The Lives of the Noble Grecians and Romanes . . . By . . . Plutarke . . . English, by Thomas North* (London, 1595), pp. 235, 243; *OED*, 'Education', 2.

10 Plutarch, p. 539; *The Romane Historie Written by T. Livius . . . Translated . . . by Philemon Holland* (London, 1600), pp. 65, 66.

grain prices jumped.[11] Yet, a grain export trade had grown up, and hence storage and shipping facilities existed, which could not be easily interrupted when dearth struck. For example, in 1606, the Venetian ambassador wrote home that English grain was being shipped overseas to Otranto, the Grand Duke, Naples, the Pontifical States, and Venice because of competitive market prices.[12] Also, an agricultural revolution was under way; a lot of land that had been arable since medieval times was now found more suitable for grazing, and pasture was being created at a fairly rapid rate. These forces tended to deprive farm labourers of work, and in years of dearth even of food itself. As a result of enclosure, the grain trade, and dearth, a discourse on the causes, effects and remedies for dearth and famine had arisen, with its own vocabulary, phrases and commonplaces.

Dearth and famine did more than create a public discourse. 'Dearth had repeatedly stimulated both [e]nclosure riots and legislation', wrote E. F. Gay.[13] 'Enclosure riots' were energetic protests against the fencing-in of arable fields, usually accompanied by tearing down hedges, throwing the new earthen embankments into the boundary ditches of the field, or knocking down stone walls. 'In areas such as the Midlands, the interests of capitalist farming and the peasantry met head-on over the issue of enclosure and conversion of land to pasture for the purposes of commercial sheep-grazing.'[14] Farm labourers were usually the main body of insurrectionists.

In 1550, when grain prices were well on their way to doubling, Robert Crowley examined the problem from both the rich and poor's points of view. If a poor countryman were asked what caused sedition, he would reply 'the great fermares, the grasiers, the rich butchares, the men of lawe, the marchaunts, the gentlemen, the knightes, the lordes . . . men that would be alone on the earth, men that bee neuer satisfied, Cormerauntes, gredye gulles . . . These Idle bealies will deuour al yat we shal get by our sore labour in our youth . . .

Better it were therfore, for vs to dye lyke men, then after so great misery in youth to dye more miserably in age.' If, on the other hand, a rich man were asked the same question, he would reply that 'the paisant knaues be to wealthy, prouender pricketh them. They knowe not them selues, they knowe no obedience, they regard no lawes, thei wold haue al men like themselues, they would haue al thinges commune . . . And if they once stirre againe or do but once cluster togither, we wil hang them at their own dores.'[15]

This, then, was the frame of the debate – the cormorant bellies on one side, the peasant knaves on the other. The language is typical of the two hostile sides: the First Citizen in *Coriolanus* uses 'cormorant belly' (1.1.119); Brutus remarks sneeringly that Coriolanus believes the people 'have their provand / Only for bearing burdens' (2.1.248–9). Coriolanus would 'hang 'em' (1.1. 179, 202; 2.3.57) or 'let them hang' (3.2.22). To Menenius, they are

---

11 James E. Thorold Rogers, *A History of Agriculture and Prices in England*, 7 vols. (1866–1902), vol. 3, 109, 113; vol. 4, 175, 180–1. The 1597 famine, which Rogers (182) did not doubt led to the Poor Law of 1601, caused deaths from starvation in all counties, particularly in Newcastle in September and October of that year (E. M. Leonard, *The Early History of English Poor Relief* [Cambridge, 1900], pp. 124–5).

12 *Calendar of State Papers, Venetian*, ed. Horatio F. Brown, vol. 10 (London, 1900; repr. Nendeln/Liechtenstein, 1970) pp. 414–15 (26 Oct. 1606).

13 E. F. Gay, 'The Midland Revolt of 1607', *Transactions of the Royal Historical Society*, 18 (1904), p. 213.

14 John E. Martin, *Feudalism to Capitalism* (Atlantic Highlands, NJ, 1983), p. 132.

15 *The Way to Wealth*, A.iii–B.iii. On 26 June 1607, the Venetian Ambassador reported that some of the Northamptonshire Leveller leaders were hanged in sight of their fellows (*Calendar of State Papers, Venetian*, vol. 11 [London, 1904] p. 8). *A Knack to Know a Knave* (1594) carries on the hostile discourse against farmers' grain-hoarding and enclosing, in four passages (C2, D1V–D2, E3, G4). Honesty, seeking a 'priuie knaue', identifies him as 'a farmer . . . which buyes vp all the corn in the market, and sends it away beyond seas, & thereby feeds the enemie'; Piers Plowman claims the farmer has impoverished him by buying up land (E3).

'clusters' (4.6.130, 136). 'Men that would be alone on the earth' is mirrored in Sicinius' angry demand, 'Where is this viper / That would depopulate the city and / Be every man himself?' (3.1.263–5).

Given the mutual despising of gentry and commons in Shakespeare's lifetime, it was inevitable that dearths and depopulation would be flashpoints. An insurrection took place in late 1596 in Oxfordshire after grain prices had tripled since 1594. The ringleaders were summoned to London, examined under torture, and attainted, and some of them hanged.[16] The insurrection of 1607 was caused by depopulation. Though 'the winter of 1606–7 was extremely severe and gave rise to a bad harvest in 1607', there was no grain shortage at market till Michaelmas (29 Sept.).[17] The trouble lay in the enclosings of fields. Husbandmen, who had lost their livelihoods because of enclosing, were calling themselves 'levellers', and assembling as early as 30 April 1607 at Haselbech, Newton, Pytchley and Rushton in Northamptonshire, and about the same time outside Northampton town, Stoke Bruerne and Ashton. By 31 May, 'there were documented riots at Haselbech, Newton, Pytchley and Rushton; in Warwickshire, at Ladbroke, Hillmorton, Withybrook, Coventry and Chilvers Coton; and, in Leicestershire, at Cotesbach and Welham'.[18] The numbers at Hillmorton were 3,000 and at Cotesbach, 5,000. On 30 May, the King and Privy Council issued a royal proclamation and found it 'now very necessary to vse sharper remedies' against the rebels and to 'suppresse them . . . be it by force of arms'.[19] These riots were actually works of destruction: 'they violently cut and brake downe hedges, filled vp ditches, and laid open all such inclosures of Commons, and other grounds as they found inclosed, which of auncient time had beene open . . . some of them were faine to vse Bills, Pykes, and such like tooles in stead of Mattocke and Spades'.[20]

On 8 June, armed gentry faced about 1,000 insurrectionists at 'Newton ffeild', as one con-temporary called it. The forces were not unknown to each other; as the Earl of Shrewsbury told Sir John Manners, Newton was 'Mr Thos. Tresham's toune'.[21] Tresham had been convicted of depopulating and sheep-farming in 1597–8, but he had since put 'the whole parish under grass' and leased it out.[22] Sir Walter Montagu and Sir Anthony Mildmay, justices of the peace, captained the gentry forces, which had to be raised from tenants because the 'trained bands' or militia would not appear. Montagu was a neighbouring enclosing landowner, and Mildmay probably another. Mildmay and Montagu 'first read the proclamation twice unto them, using all the best perswasions to them to desist that they could devise; but when nothing would prevaile, they charged them thoroughlie both with their horse and foote. But the first charge they stoode, and fought desperatlie; but at the second charge they ran away, in which there weare slaine som 40 or 50 of them, and a very great number hurt.'[23] The Revd Thomas Cox added sometime before 1640 that the levellers at Newton came to destroy the hedges and other mounds, a skirmish ensued, and 'in the fray some were killed, and wounded, and many taken prisoners, who afterwards were hanged and quartered and their quarters set up at *Northampton, Oundle, Thrapston* and other places'.[24] This signalled the end of the large-scale demonstrations.[25] On 21 June, Robert Wilkinson preached against the rebels at Northampton, finding it horrible that

---

[16] Gay, 'Midland Revolt', p. 212; Martin, *Feudalism*, p. 157.

[17] Martin, *Feudalism*, p. 162.

[18] Martin, *Feudalism*, pp. 166–7.

[19] *A Booke of Proclamations* (London, 1609), p. 139.

[20] Edmund Howes, *Annales . . . by Iohn Stow . . . Continved by Edmund Howes* (London, 1631), pp. 890–[1].

[21] Gay, 'Midland Revolt', p. 216.

[22] Martin, *Feudalism*, p. 185.

[23] Gay, 'Midland Revolt', pp. 216–17.

[24] Peter Whalley, *History and Antiquities of Northamptonshire*, 2 vols. (Oxford, 1791), vol. 2, p. 206.

[25] Martin, *Feudalism*, p. 167.

'A King of three great kingdomes must capitulate with a Tinker'.[26] (The 'Tinker' was John Reynolds, alias Captain Pouch, who was present at several insurrections and acted as a leader of sorts.) There were assemblies by mid-June in Leicestershire and Bedfordshire, and in later months at Peachley, Worcestershire; Cogges, Oxfordshire; Nassington, Northamptonshire; and Chapel-en-le-Frith, Derbyshire. Of these disaffected places, Hillmorton in Warwickshire was the worst alienated after Newton. Mary Astley had depopulated the village by enclosing 750 acres – thus depriving husbandmen of farm jobs and driving them out of town.[27] Hillmorton was struggling to survive at all; Shakespeare could scarcely not have known of the insurrection, Hillmorton being only twenty-five miles from Stratford. Moreover, he would have been in Stratford for his mother's funeral on 9 September 1608. On 28 June, King James was ready to speak again. He issued a proclamation stating that the 'meanest sort of our people' have persisted in seditious courses 'after particular Proclamations published by our Royall Authoritie'. Rebellion and unlawful assembly will be punished as treason. There will be 'execution (euen to present death) of such as shall make resistance'.[28] Slowly the large assemblies melted away; 'by mid-July, the government felt confident enough to organise royal commissions to inquire into offending enclosures. Throughout August and September the depopulation commissions for the counties concerned sat in the appropriate county towns and heard information regarding illegal enclosure.'[29]

New sufferings lay ahead for the common people. From Michaelmas 1607, the price of wheat rose almost continuously until Michaelmas of 1608. The cause was 'the autumn sowings . . . not [having] as satisfactory results as the spring sowings had'.[30] By 29 September, wheat was double in price over the previous 29 September, and remained that way on 25 March 1609. So the summer of 1608 was a summer of hunger. On 2 June 1608, King James issued 'A Proclamation for the preuenting and remedying of the dearth of Graine, and other Victuals'. This proclamation charged JPs 'to direct all Owners and Farmers, (hauing Corne to spare) to furnish the markets rateably and weekely'.[31] On the same date, William Combe, High Sheriff of Warwickshire, wrote to Robert Cecil from Warwick that the common people of the county were troubled with dearth and high corn prices, caused partly by corn speculators and partly by maltsters buying up barley to corner the market. The situation was causing the people to speak against enclosures.[32] On 5 July, another proclamation required that even bran, the coarsest portion of the ground husk, be discontinued as a source of corn starch, with the implication that it was to be made available for sale to the public.[33] 'The harvest [of 1608] is a decided failure. At first prices are very high, but they slowly decline through the year.'[34] Yet another proclamation of 12 December showed there

---

26 *A Sermon Preached at North-Hampton the 21. of June Last Past* (London, 1607), FI–[FIV]. Cf. *Coriolanus* 5.3.82–4: 'Do not bid me / Dismiss my soldiers, or capitulate / Again with Rome's mechanics.'

27 Martin, *Feudalism*, pp. 188–9.

28 *A Booke of Proclamations*, pp. 140–4.

29 Martin, *Feudalism*, p. 167.

30 Rogers, *History*, 5, 186.

31 *A Booke of Proclamations*, p. 174.

32 Edgar I. Fripp, *Shakespeare: Man and Artist*, 2 vols. (London, 1938), vol. 2, p. 706.

33 *A Booke of Proclamations*, p. 178. Cf. *Coriolanus* 1.1.142–4: 'Yet I can make my audit up, that all / From me do back receive the flour of all / And leave me but the bran.'

34 Rogers, *History*, vol. 5, p. 186; see fig. 3, Table I from Rogers, whose figures show a jump in grain prices from 37s. 6¼d. to 53s. 0½d. nationally in 1608; these sums are for 64 gallons of wheat, or 8 bushels. See also fig. 4, Table X, from W. F. Lloyd, *Prices of Corn in Oxford* (Oxford, 1830), which shows Midlands prices at Michaelmas 1608; wheat jumped to 8s. a bushel and did not decline to a more normal 4s. 2d. until Michaelmas 1609. For 8 bushels, an Oxford buyer would pay 64s. in 1608 and 33s. 4d. in 1609. The normal price was about 30s. for 8 bushels. Thus Oxford prices in 1608 were 10s. or about 20 per cent above the national average.

3   James E. Thorold Rogers, *A History of Agriculture*.

was still 'scarcity & dearth of Corne and Graine'.[35] There were no riots in 1608, but William Woodwall, preaching in Stroud, Gloucestershire, in 1609, mentioned that grain prices still remained high. 'Some', he said, 'impute it vnto vsury and extortion, for neuer was there such vsury I suppose, for heere is vse vpon vse, beside vse for the principall.' Some kept their wheat in barns so long from market that it became inedible.[36] The wheat price had declined by summer 1609.

A Commission of Enquiry into depopulations had been appointed in August 1607 to look into the Midlands enclosures. Some of the

[35] *A Booke of Proclamations*, p. 186.

[36] Woodwall, *A sermon upon the xii.xiij. and xiiij. verses of the xiiij. chapter of Ezechiel* (London, 1609), p. 22. It is easy to confuse the crisis caused by the localized rebellions of 1607 with that of the national dearth of 1608. Such seems the case with Annabel Patterson, who writes that 'the summer of 1607 saw the Midlands Rising, one of the worst agricultural protests the nation had experienced', and that 1607 also had a bad harvest (*Fables of Power: Aesopian Writing and Political History* [Durham, NC,1991], pp. 119–20). The starvation of 1608 affected many more parts of the country than the protests and hangings of 1607. Hence the 'Mutinous Citizens' in 1.1 have 'Bats and Clubs' as well as pitchforks, since they are to represent city-dwellers as well as countryfolk – both reduced by the 1608 dearth.

65

4   W. F. Lloyd, *Prices of Corn in Oxford.*

landowners were prosecuted for enclosing and depopulating, and some enclosing hedges and embankments were ordered to be levelled. In the Trinity (summer) law term of 1608, however, someone challenged the Commission's legality in the High Court, and its activities were found to be invalid on a technicality. By 12 August 1608, the Northamptonshire gentry were back at their old game of enclosing, thus 'causing discontent among the meaner sort of people'.[37]

The vocabulary of this discourse has a number of key words: dearth, bran, musty chaff, stone walls, cormorant, idle bellies, clusters, provender, depopulation; weapons, pikes, proclamations, capitulate, charges of treason; and, as punishment for riot, present death, hangings, and quarterings. The basic, time-honoured metaphor for the commonwealth or kingdom was a body with belly, limbs, veins, head, etc. – and so King James thought of it. How much of this thought and vocabulary Shakespeare borrowed from the pamphlets, sermons and proclamations that made the discourse public we cannot tell; he may simply have absorbed the small change of common talk about the enclosures, riots and dearth. Thus

---

[37] Gay, 'Midland Revolt', p. 219.

Robert Powell, writing in 1636, could refer to a depopulator's removal of arable land as 'like the biting of an Aspe, a little serpent in *Affrick*, which takes away the life of him whom it bites in a kinde of swowme'.[38] When Sicinius accuses Coriolanus of trying to depopulate Rome, he uses the same image: 'Where is this viper / That would depopulate the city and / Be every man himself?' (3.1.263–5); likewise Sicinius: 'we are peremptory to dispatch / This viperous traitor' (3.1.287–8). (The viper is the homely British equivalent of the asp – both poisonous.) Shakespeare nowhere else uses 'depopulate' or its derivatives.

The First Citizen complains, 'If they would yield us but the superfluity while it were wholesome, we might guess they relieved us humanely' (1.1.16–18). As noted, Woodwall charged 'they . . . with-draw their Corne from the poor, and keepe it in their Barnes, Rickes, or Garners, vntill it be so mouldie or fustie, that the Rats and Mice will scant eat it'.[39] The First Citizen goes on, 'The leanness that afflicts us, the object of our misery, is as an inventory to particularize their abundance; our sufferance is a gain to them. Let us revenge this with our pikes ere we become rakes' (1.1.18–22). 'The Diggers of Warwickshire' said the same thing in 1607: 'Mercyless men doe resist wth force agst our good intents . . . onely for theyr priuate gaine, for there is none of them but doe tast the sweetness of our wantes.'[40] The idea that Roman patricians and English landowners enjoyed their abundance more because of the sufferings of the poor is typical of the way Shakespeare has blended 491 BC and 1608 in Act I of *Coriolanus*. The 'pikes' (pitchforks) and 'staves' (1.1.66) were the only implements many of the levellers had, and so the Roman citizens are partly equipped with the same implements.[41]

When Menenius takes the government line ('For the dearth, / The gods, not the patricians, make it') – the First Citizen retorts, 'They ne'er cared for us yet: suffer us to famish, and their storehouses crammed with grain; make edicts

for usury to support usurers; repeal daily any wholesome act established against the rich and provide more piercing statutes daily to chain up and restrain the poor' (1.1.70–1; 77–82). Evidence survives to show that storehouses were indeed crammed with grain. William Combe, writing from Warwick on 2 June 1608, told Robert Cecil that 'the dearth of corn, the prices rising to some height, [is] caused partly by some that are well stored, by refraining to bring the same to the market out of a covetous conceit that corn will be dearer'.[42] A royal proclamation, also 2 June, said the same thing: 'The rich Owners of Corne doe keepe their store from common markets, thereby to encrease the prices therof'.[43] Woodwall mentions the usury going on at the time, and English 'edicts for usury' were debated in 1604 and 1606. In 1571, Elizabeth's parliament had passed a law against usury, setting the legal maximum rate of interest at 10 per cent, and attempts to lower this rate in 1604 and 1606 were defeated.[44] As for 'more piercing statutes daily', the First Citizen may be referring to the 1607 insurrection. He can hardly have been referring to parliamentary statutes, since Parliament was out of session from 4 July 1607 to 9 February 1609/10. The proclamations of the summer of 1607 became increasingly strident. These may be what Shakespeare had in mind. On 30 May 1607, power was given to the Lords-Lieutenants and other county officers 'immediatly to suppresse

---

38 *Depopvlation Arraigned* (London, 1636), p. 5.

39 Woodwall, *A sermon*, p. 22.

40 'The Diggers of Warwickshire to all other Diggers'. MS. Harl. 787, f. 9v. (?1607). This is not in a hand from that date, however, and may be a later copy.

41 The Earl of Shrewsbury to Sir John Manners, 11 Jun. 1607: 'thease fellows who term themselves levelers weare busily digging, but weare furnished with many half pykes, pyked staves, long bills, and bowes and arrowes and stoanes' (Gay, 'Midland Revolt', p. 216, n. 3).

42 Fripp, *Shakespeare*, vol. 2, p. 706.

43 *A Booke of Proclamations*, p. 174.

44 Norman L. Jones, *God and the Moneylenders* (Oxford, 1989), pp. 176–8.

[the assemblies] by whatsoeuer meanes they may, be it by force of Armes'. The 28 June proclamation stated that the most obstinate rebels were committing treason, and that rebels having persisted in their 'seditious courses not onely after many prohibitions by our Ministers in the seuerall Counties but after particular Proclamations published by our Royall Author-itie', the Lords-Lieutenants and other officers were authorized to destroy these assemblies 'by force of Armes, and by execution (euen to present death)'.[45] It may be that the First Citizen does not exaggerate the frequency of measures taken against the poor during the 1607 insurrections; the majority of these 'prohi-bitions' and 'Proclamations' either have been lost or are not easily accessible.

When Martius arrives, he challenges the Citizens' claim that there is enough grain in store, and adds, 'Would the nobility lay aside their ruth / And let me use my sword, I'd make a quarry / With thousands of these quartered slaves, as high / As I could pick my lance' (1.1.195–8). Shakespeare may have heard of the quarterings that followed the skirmish at Newton Field, and of the setting up of those quarters at Northampton and elsewhere. If the body quarters were on spikes, like meat on a skewer, then the comparison with a quarry or pile of deer meat was exact. In any case, no commentator on these lines has been able to suggest another case of quartered peasants set up like a quarry of meat following an insurrection. The use of the Midlands form 'pick' for 'pitch' is noteworthy. Not authorized to butcher the citizens, Coriolanus prefers to use them as recruits against the Volscians, where they can loot: 'The Volsces have much corn. Take these rats thither / To gnaw their garners' (1.1.249–50). We recall Woodwall speaking of garners and rats.

Coriolanus returns to the subject of the citizens' power in 3.1.143–64, when he urges the senators 'That love the fundamental part of state' and 'wish / To jump a body with a dangerous physic / That's sure of death without

it' to dismiss the tribunes from the senate (lines 154, 156–8). In other words, to Coriolanus Rome will die unless it receives a jolt, though the medicine may be dangerous. He is alluding to the Jacobean physicians' most risky cure; according to Philemon Holland, hellebore, ad-ministered as a decoction or inhaled, 'putteth the Patient to a iumpe or great hazzard'.[46] King James's proclamation of 28 June 1607 used the same image, again about putting down the rebellious citizens for the health of the country: 'wee are bound (as the head of the politike body of our Realme) to follow the course which the best phisitians vse in dangerous diseases, which is, by a sharpe remedie applied to a small & infected part, to saue the whole from dissolution & destruction'.[47] The parallel is close; both James and Shakespeare refer to a dangerous medicine, applied to save a patient – a country – from certain death.

The charge of treason levelled at the Mid-lands rebels is, of course, levelled at Coriolanus by Brutus and Sicinius (3.1.174; 3.3.69). Brutus pronounces him worthy of 'present death', the legal phrase used by King James on 28 June 1607. Coriolanus is charged with 'Opposing laws with strokes' (3.3.84), the same felony committed by the Midlands rebels. Some of the accusations against the desperate husbandmen appear to have been shifted to the hapless Roman hero. This is not surprising in view of the transfer of some senatorial prerogative to the tribunes. When Sicinius is giving instruc-tions to the Aediles to orchestrate the citizens' response to his verdict on Coriolanus, he remarks that the citizens will be 'Insisting on the old prerogative / And power i' th' truth o' th' cause' (3.3.17–18). The word 'prerogative' here as applied to the common people is novel (and malignant) in the play since the tribunes' authority is new. To a Jacobean audience,

45 *A Booke of Proclamations*, pp. 139, 140–3.
46 John Dover Wilson, ed., *Coriolanus* (Cambridge, 1969), p. 200.
47 *A Booke of Proclamations*, p. 143.

however, the word resonated with a current controversy because Parliament was claiming it had an old prerogative in certain matters. 'By the time James came to the throne, the popular voice in the House of Commons, hitherto disparate, had become politically articulate, skilled in the exercise of their suddenly ancient prerogative.'[48] In November 1607, John Cowell had published *The Interpreter* and in his definition of '*Praerogatiue*' wrote, 'But I hold it incontrowlable, that the king of England is an absolute king' (Ddd4). This and other entries caused offence to the House of Commons, for 'the most conspicuous exception to [the king's] complete authority was the legislative power, which he shared with Parliament. James, in describing to the Spanish ambassador the paramountcy of his position, stopped in confusion when he touched on Parliament; the ambassador tactfully pointed out that Parliament was convened and dissolved at the king's pleasure, and James gratefully agreed'.[49] Cowell appeared before the King and Council in March 1610, but could not defend the offending entries; his book was burned on 26 March.[50]

The question is, how much of all this could Shakespeare have taken from North's translation of Plutarch's 'Life of Caivs Martius Coriolanus' (1595)? Obviously, if Shakespeare could find dearth and insurrection in his major source, he need not trouble to bring in the Midlands crisis. Plutarch mentions sedition in Rome 'because the Senate did fauour the rich against the people, who did complaine of the sore oppression of vsurers, of whom they borrowed money. For those that had litle, were yet spoyled of that litle they had by their creditours, for lacke of abilitie to paye the vsurie: who offered their goodes to be solde to them that would giue most . . . they fell then euen to flat rebellion and mutinie, and to sturre vp daungerous tumults within the cittie.' Not long after, Martius stood for the consulship, wearing the customary gown of humility in the marketplace without objection, which could reveal to the citizens the candidate's wounds received in Rome's wars. Shakespeare has invented the section of 2.3 in which Coriolanus resents having to wear the gown of humility and showing his wounds.

After initial approval of Martius for consul, the citizens turned against him. Meanwhile corn shipments arrived from other parts of Italy. Martius opposed corn distribution to the poor, and attacked the idea of tribunes. A tumult followed, the tribunes sent their officers to arrest him, but the patricians 'laid it sore vpon the Aediles'. The uproar extended to a second day, but then the corn was sold cheaply, and the tribunes called for Coriolanus to answer for his speech against tribunes and resisting arrest. When he did so, he spoke threateningly, and Sicinius condemned him to die. The matter was adjourned to a trial; Martius agreed to answer charges that he wanted to be king, but was actually charged with opposing the corn dole and the tribunes, and withholding spoil. The common people voted to banish him.[51] Such is the Roman section of Plutarch's narrative, and Livy's narrative in *The Romane Historie* (1600) is much the same.

While Plutarch has a dearth, it comes *after* the insurrection in Rome over usury and the Volscian war, and the citizens are not hungry at the time of Menenius' belly-fable. The start of the troubles is the usurious cost of borrowing money; by contrast, Shakespeare's citizens never mention borrowing money. E. C. Pettet considered that the First Citizen's complaint about usury was a 'passing hit', and surprising, given the prominence of usury in Plutarch's account.[52] Yet in the sermon and pamphlet

---

[48] W. Gordon Zeeveld, '"Coriolanus" and Jacobean Politics', *Modern Language Review* 57:3 (July 1962), 325.

[49] F. D. Wormuth, *The Royal Prerogative 1603–1649* (Ithaca, 1939; repr. Kraus, 1972), p. 54.

[50] *Dictionary of National Biography*, eds Leslie Stephen and Sidney Lee; repr. 1959–60, vol. 4, p. 1300.

[51] Plutarch, *The Lives of the Noble Grecians and Romanes*, pp. 237–46; Livy, *The Romane Historie*, pp. 64–7.

[52] '*Coriolanus* and the Midlands Insurrection of 1607', *Shakespeare Survey 3* (Cambridge, 1950), p. 36.

literature on dearth and famine of the 1600s, there too usury receives only a passing hit.

Pettet notes that hunger is the chief motif of 1.1. He might have noted that the dearth rather mysteriously drops out of the play, perhaps explained by the generals' taking the Roman 'rats' to gnaw the Volscian garners (1.1.249–50) or by Brutus' reference to giving corn gratis 'of late' to the people (3.1.44–5).[53] High grain prices ended in England (for the time being) with the harvest of 1609. Shakespeare seems to have combined the insurrections of 1607 with the dearth of 1608 for 1.1 of his play, and not kept hunger as a motif after that. Perhaps he saw that the authorities were acting; in April 1608 Captain William Winter stayed a vessel full of export barley at Portsmouth, and expected to arrest other vessels. He begged 'to be allowed to sell the corn cheaply to the distressed poor'.[54] Certainly the play could not have been written before the failure of the harvest of 1608 if the First Citizen's demand for 'corn at our own price' was to be valid (1.1.10–11). The Roman plebeians wanted corn free.

Other signs point to composition in 1608. The January was bitter, and booths were set up on the Thames, some of them with cooking utensils and coals to heat them. Also in January there was a great lottery in London, with 7,600 prize-winning tickets out of 42,000 total. In February, following upon Parliament's 1606–7 amended Act 'for the bringinge of a fresh Streame of runnynge Water to the Northe partes of the Citie of London', one Sturtevant offered burnt clay conduits that were watertight and quickly made.[55] Shakespeare makes two passing references to the frost: 'You are no surer, no, / Than is the coal of fire upon the ice' (1.1.170–1), and 'chaste as the icicle / That's candied by the frost from purest snow' (5.3.65–6). Menenius guesses that 'it is lots to blanks / My name hath touched your ears' (5.2.12–13), by which he means it is pretty certain. The prize-winning tickets in 1608 were only about one in five, so evidently Shakespeare

telescopes this lottery with a famous one in 1566, which featured all winning tickets (though of course 'most "winning" lots were nearly worthless').[56]

The water-supply plan for London, which was the subject of an act in 1605–6, gave the

Lorde Maior Communalty and Citizens of the Citie of London' the authority to convey water from certain Hertfordshire springs, and 'the use and liberty of such and soe much Ground as shall conteine Tenne Foote in breadth . . . during and by all the length as the saide new Channell Cutt or River shall passe for the conveying of the saide Water from the saide Springes to the City of London, leaving the inheritance of the Newe Cutt in the Owners thereof . . . no parte of the saide Streame [may] be at any tyme after the making of the Newe Cutt without the consent of the Mayor Comminalty and Citizens of London, turned or conveyed out of the same Newe Cutt or Water course: In consideracion whereof the Maior [etc.] shall make satisfaccion or composition to and with the Lordes Owners and Occupiers of the same Groundes through which the Newe Cutt or River shalbe made, and with all such person or persons as shall sustaine any Damage Losse or Hinderance in theire Milles standing upon any of the Rivers or Streames from which the Water shall be taken through the saide Newe Cut or River, . . . in defaulte of their Agreement by mutuall Assent,

---

53 According to Annabel Patterson, the belly fable is ironic because the 'general food' is *not* being sent through the rivers of the blood to the members, and she complains that critics have not drawn the conclusion that *Coriolanus* is therefore a democratic play. However, as the hunger vanishes after Act 1, one can well see why they have 'resisted the consequences' of finding the belly fable hypocritical and then reading the whole play as an indictment of the nobles, who do not stumble again unless one counts the baiting of Sicinius and Brutus in 4.6 as anti-democratic (*Fables of Power*, pp. 118–19).

54 *Calendar of State Papers, Domestic*, ed. Mary Anne Everett Green (London, 1857), vol. 8, p. 422.

55 G. B. Harrison, *A Second Jacobean Journal* (London, 1958), pp. 68–76.

56 Eric C. Brown, 'A Note on the Lottery of Queen Elizabeth I and *Coriolanus*, 5.2', *Shakespeare Quarterly*, 50 (1999), p. 71.

such satisfaccion or recompense as shall bee limitted and appointed by the Commissioners to be assigned for that purpose ... by Commission under the Greate Seale of England or by any nyne of them, whereof Foure of them to be Citizens of the City of London.

This Act begot another in 1606–7 amending it. This time Parliament authorized 'a Truncke or Vaulte of Bricke or Stone inclosed' to carry the water.[57] This probably occurred because the king had taken up Sturtevant's invention in 1605/6; on 3 March 1607/8, Thomas Chaloner wrote to Sir Thomas Lake that in those two years Sturtevant had perfected baked earthen pipes, and asking that Sturtevant's petition to the king to start the new conduit be forwarded by Lake.[58] The 'Channell' would belong to the mayor and citizens of London, it would take water from others' rivers or streams, recompense would depend on the Commissioners, and four out of nine of those Commissioners would be London citizens.

Shakespeare evidently found matter in the 'New Cut' for Coriolanus' outrage with the tribunes' appointment (3.1.93–100):

'Shall'?
O good but most unwise patricians, why,
You grave but reckless senators, have you thus
Given Hydra here to choose an officer
That, with his peremptory 'shall', being but
The horn and noise o' th' monster's, wants not
    spirit
To say he'll turn your current in a ditch
And make your channel his?

Editors have long considered this passage to be a guide to dating the play. It seems to speak of citizen authority to cut the new ditch and their right to take others' water 'through the saide Newe Cut' or channel. The cutting of the ditch seems imminent, which was the case in March 1607/8.

For Coriolanus to have the effective first scene it does, the dearth of autumn 1608 had to have begun. The rest of the play's glancings, borrowings, and allusions to 1607–8 reinforce the impression that it was designed to make early

Rome alive and breathing to its first audience. (Of course, Shakespeare had to prevent Sir George Buc's censorship of the insurrection scenes, meaning that he could not copy the Midlands incidents too closely.)[59] J. Leeds Barroll dates Coriolanus' first performance in 'the Christmas holidays at court, 1607–8, and, for the Globe, the spring of 1608, after which the play could not be shown because of plague (except at court) for more than a year'. Plague deaths in London remained over thirty a week from 28 July 1608 to 7 December 1609, and Barroll doubts any playhouses would have been open during those months.[60] By late 1609, Shakespeare's company would have had ample time to rehearse the play while its immersion in

---

57 Statutes of the Realm, ed. A. Luders, et al.; vol. 4, pt. 2 (London, 1819), pp. 1092, 1151.

58 David George, 'Coriolanus at the Blackfriars?' Notes and Queries ns 38:4 (Dec. 1991) 490, citing PRO SP 14/31, fos. 157 r-v. The enclosed brick or stone trunk may have been a substitute for Sturtevant's clay pipes.

59 Richard Dutton points out that Tilney required the 'Ill May-Day' insurrection in Sir Thomas More to be omitted, but that Buc did not call for the removal of the insurrections in Rome (William Shakespeare [Houndmills, Hants, 1989], p. 34). Evidently the near-riot in 1.1 of Coriolanus failed to stir Buc's memory of the Midlands insurrections.

60 Politics, Plague, and Shakespeare's Theater (Ithaca, 1991), pp. 242, 225–6. Early 1608 probably saw the first performances of Pericles, however, and perhaps it is better to place Coriolanus after the hungry summer of 1608, in the late autumn (William Shakespeare: The Complete Works (Oxford, 1986), p. 1167). 'Cumulatively . . . internal evidence suggests a date no earlier than spring 1608. The play must have existed by 1609, when 2.2.101/1124 was echoed at 5.4.224–5 of Ben Jonson's Epicoene BEPD 304; (composed late 1609) and 1.1.210–11/210–11 was echoed in the address 'Ad lectorem' to Robert Armin's The Italian Tailor and his Boy (1609: STC 774; entered in the Stationers' Register on 6 February 1609) . . . It may also be significant that the Folio text contains regular act divisions: the King's Men apparently only began to make habitual use of act intervals after they acquired the Blackfriars in August 1608' (Stanley Wells and Gary Taylor, William Shakespeare: A Textual Companion [Oxford, 1987], p. 131).

the events of the two previous years would not be obsolete.[61]

While Shakespeare relied on Plutarch for his narrative and his main military and political events, he filled in passage after passage with Jacobean England. This is not so much a question of 'relevance' as an artistic method of creating immediacy for his audience and of winning their involvement. Simply, they would not have understood references to ancient Roman customs and practices. Yet so deft is Shakespeare's hand in touching on contemporary London and England that literary archaeologists have had trouble even identifying the Jacobean artefacts. Even so, the 'company of mutinous citizens' armed with a mixture of London street weapons and farm implements that bursts onto the stage in Act 1 would have been startlingly contemporary to the first audience. Their hunger and demands for cheap corn, and Coriolanus' desire to hang them, would have doubled the effect.

After Act 3, Coriolanus ceases to include passages that come from contemporary experience. Most of the thirteen scenes of Acts 4 and 5 are based squarely on Plutarch, with the exceptions of 4.3, the spy scene; most of 4.5, Aufidius' comic servants; 5.1, Cominius' report of his failed embassy to Coriolanus; 5.2, the rejection of Menenius; 5.5, the procession of victorious ladies into Rome; and 5.6, the conspirators' plot to provoke Coriolanus. Shakespeare omits the cause of the renewal of the Volscian war, the expulsion of the Volscians from the games at Rome. Volumnia's long, frigid plea to Coriolanus (5.3.95–126, 132–83) is taken almost entirely from Plutarch, versified and syntactically manipulated. Having already employed his conception of Rome as (in part) like Jacobean England, Shakespeare had to find a new way of breaking up the Plutarchan narrative when Coriolanus went to Antium. Sour humour or irony pervades much of the additional material. The narrative interest drops considerably and the sense of time is compacted, so that Coriolanus appears to die in the

same year he was a hero at Corioli. Perhaps the chief value of the last two acts is the repetition of behaviour dramatized in the first three acts: Coriolanus' military success, his mistaken submission to Volumnia's will, and his hair-trigger temper when he is accused of being a traitor. Even so, the play's vigour flags in the last two acts because so much is reported, not shown, and, as Johnson complained, there is too little bustle in the last act.[62]

Richard Wilson dates it 'earlier than the 1607 rising, though after the poetic justice of Fulke Greville's fall in 1604' ('Against the Grain: Representing the Market in Coriolanus', The Seventeenth Century 6:2 [1991], 144). Wilson's close reading includes the idea that Warwickshire politics dominate the play and hence Coriolanus is based on Sir Fulke Greville of Alcester. A London audience would not, however, be able to pick up on provincial politics and so Greville is at best a fraction of the hero. Wilson is forced to ignore Plutarch and London to achieve his local reading; however, John Ripley has amply shown the play to have been ready for the Globe or Blackfriars (Coriolanus on Stage [Madison, NJ, 1998]: 34–52). Barroll notes a drought in England in 1610–11 and therefore seriously considers these years as a possible date of composition for Coriolanus (p. 242). However, Rogers reports, under 1610–11, 'Prices [of grain] are, for the averages of the time, moderate and uniform throughout.' In 1611–12, he reports, 'Prices are rising', and they went on rising until 1614–15 (vol. 5, pp. 187–9). Wheat was not abnormally expensive until Lady-day (25 March) 1612, and even then only two-thirds the price it had been in the autumn of 1608.

61 Annabel Patterson argues that Coriolanus is 'constructed out of material already strongly grained in a certain direction', and that Shakespeare had by 1608 been brought 'to his most radical position: a belief that Jacobean England desperately needed to borrow from the strengths, as well as learn from the difficulties, of republican political theory' (Shakespeare and the Popular Voice [Oxford, 1989], p. 122). The materials out of which the play is made are 'grained' in several directions. Unquestionably Act 1 puts the hungry plebeians in a sympathetic light, but by the time Sicinius is inventing 'old prerogative' in 3.3, Coriolanus becomes the object of sympathy. Power shifts from nobles to plebeians in Act 3, and the hero is plainly abused when threatened with execution.

62 The Plays of William Shakespeare (London, 1765), vol. 6, p. 627.

SHAKESPEARE, CROSSING THE RUBICON

CYNTHIA MARSHALL

What are historical representations *representations of*?[1]

To paraphrase Hayden White, what are dramatic characters characterizations of? More specifically, how does the process of converting narrative material into dramatic form affect the shape and design, even the very concept, of character? The idea of character has fallen out of favour in the past two decades, as critics have instead pondered the birth and fashioning of subjectivity, in terms derived from Foucault and Lacan. Yet the lines demarcating the ideologically constructed, divided, and never self-authorizing subject from the authorially constructed, conflicted, and never self-actualizing character have often seemed to be unclear, and their deployment more useful to the project of directing attention past the sovereign author than to that of understanding the complicated status of dramatized beings. Indeed, a critical era attuned to social constructionism has sometimes blurred the distinction between historical subjects, shaped by colliding ideological forces, and dramatic characters, subject on several dimensions to the same forces yet fundamentally different because of being the product of a dramatist's mind and an actor's embodiment.

In this essay I engage these issues by returning to the old question of Shakespeare's relation to the Plutarchan texts recognized as the primary sources of his Roman plays. Although Geoffrey Bullough's claim that source study presents a 'way open to us of watching Shakespeare the craftsman in his workshop' depends on notions of textual and authorial autonomy that would

be difficult to support in our intertextual world, the basic recognition – that something important is happening in the passage between a clearly identified source and a later text – remains indisputable.[2] What happens, I argue, in Shakespeare's conversion of narrative into drama, is the establishment of our culture's prevailing model of character as one that is at once intensely performative and putatively interiorized. An identity that cannot be reliably narrated but must be performed will continually demand explanation, yet because its behaviours are likely to challenge or subvert whatever interpretations are attached to it, such a selfhood can only be explained by the attribution of interiority, or 'that within which passeth show'.[3] In our culture, the paradoxical link between the performative self and interiority is recapitulated in the paradigm of hysteria, instancing how, in Joel Fineman's terms, 'contemporary speculation about subjectivity repeats in a theoretical mode . . . what literature accomplishes toward the end of the Renaissance'.[4] The discourses of theory in general and of psychoanalysis in particular seek to reverse the passage from comprehensible narrative to mystifying drama. Examining the move-

---

[1] Hayden White, 'The Historical Text as Literary Artifact', *Tropics of Discourse: Essays in Cultural Criticism* (Baltimore, 1978), pp. 81–100, p. 88.

[2] Geoffrey Bullough, ed., *Narrative and Dramatic Sources of Shakespeare*, vol. 8 (New York, 1975), p. 346.

[3] *Hamlet* (1.2.85).

[4] Joel Fineman, *Shakespeare's Perjured Eye: The Invention of Poetic Subjectivity in the Sonnets* (Berkeley, 1986), p. 46.

ment from Plutarch's open form and inclusive narration to the more violent, linear designs of Shakespearian tragic drama, I will be concerned here with how relationships to the past are theorized on textual and characterological levels.

I

Because of its wide influence as a model of biographical representation, Plutarch's *Lives of the Noble Grecians and Romanes* served as a key text in the evolution of the early modern concept of character or subjectivity. Plutarch rejected other possible structures, such as chronicle history or a grouping of characters by time or type or theme, and chose instead an approach – lives of exemplary men, and direct comparisons between them – that fostered a particularly individualistic way of thinking. In a famous statement of his generic aims, Plutarch differentiated between 'histories' and 'lives', asking his readers' indulgence as he searches for signs of 'mens naturall dispositions and maners' rather than attempting a comprehensive history of designated individuals.[5] For him, a 'life' entails diversity; rather than 'declare al things at large' he will 'briefly touch divers'. Further, a moral impetus drives his work, and searching to discern 'mens vertues and vices', he places significance less on great actions and more on an underlying self, the 'naturall dispositio[n]', which may be more evident in casual events than in great ones.[6] What a later age will think of as the constitutive or inner self is already for Plutarch largely interiorized; he will 'seeke out the signes and tokens of the minde only'.[7] Indeed, the difference between 'histories' and 'lives' seems to turn on a distinction between visible action in the world ('warres, battells, and other great thinges they did') and the evidently internalized 'minde'.[8]

Yet despite his stated intention to let others write of 'warres, battells, and other great things', Plutarch's choice of biographical subjects renders impossible a strict or sole focus on the signs of moral character. His noble Grecians and Romans tend not to be contemplative types, but rather the leaders of the antique and legendary worlds, men who displayed their heroism in active, vivid ways. True to his word, Plutarch was not content with simply recounting their actions. He was primarily interested in probing the forces that produce heroic or interesting individuals, and he understood individuality to be honed through conflict, ordinarily of an overt and political sort. But in keeping with his intention to show 'naturall dispositions and maners' he also notes internal conflict, or tension within the self, especially when it moulds or even constitutes character. Plutarch's summaries of individual subjects and his comparisons between them indicate his sense of character as consistent over time and pervasive throughout the aspects of a life.[9] That character was understood as visible and durable did not, however, mean that it was self-identical or unified. Instead, episodes in the *Lives* suggest that Plutarch understood complexity or

5 Plutarch, *The Lives of the Noble Grecians and Romanes*, trans. Thomas North (London, 1579), p. 722. North's translation of Plutarch into English was from Jacques Amyot's French translation of the Greek.

6 Hermann Heuer notes that North strengthens Plutarch's moral emphasis in 'From Plutarch to Shakespeare: A Study of *Coriolanus*', *Shakespeare Survey 10* (Cambridge, 1957), 50–59; p. 53.

7 North's 'signes and tokens of the minde only' grants a slightly more cognitive emphasis to Amyot's more spiritual 'les signes des l'ame': 'nous doit-on concéder que nous allions principalement recherchant les signes des l'âme, et pariceux formant un portrait au naturel de la vie et des moeurs d'un chacun' (Plutarque, *Les Vies des hommes illustres*, trad. Jacques Amyot, ed. Gérard Walter, vol. 2 (Paris, 1951), p. 323.

8 *Lives*, p. 722.

9 Alan Wardman notes it is his 'assumption of consistency that gives Plutarch the confidence, as a biographer, to be so certain that character is knowable'. He 'only conceives of change in a very weak sense', and believed in the continuity of character over time for moral reasons, since otherwise a person would be 'politically irresponsible for his previous actions', *Plutarch's Lives* (London, 1974), pp. 132–3, 136.

depth of character to manifest the incorporation of difference, whether that appeared as diversity of ideas, emotions, or gendered influences. Conflict and internal debate seem in fact to be central elements of the fascination his subjects held for him.

In fact, Plutarch's tolerance of fluidity and even of deviance in the characters he describes marks perhaps the most striking difference between the *Lives* and Shakespeare's Roman plays. The narrative mode allows expansion, contradiction, and discussion to an extent that drama does not; moreover, Plutarch's historiographic method is inclusive and nondiscriminatory. He tends to report multiple versions of significant events in the lives of his subjects, implicitly suggesting that human experience is too complex and contradictory to be accommodated by simple formulas or categories of identity, or even, one might deduce, by exemplary plots of dramatic tragedy. Reading Plutarch, one appreciates Linda Woodbridge's description of Shakespearian tragedy and history as shaped 'by subtracting, carving from a mass of history and legend a play-sized, play-shaped plot'.[10]

The characterological material in the *Lives*, in particular, prompts complex negotiation on Shakespeare's part, involving both the overall picture of human society and behaviour in the ancient world and the representation of individual characters. On the societal level, Shakespeare's Roman plays channel the variety contained in the Plutarchan *Lives* into more definite and recognizable models of character, focusing on central tragic events and their ramifications. Frequently this entails the isolation of organized models of masculine and feminine behaviour or the intensification of outlines of sexual division found in Plutarch. These changes and omissions result to a large extent from a practical concern to streamline Plutarch's biographies into dramatic plots. Since Renaissance stage practice demanded overt, physical demonstrations of character and relationship, the result was a loading of oppositional

structures and an emphasis on sensational conflicts, so that the picture of Roman life Shakespeare handed down to us is more violent and masculinist than Plutarch's original. A sharpening of outlines is evident on the individual level as well; Shakespeare's characters are better defined, less ambiguous than Plutarch's. Here too physical violence is often the means toward clarity: characters in *Julius Caesar*, *Coriolanus*, and *Antony and Cleopatra* demonstrate self-definition through murder, war, and suicide. However, the channelling of diversity into organized forms led concurrently to the notion of internal division and conflict that forms a crucial part of what we today understand as the self.[11] The evolving Shakespearian sense of characterological depth or interiority is linked, I suggest, to Plutarch's references to ghostly others who reside within a single person, as well as to the ghostly presence in Shakespeare's Roman plays of Plutarchan material not explicitly incorporated there.

Plutarch, for all his emphasis on the knowability of character, in practice demonstrates the contradictions in individual behaviour and the unexpected divergences of identity to which they point. Narrative can fill the resulting gaps within a divergent picture of an individual; Slavoj Žižek nicely describes narrativization as 'that mode in which the contingency of past events becomes transposed into a homogeneous symbolic structure'.[12] Drama, on the other hand, introduces new gaps into the project of

---

[10] Linda Woodbridge, 'Patchwork: Piecing the Early Modern Mind in England's First Century of Print Culture', *English Literary Renaissance* 23 (1993), 5–45, pp. 16–17.

[11] As William Dodd notes, recent recuperations of characterological subjectivity understand it as the juncture of conflicting discourses. Dodd revises this notion to involve further individual agency by adding the component of moral values, 'Destined Livery? Character and Person in Shakespeare', *Shakespeare Survey* 51 (Cambridge, 1998), 147–58, pp. 150–1.

[12] Slavoj Žižek, *The Metastases of Enjoyment: Six Essays on Woman and Causality* (New York, 1994), p. 36.

conveying character: divisions between actor and character, between character and audience, between author(s) and actors. Narrative, at least in its forms prior to poststructuralism, operates under a mandate of historical continuity that applies less forcefully to performances of virtually any sort. Plutarch provides an appropriate starting point for an examination of the link between historical margins and the outlines of identity, since his *Parallel Lives*, among the least marginal of all Western historical texts, openly expresses historiographic anxiety.

The *Life of Theseus*, traditionally placed first in Plutarch's *Lives* (the first of 1175 pages in North's 1579 Folio translation) begins with a meditation on the relation between history and myth. As with the comparison of 'histories' and 'lives', Plutarch here turns his parallel method to self-conscious authorial purpose, explaining his decision to write about Theseus, a figure of distant antiquity, from a time whose record 'is full of suspicion and dout, being delivered us by Poets and Tragedy makers, sometimes without trueth and likelihoode, and always without certainty'.[13] Plutarch admits the limits of knowledge, but announces his resolve to plunge past them, designing a method for dealing with the material lying beyond the pale of 'true and certaine historie'.[14] Adopting a geographical analogy, he imagines history laid out like a map, with the unknown areas relegated to the margins. These 'unnavigable' areas escape cartographic representation, yet they nevertheless exist within the realm of language since they are indicated by 'note[s]'. The history of Theseus is unknown because historically remote, too far removed in temporal sequence – although Plutarch's analogy suggests, more insidiously, that the world known to 'trueth' and 'certainty' may be perpetually shadowed by margins. This is especially the case given that his geographical figure enfolds a generic analogy: beyond the limits of 'historie' lies the realm of 'Poets and Tragedy makers'.[15] The problem of apprehending truth is only partly a matter of chronological proximity.

Beyond dictating his choice of subjects and his formal structure, Plutarch's parallel method provides his historiographic model, for he proposes to use parallelism to tame what is marginal. The poetic domain of antiquity exists simultaneously inside and outside the historian's design, a constitutive boundary necessary to mark the edges of 'certine historie', but itself outside the control of certainty. Plutarch aims to police the boundary between truth and myth: he hopes that by comparing Theseus to Romulus, the 'inventions of Poets, and the traditions of fabulous antiquitie' might be brought into proximity and conformity with 'a true and historicall reporte'. The concept of parallels may seem to acknowledge irreducible difference and hence a state of stasis, but Plutarch's violent rhetoric suggests otherwise. The comparison of Theseus and Romulus is imaged as a battle between two champions: 'who is so bold?', 'who is he that dare defend his force?' The historian, moreover, places himself in the role of adventurer, gamely entering the realm of 'things past all proofe or challenge'.[16] Plutarch's amplification of the challenge facing the historian who would write of Theseus, and of the difficulty for any figure to measure up to Romulus, indicates that his is no innocent description of chronological history. Parallelism instead provides a technique for exerting control over marginal material that threatens by its very presence to unravel the systematic study of history. Through his logical intervention, the 'inventions of Poets, and the traditions of fabulous antiquitie [will] suffer them selves to be

---

13 *Lives*, p. 1.
14 *Lives*, p. 1. Cf. White's view of 'historical narratives . . . [as] . . . verbal fictions, the contents of which are as much *invented* as *found* and the forms of which have more in common with their counterparts in literature than they have with those in the sciences'. Plutarch anticipates White in questioning the ability of his text to serve as 'a model of structures and processes long past and therefore not subject to either experimental or observational controls' (p. 82).
15 *Lives*, p. 1.   16 *Lives*, pp. 1–2.

purged and reduced to the forme of a true and historicall reporte'.[17]

Despite his ambitious bravado, Plutarch evidently has unappeasable concerns about the likelihood of successfully banishing myth from his historical account, since he appeals to his readers to be the ultimate keepers of logical order, to 'take in good parte' what he could with 'probability' present.[18] Truth here is neither absolute nor objectively determined; it is instead a function of Plutarch's authorial purposes in writing the *Lives*. Because he came to his task as a philosopher and not as a historian, Plutarch aims simultaneously to record his subjects' characters and to encourage imitation of their virtues. Studying character could provide moral benefits, as C. P. Jones notes, for 'contemplation of virtuous deeds automatically inspired imitation: moreover, when the observer understood the motives behind them, he would acquire his own inclination to virtue'.[19] This moral purpose rendered fact itself subordinate to a conception of character. For Plutarch, who assumed a high degree of characterological consistency, probability has virtually the force of truth. In some cases the assumption deepened his analyses, since he was challenged to supply overarching explanations for what could seem irrational or contradictory actions. In other cases, he resorted to the explanation that actions were simply 'against nature'; his conception of character could not explain or even acknowledge radical personal changes.[20] Viewing character in a totalizing rather than temporalizing way, he judges the reliability of historical accounts by their likelihood, based on his understanding of an individual's character and of general patterns of human behaviour. If, on the one hand, Plutarch announces his effort to 'purge' myth in order to bring it into line with history, he accepts, on the other, the doubleness of a truth (whether historical or characterological) he sees as perpetually shadowed by its opposite. Thus his approach is intertextual, a method assuming 'that various domains of meaning are contingent upon one another' and 'that the common-sense world may be considered as a base from which other provinces of meaning are formed'.[21]

To Plutarch, bent on the moral task of providing exemplary lives and concerned to establish his credibility as a historian, myth presented a constant menace. So he repeatedly sets himself the task of judging between legendary and historical accounts – for instance, he recounts numerous versions of Romulus's birth (including one 'nothing true nor likely' involving oracular instruction for a virgin to 'have carnall companie' with a 'mans privie member' that mysteriously appears in the chimney of the King of Alba) but he grants 'best credit of all' to a report tracing the hero's paternity to Aeneas.[22] Evidently unable (or unwilling) to banish myth completely, Plutarch chooses instead to expand the compendious frame of his narrative to include stories he finds 'nothing true' alongside those he is more willing to credit. Indeed, his aim of showing the true picture of a man's life by including 'a light occasion, a word, or some sporte' necessitates the inclusion of material that defies documentation. So while Plutarch ostensibly favours the logic and control of 'historicall reporte', his method embraces much material that resists being 'purged and reduced' to that form.[23] Myth and fact remain present as irreducible doubles, interpenetrating and informing one another. Plutarch's studies have evidently left him too well aware of the diversity within any given life for the chastened form of purely credible history to seem a viable option.

II

Although Plutarch's noble Grecians and Romans lack the developed sense of interior

---

[17] *Lives*, p. 2.   [18] *Lives*, p. 2.

[19] C. P. Jones, *Plutarch and Rome* (Oxford, 1971), p. 103.

[20] Wardman, p. 139.

[21] Susan Stewart, *Nonsense: Aspects of Intertextuality in Folklore and Literature* (Baltimore, 1979), pp. 16–17.

[22] *Lives*, p. 21.   [23] *Lives*, pp. 722, 2.

consciousness that renders Shakespeare's characters so compellingly real for modern readers, the Plutarchan concept of the self is fairly complex. Plutarch distinguishes between a record of action and the evidence of moral character, and he understands performance to be contiguous with social categories shaping identity, such as gender. Because he lived and wrote in a culture that credited divine influence, Plutarch also used spiritual presences as a method for suggesting a dimensional self. Moments of crisis or indecision are frequently represented through the presence of spirits, supernatural shapes, or divine messages. For Plutarch, this nascent interior consciousness bears an implicit connection to gender difference, as evidenced in his treatment of Caesar's fateful moment of crossing the Rubicon.

This passage, recounting the action that initiated the civil wars, is crucial not only for any consideration of Roman history, but for a sense of Caesar's character: it establishes his willingness to take risks, to challenge established order, 'to execute his purpose'.[24] Like his contemporaries Lucan and Suetonius who also record this event, Plutarch emphasizes that it is a moment of personal decision. But unlike the others, Plutarch presents the decision process as an internal debate. In Suetonius's version, Caesar's conflict is conveyed through oratory: having announced the significance of crossing the river, Caesar pauses 'and stood doubtful what to do', when a strangely shaped man playing a reed appears to him and his troops.

Then Caesar: 'Let us march on', quoth he, 'and go whither the tokens of the gods and the injurious dealings of our enemies call us. The die be thrown; I have set up my rest. Come what will of it.'[25]

Virtually no emphasis is given to Caesar's own realization of the moment's importance. What matters are his words, how the moment was publicly communicated. Lucan comes closer to granting Caesar an interior consciousness. He indicates Caesar's hesitation by relating his vision of Rome as a woman in mourning, her

hair torn and her arms bare, who begs him to 'stay heare':

> This spectacle
> Stroake Caesars hart with feare, his hayre stoode up,
> And faintnes numm'd his steps there on the brincke.

While the vision is attributed to Caesar, Lucan's description makes it a public and shared experience, thus externalizing Caesar's moment of decision. Lucan also recounts the physical signs of Caesar's crisis, his upstanding hair and faint steps, and he details Caesar's duplicitous part in his conversation with the figure, his show of 'laying aside all lets of war' until he has crossed the river, only to announce 'an end of peace'.[26]

These visual and oral marks of decision-

---

24 *Shakespeare's Plutarch*, ed. T. J. B. Spencer (Baltimore, 1964), p. 54. I have used this edition when quoting from the *Lives of Julius Caesar, Marcus Brutus, Marcus Antonius*, and *Martius Coriolanus*; references are cited parenthetically. Quotations from other Plutarchan *Lives* refer to the 1579 edition (cited in note 5 above).

25 Suetonius, *History of Twelve Caesars*, trans. Philemon Holland [1606], ed. J. H. Freese (London, 1923), p. 24. Holland's was the first English translation to be published. Bullough finds 'nothing in Shakespeare's plays to prove that he had read Suetonius', but does not rule out a textual connection (vol. 5, p. 14).

26 *Lucans First Booke*, trans. Christopher Marlowe (London, 1600), sigs. B4 r–v. The likelihood that Shakespeare was familiar with Marlowe's translation is increased by its connections to members of his own publishing circle. Marlowe's translation was entered on the Stationer's Register in September 1593 a few months before his death and published by P. Short. It contains a dedication by Thomas Thorpe, the publisher of Shakespeare's sonnets, to Edward Blount, who in 1623 produced the First Folio of Shakespeare's plays with Isaac Jaggard. T. W. Baldwin finds evidence that 'Shakspeare certainly knew something of Lucan' in *William Shakspere's Small Latine + Lesse Greeke*, vol. 2 (Urbana, 1944), p. 551. Kenneth Muir notes that 'Shakespeare seems also to have been acquainted with Lucan's description of the portents connected with Caesar's crossing of the Rubicon, possibly in Marlowe's translation, although this was not yet published when *Julius Caesar* was first performed'. See *The Sources of Shakespeare's Plays* (London, 1977), p. 124.

making stand in contrast to Plutarch's description of Caesar's strictly private indecision, the 'remorse he had in his conscience', and his doubts over 'the desperateness of his attempt'. These are presented as internal debates – 'he fell into many thoughts with himself, and spake never a word, waving sometime one way, sometime another way, and oftentimes changed his determination, contrary to himself'. Although Caesar did 'talk much also with his friends he had with him' (Spencer, p. 54), Plutarch attributes an ancillary quality to such speech; it accompanies, but does not replace, Caesar's 'thoughts with himself'.

Nowhere is this Plutarchan sense of interior consciousness stronger than in the report of Caesar's 'damnable dream'. Both Suetonius and Lucan blur the line between private and shared experience of the 'visions' they report to have occurred with the passage over the Rubicon. Suetonius writes of 'a strange sight he chanced to see'. Lucan recounts Caesar's direct verbal challenge to the vision of 'fearefull Roome', but ambiguates the extent to which others witness the event.[27] Plutarch, however, significantly locates the only such vision he reports within the mind of Caesar, and certainly it is a vision of a distinctly personal sort. After at last deciding to cross over the river, Caesar does not waver, but 'before daylight was within the city of Ariminum, and took it'. At this crucial point Plutarch inserts: 'It is said that the night before he passed over this river he dreamed a damnable dream: that he carnally knew his mother' (Spencer, p. 54).[28]

To post-Freudian readers such a dream appears overwhelmingly oedipal: for Caesar to secure his destiny as leader means to take his father's place by taking his mother. But is this what Plutarch meant to suggest by reporting the dream? For the Roman dream interpreter Artemidorus (whose second-century *Interpretation of Dreams* incorporated relevant work by his predecessors), dreams were frequently meaningful, but their significance was in relation to public life, not the unconscious mind of the

dreamer.[29] Certain dreams were prophetic, some directly revelatory of future events and some allegorically suggestive. For Artemidorus, even sexual dreams were important in a public rather than a private sense; he considered incestuous dreams normal and devotes a great deal of attention to men's dreams of intercourse with their mothers. Although many factors were involved in interpreting such a dream correctly, Artemidorus wrote that a dream of 'intercourse with one's living mother is "lucky for every demagogue and public figure. For a mother

---

27 Suetonius, p. 24; *Lucans First Booke*, sig. B4r. In his modern translation of Lucan, J. D. Duff suggests that the vision is seen by all, especially since her address is directed to the 'warriors' in general:

Her mighty image was clearly seen in the darkness of night; her face expressed deep sorrow, and from her head, crowned with towers, the white hair streamed abroad: she stood beside him with tresses torn and arms bare, and her speech was broken by sobs: 'Whither do ye march further? and whither do ye bear my standards, ye warriors? If ye come as law-abiding citizens, here must ye stop.

Ingens visa duci patriae trepidantis imago
Clara per obscuram voltu maestissima noctem,
Turrigero canos effundens vertice crines,
Caesarie lacera nudisque adstare lacertis
Et gemitu permixta loqui: 'Quo tenditis ultra?
Quo fertis mea signa, viri? si iure venitis,
Si cives, huc usque licet.'
(Lucan, *The Civil War*, trans. J. D. Duff
(New York, 1928), p. 17)

In the translation by Arthur Gorges published in 1614 the vision is specifically labelled a dream:

In gloomy night there did appeare
(In dreames to him with troubling chere)
Of Italy the Image vaste.
(*Lucans Pharsalia*, trans. Arthur Gorges
(London, 1614), p. 11)

28 'Mais on dit que la nuit de devant qu'il passa cette rivière, il eut en dormant une illusion damnable: cest qu'il lui fut avis qu'il avait affaire avec sa propre mère' (Amyot, vol. 2, p. 15).

29 S. R. F. Price, 'The Future of Dreams: From Freud to Artemidorus', *Past & Present* 113 (1986), 3–37, pp. 31, 3–4. See also Michel Foucault, *The Care of the Self*, vol. 3 of *The History of Sexuality*, trans. Robert Hurley (New York, 1988), pp. 3–36.

signifies one's native country and . . . so the dreamer will control all the affairs of the city." '[30] Such an interpretation is not incongruent with a Freudian-based one, however: the dream secures an analogy between city and mother, both as objects to be possessed by the hero-in-the-making. As David Halperin cheekily suggests, if an incestuous dream indicates success in politics, success must mean 'the power to screw one's country'.[31] Through this analogy the reported dream confirms a connection between violence and sexuality. Carnal knowledge of his mother licenses or inspires Caesar to launch the attack that leads to war, so that knowledge is carnal here in sexual and militaristic senses.

The symbolic nature of the dream and its metaphysical connections elaborate what the simple fact of its occurrence suggests: in order to proceed, Caesar must acknowledge and deal with the presence of his mother within himself. The dream offers a trace of female presence, located within Caesar's consciousness and experienced as internal otherness. Thus the dream produces the sense of interior space while simultaneously attesting to the potency of the largely repressed female portion of Caesar's identity. Figuring the representative of his mother within the consciousness of Caesar creates the impression of psychological complexity: 'Rome' within is simultaneously 'room' within (pronounced the same in early modern England). The episode illustrates how Plutarch, in the translated version Shakespeare consulted, uses gender difference to create the sense of an other within the self. This early instance of assuming the interior space we now associate with selfhood or individual character corresponds to the later psychoanalytic idea of incorporation, through which an other is memorialized within the ego.

Shakespeare, of course, does not dramatize Caesar's decision to cross the Rubicon: although reference is made in Julius Caesar to several events from early in Caesar's life, the play concentrates on the events immediately surrounding his death. The trace of this important moment is evident, however, in what distinguishes Julius Caesar from Shakespeare's earlier plays, whatever their genre: its focus on the process of decision-making. As Ned Lukacher points out, in Julius Caesar, the first of his Plutarchan plays, Shakespeare 'is interested in exploring . . . "the interim" between Brutus's intention and the act' which will torment his conscience.[32] Lukacher's study of the place and development of the concept of conscience in Shakespeare's characters gives relevant testimony to William Dodd's claim of the dimensionality afforded by signs of moral character. The vexing process of moral decision-making in fact serves as the focus not only of Julius Caesar but of Hamlet, Othello, and Measure for Measure – the great character dramas of the early 1600s. These plays are followed in logical and chronological order by those that focus on the effects of tragic decision: King Lear, Macbeth, and Antony and Cleopatra. To impose a narrative of my own, Shakespeare had to cross this symbolic Rubicon, marking off the richly inventive but largely plot-driven plays of the 1590s from the deeply characterological dramas that follow, in order to take possession of his territory as a dramatist. In the next two sections, I will discuss how Shakespeare turns decision-making into a dramatic event in Julius Caesar, and then how years later, in Coriolanus, he returns to the motif of the hero choosing whether to attack his city, and to a struggle with maternal influence in making that decision.[33]

---

[30] Artemidorus, The Interpretation of Dreams, ed. R. A. Pack (Leipzig, 1963), i.79, p. 91, line 21, cited in Price, p. 21.

[31] David M. Halperin, 'Is There a History of Sexuality?' The Lesbian and Gay Studies Reader, ed. Henry Abelove, Michèle Aina Barale, and David M. Halperin (New York, 1993), pp. 416–31, p. 419.

[32] Ned Lukacher, Daemonic Figures: Shakespeare and the Question of Conscience (Ithaca, 1994), p. 204.

[33] M. W. MacCallum long ago noticed how Plutarchan material could recur unexpectedly in Shakespeare's work: 'Shakespeare often completely recasts Plutarch.

III

Even when it is pressured or shaped by social and political forces, individual choice is to some extent an expression of agency. The process of decision-making therefore offers compelling material for a plot, but it presents a challenge in terms of dramatic representation, since an individual's choices or decisions – whether understood in moral, ideological, or character-ological terms – are aspects of the inner life. To render a viewing audience acutely conscious of witnessing a decision being made is an accomplishment of phenomenology (exactly *what* are we watching when we see a decision occurring?), of dramatic timing (since the forward sweep of plot must encompass the slower moments of attention to the individual), and, not least, of acting skill.

In *Julius Caesar*, Shakespeare's portrayal of Brutus's internal struggle as he considers joining the conspiracy achieves an innovation in the representation of an inner dimension of character. Consolidated as Brutus's internal division are the warring influences figured as 'conscience' and 'fiend' in an earlier, parodic version of decision-making, Lancelot Gobbo's determination to leave Shylock's service (*Merchant of Venice*, 2.2.1–29). Plutarch describes Brutus as 'weighing with himself the greatness of the danger' and Portia as discovering 'some marvellous great matter that troubled his mind, not being wont to be in that taking, and that he could not well determine with himself' (Spencer, pp. 116–17). Shakespeare's Brutus seems unconcerned about potential danger and, as Coleridge recognized, his concerns in the soliloquy in which he resolves his ambivalence do not make political sense, because the republican Brutus would hardly need to search for justification to stop the imperialist Caesar.[34] Instead, Brutus achieves unprecedented depth as a character through his articulation of moral ambivalence: 'I would not, Cassius; yet I love him well' (1.2.84); 'It must be by his death. And for my part, / I know no personal cause to

spurn at him, / But for the general' (2.1.10–12). His conscience demands justification for the contemplated act of murder. The portrayal of Brutus accords with the intrinsic importance of moral sensibility to Western culture's basic idea of selfhood; as Charles Taylor observes, 'to know who you are is to be oriented in moral space, a space in which questions arise about what is good or bad, what is worth doing and what not, what has meaning and importance for you and what is trivial and secondary'.[35] Yet to express this moral awareness, and hence to possess this sort of selfhood, requires a split or divided self. So Brutus's pondering of the potential harm of Caesar's actions and the actual harm of his own takes shape in the soliloquy as an internal dialogue or 'quarrel' (2.1.28), as though two diverging moral influences were voiced within the single self.

In our culture, the idea of internal debate has been naturalized to the point that its dramatization seems less than remarkable. Its compelling power becomes more evident if we compare the method of showing Brutus's decision through soliloquy-as-dialogue with two other moments in the play in which significant choice is shown through exteriorized modes. In Acts 4 and 5 of *Julius Caesar*, Brutus is depleted of his carefully dialogic decision-making ability; after the assassination he becomes Caesar-like in his ruthlessness. Having sacrificed his supple powers of discrimination to the bloody cause of murder, Brutus's 'other' voice of conscience

---

But it is also true that, when he does not expressly do so, he often keeps Plutarch's statements in his mind, even when . . . he does not cite them', *Shakespeare's Roman Plays and Their Background*, 1910, foreword by T. J. B. Spencer (London, 1967), p. 612.

34 Coleridge wrote that 'nothing can seem more discordant with our historical preconceptions of Brutus, or more lowering to the intellect of the Stoico-Platonic tyrannicide, than the tenets here attributed to him – to him, the stern Roman republican' (*Lectures and Notes of 1818*, cited in MacCallum, p. 201).

35 Charles Taylor, *Sources of the Self: The Making of the Modern Identity* (Cambridge, 1989), p. 28.

becomes exterior to him – an alien, enemy voice, that of his 'evil spirit' (4.2.333). Here as frequently when Shakespeare adopts Plutarch's supernatural phenomena, he pushes their significance in a psychological direction. So Brutus's 'evil spirit' figures in Plutarch as his 'ill angel', 'a horrible vision of a man', and a 'monstrous spirit' (Spencer, pp. 100, 165), but is identified in the Folio stage direction of Shakespeare's play as 'the ghost of Caesar' (4.2.325sd). The ghost presents in embodied form the inner conflict represented verbally earlier in the play; Brutus, now gripped by guilt, is no longer the dispassionate observer of his own inner drama. Since a ghostly presence on stage figures ambiguously as internal or external to the haunted character, the 'evil spirit' will, if interpreted along plot lines as the revenging Caesar, accomplish a diminution of Brutus's character, with his suicide – 'Caesar, now be still' (5.5.50) – signalling his final capitulation to a more potent adversary. Understood structurally, the ambiguous placement and identity of this 'other' figure – who is both within Brutus and exterior to him, both his own 'evil spirit' and Caesar's 'ghost' – signals the transferential action of oedipality. Brutus's yielding to the ghost completes his embrace of an agonistic moral consciousness, which blocks the earlier complexity and creativity figured as internal dialogue. The dubious quality of Brutus's moral reasoning when he justifies Caesar's death in 2.1 of course demonstrates (and likely influenced the conceptualization of) Freud's idea of a necessary link between oedipality and ethics.[36] Before he internalizes the paternal figure (Caesar), as superego, Brutus's thoughts are morally creative, flexible, uncensored. After he internalizes that haunting figure, his thoughts are sternly ethical, anguished, self-censoring. Representing this consciousness as a ghost on stage, so that his/its demanding presence is central to viewers' theatrical experience, the play extends the oedipal structure of its plot to the audience, teaching them, with Brutus, the painful consequences of killing the father. In this sense the

ghost furthers an awareness of Brutus's inner dilemma even while it remains physically separate from him.

As for Caesar's own decisions, that his only significant choice in the play is to reject what proves sound advice and instead go forth from his home on the Ides of March reminds us of what shocks first-time readers: the title character's astonishing passivity. Caesar's choice, a cognate of the Rubicon decision, here similarly determines his movement into a new political dimension and involves interaction with a significant female figure. Where the younger Caesar grasps his future after dreaming of sleeping with his mother, the older man meets his death after dismissing his wife's canny vision of what awaits him. Shakespeare essentially follows Plutarch in attributing to Calpurnia a troubling dream and the specific awareness that it bodes disastrously for Caesar. However, he takes considerable care to transform Calpurnia's dream (uncertainly reported in Plutarch as either 'that Caesar was slain, and that she had him in her arms' or that the pinnacle on the housetop was broken (Spencer, pp. 88–9)) into the comprehensively symbolic vision of the bleeding statue, which suggests Caesar's personal and political roles (as man and statue), and the disputed relation between them (does Caesar sacrificially enrich Rome? or merely fall prey to bloody appetites?). In Plutarch, furthermore, Decius Brutus ridicules Caesar's reliance on his wife's dream but does not offer his own interpretation of it. In Shakespeare's brilliant revision, the dream takes on the status of a disputed text, and the two proffered readings of it are set side by side: Decius's and Calpurnia's,

---

[36] Freud first proposes the Oedipal complex in relation to *Hamlet*, but his several references to *Julius Caesar* in the course of *The Interpretation of Dreams* advance a personal connection and a nearly identical theme, Sigmund Freud, *The Interpretation of Dreams*, trans. James Strachey (New York, 1965), pp. 297–300, 459–61, 520–22. See also Cynthia Marshall, 'Totem, Taboo, and *Julius Caesar*', *Literature and Psychology* 37. 1–2 (April 1991), 11–33.

one from the political world and one from the domestic, one male- and one female-authored, one flattering and one simply true. Figuring Caesar's decision as one made between these two interpretations, Shakespeare weights the poles of choice, granting the moment a richly poetic but intensely oppositional significance. When Caesar finally decides to venture forth, he attributes to his wife the anxiety that made him tarry: 'How foolish do your fears seem now, Calpurnia!' (2.2.105). Obviously an act of political face-saving, the transference nevertheless works backward to code Caesar's fears as a womanly element within him.[37]

IV

As we have seen, Plutarch wrote within a tradition which attributed enormous influence to supernatural deities in the direction of human affairs. The divinely inspired visions in Lucan and Suetonius are typical of the Graeco-Roman tradition in relegating significant agency to a force outside the protagonist, but external motivation of this sort contrasts markedly with what Plutarch attributes to Caesar at the Rubicon – a struggle with his own conscience and with his internalized (m)other. Plutarch, however, has certainly not arrived at the modern idea of individuality; his gestures in this direction are tentative and sporadic. Yet he seems uneasily aware of the poor fit between the inherited model of divine inspiration and a nascent sense of human agency. In his *Life of Martius Coriolanus*, Plutarch attempts to negotiate a compromise with the Homeric model.

The meditation on human judgement and free will occurs at a crucial turning point in Coriolanus's life, which is also a crucial moment for the city of Rome. It is, in fact, Coriolanus's Rubicon, but as he is poised outside the city, about to attack, his mother makes an appeal that he is unable to reject. Coriolanus's decision is determined by his mother's influence – but what inspires Volumnia to make her appeal? Plutarch is quite

evidently troubled by such a question, for he goes to considerable length to account for Volumnia's decision. Shakespeare more fully psychologizes the relationship between Volumnia and Coriolanus, so that her motivation is located in a desire for vicarious honour through her son, and his inability to resist her plea is the final testimony to his stifled humanity, his unacknowledged need for nurturance, or his exercise of conscience.[38] But where Shakespeare places the sources for action within the experiences and developed patterns of response of the two characters, Plutarch searches for a deeper or even an ultimate source. Turning to the Homeric model, he quotes three examples of divine inspiration, among them: ' "The goddess Pallas she, with her fair glistering eyes, / Did put into his mind such thoughts, and made him so devise." ' Plutarch is aware that 'many reckon not of Homer', believing that his 'fables' slight the part of 'man's reason, free will, or judgment'. But he holds that such negative responses misread Homer, for 'things true and likely he maketh to depend of our own freewill and reason' (Spencer, pp. 349–50).

Plutarch finds in Homer a balanced model of human and divine interaction, in which the gods do not control or direct their human subjects, but offer advice and inspiration:

in wondrous and extraordinary things, which are done by secret inspirations and motion, he [Homer] doth not say that God taketh away from man his choice and freedom of will, but that he doth move

---

[37] See Coppélia Kahn, *Roman Shakespeare: Warriors, Wounds, and Women* (New York, 1997), p. 103.

[38] Interpretations of this critical moment vary: on stifled humanity, see Stanley Cavell, *Disowning Knowledge in Six Plays of Shakespeare* (New York, 1987), pp. 143–77; on blighted nurturance, see Janet Adelman, ' "Anger's my meat": Feeding, Dependency, and Aggression in *Coriolanus*,' in *Representing Shakespeare: New Psychoanalytic Essays*, ed. Murray Schwartz and Coppélia Kahn (Baltimore, 1980), pp. 129–49; on conscience, see Lukacher, pp. 207–11.

it: neither that he doth work desire in us, but objecteth to our minds certain imagination whereby we are led to desire, and thereby doth not make this our action forced, but openeth the way to our will, and addeth thereto courage and hope of success. For either we must say that the gods meddle not with the causes and beginnings of our actions; or else what other means have they to help and further men? It is apparent that they handle not our bodies, nor move not our feet and hands when there is occasion to use them; but that part of our mind, from which these motions proceed, is induced thereto or carried away by such objects and reasons as God offereth unto it. (Spencer, p. 350)

The dialogic model he outlines is unremarkable among classical texts in attributing potency to the gods without sacrificing individual human will. What *is* striking about this account of interior life is its focus on the workings of desire. Plutarch is suspicious of a model that would attribute motivation to external agency and strip human creatures of autonomy. But he is equally aware of the logical deficiencies of locating originary desire within the preordained subject: difference of some sort must create the space that desire aims to bridge. Recognizing and negotiating difference, then, is the key to Plutarch's model of human agency. North's translation renders the origin of difference wonderfully ambiguous: God (singular, for North) 'objecteth to our minds certain imagination whereby we are led to desire'. Desire begins with the introduction into the subject's mind of an object. The verb form 'objecteth' indicates the pre-objectified status of that which the subject will desire, while simultaneously suggesting the alteration of the subject worked by desire, in Lacanian terms a kind of *méconnaissance*: 'part of our mind . . . is induced thereto or carried away by such objects'. Plutarch hammers out a model of agency in which the vicissitudes of desire are foundational, and so can only be accounted for by divine inspiration.

The actual inspiration Plutarch is concerned to document is that which leads a band of Roman women to encourage Volumnia to intervene in her son's planned attack on the city. These women's prayers to the gods are answered when one among them, Valeria, 'suddenly fell into such a fancy as we have rehearsed before, and had (by some god as I think) taken hold of a noble device' (Spencer, p. 351). After Valeria speaks movingly of her inspiration – 'some god above . . . having taken compassion and pity of our prayers, hath moved us to come unto you' (Spencer, p. 351) – Volumnia agrees to entreat her son's pity on Rome. In a striking picture of female society, organization, and influence, Valeria, together with Volumnia, Martius' wife, and his children, and 'accompanied with all the other Roman ladies . . . went in troop together unto the Volsces' camp' (Spencer, p. 352).

Plutarch's 'Roman ladies' figure difference in relation to Coriolanus; they interpolate into the hero's mind a desire that is strictly counter to his previous intentions. Plutarch, on the road to a psychological understanding of free will and motivation, makes these women an intermediary force between the gods and Coriolanus's independence. Accordingly, Plutarch undercuts the concept of 'natural affection' even as he cites it as the reason for Coriolanus's defeat (he was 'overcome in the end with natural affection' [Spencer, p. 352]). The extensive, step-by-step account of how his plan to attack Rome is altered testifies to a complex set of motivations with an external origin. The women pray to the gods, who inspire Valeria, who moves Volumnia, who influences Coriolanus: Plutarch manages to grant the hero independent choice while simultaneously acknowledging a chain of external influences. When Coriolanus cries out 'Oh mother, what have you done to me?' (Spencer, p. 357), Plutarch indicates that the force exerted upon the hero can be traced back to the gods, so that he might be described as overcome with *super*natural affection.[39] Significantly, however,

---

[39] Heuer notes that the emphasis on 'nature' and 'natural' is North's.

the Roman women are intermediaries for this divine force, they 'objecteth' into the mind of Coriolanus the desire to alter his attack. Here, even more clearly than in Plutarch's account of Caesar crossing the Rubicon, women figure prominently in the hero's process of decision-making, indicating that notions of choice and internal debate can be understood in terms of gendered difference.

Shakespeare makes the influence of Coriolanus's mother the single motive force behind his internal conflict and contradictory desires. By reducing the 'troop' of 'Roman ladies' to the trio of Volumnia, Valeria, and Virgilia, Shakespeare intensifies the relationship between Coriolanus and his mother; indeed, by modern estimates, it becomes pathologically stifling. The mother-son relationship bears the weight of what Plutarch sees as divine inspiration, mediated through a company of women. The consolidation of characters reflects the practical demands of drama: Shakespeare had little need for a troop of Roman ladies to accompany Volumnia, when they could be adequately represented by Valeria alone. But the change has reverberations that affect the presentation of character: in Plutarch's version, influences on the mind are diverse and multi-dimensional, while Shakespeare limns a more fully interiorized, psychological world.

Tracing the movement from Plutarch to Shakespeare provides a useful counterbalance to strictly recursive attempts to bridge the gap between the early modern period and our own. In a compelling and influential essay, Page duBois reads *Coriolanus* as a Shakespearian meditation on the mother–son relation, partially inspired by the deaths of Queen Elizabeth I in 1603 and Mary Arden in 1608. For duBois, Shakespeare in *Coriolanus* participates in the ascendant role of the patriarchal father, and by offering a 'critique of matriarchal power' he assists 'the transition to Freud's world of the fathers'.[40] DuBois suggests that the failure of oedipal relation to order Coriolanus's world results in the 'schizophrenic' brokenness of the

hero's language, body, role, and relation to society.[41] DuBois's argument takes on greater force in light of Shakespeare's concerted move to increase Volumnia's power from what it is in Plutarch's narrative. He has made her the sole conveyer of the potency of a troop of women carrying a divine message. Volumnia's influence in the meeting with her son becomes even more remarkable when we note the structural parallel with Caesar's crossing of the Rubicon. Shakespeare, following Plutarch in his presentation of that crucial juncture, renders the moment of choice and decision an interior one that is nevertheless shaped by gender difference.

When Shakespeare's Coriolanus capitulates to his mother's demands outside the walls of Rome, no verbal explanation of his choice is offered. Indeed, the characters' words elide the actual moment of decision-making: Volumnia directs those who accompany her to kneel and then to depart; Coriolanus in his next speech refers to their encounter in the past tense:

> O mother, mother!
> What have you done? Behold, the heavens do
>   ope,
> The gods look down, and this unnatural scene
> They laugh at. O my mother, mother, O!
> You have won a happy victory to Rome;
> But for your son, believe it, O believe it,
> Most dangerously you have with him prevailed,
> If not most mortal to him. But let it come.
>
> (5.3.183 – 90)

Appearing just before these lines is the unusually expressive stage direction '*He holds her by the hand, silent,*' conflating two phrases from North's Plutarch.[42] Noting that John Bulwer's *Chironomia* (1644) cites this moment in Plutarch to illustrate the gestural insinuation of love, duty, and supplication, Michael Neill writes

---

40 Page duBois, 'A Disturbance of Syntax at the Gates of Rome', *Stanford Literature Review*, 2 (1985), 185–208, p. 206.
41 DuBois, 'A Disturbance', p. 191.
42 Philip Brockbank, ed., New Arden *Coriolanus*, by William Shakespeare (London, 1976), p. 296n.

that here 'it is *actio*, more than anything, that endows rhetoric with the active power of eloquence'.[43] A theatre audience is given to understand that Coriolanus's choice is made in the gap between Volumnia's words asking for dismissal ('Yet give us our dispatch' [5.3.181]) and her son's words asking what she has done: the choice is made during the interval in which he 'holds her by the hand, silent'. Bodily action here must convey all that is not said; the actors must somehow make comprehensible to the audience what Volumnia has done and how Coriolanus will respond. In this moment, action is rendered hysterical, for the characters' bodies must convey a knowledge that is remote from their words.[44] Her supplication and command, his capitulation and silence, are shown to be ancient postures for Volumnia and Coriolanus. And since his response appears to be one he could not explain if he tried, it may well seem to an audience that Coriolanus has been 'overcome with natural affection'.

In terms of the semiotics of character, we might ponder how his evident lack of self-knowledge and the absence of whatever explanation such knowledge might produce affects a reader's or audience's sense of who Coriolanus is. Since the hero's inner life goes so largely unrepresented in the play, the audience must itself bridge the gap between Volumnia's pleas and his accession, or more generally between his actions and a credible motivation for them. Coriolanus's mute and incomprehensible behaviours point to a reason behind or before them, and where Plutarch's second-century mind saw fit to provide a structure of external influences, Shakespeare paints a hero who remains essentially alone, one whose boundaries of self are particularly impenetrable. If a theatrical audience fails to attribute reasons, and hence an inner life, to Coriolanus, it will complain that he lacks reflectiveness and is without self; certainly the critical tradition is filled with such remarks.[45] Here we note the potential for frustration inherent in theatrical performance. Although the interior self may be represented

verbally (in narrative, in dramatic monologue, or through self-reference in dialogue), or presented on stage in exteriorized form (as with Brutus's 'evil spirit'), or suggested through symbolic choices (as with Caesar's going forth or Coriolanus's decision not to), it cannot be literally shown or visually revealed on stage. Since drama entails the acting out of what is represented through words in narrative, the genre can scarcely improve on narrative renditions of the inner self. Indeed, the paradigmatic instance of Renaissance interiority, Hamlet's claim to 'have that within which passes show' actually turns on the theatrical mode's inability to reveal what Hamlet says he has inside.[46] This means that drama necessarily complicates its audience's relationship to characters presented on stage, advertising their interior depth while unable ultimately to reveal it. Theatrical characters are thus somewhat inevitably 'all patchwork', like the early modern subjectivity Montaigne memorably describes – com-

---

43 Michael Neill, '"Amphitheaters in the Body": Playing with Hands on the Shakespearian Stage', *Shakespeare Survey 48* (Cambridge, 1995), pp. 23–50, p. 33.

44 David Bevington notes that kneeling, unlike curtseying or offcapping, 'is a profound gesture of acknowledgement of the claims of hierarchy' on the Shakespearian stage, and that it serves here as a 'visual statement [that] mocks and inverts the military might to which Coriolanus has aspired. Coriolanus' mother must kneel to him, but in doing so brings about his capitulation to her . . . The image of kneeling sharply differentiates the submission he acknowledges to his mother and that he denies to the popular will of Rome.' See *Action Is Eloquence: Shakespeare's Language of Gesture* (Cambridge, MA, 1984), pp. 164, 168–9.

45 See Cynthia Marshall, 'Wound-man: *Coriolanus*, gender, and the theatrical construction of interiority', in *Feminist Readings of Early Modern Culture: Emerging Subjects*, ed. Valerie Traub, M. Lindsay Kaplan and Dympna Callaghan (New York, 1996), pp. 93–118.

46 See Douglas Lanier, '"Stigmatical in Making": The Material Character of *The Comedy of Errors*', *English Literary Renaissance* 23.1 (Winter 1993), 81–112; and Katherine Eisaman Maus, *Inwardness and Theater in the English Renaissance* (Chicago, 1995).

pounded of various essences, influences, and interactions, and revealed at best only partially.[47]

Earlier in this essay I invoked hysteria, not as a diagnostic label for Coriolanus himself (although an interesting argument in that direction could perhaps be made), but rather as a trope for theorizing Shakespeare's relation to Plutarch's *Lives*. The Freudian understanding of hysteria proposes that what cannot be explained will be acted out. Where Plutarch's narrative mode and moralistic approach facilitated explanation, Shakespeare complicated the characterological model through an increased emphasis on individual interaction and a sceptical approach to human motivation, and, most markedly, through a conversion of narrative to drama. As I have suggested, the process of dramatizing Plutarch's narratives was in effect reversed by psychoanalysis, which attempted to explain and account for life as performed. Confronting the inconsistencies between life as enacted and life as explained or narrated, psychoanalysis systematized the gap itself as the unconscious. In the case of *Coriolanus*, Shakespeare's adaptation of the Plutarchan narrative represses the chain of divine and feminine influence on Martius's character, instead locating such influence inside him. The result is an access of depth, or at least a suspicion of it, which in the theatre can amount to the same thing. Just as hysteria was traditionally linked in medical discourse with a less solidly dense physical self, with a body whose organs were prone to wander, so there is a spatial component in the Freudian conception of hysterical character. Hysterics contained mysterious inner secrets, inner space that lent itself to narrative analysis; it was their need for explanation, I assume, that provoked Freud to write case studies of hysterics (but typically not of melancholiacs, whose inner spaces, according to Freud's theory, were overfull, replete with internalized traces of their object attachments). Critical forays into the early modern psyches Shakespeare represented will be more successful if we bear in mind the extent to which the

dramatic mode shaped his conception of character and the degree to which his model has been normalized by psychological theories of identity. Certainly it is erroneous to blur the distinction between dramatic characters in early modern texts and historical subjects from that era. Yet it may be virtually impossible to avoid doing so, since Shakespeare's characters have greatly influenced our familiar models and ideas of human identity.

His narrative mode allowed Plutarch to describe internal visions and debates that locate differences within the self, or to trace a chain of divine influence that inspires action. By contrast, Shakespeare's dramatic mode offered more restricted means for representing internal processes. The semiotic gaps between meaning and appearance inhering in drama introduce and even call for a hysterical conception of character, since what is demonstrated on stage provokes but (if the character is interesting) evades explanation. When a personal decision is conveyed in soliloquy, as in Brutus's speech beginning 'It must be by his death' (*Julius Caesar*, 2.1.10) or Hamlet's conception of the Mousetrap play, purportedly marked by his word 'Hum' (*Hamlet*, 2.2.574),[48] there are suspicious disjunctures; the words actually commemorate, rather than express, the process of making a choice.[49] In

---

47 Michel de Montaigne, *The Complete Essays of Montaigne*, trans. Donald M. Frame (Stanford, 1957), p. 244.

48 A famously disputed passage: 'Hum' appears in Q2 but not in F (on which the Oxford Shakespeare is based).

49 Luke Wilson proposes that 'Hum' 'marks Shakespeare's labor rather than Hamlet's' and that it thus 'discloses in pure form the intrusion of the temporal logic of compositional activity into the temporality of dramatic representation'. See '*Hamlet*, Hales v. Petit, and the Hysteresis of Action', *ELH*, 60 (1993), p. 25. Wilson quotes (and quibbles with) Joseph Hunter's remark that 'Hum' 'makes *prospective* what is evidently *retrospective*' (p. 24). For Wilson, 'because performance has the same convoluted temporal structure as intentional action, it conceals what it exposes in a temporal fold; the structure of Hamlet's preposterous account of his actions is the structure of an interiority that, always spatially and temporally displaced, is never quite *there*' (pp. 33–4).

theatrical practice, of course, this rarely presents a problem, because viewers assume the autonomy of decision-making as a central characteristic of the developed, considering self. Since a character can gain interiority merely through the mention, even though it be paradoxical or belated, of such 'inner' experiences as dreams, madness, or desire, one begins to understand interiority to be, almost by definition, that which can be spoken of but can itself never speak. Founded on the division of the speaking subject, interiority effects the transitivity of that subject. Such inner division is the presupposition of both characterological interiority and the psychologized self – it seems fair to say, in fact, that they are versions of the same thing.

VERNACULAR CRITICISM AND THE SCENES SHAKESPEARE NEVER WROTE

MICHAEL D. BRISTOL

VERNACULAR CRITICISM . . .

'Let us . . .for a moment, put Shakespeare out of the question, and consider Hamlet as a real person, a recently deceased acquaintance.'[1] The suggestion comes from an essay by Hartley Coleridge, first published in *Blackwoods Magazine* in 1828. It is, in a way, an interesting proposal, partly because of its tone of cosy familiarity. The part about Hamlet being 'recently deceased' is particularly ingenious; acquaintances who have died no longer have the power to surprise or to disappoint us. They 'achieve closure' as characters in the narrative of our own lives. But the key point in Hartley Coleridge's suggestion is not that Hamlet is 'recently deceased' but that he is someone with whom we can be acquainted in just the same way as we are acquainted with the real people who populate our own lives. A narrative has scope and extent beyond what is explicitly reported in a contingent text or performance. There are things that we can reliably infer about a fictional character's moral disposition, motives, beliefs and desires that derive not from explicit textual cues but from everyday background knowledge of how the world generally works. The basic competence for understanding narrative as a process of filling in or completing gaps in the contingent storytelling is acquired at a very early stage of social learning. And this competence is a basic condition for the possibility of 'getting the story'.

Hartley Coleridge's implied theory about how best to grasp a Shakespearian narrative has had remarkable persistence. In a more recent article, published in *The New Yorker* in October of 1994, David Denby compares King Lear to his own recently deceased mother.

In the years before my mother died, when she was in trouble in ways that I couldn't understand or grapple with, I had thought about 'King Lear' more than anyone would want to. She *is* King Lear, I would say angrily to my wife after an impossible phone call or visit, the joke seeming staler and less illuminating each time. She was also my mother, Ida Denby, unhappy as hell and eager to let me know it.[2]

I daresay that David Denby is not the only person ever to have harboured such thoughts about an ageing parent. And in fact I have found quite similar intuitions about this play at least as far back as Elizabeth Griffith's *Morality of Shakespeare's Drama Illustrated* (1775). Denby argues that the play is designed to suggest something personal of exactly this kind. If it does not, he claims, the story seems simply overwrought, preposterous, extravagant.

I turn finally to an even more recent example of this kind of interpretation. A flight attendant

---

1 Hartley Coleridge, *Blackwoods Magazine*, 24 (1828), 585. Cited in L. C. Knights, 'How Many Children Had Lady Macbeth?' *Explorations: Essays in Criticism, Mainly on the Literature of the Seventeenth Century* (London, 1946), p. 15.
2 David Denby, 'Queen Lear', *The New Yorker*, 70, no. 31 (1994), 89.

on an American Airlines 757 from Chicago to San Francisco broached the following theory about Lady Macbeth. Lady Macbeth has had a baby, an illegitimate child fathered by Duncan. And here I quote . . . 'That's why she hates him so much.' My aim in recounting this incident is not to get a cheap laugh at the expense of airline flight attendants, not even the ones who like to read and reflect about Shakespeare. What I like about this response to the play is not just its spontaneity and candour. I also admire the intelligence of the reasoning here, which I might briefly reconstruct along the following lines: Cold-blooded murder of a 'friend' must be prompted by powerful feelings of animosity, grievance, or resentment. What could prompt a woman to feel such intense hatred of a man? Well, Lady Macbeth speaks of a child she has nursed and whom she imagines murdering. It must be that this man Duncan has betrayed her sexually and fathered this child for whom she has such confused feelings . . .

Some of the links in this chain of inferences come from the text of Shakespeare's *Macbeth*. But additional links must be supplied from one's own background knowledge about how the world works. As David Lewis points out in his essay 'Truth in Fiction' (1983), people are often warned against 'reading into' a story things that are not 'really there' in the text. But, he maintains, this injunction is rarely followed by skilful and competent readers.[3] Most readers rely on a background of general intuitions that enable us to 'get a story' by combining elements of explicit textual content with our own default assumptions about the world. Some of the American Airlines flight attendant's intuitions are social: powerful men can and do use their power to seduce young women who are then more often than not left to manage the consequences of their seduction on their own. Other intuitions are derived from what has been called a folk psychology based on notions of motive, intention, feeling, and so on: people have reasons for what they do, and those reasons can generally be inferred from what

they say.[4] Lewis points out that this sort of 'mixed reasoning' from a combination of fictional and factual premises is a type of informal fallacy.[5] But in practice the fallacy is often not so bad, and in fact, as Lewis suggests, it may not even be possible to reason about fictions at all without reference to at least some premises that are not explicitly warranted by a text. Incidentally, historically based criticism does not provide any kind of solution to this problem. Historical criticism is based on exactly the same kind of mixed reasoning from what is true in a fiction and what is true in the known world at some moment in its previous history.

The method of interpretation practised by Hartley Coleridge, David Denby, and by the person who served me buffalo chicken salad on Flight 83 are all examples of what I am calling vernacular criticism and I want now to specify more exactly what this term means. According to the *Oxford Latin Dictionary*, vernacular comes from verna, a slave born in the master's household (typically treated with greater indulgence than other slaves). The important distinction here is most probably the difference between the native-born and the foreign slave who comes into the household either through a purchase or through military conquest. A second usage in Latin is for a 'common town-bred person'. Vernaculus, the adjective, can mean simply belonging to the household or to the country, but it was also used to mean a low-born or proletarian buffoon. Vernaculous, now spelled with an 'o', also appears as an English word meaning low-bred or scurrilous. And sure enough the originary coinage cited in the *OED* comes from the dedication to Ben Jonson's *Volpone*.

I cannot but be serious in a cause of this nature, wherein my fame and the reputations of divers

---

[3] David Lewis, 'Truth in Fiction', in *Philosophical Papers, Vol. I.* (Oxford, 1983), p. 268.

[4] Paisley Livingston, *Literature and Rationality* (Cambridge, 1991), pp. 15–48.

[5] Lewis, 'Truth in Fiction', p. 269.

honest and learned are the question; when a name so full of authority, antiquity, and all great mark, is . . . become the lowest scorn of the age; and those men subject to the petulancy of every vernaculous orator, that were wont to be the care of kings and happiest monarchs .[6]

Both the word vernaculous and its sense of 'scurrilous' are current in seventeenth-century English, but they evidently drop out of use afterwards, overtaken by the more flexible derivation in our word 'vernacular', a term that picks up the valences of the household, domestic life, and native language from its Latin sources. Vernacular can refer to material practices or things, as in vernacular architecture. And it once had the additional sense of endemic in reference to diseases.

But the principal sense of vernacular is in reference to language and specifically to what is commonly known as *langue maternelle*, mother tongue. Walter Ong's account of this term in his *Orality and Literacy* is particularly helpful here. All children learn the vernacular, principally in a domestic setting, from their mothers, their grandmothers, or from maternal caregivers.[7] In the early modern period, young boys with aspirations to social privilege were later selected to learn Latin and Greek, a language they learned only from men, in an exclusively male setting, where learning was frequently reinforced by strong forms of corporal punishment.

Vernacular can have the sense of a parochial form of speech, as in expressions like the vernacular of Montréal or the vernacular of London. It can also have the sense of a specialized or technical language, as in usage like the vernacular of engineers or the vernacular of textual scholars. But vernacular criticism of the sort I have been describing seems to have a much broader kind of appeal. It is at home with, or indigenous to a contemporary idiom of assumptions and presuppositions about how to account for the actions of ordinary people. And perhaps more important, vernacular criticism is an attempt to find an orientation in a space of

moral questions.[8] In this sense vernacular criticism is not necessarily synonymous with the interpretive amateurism practised by journalists, flight attendants, or one's own students. There are a number of influential professional critics who have found sophisticated theoretical ways to sustain this tradition – I'm thinking here of Harry Berger, Stanley Cavell, and of course Harold Bloom.[9] Inspiration for newer and more rigorous forms of vernacular criticism might come from contemporary moral philosophy – from Hannah Arendt, for example, or from the debate between Lawrence Kohlberg and Carol Gilligan, or from more recent work by Alasdair McIntyre, Charles Taylor, Lawrence Becker, and Martha Nussbaum. It helps to conjure with these names, but even without these authorities I no longer feel sure that we should be dismissing flight attendants, or students, or cab drivers for their presumption of interpretive familiarity with Shakespeare's writing.

Vernacular criticism has a venerable history in the study of Shakespeare's works, but for the past fifty years and more it has been visible mostly as the preferred scapegoat for both formalist and historicist treatments of the plays. This attitude has been powerfully codified in L. C. Knights' still influential article, 'How Many Children had Lady Macbeth?' The essay could just as well have been entitled *Cathargo delenda est* in its treatment of what I have been calling vernacular criticism, with its emphasis on folk psychology and contemporary ethical problems. Knights surveys Shakespeare criticism

---

6 Ben Jonson, *Volpone*, ed. C. H. Herford and Percy Simpson (Oxford, 1937), pp. 19–20.

7 Walter Ong, *Orality and Literacy* (London, 1982), pp. 111–14.

8 Charles Taylor, *Sources of the Self: The Making of the Modern Identity* (Cambridge, 1989), pp. 25–53.

9 Harry Berger, *Making Trifles of Terrors: Redistributing Complicities in Shakespeare* (Stanford, 1997); Stanley Cavell, *Disowning Knowledge in Six Plays of Shakespeare*, (Cambridge, 1987); Harold Bloom, *Shakespeare: The Invention of the Human* (New York, 1998).

from the time of Thomas Rymer through Dryden, Johnson, Warburton, Shaftesbury, Lady Montagure, William Richardson, Anna Jameson, Mary Cowden Clarke, Hazlitt, Coleridge, Goethe, Dowden, Ellen Terry, A. C. Bradley – the list goes on and on – as the history of error, ignorance, and irrelevance. 'The habit of regarding Shakespeare's persons as "friends for life" or, maybe, "deceased acquaintances", is responsible for most of the vagaries that serve as Shakespeare criticism.'[10] Maybe all these writers really were as stupid, not to mention bigoted and destructive, as Knights makes them out to be, though this would make them very stupid indeed. But it might also be worthwhile to take a second look at the assumption that what we know of the ordinary people who inhabit our social and personal lives might be a reliable basis for the interpretation of Shakespearian drama. Are there reasons for adopting such a belief, or does it flow only from fuzzy-headed ignorance of the teachings of I. A. Richards, as Knights seems to maintain.

The tradition of vernacular criticism flows from the recognition that Shakespeare is the creator of a great vernacular poetry. This discovery unfolds gradually in the work of many different writers and scholars of the eighteenth century, but it is most fully codified by Samuel Johnson, in the 1765 *Preface* to his edition of Shakespeare's work. Johnson was in many ways puzzled by his appreciation for Shakespeare's genius. Virtually everything distinctive in Shakespeare's works runs against the grain of Johnson's aesthetic preferences and also against some of his deepest moral convictions. The decisive achievement exhibited in the collected plays is a powerful realism of attitude, motive, and behaviour. The concreteness of Shakespearian representation, its sympathetic correspondence with everyday social reality is at once its most characteristic excellence and at the same time the source of its crucial difficulties.

It is the great excellence of Shakespeare, that he drew his scenes from nature, and from life. He copied the manners of the world then passing before him, and has more allusions than other poets to the traditions and superstition of the vulgar; which must therefore be traced before he can be understood . . . If Shakespeare has difficulties above other writers, it is to be imputed to the nature of his work, which required the use of the common colloquial language, and consequently admitted many phrases allusive, elliptical, and proverbial, such as we speak and hear every hour without observing them .[11]

For Johnson the heterogeneity of Shakespeare's language, its wide ranging familiarity with obsolete, common, and colloquial idiom as well as with foreign languages, is something of an 'embarrassment for the reader'. Nevertheless, he was astute enough to recognize that Shakespeare's use of colloquial or vernacular speech is integral to his achievement as a writer of lasting value.

Shakespeare's 'vulgarity', together with his 'ungrammatical' and 'licentious' English are not exactly praised as virtues or 'excellencies' by Johnson, but it will be his task as an editor to elucidate what has been obscured by time, rather than to correct the text in conformity with contemporary standards. As the compiler of the English Dictionary he appreciated with perhaps unusual sensitivity that a language is an immense, shared resource, equally important for the unlearned and the learned, for the 'common workmen' as well as the 'critick'. Shakespeare's works are, not incidentally for Johnson, a rich and varied printed archive of popular usage that continues to shape the language of everyday social interaction. Despite his frequently expressed distaste for vulgarity of expression and behaviour then, Johnson hopes to consider the 'whole extent of our language' with the intent to 'recover the meaning of words now lost in the darkness of antiquity'. But Johnson is really after something more than philological description here. The larger point

---

10 L. C. Knights, 'How Many Children', p. 16.
11 Samuel Johnson, *Preface to Shakespeare* (New Haven, 1958), p. 58.

revealed in Shakespeare's language is in the way it is used to work through the social and ethical exigencies of ordinary life.

One of the more significant critical explanations for Shakespeare's cultural importance begins from the conviction, emerging at the beginning of the early modern period, that everyday life has an overriding priority as a moral source. This view assigns moral pre-eminence to the regime of intimate personal relations, to the family, and to the lives of ordinary unprivileged people engaged in various forms of practical reason. Samuel Johnson identifies Shakespeare as a powerful source for articulating the moral pre-eminence of ordinary life. Johnson is a realist in his view of such unobservable phenomena as beliefs, desires and moral attitudes. He attributes the same realism about human motivation to Shakespeare. It is because Shakespeare has so much insight into both the desires and the moral sources that direct all human agency, that his works are so richly instructive. 'It was said of Euripides, that every verse was a precept; and it may be said of Shakespeare, that from his works may be collected a system of civil and oeconomical prudence.'[12] The notion of 'oeconomical prudence' here has the sense of domestic rule or household management. Although Shakespeare at times 'seems to write without any moral purpose', his lasting importance for Johnson is within the moral regime of the household and the practical demands of ordinary life.

Johnson's edition of Shakespeare, like his *Dictionary*, manifests his concern for communal life within the emerging regime we now know as Western Modernity. His well-known maxim that 'the end of all learning is piety' has to be read not as an appeal for private religiosity but rather as an apprehension about the practical importance of intellectual endeavour in the conservation of serviceable social institutions. Johnson thought that a 'system of oeconomical prudence' would be no less crucial than a common language for the repair and maintenance of such institutions.

A fuller consideration of Shakespeare's '-domestick wisdom' is reflected in the writings of his contemporary, Lady Elizabeth Montagu. Her *Essay on the Writings and Genius of Shakespeare* was, among other things, a far-reaching attempt to articulate new standards of education, learning and civility in which the gendered monopoly of classical languages would be overturned in favour of a vernacular speech and social discourse. Montagu's central claim is that Shakespeare was a great moral philosopher. Her argument redefines both the subject matter of morality and the social space in which moral enquiry is to be pursued. For Montagu the exploration of moral problems is critically linked to the question of character, conceived here in terms of what I have been calling a folk psychology. The 'moral philosophy' found in Shakespeare is a form of practical reason founded in concrete and contingent social circumstances.

The dramatis personae of Shakespeare are men, frail by constitution, hurt by ill habits, faulty and unequal: but they speak with human voices, are actuated by human passions, and are engaged in the common affairs of human life. We are interested in what they do, or say, by feeling, every moment, that they are of the same nature as ourselves. Their precepts therefore are an instruction, their fates and fortunes an experience, their testimony an authority, and their misfortunes a warning.[13]

The moral force of these depictions arises from an immediate sympathy between the dramatic character and the spectator. What makes such sympathy possible is a shared background in the complex and contradictory experience of everyday life. Shakespeare's characters are non-heroic, and even at times anti-heroic, but it is precisely the modest human scale of their depiction that makes them morally significant.

---

12 Johnson, *Preface*, p. 62.

13 Elizabeth Montagu, *An Essay on the Writings and Genius of Shakespeare, Compared with the Greek and French Dramatic Poets with some Remarks upon the Misrepresentations of Mons. de Voltaire* (London, 1769), p. 60. First Edition published anonymously.

For Elizabeth Montagu, and for many of her eighteenth-century contemporaries, morality is not a schedule of virtues, but rather a matter of more or less vivid and well-defined feelings, inclinations, dispositions. Shakespeare's 'moral philosophy' on this account is indistinguishable from his understanding of the emotional sources of will and action. Assumptions of this kind inform a wide range of critical writings: Elizabeth Griffith's *Morality of Shakespeare's Drama Illustrated* (1775); William Richardson's *Essays on Shakespeare's Dramatic Character of Sir John Falstaff and on his Imitation of Female Character* (1789); Anna Jameson, *Characteristics of Women: Moral, Poetical, and Historical* (1837); Henry Giles, *Human Life in Shakespeare* (1868); Henry Ruggles, *Shakespeare as an Artist* (1870); A. C. Bradley, *Shakespearian Tragedy* (1903); Richard G. Moulton, *The Moral System of Shakespeare: A Popular Illustration of Fiction as the Experimental Side of Philosophy* (1903).

A. C. Bradley is now often denounced or dismissed as a complacent Victorian moralist who had the further bad habit of confusing literary characters with real people. But it might be possible to get a better sense of just what Bradley was getting at by looking at his contemporary Richard Moulton. In using the term 'morals' Moulton is concerned 'with all that touches character, the ways of men, the aims, motives, impulses, whether of individuals or classes: all that is covered by the Latin word *mores*'.[14] Character, used in this way, refers not just to the fictional representation of an actual human being, but more specifically to the moral orientation or disposition adopted by any such figure. Moulton clearly grasps the difference between literary characters or dramatis personae and real people. But his central claim has to do with what we might call the experimental adequacy of fictional worlds to model human action. 'It is surely possible to survey this imaginary world from the same standpoint from which the moralist surveys the world of reality.'[15]

Principles of the kind I've just outlined are also pre-theoretical or default assumptions in Bradley's work. That is, they are assumptions that seem to receive no active justification, and scarcely any explicit formulation anywhere in his work. Now it seems evident that no matter how carefully Bradley or Moulton read Shakespeare's text, it is nevertheless the case that they are using the text to get at something that isn't the text, specifically the attitudes, beliefs, motives, and intentions of the fictional characters. And strictly speaking these 'states of mind' cannot be directly observed in texts or in real people either for that matter. Bradley's work has been dismissed as 'essentialist' because of his scrupulous attention to precisely these unobservable aspects of human behaviour. It's not really clear to me that 'essentialism' really captures what Bradley is in fact on about. But in any case it does seem that Bradley's heresy, if that's what it is, lies precisely in his robust sense of literary character and his belief in the fictional reality of unobserved states of mind.

An even more robust sense of the contingent 'realness' of dramatic character is elaborated in Gail Paster's *The Body Embarrassed: Drama and the Disciplines of Shame in Early Modern England*.[16] Paster reads early modern drama against the background of Galenic physiology. She assumes, therefore, not only that the characters represented in plays have various states of mind, like embarrassment and shame. The characters experience these states of mind because they are 'embodied selves'; they not only have bodies, they have the kind of bodies described – or constructed, if you prefer – in a late medieval and renaissance discourse of the four humours. In a way this takes the idea of vernacular criticism pretty far, because Paster's characters are not only living and breathing, they're also eating, drinking, farting, pissing,

---

[14] Richard Moulton, *The Moral System of Shakespeare: A Popular Illustrations of Fiction as the Experimental Side of Philosophy* (New York, 1903), p. 7.

[15] Moulton, *Moral System*, p. 1.

[16] (Ithaca, 1993).

bleeding, menstruating, and so on, more often than not in graphically messy ways. Paster wants to know 'what it feels like for someone to have a body in early modern society and culture'. Interestingly, the answer seems to be that it feels pretty much the way it does now: awkward, painful, gross, embarrassing, vulnerable. 'If you prick us, do we not bleed?' And of course our bodies are also a source of pleasure, through the exercise of strength and skill as in practising a sport or playing a musical instrument. But wait a minute. Isn't this pretty close to Bradley's heresy? Isn't her project also 'confusing literary characters with real people?' Literary characters don't 'have bodies' – they're just so many words on a page, aren't they? At most the characters can only temporarily borrow a body from the actors and actresses who perform their roles, but those 'borrowed embodiments' really are adventitious manifestations of what a literary character really is. But of course there's no heresy here, any more than in Bradley. Criticism recognizes that it is not true that characters have bodies or states of mind, it is only true in the fiction that these relationships exist.

The theory of vernacular criticism, as opposed to its history, is based on epistemic realism with respect to such unobservable phenomena as motives, intentions, attitudes, ethical disposition, and the like. It is not, as its detractors like to insist, a matter of confusing literary characters with real people. No one actually 'confuses' literary characters with real people. The difference between literary characters and real people is completely obvious to anyone of normal intelligence. It is of course possible that someone might hear about Sherlock Holmes or Holden Caulfield in a casual conversation and mistakenly assume that these are the names of real people. But readers of *The Hound of the Baskervilles* or *Catcher in the Rye* understand perfectly the ontological difference between their boyfriend fixing coffee in the next room and the fictional characters they are reading about. In fact I assume that other people

actually exist 'outside the text', including people I have never met personally and that their existence is independent of any discursive formation I may use to talk about them. I also assume that both lay readers and professional critics think about what characters in books are doing, that they reflect about ethical choices and ethical consequences and that they look for the reasons literary figures might have for the actions they perform.[17] Anyone might have similar kinds of thoughts about their boyfriends or people they read about in newspapers but that doesn't mean they're confused.

Of course literary characters are 'just words on a page', but the words on the page and the verbal patterns they make are not the whole story, so to speak. When someone reads *Macbeth* he has to work out just what Lady Macbeth is up to, what kind of person Duncan is, and whether or not Macduff loves his wife. Gail Paster's powerfully suggestive and historically based reference to Lady Macbeth's 'murderous weaning' of her child doesn't really differ in theory from what has been routinely dismissed as naive reading.[18] Lady Macbeth is endowed with physiological responses that are not, strictly speaking, part of the text, but are demonstrably part of the story. Paster's work suggests that, in principle at least, the interpretive practice of expert readers can be brought into a closer approximation to a vernacular criticism that still sees value in relating pragmatically to the destiny of literary characters, especially those in Shakespeare's plays.

THE SCENES SHAKESPEARE NEVER
WROTE . . .

In speaking of the scenes Shakespeare never wrote I am not proposing that we consider all

---

[17] See Gregory Currie, *The Nature of Fiction* (Cambridge, 1990), pp. 127–180; Kendall L. Walton, *Mimesis as Make Believe: On the Foundations of the Representational Arts* (Cambridge, 1990), pp. 70–106.

[18] Paster, *The Body Embarrassed*, p. 216.

the possible scenes he could have written but just never got around to. I'm not much concerned here with figuring out just what Hamlet and his friends might have done for amusement while they are attending that small college in Springfield, Ohio. At the same time, I have no wish to cast aspersions on something like Mary Cowden Clarke's *The Girlhood of Shakespeare's Heroines*, a work that is just now beginning to receive serious attention as a work of fiction from Susan Johnston, among others. Cowden Clarke's project was

. . . to imagine the possible circumstances and influences of scene, event, and associate, surrounding the infant life of his heroines, which might have conduced to originate and foster those germs of character recognized in their maturity, as by him developed . . .[19]

Susan Johnston reads *The Girlhood* narratives as a series of Gothic novellas.[20] She interprets Cowden Clarke's work against the background of nineteenth-century feminism, specifically its concern for the education of women. Cowden Clarke's discursive genre is no longer taken seriously as a form of critical thought. But her aim here does not in principle differ all that much from a more recent story about the girlhood of one of Shakespeare's heroines. I am thinking here of Gail Paster's brilliant and illuminating account of Juliet's 'late weaning' as a contemporary instance of imagining the early life of one of Shakespeare's heroines.[21]

Actually, although Shakespeare never wrote the scene of Juliet's weaning, the incident is talked about in the play. But the non-existent scenes I intend to talk about here do not belong to the category of 'prequel' or 'back-story'. I'm concerned more directly with scenes that happen during the course of the narrative action, but which are not performed on stage so that we don't see what the characters are doing or hear what they are saying. These scenes are integral to the narrative structure and to the moral plan of specific works, even though no actual textual realization for them has ever existed. They are

conspicuous by their absence, and they are very often scenes of sexual intimacy. We can't really get the story of *Romeo and Juliet* unless we have some sort of idea just what Clare Danes and Leonardo DiCaprio were doing with each other when we weren't looking. Shakespeare's verse actually gives us a more reliable sense of what that might have been than Baz Luhrmann's intrusively prurient camera. Was it a nightingale or was it a skylark they heard? Can he stay or does he have to go? Is what happened between them figured in the terrible story of Philomela (the nightingale) and Procne as rape, mutilation, and death? Or is it better represented in the iconography of the Skylark as the ascent of the soul towards heaven? Romeo and Juliet aren't quite sure about this themselves, although she is hoping it's the nightingale. The point here seems to be that even the sexual partners themselves haven't fully grasped the real meaning of their physical intimacy, even though that meaning has now become the ethical centre of their lives.

Shakespeare's realism differs significantly from that of cinema, with its sneaky all-seeing camera that can go anywhere, like Iachimo jumping out of the trunk in Imogen's bedroom. Even though we may happen to know in a general way what sex is, we never actually observe what any two lovers are to each other in their most intimate and vulnerable encounters. This is something we can only infer from their behaviour in social situations and from what we know from our background knowledge of physical intimacy. Nevertheless, it does matter. We want to understand what happened at the Sagittary on the night of

---

[19] Mary Cowden Clarke, 'Preface', *The Girlhood of Shakespeare's Heroines in a Series of Tales* (New York, [no date]), p. vii.

[20] Susan Johnston, 'The Calculus of Creativity: Normative Interpretation and *The Girlhood of Shakespeare's Heroines*', Paper present at the annual meeting of The Modern Language Association, Washington, D. C., December, 1996.

[21] Paster, *The Body Embarrassed*, pp. 220–31.

Othello and Desdemona's elopement. Were they really interrupted before the marriage could be consummated, as some critics have maintained? Or is Desdemona's ardent and over-demonstrative sexual responsiveness a hidden reason for Othello's mistrust, as Stephen Greenblatt has argued?[22] What exactly was going on when Hamlet wandered into Ophelia's chamber 'with his doublet all un-braced' and why was she so freaked out by it? And what, finally, should we make of the bed-trick that decides what happens in *Measure for Measure* and in *All's Well That Ends Well*, even though we can never see it performed on stage?

To me, the bed trick is interesting because I don't quite see how, in practical terms, anyone could actually get away with it. How dark would a room have to be to make this possible? Katherine Mansfield, in her journal entries for 1921, raises another kind of question. What would it really feel like to give yourself to a man who thought you were somebody else?

I must say Helena is a terrifying female. Her virtue, her persistence, her pegging away after the odious Bertram (and disguised as a pilgrim – so typical!) and then telling the whole story to that *good* widow-woman! And then that tame fish Diana. As to lying in Diana's bed and enjoying the embraces meant for Diana – well, I know nothing more sickening. It would take a respectable woman to do such a thing. The worst of it is I can so well imagine . . . for instance acting in precisely that way, and giving Diana a present afterwards. *What* a cup of tea the widow and D. must have enjoyed while it was taking place, or did D. at the last moment want to cry off the bargain? But to forgive such a woman! Yet Bertram would. There's an espèce de mothers-boyisme in him which makes him stupid enough for anything.[23]

I want to stress two points here. First, Mansfield's procedure is to fill in gaps in the narrative based on her own, immediate background knowledge of the social meaning of sexual intimacy. She puts herself in Helena's place in order to imagine what it would be like to enjoy the embraces meant for another woman. And she then shifts her perspective to Diana's point of view in order to imagine what it would be like to know that something of this sort is actually going on, like right now. Second, she uses these intuitions to support an evaluation of the unseen and unobservable behaviour of the characters, based on ordinary, or as we might say, vernacular ethical standards. 'I know nothing more sickening. It would take a respectable woman to do such a thing.'

Mansfield's observation of the behaviour of Shakespeare's characters is based on what she takes to be psychologically plausible. So she is puzzled by Ophelia's madness in *Hamlet*, which seems to her a grossly improbable eventuality, given the circumstances of the play.

. . . who can believe that a solitary violet withered when that silly fussy old pomposity died? And who can believe that Ophelia really loved him, and wasn't thankful to think how peaceful breakfast would be without his preaching?[24]

One feels grief and sadness over the death of a parent but after a while we get over it. So it is hard to believe that a young woman would actually kill herself just because her father died. Mansfield makes this judgement from a secure – we might even say complacent – position within her own immediate social experience, in which families assemble every morning to eat breakfast and attend to the business of life. Within the bourgeois household what matters, or what ought to matter is peace and quiet, cosiness, *gemütlichkeit*.

Now I was taught long ago not to do this sort of thing. One is not supposed to 'read into' *Hamlet* things like having breakfast that come from one's own familiar background in everyday life. To think about Ophelia eating her breakfast misrepresents the formal aim of Elizabethan poetry, which isn't based on the

22 Stephen Greenblatt, *Renaissance Self-Fashioning From More to Shakespeare* (Chicago, 1980), pp. 237–52.
23 Katherine Mansfield, *Journal of Katherine Mansfield*. ed. J. Middleton Murry (New York, 1927), p. 203.
24 Ibid., p. 205.

depiction of what's psychologically plausible. It also falsifies and distorts the culture in which Shakespeare actually wrote and in which modern forms of subjectivity didn't exist. And in post-structuralist criticism we are told that the basic assumption of subjective coherence that prompts us to look for any psychologically plausible motives or behaviours is simply false. So to be on the safe side we're not to read into the material anything that is not explicitly stated in the text, or anything derived from our own contingent background knowledge. This, at any rate, should keep us out of Ophelia's dining room. But dining rooms are not the only forbidden place Katherine Mansfield wants to go. She's after something even more intimate in her comments on Malvolio.

. . . or play with some rich jewel.' There speaks the envious servant-heart that covets his master's possessions . . . . 'having risen from a day bed where I have left Olivia sleeping.' Oh, doesn't that reveal the thoughts of all those strange creatures who attend upon the lives of others![25]

This vernacular 'reading into' *Twelfth Night* really captures a salient element in the play's structure, namely the edgy, uncomfortable relationship between domestic servants and their masters. Something else is going on in this text besides playful questioning of sexual identity. The play is about social class. Mansfield's comments should remind us that class is not just a grand political abstraction; it is actually played out in troubled, uneasy, sometimes erotically charged personal relationship.

Shakespeare didn't write any of the scenes Mansfield imagines. Still, audiences and readers are nevertheless forced to realize that scenes of sexual intimacy between Othello and Desdemona, Romeo and Juliet, Helena and Bertram are in fact part of the story, and that some kind of judgement must be rendered about them, even though they can never, in principle, be observed. I want to suggest here that these scenes are not adventitious elements in the structure of their respective plays. To the contrary, they are in every case central for under-

standing what happens in the story, and also for the intended use of the story for the practice of moral inquiry. The scenes Shakespeare never wrote raise two important theoretical issues. First, why are these moments of private intimacy privileged as a space of moral questions? Second, how is anyone supposed to make a judgement about these characters if Shakespeare deliberately withholds crucial evidence about what they do with each other? In order to pursue these matters I want now to turn to another scene that Shakespeare never wrote – the killing of Duncan by Macbeth.

There is no text of the murder of the King in *Macbeth*, and if we take literally the doctrine that there is nothing outside the text, then it seems to follow that Duncan is not really killed in this play, he just somehow becomes dead in the course of its unfolding. But of course no one really believes this. For one thing, many people have actually seen the murder happen in William Reilly's *Men of Respect* and in other film treatments. More important, even though there is no text of this scene, the text explicitly states that Macbeth murders Duncan and even explains how this deed was accomplished. But then why didn't Shakespeare go ahead and actually write the scene? After all, he was never particularly reticent in the depiction of violence. The killing of Julius Caesar, of Claudius, of Coriolanus, and of many others, all take place in full view of the audience. You probably see where I'm going with this. Shakespeare didn't never write the scene because it was violent. He did never write the scene because it takes place in a bedroom with only two people present.

Who would have thought the old man to have had so much blood in him?' Margaret Dietrich, my grade twelve English teacher at Westfield High School, thought this was a further reference to Lady Macbeth's earlier comment that Duncan 'resembled my father as

---

25 Ibid., p. 206.

he slept', an idea that seemed very plausible at the time, since we were all in the habit in those days of referring to our fathers as 'the old man'. My Grandfather Ben was of the opinion that this meant only that Lady Macbeth was surprised in a general way about how much blood there actually was in a human body. She had never killed anyone, she didn't really know what would happen if a living body was violently exsanguinated, and she didn't know what five quarts of blood would look like all over the floor. Albert Braunmuller, in his admirable new Cambridge edition of the play, acknowledges Miss Dietrich's exegesis, but he also points out that 'Lady Macbeth's surprise depends upon the conventional assumption that ageing dries the blood and diminishes its movement . . .'[26] The conventional assumption here is actually false and in this sense Lady Macbeth's remarks are an interesting, if an oblique comment on the reliability of seventeenth-century medical science. The 'experiment' of stabbing Duncan fails to confirm the results predicted by the received theory. And indeed anyone who had seen an adult male bleed to death in this way would have similar reason to question the 'conventional assumption' of humour theory. But there is more to this than simply the 'science' of exsanguination. The bloody mess Lady Macbeth finds in the King's bedchamber that she fears she will never be able to clean up is also tied to a perception of Duncan's body as somehow womanish or female.

In Mario Puzo's *The Godfather* the mafiosi often speak of 'doing the job'. To do the job on a woman is to possess that woman sexually – I did the job on her. To do the job on a man is to murder that man – I did the job on him. A man is someone who is able to do the job. But for a man to 'make his bones' it is necessary to do the job on a man.

> LADY MACBETH:. . . his two chamberlains
> Will I with wine and wassail so convince
> That memory, the warder of the brain,
> Shall be a fume, and the receipt of reason
> A limbeck only. When in swinish sleep

Their drenchèd natures lies as in a death,
What cannot you and I perform upon
Th' unguarded Duncan?   (1.7.63–70).

I don't think it's necessary to insist too strongly on the sexual resonances of Lady Macbeth's suggestion here. But why not? 'What cannot you and I perform . . .' does recall the intimate language of consenting adults, and it does hint at fantasies of including a third person. The more important point, however, is not so much about any presumptive sexual content in these lines, but more significantly to the kind of space in which Macbeth will perform something upon the vulnerable and unguarded Duncan. What makes the deed so frightful for Macbeth to contemplate and to carry out is not so much the killing itself, but the fact that he's going to do the job in the enclosed space of Duncan's bedchamber, a space in which Lady Macbeth feels very much at home. Or did, until she saw how much blood was in the old man.

Actually, what Macbeth has in mind is not, strictly speaking, a murder, but rather a political assassination – that's the actual word he uses in thinking about its potential consequences. But something rather more complicated begins to unfold as Duncan arrives at Macbeth's home.

> KING DUNCAN: This castle hath a pleasant seat.
> The air
> Nimbly and sweetly recommends itself
> Unto our gentle senses.
> BANQUO: This guest of summer,
> The temple-haunting martlet, does approve,
> By his loved mansionry, that the heavens'
>   breath
> Smells wooingly here. No jutty, frieze,
> Buttress, nor coign of vantage but this bird
> Hath made his pendant bed and procreant
>   cradle;
> Where they most breed and haunt I have
>   observ'd
> The air is delicate.   (1.6.1–9)

---

26 William Shakespeare, *Macbeth*, ed. by A. R. Braunmuller (Cambridge, 1997), p. 218.

Braunmuller glosses martlet as 'swift, but also used of the swallow or house martin (birds which build nests attached to the walls of buildings)'.[27] He then cites Peter Daly in showing that martlets 'were common emblems of "prudent trust" and "harmony in the realm."'. House martins are common and conspicuous everywhere in England during the summer months, and I like to think that they were actually flying around the eaves of the Globe theatre at the time this play was first performed in early modern London. In any case, while I don't mind Peter Daly's heraldic glosses, I do want to stress that the iconographic valences are derived from much more homely observations about these birds as 'summer guests' and their links with the prosperity of the household.

The martlets figure the patterns of a settled way of life as it is lived in the here and now, whether in medieval Scotland, or in early modern London, or yesterday afternoon in Stratford. The principal action of the play happens within what James Booth has called 'the moral architecture of the household'.[28] And this fundamentally changes the character of what Macbeth is going to 'perform upon / Th' unguarded Duncan'. Macbeth thinks first of the strategic aspects of the deed and wishes that 'this blow / Might be the be-all and the end-all . . .'But he immediately grasps that there is something even more problematic about this so-called assassination:

MACBETH. He's here in double trust:
First, as I am his kinsman and his subject,
Strong both against the deed; then, as his host,
Who should against his murtherer shut the
    door,
Not bear the knife myself.   (1.7.12–16)

We're very far here from the moral universe of heroic action depicted in the archaic warrior epics of Iceland or Mycenae. 'All truly noble morality grows out of triumphant self-affirmation' as Nietzsche reminds us.[29] Macbeth does not kill Duncan blithely and carelessly, as a

noble man conscious of his superiority. 'The noble person will respect his enemy as his mark of distinction, nor could he tolerate any other enemy than one in whom he finds nothing to despise.'[30] But Duncan is not Macbeth's enemy in this sense, certainly not a respected mark of distinction; he's about to become Macbeth's dirty little secret. The murder is not going to be performed in the grand style, and no one is going to admire him for his courage or his prowess in doing it. Nor does he believe the killing is justified, not even for strategic reasons.

What Macbeth is going to perform in that private, intimate space is not the expression of noble self-affirmation. It looks much more like what Nietzsche describes as rancour, envy, vindictive and implacable malice, in other words exactly the sort of thing captured in the figure of the witches. My reading of the weird sisters is that they are exactly what they appear to be – the projection of Macbeth's motives and desires, his inner demons as we like to say. But Francis Gentleman, in *The Dramatic Censor*, takes a rather dim view of Shakespeare's use of this device.

. . . though critically we must admire that characteristic peculiarity of sentiment and expression which distinguish the Witches, it is nevertheless necessary to remark, that exhibiting such personages and phantoms, as never had any existence but in credulous or heated imaginations, tends to impress superstitious feelings and fear upon weak minds . . . From what is thus premised, we hope, no other charge will be laid against Shakespeare, than the barbarous and credulous taste of the times in which he wrote, and to which he submitted, with possibly an oblique design of flattering the favourite opinion of James the first; yet allowing this to be really the case, it cannot exculpate his preternatural beings, as such, from rational censure for the reasons assigned above,

---

27 Ibid., p. 128.
28 William James Booth, *Households: On the Moral Architecture of the Economy* (Ithaca, 1993).
29 Friedrich Nietszche, *The Genealogy of Morals*, trans. by Francis Golfing (New York, 1956), p. 170.
30 Ibid., p. 173.

notwithstanding the author had historical tradition to countenance his introduction of them.[31]

We have a long way to go from here before we reach the more sophisticated views of Terry Eagleton, who thinks the witches embody valuable resistances to patriarchy, social privilege and entrenched political authority.[32]

Francis Gentleman is not looking for resistances to social domination. He's more worried about the dangers of superstition to 'weak' and impressionable minds. But what does superstition really mean in this context? Well, for one thing it clearly means a firm resistance to any idea that 'the devil made me do it'. Gentleman rejects any notion that actions, motives, dispositions, and so forth are caused by malevolent 'outside influences' – by the evil eye, for example, or by witches, Soviet spies, or space aliens. *The Dramatic Censor* just doesn't want to let Macbeth off the hook.

... he who does a bad action precipitately, or without knowing it to be such, may stand in some measure excuseable; but when a man has scrupulously weighed every relative circumstance in the nicest scale of reflection; and after all determines upon what nature, gratitude and justice, would avoid, he must be composed of the worst materials.[33]

What's important for Francis Gentleman is that Macbeth reflects about what he is going to do instead of just doing it. Francis Gentleman suggests that thinking about it beforehand is what makes Macbeth's crime truly reprehensible. But *The Dramatic Censor*, despite its fastidious aversion to plebeian tastes and plebeian habits, is not committed to an ethos of 'noble self-affirmation' along the lines sketched out by Nietzsche in *The Genealogy of Morals*. The analysis here is predicated on ideas of a universally binding moral rationality.

When Lady Macbeth asks her husband, 'What cannot you and I perform upon / Th' unguarded Duncan?', she intends it to be understood as a rhetorical question. It means that we have the power to do whatever we want as long as no one finds out, or as long as no one can call us to account. The question is really about power in the most immediate, intimate and personal sense, for example the power to abuse wives or children because they are weaker and more vulnerable and also because what happens in the privacy of the home can be kept secret. But what if we take Lady Macbeth's speech not as a rhetorical question, but as a plain old question in the framework of moral inquiry? 'What cannot you and I perform upon / Th' unguarded Duncan?' If this is posed as a real question it would imply that there really are things we just can't do to other people. The answer to such a question might well amount to the discovery of an essential moral truth. Of course to speak of 'essential moral truth' is to approach what has lately become intellectually dangerous ground, and therefore it might be better just to look briefly at one more passage from *Macbeth*.[34]

Macbeth always understood that the murderous betrayal of Duncan was bound up in temporality, in a *longue durée* of unforeseen consequences. The killing of Duncan can't be forgotten, it can't even be remembered, it can only be re-enacted as an interminable repetition compulsion. Macbeth finally articulates this for himself when he hears the 'cry of women' and understands that Lady Macbeth has died.

MACBETH: Tomorrow, and tomorrow, and
   tomorrow
Creeps in this petty pace from day to day
To the last syllable of recorded time,

---

31 Francis Gentleman, *The Dramatic Censor* (London, 1770), pp. 79–89.
32 Terry Eagleton, *William Shakespeare* (Oxford:, 1986), p. 2; See also Dympna Callaghan, Lorraine Helms, and Jyotsna Singh, *The Weyward Sisters: Shakespeare and Feminist Politics* (Oxford, 1994).
33 Gentleman, *Dramatic Censor*, p. 83.
34 Darko Suvin, 'Two Cheers for Essentialism and Totality: On Marx's Oscillation and Its Limits (As well as on the Taboos of Post-Modernsim)', *Rethinking Marxism*, 10 (1998), 66–82.

And all our yesterdays have lighted fools
The way to dusty death. Out, out, brief candle,
Life's but a walking shadow, a poor player
That struts and frets his hour upon the stage,
And then is heard no more. It is a tale
Told by an idiot, full of sound and fury,
Signifying nothing   (5.5.1–27)

Francis Gentleman admires this speech for its moral instruction and for its 'picture of the vanity of human life'.[35] But is this really an edifying paraphrase of the Book of Ecclesiastes? Is the speech meant to be pronounced in the biblical intonation of Orson Welles, in his film version of *Macbeth*, or is it more accurately suggested by John Turturro in *Men of Respect*? William Reilly's film is an elaborate paraphrase of *Macbeth* rewritten in the contemporary verbal and cinematic idiom of New York Mafiosi. Turturro portrays the character of 'Mikey Battaglia' with a mix of bravado, low cunning and frantic bewilderment. His tone alternates between hysterical bullying and whining self-pity. The point here seems to be that the most appalling crimes flow from reckless stupidity, a failure to think through the possible consequences of an action, to take any account of what might go wrong, or even to have any clear aim in view. *Men of Respect* empties the story of Macbeth of all pretension to tragic dignity, but in doing so it still manages to capture something immanent in the text of Shakespeare's play. The world of the heroic Scottish warlords ended long ago, if indeed such a world ever existed. What Shakespeare's play imagines is not only the heroic grandeur of this story, but its underlying and terrifyingly ordinary human scale.

It's important to sense the envious servant heart of Macbeth if we want to understand his motives. But Shakespeare never wrote the scene of Duncan's murder to accomplish another purpose. The scenes Shakespeare never wrote are there to provoke curiosity about motive and intention. But they also impose an additional burden of judgement. This is what vernacular criticism understands when it makes the inspired guess that Lady Macbeth hates Duncan because he's the father of her illegitimate child. The flight attendant on American Airline 83 to San Francisco thinks that Lady Macbeth kills out of hatred. This intuition nicely catches the banality of the crime. But Macbeth has no reason at all to kill Duncan, not even hatred, and indeed he has every reason not to kill him. What he performs upon the unguarded Duncan is done in careless indifference to the integrity and the life of another person. The scenes Shakespeare never wrote are the scenes of the most intensely personal moral experience. But although these scenes involve various forms of physical intimacy, they're not about sex, or even about power in the final analysis. They represent, if that is the right word, what we can and what we cannot perform in the co-presence of other unguarded selves.

---

[35] Gentleman, *Dramatic Censor*, p. 102.

THE SHADOW OF LEAR'S 'HOUSELESS' IN DICKENS

ADRIAN POOLE

To walk the streets of London by night, in the wind and rain, this was for Dickens the surest way to summon and greet his darkest visions. And this was how he staged himself for the readers of *All the Year Round* in one of his most astonishing pieces of non-fiction writing, the essay entitled 'Night Walks' (21 July 1860), subsequently gathered in *The Uncommercial Traveller* (1861, and later, expanded editions).[1]

Unable to sleep, he recalls, he had wandered through the night past the great enclosures of the capital, past theatres, prisons, Bank, Hospital, Parliament, Law-Courts, Abbey, Market and railway terminus. His thoughts and imaginings are suffused with Shakespearian echoes, of Macbeth's sleeplessness and Hamlet's graveyard, but the words that reverberate most persistently have their source in *King Lear*: 'houseless' and 'houselessness'. Shakespeare finds the adjective for the moment at which Lear is seized by the thought of the 'poor naked wretches' whose condition he is now about to endure feelingly for the first time. He uses the word nowhere else, but twice here in quick succession. Lear addresses 'You houseless poverty', breaks off to urge the Fool into Poor Tom's hovel, and then begins again:

> Poor naked wretches, whereso'er you are,
> That bide the pelting of this pitiless storm,
> How shall your houseless heads and unfed sides,
> Your [loop'd] and window'd raggedness, defend you
> From seasons such as these? O, I have ta'en
> Too little care of this!   (3. 4. 28–33)[2]

'In the course of those nights,' Dickens writes, 'I finished my education in a fair amateur experience of houselessness' (p. 73). His aim had been simply 'to get through the night', but there are those, he knows, mere amateur that he is, 'who have no other object every night in the year' (p. 73). Irregularly capitalized throughout the essay, the noun generalizes a condition that dissolves identity, names, stories, plots, purposes.[3] This, as we shall see, gives the figure of the 'houseless' a peculiar narrative potency – or better, a peculiarly adversarial potency in narratives primarily intent on seeking to 'house' a self, a name, a story. 'Walking the streets under the pattering rain, Houselessness would walk and walk and walk, seeing nothing but the interminable tangle of streets' (p. 74); or again, startled by 'a thing that in a moment more I should have trodden upon without seeing', the writer is pierced by 'a cry of loneliness and houselessness . . . the like of

---

1 For an easily available text see *Charles Dickens: Selected Journalism 1850–1870*, ed. David Pascoe (Harmondsworth, 1997), pp. 73–80. For other writings by Dickens references are to chapter (or book and chapter) number, the texts being taken from the Charles Dickens edition of 1867–8. References to his Letters are to the Pilgrim Edition of *The Letters of Charles Dickens*, eds. Madeline House, Graham Storey and Kathleen Tillotson (Oxford, 1965–), hereafter *Letters*.

2 References to Shakespeare are to the Riverside Edition, ed. G. Blakemore Evans (Boston, 1974).

3 The *OED* credits *Blackwood's Magazine* (1819) with a usage that for readers now immediately evokes Dickens: 'The night – the storms – the houselessness' (v. 229).

which I never heard' (p. 78). This nameless Poor Tom flees the writer's impulse of charity, leaving him with the rags out of which the creature has twisted 'like the young man in the New Testament' (p. 78). Poor naked wretch.

On 20 February 1839, William Charles Macready recorded with some satisfaction that the Queen had come to see his *Lear* and that he had pointed at her the 'beautiful lines, "Poor naked wretches!" '[4] 'Beautiful' takes some of the sting out of this gesture, and it gives a clue to the high pathos at which his performance seems to have aimed.[5] It is of a piece with Macready's sense of the play, and his audiences' taste, that the Fool whom he famously re-introduced was more delicate and pathetic than astringent. He describes the idea he had in mind of 'the sort of fragile, hectic, beautiful-faced, half-idiot-looking boy that it should be'.[6] The part was taken by the actress and singer Priscilla Horton, whose other roles included Ariel and Ophelia. J. S. Bratton concludes from a study of the cuts in Macready's acting text that his version of the play sought to subdue its political aspects rather than to promote them,[7] and the novel which Dickens began shortly after Macready's spell as manager of Covent Garden (1837–9) reflects this uncertain juncture of pathos and politics.

It was scarcely possible for first readers of *The Old Curiosity Shop* (1840–1) to ignore the parallel with Lear and Cordelia presented by Little Nell and her grandfather, even without prompting from a figure as influential as Francis Lord Jeffrey. Dickens crowed to Forster that Jeffrey was reported to be driving about Edinburgh 'declaring there has been "nothing so good as Nell since Cordelia", which he writes also to all manner of people'.[8] Nothing so good as? Even better perhaps for the novel's excision of the old man's violence and the daughter's defiance, its focus on his brokenness and her fidelity. Yet the force of the Shakespearian model is not entirely tamed, and it breaks through at exactly the moment of maximum exposure to a wider vision of destitution. In the thronging wasteland of the industrial city the

child tells the old man that they must sleep in the open air to-night. He rounds on her fiercely, only to be met with a rare firmness as the child asks him for once to consider her own suffering. This shocks him out of self-pity.

'Ah! poor, houseless, wandering, motherless child!' cried the old man, clasping his hands and gazing as if for the first time upon her anxious face, her travel-stained dress, and bruised and swollen feet.   (ch. 44)

The next moment 'a black figure' starts out of the dark recess in which they are about to take refuge. They have come face to face with one of the Poor Toms of this modern wilderness.

It was twenty years later that Dickens was moved to the black meditation on houselessness that is 'Night Walks'. This gathers together occurrences of the noun and its adjective and all they connote that are scattered throughout his earlier writings. Alfred Harbage notices as 'slightly archaic' the phrase 'houseless wretches' to be found in *Oliver Twist* and he credits *King Lear* as its source.[9] En route to deal with a fresh corpse in a vile slum, Mr Sowerberry the undertaker and the young Oliver pass some dilapidated yet not uninhabited buildings – 'even these crazy dens seemed to have been selected as the nightly haunts of some houseless wretches' (ch. 5). Yet the 'wretches' are not essential for setting off the Shakespearian reso-

---

4 *The Journal of William Charles Macready*, ed. J. C. Trewin (London, 1967), p. 132.

5 Dickens was at the first night on 25 January 1838, and although it now seems certain that he did not author the *Examiner* review a few days later on 4 February, he did review his friend's performance at the Haymarket in the *Examiner* for 27 October 1849, and was there for his final appearance on 3 February 1851. See Paul Schlicke, ' "A Discipline of Feeling": Macready's *Lear* and *The Old Curiosity Shop*', *The Dickensian*, 76 (1980), 79; and letter to John Leech, 31 January 1851, *Letters*, 6, p. 275.

6 *Journal*, p. 112.

7 *King Lear* (Plays in Performance), ed. J. S. Bratton (Bristol, 1987), p. 39.

8 Letter to John Forster [18 March 1841], *Letters*, 2, p. 238.

9 'Shakespeare and the Early Dickens', in *Shakespeare: Aspects of Influence*, ed. G. B. Evans (Cambridge, Mass. and London, 1976), p. 123.

nance audible whenever this word looms out of a Dickens text – as it does, with sufficient frequency to indicate its significance in his personal lexicon.

Take Oliver Twist again, on the road back to his birthplace, recalling himself as 'a poor houseless, wandering boy, without a friend to help him, or a roof to shelter his head' (ch. 51). Or take young David Copperfield, thankful to be tucked up in bed at Aunt Betsey's after his nightmare flight to Dover: 'I prayed that I never might be houseless any more, and never might forget the houseless' (ch. 13). This seems a particularly pointed memory of the Lear who *has* forgotten or never known what poverty means. Micawber too will echo Lear, alongside Hamlet and Macbeth, as he works himself up into his most tragical attitude: 'Welcome misery, welcome houselessness, welcome hunger, rags, tempest, and beggary!' (ch. 52). Or take young Florence Dombey, safely arrived at the Wooden Midshipman after her father has cast her into the streets, describing herself to Walter Gay as a 'houseless sister' (ch. 49). Note that while she is also called 'homeless and fatherless' and 'a homeless wandering fugitive', to be 'houseless' is to lack something more primitive than a 'home': the simplest wherewithal to shelter you from the preying elements and other creatures. The state of houselessness is one in which everyone is predator or prey or both, as a plangent paragraph in *Barnaby Rudge* about the outcast of the city intimates, 'more utterly alone and cast away than in a trackless desert', 'a houseless rejected creature' (ch. 18). Sam Weller thinks briefly of his stint in 'unfurnished lodgin's' under Waterloo Bridge, along with 'the worn-out, starving, houseless creeturs as rolls themselves in the dark corners o' them lonesome places' (*The Pickwick Papers*, ch. 16). And we can trace the incidence of the Shakespearian word right back to the street-scenes sketched by the young Boz a quarter of a century before the prestigious writer of 'Night Walks'. In 'The Streets – Morning' he observes that 'the last houseless vagrant' has coiled up in a corner; in 'The Prisoner's Van' he remarks on 'a houseless vagrant going joyfully to prison as a place of food and shelter'; and in the climactically lurid 'Drunkard's Death' he pronounces that 'in the last stage of poverty, disease, and houseless want, he was a drunkard still' (all *Sketches by Boz*).

'Shakespearian' requires qualification. The *OED* records a scattering of literary usages prior to and contemporary with Dickens, including some lines from Goldsmith in 1764, 'Where the rude Carinthian boor/ Against the houseless stranger shuts the door' (*The Traveller, or a prospect of society*, 4), and from Edward Lytton in 1829 (later to be Bulwer-Lytton, and a good friend of Dickens), 'Our home is the houseless sward' (*The Disowned*, ii. 8). To this one may add 'the poor, houseless, shivering female' who deserts the security of Goldsmith's 'sweet Auburn' for the treacherous glamour of the city,[10] and 'the houseless orphan' of Shelley's Second Citizen in the fragmentary drama of *Charles the First* (begun in 1819):

> Ay, there they are –
> Nobles, and sons of nobles, patentees,
> Monopolists, and stewards of this poor farm,
> On whose lean sheep sit the prophetic crows,
> Here is the pomp that strips the houseless orphan,
> Here is the pride that breaks the desolate heart.[11]

'Take physic, pomp': the reference to Lear on the heath is self-evident.

But the most signal appearance of the 'house-

---

10 *The Deserted Village* (1770), line 326, in Roger Lonsdale (ed.), *The Poems of Gray, Collins and Goldsmith* (London, 1969). I must thank Christopher Decker for this reference. David Womersley points out to me that a search of the English Poetry Database yields over 50 instances from 1700 to 1800, and getting on for 300 between 1800 and 1900.

11 *Charles the First*, lines 150–5, in Thomas Hutchinson (ed.), *Poetical Works* (1905). Tony Harrison cites this passage in his Introduction to *The Trackers of Oxyrhynchus* (2nd edn, London, 1991), a play in which, in the National Theatre text and production, the houseless irrupt with a vengeance (and explicit allusion to *King Lear*) at its close.

less' before Dickens is in Wordsworth's 'Tintern Abbey' (1798), where the poet's eye rests on the 'Vagrant dwellers in the houseless woods'. Jonathan Bate has some suggestive remarks about the implications of this moment. He notes that when Wordsworth wrote this poem he had recently extracted 'The Female Vagrant' from 'Salisbury Plain', his early poem of social protest.

That poem has a heath and a hovel, such phrases as 'robbed of my perfect mind' (borrowed from Lear's 'I fear I am not in my perfect mind'), and the opening line 'Hard is the life when *naked* and *unhouzed*' (my italics). 'Tintern Abbey', then, has the potential to be another poem about social conditions, to be peopled by houseless vagrants. But, in a move characteristic of his development in the late 1790s, Wordsworth turns away from political engagement and writes a poem about the self in relation to landscape. 'The still, sad music of humanity' leads him to his sister, not to a female vagrant. So it is that the allusive pattern shifts from the socially incisive moment in *Lear* to the introspection of *Hamlet*.[12]

In this context it is worth repeating the familiar thought that no matter what Dickens can be proved to have owed to his reading of Wordsworth, apart from 'We Are Seven', the children, outcasts and vagrants in Wordsworth's poetry and Dickens's fiction are bound to meet in the minds of their readers, from the 1830s through to the present day.[13] But more to my purpose is the opposition Bate draws between the associations of *Hamlet* with a turn of mind inwards towards the self and of *King Lear* with a vision directed outwards to figures of distress in a larger social landscape. I want to suggest that the 'socially incisive moment in *Lear*' continues to haunt the idea of a narrative primarily dedicated to housing the self. This is a narrative central to the nineteenth century, to which the figure of Hamlet has often been taken to stand as a great, even *the* great, sponsor.[14] Against, behind, beneath this there stands a figure of menace and guilt, embodied in what Mr Earnshaw brings back from the streets of

Liverpool, 'a tale of his seeing it starving, and houseless, and as good as dumb': this is the dehumanized child who will turn into Heathcliff.[15]

There is an interesting question about the extent of Dickens's direct indebtedness to *King Lear*, as compared with *Hamlet* and *Macbeth* in particular. But before I turn to it, let me give some further support to the emphasis I am throwing on the word 'houseless' by attending to the weather, and specifically the 'wind and rain' that typically prevail in the realm of houselessness-by-night. There is less obvious justification for hearing Shakespearian echoes in such common elements than in the image of the 'houseless'. Yet whenever they occur together there is a fair chance that they will recall the songs sung by the Clown in *Twelfth Night* and the Fool in *Lear*.[16] For Dickens the phrase naturally associates itself with the state or figure of the outcast, the vagrant, the 'houseless'. As thus for instance in *David Copperfield*, when Peggotty imagines the errant Em'ly coming

12 Jonathan Bate, *Shakespeare and the English Romantic Imagination* (Oxford, 1986), pp. 97–8.

13 In *Wordsworth and the Victorians* (Oxford, 1998), Stephen Gill writes: 'Behind Oliver and Smike and Little Nell stands the Wordsworthian child . . . Dickens's wise fools and outcasts are prefigured in Wordsworth's vagrants and old beggars.' (p. 115)

14 For extended consideration of the contrasting paradigms offered by these two plays and the uses to which they have been put over the last two hundred years, see R. A. Foakes, *Hamlet versus Lear: Cultural Politics and Shakespeare's Art* (Cambridge, 1993).

15 Emily Brontë, *Wuthering Heights*, vol. I, ch. 4 (Oxford World's Classics edn, 1995, p. 34).

16 I owe a debt here to Robert Douglas-Fairhurst's unpublished PhD thesis, 'Victorian Afterlives: Influence and Revision in Tennyson and FitzGerald' (Cambridge, 1998). Dickens seems likely to have had a hand in the article 'The Wind and the Rain' in *Household Words*, 31 May 1851, reprinted in *The Uncollected Writings of Charles Dickens: Household Words 1850–59*, ed. Harry Stone, vol. I (London, 1969), pp. 285–95. See also the passing reference to Feste's song in a letter to Forster [8 April 1862]: 'The rain that raineth every day seems to have washed news away or got it under water.' (*Letters*, 10, p. 67).

home to peep in at the window, 'like a ghost, out of the wind and rain'. (The reading he gave from this novel was his favourite; his portrayal of 'Mr Peggotty in his anguish reminded one critic of King Lear'.)[17] Or as thus in *Dombey and Son*, when an old woman sits 'listening to the wind and rain' that herald the arrival, out of the night, of her daughter Alice Marwood (ch. 34). 'Storm within, and storm without' mutters Alice much later, near the novel's end. Her own end is marked by the elements to which she has been fatally exposed: 'Nothing lay there, any longer, but the ruin of the mortal house on which the rain had beaten, and the black hair that had fluttered in the wintry wind' (ch. 58).

The combination of rain and wind comes near to rhyming with 'ruin' and 'ruined'. Such 'poetic' effects are at home in the musical prose of *Great Expectations*, where phrases fall easily into the attitudes of verse, like this for instance:

the shudder of the dying day
in every blade of grass

This haunting ballad cadence is heard in the passage describing the winter's evening on the marshes when Magwitch and Compeyson are hunted down and re-arrested: 'For there had reached us, on the wings of the wind and rain, a long shout.' It is a far cry from here to the stormy night on which Magwitch re-enters Pip's life in person, at the end of the 'second stage' of his expectations (ch. 39). But it is 'the wind and the rain' that drive away the intervening years, and carry Pip back to the churchyard where he once stood face to face with this man, 'my convict', as he does again now. It is the wind and rain to which he seems to himself to attend even more than to Magwitch: 'In every rage of wind and rush of rain, I heard pursuers.' And when he awakes to the clocks striking five, to the wasted out candles and the dead fire, it is 'the wind and rain [that] intensified the thick black darkness'. He knows himself to be 'wrecked' and 'the roof of my stronghold dropped upon me'.

Valerie L. Gager has cast doubt on the usual assumption of *King Lear*'s significance for Dickens, and its influence in particular on his representation of fathers and daughters.[18] Jerome Meckier, for example, calls the play 'A Myth for Victorian England', and identifies the relation between Lear and Cordelia at the heart of three novels in particular: *The Old Curiosity Shop*, *Dombey and Son*, and *Hard Times*.[19] Alexander Welsh has written, with reference to *The Old Curiosity Shop*, of the deep fable to which Shakespeare's play gives enduring impress, of 'truth as the daughter of a difficult old man, a daughter who will not flatter or tell lies, but whose loyalty is unswerving. This martyrdom of truth . . . is the special province of Dickens in the nineteenth century.'[20] In a later book Welsh argues for the influence on *Dombey and Son* of what he calls 'the Cordelia model of loyalty to a difficult father'.[21] John Harvey draws illuminatingly on evidence from the visual arts for the aggrandisement of the play's father and favoured daughter in the collective imagination of the nineteenth century: 'Lear and Cordelia become gigantic presences.' In literary terms these presences are to be felt above all in Dickens, in the daughters (or granddaughters) and fathers 'who shadow Cordelia and Lear (at varying distances)'. He names Madeline Bray and old Mr Bray in *Nicholas Nickleby*, Nell and her grandfather in *The Old Curiosity Shop*, Florence and Mr Dombey in *Dombey and Son*, Agnes and Mr Wickfield in *David Copperfield*, Louisa and Mr

---

[17] *Sikes and Nancy, and Other Public Readings*, ed. Philip Collins (Oxford, 1975), p. 136.

[18] *Shakespeare and Dickens* (Cambridge, 1996), pp. 11–15.

[19] 'Dickens and *King Lear*: A Myth for Victorian England', *South Atlantic Quarterly*, 71. 1 (Winter 1972), 75–90.

[20] *The City of Dickens* (Oxford, 1971), p. 170.

[21] 'Whenever Dickens required an exalted test of love and truth in his fiction, he tended to favor the Cordelia model of loyalty to a difficult father, but *Dombey and Son* is a special case.' (*From Copyright to Copperfield: The Identity of Dickens* (Cambridge, Mass. and London, 1987), p. 88.)

Gradgrind in *Hard Times*, Amy and Mr Dorrit in *Little Dorrit*, Lucy and Dr Manette in *A Tale of Two Cities*, and Jenny Wren and Mr Dolls in *Our Mutual Friend*.[22] One might for instance think of *Little Dorrit* as an inverse *King Lear*, in the sense that the frail father passes, with his devoted daughter, from the sweet wilderness of the Marshalsea into pomp and civility.[23]

Gager raises a number of objections to these claims, including a corrective glance at influential representations of fathers and daughters in models at least as close to Dickens's own hand as Shakespeare's (and Macready's) *King Lear*, such as Sheridan Knowles's *Virginius* (the title role of which belonged to Macready) and the dramatic adaptation of Mrs Opie's popular novel *Father and Daughter* (1801), known as *The Lear of Private Life; or, Father and Daughter* (1820).[24] She also points to the parallels that might be drawn for *Dombey and Son* with another Shakespeare play given a memorable production by Macready, which Dickens is known to have seen, namely *The Winter's Tale*. But her most apparently telling point is the simple statistic, based on a conscientious trawl through the texts, that explicit references to *King Lear* are very much less frequent in Dickens than to *Hamlet*, *Macbeth* and *Othello*. She notes that 'references to *Hamlet*' outnumber those to *King Lear* by almost six to one.[25]

One response to this might be to wonder what should count as a 'reference'. This, for certain, as recorded by Gager, when Jenny Wren laments of her hopeless father Mr Dolls: 'I wish I had never brought him up. He'd be sharper than a serpent's tooth if he wasn't as dull as ditch water' (*Our Mutual Friend*, III, 10). This too, for sure, though not recorded by Gager (who understandably disclaims exhaustiveness), in the number plans for *Little Dorrit*: 'Anatomize Gowan, and see what breeds about his heart.'[26] Does 'houseless' count as a 'reference'? Gager is rightly cautious about claims for the Shakespearian nuances of single words. But the cumulative evidence of the associations held by the word render its connection with *Lear*

unmistakable, especially when we think of the power of the original context.

This suggests another, more interesting question about Gager's challenge. This is the possibility that *King Lear* might play a role in Dickens's imagination no less powerful or pervasive than that of *Hamlet* and *Macbeth*, but radically different in kind – not indeed a matter of verbal allusions so much as of iconic resemblances. Dickens's references to *Hamlet* and *Macbeth* and other plays are frequently facetious, parodic, playful (which is not at all to say that they may not serve serious ends). There is Nicholas Nickleby's Romeo, Smike's Apothecary, Wopsle's Hamlet (amongst others), Quilp's Richard III, and so on. Any number of characters are associated with the milk of human kindness, transported beyond the ignorant present, marshalled the way that they were going, get amens stuck in their throat, and find that they are a man again.[27] But it is *Hamlet* which most positively promotes such playfulness. This is because its central character stands in such a resourcefully ludic relation to the story he finds himself in and the roles he might play. This is also partly true of Richard III and Iago. The opportunities for fun and games afforded by *Macbeth* are different in kind but they link up with one of *Hamlet*'s

---

22 'Shakespeare and the Ends of Time: The Illustrations', *The Cambridge Review*, 117 (May 1996), 32, 48.

23 I owe this good thought to A. D. Nuttall, whose form of words I cite almost *verbatim*.

24 Gager, *Shakespeare and Dickens*, p. 12. For a helpful account of *The Lear of Private Life*, and its effect on Victorian responses to Shakespeare's play, see J. S. Bratton, 'The Lear of Private Life: Interpretations of *King Lear* in the Nineteenth Century', in *Shakespeare and the Victorian Stage*, ed. Richard Foulkes (Cambridge, 1986), pp. 124–37.

25 Gager, *Shakespeare and Dickens*, p. 12.

26 Number plans for Book II, ch. 6, reproduced in the Clarendon Edition, ed. Harvey Peter Sucksmith (Oxford, 1979), p. 818.

27 See Gager's invaluable 'Catalogue of Dickens's references to Shakespeare', in her *Shakespeare and Dickens*, pp. 251–369.

other attractions, its hospitality to the supernatural. There is much sport to be had with ghosts and the relief from terror in laughter (as Hamlet himself so typically discovers). But *King Lear* lacks these attractions. There are no ghosts and there is not enough leisure in its plot or its language to encourage much playfulness. There is the Fool, of course, but for Dickens, his was a softened voice and in Macready's version a literally feminized one; there is Edmund, and a bit of Kent in disguise. But the kind of pain and pathos invested in the central narrative action, for Dickens and his readers, was simply not open to irony or question let alone parody.

This is where the visual life of the play in the nineteenth-century imagination is bound to qualify Gager's attention to strictly verbal references. In his valuable summary of the dominant visual images selected by artists, Harvey notes that the scene preferred by eighteenth-century illustrators was the confrontation on the heath between Lear and Poor Tom.

It is a scene of emotional and psychic upheaval, but what it most looks like, to the spectating eye, is a dramatic extreme of political upset, since it juxtaposes a poor naked wretch (we can't tell from appearances that he is the son of the Duke of Gloucester) and a raging king cast out in the wilds.[28]

Of the *Lear in the Storm* painted by Benjamin West on the eve of the French Revolution, Harvey observes: 'The fabric of the house is breaking.' At virtually the same moment as West produces this vision of the ruined patriarch, James Barry exhibits his painting of 'King Lear Weeping over the Body of Cordelia' at the opening of Boydell's Shakespeare Gallery in 1789.[29] This image is in an important sense the antidote to West's. Harvey goes on to describe the emergence in the next century of a new set of images centred on Cordelia, a 'cult' and a 'myth' about the power of a woman's love to save a man. This is a story none the less powerful for its climactic embodiment in the image of the daughter dead in her father's arms,

an ultimate sacrifice and redemption, though one not undisturbed by sexual overtones.

The point for my purposes is two-fold. First, that the life of Shakespeare's play in the imagination of Dickens and his contemporaries cannot be reduced to the limits of explicit textual reference, a matter of words alone, nor of its realization in theatrical performance. Domesticated and privatized as the unhappy story of the Lear family may seem to have been for Victorian writers and readers, there remained in the narrative nucleus bequeathed by Shakespeare two images of Lear's relationship to others that are fraught with dangerous power: the first of the king and the poor naked wretch, the second of the father and his daughter. There is an obvious sense in which this second image can be taken or made to supersede the first. The manhood that has been shaken or even shattered by the pressures of public life, as our jargon might put it, is restored on more modest terms by the faithful, forgiving woman. That Dickens and his readers were drawn to such a deep narrative paradigm goes without saying, though Gager is right to look beyond *Lear* to the still troubled but less eventually traumatic model provided by *The Winter's Tale*. But my second point is that no matter how carefully purged and de-eroticized the narrative closure afforded by the image of father and daughter restored to each other in life or in death, this cannot expunge the unresolved image of confrontation with the poor naked wretch which it seeks to supersede. The houselessness shadows the ultimate housing.

I want now to hazard a sweeping proposition about the narrative models that Shakespeare may be thought to have offered the nineteenth-

---

28 'Shakespeare and the Ends of Time', p. 31.

29 Both paintings were engraved and published by Boydell, West's by William Sharpe and Barry's by Francis Legat. Sharpe's has been called 'the most finely executed line-engraving in the Gallery', *The Boydell Shakespeare Gallery*, eds. Walter Pape and Frederick Burwick (Bottrop, 1996), p. 280.

century novelist. Let me instantly lay a great deal to one side, all question of 'characters' as such to begin with. All the women, for instance – including Cordelia – who enjoy such a lease of new life in the novelizing imaginations of Anna Jameson, Mary Cowden-Clarke, Helena Faucit and others.[30] I leave aside the great figures of passion, such as Romeo and Juliet, Othello, Macbeth and Antony and Cleopatra, who provide a powerful lexicon for the expression of desire, despair, jealousy, and guilt, for Dickens and others. I also want to skirt the argument about Shakespeare's sponsorship of the psychological realism with which in the English novel the name of George Eliot is particularly associated, an argument proposed in a weighty piece on 'Shakespeare and George Eliot' published shortly after her death, which imagines amongst other things the novel she would have made out of Helena's story in *All's Well That Ends Well*.[31] I want instead to set up as stark an opposition as possible between *Hamlet* and *King Lear*, and to suggest that the latter is for Dickens, and perhaps for others, the dark negative of the former.

That Hamlet the character is already within his play a peculiarly novelistic figure and hence the great sponsor of the creation and understanding of 'character', from Goethe's *Wilhelm Meister* to Joyce's *Ulysses*: this is an old story. It is well told by Jonathan Arac, for instance, who asserts: 'For psychology and literature alike in this period, *Hamlet* is crucial.'[32] If we want to look further than Hamlet for other young men or women in Shakespeare from whose predicament and capability novelists might take inspiration we can certainly do so, especially amongst his women. But Hamlet is rich in convenience above all others, in his readiness and his hesitation, the summary form of youth's expectations on the brink of its trial for a place and a name of its own in the grown-up world.

King Lear is not devoid of young people, or of the younger generation, amongst whom we should include Goneril and Regan, whatever their age by the clock, as well as Cordelia,

Edgar and Edmund. There is clearly an opportunity and a challenge for the novelist to rewrite this story from the point of view of one or more of the young ones, trying to make a future for themselves. Edgar or Edmund, certainly, who might help to create a new figure uncertain which of the brothers he is or might be, such as Rastignac in Balzac's *Père Goriot*. We have recently heard the version according to Goneril and Regan, as narrated by the former, from the American mid-West, in Jane Smiley's Pulitzer Prize-winning *A Thousand Acres* (1992). And there have been the rewritings in dramatic form itself, which have invariably sought to redress if not to revenge the Shakespearian centre of interest in the father, from Gordon Bottomley's *King Lear's Wife* (1911) to the *Lear's Daughters* created by Elaine Feinstein and the Women's Theatre Group (1987–8).[33]

This might suggest a fundamental difference for later artists between the models afforded by *Hamlet* and *King Lear*, and a certain kind of inevitable hostility towards the latter from which the former is largely if not wholly

30 Anna Jameson, *Characteristics of Women, Moral, Political and Historical* (1832); Mary Cowden-Clarke, *The Girlhood of Shakespeare's Heroines* (1850–2 – tales separately dedicated to Macready, Dickens et al.); Helena Faucit, *On Some of Shakespeare's Female Characters* (1887). See further Nina Auerbach, *Woman and the Demon: The Life of a Victorian Myth* (Cambridge, Mass. and London, 1982), ch. 6, and Julie Hankey, 'Helen Faucit and Shakespeare: Womanly Theater', in *Cross-Cultural Performances: Differences in Women's Re-Visions of Shakespeare*, ed. Marianne Novy (Urbana and Chicago, 1993), pp. 50–69.

31 [Peter Bayne], 'Shakespeare and George Eliot', *Blackwood's Magazine*, 13 (April 1883), 524–38. I am grateful to Philip Davis for calling this article to my attention.

32 'Hamlet, *Little Dorrit*, and the History of Character', *South Atlantic Quarterly*, 87. 2 (Spring 1988), 311–28 (314).

33 Lizbeth Goodman hails this production as 'a landmark in feminist "reinventing" of Shakespeare', in 'Women's Alternative Shakespeares and Women's Alternatives to Shakespeare in Contemporary British Theatre', in *Cross-Cultural Performances*, ed. Novy, p. 220.

exempt. The *Hamlet*-model is centred on the son's story, or rather his struggle to resist a prescribed story and to find or make one of his own to believe in. It is true that he is a son and not a daughter, but to the extent that he is not yet a *man*, there is scope to re-imagine his youthfulness as not yet irretrievably – as we have learned to say – 'gendered'. But the *Lear*-model has little such scope for re-imagining the narrative from the central character's own point of view (Randolph Stow's novel, *To the Islands* (1958) about a journey even deeper into the heath, as it were, or in this case the Australian outback, is something of an exception.) At least in terms of the family romance to which most novels find themselves committed, the model of Shakespeare's *King Lear* requires a more or less violent uprooting to liberate the stories of the figures-with-a-future. A future is just what Lear himself does not have – nor Lear-and-Cordelia.[34]

But there is more to the history of *Lear*'s re-writings than this, as Peter Conrad has recently suggested.[35] He points us to Schiller's *Die Räuber*, to Balzac and to Turgenev (*Fathers and Sons* rather than to the tale, 'A Lear of the Steppes'), and in the twentieth century to the play's after-lives in theatre, novel and film, in Tennessee Williams's *Cat on a Hot Tin Roof*, Jane Smiley's *A Thousand Acres*, Karen Blixen's *Out of Africa*, Randolph Stow's *To the Islands*, the films *Broken Lance* directed by Edward Dmytryk and *Ran* by Akira Kurosawa. (He makes no mention of Dickens.) One of the points to emerge from his useful survey is the extent to which the *Lear* narrative remains concerned with property, its possession, its lack, and its (re-)distribution. He notes the continuing significance of *land*, in Turgenev's Russia, in Smiley's mid-West, Blixen's Africa, and Stow's Australia.[36] This can of course co-exist with all kinds of family romance and nightmare, as it does in Smiley's novel, but it helps to restore or keep to the fore a political aspect to the donating narrative that excessive concentration on its psychological aspects may

serve to obscure. The politics and the psychology are not to be so easily distinguished.

This is why there is such a strong charge to the moment of Lear's exposure on the heath, and his confrontation with the figure of houseless destitution that is Poor Tom. It remains to haunt those versions of the *Lear* narrative that seek to privilege the successful accession or restoration of the self to its senses, good name, manhood and rightful property: the supposedly classic romance of the nineteenth century. One may think of the memorable effect Grigori Kozintsev creates by proliferating the figure of Poor Tom in his magnificent film (1971). The screen can manage this as the stage cannot, but the force of Shakespeare's spatial imagination is here of crucial importance. *King Lear* is the antithesis of *Hamlet*, whose Elsinore serves to inspire the interior spaces of so many Gothic novels, and beyond them, as Arac has argued, the inner space required by the whole realist novel for the imagination of 'character' itself.[37] *King Lear* by contrast moves out from inside, unhousing its central figure, and ruining all the structures on which his self, his family and his kingdom have been, as it now turns out, so

---

34 John Glavin notes of *Little Dorrit* that if Clennam tries to imagine himself as Hamlet, the novel also adapts *King Lear* as 'The Dorrits: A Carceral Family Romance'. He points out that Arac takes no interest in the latter but only in the Hamlet-model; he also reports, of the theatre group involved in devising a performance of the novel, that 'the Dorrit family plot spurred no interest at all in any of them'. (*After Dickens: Reading, Adaptation and Performance* (Cambridge, 1999), p. 156)

35 'Expatriating Lear', in *To Be Continued: Four Stories and their Survival* (Oxford, 1995), pp. 95–152.

36 See further for an argument about the play's equation between identity and property, Margreta de Grazia, 'The Ideology of Superfluous Things: *King Lear* as Period Piece', in *Subject and Object in Renaissance Culture*, eds. Margreta de Grazia, Maureen Quilligan and Peter Stallybrass (Cambridge, 1996), pp. 17–42.

37 Arac writes: '. . . the castle of Elsinore offered the model for later gothic materializations of the tragic "houses" of legend into the concrete architectural spaces that so concern the novelistic genre' ('Hamlet, *Little Dorrit*, and the History of Character', p. 320).

precariously founded. The moment of maximum exposure draws on the knowledge shared by Shakespeare and his first audiences that the difference between having or not having a roof over your head and enough clothes or mere fat on your body ('your house-less heads and *unfed sides*') may be the difference between life and death. It is a knowledge not so very far from our own, after all, however well accommodated. No wonder then that such a moment, at which you come face to face with the houseless, might shadow the stories the nineteenth century wanted to tell itself, about finding and founding your self and those you can call your own, your property.

The examples in Dickens to which I pointed earlier suggest one obvious kind of contrast between houselessness and housedness, between dreaded wakeful exposure to the elements and the night, and the security of a safe bed and sleep, watched over by a surrogate parent, better than the real thing, such as Betsey Trotwood or Captain Cuttle. But there is another kind of contrast worth considering for the role it plays in the structuring of Dickensian narrative. It is a contrast between solitude and company, between fantasy and conversation, between madness and performance. Like all such desirable oppositions, the boundary may be less certain than one would wish.

Besides 'houseless' and 'houselessness' one of the repeated words in Dickens's 'Night Walks' is 'company'. It is this for which the houseless mind yearns, he remarks, 'for any sign of company'. (It is hard not to hear the anticipations of Beckett in some of this writing.) The search fails, apart from a brief exchange with the toll-keeper on Waterloo Bridge at the start, and a weird overheard dialogue in a coffee-shop near the end. So he is thrown back on his own, and this excites a meditation on death, decay and madness worthy of the Hamlet he takes as one of his models. Explicit allusion occurs when he contemplates the emptiness of the two great theatres, and then, extraordinarily, enters one of 'these great

deserts' and surveys the auditorium from the stage:

One would think that nothing in them knew itself at such a time but Yorick's skull . . . With a dim lantern in my hand, I groped my well-known way to the stage and looked over the orchestra – which was like a great grave dug for a time of pestilence – into the void beyond. A dismal cavern of an immense aspect, with the chandelier gone dead like everything else, and nothing visible through mist and fog and space, but tiers of winding-sheets. (p. 75)

Later in his wandering he enters another massive empty structure, Westminster Abbey. This spurs him to the gothic vision of the dead rising up to overwhelm the living:

it was a solemn consideration what enormous hosts of dead belong to one great city, and how, if they were raised while the living slept, there would not be the space of a pin's point in all the streets and ways for the living to come out into. Not only that, but the vast armies of dead would overflow the hills and valleys beyond the city, and would stretch away all round it, God knows how far. (p. 78)

'Twere to consider too curiously, to consider so. But there is no Horatio at hand. There is only the thing or creature who starts up at his feet with 'a cry of loneliness and houselessness . . . the like of which I never heard'. This, and the thought of the afflicted men and women in Bethlehem Hospital whose waking fantasies match his own dreams at night, to make him wonder 'that the great master who knew everything, when he called Sleep the death of each day's life, did not call Dreams the insanity of each day's sanity' (p. 77). The great master is evidently the best company to be had when a man has none but his own. Dickens is putting on a performance for himself, or to be more exact, his writing is putting on a performance of putting on a performance for himself. And for this Shakespeare is the invaluable resource. The key figures for the language of nightmare and death are as usual provided by Hamlet and Macbeth, but there is also, at the end of the passage in the theatre, as he gazes up backstage into 'a shipwreck of canvas and cordage', an echo of Clarence's great monologue on dream and drowning and death from *Richard III*: 'Methought I felt much as a diver might, at the bottom of the sea.' (p. 75)

But it is Lear's houselessness that creates this astonishing one-man show. In his recent book on Dickens, John Glavin makes some startling claims about the novelist's fear of the theatre. Contrary to popular belief, he argues, it was not the stage in itself that Dickens loved but speech, not theatre as such but solo performance.

Dickens believes, at his most optimistic, in a theatricality that can not only exhibit, but can actually generate self. (That's why people get the sense that he loves theatre.) He also believes that theaters surely kill. (That's the part people tend to miss.) . . . Visible, misread, isolated, dead: that regress spells theater in Dickens . . . He must turn those eager prying audiences into a mirror of himself, the audiences he needs rather than the audiences who prey upon him.[38]

In other words, 'slay or be slain'. I think there is a good deal of truth in this idea of Dickens's creativity, if not enough to encompass the achievement of *Great Expectations* (as Glavin rather grudgingly admits). And it is perhaps no coincidence that 'Night Walks', with its searching reflection on the sources of its own performance, should so shortly precede the writing of Dickens's most creatively self-conscious novel (begun September 1860).[39] In the vast deserted theatre, the night-writer contemplates the dark side of the rapturous applause that greets his other self's performed Readings: the theatre as graveyard. In the asylum he contemplates the afflicted madmen and madwomen whose dreams he shares – like any Bedlam beggar.

This is where *King Lear* seems to have reached deep into Dickens's imagination to produce something more authentic than the fantasies of shaken manhood restored by loving women too easily identified with Lear and Cordelia. That is to say, the idea of a deprivation, self-loss and madness, whether in one's self or another, too sobering to be shrugged off, too grievous to be healed: something unforgettably exposed in the world, at large and at hand, of which too little care has been taken.

---

[38] *After Dickens*, pp. 67, 70, 74.

[39] On 8 August he told a correspondent that he was 'prowling about, meditating a new book' (*Letters*, 9, p. 284). To Leigh Hunt on 4 May 1855 he had described the wandering, restless state of mind he invariably endured on starting a new novel thus: 'At such a time I am as infirm of purpose as Macbeth, as errant as Mad Tom, and as rugged as Timon' (*Letters*, 7, p. 608).

SHAKESPEARIAN MARGINS IN GEORGE ELIOT'S 'WORKING-DAY WORLD'

JOHN LYON

PRELUDE

The world of the first act of *As You Like It* proves a remarkably prosaic one – literally so in the first half of the act – an entangled world in which characters are burdened by their past actions, the intricacies of past relationships, the constraints of others' actions and attitudes, inherited problems and problems of inheritance. However, as the act progresses, it emerges that this is a world which the play realizes only in order to leave it behind, its problems to be dissolved rather than resolved in the freer, transformative and Arcadian world of the Forest of Arden. Repeatedly the early dialogue records what we might call anticipatory tropes of transformation, culminating in Celia's closing pronouncement that she and the banished Rosalind now go 'in content, / To liberty, and not to banishment' (1.3.136–7). Early in the same scene the same transformation of attitude had straddled an exchange between Rosalind and Celia:

ROSALIND [. . .] O how full of briars is this working-day world!
CELIA They are but burs, cousin, thrown upon thee in holiday foolery. (1.3.11–14)

It is in this exchange that we find George Eliot's 'favorite little epithet: "This working-day world"'.[1] The little phrase was truly a favourite Eliot quotation, its brevity compensated by the sheer frequency of Eliot's use of it in a great diversity of contexts: in effect George Eliot makes the phrase her own through repeated usages which are entirely ignoring of, or hostile to, the originating Shakespearian context. Eliot's is thus a remarkable appropriation since it runs counter to the Shakespearian grain, arresting and resisting the repeated movement of *As You Like It*, pre-eminently a holidaying play. Eliot's lighting on this phrase amounts to a refusal of the Shakespearian story. As such it is characteristic of, and continuous with, George Eliot's difficult, indeed often adversarial relation with Shakespeare, a contest that has aesthetic, generic and political dimensions. Furthermore, in seizing on 'this working-day world', George Eliot is doing nothing less than again seizing the novel's birthright, the vast subject matter of the quotidian, the world of work, which is kept at the margins of Shakespearian aristocratic drama. In George Eliot's writings, there is an exemplary usage when the novelist, writing of Adam Bede, declares that there is 'no holiday-time in the working-day world':[2] Shakespearian pastoral is rebuked by Eliotic realism.

I am much indebted in this essay to my colleagues George Donaldson and Peter McDonald.

[1] George Eliot, *Letters* edited by Gordon S. Haight, vol. I (1836–51) (New Haven and London, 1954), p. 44. In his edition of George Eliot's *Essays* (New York, 1963), p. 302, note 6, Thomas Pinney records a number of Eliot's usages of the phrase.
[2] George Eliot, *Adam Bede* (first published 1859), edited by Stephen Gill (London, 1980), p. 489.

Near the close of *Middlemarch*, there is another and important swerving away from Shakespeare, typical of Eliotic narrative. Dorothea famously encounters Rosamond Lydgate and Will Ladislaw together at the Lydgates' home, and Dorothea's silent indignation at the possible improprieties of such a relationship prompts in her an energized, intoxicated, lofty madness. In effect, Dorothea plays Hamlet. In turn, Eliot characteristically deploys the down-to-earth, if complaisant Celia to register Dorothea's unreality here:

'Dodo, how very bright your eyes are!' said Celia, when Sir James was gone out of the room. 'And you don't see anything you look at, Arthur or anything. You are going to do something uncomfortable, I know. Is it all about Mr Lydgate, or has something else happened?' Celia had been used to watch her sister with expectation.

'Yes, dear, a great many things have happened,' said Dodo, in her full tones.

'I wonder what,' said Celia, folding her arms cozily and leaning forward upon them.

'Oh, all the troubles of all people on the face of the earth,' said Dorothea, lifting her arms to the back of her head.

'Dear me, Dodo, are you going to have a scheme for them?' said Celia, a little uneasy at this Hamlet-like raving.[3]

But Hamlet-like scheming is precisely and consciously excluded from George Eliot's philosophy and it is 'this working day world' which will puncture such pretension, returning Dorothea from generalizing grandeur to the stubborn complexities of the particular case:

[. . .] The objects of her rescue were not to be sought out by her fancy: they were chosen for her. She yearned towards the perfect Right, that it might make a throne within her, and rule her errant will. 'What should I do – how should I act now, this very day if I could clutch my own pain, and compel it to silence, and think of those three!'

It had taken long for her to come to that question, and there was light piercing into the room. She opened her curtains, and looked out towards the bit of road that lay in view, with fields beyond, outside the entrance-gates. On the road there was a man

with a bundle on his back and a woman carrying her baby; in the field she could see figures moving – perhaps the shepherd with his dog. Far off in the bending sky was the pearly light; and she felt the largeness of the world and the manifold wakings of men to labour and endurance. She was a part of that involuntary, palpitating life, and could neither look out on it from her luxurious shelter as a mere spectator, nor hide her eyes in selfish complaining.[4]

At the novel's climax, Dorothea finally comes to 'that question' and, with it, the Hamlet within her is compelled 'to silence'; the imagination is denigrated as 'fancy' and then dismissed. The trappings of royalty are rewritten as metaphor and – answering the Shakespearian text's invitation to the novel – interiorized as 'a throne within her'. The 'errant will' is curbed, and Hamlet's painful dilemma of action is rewritten as the need to think of others: 'Hamlet-like ravings' are supplanted as Dorothea comes to see the world as others see it. She looks beyond 'luxurious shelter', 'outside the entrance gates' as the 'selfish complaining' Hamlet all too rarely does, and sees 'this working-day world' and 'the manifold wakings of men to labour and endurance'. She sees, in Celia's terms, what she is looking at; she sees the world as it is. Or, if we are to insist that this is not the world of unmediated reality but a world with inescapable literary precedents, then it is a world which Lear rather than Hamlet glimpses (and only glimpses), the world of a homelier literary tradition, suggestive of Bunyan and Wordsworth and anticipatory of Thomas Hardy's altogether closer inspection. It is a world which refuses Shakespearian will and grandeur as illusion: what is described in *As You Like It* as Duke Senior's 'stubbornness of fortune' (2.1.19) is here to be neither sweetened nor translated, but endured.

[3] George Eliot, *Middlemarch* (first published 1871–2), edited by Rosemary Ashton (London, 1994), p. 776.

[4] *Middlemarch*, p. 788.

INTERTEXTUALITY, MARGINS AND MOTTOES

In the example from *Middlemarch* above, George Eliot rejects Hamlet (and *Hamlet*) in favour of the 'largeness of the world'. Yet this once familiar opposition – between the writerly and the real, between the literary and the actual – is one which, since post-structuralism, we have not allowed ourselves to credit. At present textuality and intertextuality are for us inescapable dominating facts of writing. It is salutary therefore to find that other historical periods, while not unaware of such possibilities, remained unexcited by them. What has come to be for us a crucial Barthesian insight is for Sir Hugo Mallinger in George Eliot's *Daniel Deronda* merely a necessary, uninteresting blindness: 'much quotation of any sort, even in English, is bad. It tends to choke ordinary remark. One couldn't carry on life comfortably without a little blindness to the fact that everything has been said better than we can put it ourselves.'[5] Writing *in propria persona* George Eliot declared 'I hate a style speckled with quotations.'[6] Because we are all intertextualists now, we underestimate how powerfully George Eliot faces down the intertextual in the interests of the prosaic, the 'ordinary remark', 'this working-day world', and we underestimate the profoundly anti-literary, anti-textual basis of her creative energy. George Eliot's creativity is in large part hostile and negative – analogous to the poetics of envy as described by René Girard[7] or the poetics of anxiety as made famous by Harold Bloom; and such hostility extends into her relationship with Shakespeare.

Writing to Maria Lewis in March 1839, the nineteen-year-old Marian Evans, in a letter turgid to the point of being well-nigh unquotable, contemplated giving up literature including Shakespeare: 'we have need of as nice a power of distillation as the bee to suck nothing but honey from his pages'.[8] Such anti-Shakespearian moments embarrass Eliot's critics and biographers, who rush to excuse, qualify,

explain and explain away, but George Eliot was to go on to make a literary and intellectual career of giving up books. Rosemarie Bodenheimer notes of these early evangelical letters, including this particular 'long set-piece essay' on the dangers of reading: 'They are manifestly adolescent; at the same time they are visibly the stuff of which George Eliot novels were to be made.'[9] The denigration of fiction is an important part of the rhetoric of realism, and thus it is customary for critics to limit Eliot's distrust of textuality to a distrust of the fictions of her immediate predecessors, those now notorious and perhaps maligned silly novels by lady novelists. Alternatively critics see Eliot's distrust as a phase which passes with her loss of, or liberation from, religious faith. However, that loss itself was effected by anti-textual means, the great challenge of history to the Bible itself – a text which even Harold Bloom will concede to be more influential even than Shakespeare – and a challenge which Eliot herself participated in as her first important contributions to intellectual life. The rejection of faith reinforces rather than contradicts the evangelical rejection of fiction. For Eliot's world was one in which the age of miracles was passed, indeed had never been, and she herself was to be one of the 'philosophical persons to make modern and familiar things supernatural and causeless' (*All's Well* 2.3.2–3). Charles Hennel's *Inquiry Concerning the Origin of Christianity* (1838) which accorded with the work of David Friedrich Strauss led George Eliot to Strauss's own *Das Leben Jesu, kritisch bearbeitet*

---

5 George Eliot, *Daniel Deronda* (first published 1876), ed. Terence Cave (London, 1995), p. 177.

6 George Eliot, *Letters*, edited by Gordon S. Haight, vol. 5 (1869–73) (New Haven and London, 1956), p. 404.

7 See René Girard, *A Theatre of Envy: William Shakespeare* (New York and Oxford, 1991)

8 George Eliot, *Letters*, edited by Gordon S. Haight, vol. 1 (1836–51) (New Haven and London, 1954), p. 22.

9 Rosemarie Bodenheimer, *The Real Life of Mary Ann Evans: George Eliot, her Letters and Fiction* (Ithaca and London, 1994), pp. 37–8.

(1835–6) and subsequently to Ludwig Feuerbach's *Das Wesen des Christenthums* (1841), the latter two works to be translated by Eliot herself: and all three works correct and revise the biblical text by reference to history and the Germanic scientific methodologies. In effect they offer to extricate truth from textuality.

Yet George Eliot does make use of the words of others, as intertextual theorists argue that she inevitably must. And she makes such use explicit in the form of frequent quotation and in the very distinctive presence in three of her novels of epigraphs as chapter headings.[10] However, the relation to the writings of others remains at base hostile and combative rather than venerating and collaborative: George Eliot's writings typically strive to efface the inescapable fact of their own textuality; to occlude or naturalize their own and others' literariness; and to conceal, contain, diminish or displace to the margins the writings of her precursors. She succeeds, to a remarkable degree, in keeping the encroaching presence of 'the *already-written*'[11] at bay. Gillian Beer recognizes as much in describing how 'George Eliot refers fugitively to other texts, or at an angle which does not at first reveal them. She engages with the work of writers she respects, or is troubled by, by means of expansion, taking the implications of words and events where they have failed to go.' Of *Silas Marner* in particular, Beer notes 'allusions [. . .] are all there to be lost and obliterated. They are part of the system of expectation and allusion which we must respond to, and dispel, if we are to reach the human directness of the work.'[12] Thus the literary is to be left behind in preference for 'this working-day world'.

In George Eliot's collected letters there are, according to Marianne Novy, 'far more quotations from Shakespeare's writings than from any other literary source except the Bible'.[13] Yet such quotations typically disappoint attention. Often in contexts which are mocking and self-conscious, the reader can hear – and often literally see – the isolating quotation marks

which are holding off the Shakespearian text rather than embracing it. Such quotations comically flaunt the quotidian inappropriateness of their new usage, and thus the *absence* of a relation with the Shakespearian drama. And the habit of quotation is typically so fastidious; it confines itself to tiny fragments, deliberately denuded of their originating context and chosen, as often as not, because of their very familiarity and commonplaceness. Usually such precisely chosen (and often repeated) snippets are truisms – variously skittish, moralized, self-deprecatory, decorative, superficial and whimsical, teetering on the verge of being inert clichés. Defused, disempowered, domesticated, Shakespeare's words become social niceties, the sparing adornment of nineteenth-century bourgeois epistolary style. In what Henry James described as the 'grayness of tone' and 'luminous brooding'[14] of George Eliot's letters, Shakespeare shrivels and all but disappears.

Henry James too detected something odd in Eliot's use of epigraphs, deeming them 'a want of tact [. . .] a trifle more pretentious than really pregnant'.[15] Yet, in sensing an inadequacy here,

---

10 For a more traditional view of Eliot's use of epigraphs than that offered here see David Leon Higdon, 'George Eliot and the Art of the Epigraph', *Nineteenth-Century Fiction*, 25 (1970–1), 127–51.

11 The phrase occurs in what amounts to a definition of intertextuality: 'Alongside each utterance [of a text], one might say that off-stage voices can be heard [. . .] in their interweaving, these voices (whose origins are "lost" in the vast perspective of the *already-written*) de-originate the utterance.' Roland Barthes, *S/Z*, translated by Richard Miller (New York, 1974) p. 21.

12 Gillian Beer, *George Eliot* (Brighton, 1986), pp. 42, 126.

13 Marianne Novy, *Engaging with Shakespeare: Responses of George Eliot and Other Women Novelists* (Athens, Georgia, 1994), p. 1.

14 Henry James, 'The Life of George Eliot' (first published 1885) in *Literary Criticism: Essays on Literature, American Writers, English Writers* (New York, 1984), pp. 994–1010 (pp. 1010 and 1000).

15 Henry James, '*Daniel Deronda*: A Conversation' (first published 1876), *Literary Criticism: Essays on Literature, American Writers, English Writers* (New York, 1984), pp. 974–92 (p. 986).

James may in fact be registering the effect which Eliot's deployment of epigraphs – or mottoes as she herself called them – characteristically strives for. In recording the fact that the 'largest single number of attributed epigraphs' comes from Shakespeare together with the telling oddity that three times as many epigraphs are anonymous and 'almost certainly Eliot's own', Marianne Novy is right to cite George Eliot's declaration that there are limits to her respect for the writings of others: 'I wish you thoroughly to understand that the writers who have most profoundly influenced me – who have rolled away the waters from their bed raised new mountains and spread delicious valleys for me – are not in the least oracles to me.'[16] Questioning whether there is truth in the oracle, Eliot's own voice is not to be cowed, even by the voice of Apollo.

Far from signalling a deference to literary authority, Eliot's use of epigraphs as chapter headings is a marginalization, and has an effect continuous with those denigrations of fiction characteristic of realism. 'The Natural History of German Life', the Eliotic manifesto which prefaced her entire creative career, had contrasted the flatness of '[a]ppeals founded on generalizations and statistics' and the dullness of 'sermons and philosophical dissertations' which 'require a sympathy ready-made', with the altogether superior representations of the social novel – the powerful, experiential and particular 'picture of human life' which realist art, 'the nearest thing to life', affords and which surprises us 'into that attention to what is apart from' ourselves.[17] In declaring their own fragmented, generalizing inadequacy Eliot's prefatory mottoes assert by implication the superior reality of Eliot's novel, the greater particularity, wholeness and truth of the body of Eliot's own texts: no less than thirty-one times the Shakespearian snippet is made to defer to the novelistic fullness of the Eliotic chapter which it prefaces.

A particularly telling example of Eliot's cavalier attitude to the use of mottoes is a usage, in

Daniel Deronda, of *The Winter's Tale*. The thirty-first chapter of George Eliot's novel has as its epigraph or motto:

'A wild dedication of yourselves
To unpath'd waters, undream'd shores.'

Shakespeare.

There is a typical casualness here in which Eliot identifies the author but not the specific play, but the passage comes from *The Winter's Tale* 4.4.566–7. At this point in Shakespeare's play Florizel finds himself at odds with his father because of his love for Perdita and, to escape his father's anger, the young couple are intent on eloping together. In turn the good counsellor Camillo helpfully suggests that Florizel take Perdita to Leontes' court and describes this course of action as:

A course more promising
Than a wild dedication of yourselves
To unpathed waters, undreamed shores; . . .

(4.4.565–7)

With this preface, chapter 31 of George Eliot's novel now proceeds to describe the marriage of Gwendolen Harleth and Mallinger Grandcourt: a brilliant and bright beginning sees the bride with 'erect head and elastic footstep [. . .] walking amid illusions'[18] and ends, a few pages later, in disillusion and pallid shrieking terror. The relation of novel and play is here of an obviousness that makes one apologize to readers for spelling it out: the romantic happiness of Florizel and Perdita is re-written, reversed and ironized, in the disastrous marriage of Grandcourt and Gwendolen. Moreover, in this predilection for the ironic and for the punishing of

---

16 Marianne Novy, *Engaging with Shakespeare*, p. 67. The quoted Eliot letter may be found in George Eliot, *Letters* edited by Gordon S. Haight, vol. I (1836–51) (New Haven and London, 1954), p. 277.

17 George Eliot, 'The Natural History of German Life' (first published 1856) in *Selected Essays, Poems and Other Writings*, edited by A.S. Byatt and Nicholas Warren (London, 1990), pp. 107–39 (p. 110).

18 *Daniel Deronda*, p. 355

romance, this revisioning is typical of Eliot's relation to earlier writings.

So far this example has seemed an unrewarding instance of the kind of tedious exposition into which Eliot's epigraphs, wanting in tact, can lead the plodding critic. What does make for interest, however, is the realization that this coming together of *The Winter's Tale* and *Daniel Deronda* represents on George Eliot's part a curious missing or wilful ignoring of an altogether more interesting intertextual opportunity. The use of Camillo's words as epigraph to chapter 31 make Gwendolen into an ironic Perdita, Eliot's heroine being lost just as Shakespeare's is about to be found. Yet in the powerful writing of the chapter's close, the terrified Gwendolen is reflected in the glass panels of her room 'like so many women petrified white'[19] and now Gwendolen may again be related to an altogether more famous and more memorable appearance of *The Winter's Tale* in *Daniel Deronda*. This is also an inversion of a Shakespearian original – not of Perdita, but of Hermione, flesh turned again to stone, just as, in the fiasco of the tableau vivant of *The Winter's Tale* in the sixth chapter of the novel, the pallid Gwendolen had also been petrified, looking 'like a statue into which a soul of Fear had entered'.[20] The chapter's epigraph, equating Gwendolen and Perdita, seems superficial and superfluous, blurring and frustrating the novel's own more internal and more subtle echoings and reworkings of Shakespeare's Hermione.

But such intertextual disappointment and frustration may be precisely Eliot's intention. The epigraph using Camillo's words and so bringing another and different facet of *The Winter's Tale* momentarily into play may serve to disrupt the intertextual dialogue, to loosen the grasp of Shakespeare's play on the larger structure of *Daniel Deronda*, to swerve away from the Shakespearian story, and thus to avoid too great a dependency on Shakespeare. All other writings, Shakespeare's included, are to be brought within Eliot's writerly powers, to be

invoked and to be ignored as and when she sees fit; and other writings, far from being oracular, are merely to serve and substantiate the greater reality of Eliot's own prose of ordinary remarks in the working-day world.

'THE POSSIBLE OTHER CASE'

The examples with which this essay began, from *As You Like It* and *Hamlet*, have already shown Eliot resisting rather than embracing Shakespeare. In her most overt novelistic engagement with Shakespeare – the appropriation in *Daniel Deronda* of the statue scene from *The Winter's Tale* – it is astonishing just how punitive George Eliot's revisioning of Shakespeare's play proves to be. Among the many diversely interesting readings of this rewriting, Jim Reilly's is surely right in seeing it as 'a radical, indeed iconoclastic revision'.[21] The reversal of the play's statue scene is punitive of Eliot's heroine, Gwendolen Harleth, punitive of Shakespeare, and – arguably – punitive of aspects of Eliot's own writing. Even its positioning early in the novel, in contrast to the play's final climactic scene, is a rebuke. It declares a hostility to aristocratic romance, to imagination and to desire, and focuses such hostility on the beautiful and 'queenly' young woman who had declared her new home a 'romantic place; anything delightful may happen in it'; who had uttered the 'glib words', 'Imagination is often truer than fact'; and who

---

[19] Ibid., p. 359.   [20] Ibid., p. 61.

[21] Jim Reilly, *Shadowtime: History and Representation in Hardy, Conrad and George Eliot* (London and New York, 1993), pp. 121–32 (p. 125). Other readings of the relation between *The Winter's Tale* and *Daniel Deronda* include U. C. Knoepflmacher, '*Daniel Deronda* and William Shakespeare', *Victorian Newsletter*, 19 (1961), 27–8; Ian Adam, '*The Winter's Tale* and its Displacements: The Hermione Episode in *Daniel Deronda*', *Newsletter of the Victorian Studies Association of Western Canada*, 9 (Spring 1983), 8–13; Adrian Poole, ' "Hidden Affinities" in *Daniel Deronda*', *Essays in Criticism* 33 (1983), 294–311; Marianne Novy, *Engaging with Shakespeare*, pp. 117–37

had announced herself in favour of the unlikely since 'what is likely [. . .] is always dull'.[22] Gwendolen, in effect, is presented as speaking, glibly and superficially, for an inversion of Eliot's realist creed, but also speaking for what Henry James described altogether more seriously as 'the something better [. . .] the possible other case, the case rich and edifying where the actuality is pretentious and vain'.[23]

In speaking up so harshly for actuality in her treatment of Gwendolen Harleth, George Eliot may be protesting too much. Eliot may be punishing her own self-contradictory reliance on the unlikely, the 'rich and strange', since, just as romance is ostentatiously dismissed from the front door of the house of Eliotic fiction, it often finds its way in by the back door, a door often left as deliberately wide as the front door is shut tight. In *Daniel Deronda*, this romantic element takes the form, as critics familiarly recognize, of the entire other plot, the story of Daniel Deronda's romantic quest. More generally there is a flaw in George Eliot's combining of realism and optimism: her own realistic concentration on the ordinary will not accommodate possibility, but threatens only dull and deadening, repetitive probability. So, if it is to be politically optimistic, her fiction, albeit through sleight-of-hand, must at some stage open itself up to enlivening romantic possibility.

The 'possible other case' in respect of George Eliot's use of *The Winter's Tale* is *Silas Marner*. George Eliot's covert, concealed but heavy reliance on Shakespeare's play – both local and structural – in this earlier fiction may explain the vehemence of her later iconoclasm in *Daniel Deronda*: the earlier debt cannot be acknowledged and thus must be denigrated and denied. But is *Daniel Deronda*'s attack on *The Winter's Tale* even necessary? So effective is Eliot's effacing of the presence of *The Winter's Tale* in *Silas Marner* that those critics who have noticed a relation have followed Eliotic practice in marginalizing such noticings: Neil Roberts and David Carroll relegate such observations to

notes, with the consequence that the question of the possible *significance* of this particular Shakespearian relation is left unaddressed.[24] Terence Cave, in his 1996 discussion of *Silas Marner*, is atypical in bringing his noticing within the main body of his discussion, but he notices the relation with *The Winter's Tale* only to dismiss it: '[T]he similarities seem only to suggest a deliberate reversal [. . .] It is important, then, not to project on to *Silas Marner* a falsely rosy image of the literary texts it alludes to.'[25]

There persists a common assumption, in the study of literary relations, that it is in the *similarities* and *continuities* that the interest lies; such an assumption has certainly made for dullness – not least in the study of the sources of Shakespeare's own works – and lends a legitimacy to Roland Barthes's contemptuous view of the uninterest of source study and the tracings of textual filiations. But, in fact, it is in the *significant differences* that the true, argumentative relations between and among texts reside. In the particular case of *Silas Marner* and *The Winter's Tale*, Eliot comments, covertly but critically, both on Shakespeare's aristocratic politics and on the philosophical evasiveness of his text's treatment of the nature–nurture debate. The Shakespearian presence, in turn, indicts the realist aesthetic which dominates Eliot's work, and puts in question the adequacy of that aesthetic in sustaining Eliot's optimism in her conservatively ameliorative politics. In

---

22 *Daniel Deronda*, p. 80; p. 26; p. 47; and p. 69.

23 Henry James, Preface to *The Lesson of the Master* (first published 1908) in *Literary Criticism: French Writers; Other European Writers; The Prefaces to the New York Edition*, pp. 1225–37 (p. 1229).

24 Neil Roberts, *George Eliot: Her Beliefs and Her Art* (London, 1975) p. 230–1 n.7; and David R. Carroll, '*Silas Marner*: Reversing the Oracles of Religion', *Literary Monographs*, Vol. 1, edited by Eric Rothstein and Thomas K. Dunseath (Madison, Milwaukee and London, 1967), pp. 167–200, notes pp. 312–14 (p. 312, note 22).

25 Terence Cave, Introduction to *Silas Marner* (Oxford, 1996), pp.vii–xxxi (p.xxiii).

Silas Marner unlikely, even tendentious, Shakespearian possibility pits itself against the ordinary and the probable. The unresolved quarrel with Shakespeare in *Silas Marner* leads, as we have seen, beyond this particular text, to Eliot's great retaliation in her altogether more overt dealings with *The Winter's Tale* in *Daniel Deronda*.

Eliot locates the inspiration for *Silas Marner* in life rather than art: 'It came to me first of all, quite suddenly, as a sort of legendary tale, suggested by my recollection of having once, in early childhood, seen a linen-weaver with a bag on his back; but, as my mind dwelt on the subject, I became inclined to a more realistic treatment.'[26] The source may be life rather than letters, but George Eliot does advertise her literary forebears, most particularly, in the opening pages of *Silas Marner*. However, such advertisement, and the *choice* of forebears to be thus advertised, are carefully controlled and controlling of readers' responses – an orientating of our reading towards the ordinary and commonplace which dictated and continues to dictate the terms of *Silas Marner*'s reception. In all we are seeing a typical effort to naturalize the literary; to foreground texts about ordinary people, texts owned by ordinary people, and the fictional modes favoured by ordinary people themselves. So Wordsworth's 'Michael' stands apart from *Silas Marner*, as introductory epigraph:

> A child, more than all other gifts
> That earth can offer to declining man,
> Brings hope with it, and forward-looking
> thoughts.

Thus the poet as ordinary man speaking to men stands at the beginning of Eliot's story, his own tragic tale of 'Michael' further excerpted and arrested, turned to a more optimistic view of the future, and the role of the child in that future, a view which Eliot's own narrative will realize in altogether fuller detail. And so, as Eliot's own narrative proper begins, we proceed, in allusive terms, to the worlds of tales, of the Bible, and of Bunyan's *Pilgrim's*

Progress. The 'Once upon a time . . .' beginning of fairy tale is invoked and corrected to the more historically situated 'In the days when the spinning-wheels hummed busily in the farmhouses . . .'[27] Silas Marner himself makes his first appearance as a type of Bunyan's 'figure bent under a heavy bag'.[28] These introductory pages partake repeatedly of biblical cadences. And, later in the tale, Eliot demonstrates her continuity with the traditions of the Bible and Bunyan and at the same time asserts her novelistic (and realistic) distance from them in the great concluding paragraph of chapter 14, which modulates repeatedly between the stark significances of the fabular ('angels', 'the hand', 'the city of destruction') and the extraneous, particularizing details of the novel ('*white-winged* angels', '*threatening* destruction', 'leads them forth *gently*', 'a *little* child's):

In old days there were angels who came and took men by the hand and led them away from the city of destruction. We see no white-winged angels now. But yet men are led away from threatening destruction: a hand is put in theirs, which leads them forth gently towards a calm and bright land, so that they look no more backward; and the hand may be a little child's.[29]

In play here are the Bible and *Pilgrim's Progress* – two texts which, if not extensively read and owned in Raveloe itself, would certainly be on the shelves in the home of the Tullivers (in *The Mill on the Floss*), and of so many families like them. And *Silas Marner* is a tale told of people who themselves tell tales. At the end of chapter 5 Silas Marner lifts the latch of the Rainbow Inn; at the beginning of chapter 7 he enters. Caught out of time, in chapter 6, and thus laying claim to timelessness and generality, and more mundanely to the typicality of repetition, this scene shows us the villagers of Raveloe

---

26 George Eliot, *Letters*, edited by Gordon S. Haight, vol. 3 (1859–61) (New Haven and London, 1954), p. 382.

27 George Eliot, *Silas Marner* (first published 1861), edited by David Carroll (London, 1996) p. 5.

28 Ibid., p. 5.   29 Ibid., p. 131.

telling themselves, yet again, the tale of the Cliffs and the Lammeters, 'real' families who have become the stuff of fable. It is a familiar tale, embellished with biblical allusion – in this case a modified quotation from the Psalms; it is an anonymous tale, shared and without the specificity of any individual originating author; a tale from life remote from the literary, and a tale which rhetorically makes claims for its own 'naturalness': as such it asserts an embedded continuity with the claims which Eliot's own *Silas Marner* strives to make for itself. In all this – even in its allusivenesses – *Silas Marner* strives to present itself as natural, as an art which 'is the nearest thing to life.'

Yet it is as plausible to see the origins of *Silas Marner* – far from being so diversely and generally spread – as highly specific and highly literary, contained in a single text, *The Winter's Tale*. The prose story's defining moment represents a conflation and correction of the two great discoveries of Shakespeare's play. Eliot brings together the finding of Perdita:

OLD SHEPHERD [. . .] Now bless thyself. Thou metst with things dying, I with things new-born. Here's a sight for thee. Look thee, a bearing-cloth for a squire's child.
> *He points to the box*
Look thee here, take up, take up, boy. Open't. So, let's see. It was told me I should be rich by the fairies. This is some changeling. Open't. What's within, boy?
CLOWN (*opening the box*) You're a made old man. If the sins of your youth are forgiven you, you're well to live. Gold, all gold! (3.3.110–20)

And the awakening, in the play's final scene, of Hermione to the belatedly outstretched hand of an agitated and afflicted Leontes:

LEONTES O, she's warm!
If this be magic, let it be an art
Lawful as eating. (5.3.109–111)

So that George Eliot's Silas, coming to after having been in his cataleptic state 'like a graven image', is also afflicted and unsettled:

to his blurred vision, it seemed as if there were gold on the floor in front of the hearth. Gold! – his own

gold – brought back to him as mysteriously as it had been taken away! He felt his heart begin to beat violently, and for a few moments he was unable to stretch out his hand and grasp the restored treasure. The heap of gold seemed to glow and get larger beneath his agitated gaze. He leaned forward at last, and stretched forth his hand; but instead of hard coin with the familiar resisting outline, his fingers encountered soft warm curls.[30]

But in *Silas Marner* Eliot is very far from being the passive recipient of *The Winter's Tale* and here her creativity manifests itself in an astonishingly precise – and sharply corrective – reconfiguration. Thus gold and the child, in Shakespeare's text, are conflated and interchangeable: Eliot prises them apart in pursuit of the precise difference in evaluations on which her tale centres. Whether Eliot's corrective clarification of the Shakespearian equivocation over human and material wealth is an enrichment or an impoverishment is a matter of taste – and perhaps of politics. In its attitude to money, *Silas Marner* can appear as Shakespeare *moralisé*.

In addition to these moments of intensity and recognition, the relation between *Silas Marner* and *The Winter's Tale* manifests itself in a number of striking local parallels, and extends far beyond these to narrative, to characterization, and to structure. Both works explicitly call attention to the sixteen-year gap between the two parts of each story. Each story moves from winter to spring. The discovery of the child in each story coincides with death – of Antigonus and Molly Farren respectively. Eliot confers novelistic inwardness and dignity on the characters at the periphery of Shakespeare's plays, and in creating Silas Marner democratizes a combination of Shepherd and Clown with the trickster Autolycus – the last mentioned, like Silas, the bearer of a burden or pack on his back, and a man whose 'traffic is sheets' (4.3.23). Dolly Winthrop is a homelier version of the forthright, officious, well-meaning

---

[30] Ibid., p. 110.

Paulina; and the whole incident of Dolly taking her child Aaron to be seen by the short-sighted Silas in the belief that 'it must do Master Marner good to see such a "pictur of a child" '[31] seems to have its origin in Paulina's more aggressive confronting of Leontes with his baby, Perdita. When we first meet him, the Shepherd in Shakespeare's play might seem to complain of the Dunstan and Godfrey Casses of George Eliot's world:

I would there were no age between ten and three-and-twenty, or that youth would sleep out the rest; for there is nothing in the between but getting wenches with child, wronging the ancientry, stealing, fighting – hark you now, would any but these boiled-brains of nineteen and two-and-twenty hunt this weather? (3.3.58–64)

Examples of such parallels and repetitions might be further multiplied. It is, however, where the two writers diverge – as in the different treatments of child and gold discussed above – that the interest of the dialogue between *The Winter's Tale* and *Silas Marner* lies. Gillian Beer has noted George Eliot's interest in foster parents, arguing that kin 'is the point of oscillation between nature and culture' and that in *Silas Marner*, in matters of parenting, 'nurture predominates over nature'.[32] Events near the tale's close emphasize such a view: Eppie discovers that her biological father is the Squire, Godfrey Cass, but remains loyal to Silas Marner, the humbler man who brought her up –

'Oh father,' said Eppie, 'what a pretty home ours is! I think nobody could be happier than we are.' [33]

This home is certainly happier than that of the other, richer father in *Silas Marner*, Godfrey Cass. In *The Winter's Tale*, Leontes has the daughter whom he had denied and had lost restored to him and he also recovers his wife, transformed from statue to warm human flesh. George Eliot's rewriting of such events for Godfrey Cass is an ironizing and realistic revision, anticipatory of the harsh reversal of *The Winter's Tale* which she is to visit on Gwen-

dolen Harleth. Too late Godfrey acknowledges, before his childless wife Nancy, that Eppie is his child:

He paused, dreading the effect of his confession. But Nancy sat quite still, only that her eyes dropped and ceased to meet his. She was pale and quiet as a meditative statue, clasping her hands on her lap.
'You'll never think the same of me again,' said Godfrey, after a little while, with some tremor in his voice.
She was silent.[34]

Eppie stays with her foster father; Godfrey's wife turns to stone – such strong interrogative revisioning of the Shakespearian original returns readers to *The Winter's Tale* with harsh and sceptical questions. Can the lost be so readily found – or replaced? Can the stony be so readily warmed? And – most precise of all – what has become of Perdita's foster family?

Little remarked in criticism of *The Winter's Tale*, Perdita's Shepherd-father and her Clown-brother are to be found, tagged on and tagging along in the company of Autolycus at the tail end of the prosaic Act 5 Scene 2. The Shepherd-father's story, the story which is to become the focus of Eliot's novelistic interest, is a vague, off-stage one in which Shakespeare has but a casual, comic interest. The Shepherd and Clown had contemplated telling Polixenes of Perdita's status as a foundling: this would have allowed them to deny any kinship with her and thus would have put them out of danger of the King's wrath. But they were tricked by Autolycus into accompanying Florizel to Sicilia where – off-stage – Polixenes had caught up with them. Off-stage the Shepherd opens the fardel which effects the reconciliation of the two royal families, royal families which now include Perdita who evinces 'the affection of nobleness which nature shows above her breeding' (5.2.36–7). Amidst such reconcilia-

[31] Ibid., p. 84.
[32] Gillian Beer, *George Eliot*, p. 130.
[33] *Silas Marner*, p. 183.
[34] Ibid., pp. 162–3.

tions, the Shepherd-father receives Leontes' thanks and 'stands by like a weather-bitten conduit of many kings' reigns' (5.2. 55–6). Shepherd and Clown then make a brief appearance before us to display their new clothes and wealth – and hence their new gentlemanly status – and to tell us how the royal families embrace them as kin. They may or may not be again silent bystanders at the coming to life of Hermione's statue in the play's last scene: Shakespeare's focus and interest are elsewhere. It is thus at the comic periphery of Shakespeare's play that George Eliot finds her more ordinary story, a once comic story now to be retold with inwardness and feeling and a story which offers a retrospective censure of Shakespeare's aristocratic politics.

If George Eliot makes much more of Shakespeare's old Shepherd, she makes much less of the great debate about art and nature which so exercises Polixenes and Perdita in *The Winter's Tale*. In the famous set piece Perdita argues for nature; Polixenes for nurture:

> You see, sweet maid, we marry
> A gentler scion to the wildest stock,
> And make conceive a bark of baser kind
> By bud of nobler race.   4.4.92–5

Yet such creations are shunned by Perdita who twice remarks that such 'slips' will never enter her garden. It is a typical Shakespearian irony that both debaters soon contradict their avowed position when the discovery of the noble Florizel's intended marriage to a humble shepherdess is made. Yet the great disappointment of *The Winter's Tale* lies in the way that the debate finally comes to nothing with the further discovery that Perdita too is of noble birth and that thus Polixenes and Perdita have nothing to argue about: the exclusivity of nobility finally goes unchallenged in Shakespeare's play.

Radically convinced of the importance of nurture, George Eliot revisions the entire debate as a common or garden matter, a practical problem easily solved:

'There, now, father, you won't work in it [the garden] till it's all easy,' said Eppie, 'and you and me can mark out the beds, and make holes and plant the roots. It'll be a deal livelier at the Stone-pits when we've got some flowers, for I always think the flowers can see us and know what we're talking about. And I'll have a bit o' rosemary, and bergamot, and thyme, because they're so sweet-smelling; but there's no lavender; only in the gentlefolks' gardens, I think.'

'That's no reason why you shouldn't have some,' said Aaron, 'for I can bring you slips of anything; I'm forced to cut no end of 'em when I'm gardening, and throw 'em away mostly. There's a big bed o' lavender at the Red House: the missis is very fond of it.'[35]

The great Shakespearian set-piece debate is thus now only ordinary novelistic conversation.

CODA

For all the sharpness of her political critique of *The Winter's Tale*, George Eliot is, as we have seen, dependent – in spite of herself – on the extraordinary in Shakespeare's play in order to secure a happy outcome for the ostensibly ordinary tale which she wishes to tell. In Shakespeare's play it is only in retrospect, as the moment of wonder gives way to disillusionment, that the mundane and the explained begin to assert themselves against the miraculous and we gradually realize that Hermione was never dead but merely in hiding, awaiting the return of her lost daughter. George Eliot's unillusioned art characteristically gets its antipathy to the miraculous under way long before its closing pages; and it is a tribute to the power of George Eliot's novelistic will to realism that, in the late nineteenth century, even those most close to the theatre, subjected one of Shakespeare's most marvellous plays to naturalizing, novelistic, Eliotic readings. Recently criticism has again noticed the Shakespearian writings of the Victorian actresses, including the essays of

---

35 Ibid., p. 139.

Helena Faucit, Lady Martin.[36] Faucit played, in company with Macready, all the celebrated Shakespearian female roles, and is declared, in her *Dictionary of National Biography* entry, to be 'the greatest [theatrical] interpreter of poetical drama that living memory can recall'. Yet the theatrical defers to the literary in a series of essays which she addressed to the likes of Browning, Ruskin and Tennyson, published individually in *Blackwood's Magazine*, and collected as a book, *On Some of Shakespeare's Female Characters*, dedicated to Queen Victoria. Although a child of the theatre – both her parents were also actors – Faucit's explanatory zeal in these writings is of a piece with the great novelistic age in which she found herself. In particular, in smoothing the improbabilities of *The Winter's Tale* into plausibilities, Faucit's narrative is, to late twentieth-century eyes, notably alien and un-Shakespearian but also remarkably akin to George Eliot – in its rhetorical questioning, its quasi-biblical cadences, its painstaking attention to the slow, uneventful passing of time, its awareness of the gradualness and partialness of things, its striving for continuity, its marvelling not at miracles but at human psychology, its scientific attentiveness and its mundane plausibility. In explaining and explaining away Hermione's sixteen-year absence, Faucit takes her dramatic cue from *The Winter's Tale* where Paulina announces that Leontes shall not marry again until his 'first queen's again in breath' (5.1.83) and then turns novelistic:

It is here the first hint is given that Hermione is still alive. How this could be, and how the secret could have been so well kept, Shakespeare gives no hint. One is thus driven to work out the problem for one's self. My view has been always this. The death-like trance into which Hermione fell on hearing of her son's death lasted so long, and had so completely the semblance of death, that it was so regarded by her husband, her attendants, and even by Paulina. The suspicion that animation was only suspended may have dawned upon Paulina when, after the boy Mamillius had been laid by his mother's side, the

inevitable change began to appear in him and not in Hermione. She would not give voice to her suspicion for fear of creating a false hope, but had the queen conveyed secretly to her own home, making arrangements, which her high position and then paramount power would enable her to make, that only the boy, and his mother's empty coffin, should be carried to the tomb. When after many days the trance gave way, Paulina would be near to perceive the first flickering of the eyelids, the first faint flush of blood returning to the cheek. Who can say how long the fearful shock to nerves and brain may have left Hermione in a state of torpor, hardly half alive, unconscious of everything that was passing around her, with a piteous look in those full eyes, so dear to Paulina, of a wounded, stricken, voiceless animal? And so the uneventful years would pass away, as such years do somehow pass with those whose lives are blanks. Gradually, as time wore on, Hermione would recognize her faithful Paulina, and such of her other ladies as were in the secret. Their tender care would move her in time to wish to live, because they wished it, and because Paulina could comfort her with the hope the oracle had given, that her lost daughter might one day be found. Upon this slender hope – the words are her own – she 'preserved herself to see the issue.' The name of Leontes is not mentioned. For a while he appears to be mercifully swept from her remembrance. She is not unforgiving, but her heart is dead towards him. Paulina feels that she dares not speak his name. It might awake too terribly the recollection of the misery he had brought upon her mistress, and in her enfeebled state prove fatal. The secret that their queen was still alive had been marvellously kept; although it had not escaped notice that Paulina had 'privately, twice or thrice a-day, ever since the death of Hermione, visited the removed house,' to which she had been secretly conveyed. Seeing the genuine contrition of Leontes, Paulina would not abandon the hope that Hermione might in time be reconciled to him. She had therefore the strongest reason to protest against the projects of marriage which were pressed upon him by his ministers.

And an event was now at hand, which could not

---

36 See, for example, Jim Reilly, *Shadowtime*, pp. 126–7; and, more generally, the writings of Nina Auerbach.

fail to bring about this reconciliation, – the arrival at the palace of the fugitive lovers . . .[37]

It is characteristically in those spaces where 'Shakespeare gives no hint', those invitations to inwardness, explanation and remembering, that the novel is driven to work out the problems – and to tell the story – for itself.

[37] Helena Faucit, Lady Martin, *On Some of Shakespeare's Female Characters* (fifth edition) (Edinburgh, 1893), pp. 383–4.

IN HER FATHER'S LIBRARY: MARGARET FULLER AND THE MAKING OF THE AMERICAN MIRANDA

PHYLLIS McBRIDE

During the late eighteenth and early nineteenth centuries, America's 'mighty evangelical churches and benevolent organizations' began a fervent crusade to educate the nation's women.[1] By financing and propagating what came to be known as 'female seminaries', these groups helped make secondary education available to more women – including middle- and lower-class women – than ever before in the nation's history.[2] Their goal was to influence 'women's supposedly unique self-sacrificial virtues' so that they might in turn guarantee 'the "salvation" of an otherwise overly expansive and competitive republic'.[3] Believing that women could exert the greatest influence in the private realm, they prepared their students to enter one of two occupations, that of wife and mother, or, 'in the case of middle- or lower-class single girls', teacher.[4] While women welcomed even these modest advances, they by no means found them sufficient. The gifted Abigail Adams, for instance, wrote that she considered the education offered her female contemporaries to be 'trifling, narrow, [and] contracted'.[5] Adams's pointed criticism was not only succinct, but also quite valid. As Faith Chipperfield has demonstrated, in even 'the best New England families', women's education 'was traditionally confined to writing and arithmetic, with perhaps a little music and dancing'.[6]

In at least some families, however, dissatisfaction with this relatively superficial education prompted those who could to educate their daughters at home. Among those who did so was Timothy Fuller, Jr. Indeed, this well-educated, well-read man tutored his daughter himself, giving her access to his library, his treasured books, and, of course, his prized volumes of Shakespeare's plays; of these, the volume which most captured his daughter's imagination was *The Tempest*.

When, as a child, Margaret Fuller (1810–50) discovered Shakespeare's *Tempest*, she found in the play – with its vivid depictions of magical books, sea storms, and shipwrecks – an exotically enchanting romance. Yet as a precocious child, she also found in the portrayal of Prospero and his young daughter Miranda a strikingly familiar scene: that of a father educating his daughter and bequeathing his library, the physical manifestation of his educational and literary tradition, to her. Consequently, it is hardly surprising that Fuller identified herself with Prospero's daughter. What is significant, however, is that she maintained – and even exploited – her identification with Prospero's daughter even as she entered her adult professional life. Her decision to do so was strategically brilliant, for Shakespeare's Miranda

---

[1] Charles Capper, *Margaret Fuller: An American Romantic Life*, 2 vols. (New York, 1992), vol. 2, p. 510.
[2] Ibid., p. 510.
[3] Ibid., p. 510.   [4] Ibid., p. 510.
[5] As quoted in Faith Chipperfield, *In Quest of Love: The Life and Death of Margaret Fuller* (New York, 1957), p. 33.
[6] Chipperfield, *In Quest of Love*, p. 33.

suggested that women could not only inherit a largely patriarchal educational and literary tradition, but also respond to it. With *Woman in the Nineteenth Century* (1845), Fuller does just that. She reads about Shakespeare's Miranda, then recasts her as the American Miranda, the female intellectual and artist. By doing so, she enables Miranda to introduce her stories – which are, of course, also her own – into the nation's educational and literary tradition, and, in the process, to transform and enrich it.

Timothy Fuller, Jr, a lawyer and politician, was, as Fuller explains in her 'Autobiographical Romance', 'a man of business, even in literature; he had been a high scholar at college, and was warmly attached to all he had learned there, both from the pleasure he had derived in the exercise of his faculties and the associated memories of success and good repute. He was, beside, well read in French literature, and in English, a Queen Anne's man.'[7] When he learned that his wife, Margarett [*sic*] Crane Fuller, was pregnant with their first child, he understandably looked forward to the day when he could pass this literary inheritance on to that child. Therefore, when on 23 May 1810 his wife gave birth to a girl, he initially expressed disappointment. However, as a faithful Jeffersonian who believed in the principle of social perfectibility, Fuller quickly decided to devote himself to providing Margaret with the same kind of education he would have offered a son. Indeed, as Fuller herself understood, 'He hoped to make me the heir of all he knew, and of as much more as the income of his profession enables him to give me means of acquiring'.[8]

Timothy Fuller began educating Margaret before she turned four, evidently hoping 'to gain time, by bringing forward the intellect as early as possible'.[9] He drew her lessons from a distinctly patriarchal educational and literary tradition. As Fuller recalls, 'I was taught Latin and English grammar at the same time, and began to read Latin at six years old, after which, for some years, I read it daily. In this branch of study, first by my father, and afterwards by a tutor, I was trained to quite a high degree of precision'.[10] Indeed, '[b]y ten she had read through most of the standard Virgil, Caesar, and Cicero, and, within another couple of years, a good deal of Horace, Livy, Tacitus, and, in translation, the Greek and Roman character portraits in Plutarch's *Parallel Lives*',[11] character portraits, of course, which focused on only men's lives and experiences.

If Timothy Fuller drew his daughter's lessons from a patriarchal tradition, he presented them by means of an equally patriarchal language, and he expected Fuller to learn that language and employ it when he quizzed her at the end of each school day. As Fuller recalls, 'he demanded accuracy and clearness in everything: you must not speak, unless you can make your meaning perfectly intelligible to the person addressed; must not express a thought, unless you can give a reason for it, if required; must not make a statement, unless sure of all particulars – such were his rules'.[12] Moreover, he required that she eliminate all conventionally feminine markers, such as qualifying words and phrases, from her speech: '"But", "if", "unless", "I am mistaken", and "it may be so", were words and phrases excluded from the province where he held sway. Trained to great dexterity in artificial methods, accurate, ready, with entire command of his resources, he had no belief in minds that listen, wait, and receive. He had no conception of the subtle and indirect motions of imagination and feeling.'[13] Consequently, Fuller explains, 'My own world sank deep within, away from the surface of my life; in what I did and said I learned to have

---

7 Margaret Fuller, 'An Autobiographical Romance', *The Essential Margaret Fuller*, ed. Jeffrey Steele (1941; New Brunswick, 1992) p. 26.
8 Ibid., p. 26. 9 Ibid.
10 Ibid., p. 28.
11 Capper, p. 47.
12 Fuller, 'Autobiographical', p. 28.
13 Ibid.

reference to other minds. But my true life was only the dearer that it was secluded and veiled over by a thick curtain of intellect.'[14]

Fuller's 'own world' of the imagination came to life after she had completed her studies for the day and recited them to her father, for it was only during these rare unstructured hours that she could do as she pleased. Because reading had by this time become both 'a habit and a passion',[15] she frequently elected to continue reading. Although '[t]here was, in the house, no apartment appropriated to the purpose of a library', there was, in her father's room, 'a large closet filled with books', and he gave her 'free access' to these.[16] Obviously, the books in her father's library reflected his tastes. As Charles Capper notes, Timothy Fuller 'admired the picaresque novels of Fielding and other male English writers because of their "wit sarcasm and satyre, and knowledge of human nature"', and he encouraged Margaret to read these.[17] However, 'the very qualities that attracted her father to the works he urged on her – their moralistic, decorative, or paternalistic aspects . . . – were the properties that were clearly not so interesting to her'.[18] Indeed, 'her father's eighteenth-century English favorites had little impact on *her* inner life, and she soon put them far down in her canon'.[19]

Yet her father also permitted her to read 'all other books' in his library, including 'the worst, or the best', except on Sundays, when he forbade her to read plays or novels, which he considered frivolous and therefore unfit reading material for such a sacred day.[20] Among these 'other books' were the works of three writers who clearly captured Fuller's imagination: '– all', she explains, 'though of unequal, yet congenial power, – all of rich and wide, rather than aspiring genius, – all free to the extent of the horizon their eye took in, – all fresh with impulse, racy with experience; never to be lost sight of, or superseded, but always to be apprehended more and more'.[21] These three writers were Shakespeare, Cervantes, and Molière. Fuller asserted that she considered Shakespeare

the greatest, and her vividly detailed account of the moment she discovered the playwright (a moment no doubt made all the more delightful since it occurred on a Sunday) certainly supports her assertion:

This Sunday – I was only eight years old – I took from the bookshelf a volume lettered SHAKSPERE. It was not the first time I had looked at it, but before I had been deterred from attempting to read, by the broken appearance along the page, and preferred smooth narrative. But this time I held in my hand 'Romeo and Juliet' long enough to get my eye fastened to the page. It was a cold winter afternoon. I took the book to the parlor fire, and had there been seated an hour or two, when my father looked up and asked me what I was reading so intently. 'Shakspere', replied the child, merely raising her eye

---

14 Ibid. In her 'Autobiographical Romance', Fuller explains that her father's insistently patriarchal instruction, while ultimately advantageous, at times proved to be both psychologically and physically deleterious: 'I had tasks given me, as many and various as the hours would allow, and on subjects beyond my age; with the additional disadvantage of reciting to him in the evening, after he returned from his office. As he was subject to many interruptions, I was often kept up till very late; and as he was a severe teacher, both from his habits of mind and his ambition for me, my feelings were kept on the stretch till the recitations were over. Thus frequently, I was sent to bed several hours too late, with nerves unnaturally stimulated. The consequence was a premature development of the brain, that made me a "youthful prodigy" by day, and by night a victim of spectral illusions, nightmare, and somnambulism, which at the time prevented the harmonious development of my bodily powers and checked my growth, while, later, they induced continual headache, weakness and nervous affections, of all kinds. As these again re-acted on the brain, giving undue force to every thought and every feeling, there was finally produced a state of being both too active and too intense, which wasted my constitution, and will bring me, – even although I have learned to understand and regulate my now morbid temperament, – to a premature grave', p. 26–7.

15 Ibid., p. 31.

16 Ibid., p. 32.

17 Capper, *Margaret Fuller*, p. 51.

18 Ibid.   19 Ibid.

20 Fuller, 'Autobiographical', p. 33.   21 Ibid.

from the page. 'Shakspere, – that won't do; that's no book for Sunday; go put it away and take another'. I went as I was bid, but took no other. Returning to my seat, the unfinished story, the personages to whom I was but just introduced, thronged and burnt my brain. I could not bear it long; such a lure it was impossible to resist. I went and brought the book again. There were several guests present, and I had got half through the play before I again attracted attention. 'What is that child about that she don't hear a word that's said to her?' quoth my aunt. 'What are you reading?' said my father. 'Shakspere' was again the reply, in a clear, though somewhat impatient tone. 'How?' said my father angrily, – then restraining himself before his guests, – 'Give me the book and go directly to bed'.[22]

Still engrossed in what she had just read, Fuller, normally an obedient child eager to please her father, hardly seemed to mind that her father had publicly scolded her. As she explains,

Into my little room no care of his anger followed me. Alone, in the dark, I thought only of the scene placed by the poet before my eye, where the free flow of life, sudden and graceful dialogue, and forms, whether grotesque or fair, seen in the broad lustre of his imagination, gave just what I wanted, and brought home the life I seemed born to live. My fancies swarmed like bees, as I contrived the rest of the story; – what all would do, what say, where go. My confinement tortured me. I could not go forth from this prison to ask after these friends; I could not make my pillow of the dreams about them which yet I could not forbear to frame. Thus was I absorbed when my father entered. He felt it right, before going to rest, to reason with me about my disobe-dience, shown in a way, as he considered, so insolent. I listened, but could not feel interested in what he said, nor turn my mind from what engaged it. He went away really grieved at my impenitence, and quite at a loss to understand conduct in me so unusual.[23]

Eager to finish reading *Romeo and Juliet* and to explore Shakespeare's other plays, including *The Tempest*, Fuller returned to Shakespeare 'at every hour [she] could command'.[24] Evidently she found in Shakespeare the presentation of a feminine sensibility missing in her father's

favourite books. 'Here', she explained, 'was a counterpoise to my Romans, still more forcible than the little garden' her mother kept.[25] Consequently, Fuller literally takes possession of Shakespeare, calling him '[m]y author',[26] just as he had figuratively taken possession of her. She explains, 'My author could read the Roman nature too, – read it in the sternness of Coriolanus, and in the varied wealth of Caesar.''.[27] 'But', she adds, 'he viewed these men of will as only one kind of men; he kept them in their place, and I found that he, who could understand the Roman, yet expressed in Hamlet a deeper thought.'[28] Clearly, Fuller found Shakespeare appealing because the play-wright comprehended and expressed the full range of human experience – the masculine (represented by the warrior's decisive acts) as well as the feminine (represented by the prince's pensive meditations[29]) – and did so in such a way as to speak to all. Indeed, Shake-speare's egalitarian impulse informs Fuller's most comprehensive plea for an egalitarian society.

This plea first took shape as 'The Great Lawsuit – Man *versus* Men; Woman *versus* Women', an essay, as Fuller later noted, that 'excited a good deal of sympathy, and still more interest'.[30] Consequently, 'in compliance with wishes expressed from many quarters', Fuller reproduced her essay, in 'modified and ex-panded' form, as *Woman in the Nineteenth Century* in 1845.[31] As Joel Myerson notes, 'The

---

22 Ibid., pp. 33–4.   23 Ibid., p. 34.
24 Ibid., p. 35.
25 Ibid. The garden, of course, is a space traditionally associated with the feminine realm.
26 Ibid., p. 35.
27 Ibid.   28 Ibid.
29 Although Fuller stops short of directly equating Hamlet with the feminine, her juxtaposition of the aggressively masculine Coriolanus with the less assertive Hamlet clearly suggests that she associates Hamlet's relative passivity with the feminine.
30 Margaret Fuller, *Woman in the Nineteenth Century* (1845; New York, 1971), p. 13.
31 Ibid., p. 13.

book sold well: all 1,500 copies went and a pirated edition appeared in England.'[32]

Although readers found the book's thesis – that women were the intellectual equals of men and should be treated as such – provocative and engaging, they found its structure baffling. For example, Boston social reformer Orestes Augustus Brownson, accustomed to reading (traditionally masculine) linear prose, criticized this structure:

The book before us . . . is no book, but a long talk. . . . It has neither beginning, middle, nor end, and may be read backwards as well as forwards, and from the center outwards each way, without affecting the continuity of the thought or the succession of ideas. We see no reason why it should stop where it does, or why the lady might not keep on talking in the same strain till doomsday, unless prevented by want of breath.[33]

Subsequent readers have echoed Brownson's criticism. However, '[t]he problem with this cumulative critical consensus', as Annette Kolodny has recently pointed out, 'is that it commits us to believing that the only woman invited as an intellectual equal into the Transcendental Club . . . was somehow incompetent'.[34] Rightly considering such a belief to be absurd, Kolodny has challenged it; she has historicized the book's project and its rhetorical strategies so that we might better evaluate their merit.

In historicizing the book's project, Kolodny, like most contemporary scholars, focuses on its feminist agenda. This focus is certainly understandable, for the book helped fuel the feminist sentiment that led to the first women's rights convention in Seneca Falls, New York, and that culminated in the first wave of feminist protest. Privileging this agenda, however, inevitably leads Kolodny to read Fuller's treatise as an address primarily to and for women. As Kolodny explains, 'if we take seriously Fuller's injunction to her female readers that they set aside the habit 'of being taught and led by men', then we understand that Fuller wanted not only to put forward a radical critique of all

'arbitrary barriers' to women's free development', but also that 'as a *woman* speaking for women', she wanted 'to put forward a treatise that would not simply replicate the strategies that might have been employed by any of her well-intentioned male contemporaries'.[35] Therefore, Kolodny concludes that 'Fuller was consciously trying to fashion a set of rhetorical strategies appropriate to the emerging feminist consciousness of her era'.[36]

When, in the preface to *Woman in the Nineteenth Century*, however, Fuller describes her philosophy, she makes it clear that she considers women and men 'two halves of one thought', and she subsequently emphasizes that she places 'no especial stress on the welfare of either'.[37] I would argue, therefore, that Fuller, who 'spoke as much with the voice of a humanist as of a feminist',[38] was attempting a project even more ambitious than what Kolodny describes. In short, Fuller was attempting to establish a set of rhetorical strategies that would enable women to communicate their experiences not only within a community of other women (which would segregate them), but also within a larger community, a community, that is, which also included men (which would integrate them). Only these strategies would enable women and

---

32 Joel Myerson, *Dictionary of Literary Biography*, 210 vols. to date (Detroit, 1978), vol. 1, p. 69.

33 As quoted in Annette Kolodny, 'Inventing a Feminist Discourse: Rhetoric and Resistance in Margaret Fuller's *Woman in the Nineteenth Century*', *New Literary History*, 25 (1994), p. 357.

34 Ibid., p. 359. The Transcendental Club, initiated in 1836, included (among others) Ralph Waldo Emerson, Bronson Alcott, W. E. Channing, Nathaniel Hawthorne, Theodore Parker, and Henry David Thoreau.

35 Ibid., p. 359.

36 Ibid., p. 361. Specifically, Kolodny argues that Richard Whately's *Elements of Rhetoric*, which Fuller used when she taught at the Greene Street School in Providence, Rhode Island, from 1837–8, informs Fuller's treatise.

37 Fuller, *Woman*, p. 13.

38 Margaret V. Allen, 'The Political and Social Criticism of Margaret Fuller', *South Atlantic Quarterly*, 72 (1973), p. 563.

men to engage in what Mikhail Bakhtin would later term a dialogue. Fuller foresaw that such a dialogue would have far-reaching implications not only in the political arena (which her treatise most directly addresses), but also in educational and literary circles, for it would give women and men a forum through which to share the riches of their respective traditions, and, in doing so, reinvigorate them. After all, as Fuller points out, 'the development of the one [man and his traditions] cannot be effected without that of the other [woman and her traditions]'.[39]

While Fuller's proposal is highly idealistic, it is at the same time shrewdly pragmatic. She realized that her project was an ambitious one and that its success hinged on her ability to persuade all of her readers, both women and men, to devote the full measure of their energy, influence, and cooperation to executing it. Therefore, she immediately requests 'a sincere and patient attention from those who open the following pages at all', and she reinforces her request by addressing both women and men in turn:

I solicit of *women* that they will lay it to heart to ascertain what is for them the liberty of law. It is for this, and not for any, the largest, extension of partial privileges that I seek. I ask them, if interested by these suggestions, to search their own experience and intuitions for better, and fill up with fit materials the trenches that hedge them in. From *men* I ask a noble and earnest attention to anything that can be offered on this great and still obscure subject, such as I have met from many with whom I stand in private relations.[40]

Fuller no doubt anticipated that the majority of her female readers would give her proposal their attention and support both freely and from the outset. Her proposal's very title, after all, suggested that she was writing on their behalf, and its central ideas – that women should have educational opportunities, egalitarian marriages, and economic independence – confirmed that. Therefore, Fuller very logically (though rather ironically, given her proposal's subject matter)

concentrates on gaining her *male* readers' support. She knew, after all, that while men might in principle agree that 'the idea of Man, however imperfectly brought out, has been far more so than that of Woman', they nevertheless might in practice resist sharing the power which would enable women to 'take [their] turn in the full pulsation',[41] enable them, in other words, to experience the opportunities that men had for so long taken for granted. Fuller's decision to curry favour with her male readers was a sound one, for it was they alone, after all, who possessed the right to vote, and, in turn, to legislate the changes that would lead to the egalitarian society she envisioned.

With this in mind, Fuller opens *Woman in the Nineteenth Century* with a rhetorical strategy designed to encourage men to empathize with women and their place in society. She presents two familiar quotations: 'Frailty, thy name is Woman' and 'The Earth waits for her Queen', and then immediately – and rather daringly – revises them: 'Frailty, thy name is Man', and 'The Earth waits for its King.'[42] By unexpectedly shifting these quotations' focus from women to men, Fuller effectively forces her male readers to experience a corresponding shift in their perspective, and, in the process, to reconsider their preconceived ideas about women's frailties and especially about their strengths. Fuller realized, after all, that effecting such a shift in perspective was essential in successfully introducing any appeal.

As Fuller's treatise continues to unfold, it becomes clear that Timothy Fuller's Prospero-like insistence that his daughter learn his language and read his books at long last benefited her. Indeed, it enabled Fuller to exhibit her familiarity with the patriarchal tradition, and, in doing so, to establish her credibility with her male readers. More importantly, however, it enabled her to identify which of men's various

---

[39] Fuller, *Woman*, p. 13.
[40] Ibid., p. 14, emphasis added.
[41] Ibid., pp. 23, 24.   [42] Ibid., p. 15.

religious, legal, and especially literary texts advanced the idea of an egalitarian society – either outright or in spirit – so that she could then either cite them as supporting evidence, or, as was more frequently necessary, subvert them to her purpose. Either way, Fuller places her male readers in an interesting quandary; they cannot argue against her text without in effect also arguing against their own texts (since her text encompasses their own), and, by extension, against some of their highest religious, legal, and literary authorities.

Fuller's ability to subvert patriarchal *literary* texts to her advantage is particularly effective, primarily because she perceives what many of her male readers almost certainly overlooked. In short, she recognizes that these texts typically present female characters as objects – the muse, the beloved, the temptress – and therefore as unimportant except as they relate to and serve the purpose of the texts' male characters. To illustrate this point, she recounts the myth of Orpheus and Eurydice. As Jeffrey Steele notes, male Romantic artists 'celebrated' Orpheus as an image of man's 'mastery over Nature, the unconscious, and woman'.[43] Fuller, however, 'knew that Orpheus' great flaw was lack of faith in Eurydice'; it was this lack of faith that prompted Orpheus to succumb to his curiosity and look back at Eurydice before they had arisen from the underworld, causing Orpheus to lose Eurydice once again'.[44] Therefore, Fuller interprets Orpheus 'as a symbol of man in general' and 'suggests that he failed to raise Eurydice (woman) up to his level'.[45] Realizing that man is unable 'to rescue woman', Fuller decides 'to reverse the process and allow woman to rescue man from his own underworld – patriarchal prejudice'.[46] Indeed, Fuller boldly asserts 'that the time is come when Eurydice is to call for an Orpheus, rather than Orpheus for Eurydice. . .'.[47] By making this assertion, Fuller suggests, in other words, that the time had come to grant the traditionally objectified Eurydice, and, by extension, the female characters and women she represents,

with subjectivity, with a speaking voice, and, in turn, with the power to initiate a Bakhtinian dialogue with the patriarchal educational and literary tradition.

With *Woman in the Nineteenth Century*, Fuller does just this. Significantly, however, she does so not by appropriating Orpheus and Eurydice or any of the other Greek myths, which deny women a voice, but by appropriating Shakespeare's *Tempest*, which offers them a voice, albeit a subdued one.[48] Indeed, Fuller, who insisted 'that the modern use of myth begins in understanding that the ideas and ideals which are represented in mythic heroes and heroines are important only insofar as they have a practical bearing on ourselves and our daily lives',[49] casts Prospero's daughter, Miranda, as her mythic heroine. In doing so, Fuller changes the tenor of Miranda's voice from questioning to assertive, even authoritative, and she underscores the need for Miranda, and, again by extension, the female intellectuals and artists she represents, to have such a voice by embedding her American Miranda myth within multiple layers of dialogue, the forum through which Fuller seeks to unite the masculine and feminine educational and literary traditions.

Because of this, Fuller's emphasis on dialogue deserves special attention. On the broadest level, of course, the whole of Fuller's treatise evokes a dialogue. As Kolodny observes, Fuller

---

[43] Jeffrey Steele, introduction, *The Essential Margaret Fuller* (New Brunswick, 1992), p. xxi.

[44] Ibid., p. xxii.

[45] Ibid.   [46] Ibid.

[47] Fuller, *Woman*, p. 23.

[48] While it is true, as Alden T. Vaughan and Virginia Mason Vaughan point out, that 'a character's importance' cannot 'be qualified' (*Shakespeare's Caliban: A Cultural History* [Cambridge, 1991] p. 7), it is nevertheless telling, as Marvin Spevack has documented, that in Shakespeare's *Tempest*, Miranda speaks only 6.242 per cent of the play's words (as noted in Vaughan and Vaughan, p. 7, fn 10).

[49] Robert D. Richardson, Jr, 'Margaret Fuller and Myth', *Prospects: An Annual of American Cultural Studies*, 4 (1979), p. 169.

'mimic[s] the polyphony of conversation' by introducing 'a variety of voices – her own, the autobiographical Miranda's, her anonymous correspondent's, and even the wholly fictive 'irritated trader' determined to maintain authority over his wife'.[50] Moreover, she suggests the 'give and take' of dialogue by including 'lengthy selections from a variety of authors – a speech by John Quincy Adams, a poem by the young transcendentalist, William Ellery Channing, and a passage from the French essayist, Suzanne Necker, among others – even when she [does] not wholly agree with the point of view expressed'.[51] Because the vast majority of these selections are from male-authored texts, Fuller puts her male readers at ease even as she begins to suggest her frustration with their dominance of the educational and literary tradition.

Because she is proposing that women be given a voice within this tradition, Fuller cleverly introduces just such a voice (her own) into her treatise. Indeed, throughout *Woman in the Nineteenth Century*, Fuller frequently shifts into first person, addressing her readers directly and thereby evoking yet another level of dialogue. Significantly, she addresses her readers most extensively when she introduces her American Miranda figure, and the way in which she organizes her address demonstrates that she knows how to use her voice effectively. She first tells her readers about her American Miranda's father, describing him as 'a man who cherished no sentimental reverence for Woman, but a firm belief in the equality of the sexes', as a man, in other words, remarkably similar to Shakespeare's Prospero and to the Prospero-like Timothy Fuller, Jr.[52] Fuller explains:

She [Fuller's American Miranda] was his eldest child, and came to him at an age when he needed a companion. From the time she could speak and go alone, he addressed her not as a plaything, but as a living mind. Among the few verses he ever wrote was a copy addressed to this child, when the first locks were cut from her head; and the reverence

expressed on this occasion for that cherished head, he never belied. It was to him the temple of immortal intellect. He respected his child, however, too much to be an indulgent parent. He called on her for clear judgment, for courage, for honor and fidelity; in short, for such virtues as he knew. In so far as he possessed the keys to the wonders of this universe, he allowed free use of them to her, and, by the incentive of a high expectation, he forbade, so far as possible, that she should let the privilege lie idle.[53]

Because this description depicts Miranda's father as benevolent and remarkably generous, Fuller continues to put her male readers at ease, even as she begins to suggest that the patriarchal educational and literary tradition Miranda's father represents is at times inflexible. Therefore, it is tempting to assume, as Elaine Showalter does, that Fuller is simply 'retelling' Shakespeare's Miranda story, and that in doing so, she is inaugurating 'a central and influential tradition of the American feminist intellectual – as motherless and isolated from other women'.[54]

But Fuller does not simply 'retell' Shakespeare's Miranda story; she appropriates it, then extends it beyond Shakespeare's script. While Shakespeare presents Miranda in her youth – sheltered, inexperienced, and questioning – Fuller presents her as an adult – daring, confident, and assertive – who possesses the self-assurance maturity brings. Indeed, Fuller's American Miranda takes her place 'easily, not only in the world of organized being, but in the world of mind'.[55] As Fuller explains,

---

[50] Kolodny, 'Inventing a Feminist Discourse', p. 367. By creating the character of the 'irritated trader', Fuller was able to incorporate the voice of a working-class New Englander alongside the voices of the educated elite.

[51] Ibid., p. 368.

[52] Fuller, *Woman*, p. 38.   [53] Ibid., p. 39.

[54] Elaine Showalter, 'Miranda and Cassandra: The Discourse of the Feminist Intellectual', *Traditions and the Talents of Women*, ed. Florence Howe (Urbana, 1991), p. 314.

[55] Fuller, *Woman*, p. 39.

A dignified sense of self-dependence was given as all her portion, and she found it a sure anchor. Herself securely anchored, her relations with others were established with equal security. . . . The world was free to her, and she lived freely in it. Outward adversity came, and inward conflict; but that faith and self-respect had early been awakened which must always lead, at last, to an outward serenity and an inward peace.[56]

While Shakespeare's Miranda follows the script written for her (by marrying Ferdinand, and, because of Jacobean marriage and property laws, subsequently forfeiting her educational and literary inheritance to him), Fuller, herself an American Miranda, makes it clear that *her* Miranda scripts her *own* role. As Fuller asserts,

She had taken a course of her own, and no man stood in her way. Many of her acts had been unusual, but excited no uproar. Few helped, but none checked her; and the many men who knew her mind and her life, showed to her confidence as to a brother, gentleness as to a sister. And not only refined, but very coarse men approved and aided one in whom they saw resolution and clearness of design. Her mind was often the leading one, always effective.[57]

To emphasize just how effective, Fuller actually transcribes the imagined dialogue she had with her American Miranda, letting Miranda speak for herself and thereby evoking yet another dialogue. This dialogue suggests, of course, that there is more than one American Miranda and that all of them, not just the privileged few, deserve access to and inclusion in the patriarchal educational and literary tradition. As Fuller's American Miranda puts it, 'I have been fortunate, and this should not be.'[58] By allowing her American Miranda to articulate her own criticism of the patriarchal educational literary traditions, Fuller vicariously yet effectively criticizes those traditions without personally alienating her male readers. After all, behind Miranda's voice is not only Fuller's own, but also Shakespeare's; because Shakespeare's voice is culturally authoritative, it lends force to Miranda's criticism.

And Miranda's criticism is pointed. As Miranda recalls, 'Religion was early awakened in my soul, – a sense that what the soul is capable to ask it must attain, and that, though I might be aided and instructed by others, I must depend on myself as the only constant friend.'[59] Miranda complains, however, that the 'self-dependence' that was 'honored' in her, 'is deprecated as a fault in most women', noting that these women 'are taught to learn their rule from without, not to unfold it from within'.[60] 'This', she concludes, 'is the fault of Man, who is still vain, and wishes to be more important to Woman than, by right, he should be.'[61] She notes, for instance, that men, 'who think that nothing is so much to be dreaded for a woman as originality of thought or character', so overload women with precepts that women's 'minds are impeded by doubts till they lose their chance of fair, free proportions'.[62] Therefore, Miranda explains, it is necessary to get women 'to the point from which they shall naturally develop self-respect, and learn self-help'.[63] Because her own father had encouraged her to develop these traits, she had once thought that all men 'would help to forward this state of things'.[64] She admits, however, that she has learned otherwise; evidently, she has come to realize that even her well-meaning male contemporaries generally assume that only men are capable of achieving any real educational and literary success.[65]

---

56 Ibid.   57 Ibid., pp. 39–40.
58 Ibid., p. 40.   59 Ibid.
60 Ibid.   61 Ibid.
62 Ibid., pp. 40–1.   63 Ibid., p. 41.
64 Ibid., p. 41.
65 Fuller reiterates this idea in a subsequent passage on p. 120. There, she explains that 'two fine figures', a husband and wife, once 'stood before' her discussing their daughter's education. 'The father', she notes, was 'of very intellectual aspect, his falcon eye softened by affection as he looked down on his fair child; she the image of himself, only more graceful and brilliant in expression'. Fuller transcribes the conversation she overheard:

Their assumption frustrates Fuller's American Miranda. Recalling a time when 'an intimate friend of the opposite sex said, in a fervent moment, that [she] "deserved in some star to be a man"', she asserts, 'Let it not be said, wherever there is energy or creative genius, 'She has a masculine mind."'[66] Fuller's American Miranda had 'faith that the feminine side, the side of love, of beauty, of holiness, was now to have its full chance, and that, if either were better, it was better now to be a woman; for even the slightest achievement of good was furthering an especial work of our time'.[67]

With *Woman in the Nineteenth Century*, Fuller does, of course, further this 'especial work'. Yet her treatise not only influences the political arena, but also the educational and literary traditions, for her treatise – with its literary borrowings, its clearly sketched characters, and, of course, its multiple layers of dialogue – suggests Fuller's impulse not only to novelize, but also, in fact, to write novels. Indeed, in 1835, 'while reading George Sand, she briefly considered such a possibility'.[68] As Fuller noted in her journal, 'These books [novels] have made me for the first time think I might write into such shapes what I know of human nature.'[69] However, she ultimately opted not to do so. 'I have always thought', she explains, 'that I would keep all that behind the curtain, that I would not write, like a woman, of love and hope and disappointment, but like a man, of the world of intellect and action.'[70] For Fuller, as Showalter explains, 'fiction was too negatively associated with the emotional and the feminine'.[71] Ironically, though, Fuller's treatise lent women's novels legitimacy; by extending Miranda beyond the confines of Shakespeare's script, Fuller provides women with a model of the female intellectual and artist, and she suggests the theme – access to and inclusion in the patriarchal educational and

literary tradition – which subsequent American Mirandas, including Harriet Beecher Stowe and Louisa May Alcott, and, in this century, Katherine Anne Porter, Madeleine L'Engle, and Gloria Naylor, would soon develop.

Perhaps on some level, Fuller realized that this was to be her role. At the close of her treatise, after all, she poses these seemingly prophetic questions: 'And will not she soon appear? – the woman who shall vindicate their birthright for all women; who shall teach them what to claim, and how to use what they obtain? Shall not her name be for her era Victoria, for her country and life Virginia? Yet predictions are rash; she herself must teach us to give her the fitting name'.[72] With Fuller's *Woman in the Nineteenth Century*, she does; it is clearly Miranda.

'I shall not have Maria brought too forward. If she knows too much, she will never find a husband; superior women hardly ever can.'

'Surely', said his wife, with a blush, 'you wish Maria to be as good and wise as she can, whether it will help her to marriage or not.'

'No', he persisted, 'I want her to have a sphere and a home, and some one to protect her when I am gone.'

Though this father clearly wants the best for his daughter, his concern that she have a 'sphere and a home' also suggests that he wants her to stay in that sphere rather than venture into the male domain. But as Fuller had earlier explained, 'the only reason why women ever assume what is more important to you [men], is because you prevent them from finding out what is fit for themselves' (*Woman*, p. 63). 'Were they free', she explains, 'were they wise fully to develop the strength and beauty of Woman; they would never wish to be men, or man-like' (*Woman*, p. 63).

66 Fuller, *Woman*, pp. 41, 43.
67 Ibid., p. 41.
68 Showalter, 'Miranda and Cassandra', p. 318.
69 As quoted in ibid., p. 318.
70 As quoted in ibid., p. 318.
71 Ibid., p. 318.
72 Fuller, *Woman*, p. 177.

THE MAGICIAN IN LOVE

JULIA GRIFFIN

Men (eternal hunters, novelty seekers, insatiable beings), men in their natural lives, pursue the concrete no less than the ideal – qualities not seldom found combined in fairy childhood.

(*Concerning the Eccentricities of Cardinal Pirelli*, p. 696)

Do you love me, master? No?
Mine would, sir, were I human.

(*The Tempest* 4.1.48; 5.1.20)

He got out his *Tempest* and tried, as a beginning, the sortes. And he went no further.

(*The Desire and Pursuit of the Whole*, p. 199)

INTRODUCTION

This essay is concerned with one small episode in the afterlife, long, rich and often strange, of *The Tempest*. At different times, to different people, the play has meant very different things: the triumph of harmony and order; the imposition of tyranny; a farewell to art. That last response is an especially persistent one. Legends of autobiography and finality have long invested the play.[1] The beleaguered author, Shakespeare/Prospero, works his magic in splendid isolation, aided only by his own powers of inspiration; the end of the play is the end of the plays. That old interpretation – so well known and so very unfashionable now among critics – is important in the background of this essay; my subject is a sort of development of this, a development into something much less familiar.

The Tempest has been many things to its recipients, but one thing it has hardly ever been

is a love story. What critic has shared Prospero's concern for Miranda's sexuality? And yet, earlier in this century, the play did offer one class of reader a parable not only about creativity but about love. Not, however, Miranda's love. For at least two writers, both once-scandalous, the relationship between Prospero and Ariel provided an image of extraordinary suggestiveness and appeal.

I. IN LONELY ENGLAND

For this little survey of magical islands, England is the starting-point. I begin with two stories with an English setting. These are not derived from *The Tempest*, but they are fantasies contemporary and related to the longer works which are (I shall argue) so derived, and thus make another kind of context and introduction for those works.

The first is an obscure short story with a famous name. 'The Priest and the Acolyte' was published anonymously by John Francis Bloxam, an undergraduate at Oxford, in 1894. In this story, there are two important characters: one is a priest, the other is a boy, and they act

---

[1] The theory has been traced back to Thomas Campbell in 1838: see S. Schoenbaum, *William Shakespeare: A Compact Documentary Life* (New York and Oxford, corr. edn 1987), p. 278. The Prologue to *The Enchanted Island*, Dryden and Davenant's adaptation, draws an implicit analogy between Shakespeare and Prospero as magicians. Prospero the colonial despot perhaps goes back to Browning's monologue, 'Caliban upon Setebos' (1864).

together against the world. They lose; for, as the author lugubriously repeats,

And whosoever shall fall on this stone shall be broken: but on whomsoever it shall fall, it will grind him to powder.[2]

The priest, Ronald Heatherington, has come to a remote curacy, and the boy, Wilfred, is his only comfort; they fall rapidly in love, meet secretly in the priest's room, and are found there, cuddling rapturously in a chair, by a senior cleric. The lovers design a beautiful *Liebestod* by drinking poison out of the sacramental chalice, and are found in all their finery next morning:

When the sun was rising in the heavens it cast one broad ray upon the altar of the little chapel. The tapers were burning still, scarcely half-burnt through. The sad-faced figure of the crucifix hung there in its majestic calm. On the steps of the altar was stretched the long, ascetic frame of the young priest, robed in the sacred vestments; close beside him, with his curly head pillowed on the gorgeous embroideries that covered his breast, lay the beautiful boy in scarlet and lace. Their arms were round each other; a strange hush lay like a shroud over all.[3]

They lose, but they also win.

The story shows some courage – the amount it takes to publish things anonymously in one's own student magazine; it is far more defiant in its story-line than anything published by its first critic, Oscar Wilde. It is also extremely crude: Wilde told Ada Leverson that it was 'to my ears, too direct: there is no nuance . . .'[4] Unfortunately for him, Bloxam, that 'undergraduate of strange beauty',[5] had produced exactly what the prosecuting counsel required, and Wilde was cross-examined closely on 'The Priest . . .' at his trial. (There he declared: 'I have read it only once . . . and nothing will induce me to read it again' (a sentiment for which all its readers will have some sympathy).)[6]

Here is another short story, better known: 'The Music on the Hill' by 'Saki' (1911). In this story, the duo of man and boy becomes a trio:

man, boy, and intrusive, voyeuristic, unwanted woman. The man, a shadowy figure known as 'Dead Mortimer', has a deep allegiance to the woods – that is, nature at its least controlled; he also has a silly young wife with the mockingly inept name of Sylvia, who has managed to marry him 'in spite of his unaffected indifference to women'.[7] On a visit to their country house, Sylvia insults the 'Wood Gods' by removing the bunch of grapes she sees that Mortimer has left in homage, and the god Pan appears to her, in the form of a beautiful, scowling boy. Unnerved, Sylvia would now like to return to town; but her husband makes no move – an immobility which signifies, in hardly disguised terms, a preference for the boy over his wife – and she is killed by a wild stag:

The antlers drove straight at her breast, the acrid smell of the hunted animal was in her nostrils, but her eyes were filled with the horror of something she saw other than her oncoming death. And in her ears rang the echo of a boy's laughter, golden and equivocal.[8]

This vicious little story and Bloxam's have, I think, deep roots in common. Saki increases the cast list without really altering it: he adds a spectator for the man's love, and a victim for

---

2 'X' [John Francis Bloxam], *The Priest and the Acolyte* (London, 1907), pp. 46, 71. The story was first published anonymously in the first and only issue of *The Chameleon* in 1894.

3 *The Priest and the Acolyte*, pp. 70–1.

4 Quoted in Richard Ellmann, *Oscar Wilde* (London, 1987), p. 404.

5 Ellmann, *Oscar Wilde*, p. 403.

6 I have taken this quotation from p. 16 of the 1907 Lotus Press reprint of Bloxam's story, which comes with a long introduction by 'Stuart Mason' [Christopher Millard] refuting the persistent belief that Wilde was the author. It should be said that, whatever his shudders here, he had urged Bloxam to publish it (Ellmann, *Oscar Wilde*, p. 404).

7 *The Complete Works of Saki* (London, 1980), p. 161. Their surname is 'Seltoun', an odd enough name to suggest that a symbolic anagram is intended: 'net-soul'?

8 Ibid., p. 166.

the supernatural power involved. 'Dead' Mortimer is unmoving himself, but Pan acts for him, liberating and revenging him. The acolyte and the wood god are both boys, both beautiful, both the object of devotion on the part of the older male protagonist – and both involved in a private, supernatural alliance.[9]

II. DEATH COMES FOR THE CARDINAL-ARCHBISHOP

Both these short stories are, in their different ways, the wish-fulfilment dreams of homosexual men in a particularly unfriendly social climate. In such a climate, Shakespeare too could offer a little warmth. The next two parts of this essay will be spent on two works – much longer, more ambitious, and more interesting than the stories – which seem to me clearly related to them, and also to *The Tempest*.

If Shakespeare has been identified with Prospero, Ronald Firbank, master of modernist camp, has been identified with his own near-ultimate hero: the eponym of his last complete work, *Concerning the Eccentricities of Cardinal Pirelli*, first published posthumously in 1926. To quote Brigid Brophy's marvellous study,

The great scarlet splurge of his Cardinal is the most tragic and the fullest of Firbank's self-portraits . . .

Shakespeare is not the obvious begetter of this work. Brophy continues:

. . . and it is a portrait of Firbank in Wilde's tragic robes.[10]

Cardinal Pirelli is Firbank, to Brophy, and he is also Oscar Wilde: 'Pirelli', she says, 'is Wilde unidealised by prudence . . .' This more familiar comparison may be taken first.

Firbank's obsession with Wilde is obvious, and its various implications have been brilliantly illuminated by Brophy; one that she surprisingly missed was Bloxam. It was to his magazine that Wilde had contributed his 'Phrases and Philosophies for the Use of the Young', of which the first is probably the best known:

The first duty in life is to be as artificial as possible. What the second duty is no one has as yet discovered.[11]

That reappears, full of new, nervous life, in *Pirelli*:

'And always be obedient, dear child,' the Cardinal was saying; 'it is one of the five things in Life that matter most.'
'Which are the others, sir?' [. . .]
'Never mind now. Come here.'[12]

Also in Bloxam's magazine was 'The Priest and the Acolyte', with all its associations for a cultist of Wilde. These are reasons for thinking that Firbank read the story; *Pirelli* itself is, to my mind, proof. Bloxam provided a dingy core for his own amazing nacre: the wan priest Ronald (a name to attract Firbank's notice) becomes the magnificent Don Alvaro Narciso Hernando Pirelli, Cardinal-Archbishop of Clemenza; and the delicate acolyte Wilfred becomes the brazen Chicklet – 'Don Wilful', as the Cardinal privately calls him.[13]

---

9 A subject like this cuts through other literary webs – either that, or it is quickly wrapped up in them. Saki's story clearly belongs to another little genre popular at the time: the 'Ariel in Mayfair' or 'A Faun in the Cotswolds' type of whimsy so cruelly immortalized by Max Beerbohm in his story 'Maltby and Braxton' (in *Seven Men* (1919)). E. M. Forster contributed – see *The Celestial Omnibus* (1911). In this sort of story, Ariel/Pan/a Faun enters and disrupts the conventional world, urban or rural, thus providing a fantasy of escape and/or revenge. It may well be that the genre was particularly popular with homosexual writers. Another of Saki's stories, 'Gabriel-Ernest', about a hen-pecked man whose life is invaded by a boy-werewolf, has affinities with it too.

10 Brigid Brophy, *Prancing Novelist: a Defence of Fiction in the Form of a Critical Biography in Praise of Ronald Firbank* (London, 1973), p. 564.

11 *The Complete Works of Oscar Wilde* with an introduction by Vyvyan Holland (London and Glasgow, rev. edn, 1966), p. 1205.

12 *The Complete Ronald Firbank* (London, 1961), p. 694.

13 Pirelli's own name seems to be patched together from pantomime and commedia dell'arte: Pierrot, Pulchinella, pirouette and, as Ellis Hanson notes, peril (see *Decadence and Catholicism* (Cambridge, MA and London, 1997), p. 361.)

In Bloxam's short story, Catholic ritual seems to represent aesthetic titillation, and also something more: civilized, semi-familiar magic.[14] In Firbank, however – a convert, but a continually lapsing one – Catholicism produced more complex, less stereotypical reflections. In the later novels it co-exists rather awkwardly with Islam, and in *Pirelli*, it overlaps with magic in its less comfortable forms:

'Perhaps a brief mass . . . We say all but the Black.'

'Oh?'

'One must draw the line somewhere!' Don Moscosco declared . . .[15]

The subject of this conversation is the baptism of a dog – the forbidden act which began the book and the ruin of the Cardinal, but is here, in the penultimate chapter, negotiable once again. Pirelli himself is described as an 'old ogre' by his witch-like opponent, Madame Poco; that is not the book's final verdict, but something of the magician clings to him even to the end.

Like Prospero, Pirelli pays for his unorthodox behaviour with exile. After the pup-christening, he 'flees the capital', and he spends the long eighth chapter at the 'slowly decaying monastery of the Desierto',[16] before facing a longer, involuntary journey to answer charges in Rome. The movement of exile and return is obfuscated, however. Pirelli never gets to Rome, and the last chapter shifts him, unexplicitly, back to his cathedral at Clemenza, where he pursues his mercenary dream-boy over urns and monuments until his heart gives way.[17] The cathedral, 'the great fane', 'God's cage; the cage of God!'[18] is the scene of his transgressions and his death, the beginning and the end of the book. The two fatal acts, the christening and the pursuit, are, from one perspective, the same: as Brophy says,

to administer to a dog a sacrament which convention reserves to another species is to spend on a boy the love which convention directs to the other sex.[19]

Instead of suffering a conventional punishment, Pirelli pays by repetition – an idea both poetic and religious.

The Desierto monastery, scene of his brief exile, is a solitary place for the Cardinal – 'It's queer, dears, how I'm lonely!' he remarks to his furniture – but also a haven: 'Lovely as Paradise, oppressive perhaps as Eden'.[20] It is different from Clemenza, but the book does not offer a contrast as sharp as that between Prospero's Island and the absent Milan. Clemenza is more crowded, but Pirelli's significant others travel, it seems, along with him: at the ruined monastery he still receives the ambiguous services of Madame Poco and the Chicklet. Madame Poco is a housekeeper of sorts, a witchy Sycorax-figure, intent on Pirelli's undoing and made the more sinister by her continued affection for him: before her mirror, she practises a 'Dance of Indictment':

Finger rigid, she would advance ominously with slow, Salomé-like liftings of the knees upon a phantom Cardinal: 'And thus I accuse thee!' or 'I denounce thee, Don Alvaro, for,' etc.[21]

---

14 Bloxam later took orders in the Church of England: see Hanson, *Decadence and Catholicism*, p. 310. This book provides extremely interesting analyses of many of the authors discussed here.

15 p. 687. Firbank's Islam is a gloriously orientalized affair which he likes to twitch brightly against the camp demure of his Church. *Valmouth* fades out with the priests waiting helplessly for the niece of an Islamic masseuse, who has run away from her wedding; in *Pirelli*, Muley, a 'negress maid', is given the end of the penultimate chapter to grieve over Pirelli's cathedral – 'a Mosque profaned' (p. 689). Blasphemy provides exoticism within the Church – sometimes within the building. In his earlier short stories, several ladies either adopt the title of saint or dream of erecting stained-glass windows to themselves: Mrs Shamefoot, in *Vainglory*, actually manages this.

16 Firbank, *Pirelli*, p. 675.

17 Like all Firbank's novels, *Pirelli* is structured with delicate care. Chapters 1–3 take place in Clemenza; chapter 4 in Rome; chapters 5–7 in Clemenza; chapter 8 in the Desierto; chapters 9–10 in Clemenza again. This forms a shape both elegant and broken – like the hero.

18 Firbank, *Pirelli*, p. 697.

19 *Prancing Novelist*, p. 564.

20 Firbank, *Pirelli*, pp. 683, 675.

21 Ibid., p. 666. Salomé is a favourite Firbankian prop, no doubt because of Oscar Wilde.

Like him, she is childless – there is no Miranda and no Caliban; but a parodic family unit is completed by the presence of the Chicklet, 'an oncoming-looking child' as he is first described,[22] who will complete Pirelli's destruction. The Chicklet is one of the heartbreaking 'dancing-choir-boys' of the Cathedral, who unite childish prettiness and disengaged knowingness in a mixture the book presents as irresistibly sexy:

And in the passing silence the treble voice of Tiny was left talking all alone.

'. . . frightened me like Father did, when he kissed me in the dark like a lion':- a remark that was greeted by an explosion of coughs.[23]

'Fairy childhood' may, as Firbank says, combine the concrete and the ideal;[24] but the combination may hurt, as Pirelli learns in his darkened cathedral, that final night:

'You'd not do that if you were fond of me, boy!' The Cardinal's cheek had paled.

'But I *am* fond of you, sir! Very. Caring without caring: don't you know?'

'So you do care something, child?'

'I care a lot!. . .'

Astride the urn of Ivy – poised in air – the Chicklet pellucidly laughed.[25]

Airy and pellucid, inhuman, the Chicklet may be, but he shares with his friends a firm grasp of the mundane. The boys like money, gifts, perfume, and prestige; they have corresponding dislikes, as we learn at their first appearance.

Low-masses, cheapness, and economy, how they despised them, and how they would laugh at 'Old Ends' who snuffed out the candles.[26]

It is his refusal to accept his beloved's own desires that does for Pirelli in the end. Their final conversation offers the Cardinal a deal he will not recognize:

'You'd do the handsome by me, sir; you'd not be mean?'

'Eh?. . .'

'The Fathers only give us texts; you'd be surprised, your Greatness, at the stinginess of some!'

'. . .?'

'You'd run to something better, sir; you'd give me something more substantial?'

'I'll give you my slipper, child, if you don't come here!' his Eminence warned him.

'Oufarella . . .'

Sarabandish and semi-mythic was the dance that ensued. Leading by a dozen derisive steps Don Light-of-Limb took the nave . . .[27]

'What is't thou canst demand?' demands Prospero, to meet the enraging, inevitable response: 'My liberty' (*The Tempest* 1.2.246). In the end, of course, it is granted:

PROSPERO My Ariel, chick,
That is thy charge. Then to the elements
Be free, and fare thou well.   (5.1.320–2)

'My Ariel, chick', discreetly manipulating for his freedom, is transformed by Firbank into the Chicklet, holding out for a better offer: 'You'd do the handsome by me, sir; you'd not be mean?'. He loses, in his own terms – the Cardinal dies without disbursing; but he escapes from the scene as lightly as any spirit:

With advancing day Don Skylark *alias* Bright-eyes *alias* Don Temptation it seemed had contrived an exit, for the cathedral was become a place of tranquillity and stillness.[28]

He leaves his pursuer behind, dead on the floor of his cathedral, clad in a mitre 'like a wondrous mustard-pot', and nothing else.[29] Ronald Heatherington lays himself out in full priestly gear; Firbank's Cardinal has finally discarded the magic of his robes.

This transformation, though by far the more subtle and complete, is not the first worked by Firbank on a Shakespeare play. Nine years before, he had made an earlier tragedy central and fatal in his novel *Caprice*, the story of a clergyman's daughter whose longing to play Juliet brings her triumph and disaster: early in the morning after her first performance, she falls

---

22 Ibid., p. 655.   23 Ibid., p. 656.
24 See the epigraph to this essay.
25 Firbank, *Pirelli*, pp. 694–5.
26 Ibid., p. 654.   27 Ibid., p. 696.
28 Ibid., p. 697.   29 Ibid., p. 691.

through a stage trapdoor into the well below the theatre. Miss Sinquier (pronounced, probably, 'Sinker'), a hapless, reckless girl, misunderstood and betrayed by her seniors, is a sort of Juliet – or a late addition to those pseudo-Juliets described by John Glavin: heroines of Victorian fiction who act Juliet and re-enact (in some form) her fate.[30] There is a certain limited similarity between Miss Sinquier and Pirelli, another self-destructive performer, unsuspecting and betrayed. *The Tempest* is not so obviously identified, but the Cardinal is no less of a victim to Shakespeare. Consider the final chapter, with its curiously contradictory descriptions of the weather.

The Cardinal, remembering that he has locked the Chicklet into the Cathedral as a punishment for chasing mice during his sermon, gazes out of the window towards the towers.

> It was a night like most.
> Uranus, Venus, Saturn showed overhead their
>   wonted lights . . .

On an amorous whim, he goes out to join the boy.

> Oh, the lovely night! Oh, the lovely night! He stood, leaning on his wand, lost in contemplation of the miracle of it.

From inside the Cathedral, however, it looks different.

> He could distinguish nothing clearly at first beyond the pale forked fugitive lightning through the triple titanic windows of the chancel.

> There was a spell of singing silence, while the dove-grey mystic lightning waxed and waned.
> Aroused as much by it as the Primate's hand, the boy started up with a scream of terror.

Is there a storm, on this final night, or not? What is a 'night like most' like? This 'fugitive', 'mystic' lightning has sufficient reality to waken the dozing Chicklet; but there is no sound, and the dawn breaks in peace:

> Through the chancel windows the day was newly breaking as the oleanders will in spring.[31]

At the start of the book, the Cardinal christened the young police-dog 'Crack'; the first chapter faded with his owner vainly calling him to heel, and thus causing an illusion of thunder: 'Crack, Crack, Crack, Crack . . .'[32] Here, at the end, an illusory tempest overwhelms Pirelli: an allusion and response to the harmless tempest controlled by the magician Prospero at the start of the play.

In his brief retreat at the Desierto, Pirelli is accompanied by his two fatal allies, but he also receives a very different visitor, whose appearance is fleeting but beautiful. After dinner, the lonely Cardinal fills and refills his wine glass . . .

> Sometimes, after the fifth or sixth bumper, the great Theresa herself would flit in from the garden . . .
> She was standing by the window in the fluttered moonshine, holding a knot of whitish heliotropes.
> 'Mother?'
> Saint John of the Cross could scarcely have pronounced the name with more wistful ecstasy.
> Worn and ill, though sublime in laughter, exquisite in tenderness she came towards him.
> '. . . Child?'
> 'Teach me, oh, teach me, dear Mother, the Way of Perfection.'[33]

That St Teresa of Avila should make a visit of mercy – albeit in his tipsy ecstasy – to this carnival Cardinal is Firbank's most daring dream, and one of his showiest triumphs of

---

30 See John Glavin, 'Caught in the Act: Or, the Prosing of Juliet' in Jean I. Marsden (ed.), *The Appropriation of Shakespeare* (Hemel Hempstead, 1991), pp. 93–110. Miss Sinquier, however, cannot really be called a victim to the 'male gaze', as all her fatal attachments are homosexual, more or less – the sort of 'gaze' Firbank preferred.

31 Firbank, *Pirelli*, pp. 691, 692, 692, 694, 697.

32 Ibid., p. 647. Firbank was perhaps borrowing from *Tristram Shandy*: chapter 17 of Book VII (the flight from Death) begins with the word 'Crack', spoken by the narrator six times (apparently referring to the coachman and his whip).

33 Firbank, *Pirelli*, pp. 683–4.

style.[34] I quote it here as a token that, in swirling the simple, tragical oppositions of Bloxam (true love against conventional hypocrisy, true Christian mercy against the merciless Church), Firbank is not writing a simple, frivolous parody of him. At the end of Bloxam's story, the priest and the boy lie together on the floor before 'the sad-faced figure of the crucifix', covered in 'a strange hush . . . like a shroud'; Pirelli's acolyte, a truer Ariel, escapes, but the difference does not express a brutal mockery. The Cardinal is accepted by the good witch, Teresa, and the bad witch, Madame Poco, gives him her blessing in the last words spoken in the book:

Fired by fundamental curiosity, the dame, by degrees, was emboldened to advance. All over was it, with him, then? It looked as though his Eminence was far beyond Rome already.

'May God show His pity on you, Don Alvaro of my heart.'

She remained a short while lost in mingled conjecture. It was certain no morning bell would wake him.

'So.' She stopped to coil her brier-wood chaplet about him in order that he might be less uncovered. 'It's wonderful what us bits of women do with a string of beads, but they don't go far with a gentleman.'

Now that the ache of life, with its fevers, passions, doubts, its routine, vulgarity, and boredom, was over, his serene, unclouded face was a marvelment to behold. Very great distinction and sweetness was visible there, together with much nobility, and love, all magnified and commingled.

'Adios, Don Alvaro of my heart,' she sighed, turning away towards the little garden door ajar . . .[35]

She finds him as tranquil as Milton's Samson – a Samson who has died alone, without hurt to the temple. The sudden protectiveness of the language – the naked word 'dead' is not spoken, and even Pirelli's own nakedness is shielded less by Sycorax's skimpy beads than by the double negative 'less uncovered' – defies both sneer and snigger. His last words are spoken twice, first to the Chicklet and after to 'some phantom image in the air': 'I have

nothing but myself to declare'.[36] It is Oscar Wilde's flamboyant boast, 'Nothing but my genius', stripped down from epigram to epitaph. Pirelli dies as he has lived, a faithful child of Wilde, but also a second Prospero:

Now my charms are all o'erthrown,
And what strength I have's mine own . . .
(5.1.Epilogue 15.1–2)

'Adios, Don Alvaro of my heart.' The witch's indulgence sets him free.

Prospero's prayer has been taken autobiographically; more data excuse the same treatment for Pirelli. By the time he finished the book, Firbank knew that he was dying.[37] The typescript was prepared at the end of April 1925; thirteen months later, he was dead. Pirelli was still unpublished: courage had failed the publisher, who rejected it on 'religious and moral grounds'; so on 23 April, 1926, one month before he died, Firbank made arrangements for producing a collected edition of his work at his own expense if he died within five years of that date. Brigid Brophy asks the pertinent question: '(Did Firbank choose the date on which Shakespeare's birthday is celebrated?)'[38] I think so.

This looks suspiciously tidy; Firbank's fictions, complexly structured, are not so, and neither is his oeuvre. Pirelli is not his last piece of writing. He left an unfinished book, The New Rhythum, which was not published until 1962, and has never been much admired. Neither, by comparison with The Tempest, have critics or audiences shown much interest in Henry VIII or The Two Noble Kinsmen. Perhaps

---

[34] St Teresa comes to the garden in search of a sheet of manuscript, and is thus, among other things, a guardian saint of literature: see Brophy, Prancing Novelist, pp. 24–6. The flowers suggest a memory of that favourite Victorian image, 'Convent Thoughts'.

[35] Firbank, Pirelli, pp. 697–8.

[36] Ibid., p. 697. The jingle is Firbank's. Brophy notes the Wildean echo, Prancing Novelist, p. 566.

[37] He had an illness of the lungs. See, for a more detailed account of this, Brophy, Prancing Novelist, pp. 566–8.

[38] Brophy, Prancing Novelist, p. 568.

the emphatic finality of *Pirelli* and *The Tempest* have something to do with it. But that finality, like so much in the two works, is a trick, a dream, an illusion.

III. VENICE DESERVED

'Sweetness' is a quality distinguished by Firbank in the face of his dead Cardinal. Pirelli does not have any personal enemies, or none of whom he is aware; the darker side of Prospero, now more popular among critics – his taste for dominance and retribution – does not find much reflection anywhere in Firbank's fiction. Though insensitive, exploitative characters are common there, they are usually undetected and never really punished; nor are they heavily abused by the author. The use made of the *Tempest* paradigm by Frederick Rolfe, 'Baron Corvo', was characteristically different. *The Desire and Pursuit of the Whole* (completed 1910; first published 1934), again a last novel, is a direct, personal fantasy of both triumph and revenge. I shall say less about this work than *Pirelli*, partly because it is less enjoyable to read (though also a stylistic wonder, and praised by Graham Greene and W. H. Auden), partly because Corvo makes his adaptation so blatant that less effort is needed to demonstrate it. The hero, Nicholas Crabbe, the usual Corvo self-idol, is in Venice, the casualty of two sets of evil exploiters in England and one apostate bene-factor in Italy. There he tries to devote himself to his books and his Catholicism (those two versions of magic). Like Corvo himself (who signed himself 'Fr. Rolfe' in some sort of hope that 'Frederick' might be taken for 'Father'), Crabbe is not really a priest, but would be so in a better world:

Of course a man with his face and manner and taste and talent and Call, ought to have been a priest . . . The fault [that he wasn't] was hardly his.[39]

The course of the book reveals to him the true monstrosity of yet another pseudo-friend, whom he nick-names Caliban. At a moment of

crisis, he uses *The Tempest* as 'sortes' – a magic text of prediction – and learns that his books, the source of his livelihood, are in danger. Fortunately, he has at his side a strange being who will defend him. This being he has rescued from a house shattered by earthquake – nearly Ariel's cloven pine – at the beginning of the book. (In this way he masters the earthquake, which, as natural disaster, is the book's own tempest.) As an adapter of the Shakespearian *Tempest*, however, Corvo cheats.

The outlines of the story run like this. Crabbe, the hero, is living, temporarily, on a boat, in which he both travels and contemptu-ously benefits the ungrateful expatriate com-munity of the city; he is generally misunder-stood and underappreciated despite being 'the most frantically interesting man alive'.[40] The element of camp there is a defensive disguise for the absolute seriousness with which Corvo/ Crabbe takes his various affronts. All the major characters in the book, bar one, earn Crabbe's loathing and obloquy (his letters to them are amazing); the only exception is his Ariel figure, 'Zildo', a figure of wonderful ambiguity – but ambiguity of a new kind. Pirelli's adored Chicklet is a child-sophisticate who seems not fully human; Zildo, or Gilda, is a girl who plays the part of a male servant and is disguised by both clothing and pronoun almost all the way through the book. She is perfectly human, but freed from any human ties by the earthquake. However, one of Crabbe's principal, self-chosen frustrations is his refusal, despite her flawless beauty and devotion, to admit love for her. In one particularly luxurious scene, Crabbe, who is ambidextrous, is shown writing an historical novel (a masterpiece, of course),

---

[39] Frederick Rolfe (Baron Corvo), *The Desire and Pursuit of the Whole*, ed. Andrew Eburne (London, 1993), p. 38. Corvo's earlier and more famous self-idol, George Arthur Rose, triumphs miraculously over all his evil detractors to become Pope Hadrian VII.

[40] Corvo, *Desire and Pursuit*, p. 43.

while receiving the most reverent kind of massage:

while he wrote in his book with one hand, the other hung down at his side, to be warmed and pressed and twisted and pinched and moulded into flexibility by the gentle force of Zildo. He deliberately submitted himself to this test, danced along this slack-wire, taking horrible, useless risks, as usual. Defiant of weakness, daring danger, he hardened himself by means of these very thrills of contact, making his citadel anew impregnable. If he thought of the effect on Zildo, he only thought of him as undergoing discipline together with his master. As a matter of fact, it was discipline for Zildo – very salutary discipline, discipline of the species which inspires kissing of the rod. Zildo quietly enjoyed his proper emotions. Nicholas permitted himself to have none.[41]

The reason why Crabbe must resist this 'test' – besides the masochistic thrill his resisting gives him – is never really explained; it simply explains itself. Gilda must be Zildo, because Crabbe wants her like that; Zildo is a boy and thus must be resisted. So the delicious tension is set up, and preserved (with teasing little lapses) until the very end.[42]

The Ariel-figure of Firbank is a boy; this Ariel is a girl. Another, and far greater, aberration from the original in Zildo is his patient, selfless love for the stoical Crabbe. Zildo wants only to serve, and to stay. At the very end, he is able to match the original benefit by saving Crabbe at the point of starvation, and his original sex is returned to him:

Zildo was on his feet, staggering, and trying not to sob hopelessly.

Nicholas seized him in his arms. 'With what did you stab your arm?' he said, using the prepotent tone of which Zildo seemed to be so hideously afraid.

'Scusi, Sior, scissors: but indeed it is nothing.'

'You gave me your blood?'

'You were dead, Sior.'

'Oh my dear, my dear, my dear, I have been hunting for you all my life.'

'Sior?'

'Gilda!'

She looked straight into his eyes.[43]

And so, as Corvo says, 'the Desire and Pursuit of the Whole was crowned and rewarded by Love'.[44]

IV. MASTER–MISTRESS

Until that final moment, Zildo/Gilda has preserved an identity which is mysterious, almost in the religious sense: she is untouchable, inexplicable, a wonder. Much is made of her difference from other people – not just the ones in the book (a gang of grotesques from whom only contrast can be expected), but other, non-Corvine characters too. One group is especially distinguished: those Shakespearian fakes, the transvestite actors with whom she might possibly be compared. Is not Zildo/Gilda really a sort of Rosalind, rather than an Ariel? Considering how best to handle her, Crabbe/Corvo deals crisply with that idea:

Shakespeare disguised a lot of his girls as boys: but that was merely his artful Jacobean stage-craft. The boy-actresses of his epoch were naturally more fitted to play the part of boy than of girl. The master made

41 Ibid., p. 125. Corvo is here using 'proper' in its archaic sense of 'own'.

42 Philip Healy, in his Foreword to the reprint by Oxford University Press (1986), points out that 'The plot requires that Nicholas's beloved is actually a girl', and he notes the scene (to me blundering and excruciating) where Crabbe finds Zildo/Gilda's rag doll and the author reflects that 'Motherhood cannot be kept from the mind of a maid' (p. xi; Eburne ed. p. 150). But Crabbe's/Corvo's opinions of 'the human female' 'as a rule' (p. 19) are lavishly and violently proclaimed: 'The form and ornament of them made him simply sick, usque ad nauseam, by reason of its vapid bunchiness and vacuous inconsequent patchworkiness . . . [etc.etc.etc.] But sometimes he did admire a young girl, at a distance, and only for her fresh wholesome youth, her lithe strength, her dainty adroitness. And, then, an appalling prevision of what she would have to hide, of what she was likely to become, made him wipe her from the mirror of his mind . . .' (p. 19). What Gilda will become, with these prospects, is unimaginable, and no doubt Corvo never did imagine it.

43 Corvo, *Desire and Pursuit*, p. 295.

44 Ibid., p. 297.

the best of his material, gave his boys their chance – sent them on, as Rosalind or Viola or Imogen, at the beginning of the play, in girl's attire, just to sign themselves and set the scene; and then let them do their real work in their own natural habiliments throughout the rest of the drama. The apparent deception was a frankly open one, which every guffin, mug, and noodle, in the audience could understand. It was of no use here.[45]

The bogus bluffness of the penultimate sentence betrays a genuine unease here, though why Corvo should feel it is a question. Is he trying to bounce his reader out of wondering what it is, exactly, that the guffins are so comfortable about? Is 'real work' a brisk way of making the flirtation of Orlando and Ganymede, say, something 'frankly open' and 'natural'? Why should Corvo write about the boys at all, if he is going to dismiss them? They are, after all, obviously different from his own character, as they are males playing girls, and she is female playing a boy.

Differences like that never are really 'obvious', of course, and no great prurience is needed to think of one reason for Corvo's train of thought. But there is more to be said, and first we need to return, once again, to Oscar Wilde. The greatest celebration ever made of the erotic potential of the boy-actors is Wilde's brilliant little essay/fantasy *The Portrait of Mr. W.H.* (first published 1889) – a work from which scholarly criticism of the sonnets has never quite freed itself.[46] The argument, offered, withdrawn, offered and withdrawn again, and finally left as a ghostly temptation to the reader, is that it was a boy-actor, 'Willie Hughes' (a name that can be found in the poems themselves), to whom Shakespeare wrote. The sonnets thus become a sincere, wholly personal act of love.

Willie Hughes! Willie Hughes! How musically it sounded! Yes; who else but he could have been the master–mistress of Shakespeare's passion, the lord of his love to whom he was bound in vassalage, the delicate minion of pleasure, the rose of the whole world, the herald of the spring decked in the proud livery of youth, the lovely boy whom it was sweet music to hear, and whose beauty was the very raiment of Shakespeare's heart, as it was the keystone of his dramatic power?[47]

This theory is shown in the story to be infectious, sometimes fatal; and Wilde has achieved the remarkable feat of influencing readers for over a century with a story that carries every warning, and declares itself untrue. When Corvo thought of boy-actors, he almost certainly thought of Wilde too, and distinguished his own fantasy sharply from Wilde's. The fact that Wilde had got there first is one possible explanation for Corvo's rejection; a better one is the hopelessness embedded in Wilde's story. His Shakespeare is fantasizing about an impossible figure, and Cyril Graham, the first man in the story to believe in Willie Hughes, is himself a lost actor, who plays Rosalind and kills himself. In Marjorie Garber's account, Rosalind's appeal seems based on this hopelessness, though the account is written in theoretical, pain-free terms:

The transvestite, the changeling boy, and the boy actor point to the impossibility of realizing [a] fantasy – and the necessity of the fantasy *as opposed* to any realisation . . . The transvestite is a figure for something fundamental to human desire yet constitutively not there . . .[48]

For Corvo, determined on a happy ending, this kind of thought was perhaps a deterrent. Zildo is 'there', even if it must be as the technically feminized, marriable Gilda. But more off-putting still, I suspect, was the very familiarity,

---

[45] Ibid., p. 49. This suggests that Corvo did not remember *Cymbeline* as well as he thought he did.

[46] For an excellent discussion of the legacy of *The Portrait* in combination with Wilde's disgrace, see Katherine Duncan-Jones' Arden edition of the sonnets (1997), pp. 32–3. See also, more generally, S. Schoenbaum, *Shakespeare's Lives* (Oxford, rev. edn 1991), part v.

[47] *The Complete Works of Oscar Wilde*, p. 1169

[48] Marjorie Garber, 'The Transvestite's Progress' in Marsden (ed.), *Appropriation*, p. 159. See also Garber, *Vested Interests: Cross-Dressing and Cultural Anxiety* (New York and London, 1992), chapter 3.

the age-given respectability, of this kind of 'cross-dressing'. And here I want to go back for a little to Corvo's 'guffins'. For Wilde, Willie Hughes was the only publishable form of a fantasy he was busily acting out in his life; however much Puritans of the early seventeenth century may have raged against them, and whatever the delight of late twentieth-century critics in their 'subversiveness', the boy-actors were an institution, and, though the playwrights may give them some suggestive lines, very little sexual scandal seems to have attached to them personally.[49] Corvo's bluster about 'noodles' is an overstatement; but his insistence that his own beloved must be more extraordinary than that may well have been sincere.

This may explain why Rosalind was not, for Corvo, sufficiently attractive to act as model. Ariel does not share her disadvantages; does he have any positive attractions of his own? Here are three possible ones. First, there is the old pull of *The Tempest*'s supposed autobiographical value: if Ariel is close to Prospero, he is close to Shakespeare himself, and fantasies about Ariel bring the fantasist closer too. Second, Ariel is no ordinary ally, but an agent of Prospero's creative life, half-identified with it; and Prospero's creative life is thrillingly analogous to the greatest literary dream of all. Third, Ariel, unlike Rosalind, has not both sexes, but neither: he is entirely not a girl, but nor is he entirely a boy. In Garber's terms, this should make him even less 'there' than Rosalind; but to someone with the emotional make-up of our authors, he might seem more immediately 'here', not encumbered with the obstacle sex nor wholly identified with the forbidden one. His sexlessness is not symmetrical, though, as these descriptions were meant to suggest. He is not at all a girl, but the rest is ambiguous. He is a spirit, but the play gives the appearance of an age and a sex: he looks young (Prospero uses diminutives for him), and he is a 'he'. He is a boy, and not a boy, in whatever combination is desired.

That desire cannot, however, be wholly fulfilled; and this is the cost of swapping Rosalind for Ariel. There is an obvious poignancy to the relationship between the spirit and his master, because Prospero cannot keep him, and must die without him. Ariel is subject to Prospero's power, but he is also its means; he is rescued from the pinetree, but he is capable of things impossible for the magician – including, we assume, immortality. The consolation is that this is a poignancy in which there is nothing special or dangerous. However close he may come to a sexual ideal, there is no disgrace – nothing unique – about not being able to possess Ariel: he is not human, and even Prospero/Shakespeare could not keep him.

And yet Corvo not only keeps him but makes him want to stay. This is to cheat with the story – and provides perhaps one more reason for his anxiety about the boy-actors. Zildo may be Prospero's agent in a world of Caliban/Antonios, but he is also, much more obviously, another Viola, orphaned, loving, obtainable, and female. But no, Corvo cries, she is *not* like this. She does not live, or look, at all like a woman: she is a boy, except that she is a girl, and above all she is a protection for the hero against 'this wicked world', thwarter of the evil Caliban and defender of the books.[50]

---

[49] Michael Shapiro, *Gender in Play on the Shakespearian Stage: Boy Heroines and Female Pages* (Ann Arbor, 1994), points out that 'there is no evidence of a coterie of male spectators whose primary interest in the representation of women by play-boys was homoerotic' (p. 39). I am trying to keep open a rather narrow path here: I am suggesting that Corvo sensed the phenomenon was not as sexless as his appeals to 'guffins' and 'noodles' pretend, but that he really did find it too conventional for his own needs. For a quick, clever speculation about the boys' appeal in terms which might have pleased all my authors, see Leslie A. Fiedler, *The Stranger in Shakespeare* (St Albans, 1974), p. 40.

[50] See pp. 49 (a boy 'excepting for the single fact that she was not a boy, but a girl'); 52 (standing between Crabbe and the cruel world); 294 (conveys the publisher's longed-for letter to Crabbe). Zildo/Gilda is unlike Viola and the others in having a doublet and hose at the centre of her disposition: she is a perfect gondolier, and would certainly have made polenta of poor Sir Andrew Aguecheek.

Their relationship is a part of Crabbe's/Corvo's identity as Prospero. Ariel's extraordinary nature might lead a would-be master to despair; but to Corvo, with his sense both of great need and of great desert, Ariel offers an unique hope: no one *else* can ever have him, for he is designed, by God – Shakespeare – Prospero himself, for no one else but Prospero.[51]

Corvo's own life in Venice makes a sad little coda to his fantasy. Alienated, eventually, by his demandingness and ingratitude, his Calibans refused to go on supporting him, and he died, four years after finishing his book, of pneumonia brought on by homelessness and hunger. There was no Gilda to help him; her 'original' was a boy, one of several young gondoliers whose very unmystical relations with Corvo were described by him in a book not published (or publishable) till long after his death.[52]

V. THINGS OF DARKNESS

To return, for one last time, to Oscar Wilde. These writers seem naturally to leave a place of honour for him; but there is no Wildean *Tempest*. Corvo's aggression was foreign to him, and *Pirelli* was beyond him, in more than one way. In art if not in life a much more conventional moralist than Firbank, he could not have offered such bold approval to the Cardinal. What he did provide was a study of what it might mean to use love and art together to turn a human being into an ideal, superhuman, Ariel figure.

In fact he offered the study twice over. First he made it short and paradoxical, *The Portrait of Mr. W.H.*; then he tried it as a full-scale tragedy, *The Picture of Dorian Gray*. In both cases, the artist, with intentions wholly pure and loving (so far, at least, as he knows), tries to make something immortal out of a young, male beauty.

Shakespeare promised Willie Hughes immortality in a form that appealed to men's eyes – that is to say, in a spectacular form, in a play that is to be looked at.[53]

What Willie thought of this we are not told; but Dorian Gray, painted to the life by Basil Hallward, soon comes to feel horror:

'How sad it is! I shall grow old, and horrible, and dreadful. But this picture will remain always young. It will never be older than this particular day of June . . . If it were only the other way!'[54]

Dorian, when he says this, is already lost to his adoring Basil; he has been seduced by the ideas of Lord Henry Wotton, an artist in a different kind. Basil has already been thwarted in his idolatry by this sinister *Doppelgänger* of himself, a man who covets the boy and leads him towards corruption. The painter's gift of immortality compounds the ruin: trying to preserve an Ariel, Basil becomes a Frankenstein. Shakespeare, in Wilde's theory of the sonnets, is thwarted similarly, by a demonic alter-ego of his own:

Marlowe was clearly the rival poet of whom Shakespeare spoke in such laudatory terms . . . No doubt, Marlowe was fascinated by the beauty and grace of the boy-actor, and lured him away from the Blackfriars' Theatre, that he might play the Gaveston of his *Edward II* . . .[55]

---

51 Another question arises from this business of cross-dressing, of a relevance rather hard to assess. *Desire and Pursuit* treats *The Tempest* as a book: the book of books, the magic book which tells the future. But when Corvo – and Firbank, and the others – saw *The Tempest* professionally performed (if they saw it performed), they almost certainly saw Ariel played by a woman. According to Stephen Orgel's edition of *The Tempest* for *The Oxford Shakespeare* (Oxford, 1987), the part was played by a woman until the 1930s (p. 70; but see note 59 below for more on this). It would be possible to make this into yet another explanation for the 'guffins' passage: what Gilda is really not-like is the boy Ariel as played by a girl; but I suspect that, for all of these writers, what the play meant was the book, and that in their own mental theatres, the spirit was always a boy.

52 The classic study of this is A. J. A. Symons, *The Quest for Corvo: an Experiment in Biography* (London, 1934). The *Venice Letters* were published in 1974; some have expressed doubts about their autobiographical value.

53 *The Complete Works of Oscar Wilde*, p. 1169.

54 Ibid., p. 34.

55 Ibid., pp. 1169–70.

If Willie and Dorian are anticipations of Alfred Douglas, both Basil and Henry, Shakespeare and Marlowe, are versions of Wilde – more truthful, perhaps, or at least more profound about that relationship than hagiolatrous critics have been.[56] Firbank, his eyes clear with love, understood: his play *The Princess Zoubaroff* (1920) includes a consolatory fantasy of Wilde and Douglas, living together in contented exile; the Wilde-figure is a lord named Henry.[57]

VI. THE MAGICIAN IN LOVE

Punishment falls heavy on both Basil and Dorian – punished, above all, for their treatment of each other. This is a far, bitter cry from the enticing, poignant, authorially-uncensored pairing at the heart of this essay. One last question before ending it is whether Firbank and Corvo really represent a beginning: that is, was anyone interested in Ariel as a love-object before them?

In a way – a rather frivolous, not very relevant way – the answer is Yes. In 1667, when Dryden and Davenant came to adapt Shakespeare's play, they filled it up with new characters who reinforce the idea of romantic harmony. One of them was the spirit Milcha, a partner for Ariel – whose own gender thus assumed, in their adaptation, a clarity which it lacks in the original.[58] But does that original, Shakespeare's spirit, have anything of the sexual at all? Prospero is anxious about the threat to Miranda's virginity that he senses from both Caliban and Ferdinand; Ariel gives him no anxiety of that kind. Does he have any other sexual possibilities? Sycorax perhaps thought so – just what her earthy and abhorred commands involved we never learn, but they sound somehow suggestive. Ariel was, of course, too delicate to perform them. But physical strength – and indeed materiality – are not required for a little flirtation.

ARIEL Do you love me, master? No?
PROSPERO Dearly, my delicate Ariel.   (4.1.48–9)

The Ariel-actor can make what he likes of this, of course, and I have never heard one make much;[59] but Ariel asks the question just after Prospero has told him about the masque he is planning for the 'young couple', Ferdinand and Miranda.[60] These humans love each other; you are human; do you love me? The thought of Prospero's feelings stays with Ariel for a while longer. The shipwrecked noblemen are in the

---

[56] Much more profound than his later *De Profundis*. Wilde himself recognized the parallel: to the fellow-prisoner who addressed him as 'Dorian Gray', he replied: 'Not Dorian Gray, but Lord Henry Wotton' (Ellmann, *Oscar Wilde*, pp. 486–7).

[57] He is Lord Orkish; his Christian name is revealed in a moment of surprise near the end of the play. For a brilliant account of the play's 'double portrait', see Brophy, *Prancing Novelist*, pp. 326–34. (But she does not mention the significance of the name 'Henry'.)

[58] There seems to have been another complication, however: according to Elizabeth Howe, the part was first played by a woman – Mary (Moll) Davis (see *The First English Actresses: Women and Drama 1660–1700* (Cambridge, 1992), p. 184). Stephen Orgel, by contrast, in his edition of *The Tempest* for *The Oxford Shakespeare* (1987), says that 'Ariel had been a male role throughout the seventeenth century' (p. 70). The existence of Milcha is probably responsible for this confusion.

[59] Ariel seems to become more metallic year by year – the result, Orgel suggests, of the reintroduction of male actors (but men, rather than boys) to play the part (*The Tempest*, p. 78). The absence of strong, coherent emotions in the play has been exploited to the limit by some film-makers: see Derek Jarman, *The Tempest* (1979) and Peter Greenaway, *Prospero's Books* (1991). An exception was the production by David Thacker for the RSC in 1995, in which Ariel was played by a woman, and appeared jealous of Miranda; to quote Peter Holland, reviewing the production for *Shakespeare Survey 49* (1996), this 'seemed like a throwback to an old theatre tradition long out of fashion', but the actress 'us[ed] her gender to create an additional layer to the master-servant relationship' (p. 247). In the same year, the production by Silviu Purcarete for the Nottingham Playhouse took the 'extreme route of denying Ariel an onstage presence at all, leaving him merely a literally disembodied voice, heard but unseen' (p. 250).

[60] I owe this observation to Dr Neil McLynn, with whom I directed a performance of *The Tempest* in Japan in January 1999.

magician's power, and the spirit reports on their plight:

ARIEL Your charm so strongly works 'em
  That if you now beheld them, your affections
  Would become tender.
PROSPERO Dost thou think so, spirit?
ARIEL Mine would, sir, were I human. (5.1.17–20)

This fascination with the human produces a fine current of something here, for which even 'flirtatiousness' might seem too earthy a description. But perhaps that current was sensed by our authors, unusually sensitive as they had to be to such things. Human beings feel love and tenderness; and Prospero is reminded of these qualities by the airy spirit that he cannot keep:

PROSPERO Why, that's my dainty Ariel! I shall miss
  thee,
  But yet thou shalt have freedom. – So, so, so. –
                          (5.1.97–8)

The books and stories here discussed were all published before 1930. There are more from that period that could be mentioned, but have not been: the most obvious of them are *Peter Pan* and *Death in Venice* – the second a story of tragic desire and pursuit to set against Corvo's vision of glory.[61] Perhaps this little tradition of the magic boy, Ariel-Amor, fades out around here: homosexual cliché has altered so much since those filmy, epicene fantasies.[62] But for the last word, I would like to jump twenty years, to something both different and similar. In *The Sea and the Mirror* (1945), W. H. Auden provided the perfect valediction for my essay, from the mouth of his own Prospero.

In this work, a luminous, illuminating series of variations on *The Tempest*, all the characters are given their say, in their own, unique styles: verse, rhymed and unrhymed, in all different metres; a dizzy prose harangue for Caliban. Prospero, of course, speaks first. He is preparing to go back to Milan, and is quite aware of all the reservations about this that any critic might think up. It will not be ideal; but he is going, anyway. Ariel is not. His last service, it seems, is to listen to Prospero's predictions about life back home.

  When I am safely home, oceans away in Milan,
    and
Realize once and for all I shall never see you
    again,
  Over there, maybe, it won't seem quite so
    dreadful
Not to be interesting any more, but an old man
  Just like other old men . . .
                      Can I learn to suffer
  Without saying something ironic or funny
On suffering?[63]

The magus speaks on, fluent and intelligent. But how much does any of it mean, really, to the ageless, unsuffering Ariel . . .? Unlike Firbank's wild romantic Cardinal, Auden's Prospero can see his situation truly, and accept it, not too tragically:

I see you starting to fidget. I forgot. To you
  That doesn't matter. My dear, here comes
    Gonzalo
With a solemn face to fetch me. O Ariel, Ariel,
  How I shall miss you. Enjoy your element.
    Goodbye.[64]

---

61 *Death in Venice* is not related to *The Tempest* as Firbank's and Corvo's books are, but belongs to the penumbra, along with Bloxam and Saki; Barrie's place is probably more central. Tadzio, the beautiful boy pursued by the magus-writer Aschenbach, is associated by him with death – an association which is half-correct (Aschenbach has an aesthetic desire that Tadzio should not live long, and does not recognize him as his own Angel of Death). Peter Pan, pursued by Captain Hook = Mr Darling = the author, is much more of an Ariel – also played by a girl on the Edwardian stage; but I have resisted the temptation to mention him (up till now), because the troubled, abstinent Barrie does not seem to me fair game in the way the others do.

62 On this point, Paul Fussell, *The Great War and Modern Memory* (Oxford, 1975), chapter VIII is extremely interesting.

63 'The Sea and the Mirror' in *For the Time Being* (London, 1945), p. 15.

64 p. 15. According to Humphrey Carpenter, ' "The section Prospero to Ariel" was listed by [Auden] as among those poems alluding to his relationship with Chester Kallman' (*W. H. Auden: A Biography* (London, 1981), p. 328.

NARRATIVE APPROACHES TO SHAKESPEARE: ACTIVE STORYTELLING IN SCHOOLS

REX GIBSON

How would you tell the story of a Shakespeare play to a ten year old? Would you leave out the casket scenes from *The Merchant of Venice?* The mechanicals from *A Midsummer Night's Dream*, Jaques and Touchstone from *As You Like It?* The Gloucester subplot from *King Lear?* Autolycus from *The Winter's Tale?* Or Sir Toby, Sir Andrew Aguecheek and Feste, together with the gulling of Malvolio from *Twelfth Night?* Would you have Antonio openly repentant, full of shame and remorse, at the end of *The Tempest,* and present the Christians in *The Merchant of Venice* in a wholly favourable light?

That's what happens in *Tales from Shakespeare* by Charles and Mary Lamb, still in print after nearly two hundred years.[1] At first hearing, these omissions and emphases seem strange, even risible. But to censure the Lambs is to mistake their endeavour. They intended their *Tales* as an introduction to Shakespeare, and an introduction is just that: something which assumes that further acquaintance will follow which fills in gaps and makes more subtle discriminations.

What more justifiably grates on a modern sensibility are the gender and social class assumptions of the Lambs' conception of that follow-up and their view of the relationship of literature and drama. For their envisaged readers, enlarged experience of Shakespeare would be mainly through their 'fathers' libraries' and 'leave of judicious friends'.[2] Unsurprisingly, most children's encounter with

Shakespeare in the early nineteenth century was an elitist affair. In the Lambs' eyes it should also be a literary affair, privileging reading over the experience of seeing the plays on stage.

These assumptions, omissions, and interpretations in the Lambs' storytelling demonstrate the need for scrutiny of the nature and function of narrative in young people's experience of Shakespeare. My purpose therefore is to describe methods currently widely used to teach Shakespeare in state (that is, publicly funded) schools in England[3] and to identify major issues which arise from that practice. Alert to the theme of this issue of *Shakespeare Survey*, 'Shakespeare and Narrative', my grounded assumption is that in school Shakespeare the two elements of that phrase are not just intertwined, they are inseparable. In schools, narrative is central to Shakespeare pedagogy, and crucial to students' learning. Indeed, for younger school students, Shakespeare *is* narrative.

The attractions of narrative are obvious. Storytelling is a familiar and congenial human activity. Story, with its chaining sequence and central concern for character, is easy to grasp

---

[1] Charles and Mary Lamb, *Tales from Shakespeare* (London, 1806). Although originally published as written by Charles Lamb, Mary Lamb wrote fourteen of the twenty tales. Charles wrote only six.

[2] Lamb, *Tales from Shakespeare*, pp. 2–3.

[3] Based on the findings of the Shakespeare and Schools project based at the University of Cambridge Institute of Education from 1986. See Rex Gibson, *Teaching Shakespeare* (Cambridge, 1998).

and recall. It does not explicitly impose analytic or evaluative demands (though each subliminally inform every telling). Storytelling is a form of communication that has universal appeal, and the younger the individual, the greater that appeal. But as will shortly become clear, schoolteachers' enthusiasm for and commitment to narrative embodies a fundamental ambivalence: storytelling is not enough.

Narrative as storytelling has long been an accepted mode of introduction to Shakespeare for school students. For most younger students, storytelling has traditionally been their major experience of the plays. The Lambs have fallen out of favour, but their modern counterparts enjoy considerable popularity. Every English primary school possesses at least one copy of some version of 'Shakespeare's stories'.[4] Whatever the version, the illustrations, presentation, language and interpretative disposition declare each to be aimed principally at younger students.

Because my concentration is on what teachers and students do in schools, I shall not address the claim that a young person's best introduction to Shakespeare is to see a production of the play. It is a claim with which Charles Lamb would not have agreed. For him, the theatre provided an all too imperfect rendering of what was on the page. His judgement, as well as his *Tales*, still survive. In 1999 a teacher removed his party of ten-year-old schoolchildren from the Royal Shakespeare Company's production of *A Midsummer Night's Dream* deeming it unsuitable for their age group.[5]

That incident has greater significance than a modern endorsement of Charles Lamb's anachronistic belief. It is more revealing in what it shows of the radical change from the Lambs' day to our own in the social class composition of young people experiencing Shakespeare and the sites of that experience. The Lambs envisaged that their *Tales* would be read by 'young gentlemen' and 'young ladies' in homes already well stocked with books. In

contrast, in England today there is a legal requirement that all school students between the ages of fourteen and sixteen will study Shakespeare.[6] Further, a recommendation in the National Literacy Strategy that ten-year-olds study a Shakespeare play 'where appropriate',[7] has increasingly been interpreted by teachers as a statutory requirement. For the great majority of students, an introduction to Shakespeare and any follow-up will be exclusively through their schools.

In practice then, Shakespeare has become a necessary part of the curriculum for all English school students. Those students typically encounter the plays in classes numbering twenty to thirty-plus, in which, for students and their teachers alike, attitudes to Shakespeare mirror those of the population at large, and notions of 'fathers' libraries' are, at best, unknown, at worst, derided. Such 'Shakespeare for all' has resulted in dramatic changes in the nature of pedagogy, in ways unimagined by the Lambs, and where 'dramatic' has both metaphorical and literal force. Teaching methods have become more active, social and collaborative,[8] with students taking part physically in some kind of enactment, and sometimes employing a technique the form of which reflects the *imitatio* that Shakespeare himself practised as a schoolboy.[9]

Today's active pedagogy is based on principles which have long been known (and urged) but have only recently effectively informed practice for most students. It recognizes that

---

[4] The most widely held and popular version is Leon Garfield, *Shakespeare Stories*, 2 vols. (London, 1985, 1994).

[5] 'Titania and Tubbies get rude awakening', *Times Educational Supplement*, 4321, 23 April 1999, p. 4.

[6] Department for Education, *The National Curriculum* (London, 1995), p. 20.

[7] Department for Education and Employment, *The National Literacy Strategy: Framework for Teaching* (London, 1998).

[8] Maurice Gilmour ed., *Shakespeare for All in Secondary Schools* (London, 1997).

[9] Park Honan, *Shakespeare, A Life* (Oxford, 1998), p. 53.

students are motivated and learn not only through listening, watching and discussing, but also by speaking and acting out Shakespeare's language. For large classes ranging widely in ability and attitude, that 'speaking and acting out' differs radically from traditional practice in which only a few students took active roles as characters. As teachers use a repertoire of techniques to enable students to take possession of Shakespeare's language, contemporary classroom methods echo the assumptions, and occasionally the rehearsal practices of experimental theatre companies.[10] Here, the play itself is the thing, rather than any prose rendering of it. 'Storytelling' becomes 'dramatic storytelling'. The student's role changes from passive listening to active participation, creating character, mood and interpretative outcome as they construct meaning from events and language.

Understanding recent developments in school Shakespeare is aided by a concept common to all types of narrative theory. Whatever the theory (and there are many), the distinction is invariably made between the events in a story and the fashioning of those events in the storytelling. As in all theoretical worlds, competing labels jostle in their claims for explanatory power, but all, like Juliet's 'rose', describe the same thing. Barthes speaks of histoire and discours;[11] Chatman's terms are story and discourse;[12] the oldest and best-known division is Propp's *fabula* and *sjuzhet*.[13] *Fabula* is what happens: the events in chronological order. *Sjuzhet* is the artist's method of relating that story: the techniques of storytelling.

Propp's terminology is unfamiliar to most schoolteachers, but their practice demonstrates that some kind of mastery of Shakespeare's *sjuzhet* is a paramount objective in every classroom. Knowledge of *fabula* alone is rarely considered a sufficient goal for any student at any age. The most obvious demonstration of that assertion is the universal injunction of secondary schools teachers to their examination students: it is never sufficient just to tell the

story. With different emphasis that precept holds for all students. For English ten-year-olds, the *sjuzhet* dimension of narrative is made quite explicit. The recommendation in the National Literacy Strategy that they study a Shakespeare play is embedded within very detailed requirements for mastery of an extensive range of language techniques.[14] Such demands for knowledge and acquisition of *sjuzhet* are the source of teachers' ambivalence towards storytelling referred to earlier: the story itself is insufficient; some analysis of its telling is required.

School Shakespeare therefore entails both *fabula* and *sjuzhet*. In practice this means that each teacher takes some account, often intuitively, and in forms deemed appropriate to the age and ability of the students, of Shakespeare's *sjuzhet*: how he tells his story. That 'telling' he intended as stage performance, as dramatic storytelling, and for school purposes it includes most obviously Shakespeare's language techniques and dramatic construction. Schoolteachers endeavour, through active pedagogy, to enable their students to perceive Shakespeare's distinctive styles of dramatic storytelling, to understand them, and to employ them to greatest effect in their own different active forms of presentation. As students grow older, greater account is taken of Shakespeare's irony, ambiguity and moral complexity; of literary and historical references and sources; and of how the plays are rooted in the social and political preoccupations of his own time.

10 See for example the interview with Simon McBurney in *On Directing*, Gabriella Giannachi and Mary Luckhurst, eds. (London, 1999), pp. 67–77.
11 Roland Barthes, 'Introduction to the structural analysis of narratives', *Image-Music-Text*, trans. by Stephen Heath (London, 1977).
12 Seymour Chatman, *Story and Discourse* (Ithaca, 1978).
13 Vladimir Propp, *The Morphology of the Folk Tale* (Austin, 1968, originally published 1928).
14 Department for Education and Employment, *The National Literacy Strategy: Framework for Teaching*, 1998 pp. 22–55.

But such matters begin with, arise from, and return to the distinctiveness of the language.

Description and analysis of Shakespeare's language take different forms depending on the level at which any enquiry or explanation is conducted. With school students and their teachers in mind it is appropriate to make a Sir Toby-like claim that language consists of five elements: imagery, repetition, antithesis, lists and verse. These few simple and discrete-seeming categories may seem to deny their essential infoldedness, and they appear far distant from the demanding catalogue of language devices that Shakespeare himself learned at school[15] or from modern scholarship on Shakespeare's language.[16] But in an era of 'Shakespeare for all' they have proved a sufficient, comprehensive and comprehensible framework for schoolteachers to devise courses and to assess how well their students have mastered the language component of Shakespeare's *sjuzhet*.

The first four components reveal a gradient of increasing potential for student enactment. Verse presents special problems for students as will be shown below. Study of imagery and repetition tends to be desk-bound, more literary than dramatic, and students' imaginative and intellectual responses yield less to physical expression. For antithesis and lists, teaching methods and students' responses become increasingly more physically active. Here I must at once disclaim any implied opposition between active and intellectual responses to Shakespeare. A fundamental assumption of active pedagogy is that it harnesses thought and action. In school classrooms, as on stage, all human faculties are in symbiotic relation.

Drawing upon Shakespeare's unrivalled richness of linguistic resource, teachers typically use short extracts to teach language skills and to develop students' imaginative writing. Shakespeare's language becomes a springboard or spur for students' creativity. For example, a single line from *The Winter's Tale* proves remarkably effective for teaching metaphor and

serves as a model for students to generate their own imagery of impossibility:

The stars, I see, will kiss the valleys first   (5.1.205)

Rosalind's reply to Celia's 'Here comes Monsieur Le Beau' is the half line 'With his mouth full of news'. Celia's similarly structured description of her father 'With his eyes full of anger', enables students, by imitation of form, to produce their own metaphors to create character: 'With her eyes full of night'.[17] The imaginative promptings of 'bearded like the pard' and 'This fell sergeant Death is strict in his arrest' are similarly productive in developing students' grasp and invention of simile and personification as they conjure up mind pictures and invite imaginative substitutions and re-creations. Some images like Viola's 'She sat like Patience on a monument /Smiling at grief' lend themselves equally to physical enactment as well as cerebral imitation and invention.

Shakespeare's frequent repetitions of sound, word, phrase and rhythm similarly lend themselves to student imitation. Characteristic language constructions and devices imitated range from the alliteration of 'Full fathom five', through the parison and isocolon of Henry VI's 'So many hours must I . . ..' (where, for teachers, students reproducing the form rather than acquiring the Latin terms is the paramount objective), to Bottom's and Flute's many parody-inviting repetitions as they play out Pyramus and Thisbe from 'O grim-looked night, O night with hue so black' to the final 'Adieu, adieu, adieu'.

---

15 The results of that learning are evident in Sister Miriam Joseph, *Shakespeare's Use of the Arts of Language* (New York, 1947).

16 N. F. Blake, *Shakespeare's Language: An Introduction* (London, 1983). Even in this introductory text, the key concept of the nominal group is unfamiliar and unused in schools.

17 School students' responses to these images from *As You Like It* and *The Winter's Tale* are given in Fred Sedgwick, *Shakespeare and the Young Writer* (London, 1999), pp. 22–4, 27–9.

The ever-present antithesis, Shakespeare's linguistic embodiment and mirror of his drama's abiding preoccupation with conflict, offers increasing opportunities for physical enactment by students as well as written imitation ('My only love, sprung from my only hate'). Antitheses lend themselves to imaginative active expression in gesture, body posture and movement, as do the oppositions which take even more compressed form in oxymoron, abundantly present in *Romeo and Juliet*: 'loving hate', 'sweet sorrow' etc. Students use a variety of activities from 'hand-weighing' or body-turning as they speak ('Fair is foul, and foul is fair'), to constructing group tableaux or mimes which physically portray the oppositions, as for example in images of deception in *Macbeth*: 'look like the innocent flower, / But be the serpent under't', 'False face must hide what the false heart doth know.'

Students similarly physically portray Shakespeare's many lists and declensions in addition to imitating them in writing. The great number and variety of such lists which occur in every play offer all kinds of classroom opportunities for enactment and creative imitation. Younger students typically begin with the always popular witches' cauldron ingredients and Jaques' 'seven ages' speech, acting and rewriting them (for example, benign ingredients, women's or school students' 'ages'). They progress to differently patterned and emotionally nuanced speeches such as the Duchess of York's sixteen-item description of her son Richard 'Tetchy and wayward was thy infancy . . .' (4.4.169–73), Rosalind's tumbling, breathless questions (3.2.215–19), or Malcolm's characterization of Macbeth: 'bloody, /Luxurious, avaricious, false, deceitful, /Sudden, malicious, smacking of every sin /That hath a name' (4.3.57–60) which affords at least fourteen different 'shows' when students take up the seven deadly sins invitation. Juliet's list of all the things she would rather do than marry Paris, often abridged or even omitted in stage productions, has been enacted in full in many

English classrooms and frequently imitated in similarly constructed 'Things I'd rather do than . . .' inventions.

Such imitations (but not enactments) echo Shakespeare's own school experience. Like his fellow students at Stratford Grammar school, he too used classical models in numerous *imitatio* activities. Now Shakespeare himself has become a model for imitation, but the demands on today's students are very different in range and intensity from those made on him.[18] As an Elizabethan schoolboy, he was expected to learn by heart over one hundred figures of rhetoric and to acquire skill in using them. Nonetheless, for all such qualitative or quantitative differences, modern forms of imitation have enhanced students' insight into and skill in creating imagery, antithesis, repetition and lists.

There is a less cheering finding for verse. Imitation and activity seem less successful in developing school students' competence in writing in iambic pentameter. For anyone who has attended a school or college Shakespeare workshop in the last dozen years, that will seem a curious claim. Almost every such workshop includes the familiar and popular 'beat out the rhythm' activity followed by the invitation to 'invent your own line in iambic pentameter': (e.g. 'I'd like to have a plate of fish and chips'). It is often assumed that these customary activities ensure acquisition of the verse form, and successes are recorded in most workshops. But the effects do not persist. In subsequent lessons, students' own verse very rarely displays sustained mastery of iambic pentameter. Similarly, popular beliefs that this metre is the natural rhythm of English and that students 'pick it up' by reading and speaking, prove ill-founded in practice. Immersion is no necessary guarantee of acquiring the skill to write in Shakespearian verse form.

Two modern pedagogical antipathies combine to inhibit students' versifying ability:

---

[18] T. W. Baldwin, *William Shakspere's Small Latine and Lesse Greeke*, 2 vols. (Urbana, Ill., 1944).

distrust of rote learning and suspicion of poetic form. To develop the capacity to write in iambic pentameter, nearly all students need directive teaching and sustained practice. Time and culture weigh against both. In teaching writing, especially in expressive modes, a majority of teachers feel that the losses imposed by the discipline of form outweigh the freedoms of free expression. For well over three decades in England the prevailing professional credo has been that emotional truth is more fully realized without the constrictions of form. Eleven-year-olds can produce lengthy and impressively empathetic point-of-view prose narratives on a Shakespeare play,[19] but any extended use of iambic pentameter is extremely rare at this age, and indeed at any stage of schooling.

It is hardly necessary to be acquainted with Chomsky's notion of deep structure to observe that even very young children draw upon complex rules of language and genre to make sense out of what they see, hear or speak. The child cannot formulate those rules, and is unaware of their existence, but they palpably govern interpretation and utterance. Such 'innate rules' (for lack of a better term) do not seem to include iambic pentameter. They might well include tetrameter, because few English students have problems with generating verbal or written utterances in that 'four beat' rhythm.

A different explanation is rooted in the ethological concept of critical periods.[20] This accepts that all known speech rhythms are in every child's genetic endowment, but which is developed is determined by the culture into which the child is born, because the critical period for learning any form is the first few years of life. After the critical period, the capacity for easy mastery fades. For all speakers of English, tetrameter is the preferred traditional form, embedded in nursery rhymes and in most publicly encountered verse from the very earliest age. In contrast, iambic pentameter is a later learned form. Most students never hear it spoken before they have passed the critical period for learning it. Just as foreign language learning becomes more difficult with age, so students lose a ready ability to master Shakespeare's distinctive verse pattern. Iambic pentameter is one element of Shakespeare's *sjuzhet* that sets his language off from everyday experience. The iamb may be culturally preferred, but the five-beat rhythm is not.

It is with the *fabula* dimension of narrative that active classroom methods come fully into their own. Traditionally, narratives of the story have been just that: the teacher telling a version of the story, sometimes speaking her own reconstruction, more usually by reading aloud a published version. More active approaches to story telling are now increasingly common in classrooms, and students find that enacting 'events' is simultaneously congenial and contextual, a source of enjoyment and learning. Such enactments afford a sense of a totality, whether of the whole play, or of a story within, tangential to, or 'outside' it.

That sense of totality is evident in the commonplace observation of schoolteachers that students possess narrative drive: telling or acting out stories with a beginning, middle, and end. The younger the student, the greater the compulsion of that narrative trajectory, especially in the desire for the closure of a happy ending. In the three-fold movement of order, disorder, order restored, equilibrium is achieved after the upheavals and turbulence of the play's 'middle'. The resolution is a rightful king for Scotland, the Verona feud genuinely ended, the villains truly repentant at the end of *The Tempest*. Only as students grow older comes irony and the satisfactions of indeterminate or downright unhappy endings in which Malcolm seems likely to prove another tyrant, the Montagues and Capulets will all too evidently soon be at each other's throats again, and Antonio,

---

19 Sedgwick, *Shakespeare and the Young Writer*, pp. 99–100.
20 K. Z. Lorenz, *The Foundations of Ethology* (New York, 1981).

Caliban, or even Ariel, threaten trouble ahead in Milan and on the island. In just the same way that modern theatre directors pay particular attention to the final image their audience will see, so the ending of any story somehow embodies and makes sense of what has gone before. It is the final destination of the narrative's journey.

The notion of narrative drive underpins active storytelling in schools. It can be seen in a typical contemporary classroom introduction to *A Midsummer Night's Dream*. The teacher selects ten episodes which represent important moments in the play and which convey an outline of the narrative sequence. Language, rarely more than a single line, is identified to express each moment:

1 Either prepare to die, [. . .] Or else to wed Demetrius.
2 The course of true love never did run smooth.
3 Ill met by moonlight, proud Titania.
4 Wake when some vile thing is near.
5 What angel wakes me from my flow'ry bed?
6 How low am I, thou painted maypole?
7 My legs are longer, though, to run away.
8 Now die, die, die, die, die.
9 And farewell friends,
  Thus Thisbe ends.
  Adieu, adieu, adieu!
10 Give me your hands, if we be friends,
  And Robin shall restore amends.

The teacher narrates a brief introduction to each episode, usually accompanying her words with actions that serve as model or inspiration for students' own actions. The students, working in pairs, speak and act out the lines, available to them on their own copy of the script or from an enlarged display on a board or screen. The first few teacher narratives convey a sense of how the lesson develops:

1 Teacher: 'All is not well in Athens. Hermia refuses to marry Demetrius, the man her father has chosen for her. Duke Theseus passes a terrible judgement on Hermia: "Either prepare to die [. . .] Or else to wed Demetrius"'. As she speaks the teacher acts both roles: a 'sentencing' Theseus, a responding Hermia. Each pair of students then steps into role to speak and show this particular moment of action. All students in the class are simultaneously actively engaged.

2 Teacher: 'Hermia decides to run away to a wood near Athens with her true love, Lysander, who tells the weeping Hermia "The course of true love never did run smooth"'. Here, the teacher's facial expression and hand gestures help to convey meaning, signalling each element in ways which have more in common with sign language for the hearing-impaired than with the conventions of the professional stage. In pairs all students again step into role and speak and act.

3 Teacher: 'Meanwhile, in the wood, Oberon, king of the fairies, angrily greets Titania, his queen: "Ill met by moonlight, proud Titania."' Once again each pair of students simultaneously strikes a pose and speak the words.

The lesson continues in similar fashion through the magic potion squeezing, Titania's awaking, Hermia and Helena's quarrel, the 'deaths' of Pyramus and Thisbe, to the final 'take a bow' moment of Puck's final appeal to the audience for applause: 'Give me your hands, if we be friends,/ And Robin shall restore amends'. In practice students experience little or no difficulty in switching between roles.

After several teacher-led rehearsals, the students work independently. They speak and act the lines using a range of techniques: performing at their own pace, promenading (each action shown in a different location), acting 'fast forwards' and slow motion versions, constructing tableaux of one or more lines. Within a one-hour lesson most students will have learned the lines, can present them in order, and can construct their own accompanying narrative.

There are obvious issues that arise from this introductory 'whole story' activity, but they are accorded different priority by teachers and by most professional Shakespearians. For teachers the very practical problem of space looms larger than the more cerebral question of which ten events and lines to select. Teachers know the activity works best in an open space with students moving freely. Where that is not possible, they adapt to classroom conditions with students seated and with suitable movements and gestures. For Shakespearians, selection of episodes and language are crucial. Teachers take comfort from knowing that any selection is contestable, that later lessons will enlarge this initial active narrative, and that the method provides a first experience of Shakespeare's dramatic construction, juxtaposing the serious and the comic, creating and resolving tension, and maintaining narrative drive to a satisfying conclusion.

Within every play are all kinds of action-filled 'self-contained' narratives which variously function to help create character, atmosphere and context, fill gaps and move the play's action forward. Such stories have become a vital part of the repertoire of teachers using an active pedagogy because they offer opportunities for groups of students to act out each event described.

Some stories tell of events that happened before the play opens. Frequently classroom-enacted examples include Hamlet's father's ghost's narration of his death, the bleeding captain's tale in *Macbeth*, Prospero's account of deposition and exile, Egeus' 'Full of vexation' complaint of how Lysander stole the love of Hermia, and Orlando's remembrance of how his brother Oliver grossly abused the terms of their father's will. Such narratives relate events that happen off stage, and are rarely enacted in professional productions.[21]

Other stories tell of events that occur within the play's own time span, as, perhaps most memorably, in the three Gentlemen's accumulating relation of how Leontes is reunited with Perdita and all the reconciliations that follow (*The Winter's Tale* 5.2.1–89). On the infrequent occasions when professional productions enact these off-stage actions, the effect is to increase students' motivation to construct their own performed versions.

Two examples illustrate the practice, one from a film extensively used in schools in video form, the second from an influential stage production much visited by organized parties of older school students. On the page, Duncan is only told of the execution of the Thane of Cawdor for treason, and how he embraced his death with impressive dignity (1.4.1–11). Roman Polanski's film portrays Cawdor throwing away his life with studied indifference. Many students have acted and written Cawdor's story: his treasons, confessions, begging pardon, repentance and stoicism in the face of death. Some students display a depressingly gruesome inventiveness in different forms of dispatching the thane. Similarly, Shakespeare does not show the scene in Alexandria of the coronation of Antony and Cleopatra, and Antony's gifts of kingdoms, provinces and islands to their children and to Cesarion (3.6.1–19). But in 1992 the Royal Shakespeare Company memorably acted out Octavius' story of the event. As Caesar described the legendary 'donations' ceremony, a dumbshow behind him portrayed just that: the two lovers enthroned in gold and surrounded by their children. The inserted mime was not critically applauded, but it was a narrative enactment that greatly appealed to students who had themselves acted out a presentation of the story.

Yet other stories recapitulate the major events of a play or an episode within it. Puck's tale of the mechanicals' reaction to the sight of the transformed Bottom begins and ends with

---

21 An entertaining exception was 'The Ballad of Sir Roland de Boys' that began the 1998 production of *As You Like It* at the reconstructed Globe on Bankside. As the ballad was sung, stage action portrayed Sir Roland declaring his will and Oliver's ill treatment of Orlando.

Titania's bewitchment: 'My mistress with a monster is in love', 'Titania waked and straightway loved an ass' (3.2.6 and 34). It contains over two dozen events that groups of students present, action by action (and *pace* the comments on verse above, it is in perfectly regular iambic pentameter).

The evident fun in Puck's tale explains why his narrative is frequently enacted by younger students. A much longer story, popular with older classes, is straightforwardly told by Friar Lawrence, Balthasar and Paris' page as they recapitulate well over forty events in *Romeo and Juliet* (5.3.231–85). Lady Macbeth's sleepwalking language recalling earlier happenings is often acted out by students of all ages who possess little knowledge of its context. It is full of opportunities for imaginative inference and action: just what does she do to accompany 'O, O, O'?

A majority of students find that narratives are often more accessible and easier to enact than dialogue. Many teachers, especially of younger students, give the stories priority because they offer many 'active' roles in which all students can participate as actors, narrators, choral speakers, mimes, providers of sound effects and so on. But less dramatic, more 'poetic' speeches pose problems. For example, Titania's 'forgeries of jealousy' (2.1.81–117) has its own narrative drive, and is a popular teachers' choice for students' performance. However, because the speech is so rich in imagery, and because imagery is more difficult than action for students physically to portray, the performance becomes more an activity in choral speaking. Students usually act out only small parts of the speech, toiling as ploughmen, hopping with increasing difficulty through the nine-men's-morris, freezing and shivering.

The level of intellectual demand is raised and narrative enactment becomes more appropriate for older adolescents when students are required to incorporate language and action from earlier scenes into their presentations. For example in the Lady Macbeth sleepwalking scene students are required to show the events, characters and language to which her nightmare language refers. Horatio's highly condensed summary of Hamlet's story makes similar demands on students when they attempt to enact each of the seven 'events' using language and action from earlier scenes:

> So shall you hear
> Of carnal, bloody, and unnatural acts,
> Of accidental judgements, casual slaughters,
> Of deaths put on by cunning and forced cause;
> And, in this upshot, purposes mistook
> Fall'n on th'inventors' heads. (5.2.334–8)

Horatio's promise of a more extended tale later is also a reminder that many plays end with a 'narrative injunction': an invitation to a character or characters to relate their stories.[22] Increasingly, school students respond to that request, stepping into role to tell the character's tale. Teachers use their acted or written accounts to judge both the students' knowledge of the whole play and their awareness of what can be called point-of-view issues: for example how much might a character legitimately know of scenes in which he or she has not appeared?

In *A Midsummer Night's Dream*, even though the mechanicals' motivation throughout is the preparation of a play for the Duke, the worlds of court and mechanicals intersect only in the final Act. Both Theseus and Demetrius promise storytelling of the lovers' adventures: 'we will hear more anon', 'let us recount our dreams' (and these injunctions are fulfilled off-stage between Acts 4 and 5). But the stories will be necessarily limited, unaware of the supernatural or mechanical worlds of the play. The story that any character tells is partial, giving that character's experience, unaware of certain characters, or of episodes in which they have not been involved.

This 'point of view' challenge for the student arises from the nature of a Shakespeare play: it is

---

22 Barbara Hardy, *Shakespeare's Storytellers: Dramatic Narration* (London, 1997), pp. 72–90.

not a story told from a single point of view, but through a series of voices. Unlike most novels, there is no omniscient narrator or single story-teller. Shakespeare does not impose his perspective or interpretation, but presents a series of differing viewpoints which shift as each character speaks, expressing his or her thoughts and feelings.

Or at least, that is the play as it lies on the page. When it is enacted or read, interpretation inevitably comes into play. Just as a director presents his or her own version of the script (even when expressing the desire to let the play 'speak for itself'), so too any telling of the story is a personal and particular view, informed and directed by conscious and unacknowledged preconceptions, values and experience. That inevitable bias has long been part of actors' folklore and anecdote, most recently displayed in *Shakespeare in Love* when the actor playing the Nurse, asked 'What's the play about?' replies 'Well, there was this Nurse . . .'

That comic moment serves to show how teachers further heighten intellectual demand by asking students to consider the truthfulness of any Shakespeare storyteller. Iago is patently untrustworthy, but students also explore the veracity of the narratives of less questioned reporters: does Benvolio give an accurate account of the initial brawl, or of Tybalt's death? Is Friar Lawrence's recapitulation of events entirely transparent? And just how accurate an account is given in that universally popular speech for school enactments, Jaques' pessimistic story of human life? The older the student, the more accuracy or justification for a character's story is required by the teacher.

Such judgement is fraught with problems because the very act of narrative provokes students into motive clarification. Shakespeare's characters do not always reveal their motivation, but in various student activities Juliet confides in her diary what she thinks of her parents, Caliban expands on his conviction that 'This island's mine', and even Coriolanus, that least inward of men, in a much favoured class-

room activity reveals his private thoughts on the student psychiatrist's couch.

These written or enacted narratives reveal that students of all ages possess some purchase on different modes of understanding and interpretation that elsewhere emerge in highly refined form as critical or literary theory. For most students these complexly fashioned analyses of the relationships of Shakespeare with feminism, psychoanalysis, neo-marxism or any other type of critical theory, are neither known nor acknowledged. But these perspectives are certainly in students' minds, albeit in untheorized form. Psychologists' reports, women's accounts, the viewpoints of the subservient or oppressed, are common elements of school Shakespeare. In blissful ignorance of theories of marginality or *aporia*, students put minor characters at the centre of their involvement with the play. Unaware of new historicism or cultural materialism, they give a voice to Caliban and other low-status characters who comment on the injustices and tyranny of their society and masters or mistresses.

The epistolary mode is a huge sub-genre of narrative form in schools. Many thousands of 'letters home' have been written by 'present' but non-speaking characters. Students choose to become one of that host of attendant lords, servants or soldiers who people so many plays. They tell of their experience as gang members or bystanders at a Verona brawl, as sailors on Alonso's ship, as soldiers in Macbeth's or Malcolm's armies, or as servants at that ghost-haunted banquet. Lady Macbeth's gentle-woman often assumes a greater presence in students' classroom work than she ever does on stage.

The exploration of silences, gaps and absences is as inventively undertaken in imaginative freewheeling school Shakespeare as by any postmodern critic. *Jouissance* is very evident as students create their own 'absent characters'. Mrs Bottom and other mechanicals' wives discuss their husbands. Juliet shares her thoughts with a teenage confidante. Fourteen-year-olds tell each other the stories that made Macbeth's hair stand on end, or write memorably as 'an evilly-disposed bat' who lives in the rafters of Inverness castle:

I watched. As Duncan was quietly eating his last supper, Macbeth quietly slipped out. He began to doubt all things that we have sorted out, the poor bugger! To think that he thought he could get out of it! It makes me sick to think of all the religious slobs there are in the world . . .[23]

Other student-invented narratives give glimpses of named characters who never appear but whose actions and personalities help to create the imaginative world of the play: Jane Shore, Cawdor, Lamord, Rosaline, the Indian boy. 'The lively Helena' tells what she knows of the Montagues and Capulets and what she saw at the party. But it is Sycorax, whose presence broods over *The Tempest*, who is the absent character most frequently acted out by students. The appeal of 'this damned witch' is obvious, and Shakespeare's *sjuzhet* provides invitations to imaginative enactment that have been readily seized in classrooms as groups of students portray her 'mischiefs manifold' and 'sorceries terrible to enter human hearing'.

Most striking is the readiness with which students take up Shakespeare's invitation to resolve what was 'the one thing she did' for which the citizens of Algiers spared her life (1.2.267–8). In the theatre the line passes quickly, unremarked by most members of the audience. In the classroom it becomes the central focus of attention, as groups discuss, rehearse and then act out what the single thing was that resulted in her reprieve.

Students' enactments of Sycorax' 'one thing' demonstrate the structural imperatives that so strongly influence human imagination and thought. The detail, the particularity, of each student portrayal has its own uniqueness (and is 'new' to the students themselves), but the generalities are limited and prespecifiable: the danger averted, the lost found, the need fulfilled. Sycorax slays the monster threatening the city, stills the storm, brings the king's daughter

back to life. This structure-revealing activity parallels that other staple of contemporary school Shakespeare in which students act out the incident that set the Montagues and Capulets at each others' throats. Here every invented story's particularities of portrayal reduce to the imperatives of sex, wealth, territory and honour.[24]

Both in these invented stories and in rewritings of speeches or scenes for active presentation, students very often create narrators quite unlike Shakespeare's few examples of the role: Rumour, Chorus, a Prologue armed, Gower. School narrators arise from the common condition of most classroom 'performances': short, for an audience of peers, abridged to fit time, space, resources and the students themselves. In these brief presentations, narrators speak invented introductions, interlinking commentary and epilogues. They put into question Barbara Hardy's claim that 'The presence of a narrator in drama is specious or misleading, deliberated to create an undramatic weight before we are released into dramatic freedom.' For Hardy, narrative, unlike drama, 'tends to be inactive, introvert, single-voiced, quiet, retrospective or prospective'.[25]

Hardy has in mind Shakespeare's and other playwrights' narrators. In contrast school narrators possess the same qualities she detects in dramatic action itself: mobile, active, extrovert, multi-voiced. They take part in the action as they invent a few sentences of introduction to a scene or episode that is about to be staged:

King Alonso's ship is sailing on the calm waters of the Mediterranean. Everyone aboard has just been a guest at the wedding of the king's daughter, Claribel, to the King of Tunis. The sailors are working at

---

[23] Peter Cochran, 'Third Year Macbeth Lessons', in Rex Gibson, *Secondary School Shakespeare* (Cambridge, 1990), pp. 46–9.

[24] Rex Gibson, ' "O, what learning is!" Pedagogy and the afterlife of *Romeo and Juliet*', *Shakespeare Survey 49* (Cambridge, 1996), pp. 141–52.

[25] Hardy, *Shakespeare's Storytellers*, p. 25.

their duties. The wedding guests are relaxing. But something is about to happen that will change all their lives for ever . . .

As they speak, the student-narrators present the ship's crew and the court party, introducing each character. In one school staging of *The Tempest* fifty ten-year-old 'chorus-narrators', sitting in two groups on either side of the stage, spoke in unison, frequently framing the action by other students who spoke Shakespeare's words. The powerful presence of such narrators is also reflected in presentations by older school students who relish inventing self-consciously ironic narration. Their style of delivery makes evident the issues which inhere in any character's narrative, because the narrator becomes in effect a character who is more than a mere describer of the actions of others.

The sonnet-form Prologue that opens *Romeo and Juliet* is a favourite for active storytelling in schools, but the *Sonnets* themselves are used selectively by teachers for acting out. Very obviously, a sonnet is not dramatic in the same way as *Hamlet* or a story within it. There is little or no action or dialogue, and instead of telling a tale, a sonnet attempts to persuade: pleading, warning, reasoning, chiding, or using some other speech mode. But a sonnet's brevity, and the 'drama' of its subject, themes and images have afforded many teachers a ready lesson-sized Shakespeare narrative experience.

Certain sonnets have proved remarkably adaptive to active storytelling by older school students. The task of student groups is to work out a dramatic presentation to accompany and illustrate individual or choral speaking. Sonnet 66 provides large groups with the opportunities to portray the living antitheses 'desert'/'beggar', 'needy nothing'/'jollity' etc. Pairs of students have acted out the implied story of sonnet 57 'Being your slave', and trios have explored the love triangle of Sonnet 42 with its forty-plus deictical referents, and Sonnet 144 'Two loves I have' with its multiple antitheses.

Sonnet 91, 'Some glory in their birth', becomes a group presentation with students portraying actions to show pride in 'birth', 'skill', 'wealth', 'body's force' etc. The nature of what or who the addressee of lines 8–14 ('one general best'), might be becomes the focus of the students' imaginative representation, producing referents that were certainly not in Shakespeare's consciousness. The traditional loved male or female gives way to an initially surprising other: a cigarette, a packet of drugs, a CD, a can of drink. The sonnet becomes a brief and unusual biography. Similarly Sonnet 29 'When in disgrace with fortune and men's eyes' has also yielded its unusual crop of unlikely representations of the 'thee' that brings 'such wealth'.

Sceptics may question the validity of such freewheeling inventions and other aspects of active storytelling described above. But compelling justifications exist for these practices in school Shakespeare. They lie not in the implicit moral agenda of the Lambs (no serious claim is made today that acquaintance with Shakespeare somehow produces better persons), but in the nature of student learning and development, and in the pluralism of Shakespeare.

Students' imaginative habitation of a play, taking parts, speaking the language, and directly experiencing characters' dilemmas, aids empathetic identification, develops awareness of moral, social and political issues, and sharpens insight into the complexity of human relationships. For those students who go on to study Shakespeare in higher education, the narrative coherence that they seek, or import into their own re-creations, prefigure the more structured understandings that later-encountered critical theories will claim to provide. Most demonstrably, the kinds of active storytelling exemplified here develop school students' language skills as they imitate, express and imaginatively extend Shakespeare's *sjuzhet*.

The second set of justifications lies in the rejection of any monolithic conception of Shakespeare. Every Shakespeare narrative takes a form appropriate to its audience and location:

here, young people and schools. Students' own re-imaginings are legitimized in the history of staging and filming the plays. The controversies which have attended particular productions ('taking liberties with the text'), reflect similar concerns about selection, addition or invention in schools. Perhaps the most striking example (certainly the one most familiar to secondary school students) is Baz Luhrmann's *Romeo + Juliet*. Its radical transpositions and language cuts provide an analogue for school Shakespeare,

empowering and giving legitimacy to students' own transformations, abridgements and inventions. It is an extreme example, but its excesses reveal key principles that are instantiated in any production, however 'conventional'. All are products of particular time and place. But in both professional stagings and in school Shakespeare, integrity is guaranteed and the charge of mere relativism avoided by due attention to Shakespeare's *fabula* and *sjuzhet*, the story and the telling.

MONSTERS, MAGICIANS, MOVIES: *THE TEMPEST* AND THE FINAL FRONTIER

RUTH MORSE

Space, of course. For mid-century America, expansion upwards seemed to offer that combination of invitation and threat, possibility and necessity, in which science fiction has thrived. It cannot be surprising that *The Tempest* should have inspired writers of science fiction as much as it inspired other ambitious recreative works of the same period. Their story – a posterity of pulp – is less well known than the one post-colonialists have told.[1] This neglect is curious, since the story is political, and involves questions of power and the responsibility of the scientist, of the definition of civilization and the 'were-I-human'. It even overlaps the post-colonial, in novels which look at the moral repercussions of what came to be called 'first contact'.[2] By contrast, however, the science fictions are less concerned with the status of the individual creative writer, of who owns the word, or of the establishment of a new national literature in a nation language.[3] It is a difficult story to tell briefly, because, in literary-historical terms, it involves descent lines which comprehend collateral branches of the family. And it is a genealogy of quarrels.

Ironies abound, since the achievements of genuinely popular authors have surpassed, in terms of reader, if not critical, attention, the theatrical aspirations of, for example, Césaire's *Une Tempête* of 1960 or Margaret Laurence's national allegory, *The Diviners* (1974).[4] To tell this story is also to question how such stories might be told, for it raises the further questions of how one recognizes a source in *The Tempest*, of just what, or just how many, allusions, and of what quality, make for intertextuality, and, ultimately, why it should have been *The Tempest* to which science fiction authors returned. The history of Caliban is a strong model of how to proceed, as well as being an example of what it describes.[5] To use a science

---

[1] Perhaps only Fredric Jameson, among outstanding cultural critics, has attended seriously to SF writers, though he has not considered their Shakespearian ley-lines. And even he only, seriously, to Philip K. Dick, to whom he has returned repeatedly. See, e.g., his *Postmodernism: or, the Cultural Logic of Late Capitalism* (London, 1991).

[2] This story could begin in 1932 with *Brave New World*, or encompass Huxley's second attempt at the theme, *Island* (1962). I will deal with these subjects at greater length in a book, *Tempests: After Shakespeare*, of which this article forms a part.

[3] On which see Jonathan Bate 'Caliban and Ariel Write Back' *Shakespeare Survey 48* (1995), pp. 155–62.

[4] Aimé Césaire's attempts to establish a 'théâtre nègre' were never popular, in the sense of being connected with the masses, though his francophone version of *The Tempest* displayed the influence of the American black power movement. Nor has Margaret Laurence achieved the audience outside Canada which she deserves. I have tried to assess her relation to the play in 'Taking the Measure of *The Tempest*: *The Diviners* and *Mama Day*' in *Variations sur la lettre, le metre et la mesure*, ed. Dominique Goy-Blanquet (Amiens, 1996), pp. 41–54. John Fowles' fascination with the play has been remarked, but less so J. G. Ballard's.

[5] All studies of the re-interpretations of the play must depend upon Alden T. Vaughan and Virginia Mason Vaughan's *Shakespeare's Caliban: A Cultural History* (Cambridge, 1991). The anecdote with which it begins (a historian's view of a character, seen independently of

fiction metaphor, Caliban is a little like a planetary moon which has escaped its orbit to become a new centre. Or one might think of the way that evolution moves by hybridity, but also by sudden genetic leaps. So authors may read or see Shakespeare directly, they may extract a name or a figure they think they know, or create by combining older motifs, almost stumbling into something quite new and different. Just as Borges insisted that even if Pierre Mesnard reinvented *Don Quixote* word-for-word his book could never be the same as Cervantes', because the world had changed (in part because of the Don), so we need to remind ourselves that assimilations of *The Tempest* absorbed books written in a world consequent upon, as well as subsequent to, Shakespeare. My quadrants, in this exploration, assume that any history of *Tempest* narratives must boldly go beyond Shakespeare's play to consider other contexts. At the same time, any study of influences must define its limits, so that something acts as a control on ostensible 'recognition'.[6] Science Fiction offers clear test cases, partly because it gives us considerable agreement about how it is to be interpreted. And, because it is so often allegorical about current anxieties, it insists upon its own decoding.

To illustrate the metaphor of moons escaping their planets, consider the way that everybody knows about 'Frankenstein monsters'. But the resuscitated cadaver has no name – it is the creator chemist who is called Frankenstein ('graves at my command / Have waked their sleepers, oped, and let 'em forth / By my so potent art'). When we call Frankenstein a scientist, we ignore the distance between natural philosophy and the white-coated boffin ('scientist', in something approaching its contemporary meaning, seems to have been coined by Whewell in 1840). Yet the question is also, metaphorically, one of family resemblances, in which later readers appear to recognize in Shakespeare anticipations of their own concerns: e.g. the control of dangerous knowledge. By genetic leaps I have

in mind the way a new creation will appear to modify something pre-existing, or add to its weight of influence, even if it is more derivative than may subsequently come to be understood. Daniel Defoe's *Robinson Crusoe* (a book of such spectacular success in so many European languages that it has itself become the source of imitation and the focus of scholarly post-colonialist study) is not usually noted as the most outstanding departure from Shakespeare's *Tempest* in the history of literature. But it is hard to imagine Crusoe ('what strength I have's mine own') without the precedent of Prospero.[7]

To claim Crusoe or Frankenstein as descendants of Prospero may appear to assume a degree of indulgence, but the links are palpable. A demonstration requires three categories of proof. First, there is the simplest: allusion,

---

the play's dynamics) is eloquent testimony to cultural memory. See now also *Constellation Caliban*, ed. Nadia Lie and Theo D'haen (Amsterdam and Atlanta, 1997).

6 When Harriet Hawkins asserts that Shakespeare's characters and situations are the ancestors of certain modern ones, she is content to notice resemblance and use it to help delineate audiences who are prepared to accept 'the supernatural', or an equivalent thereof. 'By now there are whole cohorts of thoroughly modern playgoers and cinemagoers who spent their childhoods watching "Star Trek" in America, and glued to "Dr Who" on British television, and heaven only knows how many episodes of both these popular series were directly or indirectly derived from Shakespeare's *The Tempest* . . . Shakespeare's "spirits of a gentler sort", like Puck and Ariel, have most recently been reincarnated as R2D2 and C-3PO, even as Prospero is the prototype of Obie-Wan-Kenobie – "The Force" is with them both', in 'From *King Lear* to *King Kong* and Back', in *Bad Shakespeare*, ed. Maurice Charney (N.Y., 1988), p. 45. This is too thin. One does not need heaven to list direct influence, and one must beware of overgeneralizing indirect influence. Why should we see Puck as part of another tradition of 'helpers', sometimes supernatural, sometimes animals, or both Prospero and Obie-Wan-Kenobie as a single archetype when we might add Merlin?

7 Interestingly, the Science Fiction/Science Fantasy Encyclopedias make this association without taking it further. See *The Encyclopedia of Fantasy*, ed. John Clute and John Grant (London, 1997), numerous entries.

quotation, or direct imitation.[8] Second, there is the catalogue of parallels, in which n-value counts: the more similarities the likelier it is that the second work imitates the first. But number is not everything, and the most interesting category, as well as the hardest to prove, is the third, in which original themes, questions, and attitudes find a response in a new work.[9] None of these categories exists in an isolated state of direct descent. Other works intervene. And one of these is *The Tempest* itself, as it was adapted in the seventeenth century. A 'supplemented' *Tempest*, plus Crusoe, or plus the monster, and particular ways of looking at the Folio text, are all reinforced, and the precedent of seeing Prospero as a scientist, or interpreting the arrival of the Italians on the unnamed island as a potential allegory of 'first contact', becomes as clear to one reading community as the presumed autobiographical significance of the play, or the status of Ariel as the muse (or Spirit) of poetry, once were to others.

Even when cataloguing parallels, it is clear that some are more equal than others. To insist upon a specific minimum of allusion is to raise the burden of proof too high. One might, however, sketch the following conditions: an isolated space, a powerful figure able to exert control over its inhabitants, differentiated inhabitants who might include the powerful figure's child, servant, or enemy. So the sketch contains a magician and a monster on an island. The questions of power and control (because they bring with them the limits, necessary or self-regulated, of that control), the question of that government of the self which qualifies man for government of others, also bring with them the larger question of how the question itself is to be decided. Hence government and inheritance on the island, and off it, too. Whose strict self-discipline makes him 'free'; whose 'freedom' from that discipline keeps him 'slave'? That is at the heart of what constitutes 'civilization', and a negotiable contradiction.

But the conditions of intertextuality change with time, and with accretions. We should not simply juxtapose *Brave New World* and *The Tempest*. A magician may easily become the kind of natural philosopher we would 'recognize' as a scientist; the prince assuming his right to govern becomes a man referring to the Law of God; especially after Mary Shelley raises the question of the limits of our interference in nature, issues of plot or character become issues of theme. If we turn to Crusoe we find an unaccommodated man, shipwrecked on an island, managing only with the Book of Books and the strength of his own hands until the arrival of a servant. Crusoe's experience of that Book is 'conscience raising', and his inner drama typical of Defoe's justifications for fiction. Times change: unlike the Duke of Milan, of course, the Protestant Crusoe discovers the dignity of work. And from that newly originating 'turn' we can trace the beginnings of 'first contact' novels. *Robinson Crusoe* can no more predict the dilemmas of anthropology than *Frankenstein* can outline those of science, but with hindsight both books appear to be ground-laying and, simply, suggestive.

If the premise be accepted, Defoe's variant opens a new, but not wholly new, conversation. How one is to behave once one has, as it were, landed, once one has made first contact, becomes a significant issue. When the magician has mutated into the scientist, when the scientist, perhaps modified by the great chemist whose name has slid onto the name of his monstrous creation, becomes malevolent, then Mary Shelley's 1819 contribution adds to the brew, and we find ourselves on *The Island of Dr*

---

[8] As when Poe calls his prince 'Prospero' in 'The Masque of the Red Death'; or Louisa May Alcott parallels her characters in 'Ariel. A Legend of the Lighthouse', in *A Double Life: Newly Discovered Thrillers of Louisa May Alcott*, ed. Madeleine B. Stern, Joel Myerson, Daniel Shealy (Boston, 1988). Each of these associations reinforces the recognition of magic and the supernatural in the play. The use of the 'type'-name, Miranda, tends to indicate asteroidal independence.

[9] Gloria Naylor's *Mama Day* (New York, 1988) will not be discussed here, but it is precisely this.

Moreau (1896). Just as certain mid-twentieth-century writers thought they recognized in 'Prospero' a Shakespeare-figure who represented English literature, or the right to write, or the beginnings of physical and cultural conquest, so a number of more 'popular' authors raided *The Tempest* for their own themes, themes which, nonetheless, connect them back in a long line. That the apparent similarities which stimulated attention to *The Tempest* may actually have, in some sense, begun with the play, is another of the ironies of literary history. It may also lead us to wonder if the play actually contains a bedrock of recognizable elements.

It is important to remember how far and for how long the play existed as two entities. *The Tempest* in the theatre, from soon after the Restoration, doubled the marriageable inhabitants of the island in an interpretation which had a great deal to do with inheritance and the control of sexuality.[10] Some of the early plays which borrowed motifs from Shakespeare picked up the idea of shipwreck and the fate of castaways, and helped allegorize the storm itself.[11] The theatrical effects, from flying Ariels, disappearing tables, descending goddesses, to nature at its most dramatic, offered new worlds of possible illusion.[12] Not much later, readers (as opposed to theatre-goers) began to insist on Prospero *as* Shakespeare, and on *The Tempest* as Shakespeare's farewell to his art. As a corollary of this interpretation, in eighteenth-century poetry 'Shakespeare's' relation to Ariel came to stand for his inspiration by his Muse, and Ariel then especially for the spirit of poetry itself. In this scheme, wherever the island is located, its proper home is the mind of the artist. The artist, though, is himself (that pronoun is deliberately gendered) more than a local habitation and a name, and his fine frenzy something to be taken seriously. Great power can be used for good or ill. But there is another aspect, which has only recently begun to be studied in criticism of the play, which is Prospero's relation to Sycorax. There is an opening for power, for monsters, and for

magic, which is available because the concatenation is so dangerous. The identification of Prospero with Shakespeare might easily tip over into something less attractive, as ideas of the Creator assumed darker tones.

When mapping the range of *Tempest* interpretations, we contextualize the new ones against the range of available *Tempests* and assumptions about *The Tempest* which an author, engaging with the play, might have taken for granted, as read, even normal. 'Normal' is a palimpsest. So we want to be able to think about desert islands and castaways. The empty space of the island has to be filled, not only by people, but by government, which involves the care of the land. The careful (and care-filled) paternalism of monarchy may look much more threatening if the prince appears tyrannous. But, to return to what has just slipped into the sea: *Shakespeare's* tempest was a narrative trick, at least for its first audience, something we are all too prone to forget.

To pose the question of how to identify a descendant of *The Tempest* is to suggest the following rules of thumb. There is traffic between character and plot, problem and motif, including narrative elements only implied by the source, those attractive holes which invite expansion and explanation. In the sub-genus which is now recognized under the category 'science fiction', one would expect to find a

---

[10] It is also very funny. Most recreative interpretations are not.

[11] As Michael Hattaway has recently pointed out, 'Many of the Renaissance narratives of the New World involve shipwreck. Tempest is a metaphor for rebellion in the Virginia Company's pamphlet, *A True Declaration of Virginia*, one of the principal sources for Shakespeare's play: 'the broken remainder. . .made a great shipwreck in the continent of Virginia by the tempest of dissension . . .' (Michèle Willems and Jean-Pierre Maquerlot, eds., *Travel and Drama in Shakespeare's Time* (Cambridge, 1996), pp. 183–4).

[12] See Anne Barton, ' "Enter Mariners, Wet": Realism in Shakespeare's Last Plays' in *Realism in European Literature*, ed. Nicholas Boyle and Martin Swales (Cambridge, 1986), pp. 28–49.

male character of exceptional intellectual gifts who finds himself somewhere which is or seems to be isolated, not necessarily deserted, and where he needs to exert all the authority of his power and intelligence in order to solve the problem of staying alive and subduing the recalcitrant life forms he finds. This character has been, but is not now, married. Where this 'Prospero' is accompanied by his daughter the question (or problem which is narrativized) of her marriage will arise. Food and shelter will be problems to be solved, as will intellectual work. The mechanical solution is robotic (Robbie in 1956, M4 in 1969) and may displace both Caliban and Ariel.[13] Because the 'Prospero' must erect some form of governance, the problem of sovereignty will also emerge, especially if there are living creatures (or, at least, creatures) on the island-equivalent. It might be expected that the recalcitrant beings would be co-operative and non-co-operative (that is, there must be interaction), that they might be human or not-human, communicative, communicative only to him-, it-, or them-selves, or silent.

One of the hardest things to see is always what is not there. Because Science Fiction has, largely, been an American genre, there is an absence of a servant class. That is, the new Neapolitans may be from earth or the Starship Enterprise, but even when they are in some kind of hierarchically organized armed force, they do not have human servitors. It is a striking feature of the reinterpretations of *The Tempest* just how *seldom* there are equivalents for Stephano and Trinculo. *Forbidden Planet* is exceptional in exploring a double sub-plot, with its sexual predator officer and comic enlisted man, the cook who persuades Robbie (a robotic butler) to manufacture alchohol. Science Fantasy, with its contrasting anxieties of aristocracy and abasement, offers a different sociology.

Films of *The Tempest* quickly show the influence of science fiction, as well as the other way around, as we see in the costumes of the now-

unwatchable 1960 Hallmark Hall of Fame television version of Shakespeare's play with Richard Burton as a heavily literalized web-footed Caliban as well as with other period science fiction costumes.[14] Films come with cinema contexts, their eighty-six minutes' traffic, their own traditions of reference and allusion, and in the films science fiction has never been altogether remote from the genre of the western, with its own problems of first contact, law and the frontier, asymmetries of power, knowledge, and what used to pass for civilization.[15]

Nicholas Nayfack's 'Forbidden Planet' of 1956 was the first feature-length film reinterpretation of the play.[16] It was followed by an episode of *Star Trek*, and these by a series of stories and novels which returned to the play. Not surprisingly, in both films Shakespeare's narrative template reasserts itself and gives us more traditional versions of the romance plot in which the young hero wins the magician's

---

13 One reminder of genealogical collaterals in the study of influence might invite us to consider the importance of the robot and the robots: R2D2 and C-3PO, as a pair in the original *Star Wars*, probably owe as much to *The Wizard of Oz* (specifically the Tin Man and the Cowardly Lion) as they do to Robbie and M4.

14 The Vaughans are kind to this production, but do not remark its affinities with science fiction (pp. 206–8). Daniel Mesguich's 1998 production of a play he called Shakespeare's *La Tempête* for the Comédie française appeared to have been influenced by science fiction (as well as by Peter Greenaway), at least in the sense of costumes and gadgets, including a morphing box.

15 So Zane Grey's Perdita in *The Mysterious Rider* (1921) will owe as much to the western as to Shakespeare.

16 See A. T. Vaughan and V. M. Vaughan, *Caliban: A Cultural History* (Cambridge, 1991), pp. 204–6; Tim Youngs, 'Cruising Against the Id: The Transformation of Caliban in *Forbidden Planet*', in *Constellation Caliban*, pp. 210–29 (with bibliography of film criticism); John Brosnan, *The Primal Screen: a History of Science Fiction Film* (London, 1991). For an essay on fantasy which assimilates the film to Frye's schemes, see Wolfgang Karrer, 'Fantasy-Elemente in Shakespeares *The Tempest* (1611) und MGMs *Forbidden Planet* (1956)', in *Fantasy in Film und Literatur*, ed. Dieter Petzold (*Anglistik und Englischunterricht* 59, 1996), pp. 71–82.

daughter.[17] So far from a Prospero attracting his enemies, the 'Neapolitan'-equivalents on the rescue space-ship meet only resistance from the marooned magus. The lost civilization of Altaira IV failed to govern its inner spaces, just as Morbius fails. The Caliban within, the id, destroys him as it destroyed them. So, too, changes in our explanations for human behaviour may be added to previous psychologies, and what constitutes monstrosity may inflect an old theme. How are we to live together, and what constitutes 'civilized'?

Dr Morbius, alone with his daughter on the *Forbidden Planet*, has rediscovered the power of a long-dead race of inventors whose scientific prowess undid them, offering them more intellect than the brain can handle. The film asks us to think about the power of invention, external scientific invention, and how it can turn upon its creator, but it also asks us to think in psychoanalytic terms, quite simple ones, as it emerges, about our own internalized, and not always acknowledged, mixture of good and evil. It is thus a much larger pastiche than merely one of *The Tempest*, a pastiche which reaches back to Robert Louis Stevenson's Dr Jekyll, for Hyde, the devil within, is a Calibanic monster of stellar strength who is the creation of the uncontrolled Id which overcomes Dr Morbius-Prospero. When the film's Miranda awakens to sexual knowledge she loses her invulnerability to wild beasts, a reference to the fall from innocence which the starship's captain is only too ready to recognize. That he should be called 'Commander Adams' requires no comment. Here, too, the name Miranda has become a signifier for female innocence, and pre-sexual naiveté. The story, the characters, the problems may be palimpsests, but one has also to ask, Palimpsests for whom? And admirable, yes, but only up to a point.

If the love story of *Forbidden Planet* is little more than a cliché, it is as well to remember that one might say something similar about Ferdinand and Miranda; nonetheless it is a cliché which, almost of its essence, refers to an elemental feature of *The Tempest*: youth goes to youth, though fathers rage; love promises a kind of salvation, and daughters will desert their fathers to begin a new round.[18] There is a challenge to the older generation in the captain's wooing and winning, as well as rescuing, even wresting, Alta from her father, which invites us to consider the passing of power with marriage and age. The sexual challenge is a theme emphasized in *The Enchanted Isle*, and it is still a theme when Morbius dies at the end of the film, punished by his own arrogance, and the young people beam themselves away. No sequel was expected. Thus there is not much connection with the space opera, which has a different, but related, existence from the Nayfack film or the narratives of science fiction. The exuberance of the compilation musical, *Return to Forbidden Planet*, offers different possibilities from the dark obsessions of J. G. Ballard.

Nor has the musical to cope with the pressure of next week's episode, a problem faced by television serials. My general point about the

---

[17] This is an issue in *The Magus*, too, where the 'hero' finds that he doesn't want the 'Miranda' character(s) after all.

[18] This is to the point in Tad Williams's *Caliban's Hour* (London, 1994), a book of fantasy by a big-selling science-fiction author. Caliban, now much older, escapes from the island to murder the Miranda who broke his heart many years before (now unhappily married to Ferdinand, who neglects her) – but not until he has taken his hour to tell her their story from his point of view. Her life is saved when her own daughter falls for Caliban and offers to leave with him. Here we have a rescue and recognition fantasy which owes much to the reinterpretations in which 'Caliban' becomes the name for the despised but worthy hero. Rachel Ingalls' 'Mrs Caliban' offers us a symmetrical fantasy: a housewife, disappointed in her husband, finds herself sheltering a sea-monster who takes refuge with her and makes love wonderfully, but who finally escapes back to sea. In the meantime the unsatisfactory husband is disposed of in a car crash, largely the result of his poor driving when he is struck by jealousy. See her *Mrs Caliban and Other Stories* (London, 1993).

necessity of situating a new work in its own several contexts is important here. From its inception, of course, *Star Trek* was, sometimes rather heavily, allegorical, referring to the Cold War and to American social problems – as it continues to do. Gene Rodenberry, the creator of the original *Star Trek* television series, which only ran for the three years 1966–9, liked many different kinds of literary titles, from Helen of Troy to Shakespeare.[19] In this context literary reference is a cue, an invitation to allegory. Text is public shared reference, whether it is the Bible or Sherlock Holmes, which allows the viewer to interpret; famous texts are therefore efficient.

Similarly, the early (or late) television episode, 'Requiem for Methuselah', broadcast 14 February 1969, gave us a powerful recluse who took something from Pygmalion, but also from the Inventors in *Coppélia* or *Tales of Hoffmann*.[20] The Enterprise lands on an apparently uninhabited planet in search of a cure for a virulent disease which has attacked the crew, only to find that its one powerful resident wants them to leave his hiding place immediately. Thus far *Forbidden Planet* seems a likely comparison, and 'Methusaleh' less important as a biblical reference than as another of those asteroidal free-floating labels. But titles are always important, and we neglect them at our peril. The indication in this one is that we should attend to the structural parallels: 'requiem' because Flint, who is dying, learns something from the death of his android, and decides to dedicate his great talent to mankind, rather than to continue to hide himself away. Curiously, the themes (that genius should help others, that the humane virtues are not exclusively human) are almost inconsistent with the more obvious Valentine's Day romance.

Flint (Methuselah as well as Prospero) appears to have a daughter (but so did the inventor Coppélius), the Miranda-like Rayna who falls for Captain Kirk. Rayna-Miranda's love for Kirk is a problem for Flint, because she is not his daughter, but an android whom he

hoped would fall in love with him. But although Flint could teach her, give her knowledge and intellectual stimulation, he could not awaken love. The irresistible Kirk can. Human emotions are new to the android maiden, and the pressure to choose – what Mr Spock identifies as the existential definition of freedom – between the two men she loves causes her to die, or at least to shortcircuit into

---

[19] The danger of ignoring this context is to take Shakespeare as a special case. Elaan of Troyius (broadcast 20 December 1968, in the third and last season) borrowed from the story of Iphigenia as much as it did Helen of Troy. It would be interesting to analyse how many of the seventy-nine original episodes use literary references of one kind or another. After all, the pressure to find a new, self-contained, story once a week has always proved taxing. *Hamlet* was used again in the film, 'The Undiscovered Country' (1991) where the Klingon general (Christopher Plummer) who opposes peace constantly quotes Shakespeare – and the Klingons show their more objectionable side in their belief that Klingon was the Bard's original language. The movie explores the use of Shakespeare and other cultural icons (including a Chagall Expulsion from Eden and a rule of thumb from one of Spock's ancestors, who is meant to be recognized as the denizen of 221B Baker St) to say something about the characters of characters who quote. The reference to Sherlock Holmes as an ancestor is a fine example of the looseness of reference such genres tolerate: the pleasure of recognition does not raise a resisting query about Holmes's children. As a general reference, with an excellent bibliography to 1990, see *Star Trek: an annotated guide to resources on the development, the phenomenon, the people, the television series, the films, the novels and the recordings*, compiled by Susan R. Gibberman (Jefferson, N. C. and London, 1991).

[20] This episode, available as an NTSC videocassette, was written by Jerome Bixby, produced by Fred Freiberger, and directed by Murray Golden. It is one of several episodes which refer to Shakespeare, a relationship which is the concern of a sequence of rather unreliable articles in *Extrapolation* 36.1 (Spring, 1995). There is a summary in *Star Trek 5*, by James Blish (London, 1972), pp. 95–115. The original script team, especially Bixby and Rodenberry, also used allusions to players of *Hamlet* in 'The Conscience of the King' (8 December 1966), which turned the revenge theme upside down; and *Macbeth* in 'Cat's Paw', specially written for Hallowe'en (27 October 1967).

self-destruction. It seems to be unusual for the Miranda to die, but this one is not a daughter, nor is she human. She is intended, like Pygmalion's statue, to be an immortal companion. In retrospect, there is a curious innocence in the Hallmark production (where Lee Remick is Maurice Evans' daughter) as in these two celluloid interpretations: not a hint of incest or sexual abuse. One might look at the situation, in the broad psychological sense, of *King Lear* as much as that of *The Tempest* via *Forbidden Planet*.

Four things seem striking in this episode: the first is the problem of power between the generations; the second is the problem about love and the control of sexuality which is present from the play's inception. *That* is what Kirk awakens in Rayna, and what brings her to adult consciousness. There are similar moments in *Forbidden Planet* and in *Blade Runner*. If, then, thirdly, this is remarkably like the Dryden/Davenant adaptation of *The Tempest* which co-existed with Shakespeare's play in the seventeenth century, nobody, I think, would want to suggest that the *Star Trek* writing team knew that; rather, similar problems inspire similar solutions. But in the future they will not be funny.

The structural parallels offer a fourth point, which is that Flint, who appears unable to die, has outlived – repeatedly – his human attachments. This is why he wants an android, who will not be another mortal woman loved and lost to age and time. He wants to awaken emotion in his highly educated creation. But he has himself lost the affect he seeks to find in her. That the context of the visit to this planet is plague on board ship reinforces the theme of sickness and cure – as well as of the assistance we owe each other. But above all there is the question of what constitutes civilization: it is not the pastiches of works of art by Leonardo and Brahms, fine brandy, and, of course, among Flint's books, a Shakespeare First Folio.[21] It is what we owe, and what we want. The veneer wears thin once the men (as Dr McCoy ex-

plains to Spock) descend to fighting over a woman. The competition between the older Flint and the younger Kirk is at the centre, characterized as 'a test of power'. The limits of that power fall at the compulsion to love: Flint watches the two young people change eyes as Prospero did, but so glad of this as they he cannot be. It is, however, Spock the half-human as much as Dr McCoy, who understands that the heart of civilization is choice, not force. Spock's compassion for his friend Kirk leads him to cure the disease from which Flint had suffered: the pain of loss. Nonetheless, as in a novel by Hemingway, it is the android/woman who dies.

The referentiality of science fiction films is part of film's sense of its own tradition, as science fiction novels are like other kinds of novels. New interpretations of old texts might include those texts, previous interpretations of those texts, as well as interpretations of other texts (or other media) altogether. As a final film example, there is a famous film which is *not* (or not quite) a reinterpretation of *The Tempest*. *Blade Runner*, ostensibly adapted from Philip K. Dick's novel, *Do Androids Dream of Electric Sheep?* offers a limiting case, since the film *adds* motifs associated with *The Tempest* which were not in the novel: chess; a powerful 'father' scientist whose 'daughter' Rachel is rescued by the hero Deckard (played by Harrison Ford). Deckard (married in the novel, not in the film) awakens Rachel (an android, here called a replicant) to human emotion through love (for what it's worth, given her four-year life span); there is a minor Inventor-Assistant who has built companions for

---

21 Part of the fun of these episodes was source-spotting. If I may hazard a wild guess, the source of the name for the fever, Rigellian fever, sounds as much like an opera by Verdi as the name of the planet, Holberg 917–G, does like an orchestral suite by Grieg; Rayna's surname, Kapec, is surely meant to evoke the celebrated Carel, and the locked door in Flint's laboratory is a clear reference to Bluebeard's castle: this time the other wives are duplicates of Rayna.

himself.[22] Tyrell (unmarried), who is responsible for the design and industrial development of the androids, remarks that 'a past creates a cushion for emotions. The replicants are emotionally inexperienced.' Like Morbius or Flint before him, he is the cold scientist (but less stereotyped, with his elegant dressing gown and bedroom with flounces); and like many of his predecessors, he dies at the hand of his creation. There *are* islands (the 'off-world colonies'), and they are frontiers, but the 'bad' androids have escaped from intensive labour on them ('and serves in offices that profit us') back to earth. Yet, unusually, the film is explicit that the 'bad' androids are interested not in insurrection or sovereignty, but in life itself: they do not wish to die after a mere four years. Roy, their leader (their 'king'?), ends by saying, 'It's quite an experience to live in fear. That's what it is to be a slave.' The film suppresses distractions from the 'romantic' plot, plays down Dick's own preoccupations about defining 'the human' in terms of empathy and memory (but adds the possibility that some replicants can evolve morally and emotionally), and rather offers us a world we think we recognize, in which many of the book's complexities are simply not explained.[23] Ironically, as part of the film's substitution of 'low' for 'high' culture motifs, it also erases the novel's references to Mozart's *Magic Flute*, itself probably to be associated with *The Tempest*, a play Mozart might have set had he lived.[24]

It is a cliché to remark that popular culture is often a pastiche, and movies more than most other forms. It is worth remembering how often popular imitations of Shakespeare 'correct' his inversion of a traditional plot-motif, as when the imitative plot reverts to the young man's struggle to win the girl from her Ogre/Magician/Villain father rather than retaining the old man's care for her future.[25] Yet that does nothing to answer the question why some things are more pastichable at certain times than others, and nothing to analyse how far an audience might be expected to recognize and enjoy the intertextual refer-

ences. To recur to my earlier point about efficient reference: if we search for shared icons it is because they perform some of the unifying functions of publicly available identification, giving us a shorthand reference to problems that are not only with us now, but which can be in some sense domesticated because (*mutatis mutandis*) they always have been. Nor need we always know whence the motifs have come. 'Caliban' comes to mean a monster more misunderstood than sinning, or even (as in *Forbidden Planet*) the wild, untamed, untameable, even amoral side of the self. A 'Caliban', under this definition, would be available as a mode of Man Fridays, because he (not, traditionally, she) is within us, partly, at least, human. And here, too, one must remember the complications available in the binary polarity which opposes monstrous perversion and noble savages. Concomitantly, 'Caliban' has pushed 'Ariel' out. By implication, this makes Shakespeare not more important, but less, simply one more cultural reference.

This is the connection to the descent-line of

---

22 The novel appeared in 1968; the film as originally released dates from 1982, with subsequent reissues. I refer exclusively to the 1991 Director's Cut, so I will not discuss the Voiceovers or the question of Deckard testing his own humanity.

23 These are not the only allusions: Harrison Ford's own earlier Han Solo, the evocation of Chandler's Marlowe, and Marlowe's L.A., the *High Noon* moment when Rachel kills to protect Deckard (thus demonstrating affect), and a mawkish biblical reference at the film's close, when Roy has an unexplained nail through his hand, and releases a white dove at the moment of his death. More interesting is his unmotivated rescue of Deckard ('I would, were I human').

24 This was first discussed by Alfred Einstein, 'Mozart and Shakespeare's *The Tempest*' in his *Essays in Music* (London, 1956; orig. 1941), pp. 200–7. And see also Winton Dean, 'Shakespeare and Opera', in *Shakespeare and Music*, ed. Phyllis Hartnoll (London, 1966), pp. 107–8. Both essays consider the possibility (and rightly reject it), then popular among German musicologists, that Mozart had already used *The Tempest*.

25 This would be the case in Marina Warner's disappointing fantasy, *Indigo, or Mapping the Waters* (London, 1992).

interpretations of European expansion. Caliban on the island (or the planet) also offers an opening for 'first contact' themes, in which the question of what to do with new life forms is of moment. First contact implies, and often enacts, the problem of language, also conveniently raised in *The Tempest*, whose Caliban takes his profit in curses (it is also too easy to forget that Miranda has benefited from her father's tuition as other princesses cannot have done). There is evident scope for ecological as well as human conquest. The vogue for *Tempest*-related books has given us over half-a-dozen works, some of which ought probably to be categorized additionally under the heading of 'magic realism'.[26] Just as references to *The Tempest* in science fiction films and television can include what are, in the end, instances of name-dropping, so also superficial allusions, rather than concerted, or extended, intertextual reinterpretation exist in science-fiction novels. One might expect to find Prospero, Caliban, and/or Miranda used in predictable ways as icons of power, monstrosity, and innocence. Sometimes one does, but sometimes the icons are inverted. And sometimes, to open a new category, an open reference at the beginning of an author's career may become something on which he himself rings changes, until the reference is changed out of recognition.

Outstanding among authors categorized primarily as science-fiction writers must be J. G. Ballard. Prospero and Miranda wind their ways through several of his novels, including *The Drought* (1965) and *The Concrete Island* (1974); as well as stories, such as 'The Ultimate City'.[27] Ballard's *Tempest*-allusions are associated, consistently, not with scientists but with architects; he uses a powerful father who has a daughter, physical isolation, and the problem of transfer of power from one generation to the next. Sometimes, it must be said, there is a degree of tenuousness in the connection, as if he preserved one ingredient, but only one, and not as part of a *Tempest*ian theme. His Mirandas are seldom admirable, and rarely innocent. Ballard

uses explicit literary reference, but not always to an obvious end. In *The Drought* he labels his characters as Calibans, Ariels, or Mirandas, and his architect, marooned in a drought-stricken city, has only delusions of power.

'Surprised by this brusque call, Ransom looked round at Philip Jordan, uneasy at this association between Quilter, the grotesque Caliban of all his nightmares, and the calm-eyed Ariel of the river.'

(p. 89)

In context, however, the next paragraph describes Quilter as 'a water-borne Buddha', which suggests no development through the literary references. In *The Concrete Island* a woman replaces the old magician, neither of whom is mentioned, but the marooned Maitland is an architect, and one begins to see that Ballard is ringing his changes not on Shakespeare, but on himself. On the concrete island there is a mental defective, who might, if one were looking for Calibans, fit the bill, but the subterranean reappearance of a Shakespeare play is something it would be hard to argue for if the motifs could not be traced through Ballard's career. This impression is reinforced when one turns to the long story, 'The Ultimate City', in which the architect, Buckmaster (probably an allusion to Buckminster Fuller) remains in the deserted city which has died of its own technological over-kill, pollutions, effluents, and all. His daughter, Miranda, grows flowers, but is a threat to the young

---

26 Many of the science fictions which allude to *The Tempest* name their allegiance in their titles: Phyllis Gotlieb, *O Master Caliban* (N.Y., 1976); Stephen Popkes, *Caliban Landing* (N.Y., 1987); Rachel Ingalls, 'Mrs Caliban' and Tad Williams, *Caliban's Hour* (by a science-fiction author, but not a *science* fiction) both mentioned above. But many do not: Science Fantasy offers only an opportunistic and eclectic sword-and-sorcery 'next-generation' sequel in Elizabeth Willey's *A Sorcerer and a Gentleman* (N. Y., 1995).

27 In *Low-Flying Aircraft* (London, 1976). See Gregory Stephenson, *Out of the Night and Into the Dream: A Thematic Study of the Fiction of J. G. Ballard* (N.Y., 1991).

invader of the city, who wants to bring it all back to life. What, then, are the allusions for?

Much recent theory has harnessed allusions to Shakespeare to arguments for the appropriation of high-status cultural icons in order to legitimate low-status genres. The extension of this who-owns-the-Bard argument is, of course, that the Bard functions precisely as a hegemonic symbol, which people therefore compete to use, thus, concomitantly through their competition, constantly reinscribing him at the centre of cultural capital. In science fiction this ignores the *bricolage*, the extraordinarily generous patchwork of a huge variety of inherited cultural symbols, in which Shakespeare and the Bible co-exist with cars and consumer durables as part of the *bric-à-brac* that is late-twentieth-century affluence. Shakespeare may offer a high-culture icon of reference, but one risks exaggerating his importance.

In the specific context of the *oeuvre* of J. G. Ballard, the importance of the *Tempest* allusions lies much more in the realm of anxiety over fathers, power, and sexuality, for it is the younger man's fear of the older one which evokes allusions to Prospero. For Ballard, magic is never in question, nor is extraordinary mental development. Rather, his references are like something remembered at a distance, and not recently re-read. Unlike many of the publicly available shorthand references implicit in Prosperism or Calibanity, Ballard's references to *The Tempest* belong to his private preoccupations. Indeed, once again, the popular novelist simplifies the narrative by returning it to its traditional emphasis: boy meets girl.

The discipline of manuscript derivation and editing names a principle called the *lectio durior*, the harder reading, which aims to correct the tendency of copyists to opt for easy meanings when there is something they find hard to understand. It is part of 'efficiency' of reference that it loses in nuance what it gains in speed. If we return to asteroids in new orbits, we continue to find publicly agreed meanings which have broken loose from their origins, as

Frankenstein becomes the monster rather than the chemist. Recreative interpretation has gains which may stem from the ruthlessness or simply the ignorance of interpreters' lightning raids upon the literature of the past. Caliban may be monstrous, but he is oppressed or enslaved. The arrival of Europeans on an unknown island becomes, partly via the tendency in other genres to interpret the play in terms of colonialism, a metaphor of first contact as well as of the problems of language and communication.

None of this explains why it should have been *The Tempest* which inspired science fiction. Certainly it has very good special effects. Perhaps this is an unnecessary question. Precocious readers, children whose schools inflicted Shakespeare on them young, independently floating citations, or cultural references all may introduce the unwitting to Prospero's nameless island. Children are notoriously creative interpreters, ready to recognize that science *is* magic. And imitation is not only the sincerest form of flattery, it is the most contagious. The Shaxvirus is virulent. Once there has been one recreative imitation, inertia may well take over, and in its repeated references to Shakespeare, science fiction is no different from other aspects of anglophone culture. The 'final' frontier turned out to be no more final than it was a frontier; the space odyssey retained its narrative affiliation to the horse opera. Like the *Tempest*s we now categorize as 'post-colonial', the science fiction reinterpretations demarcate their own territory, mainly that of knowledge and power, but they express their themes through the narratives of popular romance. Science fictions have always asked how we are to live. If they mark the anxiety of allegory, they continue to find in it a place to play out Gonzalo's dream.[28]

---

[28] This article originated in a talk at the University of Münster where it benefited from the scepticism of Professor Brian Gibbons. I am grateful to Dr Stefan Collini, Professor Peter Holland, and Dr Barry Windeatt for their comments on an earlier draft. See also Roger Allen, *Isaac Asimov's Caliban* (NY, 1993).

SHAKESPEARE'S SELF-REPETITIONS AND *KING JOHN*

E. A. J. HONIGMANN

Shakespeare's habit of recycling his favourite dramatic devices is generally recognized. Just about every component part of a play might be repeated – characters, episodes, 'scenic form', stage actions, thematic preoccupations, words and phrases, image clusters, and so on. How could it be otherwise? We are aware of similar self-repetition in other writers, and in composers, painters, choreographers, and think nothing of it. I want to suggest that such self-repetitions, when of sufficient quality and quantity, can serve as an authorial finger-print, with interesting applications in other fields.

For reasons that will soon be obvious, I shall focus on self-repetitions in *King John*. All are found in plays that preceded *King John* and most of them in others that came later, though I am chiefly concerned with those that preceded. *King John*, in short, is never the beginning of a series of self-repetitions in the list that follows, and usually is not the end.

(1) The most striking series involves character stereotypes. For example, scolding, aggressive and bitter women revile their enemies and/or utter long-winded lamentations (Joan of Arc in *1 Henry VI*; Duchess of Gloucester, Queen Elizabeth, Duchess of York in *2 and 3 Henry VI*, *Richard III*: compare Queen Eleanor and Constance in *King John*). This stereotype survives, in modified form, in Lady Macbeth, Cleopatra, Volumnia, Paulina. Prattling, pathetic boys are threatened with death (Rutland in *3 Henry VI*; the princes killed in the Tower, *Richard III*; Maduff's son, *Macbeth*: compare Arthur). A

Machiavellian churchman, usually a cardinal, is more preoccupied with temporal than spiritual affairs (the Cardinal Bishop of Winchester, *1* and *2 Henry VI*; Cardinal Bourchier, *Richard III*; the Archbishop of Canterbury, *Henry V*; Wolsey, *Henry VIII*: compare Pandolf). A cowardly military man who usually 'talks big' gets his come-uppance (Sir John Fastolf, *1 Henry VI*; Falstaff, *1* and *2 Henry IV*; Pistol, Parolles, Cloten: compare Austria). A princess becomes a pawn in the dynastic power-game (Bona, *3 Henry VI*; Lady Anne, *Richard III*; Katherine, *Henry V*: compare Blanche). A supporter of one of the major characters gets cold feet when asked to commit or connive at a murder (Buckingham and Hastings, *Richard III*; the Provost, *Measure*; Camillo, *Winter's Tale*: compare Hubert). See also Falconbridge (below, 10).

(2) A heroic or idealized figure from the immediate past serves as a yardstick for, and overshadows, the next generation (Henry V in *1*, *2* and *3 Henry VI*; Old Hamlet; Julius Caesar in *Antony and Cleopatra*; the dead fathers in *All's Well*: compare Richard Coeur-de-lion in *King John*).

(3) An inexperienced young prince receives instruction in *Realpolitik* from an older Machiavellian, and later defies his master (Tamora's sons and Aaron, *Titus*; Henry VIII and Wolsey; also Romeo and Friar Lawrence: compare the Dauphin and Pandolf).

(4) A play is structured around a voluntary abdication or a deposition (*3 Henry VI*, 1.1.195ff.; *Richard II*; *Lear*; and, in modified

form, *Titus* 1.1.187ff.; *Measure* 1.1.13ff.; *Pericles*; *Winter's Tale*; *Tempest*: compare *King John* 5.1.1 and 77).

(5) The siege of a city serves as focal point for a sequence of scenes (Orleans, Rouen, Bordeaux in *1 Henry VI*; Harfleur, *Henry V*; Rome, *Coriolanus*: compare Angers, *King John*).

(6) A usurper keeps his young nephew from the throne by strong possession (*King John* 1.1.40) and orders the nephew's imprisonment and murder. The king sometimes has to give way to his mother's forceful personality and is berated by his sister-in-law. Compare *Richard III*. How many other Shakespearian kings are presented with their mother, sister-in-law and nephew?

(7) An ambiguous prophecy is understood too late (Bolingbroke in *2 Henry VI* 1.4.16ff.; 'a prophecy . . . that "G" / Of Edward's heirs the murderer shall be', *Richard III* 1.1.39–40; the Weird Sisters: compare Peter of Pomfret, *King John* 4.2.147ff.).

(8) Historical events are telescoped unhistorically. In *King John* 4.2 'practically the whole span of John's reign [is] crammed into one scene and made to seem simultaneous, for the dramatic advantage of heaping up John's troubles and omens of misfortune',[1] namely events dating from the years 1200, 1201, 1202, 1204, 1213 and 1216. Exactly the same faking of historical facts, for dramatic effect, had preceded *King John* in the 'grossly telescoped history' of *Richard III*, Act 1 (1471, 1472, 1478) and 4.4.429ff. (1483 and 1485),[2] and Shakespeare continued to rearrange his source material throughout his career. The dramatic effectiveness of such rearrangement must count as one of his most distinctive artistic achievements.

(9) Scenic development can be strangely similar. Compare *King John* 2.1.1ff. and *3 Henry VI* 3.3.1ff. (a) A royal mother and her young son appeal to the French king for help against the usurping king of England (Queen Margaret, Prince Edward; Constance, Arthur). (b) The issue depends on identifying the 'true-anointed lawful king' of England (*3 Henry VI* 3.3.29), a point debated at great length in *King John*. (c) A

dynastic marriage is proposed for Bona / Blanche by a third party (Warwick; Citizen); Queen Margaret / Constance sees that this marriage would be a disaster for her cause and denounces it as 'deceit bred by necessity' (*3 Henry VI* 3.3.68) and 'False blood to false blood joined' (*King John* 2.2.2). (d) The French king and Bona / Blanche have agreed to the marriage when a messenger arrives (the 'Post', *3 Henry VI*; Pandolf, *King John*) with wholly unexpected news, a *coup de théâtre* that throws everything into reverse gear – (i) King Edward has married the Lady Grey, therefore cannot marry Bona, and (ii) Pandolf, defied by King John, orders the French king to 'raise the power of France upon his head'. (e) The French decide to invade England (*3 Henry VI* 3.3.222; *King John* 3.4.173ff.).

Here again *King John* telescopes history, which makes the repetition of *3 Henry VI* all the more significant. In Holinshed, Constance and Arthur appeal to the French for help, and a dynastic marriage is proposed to bind the French and King John together, in the year 1200. The marriage is agreed, and now the *King John* plays jump to the year 1202, when the French king commands John to restore Arthur's lands and 'began war against him', to 1205, when John and the Pope begin their quarrel, to 1209, when the Pope sends Pandolf to John, then back to 1202, when Arthur is taken captive. In *King John* all these events are crammed into a single day.[3]

The unconscious repetition of a single scene's sequence of events from *3 Henry VI* in Acts 2 and 3 of *King John* may be compared to the repetition of 'scenic form' in different plays, a phenomenon convincingly expounded by

---

[1] See my edition of *King John* (Arden Shakespeare, 1954), p. xxxi.

[2] See my edition of *Richard III* (New Penguin Shakespeare, 1968), p. 16.

[3] For Shakespeare's rearrangement of historical events see also *King John*, ed. L. A. Beaurline (New Cambridge Shakespeare, 1990), p. 202.

Emrys Jones.[4] True, a different time-scale operates in the two plays. It could be said, though, that Acts 2 and 3 of *King John*, which, I repeat, take place on a single day outside Angers, have the sweep of a single scene, modelled on the earlier and simpler scene in *3 Henry VI*. That *3 Henry VI* helped to shape the sequence of episodes in *King John* is confirmed by the curious coincidence that the two mothers (Margaret, Constance) both seat themselves on the ground, to express their sense of despair and helplessness (*3 Henry VI* 3.3.9–11, *King John* 2.2.73).

(10) One of Shakespeare's undisputed successes in *King John* is the Bastard, Falconbridge, sometimes described as a repetition of the Bastard Dunois in *1 Henry VI*. Falconbridge, however, has more in common with a more important series – high-spirited men, mostly youthful, who may be either villains (Aaron, Richard III, Iago, Edmund), or boisterous but not evil (Petruchio, Mercutio, Graziano, Hotspur). Falconbridge, clearly a member of the latter series, is nevertheless closely related to one man in the former, Richard III.

Indeed, Falconbridge is so close to Richard in so many ways that Richard must be seen as his immediate model. Both are cynics endowed with tremendous gusto, fearless fighters with exceptional 'leadership qualities', both want to rise in the world (*Richard III* 1.1.152ff.; *King John* 1.1.206, 216). Both are humorists with a similar brand of whimsy and impudence (*Richard III* 2.2.97; *King John* 1.1.233), both love to taunt their enemies, both mock conventional lovers (*Richard III* 1.2.242ff.; *King John* 2.1.505ff.) and conventional behaviour generally; Richard has a more pronounced sadistic streak, yet Falconbridge's treatment of Austria is not without sadism (*King John* 3.1.56ff.). Both ridicule the simplicity of others ('Simple plain Clarence', *Richard III* 1.1.119; 'O prudent discipline . . . Austria and France shoot in each other's mouth', *King John* 2.1.414–15). Both are called 'devil' and speak with enthusiasm of 'playing the devil' (*Richard III* 1.3.336; *King John* 2.1.135). Each is a keen analyst of motives, including his own motives, has little respect for his superiors and offers them advice unasked. Each admires his father and vows to revenge his death (*3 Henry VI* 2.1.87; *King John* 2.1.139). Each is rebuked by his mother and publicly casts doubt on her chastity (Richard with the help of Buckingham, Falconbridge in his mother's presence); the mother's 'computation of the time' (*Richard III* 3.5.87; *King John* 1.1.113) and the son's lack of resemblance to his supposed father (*3 Henry VI* 2.2.135; *King John* 1.1.79, 233ff.) are cited as evidence.

Of course, Richard and Falconbridge also differ in important respects, chiefly in their moral natures. Their similarities are nevertheless extraordinary: we may say that if Hamlet resembles Brutus, or Miranda Perdita, the 'character' of Falconbridge was quite as heavily indebted to Richard. Their family or serial connections must count as among the closest of Shakespeare's self-repetitions.

But wait: was Falconbridge not modelled on his namesake in *The Troublesome Reign of John King of England* (1591)? Could he have been modelled on two men, the Falconbridge of *Troublesome Reign*, and also Richard? This question is complicated by the fact that most of the self-repetitions noted above as (1) to (9) are, again, found in *Troublesome Reign*. Is it possible that *Troublesome Reign*, if it existed before Shakespeare began as a dramatist, influenced so many of his plays in so many different ways? That it gave Shakespeare not only the Richard-Falconbridge stereotype (10) but also other character stereotypes that remained his favourites for many years (1), structural subtleties and idiosyncrasies (2–7), the habit of rearranging historical events for dramatic effect (8) and the scenic development of *3 Henry VI* 3.3 and of *King John* 2.1 to 3.3 (9)? Is it possible that the author of *Troublesome Reign* anticipated so many of Shakespeare's dramaturgic characteristics and

---

4 Emrys Jones, *Scenic Form in Shakespeare* (Oxford, 1971).

felicities that we have to see him as, to all intents, another Shakespeare?

Here we should recall that a different view of *Troublesome Reign* has gained ground in the last half-century, prompted by a strange paradox: *Troublesome Reign*, a beautifully plotted play in its analysis of complex political manoeuvres and its dramatic control, at times appears to confuse or forget its own logic. For instance, *Troublesome Reign* brings Lady Falconbridge on stage earlier than *King John*, which means that in *Troublesome Reign* 'she witnesses the Bastard's open confession that he is the son of King Richard . . . But her presence early in the scene renders otiose the private interview that follows between her and the Bastard, for she speaks to him as if he does not know the identity of his true father.'[5] Again, as L. A. Beaurline has also shown,

the dramatic purpose of the changes common to both plays [*Troublesome Reign* and *King John*] is to focus on relationships in the first three acts, and much of the fourth, that magnify the danger of Arthur's claims to England, the opportunistic motives for French support of those claims, and John's fear of them . . . This is the selective principle for the actions of both plays: nearly everything done by John, King Philip and their entourage seems contingent upon Arthur.[6]

Yet, Beaurline went on, 'the execution of these scenes in *Troublesome Reign* is the critical evidence that the author did not realize exactly what the momentous artistic choices entail, for . . . the anonymous author failed to make much of John's order to kill Arthur'. The author of *Troublesome Reign*, said Rosalind King, 'found his own meaning in the story',[7] he wrote a play that resembles Shakespeare's in its plotting yet goes off the rails whenever it differs from Shakespeare in its plotting – 'an anti-papist polemic in the style and form of Marlowe', much more crudely anti-Catholic than *King John*.

Three of its editors have questioned the traditional view of *King John* as a reworking of *Troublesome Reign*. I have argued that *King John*,

though sometimes seen as a 'one-off' play, a play that stands apart from Shakespeare's oeuvre and refuses to fit in, has its place in the natural development of his dramatic craftsmanship, just like all his other self-repeating work. It builds on his previous successes and it makes some notable advances (Falconbridge, Pandolf, John's temptation of Hubert, 3.3.19ff., the impressive grasp of political interaction and the grand design of the play as a whole). It is particularly close to *3 Henry VI* and *Richard III*, two history plays that preceded it, in ways that have not been recognized; less obviously, it re-uses dramatic techniques that Shakespeare had tried out in other early work, and points forward to their re-use in later plays (I have cited only a few examples). It 'fits in' as an original Shakespeare play, whereas it would be an anomaly if it were the only Shakespeare play that slavishly follows the plotting of another dramatist.

Before I return to Shakespeare's self-repetitions, I want to make some further comments on the King John plays. (1) Richard III and Shakespeare's Falconbridge are so alike, and require so many similar talents in performance, that it seems not unreasonable to assume that the two roles were intended for the same actor. We know that Richard Burbage played Richard III (though not necessarily from the very beginning) – could he have been the first actor of Falconbridge?

(2) The date of the first King John play can be fixed within fairly narrow limits. Whichever came first, it was clearly an 'Armada play', and must have followed the murder of the French King, Henry III, by a fanatic monk in August, 1589 (cf. *King John* 5.6.24, 'The King, I fear, is

---

5 Beaurline, *King John*, p. 201.
6 Beaurline, *King John*, p. 202. Cf. Brian Boyd, '*King John* and *The Troublesome Reigne*: Sources, Structure, Sequence', *Philological Quarterly*, 74 (1995), 37–56.
7 Rosalind King, 'The Case for the Earlier Canon' (in *Shakespearean Continuities*, ed. John Batchelor, Tom Cain and Claire Lamont (London, 1997), 108–22).

poisoned by a monk'). The political situation in France, moreover, resembled the King John story in other ways. Henry's nobles had banded together against him in the Catholic 'League' (cf. the revolt of King John's barons). The Queen Mother, Catherine de' Medici, had been a political force for many years, dominating King Henry as Queen Eleanor dominates her son, King John (in *King John* Queen Eleanor takes charge or intervenes repeatedly as a key political player, like Catherine: 1.1.31–43; 64; 134ff.; 2.1.120ff.; 191; 469ff. She is 'An Ate, stirring [John] to blood and strife', 2.1.63).

The first King John play, then, can be dated between late 1589 and late 1591. (3) At this very time a long-standing family feud erupted at the Theatre. James Burbage, Richard's father, had built the Theatre with his brother-in-law, John Brayne; after Brayne's death, in 1586, his widow fell out with the Burbages about the receipts for the Theatre's galleries. The Court of Chancery heard the widow's complaints on 4, 13 and 28 November 1590, and the Burbages fought off the widow and her friends on 16 November, as well as other days, while theatre-goers looked on.[8]

On 16 November Mrs Brayne and her supporters stood at the gallery entrance, determined to collect her moiety (share), as Chancery had decreed. James Burbage called her a 'murdering whore' – 'hang her, whore, quoth he, she getteth nothing here!', and Mrs Burbage railed as well. One witness saw Richard Burbage in the thick of it, with a broomstaff in his hand; Burbage, laughing, said they came for a moiety, 'but', quoth he, holding up the said broomstaff, 'I have I think delivered him a moiety with this, and sent them packing.' And one ineffective supporter of Mrs Brayne deposed that Richard Burbage, 'scornfully and disdainfully playing with this deponent's nose, said that if he dealt in the matter he would beat him also and did challenge the field of him'. These events seem to be reflected in the King John plays in the family feud outside

Angers, and particularly in Falconbridge's scornful treatment of the widow's ineffective supporter, the unhistorical 'Austria', who is not present at John's interview with the French king in the chronicles (2.1.1ff.).

Yet, whether or not the battles outside Angers refer back to those outside the Theatre, the legal depositions give us a fascinating glimpse of Richard Burbage's exuberant character which, I suggest, helped to inspire Shakespeare's Falconbridge (who is briefly mentioned by Holinshed, without any hint as to his character). That in turn makes it more likely that Burbage as Falconbridge preceded his namesake in *Troublesome Reign*, a part no doubt played by a different actor for a different company, the Queen's Men.

(4) There is an unmistakable allusion in *King John* 1.1.243–4 to *Soliman and Perseda* (usually dated *c.* 1589–92). Addressed as 'thou most untoward knave', Falconbridge retorts 'Knight, knight, good mother, Basilisco-like!': compare *Soliman* 1.3; '*Basilisco.* Knight, good fellow, knight, knight – *Piston.* Knave, good fellow, knave, knave!' For this and other reasons J. Dover Wilson suggested that Shakespeare wrote an early King John play in 1590–1,[9] and E. M. W. Tillyard agreed:[10] 'as an authentic, consistent, and self-supporting composition the *Troublesome Reign* cannot pass. The masterly construction is quite at odds with the heterogeneous execution.' Accordingly Tillyard proposed that *Troublesome Reign* was not based on '*King John* as we have it', but on an earlier version by Shakespeare, later revised: *Troublesome Reign* retained the fine construction of this lost play and garbled the execution.

To sum up (1) to (4): although I do not regard these points as equally certain, I think it significant that, despite the wide-spread belief

---

8 See the Arden edition, *King John*, pp. l–lii.
9 Ibid., p. xliv, and J. Dover Wilson, ed. *King John* (Cambridge, 1936), pp. lii–liv.
10 E. M. W. Tillyard, *Shakespeare's History Plays* (London, 1944; ed. 1962), p. 216.

that *Troublesome Reign* preceded *King John*, there are reasons for dating either *King John* or an early version of this play as early as 1590–1.

(5) The curious language of *Troublesome Reign* also deserves some attention. It suffers from being grotesquely overwrought (e.g. 'Doth masserate the bowels of my soule', 142^{11}), and is overloaded with what look like echoes of Shakespeare, Marlowe, Peele and Kyd. Rupert Taylor listed most of these echoes (in 1936, before the debate about *King John* and *Troublesome Reign* had got into its stride) and concluded that 'the author of *Troublesome Reign* was a chronic imitator'.[12]

Taylor's conclusion has been stressed by those who believe that *King John* preceded *Troublesome Reign*, and largely ignored by their opponents. The opponents doubtlessly thought that close 'echoes' could have gone either way, and this is sometimes true.

(i) 'Sham'st *thou* not, *knowing whence thou art extraught*?' (*3 Henry VI* 2.2.142); 'And when *thou knowest from whence thou art extraught*' (*Troublesome Reign* 394).

(ii) '*Set down, set down* your honourable *load*' (*Richard III* 1.2.1); '*Set downe, set downe* the *load* not worth your pain' (*Troublesome Reign* 786).

Occasionally, however, an 'echoing' passage is closer to Holinshed in one text than the other – what should we make of that?

(iii)

(a) Before the days of change, still is it so.
    By a *divine instinct* men's minds mistrust
    Ensuing danger, as by proof we see
    The water swell before a boist'rous storm.
    (*Richard III* 2.3.41–4)

(b) before such great things, mens hearts of a secret instinct of nature misgiue them; as the sea without wind swelleth of himselfe sometime before a tempest. (Holinshed, 1587, iii, 721)

(c) Your Citie Rochester with great applause
    By some *deuine instinct* layd armes aside.
    (*2 Troublesome Reign* 518)[13]

Here (a) and (b) refer to the very same events, but (c) transplants 'By . . . divine instinct'

from the reign of Richard III to that of King John.

(iv) Compare also (a) *King John* 2.1.62ff. and (b) *Troublesome Reign* 485ff.

(a) With him along is come the *Mother-Queen* . . .
    With her *her niece*, the *Lady Blanche of Spain*;
    With *them a bastard of the King's deceased* . . .
    The interruption of their churlish drums
    Cuts off more circumstance. They are at hand.

(b) *More circumstance* the season *intercepts* . . .
    Next *them a Bastard of the Kings deceast* . . .
    Then is there with them Elinor *Mother Queene*,
    And *Blanch her Neece* daughter to the King *of Spaine* . . .

In *King John* the French king now exclaims 'How much *unlooked-for* is this expedition!' (line 79); in (b) he says 'I *rather lookt* for some submisse reply' (499, i.e. line 78 of the equivalent scene). Although both dramatists consulted Holinshed, one also echoed the other – and Shakespeare's 'unlooked-for' repeats Holinshed ('K. Iohn commeth vpon his enimies *not looked for*', 164 ii), whilst (b) comments on John's reply, not his unexpected arrival in France.

The echoes in (iii) and (iv) support the view that *King John* preceded *Troublesome Reign*. Yet the closeness of some of the echoes also prompts further questions. If *King John* came first, and remained unpublished until 1623, how could the author of *Troublesome Reign* reproduce so many snatches of its dialogue? I think that the answer may be that he had acted in *King John* – and, it would follow, in other plays by Shakespeare, Marlowe, Peele and Kyd. Then, to look at the problem from a different angle, if he had indeed acted in *King John* why

---

11 Line numbers refer to G. Bullough's reprint in *Narrative and Dramatic Sources of Shakespeare*, vol. 4 (London, 1962).

12 See Rupert Taylor, 'A tentative Chronology of Marlowe's and some other Elizabethan Plays', *PMLA*, 51 (1936), 643–88.

13 See my *Shakespeare's Impact on his Contemporaries* (London, 1982), p. 82.

could he not remember more of its dialogue? To get this question into focus, let us be clear that in 1591, the latest possible date for *Troublesome Reign*, the name Shakespeare had not yet appeared in print and would have little or no prestige. If *King John* already existed at this time we are not entitled to assume that the author of *Troublesome Reign* would wish to reproduce its dialogue. Quite the contrary: he favoured a very different style, the 'torrent, tempest and whirlwind' style of the popular theatre.[14] In short, he did not try to reproduce Shakespeare's dialogue because he thought he could do better.

The hypothesis that the author of *Troublesome Reign* had acted in *King John* could solve another problem – that he remembered the names of minor roles and even Shakespeare's stage directions. Others have suggested that he may have had access to a plot or scenario of *King John*,[15] which is also possible and would not conflict with my hypothesis. That actors helped to reconstruct plays as 'bad quartos' or derivative plays is not, of course, a new idea: it can be validated from the memoirs of eighteenth-century actors and producers.[16]

A date as early as 1590–1 may strike some experts as improbable. If so, they may prefer the Wilson-Tillyard theory of an earlier version of Shakespeare's play. While I would not rule this out, I think that we should take care not to postulate lost plays needlessly.[17] It should be noted, however, that whatever date we assign to Shakespeare's very first plays, it seems to be universally agreed that *King John* came a little later, after the first tetralogy, after *Titus Andronicus* and *The Shrew*. In other words, though we may argue about the *dates* of these early plays, the *order* in which they were written is not in dispute. The characteristic self-repetitions in *King John* (1–10, above), integral to the plotting of *King John* and *Troublesome Reign*, were all used independently by Shakespeare in plays written before *King John*, and this makes it unlikely that he pilfered them from *Troublesome Reign*.

I now want to return to Shakespeare's self-repetitions, and first to that of *3 Henry VI* 3.3 in *King John* 2.1.1ff. (cf. p. 176, above). For here both plays depart from Holinshed in their plotting, *3 Henry VI* a little and *King John* much more drastically (cf. p. 176) to achieve the same *coup de théâtre* – a proposed marriage and peace treaty between France and England is succeeded immediately by an outbreak of war. In Holinshed's accounts of King John and Edward IV war does not follow immediately, in the plays there is an obvious dramatic advantage in engineering such a peripeteia. Who thought of it first? There are three possibilities. Either (1) *Troublesome Reign* preceded both *3 Henry VI* and *King John*, which would mean that *Troublesome Reign* invented the quite unhistorical 'scenic development' that *3 Henry VI* later adopted directly from Holinshed. Or (2) *Troublesome Reign* came between Shakespeare's two plays and adopted its scenic development from *3 Henry VI*, which would mean that almost all my ten self-repetitions occurred in Shakespeare's plays before *Troublesome Reign* existed (even 10, since the character of Richard III was already clearly defined in *3 Henry VI*), and this, again, makes it unlikely that Shakespeare pilfered them from *Troublesome Reign*. Or, (3), the scene in *3 Henry VI*, more or less repeating the sequence of events in Holinshed, served as template for the very similar (but quite unhistorical) sequence in *King John*, and *Troublesome Reign* copied from *King John*.

In this instance either the author of *King John* or the author of *Troublesome Reign* appears to have shuffled the historical facts like a pack of cards, yet with a wonderful understanding and control of the dramatic ups and downs. Such

---

14 Cf. *Hamlet*, 3.2.6.
15 Cf. Beaurline, *King John*, pp. 206–9, and Boyd, '*King John*', p. 46.
16 See Peter Alexander, *Shakespeare's Henry VI and Richard III* (Cambridge, 1929), pp. 68–71.
17 Cf. my 'Shakespeare's "Lost Source-Plays"' *MLR*, 49, (1954), 293–307).

dramaturgic mastery cannot be acquired in a day. Even Shakespeare started as a learner, as we see by comparing the plotting skills in *3 Henry VI* (tentative), *Richard III* (a rise-and-fall plot, centring on the murder of the princes) and *King John* (a looser, more sophisticated rise-and-fall plot, centring on the supposed murder of Arthur). He had written at least seven or eight plays before *King John*, and must have learned from each of them how to improve his plotting. Are we to imagine that the author of *Troublesome Reign*, without any prior experience that we know of, reached a Shakespearian standard so quickly, a standard that Shakespeare himself made his own only after some years of trial and error?

At this point I have to stress that a dramatist's plotting may engage his very highest powers, though no doubt there are also plays that are thrown together very quickly. Shakespeare's self-repetitions may serve as an example: they are always adapted to the needs of his play, like his characterization or humour, and involved much more than the expert cobbling together of episodes. His plotting skills were called upon when he decided what to include and what to leave out, how to mingle crescendo and diminuendo, how long each scene should be – even, how long each speech should be.

It follows that the ten self-repetitions listed at the beginning of this paper are only the tip of an iceberg. Other self-repetitions form a network that links every play to the rest of the canon. And the more closely we examine Shakespeare's plotting the more clear it becomes how much trouble he took to integrate these self-repetitions in their different contexts. Thus the heroic figure from the immediate past (list 2, p. 175) reappears in the Henry VI plays as a glorious memory and rallying cry (Henry V); Old Hamlet returns 'In the same figure like the king that's dead', and seems to speak with the same voice; Coeur-de-lion is conjured up for us by his lionskin and by his son ('The very spirit of Plantagenet'). Each of the three is one of a series, and at the same

time is imagined by Shakespeare with all the particularity characteristic of his work when his mind is fully engaged.

Shakespeare's plotting, I submit, was no less characteristic of the man than his poetic style and his intellectual tolerance. His rearrangement of episodes, the multiplicity of his plot-material and his tight control of it, so that every detail counts, as also his favourite plot-devices, express his personality and distinguish him from all rivals. Except, we are asked to believe, that one, the otherwise unheard-of author of *Troublesome Reign*, had a genius for plotting marvellously like Shakespeare's own. Yet if *Troublesome Reign* did not exist, who would wish to suggest that the plotting of *King John* was not quite typical of Shakespeare? To give one more example, is it not pure Shakespeare that King John's claim to the crown is implicitly contrasted with the dispute of the Falconbridge brothers, just as, in the first scene of *Titus Andronicus*, virtuous Titus' paternal coldness is meant to contrast with wicked Tamora's maternal passion?

All too obviously, the plotting of either *King John* or of *Troublesome Reign* was copied. Which came first? It is an important question, since the dating of so many other plays depends on the answer. Let us rephrase it: one of the two plays was plotted by a master – was it a master who is never heard of again, or one who became the most admired dramatist of his age, and who had already experimented with the self-repetitions that reappear in *King John* and in so many of his later works?

How did it come about in the first place that *Troublesome Reign* was thought to be the source of *King John*? This notion was connected with the theory that Shakespeare started his career as a play-patcher. *Titus Andronicus*, *The Taming of the Shrew*, *King John*, *1*, *2* and *3 Henry VI*, even *The Comedy of Errors*, were once all held to be revisions of earlier plays. And as *2* and *3 Henry VI* appeared to follow *The Contention* and *The True Tragedy* not merely scene by scene and speech by speech but very often line by line, the closeness of *King John* to *Troublesome Reign* did not seem so surprising. Now that *2* and *3 Henry VI* are no longer seen as revisions of earlier plays we must ask whether the traditional view, that Shakespeare based *King John* on *Troublesome Reign*, the one isolated instance of his quite uncharacteristic indebtedness to a supposed source-play, is simply a hangover from an outmoded theory.

In this paper I have argued that Shakespeare's previous explorations of character, scenic development and of his drama's great variety of technical devices, would have steered him, quite independently of *Troublesome Reign*, towards a play consisting of structural elements such as those of *King John*. But why the unheroic story of King John? Reverting to the 'weak king' and other preoccupations of the first tetralogy, though now gathered together in a more typically Shakespearian plot, *King John* combines the tragedy of a family with the tragedy of England. Who, except Shakespeare, would have thought of fusing the two in the person of the Bastard, a Plantagenet who is also, it has been said, 'the spirit of England'? Who, except Shakespeare, could have *imagined* the Bastard, the crowning glory of the play, so closely related as he is to Richard III and to that other 'madcap', Petruchio (*The Shrew* 2.1.283; *King John* 1.1.84)?

Peter Alexander saw that 'powers of construction and integration' sharply distinguish the authors of *King John* and *Troublesome Reign*, 'yet it is precisely here that the author of *Troublesome Reign* is supposed to have shown the way to Shakespeare'.[18] I think that these powers are visible in the construction of the

King John story in dramatic form, the choice and rearrangement of episodes from the chronicles, and equally in the construction of characters, scenes, relationships, thematic echoes and other technical devices. Is it likely, then, that a dramatist who had already mastered the larger construction of a play, and the creation and fitting together of its minor components, needed the help of the bungling author of *Troublesome Reign* in composing *King John*? If we believe this, or that Shakespeare, once he had passed his apprentice phase, might be content to copy another man's play virtually scene by scene and sometimes speech by speech, it may be that we have not given sufficient consideration to the very personal idiom of Shakespeare's plotting.

Let us give honour where honour is due: to Peter Alexander, who was right about the King John plays seventy years ago and steadfastly refused to alter his opinion. And to 'the only Shakescene in a country', not the author of *Troublesome Reign*, for so decisively changing the course of English drama in the 1580s, an achievement that owed not a little to his quite distinctive powers of construction and integration.[19]

---

18 Quoted Beaurline, *King John*, p. 198. Compare Peter Alexander, *Henry VI and Richard III*, pp. 201–2; *Shakespeare's Life and Art* (London, 1939), p. 85.

19 For Shakespeare's exceptional 'powers of integration' see also my lecture, 'Shakespeare's mingled yarn and *Measure for Measure*' (*Proceedings of the British Academy*, 67, 1983, reprinted in *British Academy Shakespeare Lectures 1980–89*, ed. Honigmann (Oxford, 1993).

INSIDE *OTHELLO*

BARBARA EVERETT

All Shakespeare's major tragedies but one take their source from true or mythical history, whether British or classical or European. To the Elizabethan mind, not yet as relativistic about history as ourselves, this plainly invested tragedy with a special privilege, a depth and reach, a stability as of truth itself. *Othello* is the exception; it takes its story from fiction only. Cinthio's narrative of a jealous Moor in Venice, a man trapped in sexual intrigue, necessarily bequeaths to the play a yarn urban and realistic in its hard knowingness, its concise brutality, its final lack of the metaphysical. Jealousy, the very centre of the story, is nothing if not a function of love as possession and possessiveness. That Shakespeare was aware of these limiting pressures is clear from the brilliance of his evocation, in two plays, of Venice as the greatest trading-centre of Europe, its riches both extreme and vulnerable. All the many readers who have seen in *Othello* what Bradley once called its lack of universality, seen the problem of meaning in this tragedy of love-trade, are surely seeing in the play Cinthio's source: tragedy as mere narrative.

Our culture is in many ways a Restoration one. And, despite nominal political leanings, the literary–critical tone is primarily literal and literalizing, a withholding of sympathetic imagination its essential feature We see what is there. Such a school of literalism ought to be thoroughly at home with *Othello*, whose main figure declares: 'my heart is turned to stone; I strike it, and it hurts my hand' (4.1.178–9). But the Moor's words have complicated resonances and painful ironies. They suggest how far Shakespeare is from treating his materials in Cinthio's way. In the Italian fiction, a woman is bludgeoned to death; the stony heart of Shakespeare's Moor hurts differently.

In what follows, I use *Othello* to suggest the limitations of some recent approaches to Shakespeare. The tragedy's problems, both on and off the stage (the Moor is at once hero and villain to us, and in both roles is upstaged by Iago) give some sense of how much more than a narrator the poet is. What seems the simplest of the tragedies is, as a result, from some angles the hardest of them. And I want to begin from what has been made to seem one of the basic questions prompted by our environment. If Cinthio wrote about a Moor of Venice, what does that phrase mean when it is retained by Shakespeare, even in the title of his tragedy? Or, to put it in simply contemporary terms, what colour is the man who, in the second scene of the play, suddenly holds the stage, an astonishing presence lit by torches and very quiet: 'I must be found' (1.2.30)?

Chances seem strong that for the immediate future Othello will be black. By this I mean that the role will be played by a black actor. There are gaps between these two statements, and inside them as well, and I want to explore those gaps in what follows, not so much hoping to close them as testing out the echoes.

One of the best productions in years was the

1997–8 *Othello* at the National Theatre, an 'English Patient' or even 'Happy Valley' – 1930s – interpretation in design, with a fine Moor from the black actor, David Harewood. The very cogent 1999 production at Stratford had in Ray Fearon an equally impressive Othello – younger, intensely feeling, his sincerities all of the immediate moment. For a player strong enough, as Fearon and Harewood are, the role offers one solution to the professional problems of our black actors. And the situation of the African American in particular over the last two hundred years, brought to bear on the play by a black African Othello, without doubt illuminates and earns a focused sympathy for the central character.

But it is also true that an equally gifted black actor, Hugh Quarshie, has argued in a Stratford lecture that black actors should simply refuse the part.[1] Shakespeare's Othello is, to his mind, too grossly the stereotype of the black. This case would not be mine. But it offers a precedent for thinking about the whole question of the Moor's colour from a quite new and different angle. I want to follow Quarshie, and yet strongly differ from him, by suggesting that the whole issue of black actors in the part may be at best irrelevant and at worst dangerous. The actor may be good or bad, but his quality won't depend on his skin colour.

When she is fighting to stay with her as yet nominal husband (and her stance is in fact fighting, a rational but passionate 'trumpet to the world' (1.3.250)), Desdemona says to the Senators, with the obscurity of heroism, 'I saw Othello's visage in his mind' (1.3.252). The most recent of major editions of the play, the third Arden, glosses this interestingly. The editor, Ernst Honigmann, believes that Desdemona says: 'I saw (the colour of) Othello's face in (the quality of) his mind.' And he adds: 'She does not refer to his colour directly but seems to be half apologizing for it.'[2]

To call this paraphrase leading is to understate. It in fact deftly undoes what the heroine is trying to do. But this very forthrightness can also work as one of the virtues of Arden 3. It may be mentioned here that there are a good number of scholarly and critical matters involved with the study of *Othello* no more than touched on (if that) in the present essay. Luckily the two most recent editions, the New Cambridge (1984) edited by Norman Sanders and the third Arden (1997) edited by Ernst Honigmann – which I shall follow its editor in calling Arden 3 – are both of high efficiency: the New Cambridge perhaps the more cogent and lucid, Arden 3 the richer and the more absorbing. Both treat admirably such questions as text, dating, sources and theatre history, and write ably if more contentiously on such topics as characterization and tragic meaning.

Both in short can be depended on for their excellent handling of general information. But in both there is room for disagreement on local points – and I shall cite Arden 3 the more frequently, as the more provocative of the two, as well as the more recent. Both are for instance shoulder to shoulder on what seems to them the signal importance of racial issues in this tragedy. Indeed, Arden 3 so devoutly commends Stephen Greenblatt's New Historicism, which has – in the editor's words – fused ethnology and Shakespeare criticism, as to call this fusion 'a stroke almost as bold and imaginative as the writing of *Othello* itself'.[3]

There is always something to be admired in the work of Professor Greenblatt. But when one academic says such things of another something has gone badly, if conventionally and characteristically wrong, with what academics think they mean by 'imaginative'. And this is the precise matter I want to argue here. Literary scholars have always been persons, have perhaps always needed to be persons, who place a primary emphasis on fact and factuality. The

---

[1] Hugh Quarshie, 'Second Thoughts about Othello' (Chipping Camden, 1999).

[2] William Shakespeare, *Othello*, ed. by E. A. J. Honigmann (Walton-on-Thames, 1997), p. 151.

[3] Ibid., p. 27.

advent over the last twenty years of a changed, New Historical or Theoretical approach to literary study has only in fact revived a special matter-of-factness which scholars have always been praised for or accused of. The tendency is now merely more extreme, more confident, more unaware that there might be other ways of thinking about poems and plays than as quasi-historical documents. Left to itself, this scholarly New Wave has produced what might be called a literalism of approach in itself mind-boggling. Figurative language has had its day: when Othello speaks (5.2) of smelling the rose on the tree, Arden 3 reports that he 'smells' Desdemona twice.[4]

If the question of black Othellos is significant, then this is because it clarifies the degree to which the modern *Othello*, on or off the stage, is (if we allow it to be) seen from the outside, skin-deep, unimagined. Certainly Shakespeare brought the issue alive when he dramatized, embodied, Cinthio's paper text. But there is more to embodiment, and more at issue in the tragedy, than the colour of a man's skin. And when Desdemona says that she saw her lover's visage in his mind she is invoking those issues.

The very difficulty of precision on Othello's racial origins is relevant here. During the first half of the seventeenth century two great painters, Rubens and Velasquez, each showed – the first by painting a 'Negro' and the second by painting a 'Moor' – that he probably knew that these terms were not the same. But they were not poets or dramatists. Shakespeare has in *Hamlet* prevented us from defining the exact theological specifications of the Ghost; he will go on, in *The Tempest*, to create the same self-contradictions as to exactly where, as between New and Old Worlds, the island actually is. And indeed, this purposiveness is surely underlined at a factual level. I have suggested elsewhere that the dramatist conceivably took as model for his hero those Spanish Moors who as refugees flooded London at the turn of the century.[5] These were people whose genetic

origins were essentially mixed. The now nationalistic Christian Spain which exiled them, as it had the Jews, had been for so many centuries so divided between the Moor, the Jew and the white or olive-skinned 'native' – all intermarrying (the nationalistic royal family had Jewish blood) – that slogans of racial purification were then as unjust as they always are.

Shakespeare's tragedy has no answer to the question which all editors, most critics and some directors still wrestle with: as to whether Othello is Arab ('tawny Moor') or black African ('black Moor'). The play does not care. Only the play's villain appears to care much about the racial question, which fact might slow down editors more than it does. Few commentators give attention to the fact that where the source-narrative begins with years of cheerful marriage, the tragedy opens with an elopement, alluded to but mysteriously undiscussed, as it were unnoticed. Arden 3 explicitly concludes that Othello and Desdemona have eloped because Brabantio would never have accepted the Moor as a son-in-law, and drily takes Othello's belief that 'Her father loved me' (1.3.127) as either dishonest or stupid. In the play as we actually witness it, Brabantio has no pre-existing colour feeling; a foreshadowing of Othello himself, he is corrupted by Iago by being enraged into feeling that he too is a 'fixèd figure for the time of scorn' (4.2.56), robbed, diminished, humiliated. Pain and shame breed in him and are twisted in him by Iago into racial hatred.

Shakespeare's brilliant subtlety lies in showing that hatred as secondary, factitious, a part of Iago's expediency. The most immediate feeling of the play's first audience would not have been to ask whether Othello was tawny or black – no Elizabethan actor of Burbage's stature would have allowed facial expression to

---

[4] Ibid., p. 306.

[5] Barbara Everett, '"Spanish" Othello: The Making of Shakespeare's Moor', *Shakespeare Survey 35* (Cambridge, 1982); re-printed in *Young Hamlet, Essays on Shakespeare's Tragedies* (Oxford, 1989).

be covered and unreadable. And the audience's first care would have been that the part was played by the company's greatest actor, Richard Burbage: obituaries of whom later made it plain that the 'greued Moore' was perhaps his greatest role, most deeply moving, most unforgettable.[6] Othello was Burbage-coloured.

Given an actor good enough, the paint that Burbage wore, and that white actors have assumed since, has its own significance. It transforms into a vital power of metaphor. In this sense, the black actor must count the truth, the focus and the historical pathos or grandeur of his skin-colour as balanced by a loss. The painting of a Burbage's face and hands, the enrobing in that distinctive mixed-period swatch of garments Elizabethan actors took pride in, all together constitute the assumption of a role. It is the assumption of role which releases in audience or reader (reader with a power of inner theatre, audience with an inward empathy) that complicit imagination, that furious bonding sympathy which makes theatre and makes poetic drama.

As the Chorus of *Henry V* (for instance) insists to us, Shakespeare's Romantic or Gothic theatre was hugely metaphorical: it knew its ridiculous limits and it knew its sometimes sublime power to outgo them. The thing was done by using metaphorical fictions to enlarge and to deepen, to give a wholly new sense of what an art of embodiment might mean. A man may be a Moor and neither tawny nor black nor white; a love-marriage may have lasted hours or years; jealousy may have appetite but no single motive. The medium is not literal. All Shakespeare is as a result makeshift to a degree that offends natural classicists and that in its time brought down the scorn of both Voltaire and Tolstoy. Some editors have always been, understandably enough, of their party. In Variorum editions of *Othello*, it can be interesting to watch the eighteenth-century critic Steevens and even, sadly, the poet Pope agreeing in cutting the Pontic Sea image in 3.3.456 on the ground that it is an 'unnatural excursion'.[7] A

long tradition of scholars has felt the same about Desdemona's Willow Song in 4.3, similarly cut by hosts of male editors as an embarrassing uprush of female over-imaginativeness.

The tragedies close to this in time of probable first staging, *Hamlet*, *King Lear* and *Macbeth*, all understandably appeal much more than it to readers because their imaginative and metaphysical dimensions are explicit – a ghost, gods, witches, inward and cerebral explorations. *Othello* poker-facedly encourages us to agree with Iago on the Moor's 'bombast circumstance' (1.1.13); and when he says 'Mark me with what violence she first loved the Moor, but for bragging and telling her fantastical lies' (2.1.223–4), good critics and editors have been all too ready to go along with that 'bragging' and 'fantastical lies'. The tragedy has, in short, what presents itself (at the level of intrigue) as an appallingly simple narrative – reader and audience have (to quote Plath) 'boarded the train there's no getting off'.[8] But it is in fact just as difficult to say 'What happens in *Othello*' as it is to do the same for *Hamlet*. The equally poker-faced list of *dramatis personae* warns us ahead of time that Iago is 'a villain'.[9] Iago tells lies; and nothing whatever he says in the play should be trusted. Everyone else in the play, for reasons I shall come to later, is, like Othello in his marvellous narratives or autobiographies to the Senate (1.3), not lying but speaking in public, speaking defensively and to some purpose: 'I ran it through', 'It was my hint to speak', 'I did consent, / And often did beguile her of her tears', 'My story being done' (1.3.131, 154–5, 157).

---

[6] See E. K. Chambers, *The Elizabethan Stage*, 4 vols. (Oxford, 1926, repr. with corrections, 1967), vol. 2, p. 309.

[7] William Shakespeare, *Othello*, New Variorum Edition, ed. by Horace Howard Furness (Philadelphia, 1986), p. 210.

[8] Sylvia Plath, 'Metaphors' in *Collected Poems*, ed. by Ted Hughes (London, 1981).

[9] See 'Names of Actors' as listed at the end of *Othello* in the First Folio.

This apparently blazingly simple tragedy has great difficulties inside it, especially at the level of narrative. No less suggestive or figurative than its predecessor *Hamlet* is, with formidable originality it so embodies these technical depths as to seem supremely literal. Let me give one example. In the play's first scene, Brabantio exclaims to the unseen Iago, using the denigratory 'thou' of the period, 'Thou art a villain' (1.1.120); and Iago answers with a phrase universally found mysterious: 'You are a senator' (1.1.120). He is intimating that there are no 'villains' in Venice because no souls there: that this utterly worldly, moneyed, great trade Republic measures men only by status and social repute. It is notable that when Cassio later loses his 'reputation', he loses what he calls 'the immortal part of myself' (2.3.256–9).

Iago's and Cassio's General is the Moor, and the Moor is black – what, especially in the crude politics of the present moment, could be simpler? Othello has a body, and it is black: 'I strike it, and it hurts my hand' (4.1.179). It is a truism that the play affects audiences with a directness of pain and affront unique in the tragedies. There are anecdotes, some perhaps apocryphal, of audience protest and outcry, from the English Regency to the USSR of the 1930s; even for the reader, the tension is Hitchcockianly extreme, nail-biting and claustrophobic. Part of the reason is of course a pitiless manipulativeness at the level of sexual intrigue in the action, which makes use of lethal bad luck. But it has to be said too that extreme tension is created poetically as well as dramaturgically. There is on the one hand an intolerable and unremitting factuality, and on the other the power these literals have been endowed with to arouse through metaphor gigantic releases of complicit feeling and anxiety. *Othello* is, as a Restoration critic bitterly observed, 'the tragedy of a handkerchief'. And it was with some understanding of the paradoxes entailed by the play's pseudo-lucid narrative that this same critic, Rymer, concluded his wholly

hostile account with the well-known summary that this tragedy is nothing but 'a bloody farce without salt or savour'.[10]

Othello's blackness is at the centre of these dangerous simplicities, and perhaps as hard to interpret as Hamlet's Danishness is marginal. The tragedy of the Moor does not seem to this reader and play-goer 'political' in the sense that we might use the word, if we had to, of (for instance) Eugene O'Neill's *All God's Chillun Got Wings*; or even, to come nearer to Shakespeare himself, Thomas Southerne's *Oroonoko* – both the Southerne and the O'Neill serving to dramatize the cruel suffering imposed by white on black simply because he or she is black. At the same time, it is peculiarly difficult to make such distinctions of the political and the super-political at a moment when the reading of texts once believed literary has become thoroughly political, historical and externalized: a process in itself understandable as reaction from half a century's over-intense over-professional academic investigation of personal responses to literary texts.

Moreover, that obdurate externalism can make for a cheering freshness and novelty. But in the case of *Othello*, it can at the same time make for a striking degree of obfuscation. The brave logic of the Arden 3 edition of the play is genuinely helpful here, and can promote new discoveries in the reader even if in the form of indignant denial. In the same spirit as that in which he praised ethnological precision, the editor of the Arden 3 *Othello* brings to bear what he offers as a new piece of evidence concerning Othello's age. The Moor suffers it seems from 'defective eyesight', and indeed from 'weak or short sight': 'Shakespeare seems to suggest that Othello sees less clearly than Iago'. Moreover, this 'unacknowledged infirmity' suggests advancing years.[11] It has to be

---

[10] See, Thomas Rymer, 'A Short View of Tragedy', in *Shakespeare: The Critical Heritage*, ed. by Brian Vickers, 6 vols. (London 1974), vol. 2, pp. 25–59.

[11] Honigmann, *Othello*, p. 19

objected by the reader that short-sighted people in fact grow longer-sighted with age (or so oculists insist): they come to see better. That apart, there is an interesting connection here. In *Julius Caesar* Cassius explains that 'My sight was ever thick' (5.3.21); and since the dramatist presumably borrowed Caesar's falling-sickness for Othello's fit, he may have made over Cassius's eyesight too.

And yet in the case of the later tragedy something is lost by such simple literalism. Othello demands of Iago, 'Make me to see't' (3.3.369); and it is a fact that Iago is always officiously ready to notice, to be right, to explain things to his senior officer. But the reason is hardly that Othello hasn't brought his spectacles with him. The two men differ in what they mean by 'seeing'. We are in short encountering here a figure, one in itself of huge human importance, which will fully (with Gloucester's blinding) enter the moral plot of *King Lear*. In *Othello*'s briefer and more literal form, it has already affected Shakespeare's earlier work, given that the poet of the *Sonnets* was (if we wish) 'short-sighted' too: as Sonnet 113 laments, 'that which governs me to go about / Doth part his function and is partly blind, / Seems seeing, but effectually is out'. Astigmatism need not be the answer. Sonnet 112 had admitted to deafness too, given that adders were supposed to be deaf – 'In so profound abyss I throw all care / Of other's voices . . .'. Moreover, Victorian editors would propose that the lover-poet of these poems was crippled because he invited the friend to whom he was enslaved to 'Speak of my lameness, and I straight will halt' (Sonnet 89.3).

The man or woman in love will limp if thought lame, can hear nothing but the beloved, is blind to all but the beloved – because he or she is under the power of what these poems invoke as 'Thou blind fool, Love' (Sonnet 137.1). Emilia before she dies salutes Othello, with extraordinary rage and courage, as 'Thou dull Moor . . . O murderous coxcomb! What should such a fool / Do with

so good a wife?' (5.2.232 and 240–1). It may be safer, in fact, to consider *Othello* as a poem, like the *Sonnets*, than to read or stage it (or narrate it) quite literally. That said, it is of course a fact that the *Sonnets* – now, as in the biographizing nineteenth century – may be read with a painstaking misplaced literalism. Editions now sometimes reveal that the temptation to simplify and historicize these private poems has not been overcome. Shakespeare carries out his startlingly original analysis of interior feeling by using such elements as are necessary to any narrative. He appears at quite random moments to need to seem to tell a story, even a fiction autobiographical in its bearing. But the moments are not consistent, the story never properly equipped with human sense. The poet is forced by the limitations of his current techniques to speak of two kinds of love, high and low, to describe what may be the truths of Mind and Body, as if two distinct persons were confusedly involved. To read all this literally (as does, for instance, the Arden 3 *Sonnets*) is to carry out, at worst, a journalistic hunt for a pair of Elizabethan personalities, betrayed by a poet both misogynistic and climbing.

The sketchy or gestural 'story' of the *Sonnets* applies Occam's razor and lets one love sleep with the other, thus bringing in corruptions and tormented jealousies:

> Why should my heart think that a several plot
>   [i.e., a private domain]
> Which my heart knows the wide world's
>   common place?
>
> (Sonnet 137.9–10)

I quote phrases from the *Sonnets* only to suggest that work with different forms and conventions may express the same experiences. In the *Sonnets*, what is palpably a journey into the interior guides itself from moment to moment by relation to fictive styles. *Othello* comes near to reversing this. In the play, we look through the fiction (one sometimes as discontinuous or problematic as the quasi-narrative of the poems) to a degree of interior suffering which gives meaning to the whole, and yet remains always hard to explain or categorize.

The story Shakespeare had found in Cinthio is cold, competent and disagreeable. Despite the dramatist's large changes, he could never quite rid his fiction of its randomness, its mean and brutal lecheries, its vindictive destruction of a long marriage. Why did Shakespeare want it? Perhaps he was struck, as he already had been in his earlier Venetian comedy, by the hint of 'the Moor of Venice'. Perhaps the black face of the Moor, in a super-civilized society, suddenly fascinated the poet, rendered up meaning to him: an image of that mask which our interior life wears and has to wear in love, which is itself the bonding to a person and a society definitively not itself, and thereby the more desired. Cinthio's story is narrated absolutely from outside – an anecdote. But for Shakespeare, for whom the lover and the poet are (like the lunatic) interior, 'of imagination all compact' (*Dream*, 5.1.8), the story cannot be told from the outside. The lover and the poet are perhaps from outside Moors, black faces, strangers in their society, just as they are blind, deaf and lame in the bondage of their supreme and intolerable commitment. But, as well as blind, they are in love kings ('In sleep a king' (Sonnet 87.14)), souls ('A true soul / When most impeached stands least in thy control' (Sonnet 125.13–14)) and immortals ('who in thy power / Dost hold Time's fickle glass' (Sonnet 126.1–2)).

Of the two recent editions which I mentioned earlier, the New Cambridge Introduction regrets that *Othello* suffers from the lack of the 'metaphorical creation of a surrounding universe': a remark which revealingly betrays the belief that metaphors should deal with outsides not insides.[12] Arden 3, on the other hand, would like to re-value the play upwards into the status of Shakespeare's single greatest tragedy, but its Introduction, too, flatly gives up on final interpretation: 'The play was so devised that its characters and the theatre audience

cannot explain all that happens . . . after all, we cannot explain as clearly as we would like the motivation of many living men and women that we think we know.'[13]

I have been proposing that there is much in *Othello* that makes these simple literalisms at least partly justifiable. As the current (and mistaken) limiting description, 'domestic tragedy' tends to suggest, *Othello* is nearest of all the tragedies to a modern novel (Desdemona's 'house affairs', her sense of her husband 'mam'ring on' (3.3.71), Othello's 'Twill do me good to walk' (4.3.2)). And yet all this fails to account for the strange brilliance of the play, which is, after all – and unlike Cinthio – far from such reporting of marital crime as might be found in the *News of the World*. Where its literalism is strongest the work is also most painfully ironic ('But yet the pity of it, Iago. O, Iago, the pity of it, Iago!' (4.1.191–2)). Indeed, it is the complex unpitying pain of *Othello* which gives the lie to Arden 3's amiable 'honest doubt' reaction: as if tragedy can never be a 'You Never Can Tell' phenomenon, but embodies its own explanation, always, unremittingly. Hence the consistency of the play's deepening unluck everywhere, its hard humour, its savage poetry. 'Ethnology' has lost that savage poetry. Recent critical accounts of *Othello* may be too prosaic, too factual, even too newspapery, the product of a characteristically unimaginative political age.

Othello is not an easy tragedy for any age, though it has moved, excited and appalled audiences in all periods. Its difficulty lies in its contrasts, its fusion of inner and outer. In what may be his first play, *The Two Gentlemen of Verona*, Shakespeare speaks of a 'shallow story of deep love' (1.1.21). *Othello* is perhaps that story, a narrative broken and re-formed to serve as a symbol. Any reading and any production has to hold in balance its shallowness and its

---

12 William Shakespeare, *Othello*, ed. by Norman Sanders (Cambridge, 1984), p. 19.
13 Honigmann, *Othello*, p. 26.

depth, its body and its mind, its outside and its inside. Begun by Cinthio, the tragedy had to become the hardest, most colourful and most literal of the poet's dramas, a work fiercely alive in the theatre, where *Hamlet* and *Lear* and *Macbeth* also earn the devotion of readers. But the theatrical events always deepen pure theatre into pure suggestion, even poetry.

I mentioned earlier the first such expressive action in the play, non-existent in Cinthio and in fact merely imputed in Shakespeare, an element of narrative which is (significantly) only overheard or overseen through the medium of the quarrelling incoherent Iago and Roderigo: the mysterious elopement. Unclearly observed in this way, eavesdropped-on as through a thicket (and the play does borrow in plot terms from the eavesdroppings of *Much Ado*), this elopement which initiates the drama only exists to suggest, in the work's special embodying language, the lovers' unsocial furious inward life of feeling. It is an activation of the words, 'They fell in love'; and it is imagined, not seen. It joins all the more articulate of Othello's properties which are neither true nor untrue, but radiant and substantial: his account of his wooing, with his life-story at its heart; his story of the sibyl and the handkerchief; his memory of Aleppo.

This literal play begins with an unseen elopement, which I have glossed as an activation of the words 'They fell in love.' Such falling (the play seems to suggest) possibly does not afflict everybody – Othello is special from the beginning, black and royal and autonomous – but has to be taken very seriously (for good and ill) when it does. It makes human beings, as the Sonnets insist, culpably or magnificently see and hear nothing else: 'None else to me, nor I to none alive' (Sonnet 112.7) – the negatives here, in the strange and difficult 112, are idiosyncratic, even where formal tragedy is absent. Shakespeare describes many loves, and this one, while heroic and absolute, never lacks the sound of pain or danger. To high romantic love in the chivalric middle ages, loaded with

secrecy and status, the word 'Danger' was central. After the second-act storm, Cassio says proleptically of the Moor, 'I have lost him on a dangerous sea' (2.1.47). Othello himself has already voiced an anxiety in

> But that I love the gentle Desdemona
> I would not my unhousèd free condition
> Put into circumscription and confine
> For the seas' worth. (1.2.25–8)

An animal in the wild sees danger in cages.

The Moor is a human being committed by the feeling that he has chosen Desdemona; and it is the unpublic privacy, the interiority of this feeling that makes the unseen elopement more vital to the play than the assumed marriage. Desdemona herself owns to this same 'downright violence and storm of fortunes' (1.3.249). They meet, in their marvellous encounter before the Senate, in the security of Othello's magical memory, like halcyons breeding over a sea-storm; she is at home in his stories as he is in her self-giving rich beautiful Venetian belonging. This quality of self-committing consciousness in Othello, locked inward and deep and crowned by Desdemona, the worldly authoritarian Senator Brabantio, once corrupted by Iago, and abandoned by his child, thinks of as black magic; Iago calls it 'bragging' and 'fantastical lies'. If we respond to the Moor as the dramatist's gifts invite, it doesn't seem anything but believable that Desdemona calls his commitment neither magic nor lies but human love. With extraordinary delicacy of portrayal Shakespeare has made the Moor of the first act a man of superb presence, at once General and lover and fastidious poet. He has also given him a nature from which arrogance, rage and narcissism ('My parts, my title, and my perfect soul' (1.2.31)) are not absolutely lacking. Venice is here the cradle of a tragedy of romantic love.

This romantic love disseminates, in different forms, through the action, giving the dramatic world of Venice its peculiar glow, its dark and rich beauty (as in *The Merchant of Venice*). The

Cyprus of the play perhaps enacts the more desolate, dangerous and brutal endings of love. The play is a world of people relatively obtuse, and obtuse from feeling ('None else to me, nor I to none alive' (Sonnet 112.7)). Brabantio, for all his acrimony, loves his daughter enough to die with her gone; the ambitious romantic young Cassio falls into drunkenness and self-hatred as if into love, and Bianca never leaves him; Roderigo understands what Desdemona is actually like; Emilia at last defies her husband for Desdemona's sake, and as if briefly inheriting her strength. This is a play in which everyone, or everyone except Iago, can seem stupid by virtue of his or her inattention, an inability to see. And the blackness of Othello himself is perhaps – among other things more literal – an image of love as unseen, as well as unseeing – something familiar yet alien, dark and not belonging merely to social surface.

At first Othello rides a storm of which the second-act seascape is no more than splendid image. In Cyprus, the civilized securities of Venice, at once stony and safe (like a bankful of money) are left behind. External authority gone, the lovers have nothing and no one to trust or appeal to but themselves. Love, like the sea itself, gives life and destroys it; and the real storm is interior. It wrecks the Moor because something in his nature, which loves and needs Venice, has use for Iago, the city's product – a presence which appears subordinate and deferential, not equal and challenging like love. The Moor's inward self wants and needs what is outside it, a body and a city; his love wishes to be knowledge. Iago promises him that it can. When he has killed Desdemona the Moor finds himself in the realm of fact: 'I ha' no wife' (5.2.106).

Concerning Iago, Arden 3 asks the question: 'A change of emphasis, and might not the play be called *The Tragedy of Iago*?'[14] I have to admit that I wouldn't want to call it so myself, while admiring this editorial compassion; and in fact regret the now habitual co-starring, on the stage and in criticism, of Othello and Iago together (in the 1997–8 brilliant National Theatre production Harewood and Russell Beale took their bows together; in critical writing Iago all too often upstages Othello). The reason why these things happen, but also why one might not approve them, is that Shakespeare's tragedies are made what they are by their perpetual using of 'insides' to give meaning to 'outsides', their joining, if one wants, of poetry with drama, reflection with action. To be tragic, one therefore needs an inside: as under the black paint on the face there is the actor's known character, and under that, the whole potential human world of shared understanding and sympathy. But Iago, unlike Othello, has no face.

Discussions of Iago's motivation and meaning can be admirable. But they can sometimes strike a reader as provisional, hypothetical. The character is something which only a great but perhaps wearying playwright could have imagined (although Henry James also conceives persons merely public, with no other dimensions): Iago is from the very beginning, as all his strange externalizing pseudo-soliloquies manifest, a man with empty eyes, a figure of incomparable animation because so wholly without interior life. He has, one might say, no inside to his head. This is perhaps why he is so startlingly allowed at the end of his play (and critics ought perhaps to be startled by it more often) to survive most of the other main characters, even if only mute and facing severe torture. He is free never to answer because unenslaved by that hindrance, a personal intensity and a need to love.

Everything that Iago says and does has the weightlessness of the contrived as against the imagined. In 2.3 he replaces truth with facts ('Thus it is, general' (2.3.217)), making his quasi-explanation of the drunken violence procured by himself into a noose for Cassio. His intrigue characteristically puts together an

---

14 Ibid., p. 59.

airless mechanistic ballet of unreal events, where insides, or human likelihoods, are exchanged for outsides, or sheer performance. Sometimes there is power and freedom in this style, but in general the effect is very creepy. This externality of course also prevents him from telling anything that can be called the truth, a term which properly presupposes more than mere factual accuracy. It means sincerity in human communication. As a result, though critics often debate whether this or this said by Iago is true or not, their discussion strikes this reader as time-wasting. Nothing said by Iago (who prefers to obfuscate) should be taken seriously as statement, only conceivably as evidence about the character himself. Thus, the play's most outgoing and external personage is the most narcissistic and solitary. Many critics have agreed in finding Iago a fascinating enigma. He seems to me, rather, a most brilliant invention, like that great computer in Kubrick's science-fiction film *2001*: a machine that turns villain far out in space and has to be (too late) switched off, to expire alarmingly singing 'Daisy, Daisy'. Iago can be switched off; he perhaps can't die.

The question of course remains why the Moor should be so affected by a mere contrivance, and what drives Iago himself. Every now and again a critic will propose that Iago nourishes a secret and jealous passion for the Moor. This is not nonsense – Iago is clearly an unloved creature; Venice exists as a community of persons who to some degree or other have a world inside the head, and to not one of them is Iago seriously interesting. In 5.2 the Moor and Emilia within one short passage exchange the words 'thy husband' and 'my husband' (5.2.149) nine times in all, leaving the sense that neither senior officer nor wife has ever so much as looked steadily at the image they toss between them. When Othello first starts the ritual of calling Iago 'honest' (1.3.294), he plainly does it as a way of socializing his sense of the man's non-existence except as social function. When he finally returns to the theme (5.2)

with 'My friend, thy husband, honest, honest Iago' (5.2.161), the tag 'honest' now seems to struggle with some glimpsed inauthenticity of the social, the corruption of outsides.

It would make sense that Iago fights to make the Moor look at him, to fix and hold the attention of a Senior who simply is not interested: ''Tis better as it is' (looking away (1.2.6)). This is Shakespeare's coldest study of the sheer boringness, under the fun, of the power-instinct. To go further and to see Iago as yearning for the Moor is to ignore the fact that the Ancient has too little interior, for all his vitality of surface, to be in love with anybody. Nor can he see that anyone else loves or is loved: 'Blest fig's end! The wine she drinks is made of grapes' (2.1.251–2). The 'homosexual' reading is just too interesting – just as the two most distinguished Iagos in our theatre recently, Russell Beale and McKellen, have been perhaps too interesting; each of these players giving us an Iago, brilliant though different, who was all inside, all tormented twisted fascinating individual psyche. Such a reading can be wildly entertaining on stage, but it unbalances the play and makes life misery for the actor of Othello, as well as for Othello.

But certainly there is a transaction between the two men, and it involves the matter of love and sexuality. I want to finish by considering what this transaction consists in – what, so to speak, 'happens in *Othello*', what its narrative is. And I want to approach the question by turning one last time to a phrase in Arden 3, whose Introduction refers to *Othello* as 'this sex-drenched play'.[15] Such a phrase has the power of sharpening a reader's sense of how special to itself, how strange and questioning, are all this tragedy's dealings – so little sex-drenched, really – with the love of mind and body.

It needs first to be noted that there is some kind of sexual problem in this tragedy, one concealed partly in the fact that for a century

---

[15] Ibid., p. 52.

193

and a half it has struck some scholarly minds as having a 'double time scheme'. The lovers sometimes seem like an old married couple, and sometimes to have been married for so short a time as in fact to afford no one the opportunity to betray anyone. Some critics have even wondered if the marriage is actually ever consummated, or if the marriage-bed and the death-bed are not here one and the same.

Though with some sympathy for this last party, I in fact find the play constructed so as to seem quite purposively inexplicit on the subject of the married lovers' physical life. Like the enigmatic elopement, their love is 'inside', 'off-stage', no one's affair but their own. And yet marriage is indeed a public and social affair, celebrated (in the comedy *Much Ado About Nothing* for instance) in crowd-scenes, great dances. Consequently this reticence in the action, matched by a fastidiousness and privacy so obvious in Othello's will not 'to comply with heat' (1.3.264), this very containment or repression exercises a kind of discordant pressure. Like the debating Shakespeare scholars, as audience we fret, we obscurely want to know; subliminally we will some kind of awareness into the daylight, finally sharing the complicitness of Iago and the Moor.

At 4.1, Othello gibbers of 'Noses, ears and lips' (4.1.41), and falls into some kind of lapse of consciousness. A brisk malevolent Iago, like some frightful operating-theatre nurse, 'stands . . . in control' over him (Sonnet 125.14). It is hard to resist the feeling that Othello has fallen, in an almost Adamic sense, into his own body. *All's Well That Ends Well*, probably close to this play in dating, has the chaste Diana speak the truth-serving fiction, after the hero believes himself to have slept with her, 'I . . . am . . . embodied yours' (5.3.175): an image that fuses the sexual with the military. If *All's Well* is a dark comedy of embodiment, *Othello* is a harshly funny tragedy of embodiment. There is in the play a Restoration or post-modernistic mean laughter about the distraught or unbelieving innocence of the body. When Iago

undertakes his Captain's sexual education, explaining to him that his wife may have been in bed with Cassio without meaning any harm, Othello's agog and excruciated 'Naked in bed, Iago, and not mean harm?' (4.1.5) is horribly funny in a pure Wycherley or Joe Orton way. But it is that impossible thing, tragic Wycherley, tragic Joe Orton.

If there is sexuality in this play, it is largely offensive and mostly Iago's. Caring for no one, he rarely stops talking in a vein that unites mind and body falsely and grossly: he generates fantasy-sex, sex-in-the-head, cartoon-sex. 'An old black ram / Is tupping your white ewe' (1.1.88–9): from the first sexuality is used to further aggression and malevolence. The silence and darkness covering the lovers' active physical life is perfectly matched and reversed by Iago's vicious fantasies, which come to their climax with his account (3.3.415–30) of what is said to be Cassio's dream of advances on Desdemona, a dream said to be overheard by Iago while Cassio is said to be sharing a bed with him (an Elizabethan custom more expressive of shortage of beds than of erotic relations).

Iago quietens and needles an appalled, and yet perhaps obscurely excited Othello, with his 'Nay, this was but his dream' (3.3.432). At this moment, to an Othello willing to listen (and he should, of course, simply have refused at once to discuss his wife with his Sergeant-Major) Iago is converting the great dreams (of love, of art) into lies and fantasies. Othello says, 'Monstrous, monstrous' (3.3.431). In his earlier narrative of travels, he has told smilingly of meeting Anthropophagi, man-eating creatures, cannibals. Iago's dream of love has worse monsters: not because its images are (however ambiguously) homo-erotic, but because an internalized sterility of voracity is the fantasy here. The nightmare is Iago's inability really to dream for himself, is his voyueristic reportage of so-called sex from the outside: a reporting that is in its nature factitious and in its purpose vicious.

Othello listens to Iago, and there is something of seduction in this temptation scene. When the Moor turns back to his wife, it is to kill and not to love. And yet the murder of Desdemona, horrible enough in itself, is in its un-self-knowing way loving; and it is therefore, like the paint on Burbage's face, more true than Iago's bad dreams. Finding in himself at last what Emilia has called the power 'to be hurt' (5.2.169), he acts it out, dying 'upon a kiss' (5.2.369). And, though he gives it finally an actor's brilliance, it's a power inside Othello.

THE VIEW OF LONDON FROM THE NORTH AND THE PLAYHOUSES IN HOLYWELL

HERBERT BERRY

All but one of the many views of London printed during Elizabethan, Jacobean, and Caroline times show the city from the south and so can and nearly always do include places of entertainment on the south bank of the Thames. The exception calls itself *The View of the Cittye of London from the North towards the Sowth*. It does not show the south bank or its places of entertainment, but it does show at least one of the playhouses on the north side of the city, and in doing so provides the only contemporary picture of it, or them.

The *View* is a panoramic view rather than a map-view. It purports, that is, to show the city as one might see it in a photograph.[1] Its topography extends from Holywell in the northeast (on the left) to Westminster in the southwest (on the right) and is about 1039 mm wide and 96 mm high. It does not mention its artist, engraver, publisher, place of publication, or date. People who have written about it have argued that it belongs to either 1600 or some years earlier. A single copy was thought to survive, in the Library of the University of Utrecht (formerly MS 1198, f. 83, now Gr. form. 12), accompanying a manuscript account by Abraham Booth of a visit to London, 1629–30. In the summer of 1996, however, Clive and Philip Burden found another and better copy in their own collections. They deal in and collect antique maps, books, and prints at Rickmansworth in Hertfordshire.

Near the left side of the *View* is an obvious playhouse that Leslie Hotson first described in

print (1954, 1959). He declared that it is the Curtain, which had been built in Holywell in about 1577 and may still have stood at the end of the seventeenth century. Many people soon agreed: A. M. Hind (1955); the anonymous author of the catalogue for 'The Growth of London' (an exhibition at the Victoria and Albert Museum in July and August, 1964, in which the *View* was exhibited); G. E. Bentley (1968); C. W. Hodges (1968); Glynne Wickham (1972); and Rosemary Linnell (1977). Sidney Fisher, however, argued at least three times (1964, 1967, 1978) that the playhouse is the only other one in that end of London, the Theatre, built in Holywell in 1576 and pulled down during the Christmas season of 1598–9.

I dedicate this article to the memory of Professor T. J. King, who reminded me of the *View* in 1979 and invited me to join him in writing an article like this one. We corresponded, met at conferences, and collected copies of things we thought might come in handy, but we arrived at no conclusions and did no writing. Eventually Professor King abandoned the idea and sent me the copies he had collected. He died, much lamented, in 1994.

I am grateful to Mr Ralph Hyde, Keeper of Prints and Maps at Guildhall Library, for telling me of the new copy of the *View* and in general for his interest in this study. I am also grateful to Mr Philip Burden for helping me to see the new copy, to Dr Koert van der Horst, Keeper of Manuscripts at the library of the University of Utrecht, for correspondence about the Utrecht copy, and to Professor R. G. Beck for computerizing the *View*.

[1] The contemporary map-views of London show a plan of streets as modern maps do, but they also show three-dimensional buildings each of which looks as though the artist drew it directly above and to the south.

Richard Hosley has accepted the argument (1979), as have R. A. Foakes (1985), John Orrell (1988), and James Lusardi (1993). Fisher's scheme of things, virtually unchallenged, seems now to be accepted.[2]

Neither Hotson nor successors of like mind had noticed that a flag flies from a flag pole about 43 mm to the right of the playhouse. The pole apparently rises from the middle of the ridge of the pitched roof over a large rectangular building. Fisher argued that flags flew almost exclusively from playhouses. He declared, therefore, that the building from which this flag flies is the hut over another playhouse, hence that the *View* shows both the Curtain and the Theatre. He assumed that the artist drew the *View* from one place on one day. Since the obvious playhouse also has a flag, he concluded that the day occurred while plays were being produced at both places. That, he thought, would be before July 1597, because the privy council closed all playhouses then supposedly over the performance of a play, *The Isle of Dogs*, at the Swan, one of the playhouses on the south bank, and, as he also thought, the Theatre, unlike other playhouses, did not reopen. He worked out a geometrical scheme according to which he found that the *View* is 'remarkably' accurate, that the obvious playhouse cannot be other than the Theatre, and that the building with flag and flag pole to the right is the Curtain.

Fisher's case, then, requires that the *View* was drawn before July 1597 (or at least the Christmas season of 1598–9) and depends on his geometry. Neither the date nor the geometry, however, seems right. The *View*, I propose, was drawn in 1600 at the earliest and before 1613, and it was engraved in about 1610 or later. The obvious playhouse should be the Curtain, and the flagged building to the right may have to do with entertainment other than plays.

A large map-view and a small panoramic view of London may have been published as early as the 1550s. Map-views appeared often from 1572 onward, but the first readily datable panoramic view was *Civitas Londini* (1600), which was also the first large and elaborately engraved one. It led to, among others, even larger and more skilfully engraved panoramas, the much reproduced *London* of J. C. Visscher (c. 1616), and the so-called Long View of Wenceslaus Hollar (1647). Anthonis van den Wyngaerde had drawn a large panoramic view of London as early as about 1544, but it was not printed until the nineteenth century, and he may have drawn another cruder and much smaller one of *c.* 1550 that was not printed until the twentieth.

The *View* is much smaller and plainer than *Civitas Londini* or its notable successors. The topographical part of *Civitas Londini* is considerably wider than that of the *View* and more than three times higher. Visscher's topography is wider and higher still. *Civitas Londini* and Visscher's view show the Thames full of ships and boats. They have labels for many buildings and places, and decorative coats of arms, flags, putti, and angels. *Civitas Londini* has two inset

---

[2] Hotson, *The Times*, 26 March 1954, pp. 7, 14, and *The Wooden O* (London, 1959), appendices B, C; Hind, *Engraving in England in the Sixteenth and Seventeenth Centuries* (Cambridge, 1955), vol. 2, p. 114; Fisher, *The Theatre the Curtain and the Globe* (Montreal, 1964), pp. 2–6, and *An Engineer Looks at Shakespeare* (Hamilton, Ont.: McMaster University, 1967 – in the 'Humanities Lecture Series 1967: The Printed Word'), pp. 16–20, and 'Shakespeare's London and Graphical Archaeology', an essay presented at the annual meeting of the Shakespeare Association of America at Toronto in 1978, pp. 3–6; Bentley, *The Jacobean and Caroline Stage* (Oxford, 1968), vol. 6, pp. 131–2; Hodges, *The Globe Restored* (London, 1968), pp. 110–11; Wickham, *Early English Stages* (London, 1972), vol. 2, pt 2, p. 68; Linnell, *The Curtain Playhouse* (London, 1977), pp. 15, 37ff.; Hosley, 'The Theatre and the Tradition of Playhouse Design', in *The First Public Playhouse*, ed. H. Berry (Montreal, 1979), pp. 50–6; Foakes, *Illustrations of the English Stage 1580–1642* (London, 1985), pp. 8–9; Orrell, *The Human Stage* (Cambridge, 1988), pp. 30–1; and Lusardi, 'The Pictured Playhouse: Reading the Utrecht Engraving of Shakespeare's London', *Shakespeare Quarterly*, 44 (1993), pp. 202–7.

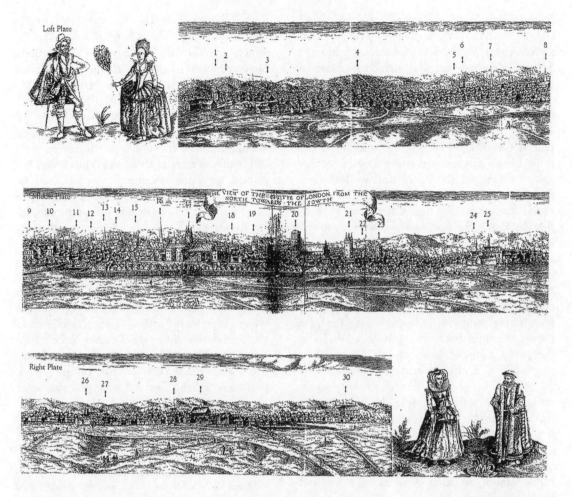

5. The Burden copy of the view of London from the North, divided to show the original places and numbered to identify buildings (see the appendix for the key).

map-views and an elaborate statement of its publication data. It has a large and beautifully engraved civic procession across the bottom, meant, apparently, to illustrate the government of London. The *View* does not show the Thames and has no labels. Instead of coats of arms and the like, it has only a banner floating in the sky in which its title is. It does have a reasonable engraving of two people standing on open ground on the left side and another of two older people standing similarly on the right side, illustrations, it seems, mainly of the gov-

ernment of the country. The procession on *Civitas Londini* is wider and higher than the whole of the topographical part of the *View*. The people on the *View* occupy less than a fifth as much space as the procession on *Civitas Londini* does and may relate to the two old people and two young people who stand at the bottom of a much printed map-view at the time, Georg Braun's and Franz Hogenberg's *Londinum Feracissimi Angliae Regni Metropolis* (1572).

Although the *View* resembles a photograph,

it is a drawing whose artist deliberately made great compromises with topography and whose engraver probably made further compromises with the artist's drawing. The artist seems first to have noted on his drawing the positions of buildings and other objects before him that he thought important and ignored much else. He next made finished drawings of many buildings, but not of some of the most famous, and then lost interest or daylight. Eventually, from a source other than London itself, he completed unfinished buildings and filled in parts of the drawing left blank. His drawings of Guildhall, St Paul's Cathedral, Westminster Abbey, and some other buildings suggest that he was not looking at those buildings when he drew them, and he treated minor buildings diagrammatically, including perhaps, some churches: drew them, that is, as they appeared in general rather than in particular. He could exaggerate buildings he thought important. The engraver added incidentals, like the people at the ends, the tiny (and often amusing) scenes in the foreground, the sky, the banner, and the lettering.

The artist's omissions are legion. Within the boundaries of the City of London, within the 600 mm or so of the *View* beginning about 220 mm from the left side, there were well over one hundred parish churches nearly all of which had towers, not to mention chapels and other buildings that also had towers. The artist should have been able to see the towers of some ninety parish churches alone. He drew perhaps twenty-five towers that seem to belong to churches. The square, pinnacled tower to the right of Guildhall illustrates the point. So far as its place on the drawing goes, it could belong to St Alban Wood Street, St Mary Aldermanbury, St Lawrence Jewry, St Mildred Poultry, St Stephen Walbrook, and no doubt other churches. It probably belongs to St Lawrence Jewry, because while the towers of all those churches were square, only that of St Lawrence had pinnacles at the corners. If the tower does belong to St Lawrence, however, the others,

including two that were closer to the artist (Sts Alban and Mary), are missing.

At first glance, the tower directly under the tower of St Paul's Cathedral on the *View* may seem to belong to St Bartholomew the Great. Even the surviving remnant of the church was (and is) a large building, and the artist should have seen it clearly. The tower probably belongs, however, to a church somewhat more distant from the artist, St Bartholomew the Less, and St Bartholomew the Great is missing. The tower of St Bartholomew the Less, unlike that of St Bartholomew the Great, had (and has) the conspicuous single window that the *View* shows in the middle of the top storey on each of the two sides that the artist could see. The crenellations also shown on the *View* do not appear on some early views, for example those of Wyngaerde and Hollar, but do on those of 'Agas' and Faithorne and Newcourt. To the right of the west front of the Cathedral the artist drew the great pinnacled tower of St Sepulchre, which survives, but not the less impressive one of St James Clerkenwell, which should be just to the left and was much closer to him. He should have seen it clearly, and he did draw the Clerkenwell ducking pond nearby.

It is tempting to suppose that the very large rectangular building 156 mm from the right edge of the *View* is Gray's Inn hall and chapel. Those buildings should have been prominent in the artists' foreground. The building on the *View*, however, does not look like the Gray's Inn buildings, which survive. Its long dimension, moreover, lies north northwest and south southeast, unlike that dimension of the Gray's Inn buildings, which lies east and west. It is probably Allington (later Warwick) House on the north side of High Holborn, where Warwick Court now is, and the buildings of Gray's Inn are probably also missing. On that side of High Holborn, according to Stow in 1598, 'haue ye many faire houses builded, . . . amongst the which buildinges for the most part being very new, one passeth the rest in largenesse of roomes lately builded, by a Widdow',

Jane Allington.[3] As the large building obviously does in the *View*, Allington House 'overshadowed' its neighbours in 1580, including apparently Gray's Inn, to which the freehold of its garden belonged. The large building is about where Allington House should be on the *View*, and, according to John Ogilby and William Morgan's *A Large and Accurate Map of the City of London* (1677), the long dimension of that house lay about as the long dimension of the building on the *View* does.[4] The buildings of Gray's Inn should be a little to the left and somewhat closer to the foreground.

The large church 250 mm from the right edge is probably St Dunstan in the West, but if it is, St Clement Danes is missing.[5] Moreover, the artist curiously omitted the buildings of Whitehall Palace, and he botched the perspective of Westminister Abbey.

The Burdens found the new copy of the *View* tipped into a copy of an early edition of John Speed's *Theatre of the Empire of Great Britaine*, whose first edition appeared in 1611. The new copy of the *View* differs from the Utrecht one chiefly in having the two people on the left end and the two older people on the right end. The Utrecht copy once had these people at the ends, too, as vestiges on both the left and right edges of that copy show. The illustration at the left end of the *View* is about 125 mm wide, and that at the right end about 131 mm wide, so that together with the topography the *View* is some 1295 mm wide.

It was engraved on three copper plates of roughly the same size: left to right 427 mm, 431 mm, and 435 mm wide and from 104 mm to 108 mm high. On the left plate are the two people at the end and topography to a little west of the Dutch Church in Austin Friars. On the centre plate is topography from there to about 45 mm west of St Etheldreda Ely Place. On the right plate is the rest of the topography and the older people.

The plates were printed separately and the resulting sheets then assembled and pasted together as appropriate. The Burden copy is much as it probably was some 400 years ago. It is in one piece and has been neither mounted onto backing nor repaired. The Utrecht copy has not been repaired or mounted onto backing either, but it is now in two pieces, the left one about 313 mm wide and the right one about 741 mm wide. The topographical parts of the plates seem not to have been changed between the printing of the sheets that comprise the two copies. The topography of the Utrecht copy, however, is bigger than that of the Burden one, the result mainly, no doubt, of how and where the sheets have been kept for 400 years and

---

[3] John Stow, *A Survey of London* (London, 1598), p. 361.

[4] The building cannot be Somerset House, which should lie behind it, because the alignments of the two buildings were quite different. The widow made her will on 15 July 1603, and her heirs proved it on 7 January 1604. They sold the house in 1607 for £2,000 to Lord Rich, a member of Gray's Inn and future Earl of Warwick. Pepys 'staid in the great hall' on 3 March 1660, 'talking with some gentlemen there'. Ogilby and Morgan (sheet 11) show Warwick House as about 45' by 90'. It has a big garden beside it on the east side and several other buildings adjoining, including a gatehouse in High Holborn that may appear at the top of Hollar's Great Map (c. 1658), reproduced in *A Collection of Early Maps of London*, ed. John Fisher (Lympne Castle, Kent, 1981). The house was pulled down in 1688 and Warwick Court built on the site. See at the PRO, PROB.11/103/ff. 68–70, and C.54/1910/m. 19 from the bottom; W. R. Douthwaite, *Gray's Inn its History and Associations* (London, 1886), p. 105; Francis Cowper, *A Prospect of Gray's Inn* (London, 1951), pp. 13–14, 60, 75–6.

[5] The church on the *View* is much closer to where St Dunstan's should be than to where St Clement's should be. Both churches had square towers: the tower of St Dunstan's was beside the nave on the north side, and St Clement's was at the western end (where it still is). The church on the *View* has a square tower at the eastern end, as St Clement's does on the inset map of Westminster on *Civitas Londini*. But attached to the southeast corner to the tower of St Dunstan's was a small tower, presumably for a stairway, with a little turret on top that rose above the main tower – according to Hollar (who dated his work 1667) and John Leake on *An Exact Surveigh of the Streets Lanes and Churches* (London, 1669), reproduced in *A Collection of Early Maps of London*. The church on the *View* has such a tower and turret at that corner of the main tower.

partly of how the original joins were made. The topography of the Utrecht copy is slightly higher and about 1.5 per cent wider than that of the Burden copy (the individual sheets of the Utrecht copy range from nearly 2 per cent to 1.4 per cent wider). The topography of the Utrecht copy is about 1054 mm wide, that of the Burden copy about 15 mm less. All the joins are less than perfect, but those in the Burden copy seem overlapped, the eastern one slightly, the western one by a little more than a millimetre.

The people at the ends of the *View* are more skilfully drawn and engraved than much else on the *View*. The two at the left end are extravagantly dressed in clothing fashionable in Jacobean times, from about 1610 until well into the 1620s. They could be King James and his wife, Queen Anne. The likenesses are reasonable, and the clothing, especially the lady's and more especially her large fan, resembles that in the familiar portraits of the two.[6] The older woman at the right end is also extravagantly dressed but in Elizabethan clothing of two decades or so earlier. She could be Queen Elizabeth. Again the likeness is reasonable, and the arrangement of hair and neckwear is that of many of her portraits. The old man wears a long robe and clutches something, perhaps a document or gloves, in his left hand. He may be a lord mayor of London, or the idea of one. Somebody may have cut these people off the Utrecht copy because they have nothing to do with topography, but more likely because they are portraits of famous people. They do not appear elsewhere among Booth's manuscripts at the University of Utrecht.

The procession at the bottom of *Civitas Londini* consists of four people afoot and twenty-one on horseback. Two municipal waits lead the procession, one playing a shawm, the other a sackbut, followed by two boys carrying wands and a military figure carrying a large sword, all afoot and all in clothing of the 1590s. Then, dressed much like the older man on the *View*, come a single horseman with a wand or

sword and twenty others riding in pairs. In 1715, John Bagford supposed that these people were 'the Cavalcade of the Lord Mayor's Show', the riders being the lord mayor and aldermen of London, and the military figure presumably the lord mayor's sword bearer.[7]

The Utrecht copy of the *View* cannot reveal when the engraver did his work, but the Burden copy can, thanks to the figures at its two ends. Because of the clothing that the two people at the left end wear, whether they are meant to be King James and Queen Anne or not, the engraver must have engraved the *View* well into, perhaps even toward the end of Jacobean times. Besides, the existence of the *View* among the papers of Abraham Booth suggests that it was available in 1629–30.

The artist should have drawn the *View* before

---

[6] One aspect of the clothing of both the man and woman that suggests a date is their neckwear, his square standing band and her semi-circular, open band. See especially the portraits of her by Marc Gheeraerts the younger and Paul van Somer and of both by Renold Elstracke for John Sudbury and George Humble. See also, for example, C. W. and P. Cunnington, *Handbook of English Costume in the Seventeenth Century* (London, 1955), pp. 37–8, 57–8, 81, etc.

[7] See Shapiro, 'The Bankside Theatres: Early Engravings', *Shakespeare Survey* 1 (1948), p. 28. The procession was engraved on only two plates. One plate has the people afoot and the leading rider. The other has six riders, but sheets printed from this plate were cut and pasted together (from the right: one complete sheet, then part of a sheet containing two riders, then two complete sheets) so that the six became twenty.

Mr Hyde has pointed out to me that both *Civitas Londini* and the *View* owe something to *The Funeral Procession of Sir Philip Sidney*, a series of engravings that Theodor de Bry issued in the Netherlands in 1587. The procession includes twenty municipal riders: a 'Sword Bearer' and 'Sr Geo: Barnes Lo: Maior' riding singly, followed by eighteen 'Aldermen Knights' and 'Other Aldermen' riding in pairs. Afoot are 'Other Cittizins called the Company of Grocers' and 'Cyttizins of London practised in Armes' led by a 'Capt' boy' with a shield and a 'Capitaneus' and a 'Locumtenens' both carrying swords and trailing pikes. Riders and horses suggest those of *Civitas Londini*, and the aldermen and Grocers wear clothes like those of the older man on the *View*.

February 1613, because he conspicuously included the unmistakable tower of the Dutch Church, whose pulling down began then.[8] He would not have drawn it before 1600 because he evidently depended on *Civitas Londini*, which appeared in that year. The artist, therefore, drew the *View* when the Curtain, but not the Theatre, still stood in Holywell.

Civitas Londini dates itself thoroughly. An inset explains that 'This description of the moste Famous Citty London Was performed in The yeare of Christe . 1600 . And in the' forty-second year of the Queen's reign (from 17 November 1599, to 16 November 1600) and the terms of the lord mayor and sheriffs of London in office from 29 September 1599, until 28 September 1600.[9] If the author of the inset used old style, therefore, *Civitas Londini* was 'performed' between 1 January or, more likely, 25 March and 28 September 1600, or, if he used new style, between 11 January and 9 October 1600. The inset adds, 'By the industry of Jhon Norden', and both inset map-views are revisions of map-views Norden had made for *Speculum Britanniae* (1593), one of London, the other (ingeniously worked into the panorama) of Westminster.

Civitas Londini and the *View* are obviously related. To argue that the *View* came before *Civitas Londini*, rather than the other way round, is in general to argue an unlikely case: that the artist of *Civitas Londini* had before him a drawing that would not be engraved, hence readily available, for a decade or more; and that the large, elaborate panorama many of whose buildings are labelled depended on the small, plain one that has no labels.

The style of engraving on the *View* is much the same as that on *Civitas Londini*. The tiny people and animals in the foreground of the *View* resemble those in the foreground of *Civitas Londini*. The sky of the *View* resembles that of *Civitas Londini* down to the cloud over the western end of London. The lettering of the *View* – especially T, C, I, S, L, A – is similar to that of *Civitas Londini*. The *View* may have

had a history like that of *Civitas Londini*. Someone who knew London well, probably Norden, made the drawing for *Civitas Londini*, and someone else who did not know London or, as I. A. Shapiro has argued, English, engraved it, perhaps in the Netherlands.[10]

The drawing of one artist is also similar in style to that of the other. And, more important here, several buildings that one artist drew suggest that he had the work of the other before him rather than London itself.

The *View* and *Civitas Londini*, for example, show the roof of Guildhall in the same uniquely mistaken way. Each has four objects of the same size and shape on the roof, one on top of each gable and two in line along the ridge, and the objects on one roof resemble those on the other. Nearly all the relatively trustworthy views that show the roof clearly up to the great fire of London in 1666 have two large objects on the ridge, and at least five also have a much smaller one on each gable. The large objects are louvres, and the small ones are finials, orna-

---

8 Over the choir of the Dutch Church was 'a most fine spired steeple, small [i.e., narrow], high, and streight, I haue not seene the like', which beautified the city: Stow, *Survay*, pp. 138–9, also the edns of 1603 (p. 178), 1618 (p. 339), and 1720 (vol. 2, pp. 114–15). The steeple is sometimes said to have fallen down in 1609 (for example W. J. C. Moens, *The Marriage, Baptismal, and Burial Registers* [Lymington, 1884], p. xxix). The idea, however, results from a misreading of a letter of 30 November 1609, in which the privy council urged the church to repair the steeple because it 'is an auncient monument' that 'giveth bewtie and ornament to the Citie, and therefore not fitt to be suffered to fall to ruine and decaie'. Just before its destruction began, it was still standing and might 'for a long time stand sound, and safe'. See J. H. Hessels, *Ecclesiae Londino-Bataviae Archivum* (Cambridge, 1897), vol. 3, pt 1, nos. 1701, 1732, 1733; *Acts of the Privy Council, 1612–13*, ed. J. R. Dasent (HMSO, 1922), pp. 67, 186–7.

9 A single copy survives, in the Royal Library, Stockholm. The London Topographical Society reproduced it in 1961 as publication no. 94.

10 'The Bankside Theatres', pp. 27–31; see also R. A. Skelton, 'A Study of the View', *London Topographical Record*, 22 (1965), pp. 14–25.

ments.[11] The louvres were installed in 1491 and remained until the fire of 1666 gutted the building. They vented smoke from the open fireplaces in each of the two rooms into which the great hall under the roof was divided. As such fireplaces were in other medieval halls, these were evidently toward the middle of each of the rooms, in front of the dais.[12] The artist of *Civitas Londini*, then, was wrong, and he of the *View* followed him, or *vice versa*. The first of them knew that there were four objects along the roof of Guildhall but could not have looked closely at them and did not know what they were. If he thought of them as louvres, he should not have put them on the gables, where chimneys would be, and if he thought of them as ornaments he should not have put them on the roof, where ornaments must add unnecessary weight. The second did not look closely, either, and simply followed the first.

The objects on the *View* look like crude versions of those on *Civitas Londini*, mostly because the objects on the *View* are too big in proportion to the length of the ridge (about 1:2) to be anything that could actually appear there. Those on *Civitas Londini* are more persuasive (about 1:5). If both views are wrong about the roof of Guildhall in the same unique way, but the *View* is more wrong, the artist of the *View* should have had *Civitas Londini* before him rather than the other way round. Norden's inset map-view of London on *Civitas Londini*, incidentally, omits Guildhall, as does his map-view of London in *Speculum Britanniae*.

Old St Paul's Cathedral on the *View* is strikingly like the one on *Civitas Londini* because both are badly drawn in the same ways. The actual Cathedral had a nave, transepts, choir, and, sitting astride the crossing, a great square tower supported by a buttress at each corner. The Cathedral on *Civitas Londini* is more elaborate than that on the *View*, but on both the tower is not on the axes of the crossing but on the side of the Cathedral away from the artist – in *Civitas Londini* on the north side and in the *View* on the south side; and on both the roof

ridge of the appropriate transept leads to a corner of the tower rather than to the middle of one side. No artist actually looking at the place could have drawn it so.

The two square towers to the left of St Paul's Cathedral on the *View* may also have to do with *Civitas Londini*. The one farther from the Cathedral has something rectangular on top. It could belong to at least eleven parish churches, all of whose towers were square. It is probably supposed to be the tower of St Botolph Aldersgate, and the rest are missing. That tower has nothing save a cross on top on other views, but two towers in about the right place on *Civitas Londini* have rectangular objects on top like the one on the *View*, and the tower of St Botolph itself has a rectangular object on top on Norden's inset map-view of London accompanying *Civitas Londini*. The tower nearer the Cathedral is bigger and has pinnacles at the corners. It should belong to St Saviour (now Southwark Cathedral) on the south side of the river, or to St Martin Vintry in Thames Street

---

11 The views are Wyngaerde's, reproduced in *The Panorama of London circa 1544*, ed. Howard Colvin and Susan Foister (London, 1996, LTS no. 151); three reproduced in *A Collection of Early Maps of London*: the anonymous one called Copperplate (*c.* 1553–9), that attributed to Ralph Agas (*Civitas Londinum* [*c.* 1562]), and Braun and Hogenberg's view; and three by Wenceslaus Hollar: his Long View (1647), *A True and Exact Prospect of the Famous City of London* 'before the fire', and a small view of London from the North (*c.* 1665). The finials appear in Wyngaerde, Braun and Hogenberg, and Hollar's Long View and *True and Exact Prospect*.

William Faithorne and Richard Newcourt's *London An Exact Delineation Thereof* (1658), also reproduced in *A Collection of Early Maps of London*, shows a single louvre in the middle of the ridge and finials at the gable ends. So does Hollar's *The Prospect of London and Westminster taken from Lambeth* before 1666 (London, 1988, LTS no. 138), but the Guildhall here may owe something to the building as rebuilt after the fire (the Guildhall in the drawing made ostensibly before the fire is identical to the one in the reworked version of about 1707).

12 Caroline M. Barron, *The Medieval Guildhall of London* (London, 1974), p. 32.

on the north side, both of which had noted pinnacled towers and are on *Civitas Londini*. The artist probably meant the tower of St Martin, because his pinnacles resemble those of that tower on *Civitas Londini*, but he drew his tower much higher than he could have seen either real tower. The main part of his tower rises well above the Cathedral roof and the pinnacles nearly to the top of the Cathedral tower. According to Stow (p. 264) and a report of 1666, the Cathedral roof was 150′ high and the tower 260′.[13] St Martin and St Saviour were on lower ground than the Cathedral and much farther from the viewpoint, St Martin nearly 550 yards and St Saviour nearly 1,200 yards. The artist evidently chose to emphasize the tower. On *Civitas Londini*, both towers are a reasonable size.

A curious link between the *View* and *Civitas Londini* is a church about 250 mm from the left edge of the *View*. It has a high, thin, improbable steeple apparently ending in a long mast and should be St Helen Bishopsgate. *Civitas Londini* has a steeple in more or less the same place, as does Visscher's view (which is also closely related to *Civitas Londini*). The steeple is un-labelled in *Civitas Londini* but is labelled 'St Hellen' in Visscher. The real church, however, did not have and has never had such a steeple, though according to Stow it should have had one. Sir Thomas Gresham (d. 1579) had promised to build one in return for a place in the church for his elaborate tomb. The church provided (and provides) the place, but Gresham did not build the steeple and neglected to mention it in his will, so that neither his widow nor anybody else built it.[14] The artists of *Civitas Londini* and the *View*, therefore, did not see the steeple in London, but the artist of *Civitas Londini* could have seen it in the editions of Stow's book in 1598 and 1599, and the artist of the *View* could have seen it there, or in a later edition, or in *Civitas Londini*.

Two prominent rectangular buildings on the right side of the *View* also suggest that the artist had *Civitas Londini* before him. They are along

the back of the city as the artist saw it, the western one some 178 mm from the right edge and the eastern one some 234 mm. They look alike: each has a pitched roof in the middle of which is a tower with a window and, on top, a dome, flag pole, and flag. Both stand well above their surroundings, and their long dimensions lie northeast–southwest. The tower above the western building is apparently round; that above the eastern one could be round or square. The western building is probably supposed to be the hall of Arundel House, and the eastern one 'the greate hall of the Middle Temple' (as Stow called it, p. 328).

While both buildings really had large pitched roofs with objects on top, the artist of the *View* could not have seen either as he drew it. Both were much less conspicuous than the buildings on the *View* are. The hall of Arundel House was and Middle Temple Hall is not only a long way from the viewpoint, but on ground well below that on which other buildings before the artist were. Moreover, the long dimensions of both halls lay mainly east and west, and the objects on their roofs were not towers with windows but louvres. Hollar, who lived in Arundel House, drew that hall on three views of London and on a little drawing, 'Aula Domus Arrundelianæ, Septentrionem versus' (Arundel House toward the north), for which he was looking straight at it from only a few yards away. His louvre is square and relatively small and has a pointed cap covered with lead.

---

13 *Survay*, p. 264; Christopher Wren, *Parentalia* (London, 1750), pp. 271, 274.

14 *Survay*, p. 133: the church 'wanteth such a steeple as Sir *Thomas Gresham* promised to haue builded, in recompence of ground in . . . [the] church filled vp, with his monument'. The remark also appears in the succeeding editions. The will is at the PRO, PROB.11/61/ff. 367–9. See also Shapiro, 'The Bankside Theatres', pp. 27–30; J. E. Cox, *The Annals of St Helen's Bishopsgate* (London, 1876), pp. 105, 219, where in 1569 the 'hole steeple' is identified as a 'cloke [i.e., clock] howse' to be 'sett . . . upon the corner of the wall so as ytt shall be borne uppon the wall and not . . . on the roofe of the Church'.

His nearby buildings are as high as, or higher than, the hall. Hollar also drew Middle Temple Hall on three views of London. His louvre here is taller than that of the hall of Arundel House and apparently has a dome on top, but it is no tower. Again, his nearby buildings are much the same height as the Hall.

On *Civitas Londini*, however, the hall of Arundel House (which is above the label 'Essex stayrs') resembles the two buildings on the *View*. It is on higher ground and is aligned as the buildings on the *View* are. It has a tall pitched roof out of which rises a round tower, though without window, flag pole, and flag. Middle Temple Hall is aligned much as it should be and looks like Hollar's drawings, except that above the dome it has a flag pole and flag.

The artist of the *View* must have thought the halls of Arundel House and the Middle Temple important or interesting enough not only to include them but to emphasize them. Since he could not see much of them from his viewpoint, he probably consulted *Civitas Londini* and for both invented an amalgam of what he saw there. It consists of the alignment and central tower of the hall of Arundel House and the dome, flag pole, and flag of Middle Temple Hall. To these things, he added a window in the towers. When Visscher came to draw a hall above 'Essex staires', he drew the building on *Civitas Londini* but added ecclesiastical windows and put a steeple on top of the tower.

Hotson argued that the *View* was drawn during the late spring or summer of 1600. He identified a large building with only two sides standing as the Fortune playhouse, which was under construction then. The building is on the northern edge of the City, just to the right of the Dutch church, and is the only apparently incomplete building. Fisher, of course, needed to demolish Hotson's argument. In 1964 he declared that, according to his geometry, the building is not close enough to where the Fortune should be. Something, however, is wrong with the calculation, for it puts the

building on the right side of the Tower of London rather than on the left, where it obviously is.[15] According to the geometry to be proposed here, the building is somewhat to the right of where the Fortune probably was, but other buildings in that part of the *View* are similarly to the right of where they were. The large building behind and to the right of the incomplete building, for example, should be Garter, later Bridgewater, House, a vast pile that was behind and to the right of the Fortune as seen from either Fisher's viewpoint or the one here.[16]

The incomplete building does not look like what the historian of playhouses would expect to see of the Fortune, or any other, playhouse. The one wall clearly visible has three two-storey windows in the bottom part and four single-storey windows in the top part. No other early representation of playhouses has such windows, and nothing in the builder's contract for the Fortune even hints at them.[17] The incomplete building, however, could be three storeys high, as the Fortune was, and seems to be square, as the Fortune also was. With the addition of the other two walls, roofs, and external staircases, the building on the *View* might seem a more credible playhouse. One should probably hesitate to endorse Hotson's idea because of the windows, but one should not dismiss it out of hand.

---

[15] Fisher must have realized that something was wrong, for he omitted the calculation in 1967, and in calculating the position of the buildings as though the obvious playhouse were the Curtain in 1978, he got the incomplete building properly on the left side of the Tower.

[16] See below and Ogilby and Morgan, *Large and Accurate Map*, sheets 8 (Bridgewater House), and 13 (the site of the playhouse in Playhouse Yard).

[17] The famous contract mentions only 'convenient' windows for the tiring house. It provides that unmentioned things be 'done' as they had recently been done at the first Globe, but nothing about that playhouse, or its successor, suggests windows like those of the incomplete building on the *View*.

To arrive at his geometrical scheme, Fisher looked first for the artist's viewpoint on a modern map. That, he thought, would be a place north of the city where a person could see the left and right ends of the topography on the *View* at an angle of about 90°, the 'normal horizontal field' that a person might 'see as a single image'. He found such a place on the north side of the Pentonville Road opposite the middle of Claremont Square, N.I., where lines to the left and right ends of the topography on the *View* form an angle of 'about' 92°. Next, he found the equivalent viewpoint on the *View* by, presumably, drawing converging lines downward from the ends to where they form an angle of 92°. On both a modern map and the *View*, he then calculated in degrees and minutes the positions mainly of five things: the site of the Theatre on a modern map and the obvious playhouse on the *View* (he assumed that the two were the same), the site of the Curtain on a modern map and the flagged building to the right of the obvious playhouse on the *View* (he also assumed that these two were the same), the Tower of London, old St Paul's Cathedral, and Westminster Abbey. He began at due north in 1964 and 1967, giving the site of the Theatre on a modern map and the obvious playhouse on the *View* as 110°. In 1978 he began from the site of the Theatre and obvious playhouse, giving both as 0°. These calculations demonstrated, he found, that things on the *View* are very close to where they should be.

Most of this logic, however, gives pause at once. Fisher's initial assumption that an artist would necessarily draw a scene spread out before him at something like 90°, is, to say the least, open to challenge. Above all, it did not occur to him in 1964 and 1967 that in making the site of the Theatre and the obvious playhouse the same place, and also the site of the Curtain and the flagged building to the right, he was begging his whole question. The idea evidently did occur to him by 1978. For then he also calculated the positions of the Tower, St Paul's, and the Abbey as though the obvious

playhouse were the Curtain and found that these figures are less satisfactory than those arrived at when the Theatre is the obvious playhouse. Even now it did not occur to him that there might be other possibilities. The site of the Curtain, for example, is not beyond dispute.[18] Besides, he could have tested his assumptions by calculating the positions of a great many more buildings.

The geometry in all this is faulty, too. The reader is evidently to think that lines northward from the ends of the topography converge at about 92° in only one place, Fisher's viewpoint. Such lines, however, converge at that angle in an infinitude of places on an arc north of the old city. Moreover, because one cannot establish on a modern map exactly where the topography on the *View* begins and ends, one can easily find other arcs that provide further infinitudes of places.[19] Fisher was right to think, however, that the person who would read the

---

[18] The Curtain was in a large enclosed former pasture on the south side of Holywell Lane, EC2, but exactly where is not known. Fisher put it on the east side of Curtain Road at Hewett Street, due south of the site of the Theatre, because Chassereau's map (1745) shows a large more or less square building there called Curtain Court. Halliwell-Phillipps had advanced the idea (1882) and J. Q. Adams had agreed (1917). But E. K. Chambers (1923) dismissed it, and Bentley (1968) and Linnell (1977) tacitly agreed with him. They put the playhouse closer to Holywell Lane and Shoreditch High Street, supposing that the 'Court' should be the site not of the playhouse but of 'the house tenemente or lodge commonlie called the Curteyne' mentioned in documents written in 1567 and 1572, before the playhouse was built, also in 1581 and, apparently, 1640. See Halliwell-Phillipps, *Outlines of the Life of Shakespeare* (London, 1882), p. 361; Adams, *Shakespearean Playhouses* (Boston, 1917), p. 79; Chambers, *Elizabethan Stage* (Oxford, 1923), vol. 2, pp. 401–2. The documents are at the PRO C.54/742/no. 34; C.54/884/m. 17–19 from the bottom; C.54/1098/m. 8 from the bottom; and at the Guildhall Library, MSS 7499, 7493 (a burial and a baptism at St Leonard Shoreditch on 31 January and 15 March 1640, of persons 'from the Curtain house').

[19] Hotson similarly guessed at a viewpoint, which he put a little west of the Angel, NI, some 300 yards east of Fisher's.

View closely should first establish a viewpoint on a modern map and its equivalent on the *View*.

Fisher measured the *View* down to a sixtieth of a degree, a minute, and so produced numbers that inspire confidence. Measuring the *View* by itself, however, can lead only to approximations and measuring it against a modern map considerably more so. I measure the *View* down to the nearest fifteen minutes, and even this diminution must suggest more exactitude than is achievable.

To begin with, panoramic views and map-views are inherently prone to error, since they are as much artistic as cartographic. John Holwell, one of the surveyors who measured and plotted London for Ogilby and Morgan's great flat map (1677), wryly observed that 'Those that are minded to draw the Map of any Town, City or Corporation, only with the Uprights of the Houses, will have no need to measure either the House, Courts or Allies thereof.' The artist of the *View* often did what artists, not cartographers, do. Each of his omissions is an example; so especially is his treatment of the most conspicuous object in the city. He made the tower of St Paul's Cathedral the middle of his drawing, left to right, although that tower actually stood well east of the middle of his topography.[20] Moreover, little on the *View* is precise or was meant to be. One cannot, for example, draw a line straight downward from the *View* with complete confidence, because lines on the *View* that should be exactly straight and parallel are not, such as its edges and its perpendiculars of buildings. One cannot even know its exact size, as the different sizes of the two known copies suggest, let alone the size of the drawing and engraving that lie behind it. Too, one must almost inevitably work with reproductions, and the lenses involved in making them will very likely introduce further distortions.

In comparing the position of a building on a view, especially a panoramic view, with that of the same building on a modern map, one must deal with an elevation on the view and a ground plan on the modern map. Should one assume (as I do) that the artist of the *View* noted the position of the top of a building and then worked downward so that the top represents the position of the building? The difference between the top of his Dutch Church, say, and the bottom is about half a degree, 30′.

The graphical archaeologist (Fisher's apt phrase) should first identify buildings on the *View* by what they look like rather than where they are. One should, that is, look for unique architectural features that a building is otherwise reliably known to have had. The most certain of such buildings on the *View* are the minaret-like tower of the Dutch church, the Tower of London, the tower of the Royal Exchange, the steeple of St Dunstan in the East, Guildhall, the steeple of St Lawrence Pountney, the tower of St Mary le Bow, St Paul's Cathedral, the tower of St Sepulchre, Westminster Abbey,[21] and St Etheldreda Ely Place.[22] Other buildings are less certain but

---

20 *Sure Guide to the Practical Surveyor* (London, 1678), p. 190. The left edge of the Cathedral tower is the exact centre of the *View*. The topography of the *View* begins south of St Leonard Shoreditch at about the western part of Calvert Avenue, E2, and ends at about the eastern part of Victoria Street, SW1. Halfway would be southwest of Ludgate Circus, EC4.

21 The tower of the Royal Exchange was at the southeast corner and consisted of three square towers one on top of the other, a loggia above the first, another above the second, and a dome above the third. St Dunstan in the East and St Lawrence Pountney had the tallest conventional steeples in the city. On top of the tower of St Mary le Bow was a curious crown-like affair. Westminster Abbey was by far the largest church west of St Paul's Cathedral (it did not have its familiar western towers until the eighteenth century).

22 On the *View*, St Etheldreda has five tall windows, a crenellated parapet, and no visible roof. It still has the windows and on the *Exact Surveigh* the parapet; it also has and had a pitched roof. Behind on the *View* is a large building, no doubt Ely House (the London house of the bishops of Ely) for which St Etheldreda was the chapel. This building has a pitched roof coterminus except on the east with the pitched roof that probably should be on the church. The artist should have seen

likely, among them the buildings of Charter-house,[23] St John of Jerusalem,[24] and the tower of St Bartholomew the Less. Many of these structures survive: the Tower of London, Guildhall, the buildings of Charterhouse, St John of Jerusalem, the tower of St Bartholomew the Less, the tower of St Sepulchre, St Etheldreda, and Westminster Abbey. Others have been rebuilt on the same site: the Dutch church, the Royal Exchange, St Mary le Bow, and, more or less, St Paul's Cathedral. The site of one is preserved (St Dunstan in the East), and another is remembered in the names of the two streets between which it was (St Lawrence Pountney).

The artist's scheme of perspective is also relevant. For churches aligned roughly east and west, he drew, from the left edge of the topography up to St Etheldreda's, something of the west side, as well as the north. He drew, for example, the north side of St Paul's Cathedral fully and something of the west front and the west sides of the tower and north transept. The viewpoint, therefore, was mainly north but also west of these buildings. He drew only the north side of St Etheldreda's, however, which was and is aligned slightly to the northeast. He drew something of the west side of the church tower that rises above the eastern half of it, which must belong to St Andrew Holborn nearby and was and is aligned somewhat to the southeast. For the only ordinary church to the right, apparently St Dunstan in the West, he drew the north side and something of the east side, not the west side. His drawing of Westminster Abbey shows neither the east side of the choir nor the west side of the nave, but incongruously it does show the west side of the north transept.

The artist is more likely to have been right in reporting that two buildings were in line vertically than in estimating the distance between them horizontally. His viewpoint, then, should have been where he could see only the north side of St Etheldreda's and, rising over the east half of it, the north side and something of the

west side of the tower of St Andrew's. To find the viewpoint on the *View*, one should first draw a line straight downward through the tower and the east half of the church. On a modern map, one should draw a similar line downward. It will be about $77°$ from due east.

To find where along this line the viewpoint was, one should look for other identifiable buildings on the *View* that lie on top of one another so that the artist could see them in that way from the viewpoint but not from other places. The unmistakable tower of St Mary le Bow rises above buildings that probably belong to Charterhouse. The northwestern edge of the tower of old St Paul's Cathedral is in line up and down with the same edge of the tower of a church that is probably St Bartholomew the Less.[25] The tower of a church that should be St

and drawn the pitched roof on the church, but had he done so he would have obliterated Ely House, the major building on the site. Hollar, I suspect, solved the same problem on the *Exact Surveigh* by omitting Ely House. See John Carter's drawing of the site in the eighteenth century, just before Ely House was pulled down: reproduced in John Britton, *Picturesque Antiquities* (London, 1830), the penultimate plate.

23 Hotson identified these buildings (without argument) as belonging to Charterhouse, but Fisher, Orrell, and Lusardi have identified them (also without argument) as belonging to the Priory of St John of Jerusalem. Hotson was probably right. By the late years of Elizabeth, the Priory was mostly gone. Some of the medieval Charterhouse was also gone, but much of it had been incorporated into a great Tudor house recently built on the site, and most of that house is still there. Of the two pitched roofs shown on the *View*, the left one is probably the library and the right one the northern building of Wash-house Court, both of which survive. See E. E. Harrison, *The History of Charterhouse and its Buildings* (London, 1990), pp. 10, 23 and *passim*.

24 St John of Jerusalem was, and what remains of it is, relatively low for a great church (see Hollar's drawings of it in Sir William Dugdale's *Monasticon* [London, 1661], vol. 2, p. 504).

25 A plan of the old cathedral carefully drawn in pencil over the plan of the new one on a copy of the Ordnance Survey map of London, 1875 (sheet VII, 65), among the maps and prints at the Guildhall Library shows the centre of the old tower at nearly the centre of the new dome. A drawing of the tower of

Martin Vintry is above a long low roof that should belong to the church of St John of Jerusalem. So on a modern map one should draw another line through the tower of St Mary le Bow and the buildings of Charterhouse. It will be about $60°30'$ from due east. To relate the viewpoint to the *View*, one should set the protractor at $77°$ on the line through the tower of St Andrew's and St Etheldreda's, then find the point on that line where a line through the Charterhouse buildings and the middle of the tower of St Mary's is at $60°30'$.

This line and the one through the tower of St Andrew's and St Etheldreda's will meet on a modern map in the Barnsbury Estate, N1, near the southwest corner of Copenhagen Street, which runs east and west, and Charlotte Terrace, which runs north and south. Copenhagen Street begins on relatively low ground north of King's Cross. After it crosses the Caledonian Road, it rises steeply up the western flank and then along the south-facing brow of Islington Hill. It reaches a peak at Charlotte Terrace, then rises a little more to Barnsbury Road and Cloudesley Road. The artist would have sat on the southwest side and just under the brow of Islington Hill. Eventually, at least, people really went to fields thereabouts to see the City.[26]

From here the artist would also have seen the towers of St Paul's and St Bartholomew the Less nearly in line and the tower of St Martin Vintry above the roof of St John of Jerusalem. All the reasonably identifiable buildings from one end of the *View* to the other are in the right order as seen from here. And all those that would have been most important and most visible to the artist, from Guildhall westward to the building that is apparently Allington House, are within a degree or so of where they should be. (See the appendix.) From St Dunstan in the East leftward, however, buildings are at increasingly greater angles than they should be. The angles range from a little more than $2°$ to $7°45'$ near the obvious playhouse – if the square tower to the right of the windmill belongs to St Mary

Matfellon and if the distant tower to the right of the playhouse is the beacon on Shooters Hill.[27] Moreover, Westminster Abbey, the only identifiable building on the far right side, is at an angle some $3°$ less than it should be, perhaps partly a result of the omission of Whitehall Palace. The leftward third of the *View* and Westminster Abbey, therefore, are closer to the centre than they should be, so that the panorama may be some 200 mm less wide than it should be.[28] The artist, that is, again did what artists, not cartographers, do. He foreshortened the parts of his drawing showing places farthest from him and in so doing made his drawing less cumbersome for him to draw and for a buyer to use. Whoever cut off the people standing at the left and right ends of the Utrecht copy made the *View* less wide and cumbersome still.

Fisher's viewpoint is several hundred yards south and a little east of the one proposed here.

St Bartholomew the Less is on the *Exact Surveigh*, and a better one of 1725 is reproduced in *The London Encyclopaedia*, ed. Ben Weinreb and Christopher Hibbert (London, 1993), p. 716.

26 See Weinreb and Hibbert, *The London Encyclopaedia*, p. 43.

27 If the tower is the beacon, it is about where it should be in relation to the Curtain. The beacon was on the main road to Dover, at an elevation of about $432'$, nearly eight miles from the viewpoint; it existed from the sixteenth century onward, and its site is in the grounds of Woolwich Memorial Hospital on the south side of Shooters Hill Road, SE18 (Darrell Spurgeon, *Discover Etham and its Environs* [London, 1992], pp. 79, 82). Another such tower on the *View* is higher and just to the right; it may be a beacon farther along the Dover road. Yet another, with a flag and flag pole, is to the left of the tower that apparently belongs to St Helen Bishopsgate. It looks like Wyngaerde's drawing (*Panorama*, p. 41) of Duke Humphrey's tower on Greenwich Hill, where the royal observatory now is. But Greenwich Hill is too far east for the tower on the *View*, which should be in Lewisham, perhaps also near the Dover road.

28 From the viewpoint here, a degree represents on the *View* about 22 mm among the buildings around the obvious playhouse, about 14 mm among the buildings directly in front of the artist, and about 17 mm at Westminster Abbey.

It is also lower. From there, an artist would have seen the tower of St Andrew Holborn as a little east of St Etheldreda, not above it, and the tower of St Mary-le-Bow as just west of the buildings of Charterhouse not above them. Neither the tower of St Bartholomew the Less nor that of St Bartholomew the Great would be in line with the tower of St Paul's Cathedral, but the unlikely twin towers of Christchurch Newgate might have been. The greatest differences between calculations made from this viewpoint and the one in Barnsbury, however, are the ends of the *View*, especially the left end, where the obvious playhouse is.

From the viewpoint proposed here, the obvious playhouse is some $10°$ to the right of the site of the Theatre but only $8°$ or less to the right of the general area where the Curtain was. So, geometrically the obvious playhouse should be the Curtain.

Except for two things, the building to the right of the obvious playhouse that Fisher thought the hut over another playhouse looks like a great many other buildings on the *View*, which are the ordinary buildings of London. It has a flag, as no other such building does. It lacks a chimney, as the hut over the obvious playhouse does; but while most similar buildings on the *View* do have chimneys, some do not, including the two nearest neighbours of this building. It is a good deal bigger than the hut of the obvious playhouse, and its flag is somewhat smaller than that of the obvious playhouse, which flies from a pole in a little crenellated tower, not in the roof ridge of the hut. Open land apparently runs up to some bushes growing under and rising above the eaves on the left side of the building, so that if the building is the hut over a playhouse, the rest of the playhouse is in an abrupt hole some 40' deep.

Its flag is the only thing about the building that could seriously suggest theatrical use. In arguing that flags flew mostly from playhouses, Fisher declared that, other than this building and the obvious playhouse, only three buildings

on the *View* have them, but many have them. Most are churches flying small things (some perhaps made of metal) from towers or steeples. But six buildings that have domes or bulbs on top also have real flags, of which Fisher noticed only two, the one that should be Warwick Inn and the Tower of London (which has flags on all four of its domes). He did not notice the flags on the domes of Middle Temple Hall, the hall of Arundel House, and two other buildings. A seventh building with a dome, the Royal Exchange, may also have a flag. Several similar buildings on *Civitas Londini* have real flags, though Fisher thought only the Bankside playhouses have them there. If players could fly flags over their playhouses, evidently the great could fly them over their halls – some of which, coincidentally, like Middle Temple Hall, could occasionally become playhouses for a few hours.

Could the building Fisher thought another playhouse be a place used for amusements other than plays? Could it, for example, be one of the 'fayre Sommer houses' that were encroaching Finsbury Fields and Moorfields in 1598, as the building on the *View* seems to do? Stow described them as 'banqueting houses' that, like bankrupts, bore 'great shew and little worth, . . . some of them like Midsommer Pageants, with Towers, Turrets and Chimney tops, not so much for vse or profites as for shew and pleasure, bewraying the vanitie of many mens mindes'. Or could it be one of the establishments that were, as Stow also noted, diminishing the custom of 'Bowyers, Fletchers, Bowstring makers, and such like' in Grub Street nearby, 'Archerie giuing place to a number of Bowling Allies and dycing houses' that are 'too much frequented'.[29]

The obvious playhouse on the *View* is an

---

[29] *Survay*, pp. 353, 354. The northern 40 per cent or so of Grub St survives, now called Milton St, EC2. In a paraphrase of Stow's remarks, Richard Johnson made the towers and turrets 'loftie' (*Pleasant Walkes of Moorefields* [London, 1607], sig. B3).

octagon three storeys high. On the northeast and southwest sides are enclosed external staircases. In the three visible sides of the octagon are a door on the ground floor that faces northwest and a window in the middle of each side of the two floors above the ground floor. Both staircases have three windows, one on the ground floor and one on each of the two floors above. The rectangular hut on top of the octagon has a pitched roof whose ridge lies east and west, and the crenellated tower is on the south side of the ridge.

This playhouse, finally, should be the Curtain if only because it doesn't look like the Theatre. For if the artist and engraver of the *View* represented it accurately, and if, as is taken for granted, the Globe was the same size and shape as the Theatre, and if the Globe had as many as sixteen, twenty, or twenty-four sides, as writers have been arguing, the playhouse cannot be the Theatre.

APPENDIX: MEASUREMENTS

The list of places below begins on the left side of the *View* and ends on the right. Each number in the first column appears directly over the relevant place on the accompanying reproduction of the *View*. The letters in the column under 'Rel.' show how reliable identifications of buildings on the *View* may be: A = based mainly on appearance recorded elsewhere; B = based partly on appearance recorded elsewhere but mainly on location from the viewpoint; C = based only on location from the viewpoint, but appearance may not be recorded elsewhere or if it is, it may not wholly agree.

The positions of buildings on the *View* are measured in general to the middle of the building, but where a part is higher than the rest, to the middle of the highest substantial part. As far as possible, the positions of buildings on a modern map are measured similarly. Calculations are in degrees (to the nearest fifteen minutes) from due east.

	Place	Rel.	Mod. map	'View'	+ or −
−	Site of Theatre	−	$c.\ 28°15'$	−	−
−	Site of Curtain	−	$c.\ 30°15'$	−	−
1	Obvious playhouse	−	−	$38°15'$	−
2	Shooters Hill Beacon	C	$c.\ 31°$	$38°45'$	$+7°45'$
3	Building with a flag	−	−	$40°$	−
4	St Mary Matfellon	C	$c.\ 35°45'$	$43°30'$	$+7°45'$
5	St Botolph Aldgate	C	$43°$	$47°30'$	$+4°30'$
6	St Botolph Bishopsgate	C	$44°$	$48°$	$+4°$
7	St Helen Bishopsgate	C	$46°45'$	$49°15'$	$+2°30'$
−	Site of the Fortune	−	$c.\ 47°45'$	−	−
8	Dutch church	A	$49°15'$	$51°45'$	$+2°30'$
9	Hotson's Fortune	−	−	$52°15'$	$+4°30'$
10	Tower of London	A	$49°30'$	$53°45'$	$+4°15'$
11	St Michael Cornhill	B	$52°$	$54°45'$	$+2°45'$
12	Royal Exchange	A	$53°$	$55°30'$	$+2°30'$
13	St Dunstan in the East	A	$53°15'$	$56°30'$	$+3°15'$

	Place	Rel.	Mod. map	'View'	+ or −
14	Guildhall	A	$56°$	$56°45'$	$+0°45'$
15	St Lawrence Jewry	B	$57°30'$	$57°45'$	$+0°15'$
16	St Lawrence Pountney	A	$57°45'$	$59°15'$	$+1°30'$
17	St Mary le Bow	A	$60°30'$	$60°30'$	Given
17	Charterhouse	B	$60°30'$	$60°30'$	Given
18	St Botolph Aldersgate	B	$61°45'$	$62°45'$	$+1°$
19	St Martin Vintry	B	$62°15'$	$64°$	$+1°45'$
19	Southwark Cathedral	−	$63°$	$64°$	$+1°$
19	St John of Jerusalem	B	$63°30'$	$64°$	$+0°30'$
20	St Bartholomew the Less	B	$66°$	$66°15'$	$+0°15'$
20	St Paul's Cathedral	A	$c.\ 66°15'$	$66°15'$	$0°$
21	St Sepulchre	A	$70°$	$69°15'$	$-0°45'$
22	Tower of Warwick Inn[30]	A	$c.\ 69°30'$	$70°$	$+0°30'$
23	St Martin Ludgate	B	$71°15'$	$71°$	$-0°15'$
24	St Bride	B	$76°45'$	$76°15'$	$-0°30'$
25	St Andrew Holborn	B	$77°$	$77°$	Given
25	St Etheldreda	A	$77°$	$77°$	Given
26	St Dunstan in the West	B	$83°45'$	$84°45'$	$+1°$
27	Middle Temple Hall	B	$86°$	$86°$	$0°$
28	Hall of Arundel House	B	$c.\ 89°$	$89°30'$	$+0°30'$
29	Allington House	C	$c.\ 90°45'$	$91°15'$	$+0°30'$
30	Westminster Abbey	A	$102°$	$98°30'$	$-3°30'$

[30] In the fifteenth century, Warwick Inn was the London house of the earls of Warwick, including the king-maker, and in the 1540s the storehouse of the King's revels. It was on the west side of Warwick Lane about where Warwick Square, EC4, is now. A tower like the one on the *View* appears at the west end of a building in Warwick Lane in about the right place on three other views: the Copperplate (the newly found plate), Braun and Hogenberg, and 'Agas' (where it is apparently made to look old). See also Henry A. Harben, *A Dictionary of London* (London, 1918), p. 613; C. L. Kingsford, 'Historical Notes on Mediaeval London Houses', *London Topographical Record*, 12 (1920), pp. 52–5, and his *Additional Notes* (Oxford, 1927), pp. 22–3.

MEASURED ENDINGS: HOW PRODUCTIONS FROM 1720 TO 1929 CLOSE SHAKESPEARE'S OPEN SILENCES IN *MEASURE FOR MEASURE*

EDWARD L. ROCKLIN

I am even willing to believe that the marriages that conclude *Measure for Measure* were not irresponsibly cobbled together because the dramatist needed a happy ending, but are appropriately disturbing at the end of a disturbing play.

(E. A. J. Honigmann, 'Shakespeare as a Reviser', p. 10)[1]

In the Preface to his edition of Shakespeare's plays, and even as he vigorously defended the playwright against attacks by other neo-classical critics, Samuel Johnson nonetheless also offered his own survey of Shakespeare's weaknesses. Among the better-known provocative remarks is his assessment of the endings of the plays:

It may be observed, that in many of his plays the latter part is evidently neglected. When he found himself near the end of his work, and in view of his reward, he shortened the labour, to snatch the profit. He therefore remits his efforts where he should most vigorously exert them, and his catastrophe is improbably produced or imperfectly represented.[2]

That *Measure for Measure*, in particular, was taken to be an example of Shakespeare's tendency to 'remit his efforts', and that these failures created problems about the ending of the play symptomatic about larger issues of genre, plot, and character is testified to by Charlotte Lennox's often-quoted criticism:

The comic Part of *Measure for Measure* is all Episode, and has no Dependence on the principal Subject, which even as *Shakespear* has managed it, has none of the Requisites of Comedy, great and flagrant Crimes, such as those of *Angelo*, in *Measure for*

Measure, are properly the Subject of Tragedy, the Design of which is to shew the fatal Consequences of those Crimes and the Punishment that never fails to attend them. The light Follies of a *Lucio* may be exposed, ridiculed and corrected in Comedy.

That *Shakespear* made a wrong Choice of his Subject, since he was resolved to torture it into a Comedy, appears by the low Contrivance, absurd Intrigue, and improbable Incidents he was obliged to introduce, in order to bring about three or four Weddings, instead of one good Beheading, which was the Consequence naturally expected.

(I, pp. 27–8)[3]

The research for this article was begun during an NEH–sponsored Folger Humanities Institute on 'Shakespeare Examined Through Performance' (1995–6), and much of the research was conducted at the Folger Shakespeare Library during a sabbatical supported by California State Polytechnic University, Pomona. I want to thank the staff of the Folger Shakespeare Library, who provided ideal working conditions. I am also pleased to acknowledge Daniel Colvin, Paul Nelson, William Slights and Jane Williamson, all of whom offered insightful criticism on earlier versions; and M. Kathleen Massey, whose own delight in conducting research has supported this endeavour.

1 See E. A. J. Honigmann, 'Shakespeare as a Reviser', in *Textual Criticism and Literary Interpretation*, edited by Jerome J. McGann (Chicago, 1985), pp. 1–22.
2 *Johnson on Shakespeare*, ed. Arthur Sherbo, in The Yale Edition of the Works of Samuel Johnson (New Haven and London, 1968), pp. 71–2.
3 Charlotte Lennox, *Shakespear Illustrated: or the Novels and Histories, On which the plays of Shakespear Are Founded, Collected and Translated from the Original Authors, with Critical Remarks. In Two Volumes. By the Author*

As we shall see, these strictures reappear in Francis Gentleman's commentary on the play in Bell's 1773 edition, and similar complaints about the ending as 'irresponsibly cobbled together' provide the cue for Honigmann's neat rephrasing of the indictment.

In this essay, I explore how some productions of *Measure for Measure* from 1720 to 1929 demonstrate that actors, actor-managers, and directors rewrote the last scene in ways that did indeed reflect a sense that the ending presented in the Folio text is 'improbably produced' or 'imperfectly represented' or both. As a means for sharpening the focus of enquiry, I will concentrate on what Philip McGuire has defined as *open silences* in Shakespeare's plays. 'Open silences' are those silences mandated by a play's text and can be distinguished, as McGuire does, from 'those [silences] that a playtext allows but does not require'.[4] *Measure for Measure* provides clear examples of both mandated and optional silences in the last scene. On the one hand, there is the *optional silence* of Isabella after Mariana completes her appeal to Isabella to join her in begging the Duke to pardon Angelo for what they suppose to be judicial murder of Isabella's brother, Claudio. As McGuire reminds us, the actress playing Isabella can choose to kneel immediately and begin the plea mandated by the words Shakespeare's text assigns to her, or she may pause, for a longer or shorter time, before beginning to speak those words. The length of any such pause cannot be determined from the text alone, however, but is rather the creative choice of the actors and director composing this production. Furthermore, such a silence will become a constitutive element in the experience of the spectators as they seek to make meaning from this act of mercy.

In contrast to this optional and delimited silence, there is the *open silence* the play mandates because no words are given to the convicted murderer Barnardine when he is pardoned by the Duke, advised to 'take this mercie to prouide / For better times to come'

and consigned to the guidance of Friar Peter (TLN 2883–4; 5.1.484–5).[5] Here Barnardine, although directly addressed, must remain silent, and yet his silence, with whatever choices the actor makes in playing that silence, must speak. McGuire himself offers this definition:

What is an open silence? . . . An open silence is one whose precise meanings and effects, because they cannot be determined by analysis of the words of the playtext, must be established by nonverbal, extra-textual features of the play that emerge only in performance. Such silences are usually required by Shakespeare's words, and they occur most often during the final scene of a play. (xv)

A focus on the open silences is particularly appropriate to this play since, as McGuire further notes, the open silences which so richly appear in the last eighty lines of the play render *Measure for Measure* one of the most 'open' plays in the canon in terms of the range of perfectly valid yet sharply divergent performances and, therefore, of coherent yet divergent, even contradictory experiences from which spectators must create meaning.

In this essay, I focus on the open silences of Isabella, Claudio, and Juliet in the last scene of the Folio text of *Measure for Measure*, as well as an earlier open silence in Act 3, Scene 1 between Isabella and Claudio, in order to trace some of the ways in which eighteenth, nineteenth, and early twentieth-century productions resequenced, repositioned and added to Shakespeare's playtext in order to close these open silences. I will also begin to delineate

---

of the Female Quixote. (London, 1753). See vol. I, pp. 1–30. Brian Vickers offers excerpts from Lennox's *Shakespear Illustrated*, vol. I and II (1753); vol. III (1754), in vol. 4 of *Shakespeare: The Critical Heritage, 1735–1765* (London, 1976), pp. 110–12.

4 Philip C. McGuire, *Speechless Dialect: Shakespeare's Open Silences* (Berkeley, 1985), p. xiv.

5 I cite the Folio text of *Measure for Measure* as the basic text giving both TLN and act–scene–line references, based on Charlton Hinman's *Norton Facsimile of the First Folio*, second edition (New York and London, 1996). Other editions will be identified as they are quoted.

another interesting feature, namely the process by which a promptbook became a performance text, and that performance text, in turn, served as the basis for a later promptbook, creating a chain that preserved theatrical innovations while rendering them available for further revision. By the end of this essay, then, I will have offered a sketch of some ways in which key revisions moved from the theatre to the performance text and, in some cases, survived for well over a century in the theatre.

Extending McGuire's definition, I would say that in most cases an open silence is initiated when one of the *dramatis personae* is addressed, and especially when that character is addressed by a speaker who seems to request, prompt, provoke, require, or insist on some response. Given this mandated silence, it is still the actor's and director's choice as to what non-verbal response, if any, that addressed character makes. Furthermore, a character may be silent not only in relation to one who addresses her or him but in relation to one or more other characters to whom she or he might be expected to respond, due either to the bonds between them or to the nature of their last encounter. As an examination of the play's last eighty lines will reveal, Isabella, Mariana and Angelo fall silent in this scene while Barnardine, Claudio and Juliet enter and maintain unbroken silences.

(1) ISABELLA. Isabella is both the first and the last character to move into an open silence during the concluding eighty lines. Manoeuvered by the Duke into a situation in which she chooses to plead for the life of the man she believes murdered her brother, Isabella falls silent after completing her plea to spare Angelo. Moreover, she remains silent when the unmuffling of Claudio reveals her brother is alive, remains silent during the reunion of Claudio and Juliet, and remains silent even as the Duke twice proposes marriage. Isabella's silence is threefold as she does not speak to her brother, her brother's wife, or the Duke.

(2) MARIANA. Married to Angelo, the man she has loved even though he not only broke off their engagement but also defamed her chastity, Mariana pleads for Angelo's life when the Duke condemns him to death for the murder of Claudio. She persuades Isabella to join her in this plea, but she falls silent, not responding verbally to Isabella, nor to Angelo's plea to be executed, nor to the Duke's pardon, nor to the Duke's exhortation that Angelo love her.

(3) ANGELO. Compelled to marry Mariana, Angelo says 'I craue death more willingly than mercy, /'Tis my deseruing and I doe entreat it' (TLN 2873–4; 5.1.472–3), and then remains silent as he is pardoned and exhorted to cherish Mariana.

(4) BARNARDINE. Previously convicted of murder, Barnardine is pardoned by the Duke (the same Duke who, disguised as a friar, had sought to persuade Barnardine to be executed not only because of his guilt but to further the Duke's own plot to save Claudio), yet he says not a word to indicate how he takes being spared execution, nor how he takes being assigned to Friar Peter's 'hand' for spiritual guidance.

(5) CLAUDIO. Claudio's open silence is also a three-fold silence: he offers no words when the Duke pardons him; nor does he respond when the Duke offers pardon while addressing Isabel; nor when, in the last speech of the play, the Duke says that Claudio should 'restore' the woman he wronged.

(6) JULIET. Juliet, who is never directly addressed but is referred to in the Duke's final speech, also has an unbroken silence: she does not speak to Claudio or the Duke, nor does she have a verbal response to Isabella.

Rephrasing this from a more performance-oriented stance, we can summarize these silences as a suite of questions:

How, if at all, does *Isabella* respond to Claudio? to Juliet? and to the Duke?

How, if at all, does *Mariana* respond to Angelo? and to the Duke?

How, if at all, does *Angelo* respond to Mariana? to Isabella? and to the Duke?

How, if at all, does *Barnardine* respond to the Duke? and to Friar Peter?

How, if at all, does *Claudio* respond to the Duke? to Juliet? and to Isabella?

How, if at all, does *Juliet* respond to the Duke? to Claudio? and to Isabella?

In this essay, my focus will be on the silences of Isabella and Claudio as enacted in five productions from 1720 to 1929, including four performance editions from 1720 to 1829 and one early twentieth-century promptbook.

The four performance editions are: (1) The edition based on the performance of 1720, with the text supplied by W. Chetwood, the prompter at the Theatre Royal at Lincoln's Inn Fields and printed by Tonson in London in 1722.[6] (2) The single-volume version in Bell's multi-volume complete Shakespeare; this edition was based on the Covent Garden promptbook, 'revised by Mr Younger, / Prompter at that Theatre', with an 'An Introduction and Notes Critical and Illustrative' which were added by Francis Gentleman, printed in London in 1773.[7] (3) A single volume edition produced by John Philip Kemble: Kemble published his first performance edition in 1794/5, and published two other similar but not quite identical performance editions in 1803 and 1815. The most important version is a promptbook which is a copy of the 1803 performance edition marked by Kemble for his part as the Duke in his production for the autumn of 1811.[8] (4) And the performance edition published by Thomas Dolby in 1824 and reissued, after Dolby's bankruptcy, as part of Cumberland's British Theatre in 1830, edited and with comments by George Daniel who signed himself 'D–G.'[9] This edition was also the basis for the promptbook created by Samuel Phelps for a production that opened in November, 1846, at Sadler's Wells, which I use as supplementary evidence.[10]

(5) Finally there is an early twentieth-century promptbook created by Henry Jewett for his Boston Repertory production which opened

16 November 1929.[11] This promptbook is *not* a marked-up printed edition but rather a bound typescript, which Jewett or an assistant created, and which clearly draws on the nineteenth-century performance editions. William Halstead, in his massive and essential compilation of acting editions, *Shakespeare as Spoken* (12 volumes) and in the *Statistical Abstract* which supplements that work (volumes 13 and 14) tersely notes 'Resemblance to Cumberland' (Halstead, 13: 601).[12]

---

6 *Measure for Measure*. A Comedy. As it is Acted at the Theatre Royal in Lincoln's-Inn-Fields. Written by Mr. W Shakespear. [With the text supplied by W. Chetwood, prompter at the Theatre.] (London, 1722.) I used the copy of the 1722 Chetwood-Tonson text at the Folger Shakespeare Library. I also used a facsimile published by Cornmarket Press (London, 1969).

7 *Measure for Measure*. As Performed at the Theatre-Royal, Covent-Garden. Revised by Mr Younger, Prompter at that Theatre. An Introduction and Notes, Critical and Illustrative, are added by the Author of the Dramatic Censor [Francis Gentleman]. (London, 1773).

8 *Shakespeare's Measure for Measure*. A Comedy, Revised by J. P. Kemble; And Now First Published as it is Acted at The Theatre Royal in Covent Garden. (London, 1803). And *Measure for Measure. John Philip Kemble Promptbooks*, vol. 6, edited by Charles H. Shattuck (Charlottesville, Virginia, 1974). This promptbook is a marked copy of Kemble's own 1803 edition of the play.

9 *Measure for Measure*. A Comedy In Five Acts by William Shakespeare. Printed from the Acting Copy, with Remarks, Biographical and Critical, by D–G. As now performed at the Theatres Royal, London (London, [1830]).

10 *Measure for Measure*. Promptbook of Samuel Phelps for the (November) 1846 production at Sadler's Wells Theatre, London. This promptbook is a marked copy of the Cumberland edition of 1830. I have used the microfilm version at the Folger Shakespeare Library.

11 *Shakespeare's Measure for Measure*. Promptbook of Henry Jewett for 1929 production of the Boston Repertory Company. Typescript based (in part) on Cumberland edition of 1830. The original typescript is in the Folger Shakespeare Library's collection of Jewett's promptbooks.

12 William P. Halstead, *Statistical History of Acting Editions of Shakespeare*. A Supplement to *Shakespeare as Spoken*, Volume 13 (Ann Arbor, Michigan, 1983). *Measure for Measure*, pp. 593–617.

Measure for Measure, perhaps surprisingly, is one of the earlier instances in which a hitherto adapted Shakespeare play text was restored to the stage performed with numerous cuts but, except for the ending, as printed in the Folio. Before this, the play had been performed in 1662, in William Davenant's *The Law Against Lovers* (the text was published in Davenant's *Works* in 1673).[13] In this version, Davenant spliced together *Measure for Measure* and *Much Ado About Nothing*, producing a radical adaptation that aimed for effects quite different from the design of the Folio text. And in 1700 the play had been performed (and published) in Charles Gildon's *Measure for Measure, or Beauty the Best Advocate*, which stripped the *Much Ado* elements out of the text, kept some of Davenant's rewriting of *Measure* (unacknowledged), and spliced segments of Tate and Purcell's *Dido and Aeneas*: the result is that Angelo watches segments of Dido's tragedy at intervals in the first four acts of *Measure for Measure*, and, almost as if he were a reformable Claudius in *Hamlet*, finds himself influenced by this opera-within-a-play.[14] Neither of these adaptations had the enduring success of Davenant's *Macbeth* and (with Dryden) *Tempest* or Tate's *King Lear*. When it is rescued from radical adaptation, the single most striking feature of the eighteenth-century performances and performance editions is the theatrical response to the open silence of Isabella in the face of the Duke's proposals. It might seem that, if they found Isabella's lack of a mandated verbal response to the Duke's sudden, twice-made marriage proposal not easily playable or foresaw that audiences might find it a bit difficult to accept on such short notice, the performers might have ended Isabella's silence by writing a speech in which she says some form of 'I do.' But in fact the players, prompters, and actor-managers whose work is embodied in the major performance editions – the Chetwood-Tonson text of 1722, the Gentleman-Bell text of 1773–4, and the Kemble texts of 1794, 1803, and

1815 – take another route: they omit the last lines of the Duke's final speech, and each substitutes a different final speech for the Duke. It is worth noting, furthermore, that while all three of these performance editions (including all three texts by Kemble) do mark the speeches so as to indicate they are *not* part of the first Folio text, this is not the case with some of the later performance editions. Thus readers of many of the nineteenth-century performance editions would have no hint that the last lines were not by Shakespeare; and of course those attending a production would have no clue from the performance of the play.

On 8 December 1720, the restored Shakespeare text was performed at Lincoln's Inn Fields Theatre, announced as 'Not Acted these Twenty Years' (*London Stage*, Part 2, volume 2, p. 603), with James Quin taking the part of the Duke (he would continue to play the role until 4 December 1750 [Hogan, 1. p. 308]) and with Mrs. Seymour as Isabella.[15] When they decided to produce this drama, the players faced the problem of what text to use, since there was no single-volume edition of *Measure for Measure* available. Whatever text was

---

13 William Davenant, *The Law Against Lovers*, in *The Dramatic Works of William Davenant*, with Prefatory Memoirs and Notes, ed. James Maidment and W. H. Logan. 5 Volumes (Edinburgh, 1872–74). *The Law Against Lovers* is in v, pp. 109–211.

14 *Measure for Measure, or BEAUTY the Best Advocate*. As it is ACTED at the *THEATRE* in *Lincoln's-Inn-fields*. Written *Originally* by Mr *Shakespear*. And now very much Altered; With *Additions* of several *Entertainments* of *MUSICK* (London, 1700).

15 I have used *The London Stage 1660–1800: A Calendar of Plays, Entertainments & Afterpieces, Together with Casts, Box-Receipts and Contemporary Comment*, ed. William Van Lenep, Emmett L. Avery, Arthur H. Scouten, G. W. Stone, Jr, and C. B. Hogan, 12 vols. (Carbondale, Illinois, 1965–1979), and Charles Beecher Hogan's *Shakespeare in the Theatre, 1701–1800. A Record of Performances in London*, 2 vols. (Oxford, 1952–7) for dates of performance and actors. And I have consulted John Genest's 10-volume compendium, *Some Account of the English Stage from the Restoration in 1660 to 1830*, 10 volumes (Bath, 1832).

used for the actual prompt-book, which apparently has not survived, a careful comparison reveals that the published text used Rowe's third edition of 1714. This was a logical choice, not only because Rowe's was the only critical edition available at that moment but because the copyright of Shakespeare's plays and of the Rowe text was owned by Jacob Tonson, who now published this edition as it was supplied by William Chetwood and 'As it is Acted at the Theatre Royal in *Lincoln's-Inn-Fields*'.

The three endings are worth reading as a set before we proceed to a more detailed analysis. Chetwood's 1722 text prints the Duke's first proposal; the ending starts with 'Th' Offense pardons itself'; prints the remaining lines of the Folio text (TLN 2934–8, 5.1.535–9); marks them for omission with an '; and adds eight new lines. On the page, the text looks like this:

> Th' Offense pardons it self. Dear *Isabel*,
> 'I have a motion much imports your good,
> 'Whereto if you'll a willing Ear incline,
> 'What's mine is yours, and what is yours is mine:
> 'So bring us to our Palace, where we'll show
> 'What's yet behind that's meet you all should know.
> Thy virtuous Goodness, which alone has Charms
> To make thee worthy of a Monarch's Arms;
> A Monarch who his peoples hearts wou'd try,
> And shrewdly turn'd a Priest to turn a Spy:
> For Empire then he quits the lower Plain
> Resumes the Scepter, and gives Laws again:
> On sure Foundations learns to fix Decrees,
> Like the Supreme, by judging what he sees.
> [*Exeunt omnes* (1722, p. 84)

The second addition comes from the 1773 edition, in a text supplied by the Covent Garden prompter, Joseph Younger (1734–84), with notes by Francis Gentleman (1728–84); it was republished in the complete acting edition version of the works by John Bell (dated 1773–4).[16]

This version cuts the first proposal, thereby making his proposal to Isabella the Duke's climactic act. His speech begins with the 'Dear

Isabel' (TLN 2933), does not print the omitted Folio text, and concludes with five new lines as follows:

> Dear Isabel, I have a motion much imports your good,
> *Shade not, sweet saint, those graces with a veil,*
> *Nor in a Nunnery hide thee; say thou'rt mine;*
> *Thy Duke, thy Friar, tempts thee from thy vows.*
> *Let thy clear spirit shine in publick life;*
> *No cloister'd sister, but thy Prince's Wife.*
> [*Exeunt.* (1773), p. 72)

The third addition develops in two phases. The new speech for the Duke appears as early as the text issued by Kemble for his Drury Lane performance of December 1794, and this final speech is also published in the 1803 text of his revival at Covent Garden Theatre. But in the promptbook for his 1811 production, which Kemble marked for his performance as the Duke on a copy of the 1803 text, he added a handwritten stage direction. Like the earlier Covent Garden adaptor, Kemble cuts the first proposal, which eliminates one of Isabella's open silences, and begins the addition a bit earlier, as the Duke finishes addressing the Provost by promising 'We shall imploy thee in a worthier place' (TLN 2930; 5.1.538). This text omits the remaining lines from the Folio, and with the marginal, handwritten stage direction – which I have inserted in the text – runs thus:

---

[16] Just as it has been suggested that James Quin supplied the extra lines for the Duke, so some scholars have wondered if David Garrick wrote this second new ending. But two points seem to weaken this speculation: first, Garrick took no interest in this play and never played the Duke; and second, the play is published as a Covent Garden version whereas Garrick was the manager at Drury Lane. On the other hand, the speculation that Kemble wrote the ending for his version seems plausible, given Kemble's work on other plays, such as his work on *All's Well* which, as Joseph Price has argued, was probably adapted and performed as a companion for *Measure for Measure*. See Joseph G. Price, *The Unfortunate Comedy: A Study of 'All's Well That Ends Well' And Its Critics* (Toronto, 1968), pp. 29–31.

DUKE . . . *For thee, sweet saint, – if, for a brother*
    sav'd,
From that most holy shrine thou wert devote to,
Thou deign to spare some portion of thy love,
Thy Duke, thy friar tempts thee from thy vow:
    [Isa. falling on her knee, the Duke prevents
    her, – kisses her hand, & 'In its right' &]
In its right orb let thy true spirit shine,
Blessing both prince and people: – thus we'll reign,
Rich in possession of their hearts, and, warn'd
By the abuse of delegated trust,
Engrave this royal maxim on the mind,
To rule ourselves, before we rule mankind.

(Shattuck, p. 68)

As readers will have noted, Kemble's revised text repeats one complete line from the 1773 edition – 'Thy Duke, thy Friar tempts thee from thy vow/s' – as well as echoing two other phrases closely, prompting the inference that whoever composed this third version was working from either the 1773 promptbook or text. I think it must have been the case that Kemble used the text of the 1773 performance edition, for the revision seems to have been shaped by at least one of the comments Francis Gentleman offered in that edition. Specifically, in discussing the new ending of the Covent Garden promptbook, which was being published for the first time, Gentleman wrote

. . . the five distinguished lines, which conclude, are an addition, by whom we know not; however, they afford a better finishing, than that supplied by *Shakespeare* . . . to royal and princely characters it offers a most valuable truth – that nothing is more dangerous, than to trust a *seemingly* virtuous statesman with too extensive powers of rule over his fellow-subjects; delegated authority being more liable to abuse, than the power which gives it.

(1773, pp. 71–2)

Not only is the content of the last four lines in the Kemble performance edition close to this observation, but the use of 'trust', 'delegated' and 'abuse' seems taken directly from Gentleman's formulation. Gentleman's commentary is also intriguing because it resonates with the commentary of Johnson and Lennox

about the problematic elements of this play noted at the beginning of this essay:

upon the whole of this play, for we cannot stile it either Tragedy or Comedy, there are several great beauties, clouded with much trifling and indecent dialogue: it must always be heavy to the majority of the audience; yet, purged of impurities and superfluities, as we hope the readers will find it, in this edition, it may be entertaining and instructive in the closet . . .

(p. 71)

Gentleman's suggestion that the revised ending offers 'a valuable truth' to 'royal and princely characters' is also an appropriate cue to note that, because the focus of this essay is on tracing how each successive acting text can be seen as responding to its predecessors, I have not sought to investigate how the different cultural and theatrical climates in which each text was produced might have influenced whoever wrote each new ending. But it is certainly the case that, in addition to the perceived intrinsic flaws of Shakespeare's ending, there were extrinsic political and religious factors which might have been at play in the consciousness and calculations of whoever composed the new dialogue; and that these extrinsic factors might have exerted a shaping pressure or offered an alluring opportunity for topical commentary. So, for example, although the first new ending was written before Robert Walpole achieved the position which made him the target for the satiric quotation of dramatic texts and the topical use of theatrical performances, the figure of Angelo as deputy and the comment about the monarch who 'Resumes the Scepter, and gives Laws again' could certainly have been heard by spectators at subsequent performances of the 1722 version as applying to Walpole. Indeed, as Michael Dobson, following Jonathan Bate, notes, it was 'one of the favourite rhetorical strategies of the Patriots' [anti-Walpole] journal, the *Craftsman* . . . [to offer] carefully chosen passages from Shakespeare (such as descriptions of Wolsey and Angelo) . . . inviting their application as prophetic portraits of Walpole'

(137).[17] Similarly, pleas to Isabella to renounce the cloister, overt in the 1773 version, more oblique in the 1794 version, could have been written to appeal to the sensibilities of the largely Protestant audience. And whether these extrinsic factors influenced those who composed them, once they were performed and published these new endings offered cues for spectators or readers to apply these words to current issues in the manner exemplified by Gentleman's discreetly nonspecific commentary on the dangers of trusting 'a *seemingly* virtuous statesmen with too extensive powers'.

Returning to the analysis of the sequence of acting editions, I would add that although there is no obvious connection between the first and second as there is between the second and third additions, it is still noticeable that each speech, in its turn, seems to offer a slightly fuller, perhaps more gallant, proposal than the preceding addition. And indeed writing one hundred years after the first addition was published, but in all probability referring only to the Kemble version, 'PP', in the 'Remarks' for Oxberry's edition (1822), presumed that this was the motive for the new speech:

It is performed with few variations from the original, beyond some necessary curtailments, and the transposition of one or two scenes; though it is curious to remark how, in the closing lines of the acting-copy, the players have thought proper to swell the *Duke's* hint of his attachment to *Isabella*, into a formal declaration of his passion. They were willing to compensate for the absence of love-scenes in the body of the play, by introducing a little courtship at the close. Perhaps the coldness with which the piece is treated, may in a great measure be placed to the account of this deficiency of love-business.   (p. vi)[18]

This comment focuses on a basic theatrical imperative to make the marriages more plausible if the play is to be performed and perceived as a comedy, and thus reinforces the idea that the players were responding to the same issues as are embodied in the critical assessments by Johnson and Lennox. PP's comment, furthermore, reminds us that Isabella's open

silence at the end can be seen as reflecting the silence of the text, which offers nothing that indicates an emerging attraction on the part of the Duke, or the Duke and Isabella, during their encounters in the last three acts. But I would suggest two other issues that may also have impelled the performers to revise the ending as they did, namely a concern for the completion of the plot in such a way as also to represent more perfectly the justice of the Duke's judgements; and a concern for character in the marriage of the Duke and Isabella.

Indeed these reshaped speeches may best be seen as being in part expressions of the two successive paradigms that dominated eighteenth-century conceptions of Shakespeare. The movement from one paradigm to another has been elegantly analysed by Jean Marsden, who demonstrates that those working in the theatre and as critics in the first half of this period (and it is important to note that, as is not true in later periods down to our own, these are often the same people), canonized a 'Shakespeare' whose genius inhered in the fables or plots, and in the thoughts of the plays. And since they believed that these elements could be expressed in different and improved language, they freely,

---

17 Michael Dobson, *The Making of the National Poet: Shakespeare, Adaptation, and Authorship, 1660–1769* (Oxford, 1994), p. 137. Jonathan Bate, *Shakespearean Constitutions: Politics, Theatre, Criticism 1730–1830* (Oxford, 1989), pp. 64–70. A portion of Gentleman's 'Introduction' also invites political applications: 'It is one of the greatest errors sovereignty can commit, to place unlimited confidence in ministers unproved; no professions, no fawnings, no fair external appearance, should prevent a watchful eye over those, who, by their rank and stations, are enabled to do much public good, or much public prejudice . . .' (Dd 2).

18 *The New English Drama, with Prefatory Remarks, Biographical Sketches, and Notes, Critical and Explanatory; being the only edition existing which is faithfully marked with the stage business and stage directions, as performed at the Theatres Royal.* By W. Oxberry, Comedian. Volume Sixteenth. Containing Every Man in His Humour. Measure for Measure. Julius Caesar. Man of the World. Every One Has His Fault (London, 1823). I have used the copy in the Library of Congress.

indeed radically, adapted the texts of the plays. Thus in this period, radical adaptation of Shakespeare's plays was almost the norm in the theatre:

Decoding the attitude toward Shakespeare's language is the key to understanding the presence of adaptation in an age which revered its 'English Homer'. The perception of Shakespeare's words as the least part of his genius, a result of the barbaric age in which he wrote rather than an example of poetic genius, gave playwrights free license to meddle with his use of language. The actual text of Shakespeare's plays was not considered sacred because it did not represent an embodiment of his genius. This genius lay instead in his ability to represent general nature, to portray universal characters, and to move an audience; these virtues, it was felt, would not be altered if the poetry were rewritten in a more modern idiom, or if the offensive puns and quibbles were quietly edited out. The assumptions concerning Shakespeare's language also governed the structural revision of his plays. As with the rewriting of Shakespeare's dialogue, the reshaping of his plot to incorporate poetic justice was seen as a change which did not alter the genius of his works. Critics argued that by adding a 'just' conclusion, in which good vanquishes evil and order is restored, an adaptation completed Shakespeare's representation of nature, for under the government of a benign deity all persons will inevitably receive their just deserts [*sic*].[19]

This need for poetic justice in order to represent a benign terrestial government and a benign celestial providence was, as Marsden notes, forcefully expressed by John Dennis in 'The Advancement and Reformation of Modern Poetry' (1712):

I conceive that every Tragedy ought to be a very solemn Lecture, inculcating a particular Providence and showing it plainly protecting the good and chastizing the bad, or at least the violent; and that if it is otherwise, it is either an empty amusement or a scandalous and pernicious Libel upon the Government of the World.[20]

In the second half of the eighteenth century, by contrast, the emerging paradigm canonized a 'Shakespeare' whose genius inheres in his sacro-

sanct words, and, in addition, is most crucially enacted not in the unity of plot but in the consistency or unity of character. Unity of character, for critics, adaptors, and theatrical professionals in this period, constituted the source of his enormous effectiveness in the theatre or the study, impelling spectators and readers to 'identify with' the characters, so that this empathetic experience moved them to heights of feeling which no other writer could elicit. These critics and playwrights radically recast the hierarchy of the parts of tragedy, reversing Aristotle, whose model had underwritten the earlier paradigm's emphasis on plot, and making character the pre-eminent element or soul of the play:

Praise of Shakespeare's characters was hardly a new topic; critics since the Restoration ... had applauded their naturalness ... Where mid-century critics differed was in the emphasis on the primary importance of character. Experimenting with new ideas but expressing them in terms of outdated theory, they created a new dramatic unity – the unity of character ... By creating a consistent and thus realistic character, the playwright allows the audience to identify with the play's action in an immediate and emotional way ... (p. 112)

In developing her analysis, Marsden necessarily focuses on the differences between the two paradigms, but I think that the three versions of the Duke's final speech suggest the overlap between the imperatives operating in each paradigm. That is, the ongoing concern with poetic justice lives on well into the second phase, even as the emphasis of Shakespeare's text and the primacy of character clearly become dominant by the time the romantic period reaches maturity. And the imperatives of both paradigms converge in the figure of the Duke with particular force in the last act. To

---

[19] Jean Marsden, *The Re-Imagined Text: Shakespeare, Adaptation, and Eighteenth-Century Literary Theory* (Lexington, 1995), p. 151.

[20] See *Critical Works of John Dennis*, ed. Edward Niles Hooker, 2 vols. (Baltimore, 1939), vol. 1, p. 200.

amplify PP's analysis, we might say that Isabella's silence emphasizes the need for the Duke to present himself more effectively not only as a lover but as a prince able to achieve justice and to articulate (in Dennis's terms, inculcate) that justice as well.

Returning to the first revised ending, written in a period (1720–2) in which the dramatic paradigm projected the plot or fable as what Aristotle had named the 'soul' of tragedy, we can see how the new lines emphasize poetic justice in two ways: first in terms of the relation of the Duke to Isabella; and second, in terms of the Duke's relation to his subjects in general.

> Th' Offense pardons it self. Dear *Isabel*,
> Thy virtuous Goodness, which alone has Charms
> To make thee worthy of a Monarch's Arms;
> A Monarch who his Peoples Hearts wou'd try,
> And shrewdly turn'd a Priest to turn a Spy:
> For Empire then he quits the lower Plain;
> Resumes the Scepter, and gives Laws again:
> On sure Foundations learns to fix Decrees,
> Like the Supreme, by judging what he sees.

In proposing to Isabella, the Duke's syntax seems to lose track of a necessary verb, but presumably spectators and readers were meant to hear the Duke as saying 'Thy virtuous goodness by itself has charms which make thee worthy of a monarch's embrace *and that is what impels me to propose marriage to you*.' The point is that Isabella, having been tested in the series of extreme demands made by Angelo, by Claudio, by the Duke-as-Friar, and by the Duke himself, has demonstrated a virtue equal to that of the 'Monarch' (a word that not only promotes the Duke but might suggest the writer inviting spectators to equate the Duke with England's own ruler) – and thus that she is worthy to be the wife of a prince. At the same time, the phrase 'alone has charms' seems to deny that the sexual desire that drove Angelo to attempt rape now moves the Duke.[21] Poetic justice, that is, will be fulfilled if Isabella, who had tentatively proposed to be a bride of Christ, now becomes the bride of a Duke who has recently performed some of the offices of a friar. Her

perfection in charity, then, seems to prove her the equal of the Duke, and as he leaves off his religious habit to resume his ducal robes, so she is invited to 'quit' the convent for the palace.

The speech moves from the issue of specific justice for Isabella to the larger political justice of the Duke as the embodiment of government in the world of Vienna. Here the speech invites spectators and readers to return to the first motives offered by the Duke in his dialogue with Friar Thomas (1.3, in a scene that is largely uncut and untransposed in this performance edition): the new ending functions to assert, more firmly than Shakespeare's text, that testing his subjects was the Duke's motive all along, and that he assumed the office of friar solely to pursue this aim – and not, say, to be a spy in the sense of voyeur or, in the play's own word, a meddler. Thus he also seems to argue that he can be a better prince, fulfilling both key functions of law-giver and magistrate necessary for justice: 'On sure Foundations learns to fix Decrees, / Like the Supreme, by judging what he sees.' Whatever actual spectators in 1720 or readers in 1722 might think (and however unwarranted the self-congratulatory rhetoric of the Duke often seems to spectators, readers, editors and critics in our own time), the claim is that because his experience as friar, plotter and providential agent has given him an opportunity to 'test the penitence' of the hearts and actions of his subjects, he now knows much more about the potential and actual discrepancies between appearance and reality. Thus he asserts that he is better equipped than ever to perform the tasks of the government of the world, or at least of Vienna. This first version, then, fills the open silence with a speech emphasizing the Duke as Prince and Isabella as an appropriate consort based on her own well-tried and demonstrated virtue – both her

---

21 We might hear the rhetoric of this speech as a miniature version of the manoeuvre by which Othello protests that it is not sexual desire that prompts him to request that Desdemona accompany him to Cyprus.

private virtue in preserving her chastity and her public virtue in placing the need for justice above any possible desire for revenge.

We do not know exactly when the second new ending was written, except that it was being performed some time before the end of 1773. However, if the *Dramatis Personae* (p. 4), with Robert Bensley (1742–1817) as the Duke and Mary Ann Yates (1728–87) as Isabella, represents the actual cast, then the ending recorded in the promptbook behind the performance edition was probably part of the production mounted at Covent Garden in the 1770–1 season, and played again in 1771–2.

> Dear Isabel, I have a motion much imports your
>   good,
> *Shade not, sweet saint, those graces with a veil,*
> *Nor in a Nunnery hide thee; say thou'rt mine;*
> *Thy Duke, thy Friar, tempts thee from thy vows.*
> *Let thy clear spirit shine in publick life;*
> *No cloister'd sister, but thy Prince's Wife.*   [*Exeunt.*

As noted, Gentleman's comment on these lines certainly demonstrates the enduring force of the imperatives embodied in the older plot-centred paradigm had not disappeared by 1773:

the five distinguished lines, which conclude, are an addition, by whom we know not; however, they afford a better finishing, than that supplied by *Shakespeare* . . . to royal and princely characters it offers a most valuable truth – that nothing is more dangerous than to trust a *seemingly* virtuous statesman with too extensive powers of rule over his fellow-subjects; delegated authority being more liable to abuse, than the power which gives it.

(1773, pp. 71–2)

The basic sequence here is the same as it is in all three endings, moving from the Duke's proposal to Isabella, with his motives indicated, to the larger issue of how his final actions achieved poetic justice through a (more) just government. This time, however, the balance, as Marsden's analysis would suggest, seems to shift away from more public, political issues to a more domestic sense of the state. For one thing, this version much more directly addresses the issue of Isabella's previous commitment as

novice to the sisters of St Clare – a point that may also indicate her costume in this scene, which would be no small issue in shaping the significance of any of the new endings. There is a tacit acknowledgment that the Duke's proposal can be seen as a *temptation*, a snare for a woman who was prepared to escape the world. Moreover in speaking of her as 'sweet saint' the Duke seems to be seeking a means for Isabella to keep her holy identify – and perhaps invoking the double office he has exercised as a justification for what might otherwise sound like an unseemly proposal. And here too the rhetoric suggests that the proposal is not about sexual desire but chaste love for the mind and spiritual virtues. Finally, the injunction to 'Let thy clear spirit shine in publick life; / No cloister'd sister, but thy Prince's Wife' is an image which represents Isabella as able to spread the same virtues that would have illuminated the convent in the wider sphere of public life. The point seems to be to persuade her to see such a marriage as an obligation consistent with her original desires: while she originally wanted to enter a purer but smaller realm, she is offered an opportunity to help purify a larger world. I would add that, as William Slights has pointed out, the logic and language here can also be heard as echoing the Petrarchan language used in Elizabethan sonnets where the praise of the lady (or, in the early sonnets in Shakespeare's sequence, the man) is an exhortation to marry so that her (or his) beauty and virtue may be transmitted to the next generation. This is also, of course, an imperative of particular significance to a prince who, until this moment, seems to have ignored the issue of succession. This second version, then, fills the open silence with a speech emphasizing the Duke as princely wooer, tempting Isabella with sonnet-like praise not because of her physical but because of her spiritual beauty. Paradoxically, that is, her 'clear spirit' which was demonstrated in her tentative commitment to religious life as a sister becomes the highest possible qualification for her commitment to public life as a wife of the Duke.

While clearly based on both the play and commentary in the 1773 performance edition, and while still concerned to establish a larger political sense of justice, the third ending can be read as embodying a stronger emphasis on character, both in its slightly fuller proposal and in its concluding focus on self-knowledge. In at least one respect it more closely resembles the first revision insofar as it places its final emphasis on the political obligations of the prince. It does so, however, in a way that seems to balance the two paradigms, for even as it responds to the need to articulate poetic justice in completing the plot it nonetheless ends by focusing as much on the character of the ruler as on his political obligations. Furthermore, this version adds a new element, namely the interpolated hand-written stage direction (again I have inserted this in the middle of the speech rather than reproduce its promptbook placement) which, while not closing Isabella's silence, nonetheless mandates an action that is a vivid response to the Duke's proposal:

DUKE . . . *For thee, sweet saint, – if, for a brother*
sav'd,
From that most holy shrine thou wert devote to,
Thou deign to spare some portion of they love,
Thy Duke, thy friar tempts thee from thy vow:
    [Isa. falling on her knee, the Duke prevents
    her, – kisses her hand, & 'In its right' &]
In its right orb let thy true spirit shine,
Blessing both prince and people: – thus we'll reign,
Rich in possession of their hearts, and, warn'd
By the abuse of delegated trust,
Engrave this royal maxim on the mind,
To rule ourselves, before we rule mankind.

The first part of this speech picks up the 'sweet saint', of the previous version and again the phrase would seem to function to emphasize the sanctity of Isabella as well as to insist that despite her earlier false confessions the Duke now vouches for her chastity – even as this version too invokes the sonnet-language derived from Petrarch, and may owe something to Romeo and Juliet's first embedded sonnet exchange. The whole phrasing of 'If

. . . Thou deign to spare some portion of thy love' seems to acknowledge that devotion to a holy shrine is higher than devotion to the Duke and the things of the Duke's world. Furthermore, he seems to request that she lower herself but also gracefully seems to acknowledge that he can ask only for a portion of her love. He thus may acknowledge the enduring bond of love for her brother – presumably a love that, especially in the theatre, urgently demands recognition at this moment not only because of the reunion but because of the suffering his plotting has forced both brother and sister to endure. Conversely 'some portion of thy love' attributes great scope or generosity to her ability to love. At the same time, Kemble's retention of 'if, for a brother sav'd' makes the Duke's own act of devotion to Isabella's cause more explicit.

Kemble's conclusion returns to issues of public rule and the Duke's own education that, as readers will recognize, dominate much twentieth-century criticism, and that seemed central to eighteenth-century spectators and critics with their own differently phrased concerns about the wisdom of monarchs:

                    – thus we'll reign,
    Rich in possession of their hearts, and, warn'd
    By the abuse of delegated trust,
    Engrave this royal maxim on the mind,
    To rule ourselves, before we rule mankind.

The last three lines in particular seek to bring closure to crucial issues about the nature of the Duke, the Duke's experience, and what he has learned from or through that experience. This third version, then, fills the open silence with a speech emphasizing the Duke as Prince, as suing for Isabella's love, which he will share with her religious devotion, and finally, as 'royal maximizer' (to employ a phrasing coined by William Slights), intent on improving self-knowledge, self-control, and therefore, his ability to rule.

If we look at the three new endings as a set, we see that while they diverge in interesting ways, they also seem to represent implicit responses to another way in which the Folio text might be thought to represent imperfectly a satisfying conclusion. For all three versions can be seen as perfecting how the Duke proposes marriage to Isabella: all three versions amplify the Duke's concluding proposal, while the second and third versions also eliminate the first proposal. Thus while none of the three supplies a speech for Isabella, they all make the Duke's proposal more extensive and more clearly the climactic act of the scene and the play. In addition, all three revisions implicitly respond to a larger political dimension, namely the question of the appropriate balance between justice and mercy, and the ways in which the ruler learns to achieve this balance, hence demonstrating his continued or perhaps even his improved fitness for the double office of law-giver and magistrate. These are, after all, the competing imperatives that are embodied in the biblical passages which the title invites spectators and readers to recall.

When we look at the revised endings in these performance editions, then, I think they demonstrate that, like Samuel Johnson, those who composed these added speeches found Shakespeare's ending both *improbably produced*, specifically in terms of the Duke's textually uncued proposal to Isabella; and *imperfectly represented*, specifically in terms of Isabella's silence in response to that proposal and, one might suspect, in the brevity of the proposal itself. Adding the speeches and, in Kemble's case, the stage direction for the actions of Isabella and the Duke, thus registers the point that for the eighteenth-century producers and the performance editors, the most troubling open silence and the one that most insistently demanded to be closed was Isabella's silence. At the same time, the endings, and especially the added action in the Kemble text, demonstrate the continued force of an imperative to maintain Isabella's virtue by maintaining her chastity, her obedience and her silence. The decision not to provide Isabella with a speech in response to the Duke's proposal becomes even more striking when we

examine performances and performance editions whose authors do, finally, provide a speech which enables her to close another of her open silences.

While these major changes in eighteenth-century editions register the sense that the open silence of Isabella in response to the Duke's proposal is the major example of how the imperfectly represented ending needed to be improved, the Gentleman-Bell text points towards another open silence, or rather linked pair of open silences, that, in the nineteenth century, and perhaps precisely because of how the 'improvements' closed this first open silence, became a focus of theatrical attention. Thus I turn to examine the silences between Isabella and Claudio. For purposes of this analysis, we need to turn back to the middle of the play, for the silence between Isabella and Claudio in 5.1 continues a silence that begins in the middle of 3.1.

In 3.1, Isabella informs Claudio that his life will be spared if she has sex with Angelo. After Claudio first agrees to die, he changes his mind and pleads with her to sacrifice her virginity. His reversal provokes a response in which, after calling him 'beast', 'Coward', and 'wretch', Isabella continues:

> Die, perish: Might but my bending downe
> Repreeue thee from thy fate, it should proceede.
> Ile pray a thousand praiers for thy death,
> No word to saue thee. (TLN 1365–8; 3.1.144–7)

And in her last speech to Claudio she insists ''Tis best thou diest quickly' (TLN 1373; 3.1.151). Given this horrific encounter, the reunion of brother and sister in the fifth act will elicit intense curiosity from spectators, especially coming after Isabella's extraordinary plea to save Angelo, the man she believes has murdered her brother and would have raped her. While the audience may hope for an immediate and complete reconciliation, they may fear that there will be a hard-to-heal or even impossible-to-heal rupture. What the performance editions and the promptbooks based on performance editions offer is the development of additions that close this open silence. This problem was also one noted by eighteenth-century critics: Samuel Johnson, for example, while he did not comment on the moment in 3.1 when the tension is created by the rupture between Isabella and Claudio, did comment on the open silence between Claudio and Isabella at the end, when the result of that rupture might manifest itself in the responses of the siblings: 'It is somewhat strange, that *Isabel* is not made to express either gratitude, wonder, or joy at the sight of her brother' (1765, I, p. 380; Sherbo VII, p. 214). Indeed, I would suggest, that this apparent omission might be one of the pieces of evidence that prompted Johnson to articulate his critique of Shakespeare's endings as 'imperfectly represented'.

The Covent Garden promptbook edited by Gentleman for Bell seems to be the first performance edition to register the open silence in 3.1 as a problem. It registers the silence, in fact, through the simple expedient of adding three words to Claudio's short speech (p. 32):

CLAUDIO Let me ask my sister pardon. Pardon,
  dearest *Isabel*; I am so out of love with life, that I
  will sue to be rid of it.   [*Exit* Claudio.

Intriguingly enough, especially given the way theatrical traditions tend to be conserved and perpetuated, being passed on from actor to actor and promptbook to promptbook, this short, effective three-word addition does not reappear in any independent later edition.[22]

The elegance of this solution is also, of course, that it removes any suspense about the later reunion if, as seems probable, Isabella offered a nonverbal response showing she accepted Claudio's apology. Indeed, with his vow ringing in her ears, her later mixture of fury and grief when she learns of his execution would be made more intense and intensely real since it would be unalloyed by any hint of guilt. At the same time, it is worth noting that

Isabella's open silence is not really ended: rather, as with the three new concluding speeches for the Duke, the problem is solved by adding words for the male character addressing Isabella.

Nonetheless, and for reasons whose contingent nature probably makes them unrecoverable, the later editions do not copy this manoeuvre. Instead, the nineteenth-century performance editions and promptbooks develop several manoeuvres, introducing added stage directions and, in some cases, added speeches to

---

22 As far as I have been able to determine, it appears only in Barker's version of the Bell edition, published after Bell had gone bankrupt and had to give up control not only of his editions of Shakespeare but of the British Poets as well. (See *Measure for Measure*, a comedy by Shakespeare, as performed at the Theatres Royal. Regulated from the prompt-books by permission of the managers. With an introduction and notes critical and illustrative (London, [n.d.]).) Barker's edition is confusing since it is issued with no date; it lists a cast headed by Kemble and Siddons, which only occurred starting in December 1794; it continues to use the frontispiece used by Bell in his single-volume issue of the play, which shows 'Mrs. Yates as Isabella', although Mrs. Yates – who had performed Isabella both at Drury Lane and Covent Garden in the 1770s and 1780s – last performed this role 1782 and had died in 1787. In fact, if the cast list means anything, it would pinpoint the time more specifically: for Hogan's lists indicate that the cluster of Barrymore playing Angelo, Charles Kemble playing Claudio, Surmount playing 1st Gentleman, Fisher playing Froth, and Hollingsworth playing Barnardine only begins 27 October, 1798, and then performs again 17 January, 19 April, and 29 November, 1799. So Barker's edition would seem to have been published, with a cast list added to the 1773 text, in 1798 or 1799. And in fact the cast list would seem to be a marketing ploy, since what Barker publishes is a version of the play that includes Juliet and uses a text with other significant differences from the first Kemble text published around the time of Kemble's first production in the 1794–5 season. Why Kemble did not avail himself of this innovation, given that he was not unwilling to add a much more substantial speech at the end of the play, is not evident. One hypothesis is that such an addition would not have harmonized with Mrs Siddons' morally lofty portrayal of Isabella and/or her dominance of the stage, but this is highly speculative.

close the open silence between Isabella and Claudio in 5.1 and 3.1. This process seems to occur in two phases, with the introduction of additions to close the open silence between Isabella and Claudio in 5.1 and then later to close the open silence in 3.1.

One simple way for the players to deal with an open silence is to add a disambiguating non-verbal action, and this is the route that Kemble apparently took in his 1794 production and in the performance edition that represented this production; repeated in his 1803 edition; and amplified in the 1811 promptbook, where he also adds handwritten stage directions for Claudio and Angelo at the beginning and end of the passage cited here (these are marked by underlining):

> L.U.E. [Claudio advances at Provost's R.]
> DUKE What muffled fellow's that?
> PROVOST This is another prisoner, that I sav'd,
>   Who should have died when Claudio lost his
>   head;
>   As like almost to Claudio, as himself.
> DUKE If he be like your brother, for his sake
>   Is he pardon'd.
>   [Claudio *discovers himself, – Isabella runs, and embraces him.*] Ang. falls on his knees, &c.
>
> (Shattuck, pp. 66–7)

Clearly, in both productions and both performance editions the aim was to establish unequivocally that Isabella has forgiven Claudio's lapse into self-preserving cowardice, and that Claudio has either overcome his own shame at having lapsed in virtue or forgiven Isabella her momentary willingness to let him die in order to save her chastity, or both.[23] It is important to note that in Kemble's adaptation, and in all the performance texts and performances that descend from it, the role of Juliet is completely eliminated. While the most telling consequence of cutting her role is the disappearance of the scene between Juliet and the Duke-as-Friar, another crucial effect of making Juliet vanish is that she is not present to provide a potentially distracting third focus during the joyous reunion between Isabella and Claudio. Elimi-

---

[23] Actually, even in the case of the two Kemble editions there is a small but intriguing difference between the two versions. The performance edition for the 1794 production (Lowndes, p. 60; there are no brackets around the stage direction in this edition) prints the moment as follows:

> PROV. As like almost to Claudio, as himself.
>   *Claudio discovers himself* and *embraces Isabella.*
> DUKE. If he be like your brother, for his sake
>   Is he pardon'd.
>   By this, Lord Angelo perceives he's safe . . .

(See *Measure for Measure: as altered by J. P. Kemble, and acted by their Majesties servants, at the Theatre Royal, Drury Lane* (London, [n.d.]).) The second Kemble performance edition (Ridgway 1803, quoted above), however, prints this:

> PROV. As like almost to Claudio, as himself.
> DUKE. If he be like your brother, for his sake
>   Is he pardon'd.
>   [Claudio *discovers himself, – Isabella runs, and embraces him.*]
>   By this, lord Angelo perceives he's safe . . .

It is, of course, not necessarily the case that this apparent reversal of who embraces whom, let alone the lack of a direction to 'run' for either Isabella or Claudio, is a distinction that makes a difference. They both might be partial attempts to deal with the problem of recording fluid stage action in the medium of the prose stage directions. Nonetheless, we might wonder if the difference does in fact record a revised action, and an action that reflects a revised imagining of the scene. For example, does it suggest different performances in which in one case Claudio and in another case Isabella is the one who is overjoyed? Or some difference as to who needs to forgive whom? who thinks she or he is in need of forgiveness? Or did Kemble think that since Claudio knows he is alive and presumes that Isabella is alive, whereas Isabella presumes Claudio is dead, it is Isabella who will be both most stunned and surprised and (perhaps) overjoyed? But the moment could also be played with Isabella so stunned that she cannot move; while Claudio, seeing her stunned, moves or runs to embrace her. As we will see, the new speech invented for this moment may also function to solve, resolve, or dissolve some of these questions – perhaps even inoculate the spectators from raising such questions in a more general rejoicing in which such nuances cease to matter. In terms of my argument, if there is an adjustment registered in this very minute difference – and not, for example, simply a difference in printing house practice or the contingent acts of the compositors – it

nating a silent character, which in a purely literary reading might seem to make no difference at all, does more than eliminate her silence: it eliminates the varied relations that performers might be prompted to invent because of that silence, and thus eliminates the suite of cascading inventions such a silence always makes possible.

But apparently, the possibility that members of the audience might speculate about the rupture between the sister and brother for a period that, by Kemble's own timing would seem to be over one hour, troubled the actor-managers who followed Kemble. (In the 1811 promptbook, Kemble gives the times for Act 3 as 35 minutes, Act 4 as 28 minutes, and Act 5 as 43 minutes: if we subtract about twelve minutes of 3.1, based on the proportion of pages, and about five minutes from the ending, we have a period of 80 minutes during which spectators might be expected to feel this tension.) The Folio text offers Claudio's speech and the Duke's reply; the Second Folio adds what is probably the exit that was simply omitted in the First Folio, so that, as the Riverside text prints it, we have:

CLAUDIO Let me ask my sister pardon. I am so out of love with life that I will sue to be rid of it.
DUKE Hold you there! Farewell. [Exit Claudio.]

But when we turn to the performance edition published in Dolby's British Theatre (1824), an edition that was soon republished in Cumberland's British Theatre (1830) – an edition that goes on to shape the sequence of editions issued by Hailes, Lacey, and French – we encounter this:

CLAUDIO Let me ask my sister pardon. [Crosses to Isabella, and kisses her hand] I am so out of love with life, that I will sue to be rid of it.
[Crosses to R.
DUKE Hold you there: farewell. – [Exit Claud. R.]
(Dolby-Cumberland, p. 33)

The added stage direction is striking enough, of course, but what is equally striking is that by introducing this stage direction the adaptor

changes the function of that speech. For when it is addressed directly to Isabella, the words become a different speech act: it is now his vow or oath to die to protect her, hence his attempt to resume the status of a gentleman she has just claimed he no longer merits. This manoeuvre preserves yet transforms the Folio speech, and it seems designed to restore or even to intensify the bond between brother and sister. The elegance of this solution – and from the point of enacting only the text of Shakespeare's play it is even more elegant than the three-word addition in Bell – is also that it removes any suspense about the later reunion if, as seems probable, Isabella indicates non-verbally, in response both to the speech and to Claudio's submissive or penitent kiss of her hand, that she accepts the apology.[24] And, of course, it would be more freely enjoyed by spectators who know the reassuring truth that she does not, namely that her brother lives.

---

would seem to be the case that Kemble is continuing to disambiguate the text, enforcing more and more effective closure on the open silences.

[24] The desire to close these open silences is not, of course, merely a phenomenon of the eighteenth and nineteenth centuries, but endures down to our own day. This need for closure is nicely represented in two citations offered by Mark Eccles in his variorum edition note on the awkward sequence in which the Duke-as-Friar summons and dismisses the Provost:

LYONS (1962, pp. 267–8): 'Why should the Provost enter only to be told to leave again? . . . Is it not possible that one function of this brief dialogue may be to draw the Duke aside and leave the stage focally to Claudio and Isabella? Most editors add a direction, as here cited, to indicate that Claudio exits immediately after the Duke's 'Farewell'. But Claudio's 'Let me ask my sister pardon' in the preceding line evokes audience anticipation which no dialogue fulfills. A brief tableau, however, can effectively cap the Isabella-Claudio prison scene. Claudio approaches Isabella and in mime asks pardon of his sister; she lovingly responds, giving her blessing to a brother penitently kneeling and now prepared for death.' Lever (ed. 1965): 'The summons leaves Claudio alone with Isabella for a mimed reconciliation.' (Eccles: 149).

The Dolby text is also the first text to offer another development of Kemble's innovation(s) in handling the open silence between Isabella and Claudio at the end of the play. For in 5.1 the Dolby-Cumberland edition prints a further development. Here, in addition to repeating the stage direction added in the Kemble text (and I note that in this text none of these added elements are marked as non-Shakespearian), the Dolby text adds a line of dialogue for Isabella:

DUKE If he be like your brother, for his sake Is he
    pardon'd.
    [Claudio *discovers himself* – Isabella *runs and embraces*
    him – Angelo *falls on his knees.*
ISABELLA (R.) O, my dear brother!   (Dolby, p. 61)

Thus this crucial open silence is transformed into speech, thereby closing, in a definitive manner, one of the troubling possibilities not explicitly resolved in Shakespeare's Folio text, namely that brother and sister might remain unreconciled at the end of the action.

As I have noted, when it is taken over and republished as Cumberland's British Theatre, the Dolby edition goes on to shape the major acting editions and performance texts that follow. So, to take one example, the Samuel Phelps prompt-book for his 1846 production at Sadler's Wells uses the Dolby-Cumberland text, and amplifies it with further stage directions. In this case, on the blank (interleaved) page facing the Dolby-Cumberland text (p. 32), we find this stage manager's note, which reiterates and amplifies the printed text:

ISABELLA comes down LC
CLAUDIO X to C. Kneels, & kisses her hand.
THE DUKE returns up C.
    (Phelps promptbook, Cumberland edition, p. 32
    and facing page)

And there are more complex examples, such as the Henry Irving Shakespeare, published 1888–90, and edited by Frank Marshall. The critical consensus is that while texts Irving was interested in and produced were shaped in part by his choices, in the rest of the canon Marshall edited without much reference to Irving. In addition, Marshall, who was ill and apparently knew he was dying, elicited the participation of other literary figures: *Measure for Measure* is edited by Arthur Symons, working from the best scholarly editions available by 1889, but with notes on staging written by Marshall. Furthermore, this text still suggests the cuts necessary for the stage or for performance of the plays as readings, and in the case of *Measure for Measure* most of the suggested cuts correspond with the Kemble text as it was transmitted by Dolby and Dolby's descendants. Here, for example, is Marshall's note on the Isabella–Claudio reunion (in the original, speeches are italic, stage directions in roman type; and ']' is omitted in the third line):

If he be like your brother, for his sake
Is he pardon'd, – [Claudio discovers himself to
    Isabella – she rushes into his arms, and then
    kneels to Angelo, –
and for your lovely sake;
Give me your hand [raising her] and say you will
    be mine;
He is my brother too: [taking Claudio's hand] but
    fitter time for that.

'The first important point to be considered is when does Isabella recognize Claudio? As the text stands, without any stage-direction, it would appear that Isabella took no notice whatever of her brother when she finds he is alive; but, as has been pointed out by other commentators, Shakespeare wrote for the stage, and this recognition of Claudio could easily take place in action without any spoken words. In the acting version it takes place after the words *Is he pardon'd*, and Isabella is made to say *O, my dear brother!* The next two and a half lines of the Duke's speech are omitted, and he resumes,
By this Lord Angelo perceives he's safe.
This, of course, gets rid of all difficulty, but to take such liberties with the text is scarcely necessary. As the passage is arranged in our text, we imagine that Claudio – who is at the right side of the stage by the side of the Provost – having thrown off his disguise, turns round to Isabella at the word *pardon'd*; she interrupts the Duke by rushing across him to embrace her brother; and then, remembering herself, kneels to express her respectful gratitude. The Duke continues his interrupted sentence, and

raises her from her knees, placing her on the left side of him. He then speaks the next line (497) holding her hand in his; at the words *He is my brother too*, turns to Claudio, giving him his hand as a confirmation of his pardon.' FAM (pp. 238b–239a)[25]

I turn now to Henry Jewett's promptbook for his Boston Repertory Company production of *Measure for Measure* in November 1929. Looking at the moments from 3.1 and 5.1, we see that Jewett's script represents an eclectic development of over 100 years of prior performance editions. In 3.1 we find

CLAUDIO Let me ask my sister pardon. (*Isabella comes forward to C*) I am so out of love with life, that I will sue to be rid of it.

When Claudio is unmuffled in Jewett's version of 5.1, the script reads:

(*Isabella runs to Claudio and embraces him*) ISABEL O, my dear brother.

And for the Duke's finale, the script includes the entire ten-line speech that first appears in Kemble's edition, but with the second line crossed out. The speech as it exists in the script thus runs as follows:

For thee, sweet saint – if, for a brother sav'd,
~~From that most holy shrine thou wert devote to,~~
Thou deign to spare some portion of they love,
Thy Duke, thy Friar, tempts thee from thy vow:
(Isabel about to drop on her knees, the Duke
prevents her, kisses her hand, and then
continues to her)
In its right orb let thy true spirit shine,
Blessing both prince and people – thus we'll
reign,
Rich in the possession of their hearts, and warned
By the abuse of delegated trust –
Engrave this royal maxim in the mind,
To rule ourselves before we rule mankind. // (all
clasp hands)
(*Flourish of trumpets and drums*)
CURTAIN

That 'Flourish' appears at least as early as the Kemble promptbook, where it is a handwritten addition to the 1803 printed text; and 'Flourish of drums and trumpets' appears at least as early as the printed text in the Dolby-Cumberland

edition. The interesting direction for the semi-circle to 'clasp hands' might be imagined as serving a double function, operating both within the fictional world of the play's 'Vienna' and in the theatrical world of a performance in Boston in 1929. Within the fictional world, it would embody a newly achieved coherence, a unity which includes not only the newly married and to-be-married couples but all those present on stage. At the same time, as a familiar gesture by which the cast of a play projects their unity in completing the performance, it would not only be a cue for the spectators to applaud but to suggest the potential for and desirability of harmony in the present world of the Jewett Company's efforts to bring Shakespeare to the Boston theatrical scene in particular.

That a stage production might need to insist on the comic nature of the ending and on prompting applause, appreciation, and connection in this fashion is something that may be attested to by the extremely hostile response of George Odell in his famous study of *Shakespeare from Betterton to Irving* (1920).[26] Here, in one of

---

25 *The Works of William Shakespeare*, edited by Henry Irving and Frank A. Marshall. Volume V (London, 1889); *Measure for Measure* pp. 161–241. I take it that 'and then kneels to Angelo' is a compositor's mistake, and that here as elsewhere Marshall or Symons was following the stage direction, whether directly from Kemble or by descent, which adds 'Ang. falls on his knees': the image of Isabella kneeling to Angelo is certainly an anomalous idea at this moment in the action. That there *are* significant typographical errors in the Irving Shakespeare and in particular in *Measure for Measure* is proved by a poignant example. For in the note in which he comments on the new ending supplied by Kemble, the line 'Thou deign to spare some portion of thy love' is actually printed thus:

Thou deign to spare some portion of toh, ev y l fo

One feels for Frank Marshall, working diligently to add to the stage history of the play. However, given that he died in December 1889, it may well be the case that Marshall never saw this mangling of his research.

26 George C. D. Odell, *Shakespeare from Betterton to Irving*, 2 volumes (New York, 1920).

the first efforts to examine the theatrical history of Shakespeare's plays in a comprehensive, scholarly fashion, and in a book published at the beginning of the decade in which Jewett staged his production, Odell bluntly announces that he finds the play indecent and revolting. Even more intriguing, Odell articulates his own preference in acting editions, and thereby suggests the ways in which some of the premises embodied in the criticism of Samuel Johnson and Charlotte Lennox were still very much alive in the early twentieth century:

Exigencies of arranging by alphabetical order bring on the second of Shakespeare's bitter comedies – Measure for Measure. This like the other – All's Well that Ends Well – has a revolting plot, and its sub-plot is even more indecent than that of its fellow play. Both comedies really deserve the stage-oblivion into which they have fallen, though Measure for Measure held a fair degree of popular acclaim during the regency of Garrick and of Kemble. This vogue I take to be attributable entirely to the assumption of the part of Isabella by several very great actresses, the most notable being Mrs. Yates, Mrs. Barry, and Mrs. Siddons. The Bell version, in which the first two probably appeared, strikes me as more satisfactory than Kemble's by just so far as it eliminates more of the offensive underworld matter of bawds and pandars and gentlemen of loose living. I believe that this subplot was necessary to round out Shakespeare's scheme, but I cannot alter my opinion that on the stage it is exceedingly offensive. In fact, I am not sure that Measure for Measure should be acted, if its rendition necessitates the retention of much, or indeed any of the Froth, Pompey, Elbow, Mrs. Overdone material.

If I am correct in this view, Bell's version of Measure for Measure is almost ideal; the character of Mrs. Overdone is entirely eliminated. The second scene of the second act omits the loose talk of Lucio and the two gentlemen, and of course the Overdone business; it starts with the entrance of the Provost, Claudio and Juliet, and with Claudio's 'Fellow, why dost thou show me thus to the world?' After this, to the close, the editor follows the original. Gentleman's foot-note is, as usual, very charming: 'There are three very slight, unworthy pages of the original most properly rejected.' A very little of the Elbow-Froth-Pompey episode, wherein they meet the Duke in the Street, is retained in Act III, Scene 2, but of the first of these scenes omitted Gentleman writes: 'Here follows no less than seven pages of absolute ribaldry, . . . the annihilation of them does credit to our author and the stage.' Otherwise the stage is fumigated free of these people, except for the necessary retention of Pompey (here called *Clown*) in the late prison scenes. It would have been well if Kemble had continued the same practice, though candour elicits the statement that he has rendered the group as little malodorous as their retention at all in the *dramatis personae* would admit. Of course the amusing scenes involving Lucio and the Duke are retained. The main plot is very well handled in Bell's edition, more of Juliet being retained than was usual in later versions . . . In general, this is an excellent acting version – its being disinfected of the gross underworld folk makes it unusually pleasing. I am glad to think that Mrs. Yates appeared in such good company. (II, pp. 23–5)

It is striking to see how Odell's words connect with Francis Gentleman's commentary from nearly 150 years earlier. (It is equally striking to see how Charles Shattuck, in turn, offers an interesting and positive analysis of how, given Kemble's premises, Kemble's adaptation might be seen to improve the play.)

It is also possible, I think, to recognize how the criticism of and hostility to the Folio text expressed by Johnson, Lennox, and Gentleman, among others, and echoed by Odell, can be seen as being supported by the radically different stagings of the play as a whole and of the ending in particular that begin around 1970. As a number of critics have noted, this shift begins with John Barton's 1970 Royal Shakespeare Company production, which ended with Isabella standing alone on stage, having *not* accepted the Duke's proposal of marriage. This was at once shocking in its rupture with the traditional staging yet illuminating in enacting an always-present yet hitherto nearly invisible potential of the play-text – and in the present context it prompts a return to the comments of Johnson, Lennox and Gentleman.[27] These earlier critics recognized the potential disharmonies in the play as written, assumed these disharmonies were the result of error or carelessness on the part of Shakespeare, and, at least in the case of Gentleman, applauded the efforts of theatrical adaptors to complete the play properly, as Shakespeare failed to do. Many of the productions of the last thirty years, on the other hand, take advantage of the openness of the ending to offer us Isabellas and Claudios who remain unreconciled and Isabellas who either flatly refuse or postpone any answer to the Duke's proposal. These productions thus demonstrate that Shakespeare's script did indeed 'fail' to mandate a fully comic ending, but then proceed to seize the opportunity offered by this openness to suggest, as some critics of the play including Honigmann now suggest, that the greatness of the play, both on the page and on the stage, is constituted precisely by its refusal to end with the flourish and the image of harmony that Jewett offered his spectators.

Indeed we might go a step further, recognizing how the disturbing endings produced by some of the more radical productions since Barton's now resonate, in ways she never could have predicted, with Charlotte Lennox's complaint that we witness 'three or four Weddings, instead of one good Beheading, which was the Consequence naturally expected'. For these stagings, at least one of which has actually begun to carry out the onstage execution of Angelo, make it appear not so much that Shakespeare had to torture his subject into a comic resolution but rather that the playwright-Duke, having chosen to psychologically torture his subjects, has found himself having to employ extreme measures to prevent the executions of Angelo, Barnardine, Claudio and Lucio – which is the consequence his victims and witnesses have been led to expect.[28]

Where Lennox saw an ending which is, in Honigmann's rephrasing 'irresponsibly cobbled together', many performers and critics now see the play's greatness as inhering in the opportunities it offers to create endings whose dissonances (which are, of course, in harmony with a dissonance-loving time) impel us to wrestle with near-tragic dilemmas as we leave the theatre. If, as Johnson claims, Shakespeare 'remit[ted] his efforts' at the end, then for two hundred and eighty years his remission has prompted those staging the play to redouble their efforts to produce more fully articulated final chords, whether those chords offered spectators the harmonies of comedy or the dissonant measures of tragi-comedy.

---

27 Asserting that a performance option of a Shakespeare playtext is 'unimaginable' or 'unthinkable' until some cultural shift has occurred is at once an appealing and a risky manoeuvre. So in this instance the idea that Isabella might refuse the Duke must be seen as a not absolutely unimaginable choice because, as Mark Eccles notes in his variorum edition, Sr St Geraldine Byrne, in a 1936 dissertation, wrote that 'It is noteworthy that in conferring his love on Isabella the Duke yet never moves to the intimate *thee*, probably because of reverence for her position and reserve. This would support the opinion that Shakespeare did not intend the Duke to marry Isabella' (97). He also quotes G. L. Kittredge, in his 1936 *Works*, who claimed that 'This conclusion of the play leaves the audience guessing – as was doubtless Shakespeare's intent' (Eccles 275).

28 The production which started and, indeed, almost completed the execution of Angelo was directed by Yossi Yzraely for the Three Rivers Shakespeare Festival, Pittsburgh, Pennyslvania; I saw two performances in July 1985. Accounts of productions which inform my conclusion are those offered by Jane Williamson in 'The Duke and Isabella on the Modern Stage', in *The Triple Bond*, ed. Joseph G. Price (Pennsylvania, 1975), pp. 149–60; Ralph Berry, in chapter 2 of *Changing Styles in Shakespeare* (London: George Allen and Unwin, 1981); Philip McGuire, in chapter 4 of *Speechless Dialect*; and Peter Holland, in *English Shakespeares: Shakespeare on the English Stage in the 1990s* (Cambridge, 1997), pp. 206–12.

SHAKESPEARIAN UTOPIAS

ROBERT SHAUGHNESSY

I

For a long time, the story goes, we supported a Victorian regime, and we continue to be dominated by it even today . . . But for decades now, we have found it difficult to speak on the subject without striking a different pose: we are conscious of defying established power, our tone of voice shows that we know we are being subversive, and we ardently conjure away the present and appeal to the future, whose day will be hastened by the contribution we believe we are making.[1]

While nothing might have been further from his thoughts when tracing the genealogy of sex in the modern period than the history of twentieth-century Shakespearian performance, the model of repression and liberation that is outlined in Michel Foucault's *The History of Sexuality* provides a striking analogy for what is said to have happened to the early modern drama on stage since the Victorian period. This story is well known: it begins around 1888 with the publication of the rediscovered DeWitt sketch of the Swan, at the time that William Poel started his long and lonely struggle against the forces of illusion and spectacle in his tireless, eccentric and even fanatical proselytizing for the platform stage. Poel's challenge was taken up by more conciliatory figures like Harley Granville-Barker in the Edwardian period, and by mavericks such as Terence Gray at his Festival Theatre; it then passed to the figure who was perhaps most instrumental in translating the dream of the open stage into a

physical reality, Tyrone Guthrie. By way of the Old Vic in the early 1930s, Kronberg Castle at Elsinore in 1937, the Assembly Rooms at the Edinburgh Festival in 1948 and finally, Stratford, Ontario in 1953 and Minneapolis in 1963, Guthrie led the way by liberating Shakespeare from the repressive confines of the proscenium arch onto the open, thrust, platform stage where, it is believed, the plays can recover their true shape, actors can enter once again into an intimate, almost mystic communion with audiences, and where the mendacity of illusion is banished by the greater truth of frank and unashamed theatricality. And so on, through the work of the Royal Shakespeare Company in its high modernist phase during the 1960s and 1970s (and especially in the work of Peter Brook, at Stratford and beyond); such was the situation as J. L. Styan assessed it in 1977, where it seemed that 'past traditions of realistic presentation are being stripped away and the spirit of Elizabethan ritual and role playing'[2] had, at last, been recovered. Since these words were written there have been the opening of the RSC's Swan Theatre in Stratford in 1986, and the reconstructed Bankside Globe. It is a story, we are told, of repression and partial liberation, of a revolutionary movement from Victorian to

---

[1] Michel Foucault, *The History of Sexuality, Volume 1: An Introduction*, trans. Robert Hurley (Harmondsworth, 1979), p. 3.

[2] J. L. Styan, *The Shakespeare Revolution* (Cambridge, 1977), p. 234.

modern sensibilities, from the deceptions and distortions of the enclosed proscenium stage to the honesty and authenticity of the open stage.

But, just as Foucault postulates that the hypothesis of repression versus sexual liberation is less a movement towards greater openness and freedom than a shift towards new discursive and scientific mechanisms of surveillance and control, so the apparent openness of the open stage may be more illusory than we think, or hope. The Shakespeare revolution has come in for something of a battering recently; it has also been argued the authenticity which is often sought from the revived or reconstructed early modern stage, for all the egalitarian talk of openness and participation, is really a focus for retrograde, nostalgic, and secretly elitist fantasies of the organic Elizabethan world order. Moreover, a range of post-Foucauldian narratives have disputed the cosily inclusive image of Shakespeare's theatre, questioning the myth of the heteregeneous but unified audience of all classes, and repositioning it as an altogether much more dangerous institution – as both the space of ambivalently licensed subversion and a site for the specular ratification of royal power. What I wish to address in a preliminary fashion here is the question of why the quest for Shakespearian authenticity continues to exert such a fascination for so many. What kind of desires does it embody, what fantasies does it entertain, what dissatisfactions does it articulate? Why do so many apparently otherwise imperturbable individuals continue to find the early modern stage so sexy? I use this term quite deliberately, for it seems to me that the scholarly and theatrical energies that circulate around this fetishized space have a libidinal quality; that there is frequently a gendered and eroticized dimension to the terminology which invites further investigation.

In the past decade or so, of course, the erotic dynamics of the Renaissance theatre have been subjected to sustained scholarly investigation, with particular attention being paid to the ambiguous and potentially subversive figure of

the 'boy actress'.[3] For the revivalist movement, however, theatrical transvestism has been a central preoccupation for far longer, to the extent that it is worth speculating whether the ostensibly antiquarian motive is of less importance than the radically transformative, carnivalesque potentialities of cross-dressing itself, as a symptom of experimentation with alternative modes of gender identity. Repeatedly, the troubling yet also potentially liberating figure of the boy-actress, in a multiplicity of gendered modes, has been at the centre of the neo-Elizabethan stage. At the turn of the century, working within the theatrical context of widespread female-to-male cross-dressing (and within a cultural context of feminist agitation), William Poel offered a variety of cross-dressed productions, to comically scandalous effect. More recently, the Bankside Globe commenced its preview season with a transvestite comedy, *The Two Gentlemen of Verona* and a one-off all-female version of Richard Edwardes' boys' company play *Damon and Pythias*; opened in 1997 with an all-male *Henry V*; and in 1998 offered another two cross-

---

[3] See for example Lisa Jardine, *Still Harping on Daughters* (Brighton, 1983); Catherine Belsey, 'Disrupting Sexual Difference: Meaning and Gender in the Comedies', in *Alternative Shakespeares*, ed. John Drakakis (London, 1985); Kathleen McLuskie, 'The Act, the Role and the Actor: Boy Actresses on the Elizabethan Stage', *New Theatre Quarterly*, 3 (1987), 120–30; Phyllis Rackin, 'Androgyny, Mimesis, and the Marriage of the Boy Heroine on the English Renaissance Stage', *PMLA*, 102 (1987), 29–41; Jean E. Howard, 'Crossdressing, the Theatre, and Gender Struggle in Early Modern England', *Shakespeare Quarterly*, 39 (1988), 418–40; Susan Zimmerman ed., *Erotic Politics: Desire on the Renaissance Stage* (New York and London, 1992); Michael Shapiro, *Gender in Play on the Shakespearian Stage: Boy Heroines and Female Pages* (Ann Arbor, 1994); Juliet Dusinberre, 'Squeaking Cleopatras: Gender and Performance in *Antony and Cleopatra*', in *Shakespeare, Theory and Performance*, ed. James C. Bulman (London, 1996); Stephen Orgel, *Impersonations: The Performance of Gender in Shakespeare's England* (Cambridge, 1996); John Russell Brown, 'Representing Sexuality in Shakespeare's Plays', *New Theatre Quarterly*, 13 (1997), 205–13.

dressed comedies, *As You Like It* and *The Merchant of Venice*. Perhaps the best-known instance, however, is a cinematic one, in Laurence Olivier's 1944 film of *Henry V*. In the first, playhouse-bound part of the film, it is, perhaps above all else, the presence of the boy player as Hostess that signals the radical otherness of its imagined stage world; the moment when the film shifts decisively from the theatrical to the realist-cinematic (and from comic to historic) mode is conclusively asserted by the change in the gender of the performer playing Hostess from male to female (a move which is reversed at the end, when Princess Katherine dwindles back into a boy player). If this gender play signals one of many ruptures within the apparently unified diegesis of Olivier's film, it is also symptomatic of its ideologically contradictory character, as it disallows the closure which the film otherwise strenuously seeks to secure. While it is true that one does not have to look very far to find instances of cross-dressing in the Elizabethan and Jacobean canon, it seems that the icon of theatrical and cultural otherness that is the boy player, and his variously gendered analogues on the twentieth-century stage, offers a particularly compelling focus not only for various kinds of transgressive (and perhaps unacknowledged) desire, but also for the sense of difference and indeterminacy that inhabits modern perceptions of the early modern stage.

But if the preoccupation with Shakespearian transvestism offers a fairly clear-cut instance of the ways in which historical research is shaped by the political imperatives of the present (in this case the politics of gender and sexuality as addressed by feminism and gender theory), there is a less immediately visible sense in which the early modern stage has been framed in both gendered and sexualized terms within scholarly discourse. As a speculative construct and absent object of, and focus for, desire, it has been conceptualized in terms which reveal interesting gender biases. Taking up Hélène Cixous' proposal that the binary pairing (or opposition) of Man and Woman 'carries us, beneath all its

figures, wherever discourse is organised', it is possible to detect, in the rhetoric of Shakespearian theatre scholarship, a metaphoric logic of masculine/feminine which further corresponds to the central differentiation, 'an absolute *constant* which orders values and which is precisely this opposition, activity/passivity.'[4] Consider the qualities repeatedly attributed to Renaissance stages: they are flexible, fluid, unlocalized, natural, neutral, free, empty, intimate and, above all, *open*: acquiescent and beguilingly seductive, the platform stage is a passive, feminized entity which is mastered, dominated and controlled by the all-male player as, energized by the phallic potency of what is referred to as a larger-than-life acting style, he walks purposefully all over it. If, as Cixous suggests, logocentrism inscribes coupledom everywhere, then the player and his stage, and Shakespeare and his theatre, have been figured as implicitly erotic as well as proprietorial relationships. Moreover, the stage which is the object of critical desire, like any romantic ideal, retains its allure and mystique by being unattainable.

If all this is largely implicit within criticism and scholarship, it becomes rather more explicit when the Elizabethan stage is reconstructed in facsimile; at the same time, however, the neo-open stage tends to exhibit a disconcerting tendency to reverse polarity in terms of gender, displaying its virility most exceptionally when it becomes 'thrust'. The Festival stage at Stratford, Ontario, for example, has been particularly prone to gendering: Robert Speaight reported that Michael Langham, Festival director from 1956 to 1967 viewed certain modifications made to the stage in 1962 as 'changing its sex . . . from masculine to feminine';[5] more recently, on the other hand, Ralph Berry has described it as 'an extremely masculine thrust

---

4 Hélène Cixous, 'The Newly Born Woman', in *The Hélène Cixous Reader*, ed. Susan Sellers (London, 1994), pp. 37–38.
5 Robert Speaight, *Shakespeare on the Stage* (London, 1973), p. 237.

stage'.[6] It could be said here that the use of the term 'thrust' (which always seems to have an air of vigorous mastery about it), particularly in relation to the early modern stage, anachronistically presupposes the picture frame as the norm against which the stage platform asserts itself. If the open stage radiates healthy, honest sexuality, the picture frame stage, conversely, has been condemned as a site of solitary vices, introverted passions and dissipated energies. William Poel implied as much in an article published when he wrote in 1893 that 'the extravagance of realism, so often thought healthy and natural, is . . . only perverse sentimentality . . . realism is exhausting and enervating in its effect, while idealism frequently avails to stimulate and fertilize'.[7] Perversity, exhaustion, enervation: as Russell Jackson observes, commenting on this passage, this certainly reveals 'the "High Victorian" terms of the debate, with Poel's attacking realism as inimical to plain living and high thinking'[8] (and, it is hardly necessary to add, purity in thought, word and deed). Seventy years on, Stephen Joseph echoed Poel rhetoric, declaring that the proscenium arch 'is now an incubus which is suffocating live entertainment'[9] (in folklore, the incubus is a demon who has sex with sleeping women).

It is easy enough to characterize the early modern stage as a focus for diverse kinds of desire, displaced and sublimated as these may be; and thence to write off the whole revivalist movement as an exercise in warped nostalgia or reactionary fantasy. But lest this should be read as a simply negative or dismissive attitude to adopt towards a century's worth of imaginative and physical reconstructive energy, I also wish to emphasize that there is a further aspect to this cultural project, which is the powerfully utopian element in the quest for authenticity. Foucault suggests that

What sustains our eagerness to speak of sex in terms of repression is doubtless this opportunity to speak out against the powers that be, to utter truths and promise bliss, to link together enlightenment, libera-

tion, and manifold pleasures; to pronounce a discourse that combines the fervour of knowledge, the determination to change the laws, and the longing for the garden of earthly delights.   (Foucault, p. 7)

For Foucault, the utopianism of the sexual revolution is naive and misplaced, and the 'natural', apparently spontaneous freedom of sex simply another subterfuge of power, another mechanism of surveillance and control. Similar things can be (and have been) said about the apparent freedoms of the open stage; despite aspirations towards democratic inclusiveness, enterprises such as the Stratford Festival and Bankside Globe are fraught with contradictions.[10] I want here simply to emphasize the element of unresolved desire: however sentimental, quixotic and contradictory, however amenable to appropriation, the aims and methods of the revivalist movement may be, they nonetheless articulate a profound (and, I stress, significant) dissatisfaction not only with the existing theatre apparatus but, more importantly, with the social order it has produced and is reproduced through it. The fantasies of organic culture that are shaped within and around the wooden O may well be described as utopian, but as Catherine Belsey points out, utopias are 'wish-fulfilments devised to supply

---

6 Ralph Berry, *Shakespeare in Performance: Castings and Metamorphoses* (Basingstoke, 1993), p. 50.

7 William Poel, 'The Functions of a National Theatre', *The Theatre*, May 1893, quoted in Russell Jackson, 'Actor-Managers and the Spectacular', in *Shakespeare: An Illustrated Stage History*, ed. Russell Jackson and Jonathan Bate (Oxford, 1995), p. 124.

8 Ibid.

9 Stephen Joseph, *Actor and Architect* (Manchester, 1964), p. 6.

10 See for example Richard Paul Knowles, 'Shakespeare, 1993, and the Discourses of the Stratford Festival, Ontario', *Shakespeare Quarterly*, 45 (1994), 211– 25; John Drakakis, 'Ideology and Institution: Shakespeare and the Roadsweepers', in *The Shakespeare Myth*, ed. Graham Holderness (Manchester, 1988); Graham Holderness, 'Shakespeare and Heritage', *Textual Practice* 6 (1992), 247–63; Denis Salter, 'Acting Shakespeare in Postcolonial Space', in *Shakespeare, Theory, and Performance*.

the deficiencies of the current order', which have 'the status of dreams, and like dreams they may be read as trivial or significant'.[11] Such Elizabethanism belongs within what Jonathan Bate has called 'a tradition which we may call Popular Shakespeare', which 'has been made to matter as a voice of radical culture, not just of established culture';[12] a Shakespeare which is not so readily aligned with reactionary values as it may first appear.

In the remainder of this paper I explore some of the implications of this claim by examining four events which have been identified as foundational moments in the history of the Shakespeare revolution. These are: William Poel's productions of *Hamlet*, in 1881 and 1900; the visit of the Old Vic *Hamlet*, directed by Tyrone Guthrie, to Kronberg Castle at Helsingor, Denmark in 1937; and the first Stratford Festival at Ontario in 1953, with particular reference to the production of *All's Well That Ends Well*. I want to consider some of the meanings which these events generated, and the contradictions within which they were implicated.

II

William Poel has been labelled a crackpot, a fanatic, a crank as (probably more) often as he has been hailed as the great pioneer of twentieth-century Elizabethanism. Even Poel's defenders have reluctantly conceded that his uncompromising adherence to the principles of Elizabethan performance rendered his experimental stagings more notable in terms of influence, of the tradition they inaugurated, than of their demonstrable achievement. The charges are familiar: that Poel's use of amateur performers inevitably generated bad acting; that his concentration on the music of verse obliterated character; that his strict adherence to period costumes and architecture was pedantic, antiquarian and unilluminating; that his Elizabethan Stage Company offered recitals rather than performances; that his practice of putting

pseudo-Elizabethan audiences on stage, and putting platform stages inside proscenium arches, was in effect a variation upon the pseudo-historicist pictorialism which he claimed to oppose; that, as a fanatic, he lacked the pragmatism of the theatre professional. What is of interest – and of potentially radical significance – in Poel's dogged pedantry is that the refusal, in certain areas, to compromise with realist theatrical norms constituted an affront to 'common sense' or, to put it another way, the dominant ideology. If reviewers ridiculed the clumsy amateurism of Poel and his inexperienced performers, they did so from a position which took for granted not only the dominant economic and social structures of the professional theatre, but also the ideology of character which its acting practice aimed to produce (it is worth remembering that there was also an element of class consciousness: Poel himself was considered too 'peevish' and 'plebeian' to rate as Hamlet[13]). Moreover, the attempt to move beyond the then dominant mode of pictorialism had its own political implications. If Victorian spectacular Shakespeare represented, by means of a conspicuously profligate visual economy, the intersection of ideologies of nationhood, individuality, sexuality and domesticity in an apparently unified scenic form, the evaporation of the naturalistic environment introduced a troubling discontinuity between character and setting; what might be termed a literal dislocation of the Shakespearian dramatis persona from his secure position as a bourgeois subject at the centre of a scene which discloses his mastery over both landscape and history. This may have been largely inadvertent, but in Poel's polemical writings on the theatre there is a consistently fierce critique of the commercial theatre,

---

[11] Catherine Belsey, *Desire: Love Stories in Western Culture* (Oxford, 1994), p. 201.

[12] Jonathan Bate, *The Genius of Shakespeare* (London, 1997), pp. 213–14.

[13] Rosenberg, *The Masks of Hamlet* (Newark, 1993), p. 156.

or, as he puts it, of theatrical capitalism, and an insistence that 'a theatre should justify its existence on the grounds that it serves the best interests of the community as a whole'.[14] His sense of the perverse extravagance of realism, to which I referred earlier, suggests a distinction between the inauthentic and alienated desires artificially stimulated by theatrical capitalism and the more substantial and lasting – and harder-earned – pleasures afforded by a more socially responsible theatre. Poel's project can be aligned with those of Ruskin and William Morris, in that his Elizabethanism might well be seen as an extension of the concerns of both the Gothic Revival and the Arts and Crafts movement. Like Ruskin and Morris, he sought to recreate early modern forms of cultural production in order to retrieve an unalienated mode of social existence, wherein labour, nature and culture were organically integrated. The result was a confrontational theatre practice to which extreme and defensive reactions were the only likely response: judged by the standards of the commercial theatre, Poel's work was almost bound to 'fail'.

Here we may turn to the 1881 and 1900 performances of *Hamlet* at St George's Hall and the Carpenters' Hall respectively. The primary interest of the first production for Poel's contemporaries lay in the provocative choice of the First Quarto text. It has been observed that Poel's pursuit of Shakespearian authenticity in staging practice ran in parallel with the Victorian preoccupation with 'authentic' texts,[15] and in this sense what was offered was a kind of facsimile performance, conspicuously estranged from familiar reading and theatregoing and therefore, apparently, more truly Shakespearian. But, as Michael Dobson has demonstrated, the editorial practices which had fashioned the editions which the textual fundamentalists reacted against were themselves ideologically overdetermined, notably in the arena of sexuality; framed in terms of the opposition between purity and corruption, the eradication of typographic, metrical, grammatical and

semantic irregularity went hand-in-glove with the 'normalizing' of sexual irregularity.[16] Moreover, in the case of the First Quarto of *Hamlet*, the text's putative proximity to Elizabethan performance conditions also implies its conjectural distance from Shakespeare's compositional genius: in almost every sense, it was (and still is) readily stigmatized as 'bad'. The terms within which this badness was constructed by reviewers of the 1881 production are not only graphically physical but implicitly sexual. Q1 was 'muddled and mangled' and 'barbarously mutilated'; it was also 'degraded' and 'corrupt'.[17] By assigning the Q1 text an aberrant, monstrous and grotesque physicality, which was seen in opposition to the wholeness and purity of spirit of the established text, the reviewers invoked a rhetoric of sexuality and the body that was recognizably of its time. This sense of the distinction between the normative and the perverse also informed critical responses to the staging and acting. The use of a bare, curtained platform was unexceptional, if novel, but elsewhere Poel's scrupulous adherence to the letter of the First Quarto generated some amusement. Poel put the Ghost, as the stage direction indicates, 'in his night-gowne', and added a veil; *The Era* reported that he looked 'like a stout female being led to the altar, to blush as a bride or pretend to'.[18] The strongest criticism, however, was directed at Poel's portrayal of Hamlet, and here the critical discourse construed his perceived histrionic failure in explicitly gendered terms. Across the range of reviews, a clear consensus emerges: Poel's

14 Poel, *What is Wrong with the Stage* (London, 1920), pp. 9–10.

15 Gary Taylor, *Reinventing Shakespeare* (London, 1991), p. 269.

16 Michael Dobson, 'Bowdler and Britannia; Shakespeare and the National Libido', *Shakespeare Survey 46* (1994), 137–44. See also Margreta de Grazia, *Shakespeare Verbatim* (Oxford, 1991), pp.77ff.

17 Quoted in Marion O'Connor, *William Poel and the Elizabethan Stage Society* (Cambridge, 1987), p. 21.

18 23 April 1881, quoted in O'Connor, p. 20.

'unmanly' portrayal was 'sure to be ridiculous', in that it alternated 'for the most part between tearful peevishness and unmanly fits of sobbing'; and, in a formulation which equates irregularity of gender identity with that of metre, and which evokes a performing body shamefully incapable of regulating its own secretions, this was 'a Hamlet who sheds tears copiously, and who would not or could not mind his stops'.[19]

Poel's second production of *Hamlet* for the Elizabethan Stage Society at the Carpenters' Hall in 1900 carried over some of the innovations of the 1881 production, although this time the text was Poel's own amalgamation of Quarto and Folio versions. It was chiefly notable for two features: the all-male casting, and its staging upon the Society's reconstruction of the Fortune playhouse. The Fortune fit-up had been a feature of the Elizabethan Stage Society since its first use in the production of *Measure for Measure* at the Royalty theatre in 1893 (which had also featured an onstage 'audience' in Elizabethan dress); the effect of the curtains and pillars had led to it being jokingly (but justifiably) described as 'Poel's four-poster.'[20] If this was another inadvertently sexualized image, then it might well have been an appropriate setting for *Measure for Measure* (or, for that matter, for *Hamlet*). Moreover, the device of putting a pseudo-Elizabethan playhouse on a proscenium stage creates an intriguing series of theatrical frames around the performance (which might have been worthy, perhaps, of *Hamlet* itself, although there was no proscenium at the Carpenters' Hall); but is also reminiscent of the metanarrative structuring which has been a recurrent tactic of utopian fiction. Clumsy as it seemed to many, the stage-within-a-stage effected a visible juxtaposition between past and present, at the very least, to demand that the spectator adopt a complexly self-conscious relationship with the theatrical spectacle and the dramatic fiction itself. As *The Times* complained of *Measure for Measure*: 'the persons of the play

. . . were merely so many abstractions, like the characters in a fairy tale'.[21] In this respect, the multiple framings of such productions rehearsed one of the central paradoxes of utopian fiction, in that the more precise and detailed the imagined world (and the detail is defined strategically or satirically against or in opposition to the existing order that is being critiqued or satirized), the more obviously a 'no-place' it becomes; characteristically, the techniques of realist mimesis work to *estrange* the real rather than endorse it. As Belsey observes, 'the alternative society is not necessarily a goal, but a hypothesis, a possibility, which clarifies the present by denaturalizing its practices' (*Desire*, p. 195). Whether it is in the form of the ancillary documentation and corroborative narratives of More's *Utopia* or in the explanatory device of the dream-framework of Morris's *News from Nowhere*, assertions of facticity and authenticity affirm both the earnestness of the utopian order and its preposterousness. The more emphatically Poel insisted upon historically accurate details of playhouse architecture, music, costume and so on in the interests of authenticity, the less seriously could they be taken; the more insistently pedantic the practice, the more (to many onlookers, hilariously) indeterminate the effect. In a sense, the amused scepticism which greeted Poel's work was a structural inevitability.

The second innovation was the all-male cast. Poel had engaged in cross-casting before, employing female performers in male roles as well as the more obviously archaeological practice of men playing women, partly following historical precedent, and partly to answer to Poel's quest for correct musical orchestration. The comments of a number of reviewers underline the

---

19 *Illustrated Sport and Dramatic News*, 23 April; *Daily News*, 18 April; *The Era*, 23 April.
20 Dennis Kennedy, *Looking at Shakespeare* (Cambridge, 1993), p. 39.
21 11 November 1893, quoted in Styan, *Shakespeare Revolution*, p. 59.

complexity (and potential instability) of gender identity as a factor in the production. The *Era*'s reviewer was vitriolic:

We never see one of these rather pedantic productions without thinking of the celebrated dinner 'after the manner of the ancients', which was given by the enthusiastic antiquarian in Smollett's novel; and we feel something of the distaste which led one of the guests to reject the archeologically correct, but actually repulsive, dish of snails ... There is no good served by reverting to the primitive practices of the early Shakespearian stage, and by the spectacle of a stalwart youth appearing as Gertrude, or a clever boy repeating in mild but masculine tones allotted to the fair Ophelia.[22]

What distinguishes this example is the extremity of the response, as cross-dressing seems to be equated with the violation of taboo, and, in particular, of the fundamental cultural distinctions between the edible and the inedible, or the raw and the cooked. But if, in this account, the contradiction between the gender characteristics of the performer and those of the character provokes a reaction of almost pathological disgust, other reviewers neutralized the potentially threatening implications through humour. Reversing the charges that had been levelled against the tearful Poel in his earlier production, the critic from *The Times* recorded that Edgar Playford's Gertrude was 'fair ... though her sobs were too manlike and tempestuous and her cheeks made one appreciate the old joke about the audience being kept waiting while the heroine was getting herself shaved'.[23] The joke, as usual, is at the expense of Poel's amateurs, as their presumed ineptitude punctures the illusion of character; but the insistent policing of masculine and feminine characteristics also reveals the instability of the gender roles that the discourse is struggling to hold in place. Tears, in particular, seem to act as a dangerously mobile and arbitrary signifier of gender, in that they can be both too feminine in one context and too manly in another. Master Bartington's Ophelia was, according to the *Stage*'s reviewer, 'truly girlish and delightful'

(1 March 1900), but his comment upon Gertrude indicates more delicate negotiations, as he asked: 'Why not have a real boy to play the Queen, not a man with a voice that reasserted his innate masculinity?' Even as the writer attempts to assert maleness as a fixed, given and immutable quality, an essence of self revealed in the grain of the voice, he subverts it with an invocation of the adolescent male, configured in terms of a more provisional masculinity which is more convincingly adaptable to the representation of the female.

What these comments point to, of course, is a deeper sense of unease and impending transformation with regard to gender roles at the turn of the century; in this respect, Poel's transvestite experiment can be seen not only within the context of widespread theatrical cross-dressing (particularly in relation to *Hamlet*) during the *fin-de-siècle* and Edwardian period, but also against the background of a growing feminist movement that was putting male supremacism to serious test.

III

I will turn now to a third *Hamlet*, the Old Vic production directed by Tyrone Guthrie, with Laurence Olivier in the lead role, which played at Elsinore in 1937. In Guthrie's own account, this was the pivotal event which led to his repudiation of the picture frame stage. Part of its appeal as a foundational myth for the open-stage movement lies in the sense that it comprised a fortuitous but also ironic series of happenings. In June 1937, at the invitation of the Danish Tourist Board, the Old Vic company visited Denmark with Guthrie's production of *Hamlet* (which had been seen in London in January), to inaugurate an annual festival of open-air productions of the play in the courtyard of the fifteenth-century Kronborg Castle at Helsingor (or, as the British press

---

22 *The Era*, 3 March 1900.
23 *The Times*, 22 February 1900.

preferred, Elsinore). The composite set from the Old Vic production was transported and reconstructed before audience seating of 2,500; floodlighting and sound amplification was installed, a crowd of extras drawn from a Corps of Officer Cadets billeted in the castle supplied; and an audience of luminaries invited, including the Danish royal family. On the afternoon of the first night, however, it began to rain, 'coming down in bellropes', in Guthrie's account.[24] A decision which, according to legend, would have crucial implications for the future of the Shakespearian theatre, was quickly made:

Miss Baylis, Larry Olivier and I held a council of war. It was, out of all question to abandon the performance, indeed the special train had already steamed out of Copenhagen. To play in the open air was going to be nothing but an endurance test for all hands. We would give the performance in the ballroom of the hotel. There was no stage; but we would play in the middle of the hall with the audience seated all around as in a circus. The phrase hadn't yet been invented, but this would be theatre in the round. (Guthrie, *A Life in the Theatre*, p. 170)

The whole enterprise is shot through with certain ironies arising from its entertainingly contradictory pursuit of authenticity. The key factor in this intercultural exchange was the idea that this was the 'real' Elsinore, home of the 'real' Hamlet, which was possibly visited by Shakespeare's own company in the seventeenth century. So this was a site-specific performance which attempted, through an oddly literal and realist understanding of what Shakespeare's Elsinore is, to harness a particular magic of place – 'the great drama enacted in its rightful setting', as *The Sphere* reported. On the evidence of the photographs published in the press at the time, however, and of the album of snapshots taken by Phyllis Hartnoll (which is lodged in the Theatre Museum), there was in actuality a startling disjuncture between set and setting. The set, taken from the Old Vic production (itself a gesture towards Elizabethan flexibility), was an unlocalized composite of platforms and

steps; in the courtyard it appears surreally truncated and open-ended, with staircases leading into the open air rather than into the wings, the whole overseen by the scene-stealing neo-classical architectural façade of Kronberg castle itself. Authenticity becomes a kind of palimpsest: we are presented with a semi-Elizabethan composite set, designed for a picture-frame stage, transposed into a pseudo-Elizabethan open-air setting, framed and, indeed validated by, the geographical reality which the play fictionalizes. Merging 'Elsinore' with Shakespeare's stage, the proposed performance was simultaneously the apotheosis of illusionistic literalism and its antithesis.

What happened next is well known: the improvised performance in the nearby hotel ballroom went ahead; it was judged, in the circumstances, a success. Although J. C. Trewin was subsequently to recall it as 'the most exciting performance of *Hamlet* I've ever seen',[25] the first-night critics made little of it at the time, preferring to review the second night (redefined as the 'real' first night) in the courtyard instead. For Guthrie, though, the experience confirmed his dissatisfaction with the proscenium stage: 'I should never have suggested staging this rather important occasion as we did if I had not already had a strong hunch that it would work' (Guthrie, *A Life in the Theatre*, p. 172). Taken together with his account of the decision quoted earlier, what emerges from all this is a strong sense not just of the spontaneity, but of the inevitability, the naturalness, the instinctiveness of the Elizabethan mode of performance: it had to happen.

There was, however, yet another layer to this event, and one which returns us to the question of sexuality. This was what has become known as Guthrie and Olivier's Freudian version of

---

24 Tyrone Guthrie, *A Life in the Theatre* (London, 1959), p. 170.

25 Quoted in Alfred Rossi, *Astonish Us in the Morning: Tyrone Guthrie Remembered* (London, 1977), p. 34.

Hamlet, in that this was the first production, under the tutelage of Ernest Jones himself, to offer an explicitly Oedipal reading of the Prince. Much more could be said about this, but I want simply to suggest a connection, for Guthrie himself at least, between the psychoanalytic reading and the drive towards the open stage. Psychoanalysis and Elizabethanism might be seen as components of a generally modernist reaction against Victorianism; Guthrie's repudiation of realism and the proscenium arch operated alongside a certain adventurousness in his treatment of Shakespearian sexualities. Following Ernest Jones, Guthrie and Olivier proposed an incestuous attachment between Hamlet and Gertrude which reverberated throughout the entire production in the form of a classic Freudian pattern of repression and revolt, one manifestation of which was an intensely athletic portrayal of Hamlet. Olivier's physical agility in the role gave emphatic embodiment to Hamlet's identification with the father and repudiation of the (passive, static, suffocating) mother. In Ernest Jones's reading of the play, the ascription of an Oedipal motive to Hamlet resolves the central enigma of the play which, according to a long critical and theatrical tradition, had been formulated at the level of characterization in terms of a paralysis of will, or inability to act, on the part of the Prince; adopting this reading, Guthrie and Jones articulated Hamlet's self-divisions in physical and spatial terms: as Olivier's dynamic, emphatically masculine energy (phallic potency abounds in the reviews, with references to his 'steely body', his 'bow-string tautness and vibrancy', and, most of all, to his virility and vitality[26]), was displayed on a set which both belonged and did not belong within the picture frame. Crucially, this restless energy was still contained within the constricting matrix of the Old Vic's proscenium arch: and in this sense the move the liberation from its repressive confines marked a kind of rebirth, an attempt (like the trip to Elsinore itself) to return to origins as a way out of the Oedipal trap.

In Guthrie's own autobiographical text, an Oedipal pattern is readily apparent, in its representation of the relations between the maternal and the theatrical, or, more specifically, between Guthrie's own mother and his theatrical career. Avowedly 'a professional, not a personal, document' (p. 72), *A Life in the Theatre* is most intriguing when the boundaries between these spheres become blurred. This happens, remarkably, in the final pages:

Just as I have gradually abandoned the idea of illusion as the aim of theatrical performance, so I have also abandoned the idea that the theatre has a moral aim: to uplift the public, to instruct it, do it good . . . For the greater part of my professional life this aim had loomed quite large. It was an attitude which I had absorbed quite unconsciously from earliest youth [from] my mother . . . like all sons of good mothers, I still, long, long after childhood, felt 'naughty' when I caught myself disagreeing with my mother, when I found that many thoughts and deeds which seemed good to her no longer seemed so to me.

(Guthrie, *A Life in the Theatre*, p. 303)

A Life in the Theatre conforms to a pattern which one theorist of autobiography has seen as typifying the classic male life story: the achievement of an autonomous and authentic masculine identity necessarily entails a repression of identification with the mother-figure.[27] This repression is linked here to the repudiation of illusion and, hence, of the picture-frame stage: this is the teleological trajectory of Guthrie's autobiography. Yet, inevitably and tellingly, the maternal cannot be expunged from the text. Guthrie concludes his Elsinore anecdote by referring to the one restraint imposed upon the ballroom performance, the refusal by the head porter to allow a particular door to be used. He subsequently discovers that it conceals 'a pair of blue-tits' and a 'little hen', and is told ' "If this

---

[26] *Observer*, 10 January 1937; *Sunday Times*, 10 January; *Daily Telegraph*, 6 January; *Sunday Referee*, 10 January.

[27] Sidonie Smith, *A Poetics of Women's Autobiography: Marginality and the Fictions of Self-Representation* (Bloomington and Indianapolis, 1987), pp. 53–4.

door had been used, she would have deserted her eggs; you wouldn't have wanted that"' (Guthrie, *A Life in the Theatre*, p. 171).

This comparatively minor instance of theatricality thwarted by maternity forms an apt prelude to what happened in 1953, in the preparations for the opening of the Stratford Festival. Guthrie's account abounds in gendered and sexualized terminology. The first season at Stratford was mounted upon a temporary stage under canvas: Guthrie tells the story of how the tent was constructed under the direction of the foreman who is strangely-but-truly-named Skip Manley, who 'referred to the tent as "she" and the hardware . . . which would raise "her" from the ground' (Guthrie, *A Life in the Theatre*, p. 295); also of the rubberneckers who 'would lurk in the spring twilight outside the skirts of the great tent' and who would, occasionally, 'lift the skirts and peek; but only surreptitiously, only occasionally' (p. 298). Finally, there is the description of rehearsals in a shed which was infested with sparrows: 'towards evening, their love life became most obtrusive . . . Scenes of unbridled bird sexuality made the life of *Richard III* seem very anaemic and suburban' (p. 294). The epithets are intriguing. There is an obvious opposition between 'anaemic' and full-blooded sexuality, but the 'suburban' sensibility which Guthrie surprisingly discovers in *Richard III* resonates precisely because of the damning in-between-ness of the term: pity the poor suburbanite crawling across the despised borderland between countryside and city, raw rural physicality and metropolitan sophistication. In the context of the current discussion this is not only ironic because, as Steven Mullaney has it, it was precisely the suburban location of the original playhouses that lent them their subversive licentiousness,[28] but also eloquently suggestive of the interconnectedness of the politics of class, sexuality and location.

This brings us, almost in the form of a coda, to *All's Well That Ends Well*, the other play in the first Stratford festival season. If we were to

seek a vindication of what Foucault calls the 'repressive hypothesis', then the cultural history of the so-called problems plays during the first part of the twentieth century might provide a good point of reference. The verdict of the Victorian and post-Victorian period was that *All's Well* was Shakespeare's worst play; largely, we might suppose, because of its combination of an excess of sexual frankness with a deficit of naturalistic respectability in terms of narrative and characterization; but since the 1950s (and directly as a result of Guthrie's production), the play has been rediscovered (or liberated). For Styan, Guthrie's was the production which, on 'a more open stage . . . proved to be the one which opened up the play.'[29] Sexual and theatrical emancipation are interconnected: the stage itself demanded a necessary sexual frankness which completely redefined the play, in a movement from enclosure, silence and concealment to dynamic openness and visibility. Indeed, Guthrie appeared to locate the play somewhere between a vaguely Edwardian milieu and postwar 'modern dress' (Foucault's resonant phrase 'we "other Victorians"' comes to mind here) but this can be read not so much as a matter of finding an appropriate sociohistorical setting as a means of negotiating its cultural history (and its audience's sexual histories) in terms of an emergence from the gloom of Victorian repressiveness. If we were looking for a route through the maze of utopian fantasy, desperate optimism, reactionary nostalgia, scholarly earnestness and blind faith that characterizes the contemporary discourse of the early modern stage, this unique conjuncture of neo-Elizabethan theatre architecture, Dionysian ritual, Victorianism and self-conscious modernity might prove a good place from which to start.

---

[28] See Steven Mullaney, *The Place of the Stage: Licence, Play, and Power in Renaissance England* (Chicago, 1988).

[29] J. L. Styan, *Shakespeare in Performance: All's Well that Ends Well* (Manchester, 1984), pp. 4-5.

SHAKESPEARE PERFORMANCES IN ENGLAND, 1999

ROBERT SMALLWOOD

Deciding on a batting order for productions to be discussed in this essay always seems rather arbitrary. Their chronological order of opening would have a sort of crude logic about it, but would offer little to the earnest essayist endeavouring to create an illusion of connectedness. My inclination as tenant of this space for the last few years has been to follow a 'Comedies, Histories, Tragedies' sort of progression in the effort to 'grow to a point'. For this, the last essay in my series, I find myself with an agenda of no histories, six comedies, six tragedies (one in two productions), and two revivals of *Troilus and Cressida*, and for no particular reason other than the desire for a change, I begin my final year with the tragedies.

Having been the subject of special articles in the last two volumes of *Survey*, this year's three Shakespeare productions at the Bankside Globe now come back within the province of this essay to find their level with the rest of the year's Shakespearian theatrical endeavour – and judged against the rest, that level is not a distinguished one. With very rare exceptions, the Globe seems to be attracting disappointingly few accomplished actors to its companies; nor have any of its directors, so far at least, had anything particularly illuminating to tell us about the plays they have presented. Indeed, the new season's programmes have banished the term 'Director' in favour of 'Master of Play' and 'Master of Verse', appellations that seem designed to warn against the hope of finding directorial vision or ideas in Globe productions.

That Globe audiences seem to be ecstatically happy with what they are being offered is part of the problem. Are they, one cannot but wonder, at the Globe as part of an itinerary that includes the major tourist attractions such as Madame Tussaud's and the Tower of London, but few, if any, other theatres? Whatever the explanation, the audience's enthusiastic pleasure, on the afternoon I saw it, in a production of *Julius Caesar* that had the qualities of mediocre am-dram writ large all over it does not encourage the hope that change is just around the corner.

With Mark Rylance as 'Master of Play', Giles Block as 'Master of Verse', and Jenny Tiramani as 'Master of Clothing and Properties', the production was played by an all-male cast in meticulously Elizabethan costume, little puffy trousers much in evidence, 'authentick' to the tips of the carefully researched hats that everyone wore; and it achieved a level of boredom hard to believe. To drain the relationships between Brutus and Cassius, Brutus and Portia, Brutus and the audience, Antony and the audience, of all genuine emotional energy is no easy matter, but it was here achieved apparently without effort. A large part of the problem lay with Danny Sapani's Brutus, a wooden, hollow, and at times inaudible performance, but there was ample support from Mark Lewis Jones's raw, unsubtle Mark Antony, a caricature of wily Welsh demagoguery, entirely predictable, and a Cassius from Richard Bremmer that was all on one note of foxy scheming, relieved fitfully by fuming despair at Brutus's tactical ineptnesses, with no glimmer of that emotional dependence upon his friend without which the quarrel scene becomes mere rant. The most interesting performance among the principals was Paul Shelley's of the title role, a younger, spryer Caesar than the norm, genially self-satisfied, a little foolish, and no threat at all to the republic. Shelley reappeared as Strato at the end of the play, giving a somewhat heavy-handed resonance to Brutus's 'Caesar now be still' – but in a production so short of directorial ideas one could not afford to be choosy when anything resembling one appeared.

The self-conscious authenticity of the staging evinced itself in several ways that cannot have helped spectators' imaginative commitment to the experience: Antony initially, and Brutus throughout, delivered their orations to the crowd from the balcony, half invisible in the shadows and imperfectly audible; the full pillar-to-pillar width of the stage was used for the intense intimacy of the scene (1.2) of Cassius's attempt to inveigle Brutus into the conspiracy; the tinny rattlings of a metal sheet – with smoke exuding feebly from the 'hut' as from a smouldering bonfire – presented the storm; Benedict Wong as Calpurnia made most bellows-mending Thisbes seem mimetic marvels (Toby Cockerell did rather better as Portia but then proceeded to camp up Octavius); a few scrawny orange trees in little baskets were absurdly hauled on by rope for Brutus's orchard and a lumpen statue (of Pompey, presumably) was awkwardly trundled in for the assassination scene; there was armour for the pre-battle scenes (the battle itself happened behind the tiring-house doors with lots of drum-beating and shouting), Mark Antony's shining like chromium plate and with long red feathers sticking out of the top of his helmet, fatally reminiscent of an ambitious Costard's presentation of Pompey in the Pageant of the Nine Worthies. But for all the elaborate authenticity of much of the event, there was flagrant ana-

chronism elsewhere: a five-minute interval was cheerily announced after every act, wrecking any hope of discovering the play's build-up of tension; Antony appeared in a sheepskin bikini for the Lupercal scene, milking the audience's wolf-whistles; the new Globe's habit of placing actors in the yard was much in evidence, with the tradesmen of the first scene, and the respondents to the orations after the assassination, in jeans and tee-shirts and baseball caps, planted among the groundlings; and, after Antony's speech, these same 'groundlings' swarmed onto the stage like a bunch of football hooligans, kicking Cinna the poet into unconsciousness and pouring a can of petrol over him. A break from the heavy hand of authenticity was welcome, of course, but the contrivance of it all seemed token, a patronizing reminder to the tourists that this four-hundredth anniversary performance was still *relevant*. How glad one was to arrive at the final jig – quite easily the most theatrical event of a long afternoon.

The same all-male company reassembled later in the season to give us their *Antony and Cleopatra*, Mark Rylance joining the ensemble to play Cleopatra and Giles Block now 'mastering' both play and verse – surely rightly, for the division seems unreal and this production, presumably as a result of combining the functions, evinced a rather firmer sense of discipline and restraint than its predecessor and for once seemed genuinely to be asking the groundlings to take the work seriously. The play, again presented in Elizabethan costume to designs by Jenny Tiramani, and again with an array of natty hats, was performed briskly, with two short intervals, opportunities for humour accepted but not indulged, direct address delivered out frankly, with rather less of that self-congratulatory currying of groundling favour than some Globe productions have so tiresomely displayed. The addition of Rylance to the company made a considerable difference, for here is an actor (whatever one makes of this or that performance) who brings undeniable presence to the Globe stage, and so it proved here. Not, however, that there was much competition. Paul Shelley's bluff, grey-bearded, sombre and ultimately uninteresting Antony offered neither a sense of past grandeur nor of being incapacitated by present passion, for in spite of a big smacking kiss between the lovers in their first scene, presumably to confront groundling titters head on, there was never the slightest sense of sexual charge between them. John McEnery as Enobarbus attempted nothing beyond the hard-bitten old soldier caricature, understated and cynical, changing sides without much apparent struggle, and dying, kneeling upright, with a sort of unsurprised resignation. Mark Lewis Jones's Pompey was pompous, loud, and boring and Ben Walden gave us a strutting, prissy Octavius, apparently less interested in Roman politics than in sartorial self-presentation – a very flashy purple cloak decorated with golden oak-leaves and a little pork-pie hat that Mistress Ford might have made the envy of all Windsor – a petulant, silly little man, accepting power with a kind of apology. The result of this down-playing of the politics of the piece, of its non-Egyptian world, was to present the play entirely to Rylance's Cleopatra.

It was accepted eagerly, for this Cleopatra was nothing if not an attention-seeker. In long black wig and a succession of lowish-cut dresses in the peasant, milkmaid, or Maid of the Mountains style, bare-footed and with a golden ankle-bangle, Rylance's Cleopatra hopped and skipped and circled, flouncing her skirts, and toying with her curls, and flashing self-consciously naughty little smiles at Antony. The care to stay in the upper registers of the slightly husky tenor voice (certainly audible, perfectly plausible, in the end a little monotonous), the constant scampering around the stage (the Globe's Artistic Director seemingly anxious to give a lesson in the value of using all of its more-than-ample space), the skittishness, the eagerness to show how filled to the brim with girlish glee she was, the calculated unpredict-ability, the hands-on-hips little tantrums, the

extraordinary battle costume for Actium that made her look like Britannia on an old penny, all produced a remarkable effect of performed performance. An she had been a woman that should have acted thus they would have – well, perhaps not hanged her, but certainly panned her for gender stereotyping. But with a few energetic exceptions, the critical response was for the most part enthusiastic. Give yourself an unnecessary mountain to climb, one might say, then sit back and wait for the lemming reviewers to praise you for partially climbing it. And in one sense it *is* an unnecessary mountain, for, with the Globe's admirable policy of ethnic diversity in casting, and thus in accents, precise replication of Jacobean conditions is clearly not the aim and we might as well have a female actor play Cleopatra and thus leave a modern audience in the same state of expectations fulfilled as their Jacobean counterparts would have been watching a male actor in the role. But we had then left unseen a wonderful (or remarkable, at least) piece of work, for what Rylance's performance achieved by showing an actor shadowing, or paralleling, the role, rather than identifying with it, was the extent to which Cleopatra is constantly performing, de-liberately presenting theatrical displays, never identifiable as herself: 'If you find him sad, say I am dancing.' It was this that made the produc-tion worth seeing – this, and one moment at the end of the 'sad captains' scene when Cleo-patra, about to follow Antony from the stage, saw Enobarbus standing alone and disconsolate and, as if intuitively realizing he was on the point of desertion (an example of sensitivity of which Antony was quite incapable), went across and kissed him gently goodbye. It was the most interesting moment of the production, and of the Globe season.

The worst moment was the hoisting of Antony up to the balcony on a rope and tackle that magically appeared from above Cleopatra's head only a few doubtful seconds after she had beckoned it to do so. Antony was helped on to a sling contraption unhappily reminiscent of the little machines for weighing babies that one used to see in old-fashioned chemists' shops and the long haul began – to the uncontrollable mirth of the audience. What made it so funny is difficult to say: perhaps it was our knowledge that the energetic pulling was being done, not by women, but by three strapping chaps – and the messenger knew all about Cleopatra's muscularity from the heavy body punch he had received for bringing bad news; perhaps it was the unfortunate hint of an interrogative with which Cleopatra said 'How heavy weighs my lord'; perhaps it was our sense that the balcony looked terribly full and here was this large horizontal addition rapidly approaching; perhaps it was the sexual possessiveness with which Cleopatra grabbed him on arrival and the apprehensiveness of his response: 'I *am* dying, Egypt.' Whatever it was, it goes down in the annals of the art of coarse acting as one of the great examples of its kind.

For the last sequence of the play Cleopatra appeared wigless, little tufts of hair sticking out here and there on a bald and scabby scalp, the gaudy dresses replaced by a white shift that looked like a hospital gown, as if the femininity that had earlier been so ostentatiously performed were now being dismantled. And after all the restless scamperings of the first half, she sat stock-still on a low, flat, golden throne. Here she received Dolabella, and Caesar, and the clown presenting his asps in a splendidly disconcerting hill-billy accent; and here she died, in robe and crown, sitting rigidly upright, to be carried from the stage at the play's end like a statue in a religious procession (her version, perhaps, of a Roman triumph), Caesar in his posh little hat fussily superintending. In a production that really had nothing at all to tell us about anything else in the play and that seemed often to be reciting the text rather than exploring it, Rylance's Cleopatra was undoubtedly worth seeing.

From quite a different direction, authentic Elizabethanism nowhere in sight, Steven Pimlott made his attempt on the difficulties of

Antony and Cleopatra at the Royal Shakespeare Theatre at Stratford. The most obvious contrast between the two productions was Pimlott's much more inclusive sense of the play's complexity. 'How does a director go about trying to strike the right note, the right tone', for a production of *Antony and Cleopatra*, he was asked in an interview for the RSC magazine (Number 18, Summer 1999, pp. 12–13). 'I think it's important not to try', was his reply, 'for the play doesn't allow it. It is defined by ambiguity, always defying expectations.' Not surprisingly, the resultant production, designed by Yolanda Sonnabend and much more eclectic than the Globe's, inevitably less clearly focused and in many ways less approachable, was in the end rather more interesting than the Bankside version.

Costumes hinted at several periods: there was armour for Antony, but his soldiers looked more likely to fight a twentieth-century war; Cleopatra's court, with cocktails and cigarettes, had a look (and sound) of the 1920s, whereas the Romans, in their austerely-cut, dark grey coats, seemed vaguely eighteenth-century; and Cleopatra's remarkable array of often very revealing gowns defied dating. The set presented a selection of oddly contrasted objects – a suspended sail, a broken classical pillar, various geometric shapes, military kit of several periods – but was dominated by three huge screens, sometimes transparent, sometimes reflective from their different angles. One was never in doubt that the central characters were on show, the observed of all observers, including themselves. It was, no doubt, from that sense of presenting a performance that the production's most controversial characteristic derived, the convention that when a character died the actor who had been playing him or her should simply walk from the stage. The conventions that they should remove themselves less visibly, in a blackout (however imperfect), or that other actors should carry them from the stage, are so much more familiar that there was much unease with this; in the end its usefulness in emphasizing the play's self-conscious theatricality was probably outweighed by the confusion it caused, particularly since the play's first death is Enobarbus', which is puzzling enough anyway for spectators unfamiliar with the piece. The choice had its compensations, however, most obviously in the poignant moment when Cleopatra tried to detain Antony, at his death-exit, toppling over in her effort to grab his hand as, in a heavy, shambling walk, he moved inexorably and for ever from her; and again, at the end, when the silence following Cleopatra's death was shattered by the braying of Caesar's brass band, and in he came, borne aloft on a golden chair, to find on the bare stage merely a forsaken golden cloak and an empty armour, like chrysalises after the butterflies have flown: this it was to conquer the world.

From the moment the production opened, with the initial duologue turned into a solo chorus and the assembled Egyptian court behind its speaker parting on 'Behold and see' to reveal Antony, head down, pleasuring Cleopatra, we were never in doubt of his thraldom, or of the fact that breaking the 'strong Egyptian fetters' was something that would never happen. Alan Bates's Antony was every inch a has-been, aware that he would inevitably be defeated, that this love-affair was his last – a hopeless prospect as ruler of the world. There was, though, a lingering charisma about him, the after-glow of a glamorous past, and the grizzled, tousled hair on the great head, the lumbering walk, the constant cup of wine, the little shrugs and snorts and wry laughs as defeat moved ever closer, had a kind of grand, grim pathos about them. He knew he was only performing (in front of her, and of the mirrors) as he pretended to be the tragic hero fighting his way back.

There was much of pathos, too, about Frances de la Tour's Cleopatra, an immensely courageous performance that presented a middle-aged woman desperately trying to hang on to her lover, her girlishness a transparent pretence, every costume she was in danger of falling out of worn in the hope of looking younger. There was about this Cleopatra's self-awareness something extraordinary: 'Cut my lace', she said, falling, and then, 'I am quickly ill and well', all in one breath, and in one movement too, down and up again. She was funny, ironic, unpredictable, physically uninhibited and emotionally stormy – and she was also, as many of the reviewers solemnly pointed out, very unregal until her final scene (though none of them specified which scenes, before the last, are those in which regality is to be demonstrated). What was more of a risk, perhaps, was that she offered the audience little opportunity to *like* her: the laughter was so often at her, sympathy kept at bay by the constant sense that nothing in this self-consciously theatrical personality was what one might safely call 'the real thing'. The connections with, and the differences from, Mark Rylance's exploration of the role's theatricality were instructive: at the Globe one enjoyed watching the skill of the male actor in creating the illusion of femininity and thus throwing light on Cleopatra's own skill in self-presentation – it was the little space between performer and role that was interesting; at Stratford there was no such space and the skill of the female actor was used to create an inveterately, overwhelmingly histrionic human being. There was something rawly embarrassing about the needy, desperate, manipulative woman that Frances de la Tour presented, and about her slightly absurd, slightly grotesque, passion for Antony. With the embarrassment, however, sympathy and pity were always mingled, and two moments in particular seemed to encapsulate the essential humanity of what she was presenting. After the defeat at Actium, and 'Fall not a tear, I say . . .', Antony struggled to his feet to make a shambling exit. She jumped onto his stooping back, her feet dragging on the floor in a hopeless failure of a piggy-back, that pathetic image of helpless ruined inter-dependence the one we took with us to the interval pick-me-up. And near the end, in the monument (to which

Antony's ascent had been mimed at stage level, a cop-out if ever there was one, but one way of avoiding the hilarities of the Globe version), as Antony sat with his usual cup of wine, the life slipping from him, she clambered awkwardly onto his lap, big bare feet flapping, desperately seeking solace like some overgrown child, before he made his exit for the dark. It was *so* undignified – which is part of the reason why it was so moving.

The dignity was found, of course, in death, but to the last the production insisted on the sense of performance. Wig-less (the production opened before the Globe's, so any influence had moved in a southerly direction), make-up-less, wearing something between a dressing gown and a monk's habit, her ashen face made to look two hundred years old through defeat and grief, Cleopatra moved, via a strangely beautiful ritual of anointing her attendants' necks, to the final performance: slowly and ritualistically she applied ghostly white make-up to her face and painted her eye-lids, then her servants dressed her in golden cope and splendid oriental crown. This was the appearance the reviewers had expected all along, and we watched it being created as we would in an actor's dressing-room. The performance over, Caesar was left to take possession of the costume, the breast we had for so long expected to reveal itself only doing so as she made the last, post mortem, exit.

It was a disturbing performance in a disturbing and uncomfortable, but never uninteresting, production of a difficult play. There were excellent performances, also, in the two main roles beyond the principals. Guy Henry brought to Octavius Caesar an admiration for Antony that was touching in its sense of lingering boyhood hero-worship, but, in their first encounter in Rome, watchful in its contained stillness and so winning all the political points from Antony's bluster. The scene was staged as a dinner party, successfully encapsulating all the awkward formality of the occasion. Control was again to the fore on Pompey's

barge, a control that he just about managed to hang on to when all about him were losing theirs, along with their trousers. There was nothing pretended about his love for his sister, or about his anger at her rejection by Antony, and this gave him a perfectly believable journey, via the hardening of his terms for Antony's surrender, to threatening Cleopatra's children if she failed to comply. But at the end, in the glimpse of his grief at his own victory, there remained a hint of the less experienced politician who began the play. 'The time of universal peace is near', and a good thing too, the production allowed us to feel, but something had had to be sacrificed to get there.

Among the sacrificial victims, of course, is Enobarbus, here presented in a remarkably impressive performance by Malcolm Storry. This wasn't the usual hard-bitten old soldier, but a man who loved Antony profoundly even as he despaired of his dwindling judgement, a choric figure foreseeing the end but powerless to prevent it, his defection as inevitable as self-destructive, his death scene a disturbing spectacle as his pounding *mea-culpa* fist seemed almost to beat the breath out of his lungs. The production thus offered us, in the very directness and straightforwardness of Storry's speaking, in the hard-edgedness, even, of his voice, an alternative emotional centre to the piece, a lover of Antony who might have led him in a different direction, but ended, instead, dead in a ditch among the troops of his enemies. What a complex play this is – and how successful this production was in compounding those complexities.

Following *Antony and Cleopatra* onto Stratford's main stage, the first time it had been seen there since 1965 (there was an Other Place version in 1980), was *Timon of Athens* in a production by Gregory Doran, designed by Stephen Brimson Lewis, with Michael Pennington in the title role. The production used a 1960s Duke Ellington score for the play and its late-night, slightly sleazy style provided an appropriately satiric mood for the rather decadent, superficial world presented in the first half of the play. Set and costumes looked vaguely seventeenth-century, sometimes more Restoration than Jacobean, but later elements were superimposed: there was something rather Dickensian about the splendid scene of the creditors milling round Timon's door; a massage-parlour was the setting for one of Timon's servants' appeals for funds; and Timon's dinner party presented the masque of Amazons as a high-camp drag show, with Apemantus, in dark glasses, addressing his acerbic commentary into a microphone, so that it, too, perhaps a little unfortunately, became just another sham performance. For the second half the stage was cleared all the way to the stunningly toplit bare brick back-wall of the theatre, with Timon down-stage centre in a hole in the floor that was cave, and gold-mine, and grave all at once – a splendidly impressive stage image.

A directorial intervention in the first half had one of the followers of Alcibiades take a particular fancy to one of the dancers in the masque of Amazons; we saw him rebuffed, then drawing a dagger as he followed his fancy from the stage; he reappeared a little later as the soldier for whose life Alcibiades pleads before the Athenian Senate. It is one of the problems of *Timon of Athens* that the role of Alcibiades is so fragmentary. Rupert Penry-Jones brought a dashing glamour to the part (though he was vocally disappointing until provided with a microphone into which to shout his orders in the final assault on the city); to have him plead for a man who has killed another for rejecting his sexual advances and to describe it as 'noble fury and fair spirit, / Seeing his reputation touched' seemed to me not only a little far-fetched, but positively counter-productive in providing what the play so obviously needs, a little more justification for Timon's commitment to the cause of Alcibiades. One also wondered about that drag-show cabaret: if the masque is indeed Timon's 'own device' might it not have been worth exploring the idea of his

sexual preference a little further? A closet desire to buy male companionship might be a way of exploring Timon's hopeless failures of judgement in choosing 'friends'. But the idea simply came and went. I was uncertain, too, about Richard McCabe's rather 'hip' Apemantus. Whether or not we are to take the Folio's 'churlish philosopher' exactly at face value, the part seems to deserve a little more weight than it here received: the shades and microphone of the first half became shades, straw hat, beach-towel, and sun-tan oil for the visit to Timon in exile, which rather robbed him of *gravitas*, though perhaps there is something to be said for the idea of Apemantus as a sort of day-tripper misogynist who really belongs in the city he pretends to despise. The supporting role that worked brilliantly was John Woodvine's Flavius, all quiet decency and dogged devotion. The final image of him standing, head bowed, after reading Timon's tombstone inscription (a textual change from the unnamed soldier, giving Flavius' role an ending though depriving Timon of the anonymity he craves), with Alcibiades astride the stage on a sort of flying bridge and Apemantus watching from his usual oblique angle, was very fine.

But after all it was for Michael Pennington's Timon that the production mattered. In the first half he showed him with an almost desperate need for companionship, an ostentatious bonhomie, and a craving for sycophantic thanks. He glowed and simpered at the little rounds of applause that his generosity provoked, like some minor monarch distributing favours and basking in the gratitude. There was something a little narcissistic about it all, something excessive, and also something oddly distancing, his gifts, perhaps deliberately, creating a space between himself and their recipients, so that the excesses, and the isolation, of the second half seemed to follow on believably from what we had seen in the first: it was not hard to suppose that such a man could flip in this way. His speaking of the great curse on Athens that ended the first half was masterly. As

6 *Timon of Athens*, directed by Gregory Doran for the Royal Shakespeare Company. Michael Pennington as Timon, Richard McCabe as Apemantus. Act 4, Scene 3.

he stood by a skeletal representation of the city's walls one watched, and heard, the character discover the power of language, every word made to count, every phrase, apparently effortlessly, sent zinging round the theatre, the great swooping rhythms ridden with tremendous power, the words, perfectly believably, metamorphosing into shrieks and howls at moments of unsuppressible emotion. It was the command of vocal variety that carried him through what could easily be the monotony of the sequence of accursed visitors to his downstage pit in the second half. The clarity, energy, and grace of his speaking as he stood there

naked but for a loin-cloth was at its most impressive in his epitaph upon himself, its sense of weary peace and willing letting-go, its poignant simplicity, making it hauntingly moving. The big two-hander with Apemantus was sizzling with verbal energy, the strange phrases they come up with seeming new-minted: 'the bleak air, thy boisterous chamberlain', 'the cold brook, candied with ice', 'women nearest, *men* are the things themselves'; and that extraordinary sequence 'if thou wert the lion the fox would beguile thee', which might easily be read as merely sardonic and contemptuous, had a sort of wistful sweetness about it that was a revelation. It was a joy to hear again in Stratford the intelligence, the variety, and the power of Michael Pennington's speaking of Shakespearian verse.

The year offered significant productions of three of what used to be called the 'major' tragedies, a *Hamlet* at the Young Vic, a *Macbeth* in the West End (a rare event indeed), and a long-overdue *Othello* at Stratford. (And as this essay goes to press there is a positive troop of *King Lear*s for the inheritor of this column to assess.) Laurence Boswell's *Hamlet*, a co-production of the Theatre Royal, Plymouth, and the Young Vic, presented a very full text, spoken with immense clarity and intelligence, on a plain black wooden traverse set designed by Es Devlin, lit with a merciless starkness. The raised platforms at either end could be joined by retractable wooden planking but were most effective in presenting the isolation, separation, or mutual hostilities of the play: Hamlet at one end staring in pained silence at Claudius and Gertrude at the other; Hamlet disbelievingly contemplating Fortinbras as he prepared his troops for Poland; Hamlet gazing yearningly at Ophelia across the unbridgeable gulf. Costumes were eclectic, medieval-looking cloaks covering Victorian style waistcoats, Hamlet and Horatio dressed indistinguishably from many a present-day student, the rapiers of the final duel replacing the pistol with which, from one platform to the other, Hamlet had threatened the praying Claudius and with which he had shot Polonius; and with it all, occasional touches of the Japanese, the Ghost (doubled, by Donald Sumpter, with Claudius) looking like a Samurai warrior, and miniature statue versions of him lining the stage like chessmen in the second half, as if in representation of the approach of the play's other armed warrior Fortinbras. The production was conspicuously well paced, its four hours never seeming to hang heavy, the sense of building to the great explosion of energy at the end inexorable. It was a remarkably well directed event.

It was extremely well acted too. Donald Sumpter's Claudius, grim and self-knowing, racked by conscience, brooding and rueful, seemed to have built his performance from the prayer scene outwards, so that his tears as he fled from the performance of 'The Murder of Gonzago' were perfectly believable and his final, frightened isolation – Gertrude would have nothing to do with him after the closet scene – strangely pitiable. Not that he was in any sense an unworthy opponent for Hamlet: his weary blink as he listened to all the stuff about man and wife being one flesh encapsulated a frightening mixture of boredom with this tiresome boy and ruthless determination to deal with him. Suzanne Bertish charted an emotional journey through the role of Gertrude that gave it remarkable poignancy and gradually increasing depth, moving from the hard-edged superficiality, butchness even, of her first scene, caked in make-up and dripping with pearls, through the growing willingness to confess to herself what she knew but wouldn't know (a willingness much increased by her shock at the idea of 'loosing' Ophelia to Hamlet), to increasingly painful isolation in awareness of her own contamination, and then to complete collapse in the closet scene, filled with disgust for herself and tenderness for her son, clutching her crucifix, her absolute separation from Claudius ending in the defiance with which, fully aware of the consequences, she drank from the cup he had poisoned. There was a blond and unstoppable Fortinbras from Todd Boyce, a nauseating creep of a Rosencrantz from Leo Wringer, a frighteningly self-assured, hard, wily Polonius from Robin Soans, a stubble-chinned epitome of gentle dependability from Richard Lintern as Horatio, and a clever attempt at Ophelia from Megan Dodds, seemingly imperturbable with her poised, china-doll beauty and Sloany voice, desperately hanging on to her dignity even after the nunnery scene, until her father's death destroyed the front utterly and the weeping started and couldn't be stopped and the elegant self-presentation was replaced by public degradation, clothes awry and indecent, shame absolute.

7 *Hamlet*, directed by Laurence Boswell for Plymouth Theatre Royal and the Young Vic. Paul Rhys as Hamlet. Act 2, Scene 2

Dominating the production was Paul Rhys's impressively moving Hamlet, his first Shakespearian role since his splendid Edgar (another feigner of madness) at the National Theatre in 1997 (see *Survey 51* (1998), 251). This was a Hamlet who moved from initial extreme imbalance, through increasing self-control, to a final calm detachment. When we first met him it seemed clear that the intense grief of bereavement had unhinged his mind and that breakdown was imminent; his eyes were red with weeping, his attempt, in the glare of the court scene, to keep back more tears, failed utterly, his voice cracked with suppressed sobs, the little flicker of a smile, the anxious twitchiness, the wide-eyed vulnerability, all making it painfully

clear that here was a young man utterly incapable of taking on the task the Ghost would assign him. He was totally out of control in the 'Remember thee' soliloquy and hopelessly groggy as Horatio and the rest swore their oaths of secrecy. But the experiences of the play hardened him. He appeared (strongly reminiscent of Mark Rylance at Stratford) in stained tee shirt and pyjama trousers through the middle scenes of the play, slowly learning the court arts of mistrust and self-preservation in the verbal contests with Polonius, Rosencrantz and Guildenstern (he hadn't the least idea which was which), and Claudius, that wan little smile of shy diffidence gradually taking on a watchful knowingness. On his return from England there was a new sense of calm resignation about him, a quiet curiosity in his examination of Yorick's skull, a certainty about his challenge to Laertes, a sort of boyish sweetness in the way he sat naked in his bath-tub – washing away the past, perhaps – scrubbing his nails (and Yorick's skull) and smiling ruefully in the awareness that the readiness is all. He died after an elegant and chivalrous fight with Laertes, sitting at last, for his final few seconds, on his father's throne, cradling his dead mother in his arms. No actor of Hamlet will ever get all that the role offers. There was little of the fiery, the frenzied, the destructive in what Rhys presented and at times he flirted with the sentimental, the lost boy in Elsinore. His speaking was always imaginative and intelligent, but there was something occasionally a little mannered about the elongation of vowels, slightly precious in the studied gracefulness of diction, and one missed a deeper register in the vocal shading. But there was so much more to admire than to cavil over: the vulnerability, the pain, the isolation, the nearness to tears, the desperate struggle to think it through, to be honest to himself, to find a route to letting be, were all movingly explored in this impressive performance.

Another young actor with a growing reputation who tackled a major Shakespearian tragic role this year was Rufus Sewell. Sadly his attempt on Macbeth fared rather less well than Rhys's on Hamlet. The production was directed by John Crowley and played for several weeks at the Queen's Theatre through the spring – the first *Macbeth* on Shaftesbury Avenue for many a year. That a relatively inexperienced director, and (in Shakespearian terms) a very inexperienced actor, should make so prominent a début with so difficult a play was obviously a risk; the result was a disappointment, though, almost by default, considerably more interesting than the disaster that many reviewers adjudged it to be. The production's most conspicuous, and damaging, feature was an apparently deliberate avoidance of any sense of the supernatural. The abstract set (by Jeremy Herbert) of red floor and open black box, reducing to a tiny cube for the pre-battle scenes of the second half – a heavy-handed hint to the audience, if ever there was one, that the psychological walls were closing in on the murderer – looked more suitable to studio Shakespeare than to a large West End stage and depended entirely on lighting for any effects that it achieved. Much of that lighting came from the sides, throwing heavy shadows that left many actors in the gloom. The witches were young women in eccentric hats and scruffy coats, nothing in the least 'weird' about them, their cauldron the pool in the floor where Macbeth had washed Duncan's blood from his hands and Macduff's son had been given his nightly bath; they had nothing to tell Macbeth that he didn't already know.

Rufus Sewell's Macbeth, virile and physically powerful, entered from the battle already obsessed, restless, angry; the witches' prophecies merely confirmed his intentions, and the news of Malcolm's elevation to the Principality of Cumberland provoked a snarling fury. Sally Dexter's Lady Macbeth knew her husband's letter by heart, her hand reaching between her legs as she yearned for his return, power through sexual domination ecstatically anticipated. Their scene together was as torrid as this

prelude suggested, his hesitations about the murder countered by her fondlings and unbuttonings, their exit with him hanging on to her hair as blatant an indication as could be of the rough sex upon which the relationship was clearly based. The murder done, her hopes of dominance were shattered; she was utterly astonished and bereft by his dismissal of her in favour of solitude until supper-time, the dress she had been so keen to fall out of replaced thereafter by a severely buttoned-up number, not an inch of skin on view below the chin, her sexuality encased and her hopes of power simultaneously destroyed, to be replaced by a frigid fearfulness and an inclination to seek solace in alcohol. The sleep-walking scene was deliberately bereft of emotion, her hands bandaged as though washed to rawness, her language apt to drift into inarticulate screams. We were, in short, being offered psychological rather than spiritual explanations for the play's central story of disintegration.

Which is why Rufus Sewell's Macbeth never evinced any sense of conflict, there being no struggle between conscience and ambition in this interpretation of the role, for of conscience he had nothing; the movement was brutally straightforward, from anger, to bitterness, to the fierce nihilism and blank, soulless despair of 'Tomorrow, and tomorrow' in one uncomplicated sweep. There were no doubts, or fears, or inward divisions; the lines were barked and shouted in a monotonous, chilling emptiness, and Macbeth immured in Dunsinane kicked the walls of his little box of confinement on 'I have lived long enough' in a fit of futile petulance. So bleak a reading was challenging and disturbing, but hardly tragic, for there was here no sense of potential virtue destroyed (virtue had never come into it), only a fiercely unsentimental study in psychological breakdown. There was outward glamour to the man, a sense of command, of military threat and ability to instil fear, but of depth of soul there was no sense, only the restless fidgeting of a small mind incapable of understanding its

present situation. One could not believe, therefore, that such a being should for so long have
expressed himself with such searing verbal
intensity – and that, in the end, was the fatal
flaw of the production, the gap between the
story it told and the language in which it told it,
for so reductive a reading of the play, however
psychologically plausible, was in conflict with
its very fabric. There were minor consolations:
some interesting 'fades' between scenes, as
when the long-hemmed cloth of the lowered
banquet table precisely hid the newly murdered
corpse of Banquo, which lay there throughout
the scene, a ghost in our minds, as in
Macbeth's; or the move from Macbeth's
vowing a future of bloody thoughts to the kids'
bath-time in the Macduff nursery, the childless
Macbeth for a crucial moment focused on the
son of his future killer as he prattled in the
bath-tub. The always difficult English scene
was illuminated by the terrible glazed-eyed
disbelief with which Declan Conlon's Macduff
tried to absorb the news of the slaughter of all
his little ones, and Peter Bayliss found an
amusing new ventriloquial way of differen-
tiating the Porter's parade of equivocators. But,
overall, the production was a disappointment, a
theatrically and spiritually reductive account of
a complex play.

Last on my tragic list was Michael Attenbor-
ough's début production on Stratford's main
stage with the RSC's first *Othello* since Trevor
Nunn's Other Place version ten years ago. It
was set, with designs by Robert Jones that
evinced much care for social realism, just
before the First War. From the misty darkness
of the opening scene, lamplight shafting
through shutters, we moved to the Senate, all
winged collars and leather chairs, and a big
golden globe showing the Empire, Othello on
the far side of it from the senators, so that he
spoke to them from the other side of the
world. Cyprus was a colonial outpost, soldiers
in scarlet tunics, women in muslin dresses,
indoor scenes created by lowering a canvas
tent wall, the herald scene a military briefing

followed by fireworks, and the brawl an officers' mess party with noisy upper-class voices
getting rowdier in a way that led inexorably to
de-bagging, and the posh young Cassio (a fine
evocation of upper-class haughtiness from
Henry Ian Cusick) smashing the high jinks as
they went too far: 'I hold him to be unworthy
of his place that does those things'. It was a
world with the strictest sense of hierarchies, in
the Senate and in the army, a world in which
the ram-rod-straight, crisply-saluting figure of
Richard McCabe's Iago knew his NCO's place
precisely, just as, with his careless sense of
superiority, Cassio knew his – 'for the lieute-
nant must be saved before the ensign', a
remark that produced a flash of the most
terrible loathing on Iago's face, replaced in a
second by the usual chirpy, phoney façade.

Given this world of recognizable social coherence Richard McCabe's meticulously
thought out, and executed, Iago necessarily had
to be psychologically explicable. He loathed
Cassio for being posh when he wasn't – 'there
is a daily beauty in his life' – for feeling that his
social superiority gave him the right to kiss
other men's wives – ''tis my breeding that gives
me this bold show of courtesy' – for believing,
unquestioningly, that he should be saved before
the ensign. Iago also seemed genuinely to
believe that Othello had cuckolded him: the
idea of getting 'even with him, wife for wife'
had a gruesome intensity. There was, too,
something horribly withered about Iago's sexuality that made him cringe from contact with
his wife – who thought, forlornly, that she
might get the kiss she craved when she found
the handkerchief, and got only the merest peck
before he disgustedly froze her out again. He
came closest to sexual excitement in the pact
with Othello: 'I am your own, for ever', was
uttered with a terrible triumph about the word
'ever'. The podgy face, the greased-down hair,
the dead eyes behind the smiley, bustling
manner, the chummy jokiness with which he
checked the adhesive qualities of the false
moustache sported by Aidan McArdle's dim,

dapper little Roderigo, the ever-so-jolly playing on the accordion at the mess-room party, but always the psychotic drive towards destruction of what he envied so ferociously – it all evinced the immense care that had been taken to create a believable human being. Only once, and deliberately outside the frame of the play, did we see him as a figure beyond psychological explanation, as a creature of that 'hell and black night' to which he once refers: at the end of the play, the stage cleared of everyone left alive, he was led off under guard, and, just as we thought we had seen the last of him, he turned, flanked by his guards, to gaze, blankly, expressionlessly (it might have been triumph, it might have been remorse, it might just have been disinterest), at the tragic loading of the bed. There, if one wished, one might have thought of him as some evil force beyond the human; but within the play itself this was a real man in a real world, his malignity far from motiveless.

Ray Fearon's Othello did not tell us that he was 'declined into the vale of years', and he wasn't, as many reviewers were so eager to point out. (He was, indeed, probably much about the age of Burbage when Shakespeare wrote the part for him.) A serious age difference between Desdemona and Othello undoubtedly adds an extra dimension to the cultural barriers that the couple have overcome before the play starts and one may regret its absence, but in no sense did it seriously inhibit the impact of the production, which left us in no doubt of the intensity of the lovers' relationship. There was a lot of innocent uninhibitedness about it, so that he seemed at times hardly able to let her go, their yearning physical desire watched embarrassedly by members of the Cyprus regiment and readily exploitable by Iago. Fearon looked splendid, his magnificent physique singling him out from his fellow-soldiers and contrasting strikingly with the corpulence of Iago, and he brought an easy, exotic dignity to the Senate scene, with his shining shaven head and glinting ear-ring, his kaftan-like shirt (generals-only-

for-the-use-of) contrasting with standard regimental trousers. 'Her father loved me', he said, 'oft invited me', and his gaze at Brabantio was accusatory and full of pain at being spurned. There have undoubtedly been Othellos with a fuller vocal range in the lower registers, but of Fearon's taking possession of the language, particularly in the later stages, and feeling the pain of his loss of control over it, there was no doubt. He also demonstrated a tremendous capacity for anger, an anger spilling over into violence: from the furious entry to stop the brawl, to an astounding episode in which he nearly drowned Iago in a zinc washing bowl as he demanded proof of his suspicions, to the ferocious blow in the face he gave to Desdemona before Lodovico, to the savage flinging of the coins in the brothel scene, to the manic strangling, was a progression of horrible believability.

He was much helped by the strength of Zoë Waites' Desdemona, a proud, strong-minded young woman in her smart Mrs Pankhurst suits, perfectly capable of the 'downright violence' of the decision she had made, as uninhibited in her physical desire for him as he for her. Some Desdemonas have seemed more vulnerable, but the great benefit of this interpretation was to present the relationship between Othello and Desdemona as absolutely reciprocal and fully self-aware, its destruction a terrible undertaking. To the role of Emilia, Rachel Joyce, too, brought some of that proto-feminist strength and independence, her clear-sighted – half-resigned, half-resentful – analysis, in the willow-song scene, of marital relations, particularly, though hardly exclusively, from the perspective of the lonely army wife, was one of the most vivid sequences in the play. She shouted too much in the final scene, but the moment of dawning revelation of the truth about the husband for whose love she has yearned, the revelation that allows her to sum up the play in one devastating line, was stark in its fierce simplicity: 'You told a lie, an odious, damnèd lie.'

I turn now to two versions of *Troilus and Cressida* that opened within a few weeks of each other in the winter and early spring. Trevor Nunn's lavish production at the Olivier Theatre in March, with a cast of forty actors, was the first with his new National Theatre ensemble, a company brought together for six productions in twelve months, two of them of plays by Shakespeare (the other was *The Merchant of Venice*, of which more towards the end of this essay). Rob Howell's bold and highly effective design presented a circular arena of a stage, a sort of bull-ring, its floor blood-red gravel; a curved wall behind, broken by six wide doors, with a cyclorama of sky above, serene blue or threatening red according to the lighting, represented the walls of Troy. Entrances were frequently by way of the long aisles of the auditorium, as well as the rear-stage doors, the combatants in the battles, physical and rhetorical, erupting into their performing arena. The Trojans wore loose robes in gleaming white, reminiscent of North African tribesmen, and went in a lot for bowls of flame standing on tripods for scenes of return from battle or meetings of the royal council; the Greeks, apart from the non-combatant Achilles and Patroclus, who were in loose kaftans, wore battered leather jackets. We were not exactly in the Ancient World, but these were very much swords-and-shields armies. With the exception of David Bamber's Pandarus, all the Trojans were played by black actors; the Greeks were all white. The total abandonment of the by-now well-established, and surely right, principle of blind casting was a surprise. The other controversial element of the production was that the actors wore microphones, the director defending the decision on the grounds that it was the only way to deal with the acoustic problems of the Olivier auditorium. They made possible the very particular staging of the overhearing scene (5.2) and were for the most part unobtrusive, but the odd moments of echo effect when actors were close to the walls, or particularly close to each other, were not a pleasant experience.

The evening began and ended with Sophie Okonedo's Cressida, much textual adjustment, obviously, being needed to achieve this. We began with Act 1, scene 2, an astute, witty, worldly Cressida, in close-fitting, low-cut white dress, and David Bamber's hand-flapping, mincing, dressing-gowned old queen of a Pandarus, with his red fez and little fly-whisk, watching the Trojan warriors return from battle down the long central aisle of the stalls. Uncle and niece were clearly both much excited by the sight of so much male flesh. Having played the text's second scene first, the third scene (the Greek council) was then played second, which meant that we had met the leaders of both sides in turn right at the top of the play; we then had the first scene and, with a few minor adjustments, the rest of the play followed in the usual order until the ending, which had Pandarus coming on accompanied by Cressida, her face smeared with lip-stick, to Peter de Jersey's Troilus, whose 'Hope of revenge' speech had just been delivered with a chilling ferocity and bleakness. His 'Ignominy and shame / Pursue thy life' was then spoken, savagely and witheringly, to both of them. Thersites then entered to return Cressida's glove and to sneer about 'wars and lechery', before Pandarus, whose obviously terminal coughing had started when Cressida left for the Greek camp, croaked and wheezed through his gloomy envoi. The play ended with us left alone with Cressida, lost and bewildered, circling helplessly in the growing darkness as the distant sound of gunfire was heard. Other wars, other spoils of war, other victims of male possessiveness and brutality, were encapsulated in that forlorn and desolate figure.

To make Cressida the play's central tragic victim required not only textual adjustment at either end of the piece, but also very particular readings of intermediate scenes. She began in energetic eagerness, much more intelligent than Troilus realized, very well aware of her blooming sexuality. She was smiling and excited in the confession of love and the vows,

8 *Troilus and Cressida*, directed by Trevor Nunn for the Royal National Theatre. Dhobi Oparei as Hector, Raymond Coulthard as Achilles. Act 5, Scene 6.

played without any sense of irony, had much of marriage about them, with the lovers kneeling and Pandarus, now in a garment that might have been mistaken for a cassock, joining their hands. At the news of the prisoner exchange she seemed inconsolable, aghast at Troilus' failure to protect her: 'O heavens, you love me not'. Her arrival at the Greek camp, a solitary black girl surrounded by threatening white men, had something of gang rape about it, with Agamemnon's enforced kiss beginning a disturbing sequence in which she was mauled by one of them after another before finding the presence of mind to mock Menelaus and then, to his fury, offering Ulysses her foot to kiss. She then managed to keep her end up in a rhythmic clapping dance in which she was flung from one to another before making an exhausted exit

on Diomed's arm. In the overhearing scene she gave in to Diomed unwillingly, resignedly, disgustedly almost, aware that moral self-destruction was the price of physical survival, her anguish undetected by the watching Troilus. Her journey from the vitality and delight of the opening, through spirited resistance and shocked acquiescence, to the misery of that final icon of abused womanhood, was at the heart of the production's intentions and very impressively presented; the extent to which interpretation had drifted towards adaptation in order to present it may be left for another occasion.

There were interesting performances throughout the production. Peter de Jersey's Troilus combined possessive romantic ardour with self-pity and intellectual perception way below the level of Cressida's, a mixture that clearly doomed the relationship from the start and made his journey one of tragic self-discovery, like hers. Dhobi Oparei was a chivalrous giant of a Hector who, somewhat naively, found himself swept up into an erotic dance with Achilles on his visit to the Greek camp, the second Trojan in the scene to find the Greeks in disconcerting dancing mood. There was a self-preening, indolent, dangerous Achilles, in pony-tail and eye-liner, from Raymond Coulthard, shockingly brutal in his murder of Hector, and a smarming Patroclus, tense and alert, from Daniel Evans. Oscar James's white-bearded Priam presided over the Trojan council scene like some Old Testament prophet, his sons having to raise their hands like schoolchildren before they were allowed to speak. The camp hand-waftings and simpering affectations of accent of David Bamber's Pandarus ('Tro-i-lus', he said, trisyllabically, all the time, alone in the play) were a front for an astute intelligence and an obsession with bringing his niece and Troilus together in order to feed his desire for the prince. Dennis Quilley made Nestor an immensely sympathetic old boy, apt to get too emotional in his memories. Jasper Britton's Thersites, wafting in and out of the play with flapping sleeves and bald, sore-encrusted head, rather reminiscent of a vulture (especially when he plundered the corpse of Patroclus), was harsher and less funny than some recent performances of the role, which gave the whole piece a much more gloomy and bitter feel. Most impressive of all was Roger Allam's Ulysses, in superb command of the verse, building the long speeches with a musician's precision, feeling the nuances of the language, marking the crescendos with unerring accuracy, occasionally using a hand gesture to explain a difficult image, or a lengthened pause to point up an important idea: 'Time . . . [pause]. . . hath, my lord'. The incisive intelligence of Ulysses was never in doubt, nor were the disgust at the failure to end the war, the brilliantly funny irony at the expense of Ajax,

the astuteness, the intellectual detachment from his fellow commanders, the sense of futility, the driving will to succeed.

The pace of the long production never slackened, scene after scene, many of them involving large numbers of actors, precisely choreographed. The Helen scene was suitably decadent, with a hookah pipe passed among the participants and much hip-wiggling from the lady (a spoil of war who luxuriated in her status, as Cressida was devastated by hers), and the overhearing scene was ingeniously staged using the whole width of the theatre, Troilus and Ulysses stage right behind the side stalls and Thersites in a similar position stage left, the sense that the audience itself was implicated in the eavesdropping made possible by the use of microphones for the watchers' whispered asides. This was a big production, impressive in its sweep and in its focus, a well oiled machine with a big score, not just of atmospheric music but of dogs barking (at one point with eerie effect, as Hector referred to the 'old common arbitrator, Time'), rooks cawing, ignorant armies clashing. It was determined to make the big Olivier space work for Shakespeare, and it did.

If Trevor Nunn's production of *Troilus and Cressida* went some way in the direction of adaptation, Michael Boyd's version for the RSC, which had opened at the Pit at the end of 1998 and was later seen in Stratford and on tour, went much further. Designed by Tom Piper, its set presented a war-ravaged interior with bullet-pocked walls, a broken stained-glass window and a statue of the Virgin Mary to one side. We were in a twentieth-century war, and a civil war too, though whether in Spain, or Bosnia, or Ireland one was probably not intended to be certain. Costumes were mid twentieth century, the Greeks all in skimped, off-the-peg grey suits, Priam in ill-fitting brown, his sons in battle-worn shirts and corduroys, except for Helenus, who appeared in dog-collar and bandolero. The women wore cotton print dresses of unbecoming design,

Cressida's in dowdy brown with a crucifix necklace at its open collar. With the exception of Thersites, who was from Ulster, the Greeks all spoke with English accents and the Trojans with Irish. The Trojan council was a family meal at a plain wooden table, Priam at one end and Hecuba at the other, Andromache and Cassandra present throughout; the Greek council was a public debate, with a microphone for the speaker. The lords of the *Iliad* and of the tales of chivalry had become peasants and civil servants fighting a savage civil war, with pistols and rifles – though about quite what it was not easy to tell.

Textual adjustments were fewer verbally than at the National, but more far-reaching in substance. The roles of Nestor and Menelaus were combined, perhaps forgivably in a touring production, but an uneasy mixture, even so, of Nestor's astuteness and Menelaus' lack of it. There were no Myrmidons, the necessary touring economy most curiously explained by presenting an Achilles with a leaning to voodoo, sprinkling chicken's blood around the stage and calling on the Myrmidons in the sky for assistance with his bloody purposes against Hector, whose heart he cut out after gunning him down. The death of Patroclus that provoked him to those bloody purposes was a mimed assassination, one pistol shot, by Diomed, organized by Ulysses, their final card in the attempt to bring Achilles back into the fray. Patroclus had been played by Elaine Pyke, a slender, girlish figure in a young man's suit, giving an extra twist of the unconventional to the sexuality of the relationship. And, as at the National, the ending was much reorganized: as guns blazed on the stage in the final battle sequence and shells were heard exploding off it, Helen appeared being used as a body-shield by Paris; Cassandra prayed and Paris wept over the corpse of Hector; and, at the end, on came Cressida too, a perhaps imagined figure standing behind Troilus as he intoned, over and over again, in a vengeful frenzy, 'I reck not though I end my life today', Pandarus' epilogue

having been given earlier, in the letter scene. A beginning and an ending with Troilus, moving from reluctant fighter and adoring lover to mad, suicidal killer, thus balanced the National's beginning and ending with Cressida and her transformation.

It was an odd, quirky production, short on respect for the text and perhaps a little long on bright ideas, but curiously watchable and exciting, with some fine performances. There was a dangerous intensity about William Houston's Troilus, an eager, raw openness that was clearly desperately vulnerable. Jayne Ashbourne's plump, round-faced Cressida, cheerful, naive, and spontaneous, yearning for physical affection, was destroyed by the transfer to the Greek camp, the 'kissing in general' again a sort of gang rape (the production preceded Trevor Nunn's), with a sinisterly orgiastic tango dance whose steps she had quickly to master or be destroyed, a drum beating all the time at the back of the auditorium to implicate us. She seemed to be in a zombie-like state as she gave in to Diomed, the stage divided between watchers and watched by a track of light at the end of which stood Calchas, her father-pimp; and for her unscripted appearance at the end of the play she was apparently unconscious. Roy Hanlon's Pandarus, in crumpled white linen suit, a distinctly passé dandy but with a hint of surviving raffishness for all his present melancholy, was very much the romantic at heart, delighted at bringing the lovers together and absolutely shattered by the defeat of his plans. Colin Hurley's smooth and dapper little Ulysses had some of the qualities of a character in a spy novel, quiet and unobtrusive and always one move ahead, confronting Achilles with compromising photographs of his relationship with Polyxena – 'All the commerce that you have had with Troy / As perfectly is ours as yours' – and organizing the shooting of Patroclus with cold-blooded efficiency. Darrell D'Silva's brutal, tattooed Achilles had the look of a Balkans war-criminal and his fight with Hector was a vicious brawl, with guns drawn by the watchers as tempers frayed. Lloyd Hutchinson's Thersites, a press reporter who presented the Prologue with a slide show of First World War battle scenes – one from the Dardanelles campaign seemed uncannily appropriate for 'In Troy there lies the scene' – haunted the play in battered bowler hat, photographing its most sordid moments and presenting his commentary on them, with all its smutty jokes, in a mock-solemn, and very funny, Ulster accent. The smuttiest joke of all, though, was Helen's, Sara Stewart presenting her posing in the position previously occupied by the statue of the Virgin Mary while hymns were chanted and she evinced enthusiastic signs of sexual pleasure, a state of affairs soon explained by Paris tumbling from under her skirts. Something was even made of the problematic role of Cassandra, Catherine Walker presenting a black-shawled little Irish girl nursing a bundle – one thought at first it was a baby but it turned out to be only rags – speaking her prophecies with a quiet intensity that was so much more effective than the usual screaming. All in all it was a curious evening, but constantly illuminating and thought-provoking.

Which is more than can be said about the first of this year's comedies. Kathryn Hunter was 'Master of Play' for the Globe's *The Comedy of Errors*, Tim Carroll 'Master of Verse', and Liz Cooke 'Master of Design'. The setting was vaguely Turkish, with middle eastern instruments accompanying the action from above, and turbaned men and veiled women peopling the world of Ephesus in a potentially interesting way. There were merchants of all sorts, too, plying their wares between the scenes, but it was the fish merchants who began to give the intentions of the production away, their special line in plastic fish proving irresistible as missiles both on stage and between stage and groundlings. The plastic fish epitomized the project. Doomed to failure before it started by the alluring but always fatal decision to double the Antipholuses and the Dromios, the production sold out, as so much of the Globe's

work seems so sadly to do, to the lowest common denominator of groundling taste. Marcello Magni is undoubtedly a very accomplished mime artist, but as a Shakespearian actor he is not an easy taste to acquire. His pillar climbing, mugging, and audience molesting were in the vein we have experienced earlier at the Globe, but as both Dromios he here had much longer to indulge them. To cast in a role for which the basic requirement is sharpness and dexterity in verbal repartee an actor whose command of spoken English is at best precarious is openly to declare that one's primary interest is not in the play's verbal texture. This was shown at its most blatant in the dialogue (2.2) between Dromio and Antipholus about time and baldness, here spoken with scarcely a word decipherable while, to the screeching delight of the audience, a game of badminton was played. Whatever became of the blue pencil if a director, or even a Master of Play, feels such contempt for a scene? No sense of the mystery of Ephesus ever emerged, and attempts to produce it were limited to such infantile moments as having a group of Ephesians sweeping the stage suddenly freeze in a bending posture holding their brushes out behind them, or the musicians in the gallery appearing in white plastic animal heads, like so many Harveys.

The acting was in the same vein of crudeness, though Robert Pickavance did attempt, in spite of groundling efforts to push in the opposite direction, to offer a serious account of Egeon's griefs and he was supported in the endeavour by Martin Turner's Solinus. Vincenzo Nicoli was not without a certain goofy charm as Antipholus, but it was at best a wooden performance, with no real distinction offered between the brothers. Yolanda Vazquez gave us one of those caricature Adrianas, standing aside from the role, as it were, and guying all its emotional extremes. Jules Melvin (a female actor) began reasonably well as Luciana, but her brother-in-law's love-verses (heavily underscored by the violin as a hint to the audience that this should be taken more solemnly than the rest of the knockabout with which they were being patronized) apparently turned her head, for she took to putting on an antic disposition and smoking a hookah in imitation of the National's Helen of Troy. Any production, certainly any stage production, of *The Comedy of Errors* that doubles the twins must inevitably destroy the play's romance ending (the prototype of *Twelfth Night* and *The Winter's Tale*) by substituting for the audience's wonder at the final miracle mere curiosity as to how the self-imposed problem will be solved. But here, just as we had come to terms with the doppelgangers and felt relief that, at last, the Abbess, at least, had been treated seriously, we had the annihilation of one of the most exquisite exit sequences in Shakespeare. Off went Antipholus and his double, but off, too, went the stand-in Dromio, leaving Magni on stage alone. The Abbess had left a cross behind at her exit and he dressed it in his coat and danced with it a little. 'I see by you I am a sweet-faced youth', he said to his dummy's facelessness and then reached round through the further sleeve of the dummy's coat and began to fondle himself. For the play's final distillment of fraternal reciprocity, of identity through relationship, was substituted this image of self-indulgence, of self-pleasuring, this – but in the fifty-third year of *Survey*'s august history I had better not be the first to use the obvious monosyllable for this swanking piece of vulgarity that provided the perfect finale to the production. The performance I saw was packed, with a long queue for returns, and it was greeted with huge applause, milked to an extent I have rarely witnessed in a series of encored jigs. It was, in every sense, a sell-out.

Two of the romance endings to which a more sensitive production of *The Comedy of Errors* might have looked forward, *Twelfth Night* and *The Winter's Tale*, were both to be seen during the year. Barrie Rutter's production of *Twelfth Night* for his Northern Broadsides company was not, however, particularly strong

on romance. It was played (in designs by Jessica Worrall) in modern dress on a plain stage empty but for two wooden cable-drums, large and rather brutal, that mostly served as tables but also provided platforms for actors to stand on at moments of particular self-display: Olivia trying to vamp Viola, Malvolio in his yellow stockings (*and* cloak) in a posture reminiscent of the paintings of Kemble as Coriolanus, the twins for the oddly matter-of-fact recognition scene, Orsino and Olivia standing between them looking up. The simplicity and directness of the staging was of a piece with the whole enterprise: this was a self-consciously crisp, no-nonsense event, the speaking brisk and to the point, the accents homely (mostly Yorkshire), the refusal ever to take a pause, let alone allow for sub-textual nuance, an article of faith. The result was a production strong on narrative energy but lacking any sense of mystery, of emotional shading, of romance or lyricism – as far as could be imagined from that Chekhovian complexity that some productions find in the play. Julie Livesey's Viola, for example, was a down-to-earth Yorkshire lass who found the unexpected gift of Olivia's ring and the need for Time to untangle the complications that it boded just a huge joke – certainly nothing to be worried or even intrigued about. Andy Wear offered an amiable goof of a Sebastian, quite untouched by the oddness of his Illyrian experience, while the roles of the Sea Captain and Antonio were combined by Kjeld Clark with no exploration at all of the nature of Antonio's emotional commitment to Sebastian. Laurence Evans's Orsino, with similar anxiety to keep things straightforward, began the play (its 'music' a company chorus of 'O Mistress Mine'), not in the usual state of wistful melancholy but in angry frustration at his failure in love.

The production's determination to avoid emotional complexity was matched by its decision to ignore the play's potent awareness of hierarchies. Costumes, like accents, homogenized social distinctions: the lilac décolleté dress

9   *Twelfth Night*, directed by Barrie Rutter for Northern Broadsides. Barrie Rutter as Malvolio. Act 3, Scene 4.

and stiletto-heeled shoes in which Olivia tried to seduce Cesario had obviously come from the same cheap high-street department store as Malvolio's lozenge-patterned pullover and Maria's Bridlington landlady's cardigan. The question 'art any more than a steward' became meaningless in such circumstances and the ambitions of Barrie Rutter's arrogant bully of a Malvolio were merely for power over the hated alcoholic Sir Toby presented by Joshua Richards; there was no sense of an assault on social barriers, for there were none to assault. One saw (or heard) nothing of the normal pathetic pretensions to gentility from this Malvolio and the aggressive dourness of his behaviour in the earlier scenes followed by the sheer absurdity of his yellow stockings (revealed by pulling on strings that hitched up the bottoms of his trousers), along with the removal of any

sense that the play's upper classes were combining to crush an upstart, deprived the scene of Malvolio's incarceration (in a curious hutch-like cage on a hospital trolley) of much of its usual sense of pain and pity. The production, in short, in its laudable search for straightforwardness and vigour, for uncluttered narrative drive, lacked depth. In its respect for the play, and for its language, it was in a completely different league from the cheapness and vulgarity of the Globe's *The Comedy of Errors*, but it, too, missed its play's romance.

Considerably more satisfactory in this regard was Gregory Doran's version of *The Winter's Tale* for the RSC's winter touring season. Robert Jones's set provided a panelled state room with a receding perspective; down the immense length of this, as the production began, ceremonially paraded Antony Sher's King Leontes, portly and bearded, wearing the diamond crown and ermine cape of a middle European monarch of the early twentieth century. The whispering we could hear over the tannoy system derived, it was apparent, not from the numerous court officials and flunkies in their frock coats, brocade waistcoats, and monocles, or from the court ladies in elegant satin and pearls, but, it seemed, from inside Leontes' own head, from his as-yet sub-conscious fear that Sicilia might be a 'so-forth'. He turned at front stage, then, accompanied by Ken Bones's Polixenes, just as formally kingly, and Alexandra Gilbreath's poised and stately Hermione, went upstage to wave in the direction of the back dock to a cheering, invisible crowd from what was clearly this kingdom's equivalent of the Buckingham Palace balcony, while Camillo and Archidamus brought us up to date with court news in a down-stage duologue of gracious elegance. These opening images, of public formality and courtesy undermined by secret, sordid imaginings, beautifully captured what was to follow in the play's next phase.

Leontes' jealousy first became known to its possessor in this production as he sat, side-stage, signing official papers (kingship was serious work in this Sicilia) and looked up to see Hermione playfully nudging Polixenes into dancing with her to music provided by an old-fashioned gramophone. Leontes' refusal of their invitation to make the dance *à trois* marked the beginning of a process of destructive self-isolation that was meticulously structured in Sher's performance. He was right downstage in intimate, rather waggish conversation with the audience as he selected candidates in the front rows for those 'cuckolds, ere now' and for 'Sir Smile, his neighbour', yet half mad with the torture of jealous grief by the end of the speech. He broke his suspicions to Geoffrey Freshwater's splendidly stolid, anxiously concerned Camillo with a nervously embarrassed little laugh, his rational self still apparently aware of the absurdity of what his self-destructive subconscious forced him into saying; but as the scene progressed, the venom took over and the repeated 'nothings', following 'Is whispering nothing?', built one upon the other in their crescendo of misery and pain. His intrusion into the homely intimacy of Hermione's scene with her women and Mamillius was remarkable in its mixture of gentleness and brutality: the speech about the spider in the cup was given fiercely, into her face; as his accusations became articulate she held out her hands to him in a gesture of love, pity, and desire to rescue him from his own aberrations; with their child screaming as he was hustled from the room, he held her in his arms, weeping, then flung her to the ground, a public humiliation before her household that was particularly shocking in this ceremonious world of royal protocol. Again her hands were held out to him, ostensibly for help in rising; he ignored her and lit a cigarette, then, degradingly for them both, went ferreting in her handbag for evidence of infidelity, the public destruction of their joint regal dignity very painful to witness.

For the 'Nor night, nor day, no rest' scene the panelled walls of the set had closed in on a Leontes discovered, in the middle of the night,

sleepless and near breakdown, unable to resist taking the infant Perdita in his arms when Paulina brought her, sobbing as he did so, then, as if forced on by his sense of misguided duty, pushing her away, manhandling Paulina and Antigonus, and collapsing to the floor in exhaustion. Exhausted still, and demented, he limped down the length of the stage for the trial scene, a terrible parody of his opening energetic entrance, stumbled up the steps of a huge throne, and made a pitiful mess of speaking the indictment against Hermione, fumbling with notes and spectacles, getting to the end with the utmost difficulty and to the excruciating embarrassment of his court. After the revelations of the oracle (presented by a priest in the robes of the Orthodox church, which seemed to be taking the Romanov-court setting somewhat too literally), and after the tirade of Paulina, we left him, sobbing, hunched on the floor, where we were to find him, still in much the same position, still attended by Paulina, sixteen years later. It was a precisely charted psychological journey that Sher presented, brilliantly executed technically but with the technique not (as in some of this actor's performances) in any way diverting attention from the emotional power of the progress to disintegration and collapse, and never allowing us to forget that there was another, a 'real', Leontes underneath this misery, that this pattern of behaviour was aberration, not evil.

The performance was splendidly complemented by Alexandra Gilbreath's Hermione, poised, confident, radiant in the opening scene; stunned by Leontes' accusations, but never losing her love for him, her sorrow and pity preparing for the final scene. Also prefiguring the ending was the extraordinary trial scene, Hermione walking onto the stage (as exhaustedly as her husband had just done) in a filthy prison shift, bloody from child-birth, her hair matted, her face ashen, her eyes staring, the entire court gasping in shock at her appearance. In a little railed dock she stood motionless, a dock that would be reinstated in the final scene, now silvered and with candles, containing its motionless, Madonna-like, Hermione and from which she would, as here in the trial, move out and extend her arms in yearning for reconciliation with her husband. The undaunted dignity of her demeanour, in spite of physical degradation, the unswerving vocal control in spite of swelling emotions, the majestic anger, were immensely impressive. There was a fine Paulina, too, from Estelle Kohler, formidable in her defence of Hermione, blisteringly fierce yet never losing her unselfconscious dignity in her attacks on Leontes, sustaining a precision of vocal clarity even in the extremes of her furious onslaught after the trial, her voice modulating into compassionate gentleness in response to his penitent sobs. The same mixture of compassion and fierceness remained, too, in the little bespectacled old lady who was still watching over him when the play returned to Sicilia for its conclusion.

Its journey to Bohemia had been marked by the roof falling in. The ceiling of Leontes' palace was a festooned white cloth which loosened and fell in sympathy with the disintegration of his world, billowing into great storm clouds for the shipwreck scene and finally looming, growlingly, over the front stalls as it shaped itself into two huge clawed paws to fall and envelope the fleeing Antigonus – another actor sacrificed to the set. The production (not unlike the author, one sometimes thinks) did less well with the Bohemian scenes, played in what was presumably a wool warehouse with hundreds of bales for actors to climb on (and they did, all the time: the proposition seemed to be that the old shepherd had turned entrepreneur following his sudden acquisition of capital). There was an admirably versatile Autolycus from Ian Hughes, shifting disguise from Church-of-England parson to rob the Young Shepherd (of everything, including his clothes, a clever, funny, but in the end long-winded scene), to Jewish pedlar with his ballads as old 78 gramophone records (they took too long to play), to Lytton Strachey look-alike for

the scene with the departing Shepherd and his son. There was much, ever so much, dancing, and lots of giggling peasant girls, and chaps in very big boots, and plentiful root vegetables in phallic suggestiveness just as at all the sheep-shearing festivals one attends. There was a splendid fit of temper from Ken Bones's Polixenes as he threw off his disguise and confronted his son, horrifyingly recalling the kingly rages of the first half and producing respondent violence from Florizel in protection of Perdita. Emily Bruni's Perdita, beautiful and charming, though vocally not always quite adequate, was doubled with a sad, pale-faced, sickly little Tsarevitch of a Mamillius, confined to a wheel-chair, an idea that made the child's death much less unsurprising than it is surely meant to be, and introduced the idea of resurrection in one place too many.

When we came to the resurrection itself, the staging echoes of the trial scene created a more subdued tone than in many productions I have seen, but a highly effective one nevertheless. Leontes, rediscovered in Sicilia seated on the ground, hunched over a book, had been knocked backwards by the return of youth and love to his kingdom, gazing at Florizel and Perdita with a moving intensity that starkly conveyed the despair of his own sense of childlessness. The offstage reunions had produced in him, by the time he entered for the statue scene, clinging to his daughter, a state of slightly disbelieving entrancement as of a man in a dream too good to be true, and this continued through the reunion with Hermione. To wonder whether Antony Sher might have done *more* as an actor is not a frequent experience, but the thought did cross one's mind here. But there was something about the choice of stillness and awed bewilderment that made one aware of the fragility of the scene's beauty and wonder and which rang true with the play's final lines. '*Hastily* lead away', he said, as if the overwhelming joy of this moment might be jeopardized if it were over-indulged; and the jeopardy derived from his preceding admission that he, like everyone else, must '*answer* to his part', in his case a part responsible for the '*wide gap* of time' through which they had all been 'dissevered'. There is guilt, and waste, within the joy and fulfilment of the end of *The Winter's Tale*, and this production found them all.

From *The Winter's Tale* to *The Tempest* is not a long step in most chronological lists of Shakespeare's plays, but the symbolic significance of Sir Ian McKellen's journey from London to Leeds to play in a repertory season at the West Yorkshire Playhouse that included Prospero in a production of *The Tempest* directed by Jude Kelly was much commented upon by reviewers. The play was offered in a grim and ugly prison-cell set by Robert Innes Hopkins, draped at the back with polythene sheeting, chains hanging from walls decorated with a daily chalk-mark to record the long months and years of Prospero's exile, piles of logs on either side, pieces of polythene strewn around, a few battered buckets, a circle of large boulders, and, centre-stage, a decayed old sofa. Since the sound-effects of wind and storm were nothing if not realistic, the requirement seemed to be that we take these visual objects at face value too, the miserable flotsam of a tide-washed island, though the polythene, it seemed (an awkward duality), had intermittently symbolic properties too, for of it Prospero's magic garment was made, from it Ariel appeared, in it Prospero became invisible, from within cones of it the goddesses spoke their amplified whispered blessings in the masque, and by its allure on Prospero's clothes-line we had to suppose that Stephano and company were diverted from their murderous purpose. The Chekhov and Coward of the rest of the company's repertoire meant that the trio of men of sin had to be played by women hardly old enough to have been actively wicked twelve years earlier, while their 'Burlington Bertie' appearance in tail-coats, and their tendency to strut and swagger like Portia practising to Nerissa for her court-room performance, robbed all their scenes of credibility and left a terrible gap in the produc-

10 *The Tempest*, directed by Jude Kelly for West Yorkshire Playhouse. Sir Ian McKellen as Prospero. Prelude to Act 1, Scene 1.

tion where the opposition to Prospero should have been. The comic scenes went for little too, though Will Keen worked hard at his wistful little stand-up Ulster comedian Trinculo.

It was, however, Sir Ian's Prospero that one had come to see. Onto the stage he shuffled as the performance began, slightly unsteady on his pins, in his battered straw hat, ragged trousers that finished half way down very white calves, ancient brogues, and moth-eaten cardigan, chuntering to himself as he inscribed this day's chalk-mark on the wall and, putting on the long polythene stole that represented Prospero's magic cloak (kissing it like a priest as he did so) and opening an ancient volume taped up against final disintegration, lit a little night-light within each of the boulders. Then he threw a toy boat into one of the buckets, began clicking a split bamboo cane over a little collection of not-very-voodooish woollen dolls, and lay back on the sofa and waited for the storm to begin. The words of the shipwreck scene were more or less inaudible for the overwhelmingly realistic sound effects, but its action was not uninterestingly eerie in a strange blue light behind the upstage polythene sheets.

Although the production as a whole was deeply disappointing, at its centre was an eccentric but fascinating reading of its principal role. McKellen presented a profoundly weary, disillusioned Prospero, crotchety and aloof and slightly dotty, though with a touching, gruff affection for his daughter. There was never any urgency about this Prospero's behaviour: it was as if he had always known that he would one day gain vengeance over Antonio and the process of achieving it was tiring and depressing. He had a habit of flapping his arms in an unco-ordinated way, as though undecided about how to proceed. Anger could still be stirred in him as he remembered past wrongs, but there was never any sense of struggle to find the ability to overcome it; to punish his enemies really wasn't worth it, for they would never learn, and, anyway, was his own earlier behaviour really beyond reproach? There were little surges of hard-won energy here and there, glimpses of approval for Paul Bhattacharjee's notably unrebellious Ariel (all in blue paint), wry half-smiles at the eagerness of Claudie Blakley's spirited if rather vulgar little Miranda, assertions of power over Timothy Walker's absurdly fang-toothed Caliban and Rhashan Stone's finely spoken Ferdinand that involved a certain amount of grim (or mock-grim) jangling of the keys which he carried to their fetters. This last, and the fact that he had Ariel and Caliban dressed in replicas of his own hat and cardigan (Caliban threw his off in glee as he subjugated himself to Stephano), were the only gestures in the direction of the recently fashionable colonial-oppressor version of Prospero. Weary old fuddy-duddy, his old brain more or less permanently troubled, was what we were mostly offered here – along with a virtuoso command of Shakespearian verse-speaking.

This was a Prospero one couldn't stop listening to – partly because some of the phrasing was so wilful that total attention was essential to stay abreast of meaning. But the sudden little spurts, the musicality with which certain phrases were slowed or speeded, language orchestrated as much as spoken, the apparent throwaway nonchalance that was in fact so precisely calculated, the mixture of the conversational and the majestic, the sheer bravura brilliance of technique unashamedly on display, were a constant source of fascination. There was a sense of bleak pathos, even doom, about 'Our revels now are ended', a detached resignation to loneliness and to every third thought being his grave which appeared again, with a lingering over the phrasing that gave an even deeper sense of world-weariness to 'Ye elves of brooks . . .'. And at the end, after his amusement at the bewilderment of the lords of Naples and Milan and their rather indecisive dismissal (had they learned anything or not?), and after a semi-affectionate pat on the head for a penitent Caliban, and with the magic polythene stole and the bamboo wand safely dispatched down the trapdoor, it was as if a weight had been lifted from him, physically and vocally, and the Epilogue had a remarkably exhilarating directness, and simplicity, and freedom, that provided a genuine climax to the piece, a Prospero earnestly begging for the audience's attention, rather than the dying fall that is one's usual theatrical experience. One had travelled to Leeds to hear a star actor speak Shakespeare and the surprises were worth the journey. Nothing else in the production was.

There was no such sense of a one-man show about the National Theatre ensemble's second Shakespeare of the year, a production, again directed by Trevor Nunn, of *The Merchant of Venice* at the Cottesloe Theatre, played in traverse mode. Hildegard Bechtler's design placed the Venetian scenes of the play in the middle of the traverse in a *Cabaret* world of thirties dance music, elegant café tables on a black and white chequered floor, much drinking of champagne, the noisy young men of the Christian community in an impressive range of well-cut suits and blacks such as Lancelot Gobbo doing the menial jobs (again the rejection of the 'blind casting' principle). At one end of the traverse, Belmont was a place of chic opulence, fashionable (and slightly sexy) murals, stiff cocktails, and Portia's first batch of suitors (the 'Neapolitan Prince' and his fellows) presented, wearing a fine selection of elegant hats, on a home cine-projector; at the opposite end was the humble, well-locked door to Shylock's house, with its photograph of Leah between candles on a little cupboard, and Jessica shouted at in Yiddish for not cleaning the pans as well as her mother used to.

We opened with David Bamber's middle-aged, pasty-faced, be-spectacled Antonio, a self-made provincial always a little nervous among the toffs and a permanent embarrassment to Bassanio, playing a melancholy tune on the café piano before Bassanio's boisterous set of pals arrived to drink champagne and flirt with the café's singing girls. Antonio's flat northern vowels (very Alan Bennett – Salerio and Solanio would later mimic his accent in describing his farewell to Bassanio), his dull, centre-parted hair, his behind-the-fashion suit, contrasted splendidly with the dashing playboy elegance of Alexander Hanson's beautifully coiffured Bassanio, more than a touch of the young Jonathan Aitken about him – and perhaps about as trustworthy. Their conversation about Portia (a photograph of her eagerly shown and wearily looked at) made clear that Antonio's forlorn sexual yearnings for Bassanio had long since been repressed (though not suppressed) and gave the impression that this was by no means Bassanio's first attempt to woo an heiress. At the end of it, Antonio was left to pay the scene's accumulated café bill, a little touch of Nunn social realism that would recur, Shylock most carefully paying, and tipping, for his glass of tea in his first scene, Salerio and Solanio, and Gratiano and company, never having a coin among them when large bills for champagne arrived.

Derbhle Crotty's Portia, an elegant and slightly world-weary society heiress, apparently capable of dealing with any of her suitors with ice-cool grace and wit, found herself surprisingly wrong-footed by the exotic poetic earnestness of Chu Omambala's splendid Morocco. In he came with his white-robed attendant in a wonderful pale grey pin-striped suit (complete with plus-fours and spats) and a demonstration of scimitar-twirling that she was not alone in finding mesmerizingly sexy. She had to hide her tears from her household at the depth of his grief when he chose wrongly. Aragon was easier, a genuinely funny caricature of moustachioed heel-clicking from Raymond Coulthard, and then the overwhelming handsomeness of Bassanio, irresistible of course, but with a most interesting hint of resentment that it should be so. There was a faint sense of tension and hesitation as they knelt (little church hassocks specially brought in) side by side to exchange vows and rings with a degree of solemnity that had a touch of foreboding about it, a mood deepened rather than dissipated by Gratiano's coarse, noisy laughter as the champagne flowed, and the jokes too, about getting sons and 'stakes down'. She and Bassanio were (contrary to the text) alone as she read out Antonio's letter at the end of the scene; when her betrothed sobbed on the word 'love', she understood the situation immediately. Her suitcase was packed the next time we saw her and when she appeared in court, her face seeming pinched and pale as if from long hours of legal study, she knew there was more than one battle to be fought.

Her ostensible adversary in the court scene was Henry Goodman's remarkable Shylock. He had first appeared in the play taking his glass of tea at a café side table, a confident if wary figure in his rather straggly beard, a large black hat over his yarmulke, a dark, slightly baggy suit, a briefcase, and a silver-topped cane. His eyes twinkled as he told the story of Jacob's sheep; there was warmth and humour here, shrewdness, and a sharp and witty intelligence, and he laughed a lot to himself before he could manage to tell them about the absurd idea of the bond. Beneath the attempts at friendliness, however, one always saw the depth of grievance. 'This *is* kind I offer' he said to Bamber's deeply hesitant, racist Antonio and for a moment, as they shook hands, a little ray of hope seemed to touch the agreement between these two lonely men. Shylock's loneliness was manifest in the little scene with Jessica, shouting at her for housekeeping failures, embracing her possessively, slapping her face when she showed too much interest in Gobbo's message, then embracing her again and forcing her to join him in a wistful Hebrew song as they gazed at the photograph of her mother. 'Fast bind', he said – and she joined in obediently on 'fast find'. The lonely widower, desperate and demanding, over-protectively clinging to his treasured child's love, was vulnerably on view here. When next we saw him he was seated (unscripted), at a café table with Antonio and Bassanio. He looked painfully ill at ease as he listened to Andrew French's Lancelot Gobbo at the cabaret microphone presenting his (transposed) story of the conflict between conscience and the fiend as a stand-up comedy turn between the singing girls. Shylock's return home through the revellers to his unanswered front door, his fumbling with his keys, his discovery of Jessica's departure (she had kissed her mother's photograph goodbye after his earlier exit), were the inevitable prelude to his cracking up at his next appearance. It was the urbane indifference to his grief of Salerio and Solanio that did it. He had greeted them eagerly, as though pleased to have their company. Their mocking callousness produced a version of 'Hath not a Jew eyes' that was eager, urgent, intended to be persuasive, and then turned very fierce, though with the tremor of grief beneath, on 'shall we not revenge?', his body tense with fury at the years of ill-treatment. It was at this point that Peter de Jersey's Salerio began to part company with Mark Umbers's implacably racist Solanio, a move that would show Salerio, by the end of the trial scene, appalled at the behaviour of his fellow

Christians and physically restraining the threatened violence of Richard Henders's loathsome Gratiano. The first half ended with John Nolan's gentle, gracious Tubal raising a deprecating hand at his friend's increasing loss of control, and Shylock vowing (from somewhat earlier in the text) 'Cursed be my tribe / If I forgive him'.

The court scene was played across the full length of the traverse stage, the Duke's desk at one end, the plaintiff and defendant half way down on upright chairs, Tubal behind Shylock, and Antonio's supporters, a Jew-baiting gang of young men in posh suits, behind him, rowdy and aggressive as a bunch of football hooligans (though in this case clearly Rugby football). The sense of physical threat to Shylock was constant through the scene. It was from it that he seemed to find the strength to resist Portia's plea for mercy. She had taken a chair to sit directly in front of him a few lines into the speech, delivering the rest of it straight to him with an earnest intensity that rivetted his attention. Never before, one felt, had a member of the Christian community spoken to him with this degree of immediacy and it was curiously welcome. At the end he agonized for several tense, painful seconds of almost unbearable suspense before a returning awareness of the Gratiano mob rekindled his resolve and he just managed to find the strength to say 'My deeds upon my head'. He was further strengthened a few moments later by the contemptible offer of thrice the money: mercy he might have been moved by, money never. The judgement given and Antonio's chest bared, Tubal rose and walked with quiet dignity from the court, absolutely dissociating himself from what seemed imminent. Shylock prayed in Hebrew; the Christians muttered 'Our Father'; Bassanio embraced Antonio who fondled his friend's face and kissed him on 'Whether Bassanio had not once a love'. And then Shylock stood, fixated and hesitant, in front of Antonio, the knife raised, his hand trembling, his eyes filling with tears, patently incapable of doing it. He

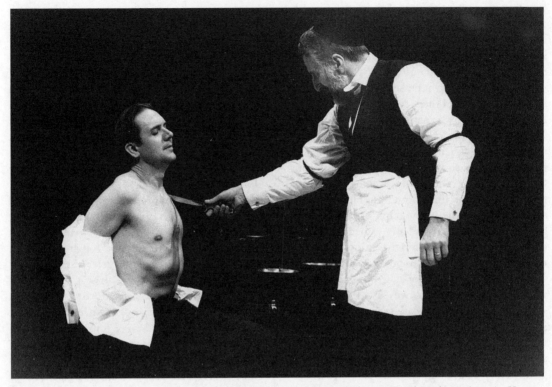

11   *The Merchant of Venice*, directed by Trevor Nunn for the Royal National Theatre. David Bamber as Antonio, Henry Goodman as Shylock. Act 4, Scene 1.

stepped back to collect himself, covering his trousers with a protective white cloth, and Portia, whose frantic searches through her law-books had produced no shred of inspiration until this moment, suddenly had the idea and rushed down the room: 'Tarry awhile', and Antonio was rescued, and Shylock too. Now the law against aliens that she had found could at last be useful, and she began to read it out, Shylock joining in with weary, contemptuous familiarity. What happened afterwards disgusted her, and Salerio, as the forces of Christian fanaticism were unleashed. Flaunting the scales, Antonio demanded that Shylock give up his religion. His accession to the appalling require-ment was resigned, bitter, ironic, as, with a mock flourish, he put his yarmulke and prayer belt onto the scales in a gesture that suggested that they might as well have taken his life, and

walked from the room to the jeers of Gratiano and his fellow yobs.

And so back to Belmont. Portia had been absolutely shattered when Bassanio's ring had been sent after her, and she took immense care over publicly humiliating Antonio in making him return it in symbolic withdrawal from her husband's life. Bamber made Antonio almost convincing (even a little peck on the cheek) in his gratitude to her for getting him some of his ships back, and then withdrew to the piano to play the same wistful little tune with which the performance had started. 'What elegant sym-metry', one thought, as three pairs of lovers stood there, somewhat uncertainly in the growing light, the first whistles from a blackbird coming in to replace the song of the night-ingale. 'It is almost morning', said Portia (from a moment or two earlier in the scene), and Gabrielle Jourdan's Jessica took a step or two away from her husband. She had seemed profoundly ill at ease ever since arriving at Belmont, looking like a refugee child, hating the cocktail she was given, much disturbed at Lancelot Gobbo's teasing, seeming to find her space invaded by the unctuous Welsh earnestness of Daniel Evans's Lorenzo, weeping bitterly as she listened to the music on the moonlit bank, and shattered by the gift of her father's property at his death. Now, as the play closed and she stood alone, stared at by the rest, she began to sing the Hebrew song she had sung with her father; and as its melancholy music took over the mood, thunder rumbled ominously in the distance and everyone froze as the lights went down. It was a stunningly effective ending to a brilliant production, a very obvious candidate for the best piece of Shakespearian theatre of the year – which perhaps, after all, it was.

That I leave that distinction to Michael Boyd's production of *A Midsummer Night's Dream* derives partly from a sense that some of Nunn's most powerful effects might be described by austere persons as adaptation rather than interpretation, and partly from the fact that its success was achieved in the always easier confinement of a studio space, while Boyd had to work on the unforgiving vastness of Stratford's main stage. At the end of his RSC production of *A Midsummer Night's Dream*, designed by Tom Piper, the strange little dance, part folk-clogging, part chorus-line, just a hint of Not-The-Full-Monty – the dance that we saw the mechanicals execute at their initial entrance, hint at in their rehearsal, and fail in, forlornly, when they arrived back in Athens without Bottom – took over the stage and included in its strangely infectious rhythms every level of society (rulers, courtiers, lovers, workmen) in a joyous celebration of community and reciprocity akin to something deep in the play's conclusion. The journey of that dance, from its tentative first appearance after the greyness and oppression of the opening scene, to its engulfing of the play of the mortals

at the end, and thence its transmutation into the footstomping fairy dance of the forest, a dance of freedom and sexuality, was the basis upon which this beautifully paced, and beautifully choreographed, production was built.

The grey rigidity of the opening, with Theseus' courtiers in long overcoats, fur hats, boots, and gloves, while frost glistened as it fell from a dark sky above the white semi-circular wall of the set, its five doors closed, took quite literally the 'hoary-headed frosts' that 'fall in the fresh lap of the crimson rose' that we were to hear about in the first forest scene. The courtiers stood obediently in a semi-circle waiting for the court session to begin. (Or was it Michael Boyd's actors standing obediently waiting for the play to begin? The production was so constantly alert to the play's own self-conscious theatricality that the question was unanswerable.) We were in a totalitarian state, buttoned up, repressive, cold. Polite applause, hollow, expressionless, greeted the utterances of Dictator Theseus and his unwilling bride-to-be. She scowled disbelievingly at the merciless treatment he inflicted on Hermia and swept furiously off with a swish of taffeta skirts when, his judgement handed down, he extended his hand to her. We were left with the lovers, still in grey, but with thoughts of escape; then the mechanicals arrived, again all in grey, but with the germ of a promise in their little dance. Then came the transformation: a magic arrow zinged into the back wall on 'hold, or cut bowstrings' – it was only a theatrical trick (pushed through from the other side), but what other sort of magic should one expect in a theatre? – followed by perky rhythms in the music, an eerie light, and the colours (the wonderfully sudden colours after all the greyness) of flowers thrusting up through the stage. And there, quite out of his court environment, stirring himself up to merriment, was the funny little bowler-hatted, bespectacled figure of Philostrate, Ronnie Corbett out of Magritte, sidling up to rub against the protruding behind of a prim, librarianly little lady picking flowers.

In a crescendo of energy that mixed annoyance and desire, pleasure and contempt, there emerged from a mutual stripping Aidan McArdle's shirtless, Irish Puck and Sirine Saba's arms-raised-always-ready, hip-wiggling Peaseblossom – and Oberon and Titania arrived just in time, else had we all been shamed.

The forest scenes were full of surprises, of flowers and fairies and ladders erupting through the floor, of beds and armchairs swinging down from the flies, of Puck administering love-in-idleness as whole plants from a wheelbarrow, complete with compost, of the alarming twitchiness of the fairy-rulers' attendants, hair-dos seriously horrible, gestures disconcertingly random. The four lovers who found themselves in this strange world were excellently contrasted: a curly-haired, goofy romantic Lysander from Fergus O'Donnell; a well-observed study in how to be broodingly handsome from Henry Ian Cusick; an only-just-over-the-top-not-altogether-dumb-blonde-in-red-shoes from Hermione Gulliford; and a fiercely managing little Hermia in tightly buttoned-up grey cardigan from Catherine Kanter. Their big quarrel-scene stayed funny, even in such athletic extremes as Hermia's upside-down mid-air exit stage left, for the very good reason that their characters gave not the slightest hint of thinking they were funny themselves, a horrible mistake that is always terminally disastrous to the scene. Nicholas Jones, in exhilarating command of the verse, offered a fine Oberon, intense, charismatic, changeable, threatening, his scalp adorned with a curiously mesmeric little hieroglyphic tattoo; and Josette Simon, sharing his strangeness, was elegant, sinuous, torrid, and sexually voracious as Titania, demanding every scrap of energetic response from Daniel Ryan's bewildered Bottom. He accepted the challenge manfully (and a bit asininely too) and their interval exit up into the flies, sighing, groaning, braying, thumping, was a tribute to their physical fitness. Still, in their next scene, as he puffed on his cigar in self-congratulation at his achievements, Titania did suggest, as she sent a fairy to seek 'new nuts' for him, that she might have tired him, just a little.

The joke can hardly be said to spring directly off the textual surface, but like so much else in the production of a more serious kind, it derived from a reading of the play that had mined it deeply. There were more such jokes in the Pyramus and Thisbe performance, in which the hammy Elizabethan costumes favoured by the self-regarding little am-dram troop were the ultimate response to those persons who phone the RSC box office to check if a play is in 'traditional costume' before divulging their credit-card numbers. Thus Thisbe's cherry lips kissed Snout's 'stones' and 'hole' as she knelt before his Wall, the not-in-the-perfectest-taste innuendos (surely authorial) appropriately noted. Directorial rather than authorial, but inspired nevertheless, was the new gloss on 'Come blade my breast imbrue': not, after all, a mere alliterative effect, but a recognition of the fact that that was all she had, dagger-handle and blade having parted company as Bottom flamboyantly drew them (it) to kill himself, a feat he then had to accomplish by gouging his eyes out with the dagger's hilt (or, in some early performances, by savaging his own throat with Moonshine's little woolly dog).

And when it was all over, and the play was found to need no excuse, came the best moment of the production, to be followed by that gloriously inclusive dance. In justifying his choice of 'Pyramus and Thisbe', Nicholas Jones had spoken Theseus' speech about 'Where I have come, great clerks have purposèd / To greet me with premeditated welcomes' in a way that made one hear it as one had never heard it before. His sense of social inter-dependence, of human reciprocity – 'Love, therefore, and tongue-tied simplicity / In least speak most, to my capacity' – brought Hippolyta, at last, to acknowledge her love for him in a kiss that she hadn't quite managed even when, in the dawn forest scene, he had, to her obvious satisfaction, over-ruled Egeus's continuing hostility. (It hadn't taken much over-ruling, for Egeus's

12 *A Midsummer Night's Dream*, directed by Michael Boyd for the Royal Shakespeare Company. Bottom (Daniel Ryan), in Pyramus costume, dances with Hippolyta (Josette Simon); courtiers and mechanicals in background, with Philostrate (Aidan McArdle) extreme right. Act 5, Scene 1.

fairy identity had already held his sleeping daughter in a forgiving embrace and he would soon be with her in the final scene exchanging harmonious banter purloined from other characters.) The play over, and also the bergomasque (the proper name, at last, for the mechanicals' special little dance), Bottom, representative of those tongue-tied subjects of whom Theseus had just spoken, one of those 'hard-handed men that work in Athens here', walked over to the bride of the monarch and put out his hand, his 'hard hand', to invite her to have the next dance with him. In the intake of breath, and the stunned silence, that followed, memories of these same two figures, in the moments before the interval, might have wafted into our conscious memories, and

perhaps into their subconscious ones too; but it was the way in which this gesture (not directly off the text, but indisputably derived from it by the art of the director and his actors) illuminated, truthfully and movingly, the scene's celebratory inclusiveness, that made its effect so powerful. After a tiny hesitation, Hippolyta accepted, and Starveling's silver moon-balloon floated free and replicated itself several times above the rear wall, and that wonderful, ecstatic dance began. For such moments of illumination of texts that one thought one knew so well one keeps going to productions of Shakespeare's plays. I can think of no more appropriate point at which to conclude, with thanks to its editors for their tolerance and generosity, my stint as reviewer for this journal.

PROFESSIONAL SHAKESPEARE PRODUCTIONS IN THE BRITISH ISLES JANUARY–DECEMBER 1998

compiled by

NIKY RATHBONE

Most of the productions listed are by professional or semi-professional companies. Productions originating in 1997 or earlier have only been included if there is new information. Details are mainly taken from newspaper reviews held in the Birmingham Shakespeare Library.

ANTONY AND CLEOPATRA

Theatre Set Up, tour of the Netherlands: June 1998–
Director: Wendy McPhee

Salisbury Playhouse and the ESC, tour with *As You Like It:* August 1998–
Director: Michael Bogdanov and Jonathan Church
Designer: Yannis Thavomis
Antony: Tim Woodward
Cleopatra: Cathy Tyson
A mix of modern and more traditional props were used for a production which was concerned with both political struggle and personal relationships. Both productions were seen at the first Bath Shakespeare Festival.

The Royal National Theatre: October 1998–
Director: Sean Mathias
Designer: Tim Hatley
Music: James Wood
Antony: Alan Rickman
Cleopatra: Helen Mirren.
Played against a huge cratered map.

Adaptation

Cleopatra by Steve Clarke and Bill Scott
Miracle Theatre Company, Heligan Garden, Cornwall: June 1998
A new play, telling Cleopatra's story.

AS YOU LIKE IT

Shakespeare's Globe, Southwark, London: May 1998–
Director: Lucy Bailey
Designer: Bunny Christie
Rosalind: Anatasia Hille
The company experimented with using the yard for the wrestling scene, and tended to play to the front of the Globe stage, resulting in poor sight lines.

Dog at a Cat Theatre Company, Barnwell Manor, Oundle: July 1998
Director: Sheila Macdonald
Music: Kendal Kirkland
A pro/am production set in eighteenth-century Ireland, using traditional Irish music.

The ESC and Salisbury Playhouse, Bath Shakespeare Festival, Hackney Empire and tour: August 1998–
Director: Michael Bogdanov
Designer: Geraldine Bunzi
Rosalind: Ivy Omere
The production examined the darker aspects of the play.

The Soho Group, tour: September 1998
Performed by a predominately female cast using modern images and exploring forbidden love, cross-dressing and sibling rivalry.

THE COMEDY OF ERRORS

The Watermill Theatre Company, Newbury and tour with *Henry V*: May 1998–
Director: Edward Hall
Designer: Francis O'Connor
A boisterous, physical all-male production making extensive use of masks in the commedia dell'arte tradition, which partly took place out of doors. Also toured to Malta and to The Other Place, Stratford.

OpenHand, in college gardens at the Cambridge Shakespeare Festival July 1998
Director Kim Gillespie:

CORIOLANUS

Loose Cannon, The Mint, Dublin: March 1998

CYMBELINE

Stamford Shakespeare Company: June 1998
Rutland Open Air Theatre, Tolethorpe Hall
This amateur company produce an annual summer season of Shakespeare in a purpose built open-air theatre.

HAMLET

Ludlow Castle: June 1998–
Director: Glen Walford
Hamlet: Martin McKellan

OpenHand, in college gardens at the Cambridge Shakespeare Festival: July 1998
Director: Simon Bell

Mouth to Mouth Theatre Company, Framlington, tour of open-air sites in Suffolk: August 1998
Director: James Holloway
A pro/am production.

The Ninagawa Company in association with Thelma Holt Ltd at the Barbican Theatre, London: September 1998
Director: Yukio Ninagawa
Designer: Tsukasa Nakagoshi
Translator: Kazuko Matsuoka
Music: Yasuhiro Kasamatsu
Hamlet: Hiroyuki Sanada
Produced as part of the BITE Festival. Played in Japanese. A two level stage was used with the upper balcony doubling as 'dressing rooms': a commentary on the theatricality of stagecraft. First performed in Tokyo, 1995.

Adaptations

Act V
QEH Theatre, Bristol: March 1998
Director: Nick Beason
An adaptation for a cast of eight played in modern casual clothes with the cast on stage observing the action.

Hamlet (the Dithering Dane)
Master Rosencrantz's Little Eyases at the Edinburgh Fringe Festival: July 1998
An adaptation played by four actors.

Hamlet in the Mirror (Hamlet en el Espejo) by Manuel Dionis-Bayer
Edinburgh Fringe Festival: August 1998
A two-hander concerning a middle aged actor and his young disciple, using material from *Hamlet* and the sonnets, played partly in Spanish.

One-Man-Hamlet by Clayton Jewne
Edinburgh Fringe Festival: August 1998
Originating in Canada where it has been playing seven years.

HENRY IV

Adaptations

Henry IV Pt 1
Volteface at the Edinburgh Fringe Festival: August 1998
A street-theatre adaptation.

Chimes at Midnight by Orson Welles
Chichester Festival Theatre: August 1998
Director: Patrick Garland
Falstaff: Simon Callow
Adapted from the 1966 film.

HENRY V

The Watermill Company, Newbury, European and British tour with *The Comedy of Errors*
See *Shakespeare Survey 52*

R. J. Williamson Company, Leeds, tour of open-air sites with *A Midsummer Night's Dream*: June 1998
Director: Geoffrey Davies
Henry: Robert J. Williamson
A traditional production presented as though by a band of travelling players, using a wagon as a raised stage.

Wales Actors' Company, tour of open-air sites in Wales: Summer 1998
Director: Ruth Garnault

Adaptation

Before Nell-After Agincourt by Peter Mottley
Stage One Theatre Company at the Phoenix Theatre, London and tour: November 1998
Director: Desmond Maurer
Nell: Steve Kyrnman
Pistol: Roy Heather
Originally two linked plays, here combined. *Before Nell* explores the position of boy actors and women. *After Agincourt* was originally a radio play.

HENRY VIII

Berengar Theatre at Barnwell Castle: July 1998
Director: Robert Hardy
A pro/am production played for brilliant spectacle, and using Elizabethan dumb show.

JULIUS CAESAR

Adaptations

Giulio Cesare
Societas Raffaello Sanzio at the Dublin Theatre Festival: October 1998
Director: Romeo Castellucci
Played in Italian and deconstructed to examine the power of rhetoric.

African Julius Caesar
A production by the Malawi National Dance Company which toured East and South Africa and was also seen at the Edinburgh Fringe Festival: August 1998
Director: Toby Gough
Storyteller: Erastus Owour

KING JOHN

The Life and Death of King John
The Original Shakespeare Company at Shakespeare's Globe, Southwark, London: September 1998
Director: Patrick Tucker
Played for one night only under supposed Elizabethan acting conditions, the actors being given only their own lines and no rehearsal.

KING LEAR

Polesden Lacey Open Air Shakespeare Festival: June 1998
Director: Peter Hahlo
The Polesden Lacey annual pro-am Shakespeare production.

Mappa Mundi at the Sherman Theatre, Cardiff: October 1998
Director: Rob Lane
Lear: Lynne Seymour
A role-reversal production with Lear's daughters played by male actors and a female Lear.

The Royal Exchange Theatre, Manchester: October 1998
Director: Gregory Hersov
Lear: Tom Courtenay

Adaptation

Le Roi Lear
Théâtre du Sycomore at the Avignon Festival
and Edinburgh Fringe Festival : August 1998
Advertised as a new translation. The players are
French amateurs, and also performed *Macbeth*.

LOVE'S LABOUR'S LOST

The Lincoln Shakespeare Company at Trinity
Arts Centre, Gainsborough and the Lawn,
Lincoln: November 1998
Director: Richard Jones
Pro/am production set in the 1970s.

MACBETH

The ESC, tour and schools workshops: January
1998
Performances for schools.

Glasgow Citizens Theatre: February 1998
Director: David MacDonald
Designer: Kenny Miller
Macbeth: Gerard Murphy
Set: three stairways, framing reflective or trans-
lucent backdrops. Roles were doubled to blur
the divide between good and evil, and the
witches were male.

Third Party Productions, tour: February 1998–
Director: Ben Benison

The Orange Tree Theatre, Richmond, Surrey:
February 1998
Director: Sam Walters
Designer: Ti Green
Macbeth: Paul Shelley
A stylised, minimalist production in the round,
praised for its psychological clarity.

Brunton Theatre, Musselburgh: February 1998
Director: David Mark Thomson
Macbeth: Liam Brennan
Played in Scots and Irish accents, using video
projections of modern warfare, and portraying
Duncan and his court as elderly civilians, in
contrast to the rebellious army.

Galleon Theatre Company at The Prince Pub
Theatre, Greenwich, London: March 1998
Director/Macbeth: Bruce Jamieson
In this production Banquo was killed by the
Witches.

The Swan Theatre, Worcester: March 1998
Director: Mark Babych
Set in a metallic steel box, with costumes
apparently indicating a progression through the
twentieth century.

Heartbreak Productions, Leamington, tour:
June 1998
Director: Donald Sumpter
Set in a Scotland inspired by the film *Braveheart*.

Frantic Redhead Productions at the Edinburgh
Fringe Festival: August 1998
A promenade production which took place on
the Royal Mile and in the Greyfriars courtyard.
Fleance reappeared as the crowned child of the
prophecy. Professional American and Scottish
actors.

OpenHand, in college gardens at the
Cambridge Shakespeare Festival: August 1998
Director: David Crilly

Hull Truck, tour: October 1998
Director: Simon Stallworthy
Costumes were a mixture of traditional and
modern with the witches in trouser suits.

Outhouse Theatre at the Riverside Studios,
London: November 1998
Director: Rosemary Bianchi.

The Wolsey Theatre, Ipswich: November 1998
Director: Andrew Manley
Video projections onto large screens were used
in a production described as futuristic.

Adaptations

Macbeth
Box Clever Theatre Company, tour: January
1998–
Touring three one-hour adaptations of *Macbeth*,
The Merchant of Venice and *Romeo and Juliet*.

Macbeth
Albion Theatre Company, tour: February 1998
Director: John Hales
Designers: William Goodman and Frances Nerini
Music: Nick Murray Brown
A winter educational project with schools workshops, playing a cut text and set in the mediaeval period.

Macbeth
Touring Lives, Wisbech, schools and colleges tour: March 1998
A professional company working with BTEC students, using an eclectic mixture of props and costumes which included mobile phones and Cossack uniforms.

Macbeth
La Licórne Théâtre, Lille, France in association with the Marlowe Theatre, Canterbury: July 1998
A production in French, using mime, puppetry and music, performed as part of the Street Level Festival.

Makbed blong Wiliam Sekspia
Adapted by Ken Campbell
The Piccadilly Theatre and Cottesloe Theatre, London: July, October 1998
A simplified version in Wol Wantok, the pidgin language of the South Seas. The production toured the South Pacific islands and other parts of the world. The actors learned all the roles and at each staging the audience chose which actors should play which parts.

Macbeth
The West-Country Theatre company, Torquay, tour of western England: August 1998
A shortened version.

Macbeth
K486 at the Edinburgh Fringe Festival: August 1998
The production was set in Brazil and used ritual dance, martial arts and voodoo ritual.

Macbeth
Théâtre du Sycomore at the Edinburgh Fringe Festival: August 1998
Amateur French teenagers. Three alternative Lady Macbeths and three interpretations of the play.
The company also performed *Le Roi Lear*.

Euro-Macbeth
Triangle Project Theatre, The Brewhouse Theatre, Taunton: September 1998
Amateur theatre groups from the UK, Spain and Portugal worked together on this project.

Television version

Macbeth
Channel 4 TV: January 1998
Director: Michael Bogdanov
Macbeth: Sean Pertwee
Lady Macbeth: Greta Scacchi
An eighty-minute version for schools set in Manchester wasteland and portraying the witches as bag ladies.

MEASURE FOR MEASURE

The Royal Shakespeare Company at the Royal Shakespeare Theatre, Stratford: April 1998
Director: Michael Boyd
Designer: Tom Piper
Music: John Woolf
Isabella: Clare Holman
The Duke: Robert Glenister

THE MERCHANT OF VENICE

The RSC at the Royal Shakespeare Theatre, Stratford: January 1998
See *Shakespeare Survey 52*.

The Belmont Players, Harlow Playhouse: January 1998
Director: Steve Hunt
A pro/am company formed for this production which characterized Portia as a ruthless schemer and Bassanio as a money-grabbing womanizer.

The Lincoln Shakespeare Company: March 1998
Director: Richard Main
Music: Joe Conway
A Dickensian production emphasizing the themes of money and debt.

The White Company at Shakespeare's Globe Theatre, Southwark, London: May 1998
Director: Richard Olivier
Designer: Jenny Tiramani
Music: Claire van Kampen
Shylock: Norbert Kentrup
Antonio: Jack Shepherd
Bassanio: Mark Rylance

Adaptations

The Merchant of Venice
Box Clever Theatre Company, the Marlowe Theatre, Canterbury and schools tour with *Romeo and Juliet* and *Macbeth*: January 1998–
Adapted for a cast of three by Michael Wicherek
Director: Andy Potter

Shylock
Adapted and performed by Gareth Armstrong, the Edinburgh Fringe Festival and tour: March 1998–
A solo performance setting Shylock in the context of four hundred years of productions of *The Merchant of Venice*, and Jewish history.

THE MERRY WIVES OF WINDSOR

Lincoln Shakespeare Company: May 1998
A pro/am production.

A MIDSUMMER NIGHT'S DREAM

The New Shakespeare Company at Regent's Park Open Air Theatre: May 1998–
Director: Rebecca Kavanaugh
Designer: David Knapman
Bottom: Ian Talbot
A re-casting of the 1997 production.

The R. J. Williamson Company, Leeds, tour with *Henry V*: June 1998–
Director/Theseus: R.J. Williamson
Music: Christopher Thomas
An open-air production partly played on a pageant wagon, with traditional costuming.

The Festival Players Theatre Company, Gloucester, tour of open-air sites: June 1998–
Director/Quince: Trish Knight-Webb
Music: Johnny Coppin

The London Bubble Theatre playing in London parks: July 1998
Director: Jonathan Petherbridge
Designer: Janis Hart
Music: Thomas Johnson
A promenade production with afternoon workshops for children.

OpenHand, in college gardens at the Cambridge Shakespeare Festival: July 1998
Director: Simon Bell

The Oxford Stage Company, Oxford Playhouse and tour: October 1998–
Director: John Retallack
Designer: Niki Turner
Music: Karl James
Set in a glass-walled cube with the cast doubling as fairies. The music was sung and hummed.

Adaptations

A Midsummer Night's Dream
The Queen's Theatre, Hornchurch, schools tour with workshops: January 1998–

A Midsummer Night's Dream
The Custard Factory, Birmingham and schools tour: January 1998–

Oberon
Music: Weber
Dialogue: James Planché adapted by John Warrack for this performance by actors from the RSC and the City of London Sinfonia. A semi-staged production at Symphony Hall, Birmingham and the Barbican, London: March 1998

Conductor Richard Hickox
Narrator: Timothy West

A Midsummer Night's Dream
Actors from the RSC and the City of London
Sinfonia at the Barbican, London: March 1998
Conductor: Richard Hickox
Mendelssohn's complete incidental music in a
semi-staged production.

A Midsummer Night's Dream
Graduates of the Birmingham Theatre School,
tour of local schools: March 1998
Director: Graham Watts
Focusing on defiance of parental authority.

The Wild Life by Kumiko Shimizu in collaboration with Peter Ellis
Artsparkle, Mile End Park, London: June 1998
An allegorical art installation commenting on
contemporary society through the characters
arranged in a tableaux with video performance.
The installation will be seen in France during
1999.

A Hard Midsummer Night's Dream by Paul Finn
Edinburgh Fringe Festival: August 1998
A sprinkling of fairy dust transports Mick's
annual birthday bash into a strange twilight
world.

Magical Midsummer Madness
A performance project for nine to eleven-year-
olds at the first Bath Shakespeare Festival:
August 1998

Bottom's Dream
The Puppet Theatre Barge, London tour:
September 1998
Puppeteers: Gren and Juliette Middleton
Designer: David Walsh

Ballet

A Midsummer Night's Dream
Choreography: Balanchine
The Pacific Northwest Ballet at the Edinburgh
Festival: August 1998

Music: Mendelssohn
Designer: Martin Pakledinaz
Advertised as the first British performance of
this ballet, choreographed by Balanchine for the
New York City Ballet, 1962. Also performed at
Sadler's Wells Theatre, February 1999.

MUCH ADO ABOUT NOTHING

Cheek by Jowl, The Everyman Theatre,
Cheltenham and tour: February 1998–
Director: Declan Donnellan
Designer: Nick Ormerod
Music: Paddy Cunneen
Beatrice: Saskia Reeves
Benedick: Matthew Macfadyen
The production was set in the Victorian period
and gave overtones of homosexuality to some
male relationships.

The Northcott Theatre, Exeter, annual open-
air production in Rougemont Gardens for the
Exeter Festival: July 1998
Director: Ben Crocker
Elizabethan period production.

OpenHand Productions, in college gardens
for the Oxford Shakespeare Festival and
Cambridge Shakespeare Festival: July 1998–
Director: David Rowan

Bickerstaffe Theatre at Kilkenny Castle,
Ireland. Open-air production for Kilkenny Arts
Week: August 1998
Directors: Maeliosa Stafford and John O'Hara
Set in the 1950s on the day of the All-Ireland
final between Kilkenny and Tipperary.
It is hoped that the Shakespeare production will
become an annual event.

Adaptation

*Much Ado About Nothing (Three Weddings and a
Funeral)* Oddsocks, tour: June 1998–
Oddsocks impersonating an Elizabethan
travelling company in a lively, physical production using circus pyrotechnics.

OTHELLO

OpenHand Productions at the Mumford Theatre, Cambridge: April 1998
An indoor production using an abstract geometric set, and costumed eclectically from various periods.

The Theatre Royal, Bury St. Edmunds and tour of the Eastern region: September 1998–
Director: Colin Blumenau
With educational workshops for schools.

TAG and Citizens Theatre, Glasgow, tour: September 1998–
Director: James Brining
Othello and Iago were portrayed as having similar possessive attitudes to women.

The New Vic Theatre, Newcastle-under-Lyme: November 1998
Director: Gwenda Hughes
Set in the twentieth century with a female Doge of Venice.

Adaptations

Desdemona: a play about a handkerchief by Paula Vogel
The Ustinov Studio Theatre, Bath Shakespeare Festival: August 1998
Billed as the UK premiere. Described as a savage and witty play in which Desdemona is as faithless as Iago suggests. Paula Vogel is an American writer.

OJ/Othello
Edinburgh Fringe Festival: August 1998
Described as a play about the price of fame, about having something everyone else wants, about love and about men who enter worlds not normally open to them.

PERICLES

The Cochrane Theatre, London: January 1998
Director: Sam Shammas

Designer: Liz Cook
A cut text.

RICHARD III

PAC Theatre Company, The Great Hall, the People's Palace, Queen Mary College, London: January 1998
Director: Ros King
With schools workshops

Northern Broadsides, Halifax, tour: January 1998–
Director/Richard: Barrie Rutter
Stamping clogs were used to symbolize battles, and Richard's departing victims hung their scarves or sashes on a wire mesh fence which eventually became a cage for Richard.

Brokenruler, Merton Abbey: July 1998
Director/Richard: Andrew Novell
Designer: David Hermon
A twentieth-century setting with a flavour of football hooliganism.

The Gavella, Zagreb, Croatia at the Edinburgh Festival Fringe: August 1998
Director: Jagoda Buic

The Haymarket Theatre, Leicester: October 1998–
Director: Paul Kerryson
Designer: Juliet Shillingford
Richard: Ian Pepperell

The RSC at the Royal Shakespeare Theatre, Stratford and tour: October 1998–
Director: Elijah Moshinsky
Designer: Robert Howell
Music: Corin Buckeridge
Richard: Robert Lindsay

Adaptations

Richard III
The Pleasance Theatre, London: February 1998
Directed and adapted by Guy Retallack and Ruth Platt

Developed at the Royal National Theatre studio and set in an East End pub in the 1960s, the period of the Kray brothers' criminal activities.

Little Richard
The Key Theatre, Peterborough: August 1998
A rock musical adapted and directed by Derek Killeen and Michael Cross featuring an Elvis-like figure as the King, and set to 50s and 60s rock music.
The latest in the series of very successful musical adaptations of Shakespeare by this amateur company.

The African Company presents Richard III by Carlyle Brown
The Riverside Studios, Richmond: August 1998
Director: Courtney Helper
Set in 1920s New York and telling the true story of a production of *Richard III* by recently freed slaves in 1821, the play dealt with issues of cultural identity.

ROMEO AND JULIET

The RSC, tour continues, including Tokyo. See *Shakespeare Survey 52* for details.

Pericles Productions, Salisbury Playhouse and tour: January 1998–
Director: Jonathan Church
Designer: Ruari Murchison
Romeo: Jasper Britton
Juliet: Jayne Ashbourne
A traditional period production played on a many-entranced curved brick set.

Traffic of the Stage, tour: February 1998–
Director/Romeo: James Reynard
Set in the Regency period, played by a cast of nine.

Greenwich Theatre, London and tour: February 1998–
Director: Rupert Goold
Romeo: Nicholas Irons
Juliet: Kate Fleetwood

A modern dress production.
The Palace Theatre, Redditch: March 1998
Director: Michael Dyer
Designer: John Plash
A modern-dress production intended for schools audiences. The parents were shown as engrossed in their own lives to the neglect of their children, who turn to the inadequate parenting of the Nurse and Friar.

Bold and Saucy Theatre Company, open-air production in Oxford college gardens for the Oxford Shakespeare Festival: June 1998

OpenHand, in Cambridge college gardens for the Cambridge Shakespeare Festival: July 1998
Director: Robert Deering

Adaptations

Romeo and Juliet
Cleveland Theatre Company, schools tour: spring 1998

Romeo and Juliet
Box Clever Theatre Company, in association with the Marlowe Theatre Canterbury, schools tour with *The Merchant of Venice* and *Macbeth*: January 1998–
Adapted by Michael Wicherek
Director/Shylock: Andy Potter
An hour-long adaptation for a cast of three.

Ballet
Romeo and Juliet
The English National Ballet at the Royal Albert Hall, London: June 1998
Choreography by Derek Deane
Designer: Roberta Guidi de Bagno
Music: Prokofiev
Romeo: Roberto Bolle
Juliet: Lucia Lucarra
The ballet was re-choreographed to take best advantage of staging in the round.

Film
Tromeo and Juliet
Tromeo Que: Will Keenan
Juliet: Jan Jensen

Directors: Lloyd Kaufmann and Michael Herz.
Production company: Troma
Screenplay: James Gunn and Lloyd Kaufmann
Music: Willie Wisely
USA release 1997, UK release 1998
Kinky violence and sex in Manhattan, with a sudden twist in the plot which results in a happy ending.

THE TAMING OF THE SHREW

Strange Fish Theatre Company, Windsor Arts Theatre and tour: February 1998–
Directors: Nick Cohen and David Bridal
Set in nineteenth-century frontier town America.

Mad Dogs and Englishmen, Colchester, tour of Essex and Suffolk: June 1998–
A flamboyant period production.

Illyria Theatre Company, tour: June 1998–
Director: Oliver Gray
Katherine: William Finkerath
The production included the Sly scenes and a male actor played Kate. A cast of five doubled four roles each.

OpenHand, in college gardens for the Cambridge Shakespeare Festival: August 1998
Director: Robert Deering

The English Touring Theatre, tour: October 1998–
Director: Stephen Unwin
A modern-dress production.

THE TEMPEST

Compass Theatre Company, Sheffield at the Theatre Royal, York and tour: January 1998–
Director: Neil Sissons
Designer: Neil Irish
Set in a circular sand pit. The six actors developed the theory that characters in *The Tempest* may be partly based on characters in Shakespeare's earlier plays. The part of Ariel was mimed.

The Royal Shakespeare Company at the Royal Shakespeare Theatre, Stratford: February 1998–
Director: Adrian Noble
Designer: Anthony Ward
Music: Stephen Warbeck
Prospero: David Calder

The New Victoria Theatre, Newcastle under Lyme: March 1998
Director: Peter Cheeseman
Chosen by the director as his last production for the New Vic.

The Stafford Shakespeare Festival, Stafford Castle: June 1998–
Director: Julia Stafford-Northcote
Prospero: Barry Foster

Adaptations

Otra Tempestad by Raquel Carrió and Flora Lauten
Teatro Buendia at the Globe to Globe International Festival, Shakespeare's Globe, Southbank, London: July 1998
Director: Flora Lauten
A dramatic meditation on colonization and autocracy explored through imaginative reconstructions based on *The Tempest; Hamlet; Macbeth* and *Romeo and Juliet*.

Storm on the Lawn
An event at the first Bath Festival: August 1998
Fifty young people working with professionals created an original piece of theatre based on *The Tempest*.

Une Tempête by Aimé Césaire
The Gate, Notting Hill, London: September 1998
Advertised as the British premiere. Black actors were cast as Caliban and Ariel in this 1968 play which explores *The Tempest* from the perspective of Caliban.

Prospero's Children by Robin Kingsland
Quick Silver Theatre, Stockport and tour: October 1998–

A production for six to twelve-year-olds, exploring the action from the perspective of Miranda. The action was somewhat confused by the inclusion of additional female characters.

Ballet

The Tempest
Cwmni Ballet, Gwent: May 1998
Director/Prospero: Darius James
Music: Jean Sibelius

TROILUS AND CRESSIDA

The New Shakespeare Company at the Open Air Theatre, Regent's Park: June 1998–
Director: Alan Strachan
Troilus: Robert Hands
Cressida: Rebecca Johnson
A First World War setting, used to develop the anti-heroic themes of the play.

The Royal Shakespeare Company at The Pit, Barbican Theatre, London, Swan Theatre Stratford and tour: November 1998–
Director: Michael Boyd
Designer: Tom Piper
Troilus: William Houston
Cressida: Jayne Ashbourne

TWELFTH NIGHT

The Royal National Theatre, schools tour: January 1998–
Director: Brigid Larmour
Designer: Nettie Edwards
School workshops followed by a promenade production.

Kaboodle Productions, Liverpool Everyman Theatre, British and Malaysia tour: February 1998–
Director: Lee Beagley
Designer: Mark Hill
Several male roles, including Feste, were played by women.
Set during the winter festival of Misrule

Kent Shakespeare Project (Deal) national schools tour, with workshops: May 1998–
Director: Luke Dixon
Also performed at the International Shakespeare Festival, Gdansk, Poland, August 1998.

Hamlet's Janitor Productions, open-air production, Colchester: June 1998
A pro/am group. The play was given a jazz setting.

The Young Vic, London: June 1998
Director: Tim Supple
Designer: Milly Still
Music: Adrian Lee

A and BC Theatre Company, Lincoln's Inn, London: August 1998
Director: Gregory Thompson
An open-air production, in modern dress.

Theatre Babel, Glasgow, tour of Scotland and Northern Ireland: September 1998–
Director: Peter McAllister
The servants played with Scottish accents, the nobility with received pronunciation.

The Crucible Theatre, Sheffield: November 1998–
Director: Michael Grandage
Designer: Christopher Oram
Maria: Una Stubbs

Adaptations

Twelfth Night
Shakespeare 4 Kidz, Edinburgh Fringe Festival and tour with *A Midsummer Night's Dream*: March 1998–
Director: Matt Gimblett
Music: Claire Gimblett
Workshops for schoolchildren culminating in performance.

Twelfth Night
Sunset Productions, the Studio Theatre, Holt Park, Leeds: October 1998
A heavily cut pro/am production for young people.

Ballet version

Twelfth Night
London Studio Centre, tour: July 1998–
Choreographer: Darius James
Music: Mendelssohn
The dancers were drawn from the Classical
Graduate year at the ballet school.
The choreographer is from Cwmni Ballet,
Gwent.

TWO GENTLEMEN OF VERONA

The RSC at the Swan Theatre, Stratford:
February 1998–
Director: Edward Hall
Designer: Michael Pavelka
Music: Mark Thomas

Rain or Shine Theatre Company (Gloucester)
Buxton Fringe Festival and national tour of
open-air sites: June 1998–
Director: James Reynard
Performed by a cast of seven.

THE WINTER'S TALE

Footsbarn at the Galway Arts Festival, Ireland:
July 1998
Footsbarn create their productions as an
ensemble and do not credit individual members
of the company. The production used masks
and chanted choruses. They hope to tour
internationally.

The RSC at the Royal Shakespeare Theatre,
Stratford: December 1998–
Director: Gregory Doran
Designer: Robert Jones
Music: Ilona Sekacz
Leontes: Antony Sher

Adaptation

The Winter's Tale
Riding Lights Theatre Company, the Bridewell
Theatre, London and tour: May 1998
Adapted by Paul Burbridge

ATTRIBUTED PLAYS

Cardenio
Attributed to William Shakespeare and John
Fletcher
The Lakeside Theatre, Essex University:
October 1998
Director: Melanie White
A postgraduate production advertised as using
some professional actors.

POEMS AND SONNETS

Dark Lady of the Sonnets
One man show created by Matthew Jenkins
and touring.
A combination of film and live performance,
first performed in 1995.

MISCELLANEOUS

Hallmarks by Reg Mitchell
Bird of Prey Theatre Company at the
Shakespeare Centre, Stratford: April 1998
A play about John Hall and Shakespeare's
daughter Susannah.

Love's Fire
The Acting Company (New York) at the
Barbican Theatre, London: May 1998–
Director: Mark Lamos
A sequence of plays and music created by the
company and inspired by the sonnets.

Shakespeare in the Dark, conceived by Tom
Morris
Royal National Theatre actors at the BAC,
Battersea: June 1998–
Extracts from Shakespeare; the closet scene
from *Hamlet*, the last scene from *The Merchant of
Venice*, soliloquies from *Macbeth*, performed in
complete darkness, to concentrate the minds of
the audience on the words.

Shakespeare's Villains: A masterclass in evil devised
by Steven Berkoff

Liverpool Everyman, the Haymarket Theatre, London and tour: June 1998–
One-man show, written, directed by and starring Steven Berkoff. An examination of Iago, Richard III, Macbeth, Shylock, Hamlet, Coriolanus and Oberon, performed with witty virtuosity by Berkoff.

The All-New Super Shakespeare Show by Michael Burrell and Nicholas Moore
The Kings Lynn Festival: July 1998
Director: Michael Burrell
A show for young people about a student writing an essay on Shakespeare, aided by two time-travelling Elizabethans. All ten characters were played by Nicholas Moore.

Enchantment
The Actor's Workshop (Bristol) at the Bath Festival: August 1998
Some of Shakespeare's most famous love scenes updated to the present day, interspersed with madrigals and presented in the round.

Shakespeare d' good stuff
Armes Production Troupe at the Edinburgh Fringe Festival: August 1998

Favourite speeches from Shakespeare presented by two punks from New York.

Shakespeare's Women by Barbara Lewis
Beyond Productions at the Edinburgh Fringe Festival: August 1998

Shakespeare's Mums
Extracts from the plays compiled and performed by Joanna Joseph, an American actress. Edinburgh Fringe Festival: August 1998

Film

Shakespeare In Love
Script: Tom Stoppard
Shakespeare: Joseph Fiennes
Viola: Gwyneth Paltrow
Queen Elizabeth: Judi Dench
USA opening December 1998
UK opening January 1999
An entertaining though unlikely plot with many witty references to Shakespeare's plays and the lives of Shakespeare's contemporaries. The Playhouse set has been stored and is expected to be re-erected in London.

THE YEAR'S CONTRIBUTIONS TO SHAKESPEARE STUDIES

1. CRITICAL STUDIES

reviewed by EDWARD PECHTER

The most significant publication in this year's critical archive is Harold Bloom's *Shakespeare: The Invention of the Human*, though as a cultural event rather than a book. Its central claim – that Shakespeare's characters furnish the self-reflexive models by which we acquire a self to reflect on – is less developed in coherent argument than asserted in a repetitive polemic. Bloom projects himself as a voice in the wilderness, warning the children of literature against the strange, resentful gods of history and politics. This amusing self-dramatization soon wears thin and detracts from the basic claim, which is neither eccentric nor new. The idea that Shakespeare invented the human was itself invented by the Romantics, whose powerful criticism contributed substantially to developing the institutional apparatus within which we still function. But simply to repeat the claims of Hazlitt, Lamb, Emerson, Herder, et al. sounds like parody (think of Bizet's Classical Symphony). Bloom does not explain why most Shakespearian work is no longer sustained by the Romantics, just inveighs against apostasy. The invective has secured him a middlebrow celebrity, but the academic excoriation may be more worrisome. Every Shakespeare session I visited at the 1998 MLA included insouciant dismissals of Bloom, 'not that I've read him', as one speaker said, and audiences responded on cue with derisive laughter, though they prob-

ably had not read him either. Abandoning 'literature', 'character' and 'the human' cannot be cost free, and even if we are prepared to pay for the privilege, the ideas that have sustained so much work over so long a period of time cannot be jettisoned by a simple act of will.

In *The Practice of Reading*, Denis Donoghue invokes Eliot's *Sacred Wood*, the 'first book of criticism that I recall reading', whose pronouncements – poetry as ' "poetry and not as another thing" ', certainly not ' "the inculcation of morals or the direction of politics" ' – have 'lodged with me for so long that I have stopped thinking of them as quotations' (p. 1), and have resulted in his conviction that 'Literature and music can be attended to only in' an 'extrapolitical, extraeconomic space'. Donoghue too is unhappy with current materialism: reading poetry or fiction, 'I should not be using the occasion to plan my next move in the class struggle' (p. 7). These foundational beliefs have roots deeper than Eliot, down into Bradley's 'Poetry for Poetry's Sake', which itself derives from the Romantic claims sustaining Bloom (the poetry-music association is part of the same package). Donoghue thus offers additional testimony for the continuing power of tradition but bears witness to its depletion as well. In the Shakespeare chapter, Othello's collapse is predicated on a wholly word-registered individual self-regard, a vulnerability to and absorption within the stylistic conventions of his own heroic language at the expense of simple truth and reality: Leavis's 'egotism' and Eliot's '*bovarysme*' all over again. *The Practice of Reading* is unfailingly responsive to the nuanced power of literary language; but whatever the value of its main critical commitments, they seem to have lost the capacity to generate urgently compelling work.

On the other hand, Alexander Leggatt's *English Stage Comedy, 1490–1990* offers abundant evidence to suggest that tradition is far from exhausted. Leggatt takes his stand with genre, but not in order to occupy an 'extrapolitical, extraeconomic space'. He insists that comedies are embedded in the details of their cultural moments, and his discussions are informed by recent social history and feminist criticism. Leggatt's main claim, however, is that 'while it does indeed matter that a play was written in the 1630s, or the 1770s, it also matters that it is a comedy' (p. 2). He emphasizes the way comedies talk to each other across history, or to an audience familiar with their conventional materials and thus enabled to enjoy their playing out, with or against generic norms: 'the playwright bonds with the audience in a common awareness of the tradition . . . aided by the theatrical habit of keeping plays in repertory'; even now 'the classic comedies are still widely available as literary texts' (p. 3). Given 'the present state of literary studies', however, Leggatt is worried how long this attenuated common knowledge can survive; we 'need . . . to reintroduce literary scholars to literature' (p. 5). He does not push the point but, in a series of interesting and smart discussions across a broad range of plays, gets on with the job.

In its showcase of exemplary comic bits, *English Stage Comedy* gives pleasure not unlike *That's Entertainment!*, those TV collections of star turns from Hollywood musicals. The material, though, is even better, and Leggatt integrates his illustrations into a powerfully critical understanding. He sees comedy as a conflicted genre: it moves us toward reconciliation but

also the anxiety of laughter; mocks the loner but adopts the loner's detachment; shows us a green world where emancipatory potentials, though, tend to be realized as madness; celebrates the renewal of social order yet tallies the cost to individuals accommodating to communal norms. (Like Tennysonian nature, comedy seems careful of the type but careless of the single life.) The book ends with 'Comedy Against Itself': *Measure for Measure*, where 'the imaginative drive towards death is more clear and compelling than its drive towards marriage' (p. 154), and Ayckbourn's *Woman in Mind*, which works 'against the communal focus of comedy' and 'locks the audience into the consciousness of a single character' whose 'isolation is painful' (pp. 156–7). By the time we get here, these 'anti-comedies' seem exemplary as well as limit cases. Leggatt's idea of comedy is not just internally conflicted but constituted by contrast – to death, pain, and individual isolation: in a word, to tragedy.

Shakespeare figures prominently in the book, but less festively or reparatively than usual. The default has shifted to the dark and problematic. Even *Dream* and *As You Like It* have their rough edges, though Leggatt is too clear-eyed to absorb them into *Measure* or *All's Well*. Jonson, too, is a major player, especially *Epicoene*, where the real eccentricity of his acerbic world gets a good showing. 'Satire' is a word Leggatt does not much use. Though it might help to fine-tune the generic complexity, especially with a Horatian-Juvenalian subdivision, it might also to lead to Polonian excess. Frye is a respected background presence but tending in Leggatt's view to turn comic ambivalence into the transcendence of romance. I missed *Roaring Girl* and *Eastward Ho* and (for 'anti-comedy') Chekhov; but Chekhov's not English, and every reader will have a list of regretted omissions. No reader, though, should wish this stimulating book any shorter.

In *Shakespeare and Social Language*, Lynne Magnusson hits on the idea of approaching Shakespeare through discourse pragmatics – the analysis of language as dialogic exchange among the differentially interested inhabitants of the same linguistic community. From this perspective, where social position is a crucially determining factor for the production and reception (both real and anticipated) of speech, Magnusson moves back and forth between theatrical and non-theatrical texts: on the one hand, rhetorical manuals and letters from bureaucrats and diplomats and merchants and friends to one another and to their superiors, at once negotiating different social interests and taking care of practical business; on the other, a variety of Shakespearian productions, including politeness formulas – 'the complex remedial strategies that serve to minimize the risks to "face"' (p. 117) – in *Henry VIII*; the 'pragmatics of repair' by which speakers protect themselves and their fragile community in *Lear* and *Much Ado* (p. 141); and the many 'competing measures' in the 'complex and variable linguistic market' that establishes credit for speakers in *Othello* (p. 164).

Insisting on the social construction of character and refusing to segregate poetic and non-poetic textual categories, Magnusson aligns herself to current critical taste. Her book, though, is revisionary as well, in regretting the way recent turns away from aesthetics to history and politics have 'drained much of the energy and interest out of language-oriented studies' (p. 5), resulting in 'an impasse' to which her own work is addressed: 'It is time to negotiate some common ground between close reading and cultural politics' (p. 7). In this negotiation, though, Magnusson remains committed to Shakespeare as a pragmatically social text, whose immediately instrumental function absorbs any residual aesthetic impact. Her sense of the plays' 'cultural work' does not include the question of a heterogeneous audience constituted chiefly by a shared theatrical interest and ignores ways (such as Leggatt's genre) in which conventional theatrical stylizations might inflect the social codes represented on stage. Magnusson's aim is to recuperate verbal analysis

for historical purposes, 'to propose taxonomies for verbal analysis that can address the place of collective invention in the production of Shakespeare's complex texts' (p. 7). In this, *Shakespeare and Social Dialogue* is resoundingly successful, offering a rich repertoire of sophisticated and productive analytical procedures by which historical critics can carry on their work. Not all will want to do so; these procedures are not conducive to grand generalizations about paradigm shifts – the 'crisis of representation' (to take one from which Magnusson politely demurs) stemming from the 'instrumental indifference' of a radically new economic formation (p. 124). Magnusson's scepticism about such claims is derived from her respect for the fine-tuned verbal articulations by which Elizabethan society maintained itself, even as it accommodated to gradual change. 'The sustained production of ordinary conversation is a remarkable social achievement' (p. 141), and in the brilliant analyses in abundance here, Magnusson shares her warm-hearted appreciation for the extraordinary beauty and strength of Renaissance language use.

In another part of the forest, far removed from the nuanced and elegantly miniatured negotiations of Renaissance English speech communities, post-colonial Shakespearians are producing thoughtful and important though very different work. *The Tempest* and *Othello* remain centre stage, the subjects of the first two pieces in *Post-Colonial Shakespeares*, a collection based on the conference 'Shakespeare–Post-Coloniality–Johannesburg, 1996'; the focuses for Thomas Cartelli in two of the three main sections in his *Repositioning Shakespeare*; and the centres for many of this year's journal articles. But this familiar material is treated in unpredictably new ways. There is little consensus about these plays or much else among post-colonial critics (even the name – hyphenated?), who keep revising their positions, exploring different territories and arguing with each other about where they have been and should be going. This volatility reflects energy and commitment, and a tendency to argument seems appropriate, given the history from which post-colonial criticism has emerged. As Margo Hendricks remarks about the tensions at Johannesburg, 'it would have been deeply troubling had the conference not ended on this note' (p. 85).

According to Jeremy Brotton, by 'dismissing the significance of the Mediterranean, or Old World references in *The Tempest*, colonial readings have offered a historically anachronistic view' of the play (p. 24). This is Derek Cohen's point, too, shifting interpretive focus from the 'history of colonialism to the older history and practice of slavery' to which the Prospero–Caliban relationship is 'more accurately and precisely' relevant (p. 260). Brotton emphasizes a political dimension as well. In their New World emphasis, 'American new historicist critics over-invest something of their own peculiarly post-colonial identities' (p. 27), thereby reproducing 'the discursive logic of a colonialist discourse' – a systematic and irresistible dominance like the structure 'they ostensibly sought to critique' (p. 26). A similar claim moves Jonathan Burton to redirect attention from *Othello*'s use of Leo Africanus to Leo himself. When 'extricated from the umbra of Shakespeare studies' (p. 45), with its 'monolithic picture of non-European peoples' as 'overpowered' (p. 43), Leo emerges not 'as a toady for European ideology' (p. 46), but as a 'wily' advocate of African civility, playing strategically to European prejudices only to establish the rhetorical ethos necessary to transform them. Leo's extraordinary impact, though, may tell us more about the horizons of his audiences – what white Christian Europe was willing to hear – than about his own intentions: it is hard to see an author beyond so much textual and historical mediation. And as for those American new historicists, who knows what ideology lurks in their hearts?

Nonetheless, these essays articulate a need felt among many post-colonialists to emphasize non-European power and traditions. Hence Martin Orkin claims that Africans in Renaissance Europe were not just impenetrable others, 'imaginable . . . only in terms of lack or absence', but 'bearers of cultures and languages of their own' (p. 15). And for Ania Loomba, 'the invocations of hybridity in most post-colonial theory' tend to 'downgrade the radical potential of notions of authenticity' (p. 147). Like Brotton and Burton, Loomba finds it useful to look away from Shakespeare: 'at first I only asked what it was doing to Shakespeare', she says of a Kathakali *Othello*, but then 'was compelled' to ask 'what the production was doing to Kathakali' (p. 151). The 'indigenous performative and intellectual histories', she concludes, constitute a more 'appropriate context' than the 'colonial heritage of English literary texts' (p. 159). For Michael Neill, on the other hand, 'Anglophone cultures have become so saturated with Shakespeare' that to 'cut oneself off from Shakespeare in the name of a decolonizing politics is not to liberate oneself from the tyranny of the past, but to pretend that the past does not exist' ('Writing away from the Centre', p. 184). Janet Suzman finds the Shakespeare text itself a source of renewal. Beginning with a funk in the UK, 'losing interest in simply doing plays for the sake of doing them' (p. 23), Suzman returns home to South Africa, still in the grip of apartheid, where *Othello* reveals itself 'quite suddenly' and '*at last*' as 'the play that might speak . . . to our anguished country' (p. 24).

Suzman speculates about the difficulty, 'now that democracy has come, to find another play with' such 'reverberations' (p. 40). This gloomy potential is realized in Orkin's account of a post-apartheid South Africa stagnant not just in terms of cultural production. He is sceptical about 'the idea of a linear, historical "progress" which the word "post" brings with it' (p. 18). In a moving and risky piece that caps off *Post-Colonial Shakespeares*, Jonathan Dollimore develops this idea about as far as it can go, dismissing the emancipatory claims of 'wishful theory' in the face of a relentlessly uniform history. The decentring of the subject,

Dollimore argues, is not the end of something (colonialism, humanism, modernity, Enlightenment), but the continuation of a restless expansionary drive that began well before the Renaissance – history without epistemic rupture, no pre-'s or post-'s anywhere in sight. It sounds like the happiest youth in 2 Henry IV who, drinking the diverse liquors in the cup of alteration, would sit him down and die. But Dollimore is neither depressed nor depressing; he maintains both his political commitments and his critical energy (the editors cite Gramsci, 'pessimism of the intellect, optimism of the will').

Post-colonial Shakespearians frequently agree on the need to analyse particular circumstances. Like 'hybridity', the value of 'Shakespeare' depends on who is using it, where, when and how. Contingency can smooth over differences but has its limits. The historical/political binary is deeply embedded in the structure of post-colonial thought – reflected, for instance, in the editors' two-part structure for Post-Colonial Shakespeares, 'the Shakespeare text "then" ' and 'later histories of Shakespeare', and nowhere more clearly than in Cartelli's overriding claim that 'The Tempest is a responsible party to its successive readings and rewritings' as an instrument of colonial rule (p. 89). Whether any text can be guilty of (or master) its own reception seems questionable. Cartelli knows about the Old World Tempest and about Shakespeare's 'complex attitude' to Prospero but takes his stand with Ngũgĩ wa Thiong'o in arguing that, since the play 'participates in a colonialist enterprise that has seldom been known to make distinctions between its colonized subjects', such manifestations of the play's 'historical distance' are 'insignificant' (p. 97). For an American academic, bound to a different kind of knowledge from a Kenyan novelist's and to a different kind of responsibility for its representation, simply to suppress his knowledge as a matter of conscious strategy sounds like a perversely literal application of the idea that blindness produces insight.

'Race', the key term among post-colonialists, can precipitate a similar kind of slippage. In a Forum on 'Race and the Study of Shakespeare', Margo Hendricks collects six pieces representing the range of interest in the topic and the controversy surrounding its interpretive value: do we emphasize the continuities or discontinuities between Renaissance meanings and our own? should 'race' be taken to describe a biologically construed otherness (Erickson), or rather 'a trope of difference' (Chedgzoy, p. 111), developed to give substance (or colour) to an otherwise empty (or white) category like national identity (Gutierrez)? In this context, Kim Hall wonders whether historicist practice seeks 'to avoid the anachronism (or the politics) of the term "race"' (p. 66), and Loomba distances herself from an essay about Othello's representation as powerful because she thinks it works 'to deny our urgent contemporary need to discuss racism' (p. 150). Such statements suggest that presumed motives or presumable consequences determine a claim's interpretive value; they seem to collapse interpretive practice into epistemological theory, as though the situatedness of historical understanding within political interest justifies understanding history as our individual interests dictate. The unpromising alternatives – obligations to the text 'as in itself it really is' within the context of history 'as it really happened' – leave us, as Michael Neill suggests, with an evidently insoluble problem. 'To talk about race in Othello is to fall into anachronism; yet not to talk about it is to ignore something fundamental' about a play that 'continues to torment us' precisely because of the way it 'refuses to align itself with either narrative' ('"Mulattos"', pp. 361 and 374).

Neill begins his essay by quoting a 'perplexed' and witty remark from Virginia Vaughan's contextual history of Othello, 'I think this play is racist, and I think it is not'. Vaughan now revisits the question in terms of a related matter, whether late eighteenth-century audiences registered the play in racial terms. The standard view (assumed, Vaughan acknowledges, in her own book) is that they did not. Now she thinks they did. As with similar revisionary claims (Jews *were* a significant presence in Shakespeare's London, women *were* a significant presence on the English stage in Shakespeare's time), the evidence is fundamentally unchanged from the material previously used to support the traditional view. According to Vaughan, William Cooke's 'denial' of racial feeling in his description of Spranger Barry's Othello 'suggests its power' (p. 64). 'Perhaps [Francis] Gentleman's seeming silence about race is not silence at all' (p. 66). These conclusions, supported by either contradictory or absent evidence, are nonetheless not implausible. They are based on the fact that late eighteenth-century England was very much concerned with racial matters (the slavery debates, a conspicuous black presence in London) and on the assumption that theatrical production is 'necessarily imbricated in the broader discourses that surround it' (p. 57). In this context, the apparent disconnection may indeed be only apparent, denial a sign of being in denial. But although disconnection can be pathological (the concentration camp guard who unwinds with Hölderlin and Brahms after a busy day at the gas chamber), without some capacity for disconnection (as the Player King in *Hamlet* suggests) we'd all be mad. Moreover, since theatre depends on disconnection, the mere fact of its existence does not give us leverage to determine its value (unless we aim to deny the power of theatre as a relatively autonomous form of cultural production). Vaughan several times refers to Othello's 'biological heritage', but the issue is precisely whether late eighteenth-century audiences understood Othello's colour in terms of an anatomically determined racial identity. If not, they would not see his blackness (it would not matter) unless the context asked them to. Nonetheless, they soon would. By the second decade of the nineteenth century, Kean's tawny make up and Lamb's and Coleridge's disgust at

a black Othello make it clear that Othello had been assimilated into the newly established norms of 'racial science'. This is the place where Vaughan's case could be most persuasive: since such assimilation does not happen all at once, late eighteenth-century silence must, arguably, signify the repression rather than the absence of racist feeling. But the issue is bound to remain irritatingly inconclusive. Even in the relatively serene context of intellectual history, 'race' is an insoluble problem.

Along with 'race', the most resonant term in post-colonial criticism is 'nation'. These terms may sound synonymous to us (*ein Volk, ein Reich*; in the Québecois version, *un peuple, une nation*), but 'nation' in the Renaissance seems to operate rather in opposition to a racially marked tribal otherness. Neill detects a seventeenth-century shift in 'definitions of alterity', with 'colour emerging as the most important criterion for defining otherness, even as *nation* becomes the key term of *self*-definition' ('"Mulattos"', p. 367). But then what constitutes the national self? 'What ish my nation?' as the Irishman asks in *Henry V* in an accent indicating that whatever his is, it is not 'ours', but leaving the question what ours is, other than not his. Several pieces take on the idea of the early modern English nation as a community imagined in linguistic terms. Alan Rosen notes that, like Shylock, the Prince of Morocco has a distinct and eccentric manner of speaking (Arragon too?). In a richly documented and strongly argued piece, Carla Mazzio examines the conflicted responses to 'the presence of foreign and "barbaric" elements within the national vocabulary' (p. 208). Some gave them welcome as a stranger, others anxiously resisted them as contaminations. The issue floats above *Merchant* 1.2, where Portia's jokes about continental outlandishness climax in the Englishman as nullity, with no language, dress or behaviour of his own. This varies on a standard joke ('there', says the gravedigger about England, 'the men are as mad as he') and seems to confirm Leggatt's point about the proximity of laughter to anxiety, here contained (both senses) in the idea of national identity as a back formation: the linguistic others who seem to threaten also serve to constitute what might otherwise be an empty category. English national identity may be 'nothing if not critical', *merely* not the Irishman's – or the Welshman's. According to Terence Hawkes in a characteristically sharp and funny piece, 'Welshness and its concerns' (p. 136) deserve as much attention as Irishness has received as one of the 'untidy exoticisms' that the history plays must 'try to shoe-horn' into the 'volatile, unstable text that is Shakespeare's "Britain"' (p. 129). These concerns can take a variety of forms, such as castrating women and magic, but chief among them is language, the sheer bodily unspeakableness to English mouths of the Welsh words so conspicuously spoken and sung in *1 Henry IV*.

Post-colonialist Shakespearians are exploring exotic new territories, even the USA. The most distinctive feature of *Repositioning Shakespeare* is a section on 'Democratic Vistas' – Emerson and Whitman, Edwin Forrest's native drama as attempt to foster 'a democratic alternative' to Shakespeare's 'aristocratic bias' (p. 36). Nineteenth-century America may be technically a colonized culture, but it is a stretch to include it with the East and West Indian and African territories on the standard grid – going all over the map in a conceptual sense. Cartelli recognizes the problem – 'postcolonial literary studies is . . . very broadly – some would say, badly – defined' (p. 4) – but sticks to his guns. Rightly so: the considerable value of his project and of the project in general is not chiefly theoretical power or coherence but inclusion. Post-colonialist Shakespearians are bringing different authors and texts into view, some with familiar names, like Shakespeare and *Othello*, but many, like Tayeb Salih's *Season of Migration to the North* and Michelle Cliff's *No Telephone to Heaven*, altogether strange (at least they are new to me).

The 1996 World Congress of the International Shakespeare Association met in Los Angeles, and *Shakespeare and the Twentieth Century*, Jonathan Bate, Jill Levenson and Dieter Mehl's edition of the selected proceedings, indicates it was an exciting event. If we understand 'Post-Colonial Shakespeare' as an inflection of 'Shakespeare and the Twentieth Century', generated out of a similarly ironic sense of continuity and discontinuity, some not wholly fanciful connections emerge. This volume's two-part structure, 'Shakespeare in the Twentieth Century', 'Twentieth-Century Readings of Shakespeare', maps easily onto Loomba-Orkin's 'then' and 'later'. Questions of 'appropriation' surface again. For Margorzata Grzegorzewska, 'twentieth-century appropriations' of Shakespeare's love poetry in Polish music 'threaten the univocality of Shakespearian verse even as they evoke it to render the authenticity . . . of love' (p. 150). Tetsuo Kishi, describing Shakespeare's transformation into musical theatre, claims that 'one has to accommodate and appropriate Shakespeare's language' to the new genre (p. 159). These doublets – threaten and evoke, accommodate and appropriate – connect to the distinction Cartelli develops (pp. 15–20) between 'appropriation' and 'emulation' as contestatory versus celebratory kinds of response. The distinction may be unsustainable – emulation is never free of aggressive competition (*Troilus*), appropriation always winds up reproducing what it seeks to repudiate (Judith Butler et al.) – but some version of it seems nonetheless indispensable for critical practice.

We have many words to describe such cultural exchanges – 'negotiation', 'dialectical' – but the apparent favourite this year is 'translation', treated by Yoshiko Kawachi in LA and elsewhere by Penny Gay, who expands the idea to include the performance of an historically remote text: 'directors and actors *always* translate the text into their contemporary tongue . . . Shakespeare is either our contemporary or he is nothing' ('Shakespeare in Translation', p. 139). Graham Bradshaw and Kaori Ashizo (we are back in LA) similarly expand the idea of translation to include all interpretive efforts to connect across difference, cultural as well as historical. 'There is no "straight" Shakespeare; we are all "translators" (p. 350). According to Gay, however (in a different piece included in the LA volume), Australians wishing to perform Shakespeare 'in their own idiom . . . must in some way subvert' the ending of *Shrew* since, 'done "straight"', it represents 'submission both to patriarchy and to text-as-imperial law' ('Recent Australian *Shrews*', p. 170). 'Straight' Shakespeare may be a fiction, but some Shakespearian translations are more bent than others.

Contributors to this sumptuous volume describe Shakespeare's nourishment of and/or cannibalization by a variety of modern cultural productions – Joyce's *Ulysses* (Reichert), film noir (Jacobs), Angela Carter's *Wise Children* (Apfelbaum), Branagh's *Much Ado* (Hattaway), among others. More generally, Stanley Cavell considers what our attitude should be to Shakespeare's continuing power. Cavell's argument with current materialism has clear affinities with Bloom (both work out of Emerson), but he is less interested in derogating the 'School of Resentment' than trying to understand and even link with it. Cavell loves the 'saturation' of Shakespeare's text (Neill's word in a different context) and understands 'praise' as the proper response – criticism as epideictic rhetoric, in effect, celebrating the 'devotion' and 'communality' Shakespeare continues 'to inspire'. Here is where Cavell finds his connection with the iconoclasts: since the 'stronger the wonder . . . the less satisfying a conventional praise', a 'contempt or fear of false praise is common ground', leaving the question whether 'such false praise is so appalling, or harmful', as to be 'called idolatry and consequently greeted with' an appropriate 'smashing' of 'its monuments' (p. 237). Cavell understands what Bloom, for all his affection for Falstaff, fails to – this is 'a question to be asked'.

Two exceptional pieces in *Twentieth-Century Shakespeare* offer exemplary resolutions of conflict, if not experiences of transcendence. Peter Womack takes on the history/politics binary,

describing a 'two-way traffic' in which 'the image of early modern theatre, as it appeared to the twentieth century, was shaped by modernist theatre practice' which was 'in turn shaped by the image' as historians developed it, producing conceptual breakthroughs in both domains. In Womack's view, historical research becomes helpful to cultural production, not by a will to power, but by being its relatively autonomous self. 'The reconstruction of the old – always an exercise of the imagination because of the paucity of evidence – was a form of self-understanding of the new' (p. 77). Ellen O'Brien focuses on the actor/director split: a residual Stanislavskian devotion to character on the one hand, an innovative *mise-en-scène* driven by theories of decentred subjectivity on the other. O'Brien nods to W. B. Worthen, who has been analysing this and related conflicts for some time, and who produced a very strong piece this year on the issue of scripted drama versus emancipated performance. In Worthen's view, these contradictions are fundamentally irresolvable, but O'Brien describes a 1995 Santa Cruz *Tempest* where things worked out. The director got his Caliban to loosen up on continuity but, in his 'moment by moment' approach (p. 129), left the actor with spots of motivational time where performance could be grounded in the character's authentic desire. O'Brien thinks there are transferable theoretical and practical models here, but success may have depended on contingency as well – a long friendship between the actor and the director, each with experience in the other's function. Even as a one-off, though, the success O'Brien describes, like Womack's piece, suggests the gratifying possibility of at least transient occasions not beset with contrariety of desire.

This seems to have been the Year of the Collection – seven, not counting the annuals. Though none is as consistently stimulating or coherent as *Shakespeare in the Twentieth Century*, all have at minimum good things on display. *Shakespearean Illuminations* is a *festschrift* for Marvin Rosenberg with the appropriate throughline, perceptible in many of the contributions, of acting – that cultural practice where literary criticism, theatrical history and performance intersect. Or fail to intersect: the 'Shakespeare' approached from and constituted by such different critical positions may have only a nominal unity. The issue is difference and translation again, though here readers have to tease it out for themselves. The editors group the first ten essays under the rubric of 'The Major Tragedies', though only two have anything to say (and only in passing) about tragedy as such. But contributors bear responsibility for occasional conceptual fuzziness as well, not always fully recognizing the acrobatics required in negotiating between the disciplines of text and performance. Hugh Richmond, convinced that *Lear* is 'the ultimate illustration of theatrical, not to say literary excellence' (p. 110), offers a hypothetical actor a miscellany of suggestions that might be of equal use indiscriminately to a reader of the play. Stephen Booth argues that acting delights us because of the 'collision' sensed between 'the actors' own identities' and 'the identities they assume in the particular fiction', but since this abstract formulation is a 'common denominator of all aesthetic pleasure' (p. 262), it applies unspecifically to any artistic experience. Jay Halio, claiming that the minimal early stage directions make 'some directorial license . . . permissible without distorting Shakespeare's design' (p. 104), leaves us to develop principles for determining the textual design and the nature and extent of a director's obligation to it.

Even some of the stronger essays leave stones unturned. Ellen O'Brien takes on the question how a textual 'role' becomes a theatrical 'character', but it is hard to see any necessary connection between her preliminary 'role-mapping' procedures and performance effects. G. B. Shand, focusing on Gertrude in Q1, describes in sharp detail the systematic erasure of Q2's and F's 'tantalizing motivational indeterminacies'. In characterizing the result as 'accomplished theatricality' (p. 34), Shand makes

claims similar to those made for Shakespeare as the only true begetter of F *Lear*. As the *Lear* argument strips 'Shakespeare' down to 'Shakespeare the Professional' (keep the action moving; no frills, no fads, no fancy stuff), so Shand implies an arguably diminished notion of theatrical value. He understands the problem, conceding at the end 'that all this spare Q1 treatment of the Queen' may amount 'to nothing more' than 'mindless patriarchal obliviousness', but he opts for 'real theatrical intelligence and craft' nonetheless (p. 45). In Sidney Homan's contribution, the issue is not the literature/theatre but the actor/director binary about which O'Brien spoke in LA. The 'director's concept', Homan remarks, provoked by his daunted Hippolyta's 'what do I do now?' is 'generally avoided by actors' (p. 280). These conflicting concerns have become the basis for a standard theatre gag (British director to American Method actor: 'don't just do something, stand there!'). Thanks to Homan's own directorial sympathy and 'the mutual role of actor and audience' (p. 294; always mutual? what kind of actor or audience?), things worked out for this production, though as with *Romeo and Ethel* (where we meet the same basic joke: 'it's about this nurse'), the convergence of such different interests seems to be the product of magic more than method.

John Russell Brown, describing two recent productions of *The Duchess of Malfi*, is less sanguine. He acknowledges the misalliance between Chekhov's stage and Webster's, but Method offers 'such assurance to actors' that directors have to respect it and can even use it to good effect, producing 'the thrill of actuality' in 'many moments' (p. 321). But there are losses as well, when actorly authenticity, 'the prevalent emphasis on *moments* of truth', interrupts the rhythm of the action and obscures 'the development of ideas, through all its repetitions, hesitations, digressions' (p. 333). No fully happy ending here, and as Lois Potter suggests, none may be possible. Potter takes off from the readiness with which we believe, in the absence of conclusive evidence, that Shakespeare was not a good actor, suggesting that we intuitively understand authorial and actorly production as incompatible. This idea is often said to originate with Lamb, but Potter's abundantly informative piece suggests it was in place much earlier than the Romantics. Barbara Hodgdon does not argue either/or, she assumes it. Describing two recent *Macbeth*s, she avoids putting them 'in relation to each other, or reading one through the other' as a way of refusing those 'paradigms that revolve around . . . "Shakespearean" textual authority' (p. 159). Performance for Hodgdon signifies in the context of other contemporary performances, theatrical or otherwise. In this *'material theatre . . . language* is only one – and perhaps not the most hegemonic – signifying practice' (p. 160). Not everyone will wish to relinquish the foundational status of the Shakespeare text, but this move enables Hodgdon to describe contemporary performance with extraordinary clarity and interpretive power.

Translation comes up again in one of the most striking contributions to *Strands Afar Remote: Israeli Perspectives on Shakespeare*. Harai Golomb quotes a nineteenth-century preface to a Hebrew Shakespeare: 'let us inflict our vengeance this day upon the sons of Albion! They have taken unto themselves our Holy Scriptures . . . Now we too shall [take] unto our bosom what they deem holy' (pp. 255–6). With Rosen's piece on *Merchant*, this early instance of the empire writing back may suggest an Israeli take on post-colonialism. Avraham Oz tries to make the connection, emphasizing 'the national project' in a brief editorial Foreword and a lengthy Afterword, but has to acknowledge that the book's 'Israeli Perspectives' are 'somewhat diffused' (p. 12). Hence in another sharp piece, Elizabeth Freund seems closer to *Tel Quel* than to Tel Aviv, analysing *Troilus* and *Lucrece* among other Shakespearian and non-Shakespearian texts in terms of the frustrated 'desire for representation' experienced by characters and audiences alike. Michael Yogev is also interested in *Troilus* and in a similar context, combining psychodynamic and language-centred poststructuralist accounts of identity formation in order 'to analyze the way in which language and "heroic" activity at once constitute and subvert the identities of the protagonists in Shakespeare's bitter drama' (p. 87). These essays work well together with David Hillman's piece, reviewed in these pages last year, on language and the body in Shakespeare's 'Gastric Epic'. In his own contribution to *Strands Afar Remote*, Hillman now transfers this method to *Hamlet*, with equally impressive results. These are all strong essays, but they tell us nothing about Israeli Shakespeare studies as such other than that it is a sophisticated and thriving enterprise.

Shakespeare studies flourishes down under as well. *Shakespeare: Readers, Audiences, Players* brings together papers from an Australian and New Zealand Shakespeare Association conference in Perth. R. S. White's helpful Introduction emphasizes the 'processes of mediation' among the kinds of interpreters listed in the title (p. 1). This may be too broad a topic to sustain a sharp focus, but the volume includes memorable pieces. Jonathan Bate describes the cultural wars of early nineteenth-century theatre, centred in Kemble versus Kean and in the Old Prices fray, as part of an argument about Shakespeare's availability to forces other than reaction. Charles Edelman turns a critical eye on the evidence of light punctuation in early texts, suggesting that subsequent tendencies to add exclamation points may be creating the false impression of a rhetorical histrionic style. Ann Blake offers an amazingly compressed review of the various claims made about boy actors, leaving herself room to argue that the effect on illusion and belief was not qualitatively different from Renaissance theatrical practice generally. Another book adding up to less than the sum of its nonetheless often engaging parts.

No focus problem exists in Gillian Kendall's collection, *Shakespearean Power and Punishment*, which occupies a clearly defined area, staked out with the signposts of 'power relations' and inhabited by the suffering bodies of subjects inscribed with the marks of an authoritarian apparatus. Nine contributors confidently implement the mature interpretive technology available to excavate this territory. The first three focus on women: the stabbed or nearly stabbed heroines of *Cymbeline* and *Philaster* who illustrate the 'attempt to eradicate female powers, both physically and politically' (Collier, p. 42), the aestheticized bodies of the Lady (*Second Maiden's Tragedy*) and Hermione, whose monumental framing deprives them of their capacity to arouse sexual or epistemological anxiety (Eaton). Ann Rosalind Jones stresses, rather, transgression: Maria in *Twelfth Night*, the Windsor wives (finally contained, she claims, within the norms of patriarchal marriage) and the more radically subversive female power dramatized in *Swetnam the Woman-Hater*. Jones's canny acknowledgement of diverse textual effects – 'contained, displaced, turned loose' (p. 23) – coincides with the late-Foucauldian emphasis in the book as a whole, power emanating not from a single source but from an array of moving positions. Hence the final three essays focus on 'The Limits of Power', including a notably vulnerable Prospero (Macdonald), and the middle three on *Measure* all work from an ironized Duke, far removed from the celebrated absolutism of a little while ago. In the book's most impressive piece, Robert Watson develops his claims in earlier work to produce a Leggatt-like version of *Measure* as an 'anti-comedy' ruthlessly exposing the inadequacy of the conventional comic closure in procreative marriage: 'subserving the survival instincts of the body politic' (p. 137), it nonetheless wholly 'fails to satisfy either our spiritual or our narcissistic cravings' for individual continuity or transcendence (p. 135) – an impotent denial of the death threat at the centre of the dramatic experience.

As this and earlier discussion suggests, gender and sexuality remain fertile sites for Shakespearian critical production. In *Patriarchy and Incest from Shakespeare to Joyce*, Jane Ford is interested in the 'resolution of the incest-threat for the father and daughter through marriage to a suitor'. She first got interested in this idea reading Joyce. Then, on the model of Freud, who 'once said of his case histories, 'I read them over and over again until they begin to speak to me''', she 'made it the central focus of my reading to seek out' this 'pattern', 'usually finding' it in some variation or other. The positive results are reported in five chapters, of which 'The Triangle in Shakespeare' is the first (the others describe 'The Triangle' in Dickens, James, Conrad and Joyce). Believing that 'the psyche of the writer reaches out to the psyche of the reader across the bridge of the written page' (p. x), Ford gives a selective sampling of items from the Shakespeare biography – 'the now notorious "second-best bed"' makes it (p. 39), but nothing about the Stratford tithes – heavily indebted to Stephen's arabesques in *Ulysses*, apparently offered with a straight face. She claims that 'variations on the father/daughter theme are central to at least twenty-one of Shakespeare's plays', but her main focus is on *Pericles* and *Tempest*. I have trouble with Ford's definite articles (*the* father, daughter, triangle, author, reader), and her bridges across text and history look unsturdy to me. Readers who do not share these concerns should get more out of this book, on the model of Freud or Ford herself. Seek and you will find, ask and it will be given to you.

Julia Walker's *Medusa's Mirrors* is a much more interesting and sophisticated book, though I had a similar kind of trouble with it. Walker builds on the belief that 'a male writer cannot perceive and construct the selfhood of a female character with the same assurance that he crafts male interiority' (p. 11). This idea is first hooked on to an elaborate and often brilliantly developed distinction between the Narcissus and the Perseus/Medusa myths (self-recognition versus the image of the female other reflected as an act of containment), then applied to Britomart, Cleopatra and Eve as less than fully realized selves. Walker acknowledges that claims about Renaissance interiority are controversial, and that Cleopatra's inner self-hood is especially hard to find (no soliloquies, always changing), but she perseveres as though coherent and purposive interiority exhausted all possibility for theatrical presence and cultural value. Since such self-possession is inevitably gendered male, the effect may be to turn Cleopatra into an honorary man and to reinforce the binaries that the play, arguably, works to deconstruct. The larger problem is over-investment in authorial control defined in anatomical terms. 'We can hardly expect this to be otherwise', she says about her heroines' inadequately represented selfhood, 'insofar as all of the authors are male' (p. 190). But cultural production cannot be so fully determined by anatomy if anatomy itself is at least partly a cultural production. Walker concedes at the end that the diminished female presence in Renaissance texts 'tells us less about the imaginations of the individual authors . . . than about the assumptions of the culture from which they grew and in which they participated' (p. 194) and in this context makes interesting connections to Elizabeth (Octavius assumes control over Cleopatra's memory in a way that reflects James's agenda for his predecessor). But the lively interpretive intelligence and historical understanding in this book never fully liberate themselves from a disabling central idea.

That biology is not destiny is central to Gail Paster's argument, carrying on from her studies of leaky female vessels to focus now on the 'unbearable coldness of female being'. Paster claims that the various versions of the single-sex theory in Laqueur, Greenblatt and Parker were fixated on bodies. It is rather the irreducible distinction between male heat and female cold that Paster sees as the 'key subtending issue' (p. 428) underlying all other attributes of gender difference, including anatomical ones. In effect, the 'caloric' or 'humoral economy' functions not like a semantics, as something to think about, but like a grammar, a structure to

think within. Like Althusserian ideology, it constitutes and limits the range of discourse. From this perspective, Paster casts a cool eye on recent emancipatory interpretations of the comedies. In *Twelfth Night*, the 'complex register of physiological and temperamental difference works to secure' rather than to destabilize 'sexual and social differences' (p. 435). She thus arrives by a very different route at Walker's conclusion – Shakespeare is perforce not a proto-feminist. The evidence is not wholly conclusive. By way of demonstrating the authority of the humoral economy, Paster describes how Helkiah Crooke 'works hard to contain the ontological possibility of female heat' (p. 427), but if the system were all-determining, Crooke would not even be able to register negative evidence, let alone feel such anxiety to refute it. According to Paster, Bacon's complaint that the 'common phrases of physicians concerning Radical Moisture and Natural Heat are deceptive' shows that the humoral assumptions were impossible to disprove (p. 418), but it can also be understood to register a pre-Enlightenment competition for scientific authority between a variety of discourses. Such quibbles notwithstanding, this essay deserves to have the same strong impact as Paster's earlier work.

The 1998 *Shakespeare Jahrbuch* devotes six pieces to 'Shakespeare's Women in a Male Theater'. For Ina Schabert, authorship is only one of many factors (actors, the plays' sources, etc.) which account for the institutional maleness of the Renaissance theatre, as a consequence of which '"women" in Shakespeare's theatre are male constructions of woman'. According to Schabert, the female actors of the Restoration changed things on stage, but by reconstructing Shakespeare as a literary text, the self-appointed male custodians of the critical institution recuperated Shakespeare as their own preserve, 'a theatre of the mind where male phantasms of woman may exist uninhibited' (p. 28). Schabert's piece connects interestingly with Roger Paulin's account of Luise

Gottsched and Dorothea Tieck and with Ann Thompson's elsewhere about Furnivall's relationship with Teena Rochfort Smith. Both call attention to the presence even within critical history of heretofore invisible women behind or at least around the big men. Schabert's piece connects in a different way with Phyllis Rackin's, for whom even Restoration actresses do not make much of an impact on male hegemony. Rackin starts from the regular practice of representing women's parts in a historically unspecific manner in contrast to the period costume for high-status men. She then connects this stage tradition with changing beliefs about the value of breastfeeding which, for all the contradictions and variations, she understands 'with the advantage of hindsight' as unified within 'the long term project of denying class difference in an ideology of universal humanity, differentiated only by gender . . . that produced the ideal of the domesticated wife' (p. 39).

Other commentators on the public/private dichotomy caution against dissolving differences into the big picture of 'the long-term project'. For Sasha Roberts, reviewing the evidence for women as early modern readers of Shakespeare and other texts, ' "the private sphere" itself is a complex domain that we should resist essentialising'. Roberts argues that 'private chambers could offer' at least some privileged women 'a degree of personal freedom . . . even as, in different discourses, privacy was used as an ideological tool to marginalize women from "public" life' (pp. 56–7). Lena Orlin goes further than this. Describing nine distinct meanings for 'closet' in Shakespeare's England, Orlin argues that 'the female closet' or 'the queer closet' may be based on stable current values anachronistically imposed on a complex and volatile situation. From this perspective, hindsight, though it is all we have, can be a disadvantage. Orlin's essay provides no big payoff in terms of interpretive conviction, let alone certainty, but the details she makes available are fascinating in themselves, and she enriches the context, astutely demonstrating theatrical values available for the 'closet scene' in *Hamlet* based on all her possible closets. This is a generously documented essay, drawing on a wealth of archival and secondary material to open up rather than close down interpretation – historical criticism as good as it gets.

In a review essay in this year's *Shakespeare Studies*, Jean Howard remarks that 'gay, lesbian and queer criticisms now have an acknowledged place' on the current scene (p. 105), a claim for which there is abundant confirmation. In 'Queer Virgins', Theodora Jankowski shifts from an exclusive focus on 'non-dominant sexualities' – a move Howard judges desirable (p. 120) – to focus on Isabella in *Measure*, among other Shakespearian and non-Shakespearian virgins who may be claimed to disrupt the heteronormative economy. In a complexly suggestive piece, Nora Johnson juxtaposes the Ganymede/Lord couple with the model of sexual desire she sees represented in *Winter's Tale* and by Renaissance theatre generally. The former allows for a kind of consequence-free sexual tourism, visiting the androgynous boy without jeopardizing the stable privileges of a distinctly male and aristocratic power. The latter, by contrast, involves 'a much more unsettling effect', a 'peculiarly theatrical breakdown of the distinctions', producing 'not only the free play of sexual desire, but also the power of that desire to adhere to subjects' (p. 211).

Two essays in this year's material focus on the 'homosocial'. Zvi Jagendorf does not use that term (or refer to Sedgwick, Girard, or Irigaray), but his *Merchant* dramatizes 'the implied competition between homosexual love characterized by debt and heterosexual love that releases treasure' (p. 20). According to Jagendorf, 'What is intriguing is the position of Portia vis-à-vis the two male points of the triangle' (p. 31), where she is at once the blocking figure and the goal of romance, a 'hybrid *Jewoman*, part Portia, part Shylock' (p. 34). Gordon McMullan looks at the Palamon–

Arcite–Emilia configuration in *Kinsmen* in at least two distinctive ways. He connects the male bond to the question of collaborative authorship, arguing that the play makes available (not as thematic or metadramatic intention) a model for understanding collaboration more useful than those currently available. In addition, he brings female desire, usually inconsequential in this critical framework, into a position of central prominence. McMullan, who does invoke the critical epithet and eminences I mentioned earlier, is responsive at once to theoretical, textual and theatrical nuance.

In the most substantial contribution to sexuality studies this year, Celia Daileader is concerned with the eroticism not just in but of Renaissance plays, their capacity to arouse as well as to represent desire. She describes how Middleton (*Women Beware Women*, *A Mad World*) and Shakespeare (*Othello*, *Romeo*) make us want to know about off-stage experiences of sexual knowledge, then shows how the literally absent female body (Maria in Fletcher's *Tamer Tamed*, Ursula in *Bartholomew Fair*) is made theatrically present. Subsequent chapters connect erotic and spiritual desire: Webster's Duchess and Middleton's Lady in *The Second Maiden's Tragedy* as sacrificial deaths; the constant bawdy in Renaissance dramatic language, illustrating Daileader's claim that the sexual replaced the sacred as area of ultimate concern. This claim is based on an idea of epistemic shift – the Reformation, discoveries about anatomy, geography, cosmography – that is bound to seem speculative. About eros itself, Daileader is also more suggestive than conclusive, oscillating between arguably incompatible models – a Barthesian intermittency, all flashes and hints, an in-your-face carnivalesque excess. Either way, Middleton looks like a misfit to me: plenty of sex, but the erotic potential diverted into commercial motivations for the characters and satiric detachment for the audience, whose desire for knowledge (of the Duke and Bianca's off-stage sex, say) is diminished by the sense

there's nothing much we *can* know, little of the Shakespearian full subjectivity with which feelingly to engage. But eroticism is like art: we know what we like, but cannot agree how to define or measure it. Daileader disarmingly abandons her deconstructive feminism whenever it jeopardizes the infectious delight she takes in the plays. Unlike the austerely de Manian Freund, for whom the desire for representation is never fulfilled, Daileader embraces the 'goal of touching the body directly' (p. 138). 'But why', she asks of Judith Butler's constructionism, '*should* sex mean anything?' (p. 141) Perhaps because, once emancipated from all cultural codes, desire is hard to talk about coherently (Leo Bersani may be an exception). At one point Daileader strings together 128 feast words from Fletcher and suggests we ought to read them out loud (pp. 64–5). In a similar predicament in the LA volume, Gary Taylor, insisting on the priority of affect in Renaissance theatrical experience, struggles to produce an appropriate methodology for interpretive action. Still, an emphasis on the erotic effects of Renaissance theatre is fully justified, and Daileader's smart, ambitious and engaging book should communicate pleasure as well as profit to a substantial audience.

The 1998 *Shakespeare Survey* collects nine pieces on eighteenth-century Shakespeare, beginning with Catherine Alexander's overview of recent criticism and research. Much more than a survey, Alexander's piece describes and locates a variety of primary and secondary materials for examining the criticism, editing, theatrical production and adaptation of Shakespeare during the eighteenth century. She is particularly detailed on the visual arts. So is the whole issue, which is lavishly illustrated with eighteenth-century theatrical portraiture and includes Desmond Shawe-Taylor's discussion of the Garrick Club holdings. People will be gratefully working out of this *Survey* and especially the generously stocked research archive of Alexander's piece for a long time to come.

According to Alexander, the field is dominated by 'the contemporary critical and cultural issues of politicization, appropriation, production, the visual image, and nationalism'. While this 'propensity to read eighteenth-century Shakespeare through the filter of late twentieth-century ideas' is 'intellectually inevitable' and 'propels eighteenth-century Shakespeare *forwards*' (p. 1), she maintains that the 'focus on materialism rather than aesthetics leaves some lacunae' (p. 14). 'Political appropriation has received more attention than literary application' (p. 15). Although such claims can be made about other areas of Shakespearian (and non-Shakespearian) study as well, they help to explain what looks like the specially strong attraction of eighteenth-century Shakespeare for current research. If we are motivated now by a desire to get underneath the aesthetic Shakespeare constructed by the Romantics, what better place to be propelled *backwards* than to the eighteenth century?

As an example of these 'lacunae', Alexander notes that 'an important anthology' like Dodd's *Beauties* 'is largely ignored' (p. 15). In an apparent exception, Sue Tweg's Perth paper speculates about the relation between Dodd as a reading anthology and a variety of eighteenth-century performance practices, from professional theatres to family productions at home. But Tweg's surprise at discovering Dodd, which she 'came across' by 'serendipity' (p. 31), and her uncertainty how to deal with it ('I had never thought much about . . . anthologized Shakespeare circulating in the same environment as a play text' [p. 32]) provide indirect confirmation of Alexander's point about the absence of an aesthetic context for current critical work.

There is more direct confirmation in the shared focus on adaptation in some of the other *Survey* contributors. Irena Cholij describes the many different musical settings of eighteenth-century *Tempests*. A. Luis Pujante finds new evidence to reinforce the belief that Theobald's *Double Falsehood* is not a forgery and therefore can give us glimpses into the lost *Cardenio*. But

it is the emphasis on 'political appropriation' in this *Survey* that provides the strongest confirmation of Alexander's analysis. In 'Daddy's Girls', Jean Marsden describes three mid-century adaptations – Garrick's *Lear*, Cumberland's *Timon* and Theophilus Cibber's *Romeo* – all of which transform Shakespearian originals to emphasize 'the icon of the daughter/subject'. According to Marsden, this self-effacing femininity, by 'furnishing England's national poet with appropriately British versions of female rectitude', produces 'a profoundly nationalistic response' (p. 26). The 'main purpose' of Sonia Massai's piece is 'to identity the ideological purposes' (p. 68) served by Lillo's updating of *Pericles* in *Marina* in a way that reinforces 'the bourgeois values of domestic virtue, chastity and industry'. In contrast to Marsden, Massai emphasizes counter-hegemonic effects as well, claiming that Lillo's transformations 'undertake a dialectic critique of those very values', basically through an ironic representation of prostitution as just another professional/commercial enterprise (p. 77). The background for Katherine West Scheil's essay is the marauding Waltham Blacks, a band of apparently high-status blacked-up poachers who represented, or were seen to represent, a Jacobist threat to the government in the early 1720s. Against this background, Scheil shows how Charles Johnson's adaptation of *As You Like It* used Shakespeare's emerging authority as the national poet to make a timely intervention on behalf of the Whig government's Black Act.

Not everyone in this *Survey* labours happily within the confines of current norms. Martin Scofield takes off from the eighteenth-century view of Richardson as another Shakespeare to develop generic, thematic and moral similarities and differences between *Clarissa* and the plays. Scofield recognizes that 'the notion of a "human nature"' underwriting such a comparison 'has become (notoriously) in recent years almost impossible to use' (p. 27) but argues that 'if we can only see where we differ from the past, and where past periods differ from each other, those differences lose their power to provoke and challenge us' (p. 43). Marcus Walsh takes on current norms directly, though unpolemically, in a piece about eighteenth-century editorial practice. Walsh acknowledges that 'appropriation' may be the right word to characterize theatrical adaptation and critical commentary but claims that editorial work operated within a fundamentally different programme of recovering original intention. He thinks that current scepticism about this programme is unjustified and tries to provide a theoretical foundation for its underlying principles in E. D. Hirsch's distinction between 'meaning' and 'significance'. Since Hirsch's distinction is easy to deconstruct, this attempt is not successful, but it does not have to be; whatever its theoretical vulnerability, the historicist *practice* of eighteenth-century editing remains fundamental to all Shakespearian commentary. Even the most robust materialist stands on the shoulders of giants like Theobald and Capell. In Walsh's essay, as in his recent book, historicist procedures do not materialize suddenly out of the ether of divine fiat or epistemic shift, like Pope's Newton or de Grazia's Malone, but develop gradually and cumulatively into the position of authority which enables them, even now, to survive routine assaults upon their putatively naive and empiricist historicism.

There were three additions in 1998 to the Northcote/British Council Writers and Their Work Series. All are lively and intelligent but in terms of format, as brief introductions designed primarily for students, they are not equally successful. Locating *Richard II* in Kiernan Ryan's 'liminal phase' of English history, 'poised between "two great epochs", neither feudal nor bourgeois' (p. 31), Margaret Healy claims that the play 'helped prepare the way for the deposition and killing of a king and the increasing democratization of government half a century later' (p. 37). This progressive analysis extends to critical history as well, in which 'the more theoretically informed and self-aware criticism of the last twenty years or so' is said to

have displaced the 'dogmatic, patriarchal literary criticism' of the past (p. 61). I am uncomfortable with this tendency to teleological triumphalism ('destined' is a reiterated word) and with what I take to be an exaggerated claim for *Richard II*'s political consequentiality. But Healy leaves plenty of room for disagreement, and given the play's stylized remoteness from current student interests, her way of 'bringing a small but important piece of the past into a meaningful dialogue with us today' makes sense (p. xi).

Sasha Roberts, writing about *Romeo and Juliet*, faces the opposite problem – not inaccessibility but overexposure. The play, she tells us in her first words, is 'familiar to the point of cliché', a situation she sets out to correct 'in the light of recent critical thinking' (p. 1), most prominently an historically inflected feminism. 'Looking beyond *Romeo and Juliet* as an icon of romantic love or an easy introduction to Shakespeare reveals a work that is multidimensional, ambivalent, and conflicted' (p. 3). Roberts' strategic defamiliarization can be questioned in terms of specific conclusions ('rather than representing a feminine ideal Juliet evokes the problematic figure of the unruly woman' [p. 53]) and general assumptions (at times she tends to exaggerate the power of social norms, as though the dominant ideology produced theatrical effects independently of emergent beliefs). But the historical material is informative and interesting in itself, including some wonderful eighteenth- and nineteenth-century visuals, and she too, like Healy, is careful to represent different views – the idea, for instance, that Romeo and Juliet mature during the action, which she recognizes as the cornerstone of 'sentimental' responses to the play. And after all, she is probably justified in her foundational claim about our over-investment in such responses. Her austerely unillusioned version serves as an effective hook to engage critical interest – and not just for student readers.

Mary Hamer's *Julius Caesar* is another matter. For Hamer, Caesar's assassination is symbolically central to the history of Rome, and Rome is symbolically central to the continuing history of Europe, so that 'if we listen carefully' to Shakespeare's version of 'that story', we can answer the question, 'Where did European civilization . . . start to go wrong?' (p. 11). The answer is, in its gender relations. 'The story of Roman marriage is . . . the story of Roman treachery and betrayal between men. The alienation from women and from their own inner lives that he has marked in showing how Roman men live within marriage, Shakespeare will track as it destroys the life of the community and its peace' (p. 59). Hamer argues for this claim in powerfully interesting ways. Her final chapter on 'The Escape from Delusion' ends with Cleopatra as Venus Genetrix, 'the missing piece in the story', the 'heart that is missing from that brutalizing institution, Roman marriage' (p. 78). This is a stronger curtain than Healy and Roberts' last sentences (drama is 'highly resistant to closure' so that '*Richard II* will never be finished' [p. 76]; *Romeo* 'will continue to provoke different interpretations and new readings' [p. 101]). Developed into a monograph, Hamer's essay might find its way into distinguished company, like Stephanie Jed's *Chaste Thinking* or Janet Adelman's *Suffocating Mothers*. But in this context, where weakly pluralist terminal gestures seem to read the audience appropriately, Hamer's strong commitment to her own views sounds too obsessive to be rhetorically effective.

This year's commentary about Shakespeare's tragedies represents, as usual, a variety of critical interests. According to Martin Orkin, the regular use of proverbial lore in *Julius Caesar* 'decentres the notion of a fixed and stable autonomy', enacting the speakers' attempts 'to attain a point of fixity they do not readily have' (p. 222). Günter Walch also treats *Caesar* in a sceptical context, 'part of Shakespeare's turn of the century theatrical exploration of power' (p. 222), an 'interrogative text' that 'does not permit any single and privileged discourse to

contain and situate the others' and thereby 'urges the reader or auditor to venture answers to questions that are raised or, more typically, suggested' (p. 224).

Following hard upon *Julius Caesar*, *Hamlet* also is characterized by proverbs and interrogation, as several pieces claim. For Manuel Barbeito, 'The Question in Hamlet' is related to a specifically Protestant sense of alienation from institutional norms. 'At the precise moment when the protagonism of the individual as subject of his own destiny looms up on the horizon of history, an abyss opens up between the subjective and the objective, the private and the public' (p. 134). For David Summers, writing in *Hamlet Studies*, aphorisms are related to an 'epistemic crisis', producing Hamlet's felt need to resist received intellectual traditions 'in order to provide a space for authentic individual virtue'. Summers concedes that the play is sceptical about the erasure of history but argues that Hamlet's ability 'to recognize his stock of commonplaces as cultural appropriation' represents at least the potential for the 'free moral and intellectual agency' of 'an autonomous self' (p. 29). Two other *Hamlet Studies* pieces give us a more traditional version of the play. Stanislaus Kozikowski's *Hamlet* is structured by three medieval topoi – *psychomachia, ars moriendi, memento mori* – which add a 'vital dimension to our understanding of the character of Hamlet' (p. 69), by allowing us to see 'how Hamlet behaves not as himself, but as the Ghost of his father' (p. 63). Robert Witt claims that the 'failure to see the duel in the last scene of *Hamlet* as a play-within-the-play has led some critics to maintain that Shakespeare departs from the conventions of revenge tragedy by not having the revenge accomplished in a play-within' (p. 50).

Yedidia Itzhaki also is interested in formal conventions, comparing 'Othello and Woyzeck as Tragic Heroes According to Aristotle and Hegel'. In this comparison, which touches in passing on the possibility of modern or plebian tragedy, Othello comes out closer to the Aristotelian norms for the tragic protagonist, but Büchner's action corresponds more closely to the 'collision of life values' which characterizes the action or tragic situation in Hegel (p. 224). Along with Cherrell Guilfoyle's treatment of romance material in the play, Itzhaki's piece is anomalous. Most *Othello* commentary continues to be fixated on sexual and racial anxieties, not just the material already reviewed but in other pieces as well: by Philip McGuire, who examines the growing explicitness in performance traditions; Richard Madelaine, who locates the play in a Renaissance dramatic context featuring sensationally eroticized death; and Jenny de Reuck, for whom 'the "moral contamination" inherent in the representation of race and gender' constitutes 'the condition of intelligibility under which the *drama* is recoverable' (p. 220).

Extravagant claims have been and are still being made about *Lear* as a radically subversive text, desacralizing majesty and sympathizing with peasant resistance to established authority, but Jerald Spotswood's strong contribution makes a persuasive case for treating such claims sceptically. The play in his view, which in effect develops the kinds of arguments in Judy Kronenfeld's book on *Lear* reviewed here last year, confirms an audience's belief in differences by never leaving us in any doubt about authentic status. It therefore 'reinforces symbolic boundaries between gentlemen and commoners, even as it reveals the performative aspects of both roles' (p. 266). This view of the play as 'social recuperation' (p. 273), however, is vulnerable to the same kind of challenge as the radically subversive version. Spotswood objects that 'the subversion-containment model' tends to represent 'social change as an all-or-nothing affair' (p. 264), but its more serious problem is a tendency to locate political values in textual rather than interpretive terms. *King Lear*, it might be argued, does not do cultural work; its audiences do, and we continue to do it in conflicting and contradictory ways to which the play is promiscuously responsive.

This year's *Macbeth* is an unrelievedly grim play. Robert O'Connor acknowledges a substantial debt to Harry Berger's view that the play leaves us with an oppressive regime fundamentally unchanged from the play's problematic inception. O'Connor associates this circularity with chaos theory. In contrast to the usual view of Shakespearian tragic process as remedial, chaos theory leaves it open to question 'whether the better succeeds the worse' (p. 193). O'Connor's interpretation coincides with Hodgdon's description of Michael Bogdanov's ESC production as violating the norms of 'Aristotelian tragedy . . . in the Bradleian mold': it offers the audience not 'a moving and instructive case-history of a good man undermined by his fatal flaw', but rather the systematic 'phallocentrism' of 'late twentieth-century military culture' (p. 149, quoting the programme notes). Polanski's *Macbeth* comes out at much the same place, although it apparently did not start there. Bernice Kliman describes in shrewd detail the process by which the film developed in production from an original 'concept of the nobly ambitious Macbeth gone bad' to the 'notion of a diseased society' within whose 'thuggish' world 'treacherous murder and rape are an inevitability'. In this 'bleak view', where 'at the end' we 'begin again the cycle of destruction', Polanski 'gives us no sense that society understands itself sufficiently to purge its rotten elements' (p. 142).

In Shuli Barzilai's psychoanalytic interpretation of *Coriolanus*, Rome seems much like Scotland – irredeemably phallocentric, unpurged and unpurgeable. Barzilai distances himself from the standard view of 'pathogenic mothering' which, by assuming the 'cause-effect relationship' of '"real" life', diminishes 'Coriolanus from the status of tragic hero to that of victim' or 'a case of infantile neurosis'. Barzilai reverses the sequence, taking his cue from Kenneth Burke who rather derives Volumnia et al. from Coriolanus himself: 'in being the kind of characters they are, the other figures help Coriolanus to be the kind of character he is' (p. 235). This elegant move might serve to recuperate the heroic protagonist for normative conventional effects, but Barzilai is too invested in current theoretical norms (and too responsive to this play's dark energies) to develop any such claims. His Coriolanus remains a victim – if not specifically of his mother then of mother Rome, 'the sociocultural context of a male-oriented world' (p. 234) and of his own internalization of these cultural values, as embodied in the repetition that pulses relentlessly through the play's action. Barzilai's argument concludes by associating this compulsive rhythm with the death wish in *Beyond the Pleasure Principle*. Another tragedy without transcendence.

Any attempt to construe these discussions is complicated by the ghostly presence, beyond Shakespeare's tragedies, of 'Shakespearian Tragedy' as an established generic object to which particular plays are referred. Though few commentators are as rigorously deductive as Witt or Itzhaki, an idea of Shakespearian Tragedy tends to shape discussion even among self-consciously innovative critics, for whom meaning and value is registered precisely as deviations from established norms. The problem, at least for anybody making historicist claims, is that these norms had not been established; Shakespeare's audience knew nothing of Aristotle and in most cases nothing about sixteenth-century Italian Aristotelians, let alone about Hegel and Bradley. In this context, where the relevance of transcendence (Bradley's 'reconciliation') is impossible to determine with certainty, its presence or absence is hard to interpret. The relevance of public or political consequentiality is uncertain in the same way. Three of Bradley's 'major four' provide it and we tend to assume its necessity for tragic experience, as in Sasha Roberts' suggestion that *Romeo* 'disrupted' the 'expectations' of 'an Elizabethan audience accustomed' to 'the more conventional gravity of opening scenes in Shakespeare's other tragedies' (pp. 11–12). But if 'domestic tragedy' (as we have come to call

it) constituted the norm, then maybe it was the still-unwritten and unwitnessed major four that caused the shock. Or maybe there was no norm in our sense of a fixed entity with recognizable topoi (anagnorisis, peripeteia) designed to achieve definite cathartic effects but merely, as Stephen Orgel suggested a long time ago, a set of flexible generative possibilities. If so, tragedy may be best left at its required minimum, the irreducible version of the fall from high to low estate signalled by the black curtain on stage – death.

This lucubration is indirectly inspired by *Tragedy*, John Drakakis and Naomi Conn Liebler's strong contribution to the Longman Critical Reader Series. The selections include some appropriately standard items (Hegel, Goldmann, Girard), but some unfamiliar writers as well (Augusto Boal, Nicole Loraux), all introduced in uncompromisingly critical essays (the General Editors say the series is designed for teachers 'urgently looking for guidance' [p. vii], but this book is not *Tragedy for Dummies*). Given the exhaustion and routinization I describe above, the fact that Shakespeare is not a central presence may make the book particularly valuable for Shakespearians: it opens the subject out beyond the familiar terrain of Hegelian and Bradleyan idealism. Though the selections begin with Hegel, the book itself begins with a head-quotation from Brecht, the familiar *Galileo* exchange about the unhappiness of the land that needs a hero, and ends with an excerpt from Derrida on the *pharmakos*, a kind of capstone to 'materialist accounts' earlier in the volume, especially feminist and psychoanalytic, that 'disturb the traditional philosophical foundations' of tragedy by focusing on 'the conflict between a metaphysically sanctioned order and those material historical forces which pose a challenge to hierarchical structures' (p. 337). This anti-metaphysical bias is useful. The 'world historical conflicts' emphasized by Hegel (and taken up even more abstractly by Bradley) represent only a part of the world, Enlightenment Europe. Materialists have their own totalizing metanarrative (liminal phases between feudal allegiance and the cash nexus of the early modern market), but this volume is designed not to get tragedy right, but to call attention to the many different localities that seem to be inhabited by the name. It can help to explain why even within Europe and even now, when differences are flattened out into a wall-less globalization, 'Shakespearian Tragedy' is different from one place to another – a point central to two of this year's essays. According to Zdeněk Stříbrný, although the West has moved on to *Lear* (and perhaps further on now to *Othello*), Eastern European theatre remains fixated on *Hamlet*. In a mordantly ironic piece, Alexander Shurbanov remarks that while the West was seizing on radically transgressive possibilities in the tragedies, Eastern Europe developed a tragic Shakespeare which was also 'irremediably politicized, though not in the way the pundits wanted him to be' (p. 143) – representing a world of acquiescence, even self-loathing.

Little or no such local variation in this year's comedy discussion; *Measure* is everywhere the play of choice. The privileged status given to it by Leggatt and by three of Kendall's contributors is reinforced by other work. R. D. Bedford notes how much text-cutting Barton and Brook required to produce an authoritative Duke. In any performance of 'the full text', it is 'hard to see' how the Duke–Lucio exchange in 3.2 'could be played without generating laughter *at* the Duke' (p. 176). Mary Crane is similarly sceptical about the Jacobean *Measure*. Claims for the play as a celebration of state power underestimate 'the unruly materiality of the subject itself' (p. 269), its 'cognitive permeability', the 'mechanisms through which the human body and embodied brain both originate and succumb to linguistic expressions of power' (p. 292). Since the 'all-too-human Duke' is subject to these mechanisms as well, 'the play insists on depicting power as it is embodied in a particular human agent who is vulnerable to the very kinds of discursive pene-

tration with which he would control his subjects' (p. 270). Crane rejects the 'Foucauldian fantasies' of earlier criticism, but her *Measure* does not replace them with any 'comforting vision' of resistance. Rather, she concludes with an interesting claim for the 'poignant' quality of the Duke as the play's figure 'who most fully understands' that 'the dilemma of embodied power' is inherently and irresolvably problematic (p. 292).

Huston Diehl is an exception to prevailing beliefs; *Measure* is not a problem for her. Taking on the many commentators for whom the play is 'deeply dissatisfying', Diehl argues that 'Shakespeare deliberately calls attention to the imperfection of his art [thereby] producing – not undermining – the play's meaning as well as its peculiar power' (p. 393). This meaning and power Diehl discovers in the explicitly Protestant effects registered by a specifically Protestant audience. 'Shakespeare deliberately cedes the reforming powers of the artist to a higher, divine authority and sacrifices the satisfaction of a comic ending in order to create a felt need for grace' (p. 410). In this strong interpretation, Shakespeare seems to be playing to a Globe audience united not just in credal allegiance but religious sensibility, void of all Catholics and of all residual Catholic feeling – a conception arguably more appropriate to the readership of Herbert's poetry.

Elsewhere, though, the dark and problematic remain as comic norms. B. J. Sokol argues that modern discomfort with Shylock's treatment is not based merely on an anachronistic imposition of liberal ideas; legal traditions available to Shakespeare's audience might have made them uneasy as well. Sokol's *Merchant* works continually to write its audience into an embarrassed sense of its own uncertainty: 'the play tempts us to lose our own ethical bearings' (p. 171). Cynthia Marshall's *As You Like It* keys on Jaques – not so much on the character as on his tone: 'a melancholy Jaques, so crucial to the play's emotional equilibrium, testifies to an undertow of sadness . . . brilliantly held at bay'.

Making use of Freud and Lacan, focusing on textual absences and ruptures, Marshall reads 'constructions of negation in Shakespeare's comedy as evincing a compensatory principle that brings about a satisfying harmony and closure' but also as leaving melancholy 'traces' that signal the 'consequences of cultural repressions' (p. 376). With Jaques moved from the margins he used to inhabit to the play's centre, *As You Like It* begins to resemble the 'anti-comedy' 'of *Measure*.

In a richly informative and powerfully argued essay, Wendy Wall reflects on 'The Sexual Politics of Domesticity' in the foundational text of English stage comedy, *Gammer Gurton's Needle*. At the centre of her discussion is a contrast between home and school: on the one hand a plebian domestic economy characterized by blurred gender roles, secured by housewifery and the English mother tongue; on the other, an elite pedagogical regime inhabited exclusively by men and boys and rigorously disciplined by Latin and the rod. Performed at Cambridge, the play nonetheless 'mocks initiating rites dependent upon the disavowal of cross-gendered domesticity' (p. 11). 'Instead of interpolating [interpellating?] the audience as Latin-speaking privileged European scholars, the play hails its audience as English speakers whose masculinity and sexuality rest on that collective identification' (p. 28). Though adapted to the different setting of the commercial theatre, Shakespeare's *Wives*, in Wall's view, works in the same line. 'Like *Gammer*, it insists on a national community' and 'rests, finally, on the common experience attributed to a world of pots and pans and the prosy English tongue' (p. 34). She distances herself from the Garter-based reading of the play, as working to relocate authority in a courtly elite (she would also, I assume, be sceptical of the view I reported on earlier, in which the Wives are contained within patriarchal marriage at the end) and winds up closer to the old-fashioned view of a play celebrating an original Englishness. But Wall's essay is nothing if not up-to-date (watching her footnotes dance

through the minefield of queer theory can take your breath away), and she does not repeat so much as get underneath the clichéd topoi of 'Merrie England' in order to show how complexly they were produced. 'These discursive ties have become so familiar to us that we can scarcely see their oddity in the Early Modern World and appreciate their emergence' (p. 30). Wall says nothing of *The Shoemakers' Holiday*, whose 'mirth' seems crucially to inflect so many of the constituents of the domestic economy into a not-yet-wholly commercial situation (and of course it has a Hodge as well). I am not complaining, just (as with Leggatt's absent Chekhov) begging for more. I hope that Wall carries on with the work of this wonderful essay, featuring Dekker or anybody she wants.

Two fascinating pieces belatedly accord his fifteen minutes' fame to Sir John Harington as a central (if subtextual) presence in *Twelfth Night* and *Much Ado*. Peter Smith argues that M. O. A. I. is an acronym for *The Metamorphosis of A IAX*. Juliet Dusinberre focuses on Harington 'as reader, writer, courtier, playgoer' as a way to 'highlight' the 'involvement' of *Much Ado* 'in the world in which it was first performed' (p. 141). Smith and Dusinberre are doing historical criticism in very different styles. As 'part of the cultural hinterland from which *Much Ado About Nothing* emerges', Dusinberre's Harington is connected to the play only in terms of hints and suggestive intimations independent of conscious intentionality or explicit effect. Smith, by contrast, declares at the beginning that his 'paper is an attempt to answer the riddle . . . decoding the puzzle' of M. O. A. I (p. 1199). But these differences blur under scrutiny. When Dusinberre tells us, say, that 'Claudio and Benedick are back from the war in the company of a noble prince, Don Pedro — a name used for one of his contemporaries in Harington's epigrams, also written some time in the 1590s' (p. 142), it is unclear why we should be interested unless the coincidences are more than just coincidental — which perforce gets us back to some kind of intentional or effective consciousness. On the other side, Smith's last paragraph seems to abandon his smoking guns and QEDs in the suggestion of a 'sobering analogy between our mission and that of the love-sick Malvolio' (p. 1222). In this witty reversal, Smith aligns himself with Jonathan Culler's claim that 'the significance of literature lies in its refusal to comply with a single interpretive shape'. So much for decoding riddles. There's a more interesting similarity as well. Both Smith and Dusinberre identify the interests of Shakespeare's audience with those of a cultural elite (who would be getting these in-jokes and covert allusions?), thereby tending to associate the value of Shakespeare with people like themselves – or, for that matter, like the author of this essay and its readers.

The most significant contribution on the histories this year is Nina Levine's thoughtful book about the 'first tetralogy' and *King John*. Levine acknowledges that Joan, Eleanor and Margaret are even more threateningly represented than in the sources but argues that the aristocratic patriarchs who self-righteously condemn this monstrous female regiment are themselves motivated chiefly by naked self-interest and thus represent an even more serious threat to the social and political order. The consequence is unresolved political conflict, corresponding to a conceptual conflict, in which none of the various 'myths of power' (p. 14) – aristocratic chivalry, patriarchal legitimacy, monarchical power – seems adequate. Levine extends the argument to the succession anxieties reflected in *John*, where 'the critique of patrilineal inheritance and royal succession' leaves us with 'the absence of any locus of authority' (pp. 138–9). This claim connects with Walch's interrogative *Caesar* (Walch in fact understands *Caesar* as a development of the dramatic impulses in the English histories), and with another piece on *John* this year, by Edward Gieskes, emphasizing *John*'s scepticism about transcendent principles of authority: in contrast to *Troublesome Raigne* where 'rank and distinction' are represented 'as inborn or pre-

ordained', Gieskes' *John* seems to make status accessible to individual initiative and achievement (p. 794). Levine's book resonates perhaps most fully with Paola Pugliatti's contention that 'instability' and 'irresolution' represent Shakespeare's most distinctive 'breach with the orthodox practice of contemporary historians'. Where the chroniclers in Levine's view dump contradictions in their readers' laps, Shakespeare 'requires [his] audience to become involved in sifting the evidence and evaluating the authority of the representations before them onstage and, by extension, in the world outside' (pp. 58–9) – writing us, in effect, into a state of informed citizenship, engaged at least conceptually or imaginatively in the political process of making the nation. This may sound suspiciously like liberal politics, but the evidence for a Shakespearian 'politics of exclusion' in service to 'the Leviathan state' is no more conclusive. Ultimately, such text-and-author judgements may be driven (yet again) by speculative assumptions about the audience – who they were, how they made use of the plays. If you follow Empson on these matters, Levine's claims will seem convincing, but even unpersuaded readers should appreciate the exceptional clarity with which she develops her argument.

In *Thwarting the Wayward Seas*, David Skeele has produced *A Critical and Theatrical History of Shakespeare's 'Pericles' in the Nineteenth and Twentieth Centuries*. The story is basically upbeat, moving from Victorian disdain to a considerable respect in our time. Skeele offers lots of reasons for the play's early unpopularity: no star turns or psychological coherence, sexual explicitness, uncertain authorship and, most important, a 'choppy, episodic, fragmented structure' (p. 11). Skeele rounds up the usual suspects from the New Shakespere Society, putting on display their purportedly scientific methods, then shifts to spatial form and myth among the Moderns (who are beginning to look almost as historically remote as Fleay and Furnivall), where the play's fortunes significantly improved, and finally to the apparently natural fit between the play and current taste, critical and theatrical, for fragmentation and pastiche.

Like much good theatre history, *Thwarting the Wayward Seas* operates with a high ratio of information to interpretation. In a different context, Theory might be evoked to justify anecdotage as the epistemologically correct response to the 'slime of history'. Skeele himself simply acknowledges that the details do not always fit into the explanatory coherence of his interpretive structure. Sometimes they have a life of their own, as in the hilariously circumstantialized description of a disastrous John Coleman performance in 1900. Sometimes the facts seem to be pointing in a different direction altogether. The play's greatest theatrical success, for instance, occurs at the wrong time, in Samuel Phelps' 1854 Sadler's Wells production, 'the biggest box office bonanza his theater ever produced, running for a record-breaking fifty-five performances' (p. 40). While two RSC productions (Terry Hands and Ron Daniels) can be described as belatedly Modernist and two more recent productions (Peter Sellars and Michael Grief) are clearly shaped by postmodern assumptions, there is little evidence to suggest that the play is achieving the theatrical status that the cultural history suggests it ought to have. Critical production does not quite answer expectations either, having 'temporarily (one can only assume)', Skeele tells us in his final paragraph, 'slowed to a trickle' (p. 145).

Pericles, it seems, while it can be fit into critical and theatrical history, does not fully have one of its own – what should we make of this? The question comes up directly in Dennis Kennedy's LA paper on 'Performing Mediocrity' which, starting with *Pericles*, tries to 'set up three chronological shifts in the attitude to the lesser plays[:] canonical inclusion, modernist recovery, and postmodern contingency' (p. 63). Kennedy claims that the last of these 'has begun to erase the distinction between the marginal and the central' (p. 69) and concludes that 'performing mediocrity undermines . . . the

rigorous classification of authorized art' (pp. 71–2). But although *Pericles* has become somewhat less inconsequential during the last two hundred years, it remains, despite everything that might seem to contribute to its canonization, an intransigently marginal production. Does the case of *Pericles*, as Skeele describes it, push us back toward the risible naivete of objective aesthetic values? You might well think so, I couldn't possibly comment.

My capacity to comment is also limited, though for different reasons, in the case of Jutta Schamp's book exploring constructions of time in the early modern period as represented in *Richard II*, *Henry IV* and *Macbeth*. Schamp challenges the sharp division between medieval and Renaissance experiences of temporal process and similarly deconstructs the binaries that have tended to shape Shakespearian interpretation: for instance, the opposition between a stable past and a disordered present in *Richard II* and *Macbeth* (yet another unredemptive version of the Scottish play). This book looks like an informed and valuable study, but I do not have the German to do more than call it to people's attention here.

In *Shakespeare's Theatre of War* Nick de Somogyi starts from the perception of a significant convergence: between 1585, when Elizabeth engaged with the Dutch against the Spanish, and 1604, when James concluded the engagement, English life was continually pressured by war and the threat of war; the same period corresponded to the high achievement of Elizabethan drama. De Somogyi explores the connection in a variety of ways. The stage represented the experience of war, including its anticipation and its consequences, as a moral, psychological, metaphysical and technological phenomenon. As siege and artillery replaced chivalric models from the past, the plays reflect an anxious uncertainty about the relevance of old conceptual models. De Somogyi focuses on the wounded soldier, a recurring stage figure who could express either the dignity of service or the disgrace of neglect, or both, and whose social reality was subject to fraudulent performance off-stage. But war was not just a subject. In discussions headed 'Playing at soldiers' and 'War games', de Somogyi describes the complicated interplay between martial and theatrical experience – the dependence on public display and pretence in war, the theatre's dependence on the military for props and costumes and its enlistment for the war effort, even occasionally impressment from among theatre audiences. A chapter on 'Rumours of War' returns to the idea of fakery or fraud, connecting the mystifications of military jargon with the newly amalgamated dramatic type of the braggart/pedant. The last two chapters focus on Shakespeare: ghosts, the uncanny presence to living memory of dead soldiers in *Henry V*; the martial background in *Hamlet*. De Somogyi suggests that Q1 *Hamlet* cuts can be explained at least partly as pre-empting censorship at a time when scepticism about the value or purpose of war would not be allowed. These arguments seem too narrowly focused to be wholly convincing; the haunting in *Henry V* may be more generally connected with historical memory in general, and there are simpler ways to explain Q1 *Hamlet*'s across-the-board cuts than such highly speculative censorship hypotheses. But the strong value of this book remains in the wealth of detail informing the discussion. De Somogyi has read intelligently over a broad spectrum of Renaissance texts (plays, military manuals, news pamphlets) as well as modern historical and critical commentary. The extraordinary learning derived from this research is made available in a generously accessible style that should enable a substantial readership to appreciate how deeply and systematically Renaissance plays reflected and shaped contemporary experiences of war – and continue to do so.

This year's archive includes three stellar – and very different – essays on the *Sonnets*. For David Schalkwyk, the tendency of commentators to focus on the *Sonnets* in 'primarily epistemological' terms has led them 'to overlook the ways in which a sonnet's conditions of address are embedded in particular social and poetical contexts of performance'. Working out of Austin and Wittgenstein, he shows how the *Sonnets* manage to negotiate the distance between speaker and addressee – change the situation. Schalkwyk's *Sonnets* 'use language . . . in a series of performances in which power relations between "you" and "I" are negotiated' (p. 251). In Lynne Magnusson's chapter on the *Sonnets* in the book discussed earlier, interiority occupies a position similar to Schalkwyk's problematic epistemology. The result is that the *Sonnets* have 'more usually been read and valued as the verbal expression of an inward state than as the verbal negotiation of an outward social relation'. Working as always out of discourse pragmatics and history, focusing on letters between Edward Molyneux (Sir Henry Sidney's secretary) and various Sidneys, male and female, which reflect and sustain 'the complex determiners of the power relations' (p. 38) that articulate a variety of different subject positions, Magnusson offers *Sonnets* that 'resemble very closely the socially conditioned strategies' (p. 52) represented in Molyneux's letters. Her point is not to deny the interiority effects produced by the poems, but to insist on their prior origins in the situation.

In contrast to these sharp and subtly nuanced views of the *Sonnets* as situated negotiations, George T. Wright's *Sonnets* represent decontextualized thought: 'speech without speech', coming 'not after but as long silence' and issuing from a 'deeply reflective speaker' who may not be 'really a speaker at all', the 'language of silent thought, unvoiced, unsounded, unperformed, the words of a consciousness (his then, ours now) silently addressing itself sometimes and sometimes an absent other?' (pp. 315–16) Such poems cannot be said to perform actions in the sense of Molyneux's letters or even of Schalkwyk's Cleopatra, inviting us to play a new language game at the end of *Antony*. Where neither speaker nor addressee is fully or stably identifiable, we cannot specify the pragmatics of the situation by which they are supposedly constituted or contained. Wright's *Sonnets* resonate richly with other recent versions by Stephen Booth and Helen Vendler, but the critical mainstream has usually flowed in the opposite direction, driven by the desire to re- rather than decontextualize, seeking to return the *Sonnets* to some explicit instrumentality. We have pretty much given up on earlier quests to provide names for WH, the dark lady and the young man, but the emphasis on 'power relations', the embeddedness in social history, may be motivated by a similar desire: if only we could put these poems back inside their original communicative circuit, summoning up the image of a readership as plausible as the one that has allowed us to believe in the 'Donne coterie' as something more than just a convenient interpretive invention. Amidst the pervasive anti-formalism of the current scene, Wright's *Sonnets* are bound to seem inadequately compelling, but something deeper may be involved. Perhaps we remain, despite all our hardnosed materialism, invested in these poems as a neo-Casaubonian key to all mythologies. It is as if we still half believe that the *Sonnets* are not just by Shakespeare but are Shakespeare.

This residual power of the author is Douglas Brooks' theme in 'Sir John Oldcastle and the Construction of Shakespeare's Authorship'. Brooks starts with an apparent coincidence: 'the first instance of an unambiguously authorial attribution to Shakespeare' in a printed playtext appears on the title page of the 1600 Quarto of *2 Henry IV*, with its shadow of the Falstaff/Oldcastle controversy, thus providing 'direct material evidence' for Foucault's claim about the connection between authorship and subjection to punitive discipline (p. 336). To this coincidence, Brooks adds many more, all richly circumstantialized and artfully woven into a tapestry representing the gradual sequence by which religious and then monarchical authority were replaced by the institution of authorship. Brooks concludes by considering the Oxford

edition's restoration of Oldcastle at a time when 'the author' is being 'displace[d] from its long-secure position as the guarantor and personification of humanist subjectivity' (p. 353). Brooks claims, as others have, that Oxford does not so much disestablish as relocate authorial sway – 'a rather nostalgic project' which, faced with the 'serious challenges in the wake of what Roland Barthes famously referred to as "The Death of the Author"', seems 'primarily interested in damage control' (p. 354).

In 'Character and Person in Shakespeare', William Dodd undertakes a recuperative project, though without nostalgia, joining with recent 'theoretically sophisticated critics who have felt a need to salvage' the concept of character 'while continuing to reject what is often called the bourgeois, liberal humanist view of the subject' (p. 147). Dodd engages thoughtfully with an impressive number of recent commentators, Shakespearian and otherwise, working especially in sociological and ethical theory (Bourdieu, Bakhtin, Charles Taylor, among many others). Chiefly, he claims the moral urgency of retaining a notion of agency. To this it might be added that the imagination of theatrical action as emerging from the will of distinct characters – rather than from the ideas of the author, say, or from ideological or cultural formations – tends to increase theatrical excitement.

A recuperative motivation may also be at work in John Russell Brown's *Survey* piece on 'Shakespeare's International Currency'. Brown sets out to explain 'why Shakespeare, who wrote four hundred years ago' (p. 193), has achieved an 'almost universal currency' on stages 'all across the world'. It cannot be the language; it must, he thinks, be a combination of speech-and-action, ceremonialized and ritualized into a rhythm that constitutes the plays' 'performative qualities, their instigation of physical, living-and-breathing realizations on a stage before an audience' (p. 203). Describing a Shanghai *Much Ado* performed in a vast open space in which 'characters would sometimes talk to each other ten or fifteen metres apart', Brown assures us that 'the narrative and comedy both survived, partly because the actors had gestures and presence to sustain them on such a scale and partly because the play is written in a demonstrative style which supplies the actors with much to do as well as to speak' (p. 197). Brown is not just claiming that the production was funny, but that it was funny in a way somehow continuous with an originating performativity: 'the comedy survived'. Survival is a key concept for Brown's sense of Shakespearian 'pliancy': the 'plays respond to major interpretations and survive all kinds of additions, subtractions, and wilful changes' (p. 200). For this claim to be fully convincing, we'd need to assume that gesture signifies like an esperanto across cultural difference. But suppose the meaning of rhythm and ceremony are no less culturally specific than language, signifying not in the context of some abstract concept of Shakespearian performativity but in terms of the local traditions and particular moments of their own productions. In this case, it makes better sense to say not that the comedy survived but that some new kind of comedy was being made, whose relation to an original potential remains problematic – no less so than textual translation. Performativity does not solve the mystery of Shakespeare's international currency, it reproduces it.

'International currency', though, seems like the right phrase, and not just to describe performance. In view of the extraordinary range surveyed here, conceptual as well as geographical, Shakespearian critical production too has become a globally negotiated commodity. I am no better off than Brown in trying to account for it. As with the collections that proliferated this year, the different parts do not cohere very easily. The persistent emphasis on translation works well enough, but the movement seems to be reciprocal, a two-way street whose originating position (Kathakali? *Othello*?) has disappeared (many two-way streets – imagine an aerial shot of the LA freeways at rush hour). To some extent, the problem reflects the artificiality of the procedure. Reading for a year-end review is very different from a normal engagement with criticism. Still, the experience should seem familiar to anyone who surfs the segmented cable TV market, hopping from the slice-prone golfers' channel to the gay dentists'. Bloom-to-Loomba may not seem so disconnected, since Shakespeare is the common interest, but it is not clear whether 'Shakespeare' has much more than a nominal significance. Web-browsing may be an even better analogy. We are all now declared to be horizontally integrated as a consequence of the new information technology, but the collapse of the walls is turning out to be a mixed blessing. Paul Werstine's LA paper gives the up side, endorsing the democratizing effect of a 'fluid' hypertext as Peter Robinson has described it. 'Editor and reader are now partners in the quest for understanding: both have access to the same materials; both may use the same tools' (p. 253). But if student-readers have no idea what to look for in this fluidity, they may wind up just wandering lost in mazes. In the logic of late capitalist Shakespearian culture, everything is flattened out into an undifferentiated freedom – just another word for nothing left to lose. But warmed over Jameson would be an ungrateful response to the enormous quantities of intelligence and knowledge on display in this year's critical archive, only a small part of which is reported on here. On the day I write, the search engine Google tells me that there are 'at least 14994 matches for Shakespeare criticism'. God's plenty. What they add up to, only God needs to know.

WORKS REVIEWED

Alexander, Catherine M. S., 'Shakespeare and the Eighteenth Century: Criticism and Research', *Shakespeare Survey 51* (Cambridge, 1998), 1–16.

Apfelbaum, Roger, '"Welcome to Dreamland": Performance Theory, Postcolonial Discourse, and the Filming of *A Midsummer Night's Dream* in

Angela Carter's *Wise Children*', in Bate et al., *Shakespeare and the Twentieth Century*, 183–93.

Barbeito, Manuel, 'The Question in *Hamlet*', *Shakespeare Jahrbuch* 134 (1998), 123–35.

Barzilai, Shuli, '*Coriolanus* and the Compulsion to Repeat', in Oz, *Strands Afar Remote*, 232–54.

Bate, Jonathan, 'Romantic Players, Political Theatres', in White et al., *Shakespeare: Readers, Audiences, Players*, 6–28.

Jill L. Levenson, and Dieter Mehl, eds., *Shakespeare and the Twentieth Century: The Selected Proceedings of the International Shakespeare Association World Congress, Los Angeles, 1996* (Newark and London, 1998).

Bedford, R. D., 'Playing *Measure for Measure*', in White et al., *Shakespeare: Readers, Audiences, Players*, 168–81.

Bloom, Harold, *Shakespeare: The Invention of the Human* (New York, 1998).

Booth, Stephen, 'On the Aesthetics of Acting', in Halio and Richmond, *Shakespearean Illuminations*, 255–66.

Bradshaw, Graham and Kaori Ashizo, 'Reading *Hamlet* in Japan', in Bate et al., *Shakespeare and the Twentieth Century*, 350–63.

Brooks, Douglas A., 'Sir John Oldcastle and the Construction of Shakespeare's Authorship', *Studies in English Literature 1500–1900*, 38 (1998), 333–62.

Brotton, Jerry, '"This Tunis, Sir, Was Carthage": Contesting Colonialism in *The Tempest*', in Loomba and Orkin, *Post-Colonial Shakespeares*, 23–42.

Brown, John Russell. 'Shakespeare's International Currency', *Shakespeare Survey* 51 (Cambridge, 1998) 193–203.

'Techniques of Restoration: The Case of *The Duchess of Malfi*', in Halio and Richmond, *Shakespearean Illuminations*, 317–35.

Burton, Jonathan, '"A Most Wily Bird": Leo Africanus, *Othello* and the Trafficking in Difference', in Loomba and Orkin, *Post-Colonial Shakespeares*, 43–63.

Cartelli, Thomas, *Repositioning Shakespeare: National Formations, Postcolonial Appropriations* (London and New York, 1999).

Cavell, Stanley, 'Skepticism as Iconoclasm: The Saturation of the Shakespearian Text', in Bate et al., *Shakespeare and the Twentieth Century*, 231–47.

Chedgzoy, Ruth, 'Blackness Yields to Beauty: Desirability and Difference in Early Modern Culture', in Gordon McMullan, *Renaissance Configurations*, 108–28.

Cholij, Irena, '"A Thousand Twangling Instruments": Music and *The Tempest* on the Eighteenth-Century London Stage', *Shakespeare Survey* 51 (Cambridge, 1998), 79–94.

Cohen, Derek, 'The Culture of Slavery: Caliban and Ariel', in White et al., *Shakespeare: Readers, Audiences, Players*, 260–71.

Collier, Susanne, 'Cutting to the Heart of the Matter: Stabbing the Woman in *Philaster* and *Cymbeline*,' in Kendall, *Shakespearean Power and Punishment*, 39–58.

Crane, Mary Thomas, 'Male Pregnancy and Cognitive Permeability in *Measure for Measure*', *Shakespeare Quarterly*, 49 (1998), 269–92.

Daileader, Celia R., *Eroticism on the Renaissance Stage: Transcendence, Desire, and the Limits of the Visible*, Cambridge Studies in Renaissance Literature and Culture, 30, (Cambridge, 1998).

Dodd, William, 'Character and Person in Shakespeare', *Shakespeare Survey 51* (Cambridge, 1998), 1998, 147–58.

Dollimore, Jonathan, 'Shakespeare and Theory', in Loomba and Orkin, *Post-Colonial Shakespeares*, 259–76.

Donoghue, Denis, *The Practice of Reading* (New Haven and London, 1998).

Drakakis, John, and Naomi Conn Liebler, eds., *Tragedy*, Longman Critical Readers (London and New York, 1998).

Dusinberre, Juliet, 'Much Ado About Lying', in White et al., *Shakespeare: Readers, Audiences, Players*, 140–67.

Eaton, Sara, '"Content with art"?: Seeing the Emblematic Woman in *The Second Maiden's Tragedy* and *The Winter's Tale*,' in Kendall, *Shakespearean Power and Punishment*, 59–86.

Edelman, Charles, '"What Is Asking and What Is Wondring": Dramatic Punctuation in Shakespeare', in White et al., *Shakespeare: Readers, Audiences, Players*, 106–20.

Erickson, Peter, 'The Moment of Race in Renaissance Studies', *Shakespeare Studies*, 26 (1998), 27–36.

Ford, Jane M., *Patriarchy and Incest from Shakespeare to Joyce* (Gainesville, 1998).

Freund, Elizabeth, '"I See a Voice": The Desire for

313

Representation and the Rape of Voice', in Oz, *Strands Afar Remote*, 62–86.

Gay, Penny, 'Recent Australian *Shrews*: The "Larrikin Element"', in Bate et al., *Shakespeare and the Twentieth Century*, 168–82.

'Shakespeare in Translation: The Trial Scene in *The Merchant of Venice*', in White et al., *Shakespeare: Readers, Audiences, Players*, 131–39.

Gieskes, Edward, '"He is but a bastard to the time": Status and Service in *The Troublesome Raigne of John* and Shakespeare's *King John*', *English Literary History*, 65 (1998), 779–98.

Golomb, Harai, 'Shakesperean Re-Generations in Hebrew: A Study in Historical Poetics', in Oz, *Strands Afar Remote*, 255–75.

Grzegorzewska, Margorzata, 'Wooing in Festival Terms: Sonneteering Lovers, Rock, and Blues', in Bate et al., *Shakespeare and the Twentieth Century*, 148–56.

Gutierrez, Nancy A., 'King Arthur, Scotland, Utopia, and the Italianate Englishman: What Does Race Have to Do with It?' *Shakespeare Studies*, 26 (1998), 37–38.

Halio, Jay L., 'Staging *King Lear* 1.1 and 5.3', in Halio and Richmond, *Shakespearean Illuminations*, 102–9.

and Hugh Richmond, eds., *Shakespearean Illuminations: Essays in Honor of Marvin Rosenberg* (Newark and London, 1998).

Hall, Kim F., '"These Bastard Signs of Fair": Literary Whiteness in Shakespeare's Sonnets', in Loomba and Orkin, *Post-Colonial Shakespeares*, 64–83.

Hamer, Mary, *Julius Caesar* (Plymouth, 1998).

Hattaway, Michael, '"I've processed my guilt": Shakespeare, Branagh, and the Movies', in Bate et al., *Shakespeare and the Twentieth Century*, 194–211.

Hawkes, Terence, 'Bryn Glas', in Loomba and Orkin, *Post-Colonial Shakespeares*, 117–40.

Healy, Margaret, *Richard II* (Plymouth, 1998).

Hendricks, Margo, '"'Tis not the Fashion to Confess": "Shakespeare–Post-Coloniality–Johannesburg, 1996"', in Loomba and Orkin, *Post-Colonialist Shakespeares*, 84–97.

ed., 'Forum: Race and the Study of Shakespeare', *Shakespeare Studies*, 26 (1998), 19–79.

Hillman, David, 'Hamlet's Entrails', in Oz, *Strands Afar Remote*, 177–203.

Hodgdon, Barbara, '*Macbeth* at the Turn of the Millennium', in Halio and Richmond, *Shakespearean Illuminations*, 147–63.

Homan, Sidney, '"What Do I Do Now?" Directing *A Midsummer Night's Dream*', in Halio and Richmond, *Shakespearean Illuminations*, 279–96.

Howard, Jean E., 'The Early Modern and the Homoerotic Turn in Political Criticism', *Shakespeare Studies*, 26 (1998), 105–20.

Itzhaki, Yedidia, 'Othello and Woyzeck as Tragic Heroes According to Aristotle and Hegel', in Oz, *Strands Afar Remote*, 204–31.

Jacobs, Alfred, 'Orson Welles's *Othello*: Shakespeare Meets Film Noir', in Bate et al., *Shakespeare and the Twentieth Century*, 113–24.

Jankowski, Theodora A., 'Pure Resistance: Queer(y)ing Virginity in William Shakespeare's *Measure for Measure* and Margaret Cavendish's *The Convent of Pleasure*', *Shakespeare Studies* 26 (1998), 218–55.

Johnson, Nora, 'Ganymedes and Kings: Staging Male Homosexual Desire in *The Winter's Tale*', *Shakespeare Studies*, 26 (1998), 187–217.

Jones, Ann Rosalind, 'Revenge Comedy: Writing, Law, and the Punishing Heroine in *Twelfth Night*, *The Merry Wives of Windsor*, and *Swetnam the Woman-Hater*', in Kendall, *Shakespearean Power and Punishment*, 23–38.

Kawachi, Yoshiko, 'Gender, Class and Race in Japanese Translations of Shakespeare', in Bate et al., *Shakespeare and the Twentieth Century*, 390–402.

Kendall, Gillian Murray, ed., *Shakespearean Power and Punishment: A Volume of Essays* (Newark and London, 1998).

Kennedy, Dennis, 'Performing Mediocrity', in Bate et al., *Shakespeare and the Twentieth Century*, 60–74.

Kishi, Tetsuo, 'Shakespeare and the Musical', in Bate et al., *Shakespeare and the Twentieth Century*, 157–67.

Kliman, Bernice W., 'Gleanings: The Residue of Difference in Scripts: The Case of Polanski's *Macbeth*', in Halio and Richmond, *Shakespearean Illuminations*, 131–46.

Kozikowski, Stanislaus J., 'The Three Medieval Plots of *Hamlet*: *Psychomachia*, *Ars Moriendi*, *Memento Mori*', *Hamlet Studies*, 20 (1998), 63–70.

Leggatt, Alexander, *English Stage Comedy 1490–1990: Five Centuries of a Genre* (London and New York, 1998).

Levine, Nina S., *Women's Matters: Politics, Gender, and Nation in Shakespeare's Early History Plays* (Newark and London, 1998).

Loomba, Ania, '"Local-Manufacture Made-in-India Othello fellows": Issues of Race, Hybridity and Location in Post-Colonial Shakespeares', in Loomba and Orkin, *Post-Colonial Shakespeares*, 143–63.

and Martin Orkin, eds,. *Post-Colonial Shakespeares* (London and New York, 1998).

Macdonald, Ronald R., 'The Unheimlich Maneuver: Antithetical Ways of Power in Shakespeare', in Kendall, *Shakespearean Power and Punishment*, 197–209.

Madelaine, Richard, 'Putting out the Light: A "Snuff" Variant?' in White et al., *Shakespeare: Readers, Audiences, Players*, 207–19.

Magnusson, Lynne, *Shakespeare and Social Dialogue: Dramatic Language and Elizabethan Letters* (Cambridge, 1999).

Marsden, Jean I., 'Daddy's Girls: Shakespearian Daughters and Eighteenth-Century Ideology', *Shakespeare Survey 51* (Cambridge, 1998), 17–26.

Marshall, Cynthia, 'The Doubled Jaques and Constructions of Negation in *As You Like It*', *Shakespeare Quarterly*, 49 (1998), 375–92.

Massai, Sonia, 'From *Pericles* to *Marina*: "While Women are to be had for Money, Love, or Importunity"', *Shakespeare Survey 51* (Cambridge, 1998), 67–77.

Mazzio, Carla, 'Staging the Vernacular: Language and Nation in Thomas Kyd's *The Spanish Tragedy*', *Studies in English Literature 1500–1900*, 38 (1998), 207–32.

McGuire, Philip C., 'Whose Work Is This? Loading the Bed in *Othello*', in Halio and Richmond, *Shakespearean Illuminations*, 70–92.

McMullan, Gordon, 'A Rose for Emilia: Collaborative Relations in *The Two Noble Kinsmen*', in Gordon McMullan, *Renaissance Configurations*, 129–47.

ed. *Renaissance Configurations: Voices, Bodies, Spaces, 1580–1690* (Basingstoke, 1998).

Neill, Michael '"Mulattos", "Blacks", and "Indian Moors": *Othello* and Early Modern Constructions of Human Difference', *Shakespeare Quarterly*, 49 (1998), 361–74.

'Post-Colonial Shakespeare? Writing Away from the Centre', in Loomba and Orkin, *Post-Colonial Shakespeares*, 164–85.

O'Brien, Ellen J., 'Civil Wars in the Rehearsal Room: Conflicting Theories in Collaborative Praxis', in Bate et al., *Shakespeare and the Twentieth Century*, 125–36.

'Mapping the Role: Criticism and the Construction of Shakespearian Character', in Halio and Richmond, *Shakespearean Illuminations*, 13–32.

O'Connor, Robert F., 'The Better Concludes a Worse?: Shakespeare, *Macbeth* and Disorder', in White et al., *Shakespeare: Readers, Audiences, Players*, 182–94.

Orkin, Martin, 'Proverbial Allusion in *Julius Caesar*', *Pretexts: Studies in Writing and Culture*, 7 (1998), 213–34.

'Whose *Muti* in the Web of It?: Seeking "Post"-Colonial Shakespeare', *Journal of Commonwealth Literature*, 33, 1998, 15–38.

Orlin, Lena Cowen, 'Gertrude's Closet', *Shakespeare Jahrbuch* 134 (1998), 44–67.

Oz, Avraham, Afterword: '"Prosper Our Colours": A Case/Noncase for National Perspectives on Shakespeare and his Contemporaries', in Oz, *Strands Afar Remote*, 276–300.

ed., *Strands Afar Remote: Israeli Perspectives on Shakespeare* (Newark and London, 1998).

Paster, Gail Kern, 'The Unbearable Coldness of Female Being: Women's Imperfection and the Humoral Economy', *English Literary Renaissance*, 28 (1998), 416–440.

Paulin, Roger, 'Luise Gottsched und Dorothea Tieck: Vom Schicksal zwerer Uberzetzerinnen', *Shakespeare Jahrbuch*, 134 (1998), 108–122.

Potter, Lois, 'Killing Mercutio: Or, Is There Such a Thing as an Actor-Playwright', in Halio and Richmond, *Shakespearean Illuminations*, 267–78.

Pugliatti, Paola, 'Shakespeare's Historicism: Visions and Revisions', in Bate et al., *Shakespeare and the Twentieth Century*, 336–49.

Pujante, A. Luis, '*Double Falsehood* and Verbal Parallels with Shelton's *Don Quixote*', *Shakespeare Survey 51* (Cambridge, 1998), 95–105.

Rackin, Phyllis, 'Dating Shakespeare's Women', *Shakespeare Jahrbuch*, 134 (1998), 29–43.

Reichert, Klaus, 'Shakespeare and Joyce: Myriad-minded Men', in Bate et al., *Shakespeare and the Twentieth Century*, 103–12.

de Reuck, Jenny, 'Blackface and Madonna: Race and Gender as Conditions of Reception in Recovering *Othello*', in White et al., *Shakespeare: Readers, Audiences, Players*, 220–32.

Richmond, Hugh, 'A Letter to the Actor Playing Lear', in Halio and Richmond, *Shakespearean Illuminations*, 110–30.

Roberts, Sasha, *Romeo and Juliet*, (Plymouth, 1998). 'Shakespeare "creepes into the womens closets about bedtime": Women Reading in a Room of their Own', in Gordon McMullan, *Renaissance Configurations*, 30–63.

Rosen, Alan, 'The Rhetoric of Exclusion: Jew, Moor, and the Boundaries of Discourse in *The Merchant of Venice*', in Oz, *Strands Afar Remote*, 38–50.

Schabert, Ina, 'Männertheater', *Shakespeare Jahrbuch* 134 (1998), 11–28.

Schalkwyk, David. 'What May Words Do? The Performative of Praise in Shakespeare's Sonnets', *Shakespeare Quarterly*, 49 (1998), 251–68.

Schamp, Jutta, *Repräsentation von Zeit bei Shakespeare: 'Richard II', 'Henry IV', 'Macbeth'* (Tübingen, 1997).

Scheil, Katherine West, 'Early Georgian Politcs and Shakespeare: The Black Act and Charles Johnson's *Love in a Forest*', *Shakespeare Survey 51* (Cambridge, 1998), 45–56.

Scofield, Martin 'Shakespeare and *Clarissa*: "General Nature", Genre and Sexuality', *Shakespeare Survey 51* (Cambridge, 1998), 27–43.

Shand, G. B., 'Gertrud, Captive Queen of the First Quarto', in Halio and Richmond, *Shakespearean Illuminations*, 33–49.

Shawe-Taylor, Desmond, 'Eighteenth-Century Performances of Shakespeare Recorded in the Theatrical Portraits at the Garrick Club', *Shakespeare Survey 51* (Cambridge, 1998), 107–23.

Shurbanov, Alexander, 'Politicized with a Vengeance: East European Uses of Shakespeare's Great Tragedies', in Bate et al., *Shakespeare and the Twentieth Century*, 137–47.

Skeele, David, *Thwarting the Wayward Seas: A Critical and Theatrical History of Shakespeare's 'Pericles' in the Nineteenth and Twentieth Centuries*. (Newark and London, 1998).

Smith, Peter J., 'M. O. A. I. "What should that alphabetical position portend?" An Answer to the Metamorphic Malvolio', *Renaissance Quarterly*, 51 (1998), 1199–224.

Sokol, B. J., 'Prejudice and Law in *The Merchant of Venice*', *Shakespeare Survey 51* (Cambridge, 1998), 159–73.

de Somogyi, Nick, *Shakespeare's Theatre of War* (Aldershot and Brookfield, Vermont, 1998).

Spotswood, Jerald W., 'Maintaining Hierarchy in *The Tragedie of King Lear*', *Studies in English Literature 1500–1900*, 38 (1998), 265–80.

Stříbrný, Zdeněk, '*King Lear* versus *Hamlet* in Eastern Europe', in Halio and Richmond, *Shakespearean Illuminations*, 93–101.

Summers, David, '" – the proverb is something musty": The Commonplace and Epistemic Crisis in *Hamlet*', *Hamlet Studies*, 20 (1998), 9–34.

Suzman, Janet, 'South Africa in *Othello*', in Bate et al., *Shakespeare and the Twentieth Century*, 23–40.

Taylor, Gary, 'Feeling Bodies', in Bate et al., *Shakespeare and the Twentieth Century*, 258–79.

Thompson, Ann, 'Teena Rochfort Smith, Frederick Furnivall, and the New Shakspere Society's Four-Text Edition of *Hamlet*', *Shakespeare Quarterly*, 49 (1998), 125–39.

Tweg, Sue, 'Readers, Audiences, Players and the *Beauties of Shakespeare*', in White et al., *Shakespeare: Readers, Audiences, Players*, 29–46.

Vaughan, Virginia Mason, 'Race Mattered: *Othello* in Late Eighteenth-Century England', *Shakespeare Survey 51* (Cambridge, 1998), 57–66.

Walch, Günter, 'The Historical Subject as *Roman Actor* and Agent of History: Interrogative Dramatic Structure in *Julius Caesar*', in Halio and Richmond, *Shakespearian Illuminations*, 220–41.

Walker, Julia M., *Medusa's Mirrors: Spenser, Shakespeare, Milton, and the Metamorphosis of the Female Self* (Newark and London, 1998).

Wall, Wendy, '"Household Stuff": The Sexual Politics of Domesticity and the Advent of English Comedy', *English Literary History*, 65 (1998), 1–45.

Walsh, Marcus, 'Eighteenth-Century Editing, "Appropriation", and Interpretation', *Shakespeare Survey 51* (Cambridge, 1998), 125–39.

Watson, Robert N., 'The State of Life and the Power of Death: *Measure for Measure*', in Kendall, *Shakespearean Power and Punishment*, 130–56.

Werstine, Paul, 'Hypertext as Editorial Horizon', in Bate et al., *Shakespeare and the Twentieth Century*, 248–57.

White, R. S., Charles Edelman, and Christopher Wortham, eds., *Shakespeare: Readers, Audiences, Players* (Nedlands, 1998).

Witt, Robert W., 'The Duel in *Hamlet* as Play-within', *Hamlet Studies*, 20 (1998), 50–62.

Womack, Peter, 'Notes on the "Elizabethan" Avant-Garde', in Bate et al., *Shakespeare and the Twentieth Century*, 75–84.

Worthen, W. B., 'Drama, Performativity, and Performance', *PMLA*, 113 (1998), 1093–1108.

Wright, George T., 'The Silent Speech of Shakespeare's *Sonnets*', in Bate et al., *Shakespeare and the Twentieth Century*, 314–35.

Yogev, Michael, '"War and Lechery Confound All"': Identity and Agency in Shakespeare's *Troilus and Cressida*', in Oz, *Strands Afar Remote*, 87–112.

2. SHAKESPEARE'S LIFE, TIMES, AND STAGE

reviewed by ALISON FINDLAY

I

It is ironic that the Bard voted 'Man of the Millennium' in Britain has simultaneously been increasingly associated with a subversive Catholic minority in early modern England. This year has seen a growing tide of interest in Shakespeare's connection with the culture of the Counter-Reformation. Biographical studies by Honan and Holden note that the theory that Shakespeare spent time in Lancashire in the service of the Catholic de Hoghton family is the most likely explanation for the so-called 'lost years'.[1] Manchester University Press has reprinted Honigmann's *Shakespeare: The 'Lost Years'*, the pioneering book that revived the theory in the mid-1980s. The new edition is very welcome, as this remains the best book-length collection and analysis of the evidence; it was frequently cited at *Lancastrian Shakespeare: Region, Religion, Patronage and Performance*, an international conference held at Hoghton Tower and Lancaster University (21–4 July 1999). Honigmann's new edition contains a second preface, citing Richard Wilson's recent research on the Lancashire theory. In 'Shakespeare and the Jesuits: New Connections Supporting the Theory of the lost Catholic years in Lancashire', Wilson draws striking links between John Cottom, schoolmaster at Stratford Grammar School, the de Hoghtons, and the Sodality of young Jesuit priests who were recruited by Edmund Campion.[2]

Campion's visit to Hoghton Tower, just before his arrest, puts the de Hoghton household at the heart of Counter-Reformation plots. Wilson proposes that Shakespeare may have been a potential recruit to the priesthood, but shied away from the fate of Campion and his followers in favour of a career in the theatre, thus appearing in Alexander de Hoghton's will as the 'William Shakeshafte now dwelling with me' who is recommended to Thomas Hoghton along with a bequest of 'instruments and play clothes'.[3]

Wilson provides more evidence to support the theory of Shakespeare's continued preoccupation with the Jesuit brotherhood, in an article 'A Bloody Question: The Politics of *Venus and Adonis*', which argues that the poem is 'a critique of martyrdom' (p. 164). Wilson traces a literary relationship between Shakespeare and his cousin and fellow poet, the Jesuit Robert Southwell. By reading Southwell's *Saint Peter's Complaint and Saint Mary Magdalen's Funeral Tears* as a critical commentary on *Venus and Adonis*, Wilson uncovers a network of religious politics in the world of its dedicatee Henry Wriothesley. The poem is 'constructed like one

---

1 Park Honan, *Shakespeare: A Life* (Oxford, 1999 to be reviewed in the next issue of *Survey*), Anthony Holden, *William Shakespeare: His Life and Work* (London, 1999)

2 *Times Literary Supplement*, 19 December 1997, pp. 11–13.

3 Ernst Honigmann, *Shakespeare: The 'Lost Years'* p. 136.

of those secret "musits" or priest-holes through which outlawed Catholics evaded capture' (p. 165), Wilson shows, proposing that the overbearing queen of love figures Elizabeth I; the savage boar, her priest-hunter Burghley, and the stubborn Adonis 'the self-immolation of an entire generation of Catholic emigres' (p. 174). It is to be hoped that Wilson's book-length study will reveal more exciting material and elegant analysis like this.

Anthony Holden's biography *Shakespeare: His Life and Work* contains a chapter on the Lancashire household context, a theory to which Holden admits he is positively biased by his own Lancashire origins. Unlike Honan's drier biography, this book self-consciously flourishes its delight in reconstructing Shakespeare after its author's own image. Its attempt to 'put him back together again' (p. 1), after the onslaughts of heavily historicized and politicized critiques, seems designed to appeal to a non-scholarly audience. This is not to say that it is lacking in detailed research. On the contrary, each episode of Shakespeare's life is recounted with the help of a mass of material, and accompanied by photographs of the signatures, legal documents, title pages, and pictures. As the title of the book indicates, details from the life are interwoven with discussions of the works, producing a rich, multi-textured narrative. Holden's fear that such connections may be seen as 'heresy' (p. 3) is unfounded. He is acutely sensitive to 'Shakespeare's ghost cackling at the literalmindedness of scholars' and biographers (p. 142). With this cautionary spirit of mockery always in mind, he suggests some interesting connections between life and work: the death of Hamnet and the grief of Constance in *King John*; the possibility of adultery on the part of Shakespeare's landlady, Lady Mountjoy, inspiring *Othello* (p. 218); the threat of his recusant connections returning to trouble him, and producing reworked versions of the Gunpowder plot in *Macbeth* and *King Lear*. What is perhaps more problematic from a scholarly point of view, is Holden's determination to

'spare the reader' the trouble of footnotes (p. 5), when he runs the risk of juxtaposing different kinds of source material, including the more fanciful ideas of Anthony Burgess (pp. 66–7). In fact Burgess shadows Shakespeare, at key moments, as another Holden hero. The weaving of fact and fiction is inevitable in an attempt to 'pin [Shakespeare] firmly to the page, no matter how hard he has struggled to escape' (p. 4), and this Shakespeare is an entertaining, valuable read, especially for those ready to unpick the 'worm-eaten tapestry' (*Much Ado* 3.3.132) and distinguish the strong threads from the weaker ones.

The overwhelming desire to recover a 'genuine' Shakespeare reached fantastic extremes when 'Believers' eagerly accepted the forgeries of William Henry Ireland. In *Reforging Shakespeare* Jeffrey Kahan gives a much-needed re-evaluation of the scandal, tracing back to the sources. By placing *Vortigern* in its theatrical context for the first time, Kahan shows that 'forging Shakespeare was probably the only way to ensure a positive response for a new tragedy written in the 1790s' (p. 21). The book's Sherlock Holmes style of detective investigation makes it fun to read, but it has a serious argument to make: that, far from being a naïve dreamer, William Henry was 'a deliberate and calculating fraud' (p. 44) whose forgeries were all part of a money-making master plan. *Vortigern*, Kahan shows, was 'deliberately informed by the literary and artistic life of the eighteenth century' (p. 81). The tortuous process whereby it reached the stage is wittily outlined, complete with diagrams, like a parody of the transmission of a Shakespeare play from foul papers to variant printed texts. Throughout this immensely entertaining book, one gets a strong sense of the theatrical culture of the eighteenth century and the market value of Shakespeare.

The religious associations surrounding Shakespeare himself are the subject of Péter Dávidházi's *The Romantic Cult of Shakespeare: Literary Reception in Anthropological Perspective*. The author re-examines the growth of bardolatry in England and in Hungary as a cult 'whose psychology, ritual and rhetoric reveal latent religious patterns' (ix). He argues for an 'agnostic suspension' of value judgements, in order to appreciate the phenomenon more fully than previous studies, which have emphasized the political and social aspects of the Shakespeare cult (p. 23). The book explores religious psychology through discussion of the bardolaters' specific attitudes, their different rituals and their use of language. Dávidházi argues that the Garrick jubilee of 1769 implicitly relied on the ancient religious idea of *yobel* as a time of liberation from bondage and spiritual restoration. Drinking from the mulberry goblet, made out of the tree supposedly planted by Shakespeare, became a form of Eucharist at the Jubilee, revealing 'an unconscious yearning for the bond of *communitas*, something immediate and without hierarchy' (pp. 41–2). Chapter 3 traces a parallel case study of the development of the Shakespeare cult in Hungary, giving new insights into the work of Vörösmarty, Petofi, and Emilia Lemouton, among others. The alternative focus on religious psychology is not fully achieved, however, since the book tends to get bogged down in detail (and some repetition), rather than following through the very interesting ideas it opens up. This is unfortunate since Dávidházi's approach has cast new light on the Romantic recreation of Shakespeare as a god.

The Catholic contexts in which Shakespeare wrote are explored in Elizabeth Hanson's *Discovering the Subject in Renaissance England*, a fine study of the growth of subjectivity in apparently hostile conditions, focusing on conscience, faith and the context of religious persecution and torture. Hanson identifies 'an alliance between inwardness and agency in the service of self-interest' which gives the subject an unnerving 'leverage against his world', even when being subjected by the authority of the State (pp. 16–17). She explores this curious power in four specific sites: firstly, the persecution of Jesuit priests, whose torture produced 'hybrid' confessions which opened 'the secrets of the Catho-

lics' consciences' to the interrogator in terms of their earthly sins, but simultaneously concealed and prioritized the inner 'truth' of their souls, thus publicizing an inviolable interiority (p. 51). In chapter 3, Hanson relates this model of secrecy to a wider context, to examine 'the ways in which fears about specific concealed identities could fuse with more general anxieties about place-changing' (p. 86), in examinations of *Othello* and *Measure For Measure*. Both these chapters have appeared previously, in journals, but the power of their arguments is strengthened by their inclusion alongside new chapters on authorship, and on Bacon's 'self-discovering subject'. The strength of Hanson's analyses lies in her careful attention to detail. Like an expert inquisitor herself, skilled in the use of theoretical instruments for eliciting the 'truths' she seeks to expose, she interrogates the texts with real flair and the results are impressive.

Megan Matchinske's *Writing, Gender and State in Early Modern England* also concentrates three of its four chapters on religion as a vital point of connection and contradiction between the subject and the State. Matchinske argues powerfully for the need to reread women's writings in order to illuminate the forms of resistance and difference that are obscured in accounts of the Reformation, Counter-Reformation and the religious climate of the Civil War. This method works well to resituate the eccentric writings of Eleanor Davies (discussed in chapter 4). In the earlier chapters, Matchinske reads Anne Askew as a figure who embraces the notion of Protestant privacy to 'construct a separate and interior space from which to imagine her subjectivity' (p. 49). Chapter 2 goes on to examine the Catholic martyr Margaret Clitherow, as a figure who fulfils the role of ideal Elizabethan housewife by remaining silent in her trial for harbouring priests, but whose performance of that role is essentially subversive. Behind the closed doors of the Catholic household, Clitherow was able to generate a secret but powerful form of agency. Although her martyrdom undoubtedly served the Catholic mission well, it may also 'have had a direct impact on the way other married women of Clitherow's status and belief took up religious positions' (p. 82). Clitherow left no personal record of her trial and one of the real strengths of Matchinske's analysis is her exploration of ways of reconstructing the voices of her subjects. She takes trouble to outline the advantages and potential hazards of her own methods, thereby providing an excellent model of working practice for other scholars of women's writing.

II

The philosophical contexts on which Shakespeare drew are examined in three new books. Nick Davis's *Stories of Chaos* draws on the ideas of Plato, Aristotle and Pythagoras alongside those of Freud and Lacan to suggest that early modern imaginative literature is preoccupied with the fragile relationship between reason, chaos and narrative. The different elements of the theoretical framework are not always brought together clearly, but the book offers an exciting, original angle by considering mathematics as a mode of 'systematic thinking' (p. 15) that simultaneously displays irrational or chaotic elements. Davis uses this innovative approach to read *Sir Gawain and the Green Knight*, *The Fairie Queene*, *King Lear*, and *Paradise Lost* as key imaginative texts that demonstrate the emergence of narrative at the point where reasoning breaks down. The chapter on *King Lear* offers new insights into the play's interrogation of 'nothing'. Davis argues that Shakespeare's awareness of the modern form of decimal 'reckoning' is set against the abacist style of calculation and can be mapped onto the play to expose the different philosophical positions of the older and younger generations. Lear and Gloucester fail 'to grasp the bivalence of arithmetical 'o' as multiplying placeholder and indicator of emptiness' (p. 137), while the play dramatizes the collapse of a system where 'numbers are solid, integral things, moved about by straightforward

rules in public view, and not subject to the manipulation that exploits the "new" numbers' capacity to multiply and evaporate under the pen' (p. 137). Original arguments such as these sometimes appear to get lost in a wealth of other details and asides in the book, partly as a consequence of its ambitious scope. Nevertheless, Davis's thesis is exciting; it illuminates the literary articulation of an important dimension of early modern thinking.

Geoffrey Aggeler's *Nobler in the Mind* explores the relationships between different philosophical and religious ideas, to reveal 'how much common ground a Calvinist Protestant could find with an ancient Stoic' (p. 31), and how the scepticism about man's reason brought together diverse thinkers like Luther, Calvin and Montaigne (p. 38). Intertwined patterns of belief are then examined in the protagonists of Renaissance tragedies, who shift between Stoic and Sceptic stances, even combining them. Aggeler devotes close attention to the systems of divine and human justice in Kyd's *The Spanish Tragedy* to conclude that it is 'a pagan humanistic skeptical tragedy' (p. 71). Marston's 'Calvinist Neostoic' philosophy is demonstrated, and a further complexity to the Stoic-Sceptic dialectic is analysed in Chapman's *Bussy* plays. Aggeler rightly re-evaluates *The Revenge of Bussy D'Ambois* as an important 'critique as well as a celebration of the Stoic ideal' (p. 141). Throughout these very readable chapters, the opinions of other critics are animated in a lively critical debate. The dust jacket's résumé of the book claims that the early chapters may be seen as 'parts of an extended preface to the discussion of *Hamlet*'. His analysis does explore the complex spiritual and intellectual journey the protagonist takes, concluding that 'for Hamlet, as for Job, skeptical questioning that undercuts conventional assumptions and canned wisdom finally refutes itself and prepares the way for faith and acceptance' (p. 157). However, it is disappointing that many of the issues raised earlier, such as the questionable ethics of revenge, are not addressed.

An important literary influence on Shakespeare is explored in Margaret Tudeau-Clayton's *Jonson, Shakespeare and Early Modern Virgil*. As the title implies, she discusses how Jonson and Shakespeare's works are associated with two different models of Virgil, which promote opposing political positions. The first two chapters provide excellent outlines of the elitist 'learned man's Virgil' associated with 'a traditional "Catholic" structure of hermeneutic authority' (p. 31), and the less esoteric 'schoolboys' Virgil'. Because both Virgil and Shakespeare are celebrated as 'figures of equal, absolute value' central to a canonized 'structure of literary history' (p. 3), it is inevitable that Shakespeare should also be associated with the authoritarian image of the poet. However, Tudeau-Clayton argues that it is more appropriate to identify Shakespeare with a sceptical mode associated with what she calls the 'Protestant Turn', a position which entails 'dis-placing the received Virgilian mediations as groundless fictions of the past' (p. 10), and dismantling the structures of authority and the hierarchy of privilege which those 'sacred' texts perpetuate. Her discussion of *The Tempest* begins by criticizing previous studies of the play's Virgilian echoes for failing to take account of the political significance of Virgil as icon of established authority, an educational tool to fashion colonialist superiority. She goes on to explore how Caliban and Miranda's language 'aspires to reproduce the "noise" of nature and so erase from within the distinctions of the symbolic order' (p. 201). The civilizing 'Father tongue' may be critiqued by the Boatswain too, but in Tudeau-Clayton's view, the play is finally 'coerced to underwrite the restoration of the master[s]' Virgil, Prospero and Shakespeare (p. 243). This fails to take account of the epilogue's complete reliance on the wider populace of spectators to 'set me free' (Epilogue 20). Although readers may disagree with elements of the book's analyses, it undoubtedly succeeds in reanimating the early modern Virgil as a significant political phenomenon.

In the case of Jonson, Tudeau-Clayton argues that the masques appropriate the voice of Virgil to underwrite monarchical authority, and that his staging of Virgil in *Poetaster* (1601) characteristically promotes a politics 'no more egalitarian' (p. 168) than an education system through which only exceptional figures like Jonson could rise. Julie Sanders takes issue with such categorizations of Jonson in *Ben Jonson's Theatrical Republics*. This subtle and well-nuanced assessment argues that Jonson's plays 'are not manuals for political activism, but neither are they royalist propaganda that dismisses the politics of the masses' (p. 27). The early modern myth of Venice as a *stato misto*, a paradox of quasi-monarchical power (the Doge) within an ostensibly republican state, proves a useful means of reading the schizophrenic energies of *Volpone*. In the second section of the book Sanders moves on to argue that Jonson's sense of republicanism is more accurately located in drama itself. Her chapter on Jonson's depiction of women, drawing on *Epicoene, Catiline* and masques sadly doesn't make much of the theatrical contexts, but the following chapter on *The Alchemist* neatly demonstrates how 'the paradox of the stage republic' is played out (p. 77). *Bartholomew Fair* speaks both to courtly and popular taste, Sanders argues, its ambivalence linked to Jonson's consciousness that 'the nature, composition, and reception of any one audience' changes the performance (p. 96). A final section of the book focuses specifically on Jonson's representation of communities, and pays attention to some of the later works. Throughout, Sanders writes with an engaging style. Her reassessment of complex political negotiations in the plays makes a significant contribution to Jonson studies.

The theatrical dimensions of Jonson's texts receive new attention in *Ben Jonson and Theatre*, by Richard Cave, Elizabeth Schafer and Brian Woolland. The 'venture tripartite' makes a conscious effort to stage a dialogue between academics and theatre practitioners, drawing from the authors' experiences of an interdisciplinary conference held at Reading University. Their project succeeds admirably. In the first section, Richard Cave makes succinct points about the theatrical dimensions of Jonson's texts and the challenges of realizing these on stage. References to recent productions and to the opinions of actors John Nettles and Simon Russell Beale lend additional authority to this examination of performance possibilities. The central section, by Brian Woolland, takes a closer look at the connections between rehearsing and teaching Jonson, clearly demonstrating the value of practical work as a way of dispelling the myth that Jonson's texts are inaccessible to modern sensibilities. It is full of intelligent, practical suggestions as well as a pertinent essay on literary value judgements by Mick Jardine. Elizabeth Schafer contributes a section on even more 'marginalized' Jonsons, namely his interpretation by women and in an Australian production. Gender politics and performativity receive attention here. It is good to see reference to plays like *The Devil is An Ass, The Magnetic Lady* and *The New Inn*, running throughout the book, whose debates between academics and theatre practice prove, in Gina McIntosh's words, 'you do get a very extraordinary kind of spark' (p. 145) from Jonson's texts.

Discussion of a 'source' for Jonson's *Alchemist* is the starting point for an impatient critique of source studies in an article by Richard Levin. He argues that an incident identified by Sissons as a source for the plot involving Dapper and the 'Fairy Queen', cited by subsequent editors, bears little similarity to the play. Having outlined details of potentially stronger 'source' material in pamphlets involving a deceiver called 'Doll', Levin goes on to accuse historicist critics of being over-zealous in their attempts to identify topical allusions in plays. According to Levin, the enthusiasm of source hunters leads easily into Fluellen-like misinterpretation, whereby 'he [*sic*] selects only the similarities between the two objects and ignores all the differences', ignoring other dimensions of both

text and context (p. 221). Levin gives a good cautionary reminder about the use of other documents, but to suggest that 'we do not need them to understand and appreciate those plays' (p. 230) ignorantly disregards the insights that have been gained in critical writings which acknowledge the tangential relationship between texts.

Critics seeking more contextual material for *The Alchemist* are spoilt for choice in the detailed treasure trove of *A Dictionary of Alchemical Imagery* compiled by Lyndy Abraham. It outlines the symbolism of alchemy with a particular (though not exclusive) reference to texts and pictures of the sixteenth and seventeenth centuries. A definition of each symbol details its physical and figurative meanings, and is accompanied by quotations from literary and intellectual writings. Amongst the 220 pages there are some surprising entries. For example, the word 'worm' is defined as 'the mercurial waters of life and death' (p. 220). One would be hesitant about suggesting a new 'source' for *Antony and Cleopatra*, of course, but editors of Shakespeare will find many intriguing possibilities in this wonderful reference book.

Another of Shakespeare's contemporaries is discussed in Ian McAdam's *The Irony of Identity*, which explores the failure of self-fashioning in Marlowe's plays as the result of a conflict between self-assertion and self-surrender. McAdam points out that Marlowe 'seems obsessed with religious ideas to a greater degree than any other major dramatist of the period' (p. 17) and argues strongly for a reassessment of Marlowe's own psychology as informed by Augustinian religious sympathies, and unease at his own homosexuality. This is a brave approach, and McAdam registers his difference from much recent critical methodology in the lucid introduction. His subsequent analyses of the plays chart different phases of an increasingly desperate Marlovian imagination. Thus, *Dido, Queen of Carthage* is explored as a crisis of masculinity caused by the hero's narcissism, for example, and *Tamburlaine* as a deeply ambivalent text in which the hero's self-shaping as a god involves an incomplete suppression of homosexual longings. At the heart of the book lies a remarkable reading of *Doctor Faustus* as a psychological drama. McAdam analyses Faustus's fear and erotically charged passion in his relationship with God, as the expression of Marlowe's attempt 'to free himself psychologically, by directly facing and thus exorcizing his own desire for religious surrender and self-subordination' (p. 113). This is stirring stuff, and the book will certainly make its mark as a powerful reading of Marlowe.

The whole dramatic period in which Shakespeare worked is covered in G. K. Hunter's *English Drama 1586–1642*. It is impossible to do justice to this monumental volume in the short space allowed here, but its overall structure serves the material well. Hunter concentrates on printed texts and groups them round the organizing principles of generic likeness. Broad categories like 'Early History Plays' and 'Later Comedy' contain smaller groupings such as 'prodigal plays' or 'domestic tragedy'. *All's Well* is interestingly grouped with other 'prodigal' plays (pp. 385–6). Plays which innovate such movements are prioritized in discussion, even though they are not always 'the literary favourites' (p. 5). I was therefore sad to see that, even though Elizabeth Cary's *The Tragedy of Mariam* (*c.* 1605) is mentioned as an example of tragedy based on the Herod and Mariam story, it is simply relegated to the category of 'closet drama', in favour of Markham and Sampson's later play which is discussed in more detail (p. 459). Henrietta Maria's involvement in masques and courtly entertainments is not mentioned at all, so we obviously still have a long way to go to integrate female dramatic production into the canon. The exception to Hunter's principle of generic organization is an informative chapter on the boys' companies, which he reads as sites of self-conscious innovation. Interestingly, he proposes that *Troilus and Cressida* may have been written for boy actors. My feminist disappointments aside, I found this an

admirable book in which the brief analysis of texts is unfailingly sound.

Paulina Kewes gives a later history of Shakespearian production in her *Authorship and Appropriation*, a carefully worked out reading of the development of original creativity as the criterion dictating authorship in the later seventeenth century. Although Laura Rosenthal has published a similar study, this book is to be welcomed for the breadth of its focus and its wealth of illustrative detail.[4] Kewes considers, for example, how models of appropriation worked differently in the popular genres of romance and history since history as 'common cultural heritage', was not an 'authored' text in the same way as a romance (p. 88). Shakespeare and attitudes to his plays receive detailed attention in the book, where the adaptations of Dryden, Davenant, Otway, Tate and Cibber are discussed. Whereas Shakespeare's work was authorized through Restoration adaptations in the 1660s and beyond, towards the turn of the century, theatrical refinements of Shakespeare began to come under attack when 'ownership of language came to be circumscribed in print' (p. 92). Kewes makes a thorough study of the field; her book is a valuable addition to scholarship of later seventeenth-century drama.

Studies of the immediate cultural context in which Shakespeare worked are provided in Ilona Bell's *Elizabethan Women and the Poetry of Courtship* and David J. Baker's *Between Nations: Shakespeare, Spenser, Marvell and the Question of Britain*. Bell's wonderful book focuses on the personal, her analyses proving beyond doubt the importance of reading Elizabethan love poetry as an active form of emotional interaction and negotiation between early modern men and women. Little-known texts such as *The Autobiography of Thomas Wythorne* and poems surrounding the courtship of Anne Vavasour and Henry Lee are explored in fasci-

---

[4] Laura Rosenthal, *Playwrights and Plagiarists in Early Modern England: gender, authorship and literary property* (Ithaca and London, 1996).

nating detail. By paying attention to women's responses, in prose, poetry and speech, Bell creates the dialogue which Maureen Quilligan called for to 'complete the conversation' between canonized male-authored texts and women's writings.[5]

In contrast to Bell, Baker focuses on the national picture, beginning with a lengthy chapter on *Henry V*. He brings new light to bear on Macmorris and the tensions surrounding Essex's failed campaign by looking at the figure of Christopher St Lawrence, an Irish captain serving under Essex. St Lawrence appeared, like the character, to 'slide between the various definitions the "British" was attempting to subsume' (p. 35). Anxieties over Welsh subversion are figured in Fluellen, Baker goes on to argue, drawing on Christopher Highley's arguments.[6] Fluellen's Anglo-Welsh speech, indicating both sameness and difference, is a troubling presence on the stage since it alludes back to the Welsh origins of English monarchy (p. 61). Baker's new insights into polysemy as an indicator of national uncertainty make this an important reading.

The cultural ambiguity of Wales is also the subject of Garrett A. Sullivan's discussion of *Cymbeline* in his book *The Drama of Landscape*. His timely reminder of the setting enhances understanding of the play, by pointing out that Wales is both a foreign country and a 'shadow' that 'seeks to promote the cultural centrality of London and the court' (p. 146). In other chapters, Sullivan skilfully charts the use of urban, private and national territory in *2 Henry VI*, Heywood's *Edward IV*, *Arden of Faversham*, *Woodstock*, and Brome's *A Jovial Crew*, arguing that these texts stage 'complex relations between landed property and a range of social practices from which it is inseparable' (p. 13). Sullivan proposes that Shakespeare's use of maps in *Richard II*, *1 Henry IV* and *King Lear* explores early modern encounters with a new textual form 'that posed unsettling interpretative or epistemological questions' (p. 95). His discussions are uniformly clear, making this an informative book for the undergraduate as well as for more senior scholars.

Territories further afield are explored in Joan Pong Linton's *The Romance of the New World*, which seeks to combine the personal and the national, in a comparative study of colonial exploration and popular romance narratives. Her aim of reading the colonizing English explorer as a macrocosmic translation of the husband of romance narratives seems promising since its focus on gender, manipulation and violence characterizes both genres. In discussions of Shakespeare's plays the model does not always fit perfectly. The author argues that in *Troilus and Cressida* 'the New World leaves its trace on an old romance' (p. 134) and general features of romance are certainly to be found in the play's display of commodified women, its preoccupation with inconstancy. Overlaying comparisons with the Jamestown's narratives seems strained however. Linton's approach works infinitely better when she reads *The Tempest*. She uses the Pocahontas story to give an impressive postcolonial reading of the threat of rape, the importance of education, and the exploitative art of husbandry as vital tropes in the play, demonstrating how 'the propriety of the husband is undercut' when 'the preacher and colonial promoter begins to pander like a failed rapist' (p. 183).

III

Pauline Kiernan prefaces her book *Staging Shakespeare at the New Globe*, with a reminder that her findings are only 'an early sketch' (p. ix) of the possibilities offered by that space, based on early work there. The provisional nature of the findings is emphasized by the book's organization, a collocation of different voices, opinions, ideas, from both past and

---

[5] Maureen Quilligan, 'Completing the Conversation', *Shakespeare Studies* 15 (1997), 42–9.

[6] Christopher Highley, *Shakespeare, Spenser and the Crisis in Ireland* (Cambridge, 1997).

present, as seems highly appropriate to a volume on the paradoxical new/old theatre (p. 3). Kiernan's overview draws on references to playgoers, players and theatre spaces in Renaissance texts alongside anecdotal evidence from new Globe performances. The lengthy central section then details the process of mounting an 'authentic' production of *Henry V*, and is set out as a diary using bullet points and numerous sub-headings. Interviews with the actors make up a final section; their candid responses to playing the new Globe fully testifies to Kiernan's belief in the value of recording initial responses to the space. The 'spontaneous' rather than studied style of the book means that there is frequent repetition of material – in terms of ideas and impressions. However, the babel of enthusiastic opinions conveys an inspiring sense of excitement. Kiernan's book puts a polyphonic sound into the theatre space; it fills the architectural wooden O analysed in Shewring and Mulryne's *Shakespeare's Globe Rebuilt*, with living theatre practice.[7]

Attending to the 'O' factor is the aim of Bruce R. Smith's brilliant book *The Acoustic World of Early Modern England*. Smith opens with a series of exercises not unlike those in Cicely Berry's *The Actor and The Text*[8] but he historicizes the physicality of language with reference to early modern physiologists and theorizes it with reference to Derrida, Lacan and Barthes. Early modern sensitivity to the relation between orality and literacy is demonstrated so as to show that aural signifiers of the period probably functioned as indices 'with a natural or metonymical connection between the sign and what it represents' (p. 129). Smith points out how sound was a means to mark boundaries and to 'maintain communal self-identity' (p. 43) for the early modern population. He gives a series of vivid soundscape tours of the city, the countryside round Kenilworth and the bustling world of the court. The combination of imaginative insight and scholarly research is highly effective.

Music is a prominent feature of the book but rather than analysing only court or religious music, Smith offers a cacophony of festive noises ranging from Robin Hood games and street cries to ballads. Especially interesting is his view of ballads transformed from plays (pp. 201–5). Smith then moves inside the Wooden O (and the indoor theatres) to discuss the effects of sound in relation to architecture and the contrasting voices of man and boy actors. He wisely avoids trying to reconstruct an early modern accent, choosing instead to consider the variations in pitch and timbre in scenes from *Richard III*, *Twelfth Night*, *The Tempest* and *Antony and Cleopatra*. While these analyses may seem over-schematic, they are vital in reminding us how acoustic equivalents of visual scenes are built into the texts. We may not wholly agree with Smith that Shakespeare's immortality rests on his 'genius as an artist of sounds' (p. 278) but we do well to observe this dimension. *The Acoustic World of Early Modern England* will surely remain an invaluable text since it opens up the aural panorama with such perfect pitch.

The relationship between festive celebration and theatre is taken up again in *Playing Robin Hood*, edited by Lois Potter. Alexandra F. Johnston's essay, which draws on material from across the REED records, shows that the Robin Hood of the festivals was a fundraising role for parishes in the Thames Valley and west of England. Edwin Davenport, Jeffrey L. Singham and Michael Shapiro discuss the use of Robin Hood in Elizabethan history plays, concentrating on performativity. Shapiro's essay outlines the tradition of cross-dressing in the role of Maid Marion, arguing that in the Rose theatre, plays were staged which supported both sides of the debate on cross-dressing and the traditional pastimes associated with it.

The contexts of early indoor entertainments are examined in Greg Walker's *The Politics of*

---

7 J. R. Mulryne and Margaret Shewring, eds., *Shakespeare's Globe Rebuilt* (Cambridge, 1997).

8 Cicely Berry, *The Actor and The Text* (London, 1993).

Performance in Early Renaissance Drama. Walker locates plays by Heywood, Sir David Lindsay, Nicholas Udall and Norton and Sackville within the great hall or court, as arenas that inevitably politicize the performances. Far from being sycophantic, interlude drama exhibits an intellectual freedom, showing a 'curiously ambivalent attitude to royal and noble authority' (p. 51). Nicholas Udall's *Respublica* is read as 'a play constructed out of the poverty and social distress of the mid-Tudor period' (p. 178), for example. The last chapter on *Gorboduc*'s relation to the politics of Elizabeth I's potential marriage prospects doesn't add to what has already been published (by Walker and others) following the discovery of Richard Beale's interpretative account of a performance. Nevertheless, by bringing together readings from diverse geographical contexts, the book makes a strong overall case for the politicized nature of early great house drama.

Later private performance is considered in John H. Astington's *English Court Theatre*, a painstakingly researched book which brings together details on architecture, administration, audiences and the sense of occasion which informed performances at court. The opening chapter usefully outlines the relationship between the different royal offices responsible for the management of mirth: the Revels and the Works. Spanning a broad period from the mid sixteenth century to 1642, Astington considers the venues in which performances were staged. The various royal palaces and the specific playing spaces are discussed with reference to plans to reveal surprising contrasts in size and shape of theatre. The chapter on artists and artisans argues that Anthony Toto 'was directing the painted design of scenery and making costume designs for tailors well before Inigo Jones engaged in similar work' (p. 129). Astington usefully pinpoints the special nature of courtly audiences, identifying their constantly changing configuration and their likeness to spectators 'for a school or college play' because of their involved and intimate relationship with the performance (p. 161). In contrast to our usual perception of the monarch being central to the entertainment, Astington shows how, in 1624, the Christmas revels were 'taken up by the court itself' in James's absence (p. 180). He also makes some important points about the significant influence of women, not only the Queens, on courtly festivities. The book is packed with factual detail. What is missing, unfortunately, is any sense of the dangerous excitement that must have surrounded many of these high-powered entertainments. The political implications of masques have been studied elsewhere, it is true, but more reference to those dimensions would have given additional sparkle to this valuable source of information.

There are two essays on courtly entertainments in Volume 10 of *Medieval and Renaissance Drama*, edited by John Pitcher. Timothy Taylor gives a survey of the possible authors of *The Essex House Masque*, given by Viscount Doncaster on 8 January 1621, and recently rediscovered by Taylor in manuscript. Michael Leslie's interesting essay on country house entertainments for Queen Elizabeth argues that they made conscious use of unfamiliar space to reverse the usual power relations of the court masque. Nowhere is this more obvious, Leslie argues, than in the Cowdray entertainment of 1591 at the home of the Roman Catholic Lord Montague. Montague's entertainment capitalizes on the Queen's uncertainty in unfamiliar territory to coerce her into publicly acknowledging him as a loyal subject, while attacking her attendant courtiers. Other essays in this volume deal with the political subtext of the Christmas court revels in 1551–2 (pp. 19–46), and the professional theatre. S. P. Cerasano questions the evidence surrounding Alleyn's retirement, and Mary Bly gives a perceptive reading of the first boys' company at Whitefriars. Herbert Berry re-examines the documentation on playhouses in Folger MS VB 275 to conclude that it is 'probably a fraud', at least as far as its claims to offer primary evidence about events up to 1658 (p. 287). In addition the volume contains essays on *Arden of Faversham*, *Women Beware Women* and *The Tragedy of Mariam*.

Later theatrical history is illustrated in *John Bell: Patron of British Theatrical Portraiture*, a catalogue of portraits taken from his edition of Shakespeare's Works and from *Bell's British Theatre*. This comprehensive reference book has been carefully edited by Kalman A. Burnim and Philip H. Highfill Jr, who give prefatory essays with brief information about the editions and the theatrical styles which informed the representations. Most of the items in the catalogue are illustrated in small well-produced plates, each with details of the performer, artist, engraver, edition, date, location of the original and provenance. The images parade a wonderful display of Shakespearian characters as conceived by eighteenth-century imaginations. As well as familiar figures like Macklin's Shylock, complete with knife and scales (p. 65), there are some unusual images, such as a picture of Priscilla Hopkins (later Mrs Kemble) as Lavinia, a role she did not act in London (pp. 57–8). Samuel Reddish as Edgar's Poor Tom (p. 72) and Jane Lessingham as Ophelia (p. 64) give an impression of neatly ordered madness, while images from other popular productions of the eighteenth century set the Shakespearian characters in context. Apparently Bell declared that his revival of *British Theatre* would 'challenge the admiration of the World' (p. 15). *This* revival will certainly command the respect and interest of those researching theatre of the late eighteenth century.

Theatrical histories of *Hamlet* and *Antony and Cleopatra* appear in two new volumes in the Shakespeare in Production series. Faced with the daunting task of compiling a volume on Hamlet, Robert Hapgood states that he has concentrated on live performances and on the title role, yet his critical introduction covers an amazing breadth of material. He outlines turns in the definition of 'princeliness' via key figures like Burbage, Betterton, Kemble, Kean, Macready, Booth, Irving and Sarah Bernhardt. 'Hamletism' as a phenomenon is not discussed,

so leaving space for some twentieth-century Hamlets, including Gielgud, Olivier and John Barrymore. (On the latter, it is very pleasing to see that a paperback version of Michael A. Morrison's wonderful biography has now been published.) Hapgood gives an insight into modern conceptions of the play by focusing on some productions striking for their design concepts, and politicized versions of the play in East Germany and Moscow. Even Gertrude, Claudius and Ophelia are the subject of well-focused attention. The text which follows has some unusual details in the performance notes. For example, the rhythmic inflection of Garrick's 'To be or not to be', as observed by Steele, is given in musical notation. Obviously, choosing from a wealth of excellent interpretations for almost every line is difficult, but Hapgood's choices prove his point that 'Hamlet has led a virtually continuous life in the theatre' (p. 1)

Richard Madelaine argues that *Antony and Cleopatra* has had a strange stage life due to the difficulties and expense of producing it, one of the main problems being the infinite variety of each protagonist, problematic for a single actor to realize in performance. In addition, 'the relationship between the performance of actresses and the cultural construction of femininity' (p. 4) have made the role of Cleopatra especially difficult for female actors, the editor argues. It is performances by actresses rather than actors which dominate his introduction, although the play's connections with Orientalism and the long tradition of spectacular effects are also discussed. In keeping with the bias of the introduction, the most extensive notes in this edition are on Cleopatra's scenes, which is a shame for Antonys-to-be.

Detailed study of a single production is offered in Robert Lyons' *Swedish Midsummer in Shakespeare's Dream* which analyses the creative process behind Eva Bergman's 1989 production at the Backa Theatre, Goteborg. Lyons gives an exhaustive account: from the cultural, theatrical and architectural contexts of the production, through the rehearsal process, costume and music, to its reception. The careful statement of aims and ideas, typical of a postgraduate thesis, do slow the book down at times, but a sense of immediacy about the production is recovered by blocking plans, interviews and illustrations, which are discussed intelligently by Lyons. Especially interesting is the section on Eva Bergman's own influences. Her decision to depart from the style of her father Ingmar, to work in 'another mode, the epic, for a primarily different audience, the young' (p. 165), and to adopt different working methods and a less 'faithful' attitude to the 'original' scripts (p. 169) illuminates the production within the context of Swedish national theatre.

Journeys taken by daughters from the 'fatherly' text are examined in the provocatively titled *Ms-Directing Shakespeare* by Elizabeth Schafer. This inspiring book shows how by 'misdirecting' or 'Msdirecting', women assert 'their right to bring their own, very distinctive wisdom to the Shakespeare canon' (p. 7). Importantly, Schafer devotes the last section of the book to a marginalized tradition of female directors, including Madame Vestris, Edy Craig and many lesser-known figures. In the first two sections, Schafer explores the work of nine modern directors. Jane Howell's significant contribution to televized Shakespeare, and Joan Littlewood's radical experiments are properly reassessed within a context of rewriting theatrical history. The directors are frequently allowed to speak for themselves in transcripts of interviews here and in the second section on the plays. Schafer is to be warmly congratulated for making this material available as an introduction to the field and a source for future studies.

Modern revivals of other Renaissance plays are considered in *Renaissance Drama in Action* by Martin White. Designed primarily for a student audience, the book steers the reader through some important aspects of dramaturgy in chapters on the rehearsal process, acting styles, indoor and outdoor venues, and difficult juxta-

positions of mood. One of its great strengths is the number of points of access it offers to readers to engage with the ideas and texts. In chapter 6, for example, the bizarre blurring of comedy and horror in much Renaissance tragedy is explored with reference to (among others), Hamlet, El Greco, Peter Greenaway, Joe Orton and Dennis Potter, before moving on to exemplary scenes in *The Duchess of Malfi* and *Titus Andronicus*. White's long experience of working practically on the texts and seeing them in production shines through in the astute analyses of such moments. In spite of his obvious expertise, however, his authorial style is not the least intimidating; his use of the personal pronoun welcomes readers. His acknowledgement of the difficulties as well as the pleasures of the texts also makes the book accessible to undergraduates. The final chapter gives a useful potted history of theatrical taste, and here, as elsewhere in the book, the author's passionate commitment to theatre is accompanied by an awareness of its social responsibilities.

Players of Shakespeare 4 edited by Robert Smallwood covers work by actors in the Royal Shakespeare Company between 1992 and 1997 with a special focus on Shakespeare's clowns. Actors' fears of these roles, and the sheer hard work of interpreting the text for a successful performance is combined with a genuine sense of discovery in some of the essays. In particular, David Tennant gives a delightfully funny account of his horror at being cast as Touchstone when he went to audition for Orlando, and then examines how he came to enjoy the role having 'gradually discovered that Shakespeare's clowns are funny' (p. 44). Christopher Luscombe's remarks on his Lancelot Gobbo and the small role of Moth makes explicit the point that lies behind all such postproduction analysis: 'most of what I did in these plays was less rational than it may now appear, and it's only with hindsight that I can find ways of justifying myself' (p. 19). What this volume, like its predecessors, proves, though, is that self-examination or justification is not just a continuation of the learning process for the actor. By making available an 'autobiography' of the life of a part, these essays remind us of the particularity of these roles. Jane Lapotaire's sensitive essay on Queen Katherine in *Henry VIII* and David Troughton's commentary on playing Richard III as an evil jester are especially impressive examples from the current volume.

Eastern stages for Shakespeare are considered in two new books: *Shakespeare and the Japanese Stage*, edited by Takashi Sasayama, J. R. Mulryne and Margaret Shewring, and *Theatre, the Audience and Asia* by John Russell Brown. The former explores Shakespeare production as a particular manifestation of the complex relationship between East and West. There are seventeen essays, by Japanese and Western contributors, and a helpful chronology of Shakespeare productions in Japan from 1866 to 1994. The essays give intelligent readings of the engagement of traditional Japanese forms, Kabuki, Kyogen, Bunraku and Noh with Shakespearian texts, and the wider cultural implications behind these reinterpretations. The first two chapters chart the development of Japanese Shakespeare: the deference to Western models and the growth of a self-consciously politicized theatre through the work of Koreya Senda. Sasayama's comparison of Shakespeare and the playwright Chikamatsu draws attention, among other things, to the ways in which Bunraku puppet forms can illuminate the narrative aspects of Shakespeare's plays (pp. 151–2). Yoko Takakuwa gives an illuminating discussion of the performance of female identity by boy actors in England and the transvestite *onnagata* who ' "fictions" the symbolic identity of "woman" on stage' in Kabuki theatre (p. 202). The work of remarkable individuals is also considered. Tadashi Suzuki's art, 'both culturally inclusive and culturally specific' (p. 93) receives welcome attention, as does that of Hideki Noda. This impressive collection offers a valuable, authoritative source of information on its subject.

John Russell Brown's book is much more personal in tone, but also argues that in some ways, 'Asian theatres offer a better site than the new Globe for reconsideration and reform' (p. 191). Via unusual comparisons between his experiences of Japanese and Indian theatre and moments from Shakespeare's plays, he raises questions about pacing, the importance of entrances and exits, audience participation of various types. He proposes 'Jatra', Indian touring theatre, as a company model for the Admiral or King's Men, and advocates a return to such communities where 'actors are intended to remain in charge' (p. 171). The most powerful influence, a 'Kutiyattam' performance in India, which combined intimacy and sacred, heightened artistry (p. 81), leads John Russell Brown to re-examine powerful moments in Shakespearian tragedy, in which the actor and audience are melded by their creative constructions of human experience (p. 85). Informed by the author's sensitivity and intelligence throughout, the book intriguingly questions what kind of actor and acting style can 'serve Shakespeare well' (p. 180).

Shakespeare on film and in electronic media is discussed in Robert Shaughnessy's New Casebook *Shakespeare on Film* and Richard Burt's remarkable *Unspeakable Shaxxxspeares*. The former is a well-chosen selection of published work illustrating the shift from traditional liberal–humanist readings of film to politicized cultural materialist interpretations. Pieces by Jack Jorgens and Anthony Davies are offered as examples of the best kind of traditional criticism which the editor, somewhat surprisingly, feels 'has been dominant in the field of Shakespearian film criticism in recent years' (p. 8). Belsey's essay gives a retrospective critique of such readings. The rest of the essays, which are necessarily only a small proportion of what has been published, demonstrate how recent film criticism has variously repositioned itself within a theoretically informed discourse. There are good examples of psychoanalytic, cultural materialist and feminist readings in practice, and

Douglas Lanier's postmodern analysis explores how Greenaway's *Prospero's Books* 'meditate[s] upon the status of Shakespeare in an age of electronic performance' (p. 182).

It is this virtual or 'unspeakable Shaxxxspeare' which Richard Burt's book scrutinizes with wit, intelligence and deadly seriousness. Burt compiles an archive of contemporary allusions to Shakespeare in film, television, video, internet sites and CD-ROM to show how the Bard has become 'a symptom of an unconscious and vestigial American postcolonial identification with British colonial culture' (p. 11). Burt's use of Lacanian psychoanalysis and queer theory produces some sensitive readings, such as his analysis of vocal absence and presence in *Prospero's Books* (pp. 189–96). The book is not really about analysing individual reinterpretations, though. It rather uses them to ask pressing philosophical and social questions. In particular, the book explores how Shakespeare is both 'cool' and 'uncool' for youth culture in the States. The proliferation of Shakespeare into popular forms like television soaps, cartoons and Hollywood films is not necessarily celebratory, Burt observes. He paints a depressing picture of how 'kiddie' culture engages in a process of 'dumbing down' Shakespeare as a symptom of immature and infantile regression 'in the 1990s context of diminishing expectations' (p. 9). This is not critical overkill, as Burt anxiously suspects; his book obliges us to stop and think, to ask, is this Shakespeare the man of the next millennium?

WORKS REVIEWED

Abraham, Lyndy, *A Dictionary of Alchemical Imagery* (Cambridge, 1998).

Aggeler, Geoffrey, *Nobler in the Mind: The Stoic-Skeptic Dialectic in English Renaissance Tragedy* (Newark, 1998).

Astington, John H., *English Court Theatre 1558–1642* (Cambridge, 1999).

Baker, David J., *Shakespeare, Spenser, Marvell and the Question of Britain* (Stanford, 1997).

Bell, Ilona, *Elizabethan Women and the Poetry of Courtship* (Cambridge, 1998).

Brown, John Russell, *New Sites for Shakespeare: Theatre, The Audience and Asia* (London and New York, 1999).

Burnim, Kalman A. and Highfill, Philip H. Jr, *John Bell, Patron of British Theatrical Portraiture: A Catalog of the Theatrical Portraits in His Editions of Bell's Shakespeare and Bell's British Theatre* (Carbondale and Edwardsville, 1998).

Burt, Richard, *Unspeakable Shaxxxspeares: Queer Theory and American Kiddie Culture* (Houndmills, 1998).

Cave, Richard, Schafer, Elizabeth and Woolland, Brian, *Ben Jonson and Theatre: Performance, Practice and Theory* (London and New York, 1999).

Dávidházi, Péter *The Romantic Cult of Shakespeare: Literary Reception in Anthropological Perspective* (Macmillan, 1998).

Davis, Nick, *Stories of Chaos: Reason and its Displacement in Early Modern English Narratives* (Ashgate, 1999).

Hanson, Elizabeth, *Discovering the Subject in Renaissance England* (Cambridge, 1998).

Hapgood, Robert, ed., *Hamlet, Prince of Denmark*, Shakespeare in Production (Cambridge, 1999).

Holden, Anthony, *William Shakespeare, His Life and Work* (London, 1999).

Honigmann, E. A. J., *Shakespeare: The 'Lost Years'* (Manchester, 1998).

Hunter, G. K., *English Drama 1586–1642: The Age of Shakespeare* (Oxford, 1997).

Kahan, Jeffrey, *Reforging Shakespeare: The Story of a Theatrical Scandal* (Lehigh University Press, 1998).

Kewes, Pauline, *Authorship and Appropriation: Writing for the Stage in England, 1660–1710* (Oxford, 1998).

Kiernan, Pauline, *Staging Shakespeare at the New Globe* (Houndmills, 1999).

Levin, Richard, 'Another "Source" for *The Alchemist* and Another Look at Source Studies', *English Literary Renaissance*, 28 (1998), 210–30.

Linton, Joan Pong, *The Romance of the New World: Gender and the Literary Formations of English Colonialism* (Cambridge, 1998).

Lyons, Robert, *Swedish Midsummer in Shakespeare's Dream: A Study of the Creative Process Resulting in Eva Bergman's 1989 Production of 'A Midsummer Night's Dream' at Backa Theatre, Goteborg, Sweden* (Goteborg, 1998).

Madelaine, Richard, *Antony and Cleopatra*, Shakespeare in Production (Cambridge, 1999).

Mahood, M. M., *Playing Bit Parts in Shakespeare* (London and New York, 1998).

Matchinske, Megan, *Writing, Gender and State in Early Modern England* (Cambridge, 1998).

McAdam, Ian, *The Irony of Identity: Self and Imagination in the Drama of Christopher Marlowe* (Newark, 1999).

Morrison, Michael A., *John Barrymore: Shakespearian Actor* (Cambridge, 1997), reprinted in paperback, 1999.

Pitcher, John, ed., *Medieval and Renaissance Drama in England*, vol. 10 (Madison Teaneck, 1998).

Potter, Lois, ed., *Playing Robin Hood: The Legend as Performance in Five Centuries* (Newark and London, 1998).

Sanders, Julie, *Ben Jonson's Theatrical Republics* (Houndmills, 1998).

Sasayama, Takashi, Mulryne, J. R., and Shewring, Margaret, eds., *Shakespeare and the Japanese Stage* (Cambridge, 1998).

Schafer, Elizabeth, *Ms-Directing Shakespeare: Women Direct Shakespeare* (London, 1998).

Shaughnessy, Robert, ed., *Shakespeare on Film*, New Casebooks (Houndmills, 1998).

Smallwood, Robert, ed., *Players of Shakespeare 4* (Cambridge, 1998).

Smith, Bruce R., *The Acoustic World of Early Modern England: Attending to the O Factor* (Chicago, 1999)

Sullivan, Garrett A., *The Drama of Landscape: Land, Property and Social Relations on the Early Modern Stage* (Stanford, 1998).

Tudeau-Clayton, Margaret, *Jonson, Shakespeare and Early Modern Virgil* (Cambridge, 1998).

Walker, Greg, *The Politics of Performance in Early Renaissance Drama* (Cambridge, 1998).

White, Martin, *Renaissance Drama in Action: An Introduction to Aspects of Theatre Practice and Performance* (London and New York, 1998).

Wilson, Richard, 'A "Bloody Question": The Politics of *Venus and Adonis*', in *Astraea, 9: William Shakespeare, Venus and Adonis: Nouvelles Perspectives Critiques* (Montpellier, 1999).

3. EDITIONS AND TEXTUAL STUDIES

reviewed by ERIC RASMUSSEN

I TEXTUAL STUDIES

Whereas previous generations of editors blamed the early printers as the agents responsible for the errors in Shakespeare's texts, today's editors tend to blame previous editors. The fault, it turns out, is not in the compositors but in ourselves. In the textual studies under review here we are told that the New Bibliographers created 'a clairvoyant world, where the metaphysics of presence endorsed editorial decisions', that the Oxford Shakespeare 'dematerializes the text', that 'much of what editors have done is an obstacle to staging the work', that 'the texts of Shakespeare have been occluded by the labours of privilege', and that 'the most difficult problem' for editors working today is 'how to shake off the eighteenth-century hand of Nicholas Rowe and those who have followed him'.[1]

Given the current critical climate in which early editors are more likely to be reviled than revered, the appearance of the Pickering & Chatto seven-volume facsimile of Rowe's 1709 edition presents something of a problem. Should we clasp the hand of the past, shake it off, or engage in some intermediate, compromise gesture? Peter Holland's introduction asserts Rowe's claim to importance as 'the single greatest determinant' of the way Shake-

---

[1] These comments are all drawn from essays in the *Textual Formations and Reformations* collection, edited by Laurie Maguire and Tom Berger. Their authors are A. R. Braunmuller, David Scott Kastan, Ralph Alan Cohen, Valerie Wayne, and Barbara Mowat, respectively.

speare's plays appeared in edited versions for nearly three centuries: 'From the names by which we know some of Shakespeare's characters, the definition of where scenes take place, the list of characters or the act and scene divisions to the spelling, along with hundreds of emendations to the text and the way in which Shakespeare's language is punctuated, Rowe's work defined the methods and the details by which we think we know Shakespeare in print' (p. viii). By deftly slipping *we think we know* into the final clause of his sentence, Holland infuses his description of Rowe's achievement with indeterminacy, implying that subsequent editors may have been mistaken in the foundation they built upon. Holland reminds us of how many of the things we think we know about Shakespeare were, in fact, Rowe's innovations: 'Were it not for Rowe, we probably would not talk of a character named Puck or believe that Lear goes out onto a heath in the storm, we would not say "Some are born great", quoting Malvolio reading from the letter, or assume that Shakespeare wrote all his plays in five acts' (p. viii).

Holland observes that Rowe was 'the first editor to create a Shakespeare play by conflating the quarto and folio traditions of texts and it was not until 1986, in the Wells-Taylor edition, that the effect of that process and practice of conflation, as it affected *Hamlet*, and, especially, *King Lear*, was finally reversed' (p. xii). But Holland's account of a homogeneous tradition of conflation may need to be diversified in order to make room for the many editors before Wells & Taylor who published Folio-based texts of *Hamlet* (e.g. Caldecott in 1819, Knight in 1841, MacDonald in 1885) and the reversal may need to be revisited in light of the 1997 *Norton Shakespeare*, which, despite being based on the Oxford text, re-conflates both *Hamlet* and *King Lear*.

The anonymous engravers of the plates that adorn Rowe's edition 'inaugurated the whole tradition of Shakespeare illustration', and Holland encourages us to admire their 'gentle

attainment'. Holland draws attention to Charles Gildon's much-neglected essay that was appended to Rowe's edition in 1710 – 'Remarks on the plays of Shakespeare' – as an 'inaugurating moment' in Shakespearian commentary; he praises Gildon's work as 'a measured advocacy of Shakespeare, a cautious recognition of what he was prepared to admire and an equally determined refusal to indulge in what would later become the cult of bardolatry' (p. xxvii). Holland's prose sparkles with well-chosen adjectives as it glides along builded crescents of syntax. Unfortunately, the facsimile itself is not nearly as elegant. The dark and blotchy reproduction of the plate that accompanies *Venus & Adonis* is indescribably poor. Moreover, a stray ink-mark appears about a third of the way down on the verso pages throughout volume 7; the fact there is no corresponding bleed-through mark on the recto pages indicates that the recurring spot does not appear in the original but was probably caused by a flaw in Pickering & Chatto's plates. In other instances, flaws in the original copies (the British Library copy of the six volumes of Rowe's 1709 edition and the Trinity College Library copy of the 1710 volume of poems) are responsible for obscured readings in the facsimile: a smudge renders two lines of text unreadable on page 6 of *The Tempest* (volume 1); 'your' is crossed through in pen and ink on the second line of page 1540 (volume 4); and the inking is so heavy at the top of page 1722 (volume 4) that the first five lines of text are nearly unreadable. Although one might have hoped for fewer blemishes in a facsimile priced at £475/$760, the set nevertheless deserves a place in every research library that does not possess a copy of the original.

Future editors may find a useful companion-piece to the Pickering & Chatto facsimile in Barbara Mowat's contribution to *Textual Formations and Reformations*, a collection of essays edited by Laurie E. Maguire and Thomas L. Berger in honour of George Walton Williams (although perhaps because of the reluctance of academic publishers to admit that a Festschrift is a Festschrift, the honorand is not acknowledged in the title of this volume). Mowat's essay details her editorial attempts to unemend some of Rowe's character names. In *The Merchant of Venice*, for instance, Rowe called the younger Gobbo 'Launcelot' whereas all early texts identified him as 'Launcelet' or 'Lancelet' – a little lance, rather than a figure from King Arthur's court. Because Rowe edited *Hamlet* primarily from F4 rather than Q2, Hamlet's mother has since been known as 'Gertrude' rather than 'Gertrard'. Mowat and Paul Werstine became the first editors to restore 'Lancelet' in their 1992 Folger Shakespeare edition of *The Merchant of Venice*, but they apparently did not have the courage of their convictions when it came to Gertrude. As Mowat explains, 'editors deeply committed to following Q2 *Hamlet* as copytext have continued to use F's 'Gertrude'. They do so, I suspect, for the same reason that Paul Werstine and I do in the New Folger *Hamlet*: namely, because it is as Gertrude that she exists and has existed for nearly three hundred years' (p. 142).

Invoking the weight of editorial and cultural tradition to challenge the authority of the early printed texts is nothing new. In 1861, R. Grant White noted that 'Launcelet' is the 'invariable spelling' in the quartos and folios and 'warrants the belief that such was its original form' but White concluded that 'as the present name has been in the text for a hundred and fifty years it is not worth while to make a change in so trivial a matter'.

Editorial re-naming of Shakespeare's characters emerges as a leitmotif in *Textual Formations and Reformations*. David Scott Kastan weighs in on the Oldcastle vs. Falstaff debate with 'Killed with Hard Opinions: Oldcastle, Falstaff, and the Reformed Text of 1 *Henry IV*'. Kastan agrees with Gary Taylor that restoring *Oldcastle* effectively rehistoricizes the character of Sir John, but observes that since all the authoritative texts print *Falstaff* and none prints *Oldcastle*, the restoration of *Oldcastle* 'effectively dehistoricizes

and in the process dematerializes the text in which he appears' (p. 218).

A. R. Braunmuller interrogates the rationale behind the differences in editorial treatment of geographic place-names (which are traditionally modernized) and personal names (which are not) in *Macbeth*. Braunmuller ranges brilliantly over this topic, suggesting pragmatic possibilities – 'place-names are more familiar to editors and modern readers than the names of eleventh-century Scottish noblemen' – as well as philosophical food for thought: 'If editors reproduce the early spelling or pronunciation, they grant these figures historical subjectivity, individuality, and thus retain their own (modern) subjectivity and individuality' (p. 118).

Charles B. Lower presents a variation on the theme of re-naming characters by insisting that sometimes naming characters *at all* constitutes unwanted editorial interference. Given that the original theatre audience would have had 'no access to what is so familiar and inescapable to us as readers today – a list of characters, stage directions, and speech prefixes . . . Critics in their discussions have frequently misled because they have given prominence to a character name unknown to a theatre audience' such as Escalus in *Romeo & Juliet* or Claudius in *Hamlet* (pp. 232–4). Lower argues that there was 'likely purposefulness' behind the fact that the audience never learns these names; he sets out to 'preach to future editors' that 'a Shakespeare edition, in the imperfect mode of only printed words, should seek accord with the aural and visual experience of a theatre audience, and in *Hamlet* the speech prefix *King* [instead of *Claudius*] fosters this accord' (p. 236).

Lower fails to acknowledge what is for many an important distinction between the reading audience and the theatrical audience. A reader of early modern dramatic texts is often in a privileged position: one thinks of the *dramatis personae* list in Jonson's *Epicoene* where the reader receives the critical information at the beginning of the play that Epicoene is '*a young gentleman, suppos'd the silent woman*', whereas the theatre audience is not aware of this until the play's conclusion. Clearly, some characters' names are unavailable to a theatre audience, but to change copy-text stage directions and speech-headings in order deliberately to conceal those names from the reading audience as well seems to me an unnecessary sort of affirmative action.

Paul Werstine's 'Touring and the Construction of Shakespeare Textual Criticism' ably deconstructs the widespread belief that the so-called 'bad quartos' represent deliberate abridgements made for touring in the provinces. Werstine suggests that the 'performance-text bad quarto' narrative originated in Alfred W. Pollard and J. Dover Wilson's deeply held belief in the superiority of London to provincial theatre coupled with the related assumption that provincial taste was bad. In Pollard and Wilson's seminal 1919 *TLS* article, they claim that 'these abridgements can only have been made for audiences in the provinces, where the conditions of performance and the smaller number of actors, as compared with the fuller London companies, compelled drastic excisions'. Rather remarkably, Pollard and Wilson go on to suggest that the provincial audience would lack the sophistication of even 'the groundlings of a London theatre [who] would have had a good deal to say if, after paying for an afternoon's entertainment, they had been fobbed off with anything less', and thus 'abridgements made for provincial representation . . . would be useless for London performances'.

There is no external evidence that would support the claims that the early quartos represent abridgements for touring and the evidence that Werstine marshals here renders these assumptions untenable. Greg's hypothesis that travelling troupes performed with no 'book' or with an unauthorized book that they had memorially reconstructed, for instance, is challenged by an entry in the Hall Book of Leicester dated 3 March 1583/4 which reads that 'No

play is to bee played, but such as is allowed by the sayd Edmund [Tilney], & his hand at the latter end of the said booke they doe play' (p. 56). The Greg datum that a travelling troupe would constitute only a fraction of the London company may well be true, but analysis of the 'bad quartos' of *2* and *3 Henry VI* reveals that these texts require 'casts' of over twenty-four and Werstine observes that none of the recorded counts of travelling troupes before 1600 exceeds ten. As Werstine acknowledges, 'the gap does not prove that the bad quartos cannot be touring texts, but it does prove that the 'bad quartos' cannot be *shown to be* touring texts' (p. 58).

In a coda to his essay, Werstine challenges the view that successful recent stage productions of the First Quarto text of *Hamlet* serve to confirm that Q1 represents a version of the play that was streamlined for performance. Werstine sees a circularity in which scholarly opinion about the nature of Q1 has exerted a strong influence upon directors, actors, and reviewers. Nicholas Shrimpton, for instance, reviewing the 1985 Orange Tree Theatre production for *Shakespeare Survey*, observed that 'the brevity of the text proved ideally suited to the kind of small-scale performance for which it was, very probably, originally intended. Regional repertory companies who shrink from the cost of a conventional *Hamlet* might well consider this alternative' (p. 61). 'The enthusiastic reception of this production', Werstine concludes, 'cannot logically be reduced to a confirmation of the reigning scholarly belief that the quarto is a performing text; it would be more accurate to suggest that the reception has been produced by the belief it is supposed to have confirmed' (p. 61).

Michael Warren's 'Greene's *Orlando W. W. Greg Furioso*' offers 'a suspicion that should be entertained' that the one extant actor's manuscript part, apparently used by Edward Alleyn for the title-role in Greene's *Orlando Furioso*, may not be representative of that category of document but was perhaps 'originally unfinished and imperfect, for some reason unused and rejected' (p. 77). Richard Proudfoot argues that *The London Prodigal* 'represents the workmanlike norm of playwriting for the King's Men in the early years of the reign of James I'. Championing *Prodigal* as a work 'of real interest and modest achievement', Proudfoot contends that it 'has been devalued as a result of its unhappy association with "our greatest poet's name" and of the critical unease that has resulted from the assumption that we need to be confident where we stand on the issue of authorship before we can engage with the play' (p. 157).

In introducing the *Textual Formations and Reformations* volume, Laurie Maguire observes that 'one of the most welcome advances in textual criticism in the last twenty years has been its readability' (p. 13). The superb work on display in this collection is clearly accessible to a great variety of readers, and Maguire hails the willingness of her authors to range beyond the traditional, presumably arcane concerns of their discipline. Textual criticism, she writes, is no longer 'simply about compositor analysis, watermarks, and editing, it is also about ideology, politics, feminism, theory, literary criticism' (p. 13). But the shift in focus is rather more radical than Maguire suggests: neither 'compositors' nor 'watermarks' even merits an entry in the index. However much we may admire these marvellous essays, when we are told that they were selected, in part, 'for their stylistic verve', is it fair to wonder if more prosaic discussions of bibliographical evidence were therefore excluded from the collection?

The technical elements of analytical bibliography that find no place in *Textual Formations* are everywhere in evidence in Richard F. Kennedy's essay on 'Speech Prefixes in Some Shakespearian Quartos', which may prove to be this year's most lasting contribution to Shakespearian textual study. Kennedy engages the debate over editorial re-naming by proposing that variant speech-headings in early printed texts may not be signs of an author 'in the heat

of composition', but are rather to be understood as indications of a compositor switching speech-headings because of a type shortage. Kennedy's detailed analysis of type shortages in Q1 and Q2 *A Midsummer Night's Dream*, Q2 *Titus Andronicus*, Q1 *The Merchant of Venice*, Q1 *1 Henry IV*, and Q2 *Hamlet* proves this thesis rather conclusively. He argues that the manuscript copy for *The Merchant of Venice* had the speech-heading '*Iew*' for Shylock throughout and that the compositors altered this to '*Shy*' when they ran out of italic *I*'s; similarly, it appears that the compositors changed the speech-heading '*Clown*' to '*Launce*' due to a shortage of italic *C*'s. Kennedy's findings have important implications for all editors: those who follow the traditional practice of normalizing and regularizing speech-headings in a critical edition, and especially those who are contemplating blazing new trails by retaining variant speech-headings in the interests of preserving what they perceive to be ideological differences and indeterminacies in the early texts.

II EDITIONS

Despite the calls for editors to sever all ties with Nicholas Rowe, the Arden 3 edition of *The Tempest*, edited by Virginia Mason Vaughan and Alden T. Vaughan, actually strengthens its textual connection to Rowe. The Vaughans' is the first critical edition to collate the British Library's unique copy of a trial-sheet of the first eight pages of *The Tempest: A Comedy*, 'Printed in the YEAR 1708', a preliminary sample of the octavo format that Jacob Tonson intended to use for Rowe's edition in 1709. For this trial Rowe derived his text from F2, whereas for the final edition he used F4 throughout. Peter Holland observes that the 1708 trial-sheet 'projects a distinctly more old-fashioned text of Shakespeare'. Words like 'Schreen', 'Carkass' and 'Stomacke' in the 1708 trial, for instance, become 'Screen', 'Carcass' and 'Stomach' in the 1709 edition (Pickering & Chatto facsimile, pp. xiii–xiv). The Vaughans rightly regard the eight-page trial-sheet as an independent, if fragmentary, edition.

Following in the distinguished footsteps of Frank Kermode's Arden 2 edition of the play, the Vaughans' edition distinguishes itself as a veritable cultural history. Their introduction details various attempts to locate the play in a specific geographical setting, with Caliban emerging as the poster-boy for multiculturalism (literally so in the splendid art-deco advertisement for the 1916 Shakespeare Tercentenary Celebration reproduced on page 97). The Vaughans explore Caliban's many possible identities: a native Carib, an American Indian, an African, a cannibal (as suggested by the anagram of his name), and even an 'uncouth, unlettered, rebellious and intoxicated' Irishman (p. 52). A five-page discussion of narratives from the New World is curiously undercut, however, by the conclusion that 'the bulk of information in the Bermuda and early Virginia tracts is not directly relevant to The Tempest, and there is little scholarly consensus on Shakespeare's indebtedness to any specific text or passage' (p. 43).

In a particularly rich introductory section entitled 'The Afterlife', the Vaughans observe that during the period from 1611 to 1898 critical commentary on The Tempest rarely emphasized its possible American sources or resonances. Rudyard Kipling inaugurated a popular trend by insisting that Bermuda was, in fact, the play's location. The Vaughans trace the evolution of colonial themes in modern productions in some detail, but the evolution of critical discourse receives somewhat less attention; the 'New Historicist insistence on The Tempest's colonialist inspirations and controlling energy' is dismissed out of hand for 'underestimating the play's classical roots and European contexts' (p. 124).

This edition is fascinated by the passage of time in the world of the play and in the theatre. Prospero's instructions to Ariel make it clear that the plot consumes the hours between 2 p.m. and 6 p.m. and the Vaughans suggest that with the addition of musical interludes between the acts The Tempest would have lasted approximately four hours (p. 14n). This interest in temporal precision is further pursued in calculations of Caliban and Miranda's ages, which are established to be 24 and 15 respectively (pp. 34, 135–6, and 169). This may be useful information, but is it perhaps too curious to consider that 'Caliban's assault on Miranda presumably did not occur until she reached puberty at approximately 13'?

The textual introduction might be said to lack precision. The purely hypothetical manuscript printer's copy behind the Folio text appears in the Vaughans' presentation to have a material existence: 'The manuscript used by the compositors has been identified as one of six prepared in the early 1620s by the legal scrivener Ralph Crane' (p. 126). Their account of the apparently accurate casting-off of copy throughout the Folio text of the play – 'there seems to have been little difficulty in dividing up the text so that it came out fairly evenly and clearly' (p. 126) – does not account for the instance at the foot of sig. A6v in which four lines of prose are expanded to nine lines of quasi-verse, presumably because the compositor needed to fill out the page. In discussing the disputed speech-heading for Miranda's angry denunciation of 'Abhorred slave' Caliban, the Vaughans claim that 'beginning with Dryden and Davenant [in 1670] and for the next two and a half centuries, editors reassigned this speech to Prospero, principally because it seemed to them indecorous for a young lady to speak so frankly' (p. 135). This misleading generalization effectively erases a number of significant editors – including Rowe, Pope, and Staunton – who retain the 'Miranda' speech-heading.

The most celebrated textual crux in The Tempest is, of course, the question of whether at 4.1.122–4 Ferdinand exclaims 'Let me live here ever! / So rare a wondered father and a wise / Makes this place paradise' or 'So rare a wondered father and a *wife*'. Although the Folio text apparently reads 'wise', Rowe's emendation, 'wife', was adopted by every edition through the middle of the nineteenth century; since that time most editions, with a few notable exceptions, have read 'wise'. In 1978, Jeanne Addison Roberts argued that the apparent long 's' was actually a broken 'f' which can be seen intact in a few early impressions before subsequently losing half of its crossbar. Feminists hailed the new reading's acknowledgement of Miranda's importance in this male-dominated play. However, after examining all relevant instances of the key letter in the Folger's extensive Folio collection under 200x magnification, Peter W. M. Blayney reported that the letter in question appears to be an 's' in all instances; in the few impressions in which Roberts had seen an 'f', blotted ink rather than a broken crossbar encouraged these readings. In an essay in the *Textual Formations* collection, Valerie Wayne argues that feminist readers need not necessarily defer to the scientific claims that Blayney makes ('scientific discourse . . . is usually gendered as male') any more than they would defer 'to the weight of a masculinist editorial tradition' (p. 187). (This masculinist tradition apparently does not include those editors who emend 'wise' to 'wife' – Rowe, Pope, Theobald, Warburton, Johnson, Steevens, Malone, Knight, Bevington, Orgel – only those who do not.)

With the ideological battlelines thus drawn and expectations high, the Vaughans have decided to retain 'wise' in the Arden 3 text, arguing that 'Ferdinand's image of paradise may have been (however implausible to modern sensibilities) inhabited exclusively by himself and his seemingly omnipotent, omniscient new father-in-law' (p. 137). They acknowledge that the 'wife' reading is 'syntactically and logically sound' and that Shakespeare's original 'wife' may have been altered to 'wise' in the process of the text's transmission from authorial manuscript to scribal transcript to compositorial typesetting, but the Vaughans ultimately opt for the

Folio's 'wise', finding 'no compelling reason to alter a word that is as plausible as the alternative in syntax and logic, more feasible in rhyme and more compatible with the technology of Jacobean type-founding' (p. 138).

The Vaughans observe that Jaggard's shop gave 'special care' to proof-reading the Folio text of *The Tempest*, the first page of which was corrected against proof at least four times. This edition might have profited from more attention in this regard. I have found two substantive errors in the text – at 3.2.20–1 for 'if thou be'st good mooncalf' read 'if thou be'st a good mooncalf'; at 5.1.277 for 'Is this not Stephano' read 'Is not this Stephano' – and a few more in the notes.[2] At 3.3.33, FI's 'humaine' is emended to 'human' without collation; so too, FI's 'bass' is silently emended to 'base' (3.3.99). The stage direction '*Drinks*' is enclosed in parentheses at 2.2.54.1 whereas the same direction ten lines earlier is not. The Vaughans set the Folio's prose as verse without collation at 2.2.114–16, 3.2.41–2, and 3.2.81–2; conversely, they set the Folio's verse as prose without collation at 2.1.18–19, 2.1.30–1, 2.2.155–6, 3.2.74–5, 3.2.128–9, and 3.2.131–2. It is unclear why the expansion of FI's '&c' to '*and others*' at 3.3.0.2 is flagged by an asterisk signalling an editorial emendation worth special notice when the editors have simply translated the Latin abbreviation *et cetera*. Finally, despite series guidelines which dictate that 'editorial notes of location should be omitted from the text', surely a place could have been found in the Arden 3 text for FI's 'The Scene, an vninhabited Island' – wonderfully ironic in its Folio context at the head of the *dramatis personae* list of the island's inhabitants – which now languishes in the obscurity of the collations.

In terms of textual recognition, it is apparently sometimes better to be vile esteemed. Because the 1594 text of *The Taming of a Shrew*

---

2 In the collation note to 2.2.86 quoting the Folio reading for 'I' read 'It'; 3.2.70 for 'F²' read 'F2'; 3.2.153 for 'Stephano' read '*Stephano*'.

is no longer viewed as a 'bad quarto', it was excluded from the 1981 Allen and Muir facsimile edition of *Shakespeare's Plays in Quarto* (an unfortunate omission from a collection made up of quartos from the Huntington Library, which owns the unique copy of the *A Shrew* quarto). With the appearance of Stephen Roy Miller's new edition of the play in Cambridge's Early Quartos series, *A Shrew* reasserts its right to be studied by all who are interested in Shakespeare's plays in quarto.

Students of the *Shrew* play(s) will no doubt welcome the first modernized edition of *A Shrew* to appear in ninety years. Miller's introduction offers an extraordinarily detailed comparison of *A Shrew* and *The Shrew* running to over fifty pages and ranging widely over their similarities and differences, their sources, and their intertwined stage histories (a version of Miller's introductory essay also appears in the *Textual Formations* volume). This densely written synthesis of critical commentary on the relationship between the two plays is invaluable, but the text of the edition is a disappointment. There is some confusion about whether the exact form of the title is 'A Pleasant Conceited Historie, called The taming of a Shrew' (p. 31) or 'A Pleasant-conceited Historie, called *The Taming of a Shrew*' (p. 60). The text of the play mistakenly reads 'Not lambs to lions' for QI's 'Nor lambs to lions' (4.121). QI's 'his selfe' is rendered 'hisself' (4.41). The QI reading 'champion' is silently emended to 'champaign' (13.84) as is QI's 'pompered' to 'pampered' (14.114). These alterations may represent modernizations of spelling rather than substantive emendations, but a note to that effect would have been helpful, as would notes on the apparent modernizations of QI 'key' to 'quay' (3.28) and QI 'faste' to 'faced' (10.32 and 10.34). Miller notes that 'silver-scaled dolphins' (11.43) is an obvious error but does not record Geoffrey Bullough's emendation of 'scaled' to 'sealed'. QI's 'omnes' has been silently deleted from the stage directions at 1.86, 5.119, 9.65, 10.65, 11.77, 12.55, 13.126, 15.23. This was

certainly done intentionally, but it is unclear why, since 'omnes' is retained in the stage directions in other volumes in the Early Quartos series. QI '*Exit*' is silently changed to '*Exeunt*' without collation at 3.184, 3.308, 4.94, 5.82, 5.119, 6.32, 13.136, 14.153, 4.161.

Miller resets much of QI's verse as prose without collation (1.5–7, 1.81–4, 2.28–9, 3.186–193, 3.206–16, 3.218–25, 3.253–55, 5.1–36, 5.44–6, 6.1–16, 6.23–25, 8.1–22). No one would deny that *A Shrew* is a prosaic play (in all senses of the word); as such, Miller's alterations have a certain validity. But the quasiverse of QI – which does not contain a line of prose – might be viewed as an important idiosyncratic feature of that text, one that perhaps ought to have been preserved in an edition entitled *The Taming of a Shrew: The 1594 Quarto*. Even if the prose/verse discrepancies are ironed out in the interests of making the text accessible to a wide audience, Miller ought to have recorded these changes in the collation notes to provide serious students of the text with the necessary tools they need to evaluate this peculiar quarto.

Richard Proudfoot has recently made the trenchant observation that editions of *The Two Noble Kinsmen* published in 'Complete Shakespeares' as 'by William Shakespeare and John Fletcher' enjoy a commercial advantage over those that adopt the 1634 quarto's attribution to 'John Fletcher and William Shakespeare' and are published independently of such series ('Shakespeare's Most Neglected Play', p. 149). This privileging and positioning is manifest in Jay L. Halio's new edition of *King Henry VIII* in the Oxford Shakespeare series, which bears a title-page attribution to 'WILLIAM SHAKESPEARE AND JOHN FLETCHER' and, unaccountably, nowhere acknowledges or even mentions Fredson Bowers' edition of the play in *The Dramatic Works in the Beaumont and Fletcher Canon* (Volume 7, Cambridge University Press, 1989).

This unfortunate slight (or oversight) notwithstanding, Halio's edition is a solid achievement. The text is the most error-free of any of the editions under review.[3] Halio's commentary notes are full, helpful, and punctuated by moments of quiet humour: the gloss on 'Paris Garden' (5.3.2), the bear-baiting ring near the Globe, suggests that readers will find an apt analogy if they 'cf. modern football crowds'. The only crux in the play that has occasioned much recent comment is its title. The title used in the Oxford *Complete Works*, *All is True (Henry VIII)*, is here chiastically reordered to *King Henry VIII, or All is True*, and Halio provides a balanced discussion of the question of whether *All is True* represents the play's original or alternative title. His introduction presents an overview of historical scholarship and an enthusiastic apologia for a play that is often excluded from the standard studies of Shakespeare's work, even studies devoted to the history plays. Faced with Norman Rabkin's arguments that the play is 'a half-hearted and unconvincing piece' with a 'cynically arbitrary' structure, Halio can probably be excused for responding with what might be characterized as Hotspurian insistence: 'The play's structure is far from merely arbitrary and its themes are important' (p. 25).

In light of the current discourse on editorial re-naming, two of Halio's minor emendations deserve comment. Lord Sands appears in the FI stage direction at 2.1.54 as '*Sir Walter*' whereas in Holinshed his name is 'William'. At 4.1.34, the place where Queen Katharine is held after her divorce is termed 'Kymmalton' in FI whereas it appears as 'Kimbalton' in Holinshed. In his Arden 2 edition of the play, R. A. Foakes retained the FI readings in both instances. Halio, however, emends 'Walter' to 'William', in deference to Holinshed, and opts for the F3 reading 'Kimbolton', but notes that the FI spelling 'conveys the pronunciation, accenting the first syllable'. An especially attentive member of an audience might possibly be able to detect a difference between 'Kymmalton' and 'Kimbolton' spoken onstage, but 'William' will never be heard since Lord Sands' Christian

name appears only in a stage direction (although a *Sir William Sands* may well appear in the cast list of some future programme of a production using the Oxford text). Setting aside the theoretical issues of rehistoricizing characters and dehistoricizing the text, one might ask, more simply, in what ways theatre and reading audiences are better served by the emended Oxford text than they are by the unemended Arden?

III MONOGRAPHS

An Index of Characters in Early Modern English Drama: Printed Plays, 1500–1660, compiled by Thomas L. Berger and Sidney L. Sondergard, a revised and expanded edition of *An Index of Characters in English Printed Drama to the Restoration*, edited by Berger and William C. Bradford, originally published in 1975, is a useful research tool as well as a fascinating study of what constitutes a 'character'. In indexing over a thousand printed plays, Berger and Sondergard have cast what can only be described as an extraordinarily wide net: 'In addition to the entries for his or her given name and surname, the character may have an entry for his or her nationality, occupation, religious proclivity, and/or psychological state . . . Our intent is to include all characters who appear on stage, even if a character does not appear alive, all in one piece, or as himself . . . We have included all animals appearing in the plays as well as inanimate objects whose roles are taken by actors' (pp. 2–6).

This monumental work of scholarship will certainly become a standard reference work for students and researchers. Despite its seemingly limitless scope, however, the index has some limitations. The failure to distinguish between personal names and geographical locations, for

---

[3] In the commentary note for 2.2.84 for 'comma' read 'semi-colon'; the (rejected) emendation of 3.1.119 should properly be credited to F4 rather than Rowe; at 5.2.109 the text's 'faulty' should be collated as the F2 correction of FI's 'faultly'.

instance, results in an entry for 'Arden' that lists both *Arden of Feversham* (for the character) and *As You Like It* (for the forest). The entry for 'Kent' lists *2 Henry VI*, presumably because Alexander Iden identifies himself as 'A poor esquire of Kent', but I remain puzzled by the listing of *2 Henry IV* in which I cannot find a character with a Kentish connection. One can imagine a scholar interested in researching various dramatic portrayals of the earl of Kent becoming frustrated by the entry that sends her to *The Spanish Tragedy* and *Michaelmas Term*, in neither of which does a character named 'Kent' appear.

The compilers of the *Index* observe that 'modern editions of Renaissance plays frequently make emendations of characters' names significant enough to merit inclusion in the index'; they have endeavoured to include in their listing the names as they appear in the original texts *and* any significant editorial emendations of these names: 'we include *Claudio* and *Varrus* from the First Folio text of Shakespeare's *Julius Caesar*, even though subsequent editions have changed their names to *Claudius* and *Varro*, names we also index . . . We enter *Semus* as his name appears in the first two quartos of Middleton's *A Mad World my Masters*, even though one editor has determined that his name is a misprint for *Servus*, whom we also include' (p. 4). In point of fact, however, editorially emended names often supplant the original names of the characters in the *Index*: there is an entry for Rowe's 'Lancelot' Gobbo but none for FI's 'Launcelet'; an entry for 'Gertrude' but none for Q2's 'Gertrard' (even though the latter is often viewed as a misprint for the former occasioned by compositorial *a:u* misreadings of Shakespeare's foul paper manuscript); the names 'Humphrey' and 'Sinklo' in the Folio text of *3 Henry VI*, sometimes omitted from editions of the play because they are thought to refer to specific actors rather than fictional characters, are similarly omitted from Berger-Sondergard.

Linda McJannet's *The Voice of Elizabethan Stage Directions: The Evolution of a Theatrical Code* traces the history of the stage direction from its non-beginnings in classical drama (in which stage directions are virtually non-existent), to the first attempts to distinguish directions from dialogue in the rubricated margins of medieval manuscripts, to the recognizable italic formula in Renaissance dramatic texts – *Enter the King* – with its inverted grammar and uninflected verb. McJannet's careful attention to this largely neglected subject yields some insights. She finds, for instance, that temporal and spatial markers often figure in stage directions in sixteenth-century texts but not in those of the early seventeenth century. Thus the old-fashioned marker '*Here*' appears in the 1597 quarto of *Richard III*, '*Here she lets fall the sword*' but has been eliminated from the Folio, which reads '*She falls the sword*'. Similarly, the 1598 quarto of *1 Henry IV* has '*Here they embrace*' for which the Folio substitutes '*They embrace*' (pp. 121–3).

Had McJannet's survey been comprehensive in its scope, it might have produced a work of great value. In the event, however, McJannet's findings are severely compromised by the meagreness of her research sample. The analysis of the visual conventions governing printed plays 'relies chiefly on twenty-nine plays published in quarto between 1593 and 1661' (p. 89). 'A small sample thoroughly digested', McJannet writes, 'seemed preferable to a large one that might prove unmanageable' (p. 90). But given that there are more than seven hundred extant play quartos from this period (not including reprints), a sample of twenty-nine (less than five per cent) cannot possibly be construed as representative. As a result, many of the generalizations McJannet derives from this sample are suspect. She concludes, for instance, that printed plays associated with the London theatres almost invariably indent speech-headings: 'In the early editions surveyed for this book, I have encountered only one in which the practice of slightly indenting the left-hand prefix is not consistently observed, namely the 1599 quarto of *George a Green*' (p. 65). Although

McJannet includes Q2 *Hamlet* in her list of twenty-nine plays, she does not observe that the speech headings are set flush with the margin on signatures B1r, B1v, F1r, F2v, and F3r of that text, as they are in the 1595 text of *The True Tragedy of Richard Duke of York* from signatures C5v through E8r. Are these exceptions that prove McJannet's rule, or do they call the rule itself into question?

IV UN-EDITING

Michael Warren, Randall McLeod, and others have long called for the 'unediting' of Shakespeare, a radical stripping away of 'editorial encrustation' (to use Gary Taylor's happy phrase), relying instead upon photographic facsimiles of the early texts. The uncritical acceptance of a facsimile, however, can be as dangerously misleading as the reliance upon an editorially constructed text. Even the most sophisticated reproductive technologies cannot prevent an occasional birth defect: witness the new Routledge facsimile of the First Folio. In introducing this facsimile, billed as 'an affordable tool for actors and theatre people', Doug Moston asserts that 'the First Folio is by no means so error ridden as has been argued' and that no matter how much 'scholarship advances from decade to decade, the text in the Folio is eminently more actable than in any later edited editions' (p. vii). Had Moston consulted some of that scholarship he could have saved himself and his publisher considerable embarrassment.

Moston's is not a facsimile of an actual First Folio, but a reproduction of the notoriously unreliable facsimile prepared by J. O. Halliwell-Phillipps in 1876. The pen-and-ink 'doctoring' of the Halliwell-Phillipps facsimile is well-attested, having been described in some detail by Charlton Hinman, who found 'deliberate tampering' on almost every page.[4] Among the thousands of changes in the volume, Hinman pointed to the manifest error on page 74 in the Comedies where 'Tunne-dish' is changed in the facsimile into the meaningless 'Tunnerdish'.

'The tampering is sometimes so inept as to be downright amusing', Hinman observed, pointing to the pen-and-ink page numbers that are supplied for the unpaginated pages of *Troilus and Cressida*. I notice that the colophon on the final page of the Folio has disappeared altogether. Any actor contemplating using the Routledge facsimile in place of an edited text ought first attempt to speak the speeches on page 51 of *1 Henry IV*, in which Hotspur emerges 'Baeathlesse' from battle, complains of seeing the messenger 'shide' so brisk, and cries 'let my soul Waht mercy'. Get thee to a Norton facsimile.

V *reviewed by* DAVID BEVINGTON[5]

Frequently of late, seminars at the annual meetings of the Shakespeare Association of America produce collections of essays that find their way into print. The result can be a usefully focused study of a specific topic. *Reading Readings: Essays on Shakespeare Editing in the Eighteenth Century* is a case in point. The seminar was conducted by Bernice W. Kliman, who also contributes an essay. The volume has been edited by Joanna Gondris, who theorizes the topic engagingly in an introductory essay. The title, *Reading Readings*, though not very felicitous or memorable in my judgement, is meant to place this exploration of eighteenth-century editing in the larger context of Shakespeare's 'afterlife' – the ever-changing face of Shakespearian interpretation. The Shakespeare edition is a new phenomenon in the eighteenth century, one that was destined to shape the way we read Shakespeare, for better and for worse.

To say that 'the Shakespeare edition' is a new thing after 1700 is, of course, to subscribe at

---

4 'The "Halliwell-Phillipps Facsimile" of the First Folio of Shakespeare', *Shakespeare Quarterly*, 5 (1954), 395–401.

5 *Reviewer's note*: Because I was a contributor to the *Reading Readings* collection of essays, in the interests of objectivity I have invited Professor David Bevington to review the volume here. E. R.

least implicitly to the view that the various quartos and folio editions preceding that date are not 'editions' in the commonly received sense of having been newly presented by an editor, with emendations, stage directions, biographical information, textual and commentary notes, and so on. Eric Rasmussen nicely complicates this distinction by reminding us that Heminges and Condell were certainly editors in their choice of texts and in many other features of presentation. Rasmussen also calls our attention to the virtually forgotten F5, a republication of the fourth folio of 1685 some time after 1700 with seventy reset pages, evidently to make up shortages in the supply of those pages as the book continued to sell. The resetting introduced a striking number of alterations that need to be noted by modern editors, since a number of emendations regularly attributed to Nicholas Rowe and others were first introduced in F5 in plays like *Troilus and Cressida*, *1* and *2 Henry VI*, *Henry V*, and *Coriolanus*. I cringe to discover that this deficiency can be found in my recent Arden *Troilus and Cressida*. Nonetheless, by and large one can still venture the claim that the Shakespeare 'edition' sprang from the forehead of Nicholas Rowe. He was soon followed by imitators and competitors. One of the most fascinating stories to emerge from this collection of essays has to do with this struggle for the 'ownership' of Shakespeare – a competition that was at once commercial, ideological and personally self-aggrandizing. The story is not told consecutively and must therefore be gleaned from discussions here and there, and certainly not all of it is new, but it has many telling things to say about the personalities of the players and about the momentous consequences for the way we read Shakespeare today.

I share with Peter Seary and Caroline Roberts the view that Lewis Theobald is the misunderstood and indeed reviled hero of the story. The scholarly methods he introduced, and the detailed information he presented, were plundered outlandishly by his competitors.

Alexander Pope's gleeful animus directed at his chief Dunce is of course notorious; less well known is the extent of Pope's liftings. At least, as Seary charitably allows, Pope stole openly, so much so that a learned reader could be expected to see how much he had taken. William Warburton's pilferings were of a different order of mendacity in that he presumably knew he would remain undetected so long as Theobald's correspondence with him remained unpublished. Warburton emerges as the moustache-twirling villain of this serio-comic operetta. 'Until finally overcome by senility', writes Seary with richly deserved acerbity, 'Warburton was motivated throughout his career by naked ambition' (p. 105). We catch numerous glimpses of what it must have been to be a dilettante clergyman scholar in that era. Warburton is the pedantic ancestor of Dr Casaubon in *Middlemarch*, pompous, shallow in learning, vain of his own scribblings, hypocritically pretending not to care about their publication, vindictive and jealous toward rivals – most of all toward the vastly more capable Theobald. If this volume of essays does nothing more than to resuscitate Theobald's reputation as editor, it will have laboured fruitfully.

Yet the damage was done, by Pope and Warburton. Samuel Johnson said some very mean-spirited things about Theobald, perhaps out of envy for a scholar who had anticipated his own scholarship to an extent, perhaps out of deference to Pope's cruel ridiculing. Edmond Malone followed Johnson's line of denigration, though he also castigated Warburton for limitless caprice. Other major players in this serio-comic battle of the books include the bookseller Jacob Tonson and the editor Thomas Hanmer. Bernice W. Kliman has some very perceptive things to say about these figures. I'm not sure I'm entirely convinced that Tonson hired Dr Johnson in 1745 to identify the sources of emendation for the so-called Oxford University edition that Hanmer had brought forth in 1744, at a time when Johnson was in such desperate financial straits that he needed to do hack work (indeed, Kliman puts this idea forth only as an intriguing possibility), but Kliman's essay nicely clarifies some commercial aspects of the competition. Because Tonson was ruthlessly determined to appropriate Shakespeare as his intellectual property, he was alarmed by the appearance in 1744 of the Oxford edition, anonymously presented but known to be by Hanmer, in six large, handsome quarto volumes. Tonson's response was to co-opt it in an edition of his own, duplicating the Oxford format in octavo and using Hanmer's text, along with assigning credit for the emendations. He also paid some writer, perhaps Johnson, for additional commentary notes. The tactic succeeded: when Warburton, having become the designated literary heir of Pope after establishing a collaboration with Hanmer, finally edited his version in 1747, he assigned all rights to Tonson. Samuel Johnson's 1765 edition was published by Tonson. This is the chap who invented tenure.

In a helpfully related essay, Alan R. Young shows how the art of illustration entered the fray. Hanmer's had been an expensive edition, out of the reach of many readers; Irene Dash, in her informative essay on Hanmer's *Winter's Tale*, aptly characterizes it as an elegant production aimed at a 'culture-hungry, increasingly affluent, Puritan-oriented, merchant class' (p. 268). Pope's edition was also a luxury item. But cheaper editions were at hand, often of single plays sold in the playhouses. In the later century, editions by Bell, Harding and Bellamy satisfied a public demand for inexpensive editions with numerous illustrations. Young's contention is that more attention needs to be paid to ephemeral editions to correct a mistaken impression we get from focusing on the illustrations of Rowe and the better-known editors of the century.

The advent of 'the Shakespeare edition', chronicled in such interesting detail in this collection, was of course not an unmixed blessing. As though to trumpet this deconstructive view of editing, the volume (after its introduc-

tion) leads off with a lengthy, playful, serious, outrageous, stimulating, maddening, critically important diatribe against the whole enterprise of editing by – guess who – Random Cloud, a.k.a. Randall McLeod, the poor man's James Joyce (or do I mean Peck's Bad Boy) of the textual world. The thrust of the argument will be familiar to any reader of this engaging and necessary gadfly-critic: textual editing, by its very nature, tampers with fascinating and endlessly revealing evidence of the text as originally printed. Earlier essays by Cloud have shown us how much there is to discover, for example, from kerning of letters in original type face. The present essay aptly chooses as its material the gibberish or 'Choughs language' employed in Act 4 of *All's Well* to interrogate and terrify the captured Parolles. The evidence of the 1623 Folio text about 'u/v' interchanges in marvelous nonwords like 'mououfus' and 'vauvado' leads Cloud into a fresh and important narrative about shifts in the early seventeenth century in compositors' use of 'u/v'. Cloud hectors the reader with pert questions ('am I right?' 'Pronounce them, then, will you?'), he spells 'Shakespeare' every way known to the Renaissance and then some, and dazzles us with computer-driven visual effects that cumulatively demonstrate what he means by his title, 'Babel'. He takes irreverent and even obscene pot shots at presumed big-time editors ('Do I sound bitter? Just because I didn't become some fucking big-bucks editor?' (p. 17) – this just after he has been horsewhipping Gary Taylor and David Bevington). I like everything he says, and I also remain unrepentant. Cloud brilliantly demonstrates how we need to go back to the originals. I would argue only that there is a place for edited texts of various sorts in varying situations of classroom and personal reading, and that one response to our postmodern world's call for a multiplicity of texts is to provide just that to our readers – edited and unedited, old-spelling and new, annotated and not. As Fred Bowers liked to say, You pays your money and you takes your choice.

I do not have space to go into extensive detail on the many essays in this stimulating and significant collection. A few do not succeed for me. The essay by Irene Fizer (who was not a seminar member) on the editing of bawdry in Shakespeare makes the serious mistake, in my view, of lumping all editors together as though they were all Thomas Bowdlers. I found all this to be old news. Some other essays are solid enough but predictable in method, walking us through eighteenth-century editions (e.g. Margaret Maurer on *Twelfth Night*, though the essay does argue for some FI readings over emendations and suggests that Rowe may have been influenced by *Sauny the Scot*). Perhaps the editor of the volume has tended to be too loyal to the membership of the seminar – evidently only two participants did not have their essays included – and not encouraging enough toward non-participants, since there's no inherent likelihood that all the good people on eighteenth-century editing would have gathered in one room. I would have been glad to hear, for example, from Barbara Mowat and Paul Werstine.

On the other hand, there are many fine pieces. Ann Thompson's essay on eighteenth-century grammatical emendation, especially in *Cymbeline*, shows how editing was (and in some cases remains today) far too ready to obliterate what the original can show: a distinctive new phase in Shakespeare's late style. Linda McJannet offers revealing observations on what was likely to happen to the stage direction in the eighteenth century – that is, how the Elizabethan form of the stage direction that had evolved over time remained durably in place for the most part, along with some radical changes. Her examples are drawn from *Henry VIII*. Joanna Gondris looks at the eighteenth-century Variorum page as a critical structure. Richard Kennedy provides useful insights into the two editions in 1765 of Johnson's edition published by Tonson, arguing that Johnson did not revise his text for the second edition of that year, at least in *A Midsummer Night's Dream*.

Frank (Nick) Clary chooses Hamlet's Mousetrap as an illuminating paradigm of the way eighteenth-century editors under-appreciated Shakespeare's 'conservative originality' (p. 180) in his uses of sources such as Plutarch. Hardin Aasand leads us through the devices by which editors transformed Ophelia's madness 'into an occasion for explicating and elucidating both the madness and the love that begets it' (p. 239). Paul Nelsen introduces a usefully complementarity of method by studying the reading habits of an avid note-writer, John Howe, Baron Chedworth, whose belief in his own perfected reading of the plays constitutes for him an idealized reflection of Shakespeare's 'genuine intent' (p 161). Laurie Osborne surveys eighteenth-century editions of *Twelfth Night* in order to argue that FI's wording of Viola's speech at 2.2.31, 'Alas, O frailtie is the cause, not wee', makes good sense and should not be emended to 'Alas, our frailty' as in modern editions generally. Catherine Alexander follows the fortunes of the poems in the eighteenth century as they are first excluded by Rowe and later comprehensively included by Malone. All in all, the volume provides amplitude and depth. It offers significant commentary on most of the major editors of the century. And its implications for modern editing are consistently stimulating.

WORKS REVIEWED

Berger, Thomas L., William C. Bradford, and Sidney L. Sondergard, eds., *An Index of Characters in Early Modern English Drama: Printed Plays, 1500–1660*. Revised Edition (Cambridge, 1998).

Gondris, Joanna, ed. *Reading Readings: Essays on Shakespeare Editing in the Eighteenth Century*, (Madison and London, 1998).

Kennedy, Richard F., 'Speech Prefixes in Some Shakespearian Quartos', *Papers of the Bibliographical Society of America*, 92 (1998), 177–210.

McJannet, Linda, *The Voice of Elizabethan Stage Directions: The Evolution of a Theatrical Code*, (Newark, 1999).

Maguire, Laurie E., and Thomas L. Berger, eds.

Textual Formations and Reformations (Newark, 1998).

Miller, Stephen Roy, ed., *The Taming of a Shrew: The 1594 Quarto*, New Cambridge Shakespeare: The Early Quartos (Cambridge, 1998).

Shakespeare, William, *Mr. William Shakespeare's Comedies, Histories, & Tragedies. A Facsimile of the First Folio, 1623*, Introduction by Doug Moston (New York and London, 1998).

The Tempest, ed. by Virginia Mason Vaughan and Alden T. Vaughan, Arden 3 (Walton-on-Thames, 1999).

The Works of Mr. William Shakespeare, ed. by Nicholas Rowe. A facsimile edition. Introduction by Peter Holland, 7 vols (London, 1999).

Shakespeare, William, and John Fletcher, *King Henry VIII, or All is True*, ed. by Jay L. Halio, Oxford Shakespeare (Oxford, 1999).

BOOKS RECEIVED

This list includes all books received between September 1998 and September 1999 which are not reviewed in this volume of *Shakespeare Survey*. The appearance of a book in this list does not preclude its review in a subsequent volume.

Boitani, Piero, *The Bible and Its Rewriting*, trans. by Anita Weston (Oxford, 1999).

Clare, Janet, '*Art Made Tongue-Tied by Authority*', 2nd edn (Manchester, 1999).

Garber, Marjorie, *Shakespeare's Ghost Writers: Literature as Uncanny Causality* (London, 1987; repr., 1999).

Heale, Elizabeth, *The Faerie Queene: A Reader's Guide*, 2nd edn (Cambridge, 1999).

Marlowe, Christopher, *Tamburlaine*, ed. by J. S. Cunningham, 2nd edn (Manchester, 1999).

Marston, John, *Antonio's Revenge*, ed. by W. Reavley Gair, 2nd edn (Manchester, 1999).

Pitcher, John, ed., *Medieval and Renaissance Drama in England*, vol. 11 (London, 1999).

Thomas, David, ed., *Six Restoration and French Neoclassic Plays* (Basingstoke, 1998).
– *Four Georgian and Pre-Revolutionary Plays* (Manchester, 1998).

Thomson, Peter, *Shakespeare's Professional Career* (Cambridge, 1992; repr. 1999).

Shakespeare, William, *King Henry IV Part 1*, ed. by Rex Gibson (Cambridge, 1998).
– *King Henry IV Part 2*, ed. by Rex Gibson (Cambridge, 1999).
– *Macbeth*, audio CD (Cambridge, 1999).
– *Romeo and Juliet*, ed. by Rex Gibson, 2nd edn (Cambridge, 1998).
– *The Winter's Tale*, ed. by Elizabeth Huddlestone and Sheila Innes (Cambridge, 1998).

Stephens, Dorothy, *The Limits of Eroticism in Post-Petrarchan Narrative: Conditional Pleasures from Spenser to Marvell* (Cambridge, 1998).

INDEX

INDEX

INDEX

INDEX

INDEX

INDEX

INDEX

INDEX

354

INDEX

INDEX

INDEX

357